BPB's

COMPUTER COURSE

WINDOWS 10 WITH MS OFFICE 2016

Complete book for learning better and faster

by

Satish Jain
B.Sc., B.E.(IISc), M.E.(IISc), M.Tech.(IIT Kanpur), Wing Commander (Retd.)
Ex-Professor of Information Technology, Institute of Information Technology & Management GGS Indraprastha University, Delhi.

Shashi Singh
MCA, M. Phil

M. Geetha
B. Com., Dipl. Computer Science

REPRINT 2026
FIRST EDITION 2018

ISBN :978-93-8728-401-2

LIMITS OF LIABILITY AND DISCLAIMER OF WARRANTY

Distributors:

BPB PUBLICATIONS
20, Ansari Road, Darya Ganj
New Delhi-110002
Ph: 23254990/23254991

BPB BOOK CENTRE
376 Old Lajpat Rai Market,
Delhi-110006
Ph: 23861747

MICRO MEDIA
Shop No. 5, Mahendra Chambers, 150
DN Rd. Next to Capital Cinema, V.T.
(C.S.T.) Station, MUMBAI-400 001 Ph:
22078296/22078297

DECCAN AGENCIES
4-3-329, Bank Street,
Hyderabad-500195
Ph: 24756967/24756400

Published by Manish Jain for BPB Publications, 20, Ansari Road, Darya Ganj, New Delhi- 110002 and Printed him at Manipal Technologies Limited, Manipal

Dedicated to

Sri Raja Rajeshwari, Sri Sharda Devi and Sri Sai Baba

Whose blessings will overcome all the hurdles in life

PREFACE

The objective of BPB's Windows 10 with MS Office 2016 is to meet the growing need of PC users to learn and become proficient in using Computer fundamentals, Operating system and Internet as well as software packages namely, MS Office 2016. This course is based on step-by-step learning methodology.

Chapters 1 and 2 discusses the basics of Computer fundamentals and Windows 10, the latest operating system used in PCs. Chapter 3 to 17 pertains to MS-Office 2016. These chapter describes Word, Excel, PowerPoint and OneNote with ample number of examples and large number of screens.

Chapter 18 Internet and E-mail concepts and their applications are discussed in a simple way. Each concept is explained with diagrams. The PC user will be able to connect to the Internet for sending/receiving E-Mail.

Chapter 19 to 22 discusses Time Management, Manage Files and Fonts, Up-to-Date Secure and More Office Apps in simple English language. These chapter discusses with Time management how to organize your daily activities to remind your tasks and events and it also discusses how to store and manage the files that constitute the documents and the fonts, when it use to share documents with other users and also take the advantage of Office updates to protect your documents and secure your system with OneDrive.

A special feature throughout this book is that the salient and crucial information has been encapsulated within parallel and horizontal lines with a (☞) mark to draw attention of the reader.

We shall feel obliged to the readers if they send us their critical opinion regarding the presentation, readability and coverage in this book and request them to mail their suggestions, if any, to improve the subject matter.

4th April, 2018

Authors

Contents

BPB COMPUTER COURSE

Chapter 1. Computer Fundamentals 1

1.1 **Introduction** 1
1.2 **What is a Computer?** 1
- Characteristics of Computer 1
- History of Computer 2
- Generations of Computer 3
- Applications of Computer 5
- Types of Computers 6
- Concept of Computer System 7

1.3 **Components of Computer System** 7
- Input Unit 7
- CPU (Central Processing Unit) 8
- Output Unit 8

1.4 **Input/Output Devices** 8
- Input Devices 8
- Output Devices 12
- Printer 13
- Plotter 15
- Multimedia Projector 15
- Speech Synthesizer 15
- Speakers 15

1.5 **Main Storage Devices** 16
- Random Access Memory (RAM) 16
- Read Only Memory (ROM) 17

1.6 **Secondary Storage Devices** 17
- Magnetic Tape 17
- Hard Disk 18
- Optical Disk 18
- DVD 19
- Zip Drive 19
- Pen Drive/USB Flash Drive 19
- Blu-Ray Disk 20

1.7 **Memory Units** 20
1.8 **Concept of Data Processing** 20
- Basic Tasks in Business Data Processing 20

Chapter 2. INTRODUCTION TO WINDOWS 10 22

2.1 **Introduction to Windows 10** 22
- System Requirements 22

2.2 **Getting Started** 22
- View Account Commands 23

2.3 **The Desktop and Taskbar** 23
- Start Button 23
- Search Box/Cortana 24
- Task View 24
- Microsoft Edge 24
- File Explorer 25
- Store 26
- Notification Area 26
- Opening the Action Center 26
- Taskbar 27
- Configure the Taskbar 27
- Move the Taskbar 27
- Change the Taskbar Height 27
- Pin an Application to the Taskbar 27
- Unpin an Application from the Taskbar 27

2.4 **Working with Apps** 27
- Windows 10 Apps 28
- Manage Start Screen Tiles 28
- Uninstalling Applications 29
- Viewing All Apps 30
- Searching for Apps 30
- Using Windows Store 30
- Closing Apps 30
- Buying Apps 30
- Using Live Titles 30

2.5 **Basic Controls** 30
- Menus 30
- Dialog Boxes 31
- Working with Multiple windows 31

2.6 **Customizing Windows** 32
- Using Themes 32

2.7 **File Explorer** 34
- Libraries 34
- Sorting and Grouping Files 36

2.8 **Managing Files and Folders** 36
- The File Explorer Ribbon 36

2.9 **Microsoft Edge Browser** 36
- Open Edge 36
- View Favorites 37
- Add a Webpage Favorites 37
- Use Reading Mode 37
- Microsoft Edge's Secret History 37

2.10 **Digital Life Style** 37
- Using OneDrive 37

2.11 **Media Management** 38
2.12 **Keeping in Touch** 38
- Working with Mail 38
- Composing email 39
- Reading and Replying to Messages 39
- Finding People 39
- Chatting with Skype 39

OFFICE 2016

Chapter 3. Introducing Office 2016 40

3.1 **Introduction** 40
3.2 **Office 2016** 40

3.3 Installing Requirements for Office 2016 40
3.4 Start an Application 40
- The Application Window 41
- Understanding OneDrive 42
- Working with Ribbon 42
- File Extensions 43
- Office Documents Types 43
- Compatibility Mode 43
- Convert a Document 43
- Quick Access Toolbar 44
- Dialog Box Launchers 44

3.5 Creating Word Documents 44
- Creating a New Blank Document 44
- Opening an Existing Document 44
- Saving a Document 45
- Saving and Opening Files in OneDrive 45
- AutoRecover 45
- Select Recently used files 46
- Print and Previewing a Document 46
- To Preview Design Template 47
- To Create a New document from a Template 47
- Closing and Quitting Word 2016 47
- Sharing Documents 47
- Exporting Documents 48
- Different Views in Documents 49

3.6 Getting Help on Tell Me Feature 50

Chapter 4. Word 2016 51

4.1 Text Basics 51
- Enter Text 51
- Select Text 52
- Edit Text 52
- Copying and Moving Text 52
- Cut, Copy and Paste Text 52
- Drag and Drop Text 52
- Undo Redo 53
- Zooming In or Out a Document 53

4.2 Formatting Text 53
- Change Font and Font Size 53
- Change Color 54
- Use Bold, Italic and Underline Commands 55
- Change Text Case Command 55
- Text Alignment 56

4.3 Indents and Tabs 56
- Indenting Text 56
- Indent Markers 57
- Indent Commands 57
- Tabs and Tab selector 57
- Removing Tab stops 58

4.4 Line and Paragraph Spacing 58
- Paragraph Spacing 58
- Working with Lists 59
- Create Bullets Lists 59
- Create Number Lists 59
- Understanding Hyperlinks in Word 61

4.5 Find and Replace 62
- Finding Text 62
- Replacing Text 62

4.6 Checking Spelling and Grammar 62
- Automatic spelling and Grammar Checking 62
- Hide Spelling and Errors in a document 63
- Correct Proofing Errors 63
- Change Proofing Settings 63
- Word Count 65

Chapter 5. Layout and Printing 66

5.1 Introduction 66
- Page Orientation 66
- Page Size and Margins 66
- Printing Documents 68
- Insert Columns 68
- Headers and Footers 69
- Page Numbers 69
- Macros 70

Chapter 6. Working with Objects 72

6.1 Working with Graphics 72
- Inserting a Picture 72
- Text Wrapping 73
- Formatting Pictures 73
- Creating Text Boxes 74
- Aligning and Grouping Objects 75

6.2 Working with Tables 76
- Inserting a Table 76
- Modifying Tables 77
- Merging and Splitting Cells 77
- Aligning Text in a Table Cell 79
- Convert Text to a Table 79
- Formatting Table Styles 79
- Adding Borders 80
- Sorting the Contents of a Table 80

Chapter 7. Creating Mail Merge 81

7.1 Using Mail Merge 81
- Creating a Mail Merge Letter 81
- Starting Mail Merge 81
- Saving the Master Document 83
- Printing the Merged Letters 84

Chapter 8. Complex Documents 85

8.1 Start a Booklet 85
- Create a Booklet 85
- Choose Page Arrangement 85
- Import Text 86
- Insert Illustrations 87
- Add Captions 87
- Table of Contents 88
- Update Table of Contents 88
- Table of Illustrations 88
- Insert Preface 89
- Decorate the Page 89
- Publisher 90

- Create a Publication ... 90
- Print the Publication ... 91

Excel 2016

Chapter 9. Excel 2016 92

9.1 Introduction to Excel 2016 ... **92**
9.2 Basic Excel Concepts ... **92**
- Electronic Spreadsheet ... 92
- Excel 2016 Terminology ... 92
- Working with Excel 2016 ... 92

9.3 Starting Excel 2016 ... **92**
9.4 Excel 2016 Interface ... **92**
9.5 Creating and Opening Workbook ... **93**
- Creating a New Workbook ... 94
- Opening an Existing Workbook ... 94
- Saving and Sharing Workbook ... 94
- Closing a Workbook Window ... 96

9.6 Quitting Excel 2016 ... **96**
9.7 Getting Help on Tell Me ... **96**

Chapter 10. Working with Cells and Sheets 97

10.1 Cell Basics ... **97**
- Understanding Cells ... 97
- Cell Content ... 98
- Copy and Paste Cell content ... 99
- Drag and Drop Cell ... 99
- Quick Fill ... 100
- Workbook Views ... 100
- Controlling the Display of Sheet Tabs ... 101

10.2 Formatting Cells ... **101**
- Change Font and Font Size and Color ... 101
- Cell Borders and Fill Colors ... 102
- Cell Styles ... 103
- Text Alignment ... 103

10.3 Modifying Columns, Rows and Cells ... **104**
- Modify Column Width ... 104
- Modify Row Height ... 104
- Modify All Rows or Columns ... 105
- Inserting Cells, Rows or Columns ... 105
- Deleting Cells, Rows or Columns ... 106
- Clearing Cell Contents ... 107
- Hide and Unhide Columns in a Worksheet ... 107
- Wrapping Text and Merging Cells ... 108

10.4 Understanding Number Formats ... **109**
- Why use Number Formats? ... 109
- Enter Number Formats Correctly ... 109
- Entering Data and Time in a Worksheet ... 110

10.5 Working with Multiple Worksheets ... **110**
- Inserting and Deleting Sheets ... 111
- Copying and Moving Worksheets ... 111
- Renaming a Worksheet ... 112
- Grouping and Ungrouping Worksheets ... 112

10.6 Using Find/Replace Feature ... **113**
- Find Command ... 113
- Replace Text ... 113

10.7 Page Layout and Printing ... **114**
- Printing Sections of a Worksheet or Multiple Worksheets ... 114
- Adjusting Content ... 115
- Print Tiles ... 115
- Headers and Footers ... 116
- Zooming on the Previewed Worksheet ... 116

Chapter 11. Formulas and Functions 117

11.1 Introduction ... **117**
- Creating Formulas ... 117
- Sum and Differences ... 118
- Entering Cell References ... 119
- Using Operators in Formulas ... 119

11.2 Functions in Excel 2016 ... **120**
- Creating a Function in a Worksheet ... 121
- Using the Insert Function ... 123
- Freezing Rows and Columns ... 123

11.3 Goal Seeking ... **124**

Chapter 12. Tables and Charts in Excel 2016 126

12.1 Introduction ... **126**
12.2 Formatting Tables in Excel 2016 ... **126**
- Create a Table ... 126
- Import a List ... 126
- Add Totals to Table ... 127
- Computed Column ... 128
- Table Lookup ... 128
- Manage Data using Access ... 129
- Adding Records ... 130

12.3 Protecting Workbook ... **130**
- Protecting and Unprotecting Sheets ... 130
- Group of Sheets in a Workbook ... 131

12.4 Creating a Chart ... **131**
- Changing Location of a Chart ... 132
- Sizing and Positioning a Chart ... 132
- Changing the Type of Chart ... 132
- Changing Data Source ... 133
- Inserting Chart Elements ... 133

12.5 Chart Terminologies ... **134**
12.6 Standard Chart Types ... **134**
- Column Chart ... 134
- Line Chart ... 134
- Bar Chart ... 134
- Pie Chart ... 135
- XY (Scatter) Chart ... 135
- Area Chart ... 135
- Radar Chart ... 135
- Bubble Chart ... 136
- Surface Chart ... 136
- Stock Chart ... 136

- Waterfall Chart 136
- Box and Whisker Chart 138
- Histogram Chart 141

12.7 Using Sparklines 143
12.8 Previewing Charts 143
12.9 Templates 143
12.10 Manage Data 144
- Import Data 144
- Sort 144
- Filters 145
- Number Filters 146

12.11 Pivot Table 146
12.12 Using Slicers 148
- PivotCharts 149

PowerPoint 2016

Chapter 13. PowerPoint 2016 150

13.1 Introduction 150
13.2 Starting PowerPoint 2016 150
- Understanding the Screen Elements 150
- The PowerPoint 2016 Interface 151
- Understanding OneDrive 152

13.3 New Features in PowerPoint 2016 153
- Quick Shape Formats 153
- Screen Recording 153

13.4 Managing Slides 153
- Normal View 153
- Slide Sorter View 153
- Notes Page View 154
- Slide Show View 154
- Reading View 155

13.5 Creating a Presentation 156
- Create a New Presentation from a Template 156
- Open an Existing Presentation 156
- Pin a Presentation 156
- Compatibility Mode 157
- Saving the Presentation 157
- Using AutoRecover 158
- Exporting Presentations 158

Chapter 14. Working with Slides 160

14.1 Introduction 160
14.2 Insert a New Slides 160
- Adding Text in a Placeholder 160
- Expand the Slide 161
- Creating Text Outside a Placeholder 161

14.3 Text Basics 161
- Moving Text 161
- Deleting Text 161
- Drag and Drop Text 161

14.4 Formatting Text 161
- Aligning Text in a Slide 161
- Changing Fonts 162
- Changing the Text Size 162
- Adding Special Effects to Text 163
- Changing text Color 163
- Bullets and Numbering 163
- Removing Bullets and Numbering 164
- Tabs 164
- Set Paragraph Indents 164
- Adding Background Colour 165
- Using the Spelling Checker 165

Chapter 15. Working with Tables and Objects 167

15.1 Introduction 167
15.2 Inserting a Table Slide 167
- Entering Text in a Table 167
- Editing a Table 167
- Changing a Table Style 169
- Adding Borders and Fills 169

15.3 Creating Charts in PowerPoint 170
- Insert a Chart in a Presentation 170
- Creating charts with existing Excel data 171
- Changing Data in an Existing Chart 171

15.4 Creating a SmartArt Graphic 171
- Insert SmartArt Graphic 171
- Apply a SmartArt Style to a SmartArt Graphic 172

15.5 Inserting Graphics 172
- Modifying Pictures 173
- Rotating and Flipping Objects 173
- Duplicating and Deleting Slides 174
- Printing the Presentation 174

Chapter 16. Customizing Your Presentation 176

16.1 PowerPoint Theme 176
- Applying Themes 176
- Slide Master View 176
- Customizing text formatting 177
- Using Notes Pages 177
- Printing the Notes Pages with Slide Thumbnails 177
- Using Handouts for Presentation 178

16.2 Overview of Layouts 178
- Custom Layouts 178
- Insert a New Slide Layout 178

16.3 Creating and Presenting a Custom Show 179
- Basic Custom Shows 179
- Creating a Basic Custom Show 179
- Hyperlinked Custom Shows 180
- Using Shapes Action Buttons 180
- Add Transitions between Slides 181

16.4 Animate Text and Objects 182
- Using Animations 182
- Animation Effects 182

16.5 Running a Slide Show 183
- Starting the Slide Show 183

16.6 Rehearsing and Recording the Presentation 183

- Rehearsing Slide Show Timings 183
- Recording your Slide Show 184

16.7 Package for CD **184**

OneNote 2016

Chapter 17. OneNote 2016 186

17.1 Introduction to OneNote 2016 .... **186**
- Why Use OneNote? 186
- OneNote 2016 Interface 186
- Creating a New Notebook 187
- Opening and Closing Notebooks 188
- Add Sections 188
- Add Pages 189
- Make Notes 189
- Insert Images 190
- Capture Snippets 191
- Create Tables 191
- Record Audio 192
- Page Templates 193
- Quick Notes 193

Chapter 18. Internet 195

18.1 Introduction to Internet **195**
- Applications of Internet 195
- Advantages/Disadvantage of Internet 195

18.2 Internet Services **195**
- World Wide Web 195
- Web Browser 196
- Web pages vs Websites 196
- Uniform Resource Locator (URL) 196
- Benefits of Search Engines 197
- Commerce on Internet 197
- Impact of Internet on Society 197
- Use of Search Engines 198

18.3 Methods of Connecting to the Internet **198**
- Broadband Connections 198
- Wi-Fi Connections 198
- Satellite Broadband 198
- Cellular 198

18.4 INTERNET PROTOCOLS **198**
- TCP/IP 199
- FTP 199
- HTTP 199

18.5 E-Mail **199**
- Starting Outlook 199
- Your First Messages 200
- Turn Off Reading Pane 200
- Create a Message 201
- Insert a Signature 201
- Message Tags 201
- Receive a Message 202
- Save All Attachments 203
- Print the Message 203
- Reply to the Message 204
- Add Address to Contacts 204
- RSS Feeds 205
- Spam and Phishing 205

18.6 Using Instant Messaging **206**

18.7 Mobile Adhoc Networks **206**
- Types of MANET 207

18.8 What is Security? **207**
- Need of Computer Security 207
- Inbuilt PC Security 207

18.9 Network Security Concepts **208**
- Virus 208
- Worms 209
- Trojan Horse 209
- Spams 210

18.10 Cyber Crime **210**
- Reasons for cyber crime 210
- Prevention of Cyber crime 210

18.11 Data Security and Protection **210**
- Concept 210
- Creating Strong Password 211
- Identify Secure Website 211
- Clear Cookies 211
- How to Delete Cookies in Chrome 211

18.12 Discover Network **211**
- Networking Components 211
- Hubs 211
- Switches 211
- Routers 212
- Bridges 212
- Modems 212
- Cables and Connectors 212
- Network Interface Card 213
- Network Sharing Center 213
- Sharing Files and Folders 215
- Join Homegroup 216
- Network Troubleshooting 217

18.13 System & Security **217**
- System Properties 217
- Clean up your disk 218
- Windows Update 218
- Backup and Restore Data 219
- Restoring from Backup 221
- System Restore 221
- Malware Protection 222
- Windows Firewall 223

Chapter 19. Time Management 224

19.1 Outlook Calendar **224**

19.2 Schedule an Appointment **224**

19.3 Change Appointment Details **225**

19.4 Recurring Appointments **225**

19.5 Create a Meeting **226**

19.6 Respond to an Invitation **227**

19.7 Add Holidays **227**

19.8 Report Free/Busy Time **228**

19.9 Schedule a Meeting **229**

19.10 Creating Tasks **229**

19.11 Assigning Tasks **230**

19.12 Accepting Task Requests 230
19.13 Finishing a Task 230
19.14 Outlook Notes 230
19.15 Journal 231

Chapter 20. Manage Files and Fonts 232

20.1 Windows Versions 232
20.2 Library Location 232
20.3 Finding Files 232
20.4 Recent Documents 233
20.5 Change File Type 234
20.6 XML File Formats 235
20.7 Save As PDF or XPS 235
- Make changes to an XPS file 236

20.8 Fonts in Office 2016 236
- Create and Run ListAllFonts 237

20.9 Document Recovery 238

Chapter 21. Up-to-Date and Secure 240

21.1 Enable and Disable Updates 240
21.2 Apply Updates 240
- Change Settings 242

21.3 Office Help 242
21.4 Developer Tab 243
21.5 Remove Personal Information 244
21.6 Protect Your Documents 246
- Encrypt with Password 246
- Remove the Encryption 247

21.7 Restrict Permission 248
- Remove the Restriction 249

21.8 Trust Center 249

Chapter 22. More Office Apps 10 251

22.1 Office Tools 251
- Office 2016 Language Preference 251
- Upload Center 251

22.2 Office Online 252
22.3 Office For Android 253
22.4 Sway Storytelling 253
22.5 Visio Diagrams 253
22.6 Project Management 254
- Switching Task 255

22.7 Business Products 255
- Microsoft Exchange Server 255
- SharePoint Online 255
- OneDrive for Business 255
- Skype for Business 255
- Yammer 256
- Power BI 256
- Microsoft Dynamics CRM 256

Appendix 257

CHAPTER 1

Computer Fundamentals

1.1 INTRODUCTION

Nowadays, computers became an integral part of our lives. Ever since its invention, the power of computer has been growing rapidly. Strangely enough, the cost of hardware has been declining by the year. A large number of application software packages are now available that make computers highly productive, versatile and easy to use.

The use of computer is spreading to more virgin areas of human activities to make life more comfortable and leisurely. They are used for the reservation of tickets for airplanes and railways, payment of telephone and electricity bills, deposit and withdrawal of money from banks, processing of business data, forecasting of weather conditions, diagnosis of diseases, searching for information on the Internet, etc. A computer is also used extensively in schools, universities, organizations, music industry, movie industry, scientific research, law firms, fashion industry, etc.

1.2 WHAT IS A COMPUTER?

A computer is an electronic device that is designed to work with information. The term computer is derived from the word "computer", which means to calculate. It also refers to the Central Processor Unit and Internal memory. It cannot do anything without a Program.

A computer is an electronic machine that takes raw data as input from the user and processes these data under the control of set of instructions (called program) and gives the result (output) and saves output for the future use. It can perform both simple and complex operations, with speed and accuracy. A computer components are divided into two major categories namely, hardware and software. Hardware is the machine itself and its connected devices such as monitor, keyboard, mouse etc. Software are the set of programs that make use of hardware for performing various functions (See Figure 1.1).

Figure 1.1 Parts of computer system

☞ *The first mechanical computer was designed by Charles Babbage was called Analytical Engine. It use read-only memory in the form of punch cards.*

1.2.1 Characteristics of Computer

The common characteristics that make computers of all sizes powerful machine are speed, accuracy, and reliability, storage capacity ability to operate automatically, diligence, scientific approach and versatility. Some of the important characteristics are described below: (See Figure 1.2)

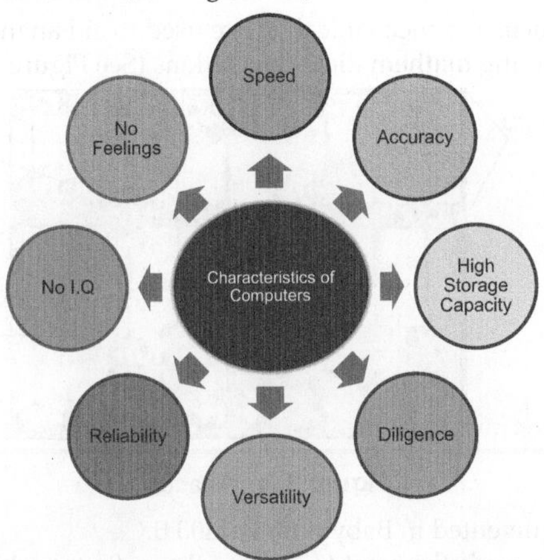

Figure 1.2 Characteristics of Computer

- **Speed:** As you know computer can work very fast. It can perform large amount of work in a few seconds and measured in microseconds (10^{-6}), nanoseconds (10^{-9}) and pico seconds (10^{-12}).
- **Accuracy:** Computer provides a high degree of accuracy depending upon its design. For example, the computer can accurately give the result of division of any two numbers up to 10 decimal places.
- **High Storage Capacity:** The computer has an in-built memory where it can store a large amount of data. You can also store data in secondary storage devices such as flash drive and external hard drive which can be kept outside your computer and can be retrieved whenever required.
- **Diligence:** The computer is a machine, which doesnot suffer from the human traits of tiredness, nor does it loses concentration even after working continuously for a long time.

- **Versatility:** It means the capacity to perform completely different type of work. At one moment you can use the computer to prepare payroll slip and in next moment you can play music or print a document.
- **Reliability:** Computer provide very high speed accompanied by an equality high level for reliability. Thus, computers never make mistake of their own accord.
- **No I.Q.:** A computer is a magical device. It can only perform tasks that a human being can. The difference is that it performs these tasks with unthinkable speed and accuracy. It posses no intelligence of its own. Its I.Q is zero atleast till today. It can only perform what is programmed to do. Hence, only the user can determine what tasks a computer will perform. It have no sense of meaning, cannot perceive and are only able to make simple decision about the data they receive.
- **No Feelings:** It does not have feelings or emotion, so the given instruction given to them in the form of programs that are written by us (human beings).

1.2.2 History of Computer

The history of computers starts as far back as 5000 BC.

Abacus

- An abacus is a mechanical device used to aid an individual in performing mathematical calculations (See Figure 1.3).

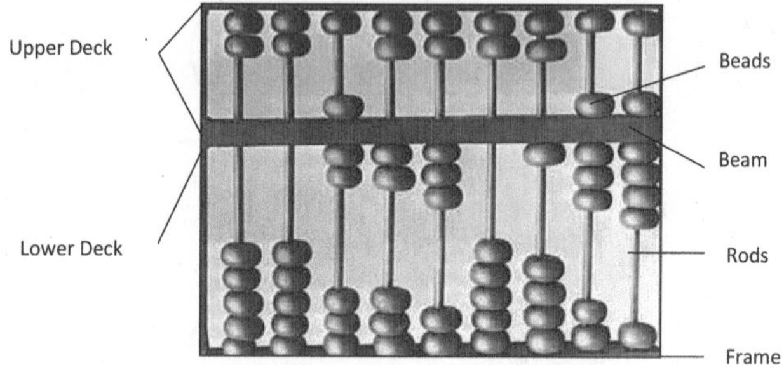

Figure 1.3 Abacus

- It was invented in Babylonia in 2400 B.C.
- The abacus is the most familiar and was first used in China in around 500 B.C. It is used to perform basic arithmetic operations.

Napier's Bones

- John Napier developed the logarithms rules which are very useful in mathematics and computer technology (See Figure 1.4).
- Operations such as multiply, divide and square and cube roots are performed by moving the rods and placing them in constructed boards.

Pascaline

- The first mechanical adding machine was invented by Blaise Pascal in 1642.
- Its limitation was addition and subtraction.
- It is too expensive.

Figure 1.4 Napier's Bones

Stepped Reckoner

- This machine was further improved by Baron Gottfried Wilhelm von Leibniz of Germany in the year 1671.
- The machine can add, subtract, multiply and divide automatically.
- He discovered that computing processes can be done much easier with a binary number coding.

Jacquard Loom

- Joseph Marie Jacquard (1752-1834) was a French silk weaver and inventor.
- It was an automatic loom controlled by punched cards.

Arithmometer

- A mechanical calculator invented by Thomas de Colmar in 1820.
- The first reliable, useful and successful calculating machine. The machine could perform the four basic mathematical functions.

Different Engine and Analytical Engine

- It was an automatic, mechanical calculator designed to tabulate polynomial functions (See Figure 1.5).
- Invented by Charles Babbage in 1822 and 1834.
- It is the first mechanical computer.

Difference Engine

Analytical Engine

Figure 1.5 Different engine and analytical engine

First Computer Programmer

- In 1840, Augusta Ada Byron suggests to Babbage that he use the binary system.
- She writes programs for the Analytical Engine.

Tabulating Machine

- Tabulating machine uses punched cards as a data input mechanism invented by Herman Hollerith in 1890 which merged into an organization that would grow and evolve into the International business machine (IBM) company.

Havard Mark 1

- Also known as IBM Automatic Sequence Controlled Calculator (ASCC).
- Invented by Howard H. Aiken in 1943.
- The first electro-mechanical computer.

Zuse's Z1

- The first programmable computer.
- Created by Konrad Zuse in Germany from 1936 to 1938.
- The program Z1 required that the user insert punch tape into a punch tape reader and all output was also generated through punch tape.

ENIAC

- ENIAC stands for Electronic Numerical Integrator and Computer.
- It was the first electronic digital computer completed in 1946.. Developed by John Presper Eckert and John W. Mauchl.
- This machine was thirty times more powerful than the earlier machines.
- It contained about 18,000 electronic valves. It could perform 5,000 additions per second and consumed 150 K watts of power.

UNIVAC-1

- The UNIVAC (UNIVersal Automatic Computer 1) was the first commercial computer, designed by J. Presper Eckert and John Mauchly.
- This machine used magnetic medium for data input and output.
- These computers used valve technology and had the main limitations of heavy power consumption and very high unreliability in operations.

EDVAC

- EDVAC stands for Electronic Discrete Variable Automatic Computer.
- The first stored program computer. Designed by Von Neumann in 1952.
- It has a memory to hold both a stored program as well as data.

1.2.3 Generations of Computer

A generation refers to the state of improvement in the product development process. Each generation of computers is characterized by major technological development that fundamentally changed the way computers operate, cheaper, more powerful, more efficient and reliable devices.

There are five computer generations known till date. Each generation has been discussed in detail along with the time period, technology and characteristics.

First Generation (1942-1955)

- **Hardware Technology:** It uses vacuum tubes as the basic components for memory and circuitry for CPU. Input was based on punched cards and paper tapes, and output was displayed on printouts (See Figure 1.6).

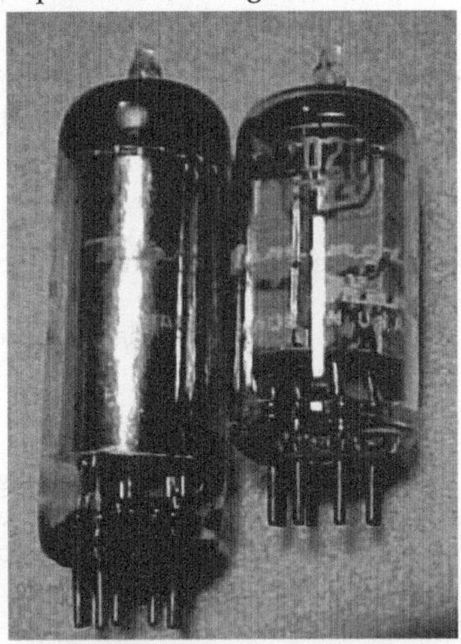

Figure 1.6 Vacuum tube

- **Software Technology:** The instructions were written in machine languages and uses 0s and 1s for coding.
- **Examples:** Universal Automatic Computer (UNIVAC), Electronic Numerical Integrator and Calculator (ENIAC), and Electric Discrete Variable Automatic Computer (EDVAC).

The main characteristics are:

- Size of machines was big
- Very expensive
- Lot of heat is generated so it need air conditioning
- Consumed lots of electricity
- Required large amount of energy for processing
- Not reliable
- It is used for mostly scientific applications

Second Generation (1955-1964)

- **Hardware Technology:** Transistors was replaced by vacuum tubes. The Transistors allows computers to become smaller, faster, cheaper more energy efficient and reliable. Magnetic cores were used as the primary memory and magnetic tape and disks as secondary storage devices (See Figure 1.7).
- **Software Technology:** High-level programming languages like FORTRAN, COBAL were used.
- **Examples:** IBM 7094, CDC 1604 and UNIVAC LARC.

Figure 1.7 Transistor

The main characteristics are:

- Compared to G1 computer, less expensive and smaller in size
- Fast in speed
- Need lower power consumption
- Portable
- Required less maintenance than the first generation computer.
- It is used for scientific and commercial purposes

Third Generations (1964-1975)

- **Hardware Technology:** 3G is used as Integrated Circuits (ICs) in place of transistors. A single IC has many transistors, registers and capacitors on a single silicon chip. The use of IC chip increased the speed and the efficiency of computer, manifold (See Figure 1.8).

Figure 1.8 Integrated Circuit

- **Software Technology:** Multi-programming operating system were used. High level programming language such as FORTRAN, COBOL, Pascal and BASIC.
- **Examples:** IBM System 360/370, PDP-8/11 (Personal Data Processor), CDC 6600

The main characteristics are:

- Smaller in Size, Faster
- Low power consumption and generated less heat
- Easy to operate
- Supported high-level language
- Input device introduced and that make user easy to interact with keyboard and mouse.
- It is used for scientific, commercial and interactive online applications.

Fourth Generations (1975-1989)

- **Hardware Technology:** They use the Large Scale Integration (LSI) and the Very Large Scale Integration (VLSI technology). Thousands of transistors on a small silicon chip using LSI technology. VLSI allows hundreds of thousands of components to be integrated in a small chip. Microcomputers came in to existence, and gave rise to personal computers in this generation. In this generation, time sharing, real time networks, distributed operating system are used. You can also saw the development of pointing devices and handheld devices (See Figure 1.9).

Figure 1.9 Microprocessor

- **Software Technology:** Operating Systems like MS-DOS and MS-Windows developed during this time. It also supports Graphical User Interface. It is a user-friendly interface that allows user to interact with the computer via menus and icons. Programs are written in high-level programming languages such as C, C++, DBASE etc.
- **Examples:** VAX 9000, PDP 11, CRAY-1, 2 (Super computer), CRAY-X-MP

The main characteristics are:

- Smaller in size.
- They have very high speed of processing; they are accurate, reliable, diligent and versatile.
- Great developments in the field of networks.
- For general purpose
- More external storage mediums are introduced like CD-ROM, DVD-ROM.
- It is used for commercial and network applications.

Fifth Generations (1989- Present)

- **Hardware Technology:** Fifth generation use ULSI (Ultra Large Scale Integration) chips. Millions of transistors are placed in a single IC in ULSI chips. The use of parallel processing and super conductors is helping to make artificial intelligence a reality.
- **Software Technology:** Programming was done in High level programming language such as Java, Python and C#.
- **Examples:** IBM notebook, Pentium PCs, SUN Workstations, PARAM 10000

The main characteristics are:

- Portable computers, powerful, cheaper, reliable and easier to use desktop machines
- There are some applications, such as voice recognition, that are being used today.

- The goal is to develop devices that respond to natural language input and are capable of learning and self-organization.
- More user-friendly interfaces with multimedia features
- It is used for commercial, interactive online multimedia (i.e. graphics, audio, video) and network applications.

1.2.4 Applications of Computer

The applications of computer in various fields. Some common uses of a computer are shown in Figure 1.10 which are discussed below.

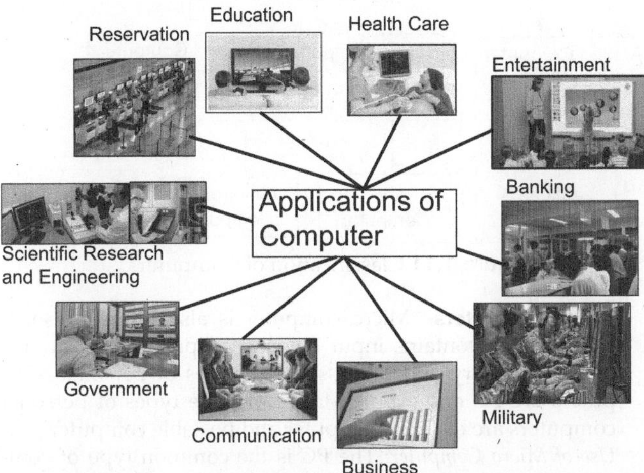

Figure 1.10 Applications of computer in various fields

- **Education:** With in recent advancement in the education industry, the use of computers in education has become relevant. It play a great role in helping students to learn faster. Students can learn using visual illustrations such as smart whiteboards, iPads and Projectors. Many universities and colleges have added online education on their curriculum and they enrol students from all parts of the world (See Figure 1.10).
  Various applications of computer in Education are:
  - Video conference
  - Distance Learning
  - Research
  - Taking online courses
  - Online examination
- **Health and Medicine:** Most of the medical information can now be digitized from the prescription to reports. Computation in the field of medicine allows us to offer varied therapies to the patients. ECG's, radiotherapy was not possible without computers. Now a days, computers are also used in performing surgery.
  Various applications of computer in Health and Medicine are:
  - Patient monitoring
  - Patient records
  - Diagnosis purposes
  - Hospital administration
  - Medical history records
- **Entertainment:** Computers are widely used in the entertainment industry. The user can download and view movies, play games, watch live matches on the internet.
  Various applications of computer in Entertainment are
  - You can compose music and other sound effects using external devices such as electronic keyboard.
  - Download different songs, movies
  - Digital video and sound editing
  - Drawing and other artistic programs
- **Reservation:** A computer reservation system is a computerized system used to store and retrieve information and conduct transactions related to air travel, hotels, car rental and other activities.
- **Scientific Research, and Engineering:** Supercomputers have especially revolutionized the scientific process and are used in meteorology to molecular biology to astronomy to environmental science and engineers use computers for performing complex scientific calculations, for designing and making drawings (CAD/CAM applications) and also for simulating and testing the designs.
  Various applications of computer in Engineering Design and Scientific are:
  - Structural and industrial design such as design of ships, airplanes.
  - Complex data analysis
  - Astronomical function
  - Robot for atomic research
  - Satellite
  - To predict about the effects of earthquake on buildings in a particular area.
- **Government:** The government uses computers to manage its own operations and also for e-governance. The websites of the different government departments provide information to the users. Computers are used for the for the access of land record details, etc. The police department uses computers to search for criminals by using fingerprint matching, etc.
  Various applications of computer in Government are:
  - Computerized of PAN Card
  - Filing of income tax return and paying taxes
  - Income and Sales tax departments
  - Online submission of water and electricity bills.
  - Used to track population and collect census data
- **Communication:** Communication means to convey message, an idea, a picture or speech that is received and understood clearly by the person for whom it is meant for.
  Various applications of computer in Communication are:
  - Chatting
  - E-mail
  - Usenet
  - Video-conferencing
- **Military:** A computer are the main tools which help in developing missiles and other equipment in the defence system. Construction of weapons and controlling their functions is not possible without the aid of computers.
  Various applications of a computer in Military are:
  - Controlling VAV or unmanned air-crafts an example in Predator.

- They are also used on Intercontinental Ballistic Missiles (ICBMs) that uses GPS and computers to help the missile get to the target.
- **Business:** Computers are the essential part of any business organization. Computers are used in business companies for performing different tasks like Record Maintaining, Stock management, Pay roll system, Business correspondence and Business communication etc.
  Various applications of computer in Business are:
  - Use computers for marketing their products.
  - Stock exchange
  - Banks are using computers to record daily customer transactions.
  - By E-mail, you can send and receive messages.
  - Payroll system is used to maintain pay accounts of employees, easily and quickly.
- **Banking:** Today banking is almost totally dependent on computer. It is easier for customers to manage their money is through Internet banking. Customers can view their balances, and setup payments from their own computer, at any time of day.
  Various applications of computer in Banking are:
  - Electronic bill payments
  - Ordering cheque books
  - Fund transfers

1.2.5 Types of Computers

The Three basic types of computers
(a) Analog
(b) Digital
(c) hybrid

Analog Computers

Analog computer is used to measure continuous values. It measures a physical property like voltage, pressure, speed, time and temperature. An analog computer takes input in analog form and gives output is usually displayed on a meter or scale. Analog computer is mainly used in the field of engineering and medicine.
Examples are: Thermometer, Speedometer, Analog clock

Digital Computers

Digital computer uses binary number system consists of only two digits 0 and 1. It represents data in digital signals. A 0 represents OFF and a 1 represents ON. Digital computer performs arithmetic and logical operations on data. It gives output in digital form. Digital computers are very fast and they have large Memory (that is data storing capacity). Today most of the computers used in offices and homes are Digital computers.
Examples are: Personal Computer (PC or Micro Computer), Digital Score board and Digital watch

Hybrid Computers

A hybrid computer is a combination of both analog and digital computer. Hybrid computer can handle both analog and digital data. A hybrid computer combines the best characteristics of both the analog and digital computer. It can accept data in both analog and digital form.
Examples are: It is used in hospitals to calculate patient's heart function and blood pressure monitor, spaceships and missile system.

Classification of Computers

Computers are classified into the following types based on the size and the speed of working: (See Figure 1.11).

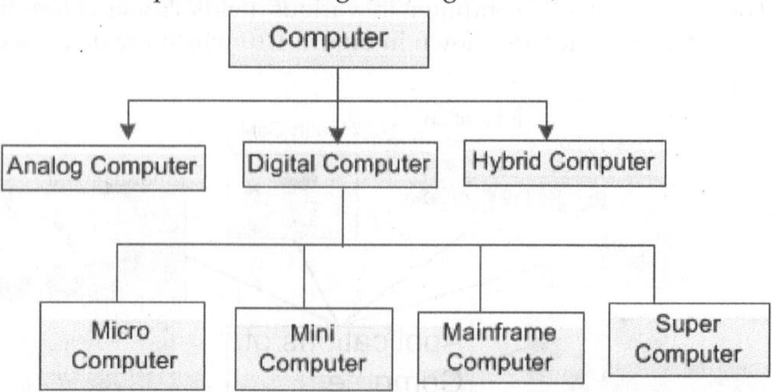

Figure 1.11 Classification of Computers

- **Micro computers**– Micro computer is also called personal computer. It contains input devices, output device, storage device, memory and processor. Examples of personal computers are PC and Apple Macintosh. The types of personal computers are desktop computer and portable computer.
  Use of Micro Computer: The PC is the common type of computer used in the office. It is now widely used in homes, business and engineering application.
  - *Desktop Computers*–It is most common type of microcomputer. It can easily fit on a table or desktop. It consists of three units –keyboard, monitor, and a system unit containing the CPU, memory, hard disk drive, etc. It is not very expensive and is suited to the needs of a single user at home, small business units, and organizations.
  - *Portable Computer*–Portable is a personal computer that can be carried from one place to other easily. Notebook computer and handheld computer (smart phone) are examples of portable computers. Notebook computer is also called laptop computer. Laptop computers are very small in size and can be placed easily on lap.
  - *Handheld Computer or Personal Digital Assistant (PDA)*–It is a small computer that can be held on the top of the palm. It is small in size. Instead of the keyboard, PDA uses a pen or a stylus for input. PDAs do not have a disk drive. They have a limited memory and are less powerful. PDAs can be connected to the Internet via a wireless connection. Casio and Apple are some of the manufacturers of PDA.
  - *Smart Phones*– Cellular phones that function both as a phone and as a small PC. They may use a stylus or a pen, or may have a small keyboard. They can be connected to the Internet wirelessly. They are used to access the electronic-mail, download music, play games, etc. Blackberry, Apple, HTC, Nokia and LG are some of the manufacturers of smart phones.

- *Tablet PC*–A *tablet PC* is a medium-sized mobile computer integrated into a flat touch screen using stylus, digital pen with a virtual onscreen keyboard. It is a touch-pad device that combines the features and qualities of a smart phone and a laptop.

- **Mini computers**–Minicomputers are digital computers, generally used in multi-user systems. They have high processing speed and high storage capacity than the microcomputers. It can execute five million instructions per second. It generally consists of two or more processors. Mini computer can serve up to 4000 connected users simultaneously. Examples of mini computers are: VAX-8800 and AS 400.
  Uses of Mini Computers: It is used by small and medium-sized companies to provide centralized store of information.
- **Mainframe Computers**–A mainframe computer is a very large computer in size. It is more powerful than mini computer. It consists of multiple processors. It is designed to perform multiple tasks for multiple users at the same time. The users access a mainframe computer through terminal or personal computer. A typical mainframe computer can execute 16 million instructions per second.
  Examples of mainframe computers are NEC 610 and DEC 10
  Uses of Mainframe Computers: It used in large organizations. For example, airlines use these computers for ticket reservation system.
- **Super Computers**–Super computer is the fastest computer. It is the biggest in size and the most expensive in price than any other computers. It has a very large storage capacity and very expensive. It can process trillions of instructions in one second. Super Computer is the fastest and most powerful computer of a time. It is used for highly calculation-intensive tasks. Super computers are used for specialized applications that require immense amounts of mathematical calculations. Examples of supercomputers are IBM Blue gene and Intel ASCI red. PARAM is a series of supercomputer assembled in India by C-DAC (Centre for Development of Advanced Computing), in Pune.
  Uses of Super Computers: Weather forecasting, climate research (global warming), biological research, nuclear research and aircraft design etc.

1.2.6 Concept of Computer System

A computer system consists of four parts:

1. **Hardware**
   The physical components of a computer are known as hardware. The physical parts or components of a computer such as the monitor, mouse, keyboard, computer data storage, hard drive disk (HDD), system unit (graphic cards, sound cards, memory, motherboard and chips), etc.
2. **Software**
   Software is the set of instructions given to computer to perform a task. System Software like operating systems are used to manage components and operations of computer. Application Software like MS Word and MS Excel are used to solve specific problems of the user, for example creating documents or preparing Student Result Sheet etc.
3. **Data**
   Data is a collection of raw facts. Computer processes data in many ways to convert them into useful information. For example, 31 January 1994 are processed by the computer to give the data of birth of a person.
4. **Users**
   Users are people who write computer programs or interact with the computer. They are also known as skinware, liveware. For example, in a grocery shop a computer operator feed the items price in the Excel software.

1.3 COMPONENTS OF A COMPUTER SYSTEM

All types of computers follow the same basic logical structure and perform the following five basic operations for converting raw input data into information useful to their users. A block diagram of the basic computer organization is shown in Figure 1.12.

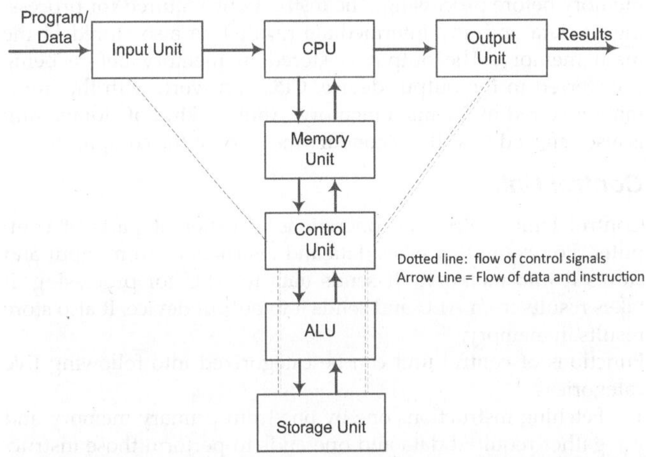

Figure 1.12 Block diagram representation of a computer system

Inputting: The process of entering data and instructions into the computer, by the user using an input device, such as keyboard.
Storing: The input data and instructions so that they are available for processing as when required.
Processing: The computer processes the input data. For this, it performs some actions on the data by using the instructions or program given by the user. The action could be arithmetic or logic calculation. During processing, the data, instructions and the output are stored temporarily in the computer's main memory.
Outputting: It is the process of produced useful information or results for the user, such as printed report or visual display.
Controlling: Refers to directing all the above processes, in coordination. The control unit will control operations and components of a computer.

1.3.1 Input Unit

The user interacts with the computer via the I/O unit. The Input unit accepts data from the user. The Input unit converts the data that it accepts from the user, into a form that is understandable by the computer. The input is provided to the computer by using input devices like keyboard, trackball and mouse.

1.3.2 Central Processing Unit

The CPU is the brain of a computer. It performs all types of data processing operation. It stores data, intermediate results and instructions (programs). It controls all activities of different parts of a computer.
CPU itself has the following three components:

- Memory or Storage unit
- Control Unit
- ALU (Arithmetic Logic Unit)

Memory or Storage Unit

Memory unit stores data, instructions, intermediate results and output, temporarily, during the processing of data. This memory is also called the main memory or primary memory of the computer.

The input data that is to be processed is brought into the main memory before processing. The instructions required for processing of data and any intermediate results are also stored in the main memory. The output is stored in memory before being transferred to the output device. CPU can work with the information stored in the main memory. Another kind of storage unit is also referred to as the secondary memory of the computer.

Control Unit

Control Unit controls all operations of different parts of computer. For example it takes data and instructions from input and stores it into memory. It sends data to ALU for processing. It takes results from ALU and sends it to output device. It also store results in memory.
Functions of control unit can be categorized into following five categories

1. Fetching instructions one by one from primary memory and gather required data and operands to perform those instructions.
2. Sending instructions to ALU to perform additions, multiplication etc.
3. Receiving and sending result to operations of ALU to primary memory.
4. Fetching programs from input and secondary memory and bringing them to primary memory.
5. Sending results from ALU stored in primary memory to output.

Registers A registers is one of a small set of data holding places that are part of ALU. It holds instructions and data as along as it is being processed by CPU. When instructions and data is fetched from memory then it is stored in a register. A register must be large enough to hold an instruction. For example, in a 32-bit computer, a register must be 32 bits in length.

Arithmetic Logic Unit

ALU is a digital circuit used to perform arithmetic and logic operations. It represents the fundamental building block of the CPU of a computer. ALU performs data processing according to given instructions. According to their function ALU may be further categorized in two sections these are:

- *Arithmetic section*–It performs arithmetic operations like addition, subtraction, multiplication and division.
- *Logic section*–It performs logical operations like comparison between two valves. For example, 8>4 will give TRUE. And 3<1 will give FALSE. Control unit sends data and instructions to perform calculation on the data to the ALU. Then ALU performs this calculation.

1.3.3 Output Unit

The Output unit provides the processed data i.e. the information to the user. Similarly, the Output unit provides the output in a form that is understandable by the user. Some of the commonly used output devices are monitor and printer.

1.4 INPUT/ OUTPUT DEVICES

These devices are used to enter information and instructions into a computer for storage or processing and to deliver the processed data to a user. Input/Output devices are required for users to communicate with the computer. In simple terms, input devices bring information INTO the computer and output devices bring information OUT of a computer system.

1.4.1 Input Devices

Input devices are those devices which are used to enter information into a computer or other data processing devices. These devices are:

(a) Keyboard
(b) Mouse
(c) Joystick
(d) Touch screen
(e) Light pen
(f) Scanner
(g) Voice Input and Recognition System
(h) Optical Mark Reader
(i) Bar-code Reader
(j) Magnetic Ink Character Recognition
(k) Web Camera
(l) Video Camera

Keyboard

Keyboard is a common input device which helps to input data to the computer. A keyboard is similar to the keyboard of a typewriter. It contains alphabets, digits, special characters, function keys and some control keys. When a key is pressed, an electronic signal is produced which is detected by an electronic circuit called *keyboard encoder* (Figure 1.13).

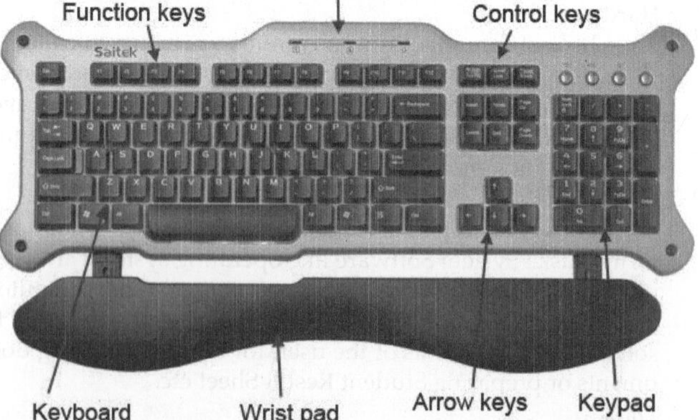

Figure 1.13 Keyboard depicting different keys' functions

Types of keys on keyboard

- *Alphanumeric keys:* It includes all the numbers and letters on the keyboard. e.g., A-Z and 0-9.
- *Functions key:* Keys from F1 to F12.
- *Punctuation keys:* These include comma, semicolon and brackets.
- *Special keys:* These includes controls keys, Arrows key, Caps lock key, Delete key.

Advantages: Keyboards have special key that perform specific functions. Keyboard is less expensive.

Disadvantages: Not much useful for enlarging or changing sizes of windows on screen. Not entering some specific type of data, for example, pictures, games, etc.

Mouse

Mouse is an input device used to control motion of pointer on screen. It is used to position the cursor on screen, move an object by dragging, or select an object by clicking. It is a small hand-held device having two or three buttons on its upper side. In addition to the buttons, mouse also has a small wheel between the buttons. The wheel of the mouse is used for the up and down movement, for example, scrolling a long document (See Figure 1.14).

Figure 1.14 Mouse

A mouse has two types one is mechanical and another is optical. Mechanical mouse has a rubber ball on the bottom side that protrudes when the mouse is move. It requires a smooth, dust free surface, such as a mouse pad, on which it is rolled. In a physical mouse, rollers and sensors are used to sense the direction and rate of movement of mouse.

Optical Mouse uses a Light Emitting Diode (LED) and a sensor to detect the movement of mouse. Optical mouse requires an opaque flat surface underneath it. When an optical mouse is moved, a beam of light is reflected from its underside.

Techniques for using a mouse

Five essential techniques for using a mouse are discussed below:

(a) *Pointing:* It means to move the cursor to the icon or a menu item.

(b) *Clicking:* It means to press and release the left mouse button once.

(c) *Double clicking:* It means to press and release left mouse button twice in rapid succession.

(d) *Dragging:* It means to hold the left mouse button as you move the pointer.

(e) *Right clicking:* It means to press and release the right mouse button.

Advantages: The mouse gives the computer user the freedom to move cursors in any direction.

Disadvantages: They need a flat surface or else they won't function. A mouse cannot easily be used with a laptop or a note book or a palmtop computers.

Joystick

Joysticks are used to control video games. A joystick has one or more push-buttons, called switches, whose state can also be read by the computer. (See Figure 1.15).

Advantages: They give better gaming experience for racing for flying styles of computer games.

Disadvantages: Joystick are not particularly robust and can break easily if too much force is used on them.

Figure 1.15 Joystick

Touch Screen

A *touch screen* is a computer display screen that is sensitive to human touch, allowing a user to interact with the computer by touching pictures or words on the screen. Touch screens are used with information kiosks, computer-based training devices and systems designed to help individuals who have difficulty in manipulating a mouse or keyboard (See Figure 1.16). The use of touch screen are on smart phones and modern tablet computers. Each 'app' is accessed by an icon on the touch screen.

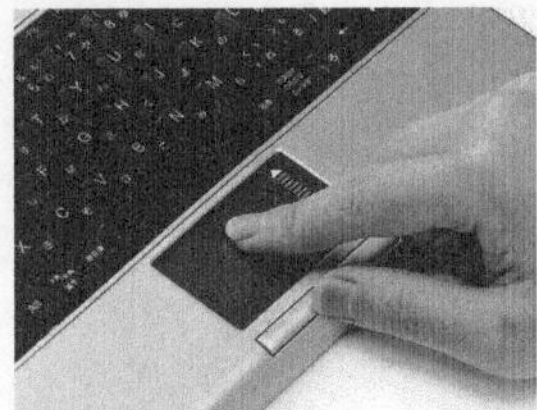

Figure 1.16 Touch Screen

Advantages: For people new or uncomfortable with normal desktops, touchscreens are easy to use, thus more people get used to using computers.

Disadvantages: The screen has to be big enough to be able to touch the buttons without missing. The screens will get very dirty. In direct sunlight it is less efficient and very difficult to read the screen.

Microphone

An input device that converts sound into a signal that can fed into a computer. The signal from a microphone is usually analogue before it can be processed by a computer. An Analogue-to-Digital Convertor (ADC) (usually built into the computer's sound card) is used for this purpose converted into digital data. Many headphones now come with microphones to allow them to be used with chat and phone applications (See Figure 1.17).

Advantages: Voice recognition software can be used to convert your voice into text or to control menu options on a phone system.

Disadvantages: Stored audio files can take up a lot of memory.

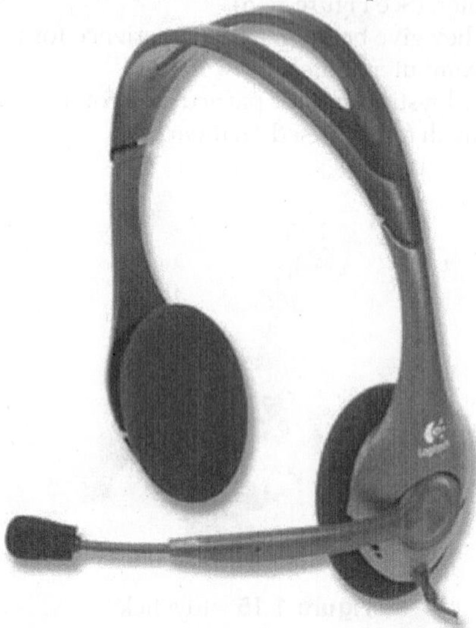

Figure 1.17 Microphone with earphone

Scanner

Scanners are a kind of input devices. They are capable of entering information directly into the computer. The main advantage of direct entry of information is that users do not have to type the information. This provides faster and more accurate data entry (See Figure 1.18).

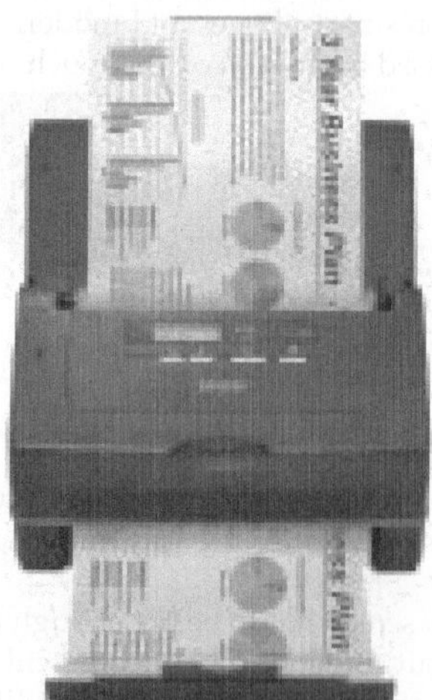

Figure 1.18 Scanner

Types of Scanners Different types of scanners are used for different applications. The capability and cost of scanners differ from type to type. The scanners required for industrial purpose are different from scanners meant for use at home or in small offices. Scanners are of three types. They are:

(a) *Flatbed scanner:* A flatbed scanner is also known as a desktop scanner and it works just like a photocopier. This scanner allows the user to place a full piece of paper, book, magazine, photo or any other object onto the glass surface of the scanner. It has the capability to scan that object and convert it into digital form.

(b) *Sheetfed scanner:* A sheetfed scanner is also known as a rollerfed scanner. It works like a fax machine. The image is passed over a roller where it is captured. A Sheetfed scanner is very versatile in scanning loose sheets of paper.

(c) *Handheld scanner:* A handheld or portable scanner is an optical scanner which is designed to be moved by hand across the object or document being scanned. Today, a hand scanner is extensively used with a PC or a word processor as an image inputting device. It is used for optically reading images or data from a document. It is operated by hand.

Optical Mark Reader (OMR)

Optical Mark Readers are special scanners used for recognizing a pre-specified type of mark made by pencil or pen. For example, in the objective test paper of competitive examinations, you mark your answers on a special sheet by darkening a small square, using a pen or pencil.

Bar-code Reader

A Barcode reader is a hand-held input device used to capture and read information contained in a barcode (Figure 1.19). A barcode reader consists of a lens, light source and a light sensor translates optical impulses into electrical ones. All barcode readers consists of a decoder circuitry that analyzes the barcode's image data provided by the sensor and sends the barcode's content to the scanner's output port.

Advantages: Faster in data entry. less data entry error. Enables automatic stock control.

Disadvantages: It is relatively expensive to setup, Works with computers or POS terminals.

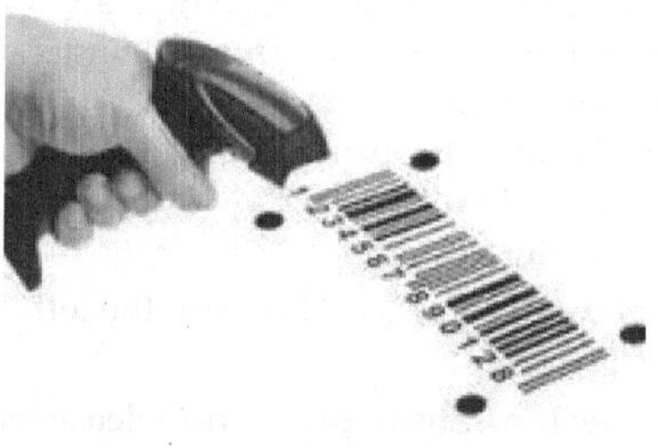

Figure 1.19 Bar code Reader

Magnetic Ink Character Recognition (MICR)

The MICR detects the special encoded characters on bank cheques and deposit slips. After detecting the encoded characters, the MICR converts them into digital data for the computer. Figure 1.20 shows a bank cheque which will be processed by using a MICR device.

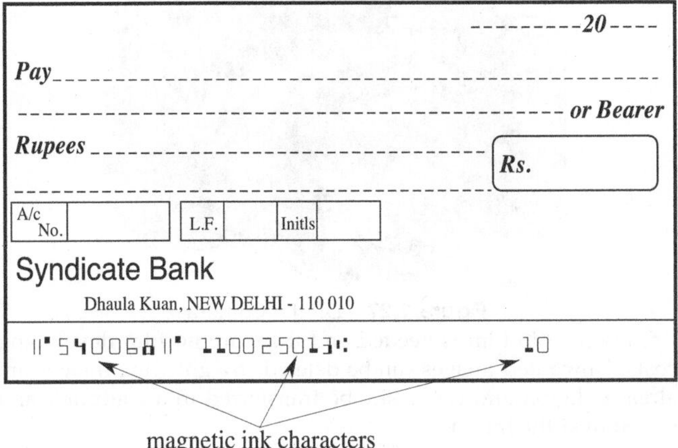

Figure 1.20 A bank cheque that is processed using a MICR device

Advantages: The major advantages of MICR is accuracy and its speed.

Disadvantages: The number of characters that can be recorded with present techniques is very limited. Also, the characters cannot be read repeatedly without losing their magnetism.

Optical Character Reader (OCR)

Optical character readers is technique for inputting text into a computer by means of a document reader. In other words, an OCR converts images into actual text, which can be edited using word processors. There is also an advanced OCR, which can even read handwritten text. Figure 1.21 shows functioning of OCR. OCR is used, for example, by gas and electricity companies to input data collected on meter-reading cards, and by personal digital assistants to recognize user's handwriting. (See Figure 1.22)

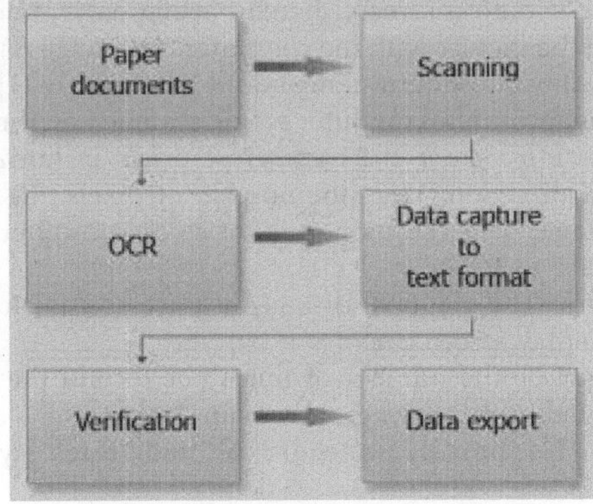

Figure 1.21 Functioning of OCR

Figure 1.22 OCR

Advantages: It makes data entry simple and faster using scanners. It also reduces workload for people who have to feed large amounts of data into computers on a regular basis.

Disadvantages: It is not completely accurate and text would need proof-reading afterwards. You will need to buy a scanner and OCR software which are expensive.

Card Reader

A card reader is a device that reads punched cards. A punched card is a storage medium made of thick paper card that holds data in the form of punched holes. The holes are punched into the card by a key punch machine or card punch peripheral device connected to a computer.

The punched card code is detected by patterns of light passing through the holes in the cards.

Another card reader, called magnetic card reader, is used for reading the magnetic strip on the back of credit cards and transferring data sent through the card. (See Figure 1.23).

Figure 1.23 Card Reader

Biometric Sensor

Biometric Sensor is the device that is used to identifies fingerprints, DNA identification, eye retinas and irises, voice patterns, facial patterns, hand measurements, face shape and signature verification (See Figure 1.24). They are used for security purposes to identify the persons who are permitted to enter the organization.

Web Cameras

This is a very basic video camera used to feed live video into a computer. The video data from a web cam is of low quality as compared to a full video camera. However, it is good enough for web chats (e.g. using a messenger application such as MSN messenger or Skype). It is usually a web cam is clipped to the top of a monitor, but many laptops now have web cams built into the edge of the screen (See Figure 1.25).

Advantages: Able to interact with people across long distance. Both sound and video is used, making the communication more sophisticated.

Figure 1.24 Biometric Sensor

Disadvantages: Feed when video chatting can be choppy/pixelated. It can be used to film inappropriate/illegal videos. Privacy in computer uses is decreasing. Hackers can enable webcams even when the owner is not aware.

Figure 1.25 Web Camera

Video Cameras

A device that captures moving images, or video. Like a digital camera, most video cameras do not directly input data into a computer. The captured movies are stored on videotape or memory cards and later transferred to a computer (See Figure 1.26).

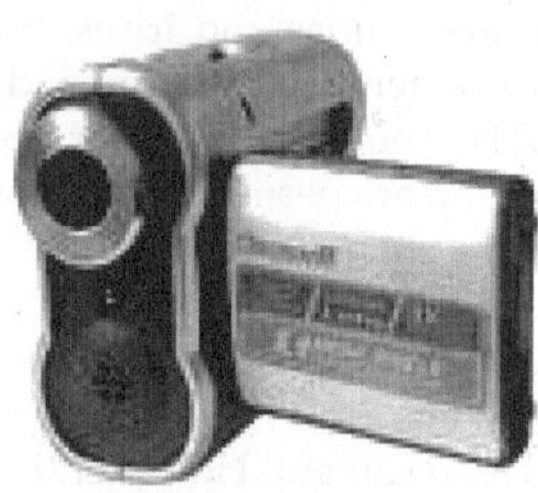

Figure 1.26 Video Camera

Advantages: Portable and more resolution compared to webcams. Rich features like zoom, video editing etc. Both the online and offline capability.
Disadvantages: Expensive as compared to webcam.

Digital Camera

A *digital camera* records and stores photographic images in digital form that can be fed into a computer as the impressions are recorded or stored in the camera for later loading into a computer (See Figure 1.27).

Figure 1.27 Digital Camera

Advantages: No film is needed and there are no film developing costs. Unwanted images can be deleted straight way. Images are already digital and can easily be transferred to a computer and edited over the Internet.
Disadvantages: Images often have to be compressed to avoid using up too much expensive memory.

1.4.2 Output Devices

Output devices are those devices of a computer system that supply information or results either in the form of hardcopy (printer) or softcopy (monitor). Some of the common output devices are as follows:

(a) Monitor
(b) Printer
(c) Plotters
(d) Multimedia Projector
(e) Speech Synthesizer
(f) Speaker

Monitor

A computer monitor, technically termed as a VDU, can be plainly described as an electronic device that transmits information from the computer onto a screen, thereby acting as an interface and connecting the viewer with the computer. An image on the monitor is created by a configuration of dots, also known as pixels. The clarity of image on the computer screen depends on three factors.

- *Resolution of Screen*–the number of pixels in horizontal and vertical direction. More the number of pixels, the sharper is the image. The common resolution of computer screen is 800x600 and 1024x768,
- *Dot Pitch*–The diagonal distance between two colored pixels on a display screen, and
- *Refresh Rate*–the number of times per second the pixels are recharged so that their glow remains bright.

They can be broadly categorized into three types. (See Figure 1.28)

Figure 1.28 Types of monitor

Cathode Ray Tube (CRT):

These monitors employ the CRT technology used most commonly in the manufacturing of television screens. A cathode ray tube is a basically a vacuum tube containing an electron gun at one end and a fluorescent screen at another end. From this electron gun, a process called thermionic emission generates a strong beam of electrons.

There are several advantages of using CRT monitors. These are:

- Firstly, these monitors are highly reliable and efficient and are capable of generating a resolution of up to 2048 x 1536 pixels, thereby providing a clear picture quality. Also, CRT monitors that are now available are capable of producing thousands of different colours.
- Secondly, CRT monitors are affordable and cost effective.
- Modern technological advancements have resulted in the development of flat screen CRT monitors that reduce the glare and are good for the eyes.

Liquid Crystal Display (LCD): Liquid crystal display, also known as liquid crystal diode, is one of the most advanced technologies available at present. Typically, an LCD monitor consists of a layer of colour or monochrome pixels arranged schematically between a couple of transparent electrodes and two polarizing filters.

At present, there are two types of LCD technologies available. These include the active matrix or TFT and a passive matrix technology. Among these, TFT technology is more secure and reliable, and generates better picture quality.

Some major advantages of using an LCD monitor include:

- These monitors are compact, lightweight, and do not consume much desk space.
- Secondly, these monitors do not consume much electricity and can even be operated by using batteries.

However, LCD monitors have certain disadvantages. These monitors are very expensive. Secondly, the image quality is not constant when viewed from different angles. An LCD monitor's resolution is always constant.

Light-Emitting Diodes (LED): LED monitors are the latest types of monitors in the market today. Like LCD, it is a flat panel display making use of light-emitting diodes for back-lightning instead of Cold Cathode Fluorescent (CCFL) back lightning is used in LCDs. Primarily, the display is of LCD only but the back lightning is done by LEDs. LED monitors use much lesser power than CRT and LCD.

Some advantages of LED monitors are:

- They produce images with higher contrast
- The lifespan and durability of LED monitors is more than CRT or LCD monitors because of the technology, the monitor panels can be made very thin
- They do not produce much heat while running

TFT-LCD Monitor

TFT-LCD (thin film transistor liquid crystal display) is a variant of liquid crystal display (LCD) which uses thin film transistor (TFT) technology to improve image quality. TFT-LCD is one type of active matrix LCD. It is used in televisions, flat panel displays, projectors, etc.

TFT-LCD has a sandwich-like structure with liquid crystal filled between two glass plates. TFT Glass has as many TFTs as the number of pixels displayed, while a Colour Filter Glass has colour filter which generates colour. Liquid crystals move according to the difference in voltage between the Colour Filter Glass and the TFT Glass. The amount of light supplied by Back Light is determined by the amount of movement of the liquid crystals in such a way as to generate colour.

1.4.3 Printer

A printer prints the output information from the computer onto a paper. Printers are generally used to print textual information, but nowadays printers also print graphical information. The print quality of the printer is determined by the resolution of the printer. Resolution is measured in dots per inch (dpi). Printers with a high resolution (more dpi) provide better quality output. Different kinds of printers are available for different types of applications (See Figure 1.29).

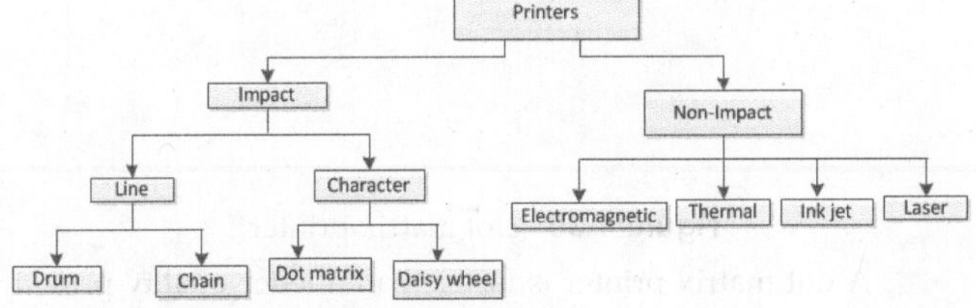

Figure 1.29 Different kinds of printers

The printers can be classified as:

(a) Impact printers
(b) Non-impact printers

Impact printers Impact printers use the typewriter approach of physically striking a typeface against the paper and inked ribbon. Impact printers can print a character or an entire line at a time. Impact printers are low-cost printers useful for bulk printing. The impact printers are further classified into the following categories:

(a) Line Printers
(b) Character Printers

Line Printers: A Line printer is a high-speed printer that prints an entire line at a time. The speed of a line printer is measured by the no of lines per minute. They can typically print the range of 1,200 to 6,000 lines per minute. Different types of line printers are–*Drum printer* and *Chain printer*.

- **Drum Printer:** An old line printer technology that used formed character images around a cylindrical drum as its printing mechanism. When the desired character for the selected position rotated around to the hammer line, the hammer hit the paper from behind and pushed it into the ribbon and onto the character.
- **Chain Printer:** Use type slugs linked together in a chain so as its printing mechanism. The chain spins horizontally around a set of hammers. When a desired character is in front of the selected print column, the corresponding hammer hits the paper onto a ribbon and onto a character in chain. It is one of the fastest impact printers that can produce up to 400 to 3000 characters per second. Chain printer also called band printers.

Character Printers (Serial Printer): A character printers print one character at a time. They are low-speed printers. Their printing speed lies in the range of 30-600 characters per second. Different types of character printers are–*Dot matrix printers* and *Daisy wheel.*

- **Dot Matrix Printer:** A dot matrix printer is the most popular serial printer (See Figure 1.30). The printhead contains a vertical array of pins. As the printhead moves across the paper, selected pins fire against the ribbon to form a pattern of dots on the paper.

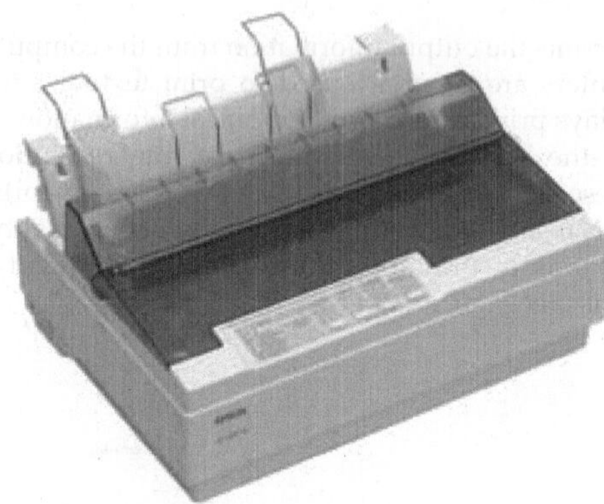

Figure 1.30 Dot matrix printer

A dot matrix printer is faster than a letter quality printer. These printers operate at two or three speeds. The lower the speed the better is the printing quality. Higher speed is for draft printing and lower speed is for Near-Letter Quality (NLQ) printing.

Advantages: In-expensive, Low per page cost, Energy efficient.

Disadvantages: Noisy, Low resolution, Limited fonts flexibility, Poor quality graphics output.

- **Daisy Letter printers:** Daisy Wheel Printers print one character at a time. They produce letter quality document which is better than a document printed by a dot matrix printer. The speed of daisy wheel printers is about 100 cps. The print head of the printer is like a daisy flower. These printers are slow, can only print text (not graphics), and are costly in comparison to dot matrix printers. Daisy wheel printers are used where high quality printing is needed and no graphics is needed.

Non-impact printers An non-impact printer prints characters and graphics on a piece of paper without striking the paper. These printers are categorized as:

(a) Electromagnetic Printer
(b) Thermal Printer
(c) Inkjet Printer
(d) Laser Printer

Electromagnetic Printer: This printer uses magnetic recording techniques. By using this technique, the required output is written on a drum surface. Then this surface is passed through magnetic powder which adheres to the charged areas. The powder is then pressed onto the paper.

Thermal Printer: This type of printer uses a special heat-sensitive paper. These papers have a special heat-sensitive coating. When a spot on the paper is heated, it becomes dark. A character is printed with a matrix of dots. These printers have a speed of 200 characters per second.

Ink-Jet Printers

Ink-jet printer is a type of non-impact printer. It creates output on paper by spraying tiny drops of liquid ink. It has print-head that can spray very fine drops of ink. It consists of print cartridge filled with liquid ink and has small nozzles in form of matrix. These printers produce better quality of text and graphics and are faster. The ink-jet printers have low price than laser printer. They are also slower and have low print quality than laser printer. However, they are faster and have high print quality than dot matrix printers. The printing speed of ink-jet printer is from 1 to 6 pages per minute. A standard ink jet printer has a resolution of 300 dots per inch (See Figure 1.31).

Advantages: Low cost, High quality of output, easy to use, No warm up time.

Disadvantages: Print head is less durable, prone to clogging and damage, Not good for high volume printing, speed is not as fast as laser printers, Expensive replacement ink cartridges.

Figure 1.31 Inkjet printer

Laser Printer

Laser printers are non-impact type printers. Laser printers provide highest quality of text and graphics printing. Laser printers process and store the entire page before printing and are also known as page printers. The laser printer can print 5–24 pages of text per minute and their resolution ranges from 400 to 1200 dpi. They are faster and expensive than impact printers. Laser printers are used in applications requiring high quality voluminous printing. They are mainly used for desktop publishing work. Figure 1.32 illustrates a laser printer.

Advantages: Fast, good image quality, reliable, durable water resistant image, excellent quality color.

Disadvantages: Expensive cartridge, single copy at a time, Expensive hardware, need warm-up time.

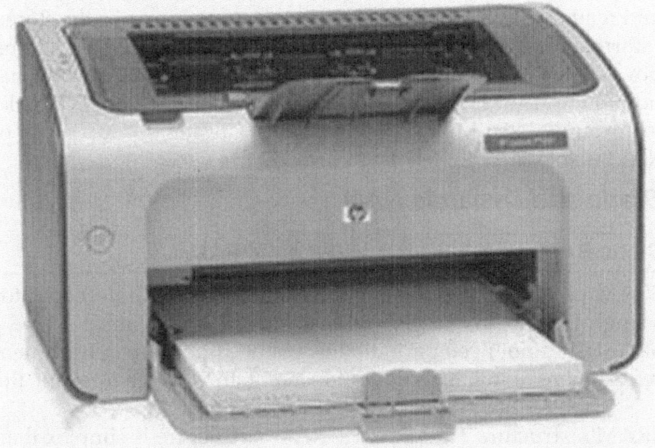

Figure 1.32 Laser printer

3D Printers

3D printing is a form of additive manufacturing technology where a three-dimensional object is created by laying down successive layers of material. It is also known as rapid prototyping and is a mechanized method whereby 3D objects are quickly made on a reasonably sized machine connected to a computer containing blueprints for the object. This method is used for creating 3D models with the use of inkjet technology saves time and cost by eliminating the need to design, print and glue together separate model parts. Now, you can create a complete model in a single process using 3D printing. The basic principles include materials cartridges, flexibility of output, and translation of code into a visible pattern.

1.4.4 Plotter

Plotters are output devices. A plotter (Figure 1.33) is used for vector graphics output to draw graphs, maps, blueprints of ships, buildings, etc. Plotters use pens of different colors (cyan, magenta, yellow and black) for drawing. Plotters draw continuous and accurate lines, in contrast to printers where a line is drawn as closely spaced dots. Plotter is a slow output device and is expensive.

Pen plotters may be classified into the following four types:

(a) Drum plotter
(b) Microgrip plotter
(c) Flat-bed plotter
(d) Inkjet plotter

Each type is used depending on the quality of graphic work needed.

1.4.5 Multimedia Projector

A Multimedia Projector is an output device connected to a PC and used to project information from a computer on to a large screen (a cloth screen or wall). The information is thus viewed by a large number of people. It is widely used for giving presentations. The presenter can directly point to, mark or edit the displayed information to make it more understandable. Audio, video, image and animation can be prepared on a PC and using a multimedia projector the presentation can be made more lively and interesting (See Figure 1.34).

Figure 1.33 Plotter

Figure 1.34 Projector

1.4.6 Speech Synthesizer

Speech Synthesizer is an output device that converts textual data into spoken sentences. To produce the speech, basic sound units called *phonemes* are combined. The sequence of words in a text are combined into phonemes, amplified and outputted through a speaker attached to a computer (See Figure 1.35).

Figure 1.35 Speech Synthesizer

1.4.7 Speakers

Speakers are hardware devices connected to a computer's sound card that outputs sounds generated by the card. A speaker makes sound by being fed on electrical signals which is changed or modulated, corresponding to the sound that is to be made. The speaker converts the changes or waves in the electrical signal to matching sound waves, which we hear. There is no volume control in the PC, since it was not intended to produce sophisticated sounds. Speakers are further attached to the system to enhance the sound quality. (See Figure 1.36)

Figure 1.36 Speakers

1.5 MAIN STORAGE DEVICES

A computer needs memory to store data. It also needs memory to perform arithmetical operations and storing programs and pictures. Computer memory is of two types: (See Figure 1.37)

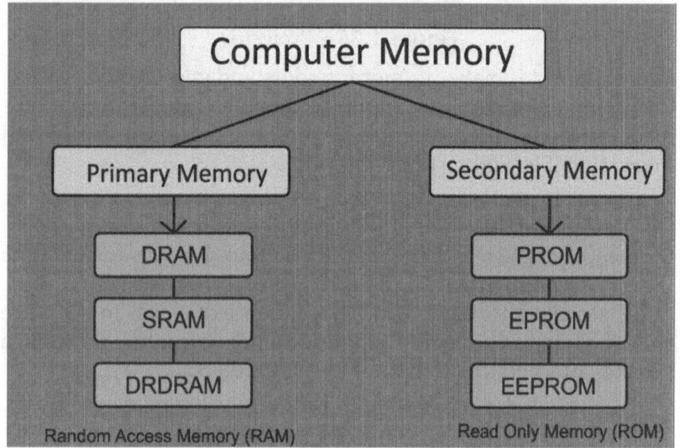

Figure 1.37 Types of Memory

(a) Primary Memory
(b) Secondary Memory

Primary storage is also called internal storage or memory. It is used to store programs and data currently being processed by CPU. Primary storage circuits like light bulbs need electricity to stay on. If the power to the computer is turned off, all the circuits will turn off and all data in primary storage will be lost. When computer is turned back on the data will not reappear. The data is lost forever.

Primary memory can be divided into the following two types:

(a) RAM
(b) ROM

1.5.1 Random Access Memory (RAM)

RAM is a read/write memory. Information can be written into and read from a RAM. It is a volatile memory. It retains the stored information as long as it is supplied with power supply. When power supply is switched off or interrupted, the stored information in the RAM is lost. RAMs of various capacities are available, for example, 256 MB, 512 MB, 4 GB, 8 GB and so on. Types of RAM is shown in Table 1.1.

Static and Dynamic RAM

Static RAM	Dynamic RAM
SRAM uses transistor to store a single bit of data.	DRAM uses a separate capacitor to store each bit of data.
SRAM does not need periodic refreshment to maintain data.	DRAM need periodic refreshment to maintain the charge in the capacitors for data.
SRAM's structure is complex than DRAM.	DRAM's structure is simplex than SRAM.
SRAM are expensive as compared to DRAM.	DRAM's are less expensive as compared to SRAM.
SRAM are faster than DRAM.	DRAM's are slower than SRAM.
SRAM are used in Cache memory.	DRAM are used in Main memory.

SDRAM (Synchronous Dynamic Ram) SDRAM (synchronous DRAM) is a generic name for various kinds of Dynamic Random Access Memory (DRAM) that are synchronized with the clock speed that the microprocessor is optimized for. This tends to increase the number of instructions that the processor can perform in a given time. The speed of SDRAM is rated in MHz rather than in nanoseconds (ns). This makes it easier to compare the bus speed and the RAM chip speed.

RDRAM (Rambus Dynamic Random Access Memory)
RDRAM (Rambus Dynamic Random Access Memory) is a memory subsystem that can transfer up to 1.6 billion bytes per second. Rambus is intended to replace the current main memory technology of Dynamic Random Access Memory (DRAM). Much faster data transfer rates from attached devices such as video-games using FireWire and the Accelerated Graphics Port (AGP) make it important to reduce the bottleneck in getting data into the computer. Direct Rambus (DRDRAM) provides a two-byte (16 bits) bus rather than DRAM's 8-bit bus. At a RAM speed of 800 megahertz (800 million cycles per second), the peak data transfer rate is 1.6 billion bytes per second. The components that are inserted into motherboard connections are called Rambus in-line memory modules (RIMMs). Such components can replace conventional dual in-line memory module.

DDR RAM Double-Data-Rate Synchronous Dynamic Random Access Memory, also known as DDR SDRAM or DDR RAM for short, is a type of very fast computer memory. DDR RAM is based on the same architecture as SDRAM, but utilizes the clock signal differently to transfer twice the data in the same amount of

Table 1.1 Types of RAM

Static RAM/ SRAM	Dynamic RAM/ DRAM	Enhanced version of RAM
Requires constant power flow to hold information	It stores its information in cell called capacitor and transistor	EDORAM Extended data output random access memory.
Expensive and faster	Less expensive and slower	SDRAM: Synchronous dynamic random access memory.
More power is required	Less power is required	DDR SDRAM: Double data rate synchronous dynamic random access memory.

Table 1.2 Types of ROM

PROM	EPROM	EEPROM
Programmable read only memory	Erasable programmable read only memory	Electrically erasable programmable read only memory
Information cannot be altered once written	Information can be changed by exposing to ultraviolet light	Information can be erased and reprogrammed by using electric charge.

time. In a computer system, the clock signal is an oscillating frequency used to coordinate interaction between digital circuits. Digital circuits designed to operate on the clock signal may respond at the rising or falling edge of the signal. SDRAM memory chips utilized only the rising edge of the signal to transfer data, while DDR RAM transfers data on both the rising and falling edges of the clock signal.

EDO RAM EDO (Extended Data Output) RAM is a type of Ran- dom Access Memory (RAM) chip that improves the time to read from memory on faster microprocessors such as the Intel Pentium. EDO RAM was initially optimized for the 66 MHz Pen- tium. For faster computers, different types of Synchronous Dynamic RAM (SDRAM) are recommended.

1.5.2 Read Only Memory (ROM)

ROM stands for Read Only Memory and it is a permanent type memory. Its contents are not lost when power supply is switched off. The user cannot write into a ROM. Its contents are written at the time of manufacturing. ROMs store permanent programs and other types of information which are needed by the computer to execute the programs. When you turn on a PC, you will usually see a reference on BIOS (Basic Input output System). This is part of the ROM chip containing all the programs needed to control the keyboard, monitor, disk drive and so on. Types of ROM is shown in Table 1.2.

Programmable ROMs (PROMs)

Programmable ROMs called PROMs are also available. Further, different types of PROMs, such as erasable PROM called EPROM, electrically erasable PROM called E^2PROM are also available. Users can write information in PROMs, EPROMS and E^2PROMs. Once programmed the recorded information into an EPROM or E^2PROM can be erased to record different information, whereas in a PROM the information once written by the user cannot be changed.

Erasable PROM (EPROM)

An EPROM is an erasable PROM. The stored data in EPROMs can be erased by exposing them to high intensity short wave ultraviolet light for about 12 minutes. When an EPROM is exposed to ultraviolet light the entire data is erased. EPROMs are cheap, reliable, and hence they are widely used. EPROMs are used to store programs which are permanent but need updating. The permanent programs which are at the research and development stage also need to be stored in EPROMs because they are modified several times. Where updating or changes in programs at the development stages are required, EPROMs are far more economical than PROMs because they can be reused. An example of EPROMs is Intel's 87C257.

EEPROM (E 2 PROM)

This is an electrically erasable PROM. The chip can be erased and reprogrammed on the board on a byte to byte basis. It requires much shorter time, a few seconds as compared to 10-20 minutes for EPROM. Intel 2816A is a 16K (2K x 8) EEPROM available commercially.

☞ *E^2 PROM requires 21 Volts pulses for writing or erasing and 5V for read operation.*

1.6 SECONDARY STORAGE DEVICES

Secondary memory is employed for bulk storage (mass storage) of programs, data and other information. It has much larger capacity than the main memory. Any data or programs stored in secondary storage stays there, even with the computer power turned off, unless someone erases them. The secondary memory is non-volatile in nature. Examples of storage devices include hard disk, CD and DVD etc.

There are two methods for accessing data from it:

1. *Sequential Access*–This is the method in which we search the data sequentially or line by line until you find the desired data. Magnetic tape is an example of sequential access device.
2. *Direct Access*–This is the method in which computer can go directly to the information that the user wants. Magnetic disks and optical disks are examples of direct access devices.

1.6.1 Magnetic Tape

Magnetic tape is a plastic tape with magnetic coating (Figure 1.38). It is a storage medium in a small cartridge or cassette (like a music cassette). Magnetic tapes are cheaper storage media. They are durable, can be written, erased, and re-written. Magnetic tapes are sequential access devices, which mean that the tape needs to rewind or move forward to the location where the requested data is positioned in the magnetic tape.

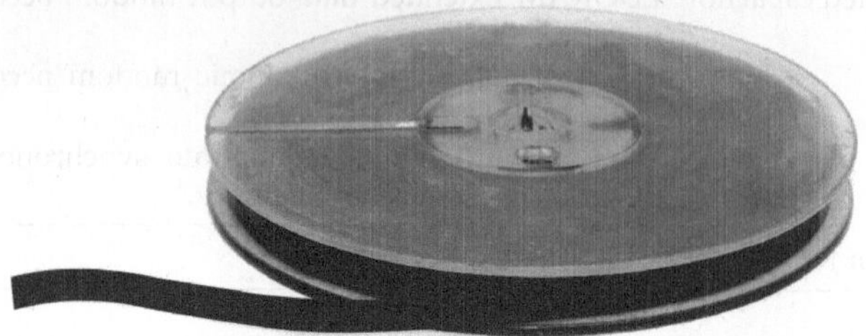

Figure 1.38 Magnetic tape

The features of magnetic tape are:

- Inexpensive storage device
- Can store a large amount of data
- Easy to carry or transport
- Not suitable for random access data
- Needs dust prevention, as dust can harm the tape

1.6.2 Hard Disk

A hard disk, or hard disk drive, consists of several inflexible, circular platters that store items electronically. A platter in a hard disk is made of aluminium, glass, or ceramic and is coated with a material that allows items to be recorded magnetically on its surface. Each platter has two read/write heads, one for each side. Because of the stacked arrangement of the platters, the location of the read/write heads often is referred to by its cylinder, which is the location of a single track through all platters. Some computers improve hard disk access time by using a disk cache, which is a portion of memory that the processor uses to store frequently accessed items. A hard disk can be divided into separate areas, called partitions, each of which functions as if it were a separate hard disk drive (See Figure 1.39).

The features of magnetic tape are:

- Hard disk is a fixed disk. The disk is not removable from the drive.
- It is a single unit.
- Hard disk can store much more data than floppy disk. The data in hard disk are packed more closely (because fast spinning uses smaller magnetic charges) and they have multiple platters, with data being stored on both sides of each platter. Large capacity hard disks may have 12 or more platters.
- The read/write head of hard disk does not touch the disk during accessing.
- Hard disk can spin at the speed of up to 10,000 revolutions per minute and have an access time of 9–14 ms. It stores 512 bytes per sector.
- Nowadays, hard disks are available that can store up to 500 GB of data. Generally, PCs come with 160 GB hard disk.

The specific functions of the storage unit are to store the following:

(a) All data and instructions to be processed,

(b) Intermediate results of processing, and

(c) Final results before sending them to output devices.

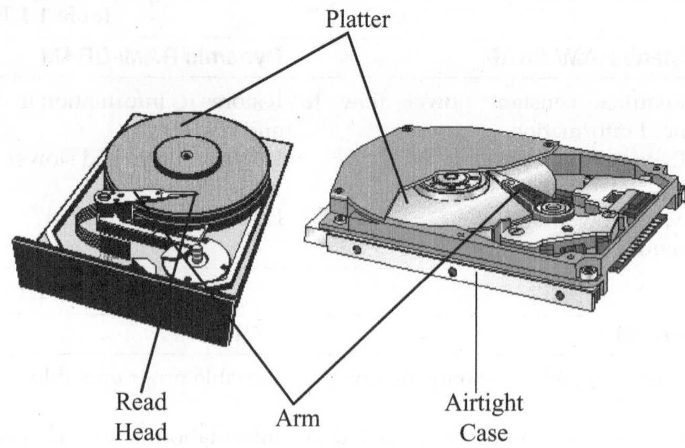

Figure 1.39 Hard disk

Hard disks are available in the capacity of 1 TB. Depending on the type of programs being used, one can store very large-sized database in these hard disks.

1.6.3 Optical Disk

It is an optical Read Only Memory (ROM). The disk is made up of a resin, such as polycarbonate. It is coated with a material which will change its reflecting property when a high intensity laser beam is focused on it. The coating material is highly reflective, usually aluminium. The high intensity laser beam forms a tiny pit along a trace to represent '1' and the surface without a pit known as 'land' represents '0'.

The main types of optical disk are CD-ROM, CD-R or WORM, CD-W, DVD-ROM, DVD-R, and DVD-W.

CD/ CD-ROM

CD stands for Compact Disk, and ROM stands for Read Only Memory. A CD-ROM disk can read an optical read-only CD-ROM disk. The CD-ROM disk is a very high capacity disk. The data stored on CD-ROM can only be read (See Figure 1.40).

Figure 1.40 Compact disk

The CD is made out of a clear piece of polycarbonate plastic. The CD has different layers that enable the CD drive to read data from the CD. The layers that make up the CD depend on the type, and the number of times that you can write data on the CD.

The basic layers of the CD are:

- Polycarbonate plastic–layer of the disc
- Aluminium–Reflects the laser beam from the CD-drive like a mirror that reflects light.
- A crylic–Protects the CD layers
- Label–Enables you to name the CD for identification.

The advantages of CD-ROM are its high storing capacity, mass copy of information stored, removable from the computer, etc. Its main disadvantages is longer access time, as compared to magnetic hard disk. It cannot be updated because it is a read only memory.

Compact Disc-Recordable (CD-R) OR WORM (Write Once Ready Many)

In CD-R (Compact disc Recordable) text once written cannot be erased. The CD-R is useful to backup data. The CD-R is also used to create music CDs that can played on music systems.

Most common CD-Rs nowadays store 700 MB information and 800 MB CD-Rs are also widely available. Maximum capacity of a CD-R nowadays is 860 MB. Actually, maximum capacity of a CD is not strictly defined, depending of production technology and the quality of the disk the maximum capacity could be pushed up to about 875 MB (See Figure 1.41)

☞ *CD-R disc are useful for backing up data that must not be modified.*

CD-Rewritable (CD-RW)

The CD-RW disk enables you to rewrite data, to the disc. The data when not required can be erased from the disc (See Figure 1.41).

The CD-RW disc are useful for transferring data from one system to another, or for storing files that are to be updated regularly .

CD-R

CD-RW

Figure 1.41

1.6.4 DVD

DVD stands for Digital Video Disk. A laser beam with a short wave length is used to create very very small holes on the surface of disk. So there are much more tiny holes on the surface of DVD as compared to that of CD. Therefore, storage capacity of DVD is much larger than CD. It can store up to 17 GB or more data.

DVD-ROM

DVD-ROM (Read Only Memory) was the first DVD standard in the market and is a read-only format. These discs cannot be written to and DVD-ROM drives are only players. It is capable of storing 4.7 GB to 17 GB and access rates of 600 KBps to 1.3 MBps. DVD-ROM drives can read audio CD's, CD-ROM's, CD-R's and CD-RW's.

DVD-RAM

It stands for "Digital Versatile Disc Random Access Memory." DVD-RAMs are writable DVDs that can be erased and rewritten like DVD-RW and DVD+RW discs.

DVD-R (DVD-Recordable)

DVD-R similar to CD-R's allow users to write on the disc once but read it may times (Figure 1.42).

DVD-RW (DVD-Rewritable)

Most writable DVD drives are DVD-RW. You can erase and read many times, because of enormous capacities, they are replacing CD technology (See Figure 1.42).

DVD-R DVD-RW

Figure 1.42

The main difference between DVD-R and DVD-RW or DVD+R and DVD+RW is that the R disc formats can only be written to once, and then it is only readable and can't be erased. While RW discs can be written to and erased many times, they are both readable and writeable.

1.6.5 Zip Drive

A *Zip drive* is a removable storage device that securely stores all your important computer data magnetically. Zip drives and Zip disks are durable, portable, easy-to-use, and extremely efficient. A zip disk of 250 MB capacity can store the same amount of data as 173 floppy disks. Zip disk are available in 100 MB, 250 MB or the 750 MB capacity. You can choose between built-in (internal) or portable (external) versions of the reliable Zip drive, depending on your needs.

1.6.6 Pen Drive/ USBFlash Drive

A thumb drive, also known as flash drive, pen drive, memory stick or USB drive is a small portable device in the shape of the thumb, which can be connected to the USB port of a computer, which stores, transfer data quickly and easily. The main components of a thumb drives is flash memory. Flash memory is a special type of memory which can retain data even when there is no current passing through it. It is somewhat like an external hard drive. They are cheap resistant and came in different size. (See Figure 1.43)

Normally pendrives are at the range of 1GB, 2GB, 4GB, 8GB, 16GB, 32 GB and 64GB available in the market like HP, Kingston, SanDisk and Transcend etc. Some of the Pen Drive comes along with built-in Anti-virus which are very helpful for the users.

Figure 1.43 Pen Drive

Advantages of Pen Drive

Pen drives offer potential advantages over other portable storage devices such as floppy disk. These advantages are as follows:

(a) It is more compact, faster, hold more data, and are more reliable due to their lack of moving parts, and more durable design.

(b) It uses the USB mass storage standard, supported natively by modern operating systems such as Windows, Linux and Unix.

To access the data stored in a pen drive, the drive must be connected to a computer by plugging it into a USB host controller built into the computer Pen drives are active only when plugged into a USB connection and draw all necessary power from the supply provided by that connection.

Cloud storage

Cloud storage is ideal for students and business as you can access all your data from any device. Your important files are encrypted, stored online and can be accessed from any of your online devices, anywhere in the world.

1.6.7 Blu-Ray Disk

A Blu-ray Disc is a high density optical disc storage medium, which is used for the storage of all high-definition digital formats like audio, video, and play-station games and so on. The name BLU-RAY is actually a combination of the colour blue and ray. Here blue refers to the blue colour of the laser that is used for its reading and ray refers to the optical ray.

1.7 MEMORY UNITS

All information in the computer is stored using electronic components such as integrated circuits. Two symbols used to represent the two binary states are 0 and 1. These are known as BITS (an abbreviation for Binary Digits). In this, 0 represents the absence of a signal, 1 represents the presence of a signal. A BIT is, therefore, the smallest unit of data in a computer.

The binary number system works like the decimal number system with the following exceptions:

- The decimal number system uses a base 10, on the other hand the binary number system uses base 2.
- The decimal number system uses digits from 0 to 9 but the binary number system uses only two digits 0 and 1. Any other digit is considered to be invalid.

Some important terms in binary number system are:

- **Bit**–A bit is the smallest unit in digital representation of information. A bit has only two values, ON and OFF where ON is represented by 1 and OFF by 0.
- **Nibble**–A group of 4 bits are referred to as a nibble. For example, 1001
- **Byte**–A group of 8 bits is called byte.
- **Word**–A word like a byte, is a group of fixed number of bits processed as a unit, which varies from computer to computer but is fixed for each computer.

The following main memory of storage units:

Byte–A byte is a unit of data that is eight binary digits (0 and 1) long (1 byte = 8 bits).

Kilobyte (KB)–A kilobyte (KB) is actually 2^{10} = 1024 bytes. or 1 KB = 1,024 bytes (Approx. 1,000 bytes and hence the name)

Megabyte (MB)–A megabyte (MB) is 2^{20} byte or 1,048,576 bytes in decimal notation. or 1 MB = 1,024 KB (Approx. 1,000 KB)

Gigabyte (GB)–A gigabyte (GB) is 2^{30} byte or 1,073,741,824 bytes in decimal notation. or 1 GB = 1,024 MB (Approx. 1,000 MB)

Terabyte (TB)– A terabyte is a measure of computer storage capacity and it is equal to the 2^{40} bytes. or 1 TB = 1,024 GB (Approx. 1,000 GB)

Petabyte (PB)–A petabyte is 2^{50} byte or approx. 1,125,899,900,000,000 bytes in decimal notation. or 1 PB = 1,024 TB (Approx. 1,000 TB)

Exabyte (EB)– A exabyte is 2^{60} byte. or 1 EB = 1,024 PB (Approx. 1,000 PB)

Zettabyte (ZB)–A Zettabyte is 2^{70} byte. or 1 ZB = 1,024 EB (Approx. 1,000 EB)

Yottabyte (YB)–A Yottabyte is 2^{80} byte. or 1 YB = 1,024 ZB (Approx. 1,000 ZB)

1.8 CONCEPT OF DATA PROCESSING

Data is a collection of facts that are to be organized and manipulated to become useful information. A collection of sales order, class attendance cards are a few examples. But, *processing* is a series of actions or operations that converts input data items into useful output information. Hence, *data processing* is defined as a series of actions or operations that converts data into information. *Data processing* comprises of the following steps:

(a) Capturing data

(b) Storing data

(c) Updating and retrieving data and other useful information

☞ *Manipulation of raw facts into useful information is called **data processing**. Data processing may be carried out using manual or electronic methods.*

1.7.2 Basic Tasks in Business Data Processing

Business data processing is the manipulation of raw facts using electronic machines. The main purpose of Electronic Data Processing (EDP) is to do complex jobs of processing at incredible speed.

Sometimes, a part of the data processing job may be done using manual methods. As an example, a class teacher may prepare the list of marks manually for further processing by a computer to award students the grades and merit position in the class. The latter part is faster and more accurate when done on an electronic machine such as a digital computer.

Since electronic machines are accurate and fast in operations as well as cheaper in price, one may prefer them over manual methods. A business data processing cycle consists of three basic steps (See Figure 1.44). These are:

(a) Input cycle,

(b) Processing cycle, and

(c) Output cycle

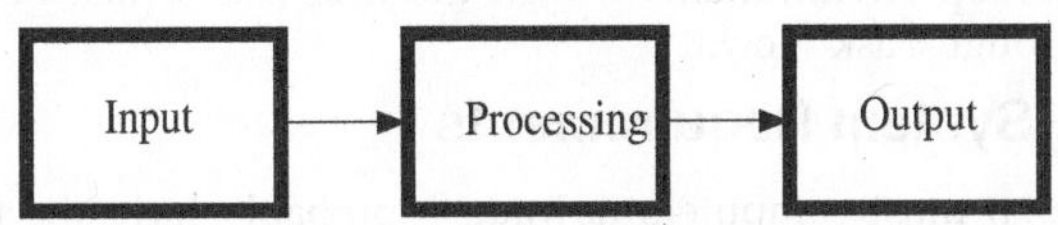

Figure 1.44 Block diagram of a basic data processing cycle

Input Cycle

In this phase, data are prepared in some convenient form and on a storage medium most suitable for entry into a processing machine. For example, in a manual system, we may prefer to write data in a tabular form on a sheet of paper such as the marks sheet of students of a class. We do so, because it is very convenient to read the marks written in tabular form. In case of electronic data processing machines, we may store data on a floppy disk or a zip disk or a compact disk.

Processing Cycle

In this cycle, we manipulate or combine the input data with other data as per the instructions. For example, in a manual processing cycle, a class teacher adds the marks secured by each student in different subjects. The teacher divides this addition by the maximum marks and calculates the percentage of marks. The teacher can also award a grade, based on the percentage of marks. In an electronic data processing system, these actions are performed automatically in accordance with a series of instructions called a *program*, which is stored in the computer. The computer will do exactly the same job as is told to it by the set of instructions or program.

Output Cycle or Managing Output

Once data are processed, the results are to be brought out in a form most suitable for the user. This is called the *output cycle*. For example, in the marks processing case, the marks of each student for each subject are transferred to print report cards. Remarks about pass/fail are also recorded on this report along with the merit and the grades. This job is done by a class teacher in a manual data processing system and by a computer using printer in an electronic data processing system.

CHAPTER 2

Introduction to Windows 10

2.1 INTRODUCTION TO WINDOWS 10

An Operating System (OS) is a software program that controls the internal activities of the computer hardware and provides user interface. Application programs need to interact with the operating system for using hardware resources.

OS is the first program loaded (copied) into the computer's main memory after the computer is switched on.

☞ *One of the primary functions of the Operating System is to provide an interface between the user and the hardware. This interface enables a user to use hardware resources efficiently.*

Windows 10 is the most recent version of the operating system from Microsoft. Officially it was released in 2015 and was initially offered free of charge to legitimate users of Windows 7 and Windows 8.1. This new version combines features from those two previous instalments to suit the users in a better way for both desktop/laptop computers as well as mobile devices. The most notable change in Windows 10 is that Microsoft replaced the Start screen tiles from Windows 8, and brought back the Start Menu. They also removed the vertical toolbars (charms) that appeared from the sides of the screen. These changes make this Windows version easier to use for users of both desktop/laptops and mobile devices.

Windows 10 expanding on Metro-style apps and these apps can be designed to run across multiple MS product families including PCs, tablets, smartphones, embedded systems, Xbox One, Surface Hub and HoloLens. The Windows user interface was revised to handle transitions between a mouse-oriented interface and a touchscreen-optimized interface based on available input devices – particularly on 2-in-1 PCs; both interfaces include an updated Start menu that blends the elements of Windows 7's traditional Start menu with the tiles of Windows 8. The first release of Windows 10 also introduces a virtual desktop system, a window and desktop management feature called Task View, the MS Edge web browser, support for fingerprint and face recognition login, new security features for enterprise environments, and DirectX 12 and WDDM 2.0 to improve the operating system's graphics capabilities for games.

☞ *Windows 10 is the latest OS version from Microsoft.*

Some Windows 10 features:

- The familiar Start Menu is back.
- The Metro interface, with its Live Tiles, is accessible from a panel to the right of the Start Menu.
- Users can toggle between touchscreen and keyboard interfaces on devices that offer both.
- The OS runs on desktops, laptops, smartphones, tablets and embedded devices.
- The final release is expected to detect touch or keyboard input and seamlessly switch apps from one to the other accordingly.
- Integrated search makes it possible for users to search all local locations as well as the Web.
- A virtual desktop feature enables the creation of multiple desktop environments, which the user can switch between through Task View.

2.1.1 System Requirements

Although most computers nowadays probably have the necessary requirements for Windows 10. It will certainly be useful to know them in case you want to upgrade from an older system. The main requirements are:

- A processor (CPU) with a clock rate of at least 1GHz.
- At least 1 to 2GB of memory (RAM), but Microsoft recommends 4GB.
- At least 16GB space in your hard disk.

☞ *The installation process itself will verify your computer hardware and let you know if it qualifies for a Windows 10 upgrade or not. If not, then you will need to upgrade your hardware.*

2.2 GETTING STARTED

Get started using Windows 10, we look at the Windows user interface elements that we encounter in every Windows session the Lock screen, the Welcome screen, the desktop, the taskbar, the Start screen, and the Start menu.

Start screen that introduced in Windows 8 and the Start menu that was in Windows 7 and previous versions of Windows have been combined and are both available, all the time in Windows 10. So, we have the choice of two Start screen configurations:

- A full-screen Start screen with the Start menu collapsed on the left side.
- A partial-screen Start screen with the Start menu always visible on the left side. The partial-screen configuration is the default.

The default Start screen configuration always displays the Start menu. In either configuration, the Start menu displays predefined content, and the Start screen displays tiles. In contrast to earlier versions of Windows in which you could add shortcuts to specific apps to the Start menu, you now choose only the types of content you want Windows to display on the Start menu, and add custom content only to the Start screen.

Once you have switched on your computer you will get a Welcome Screen with the time and date. Windows 10 lock screen (See Figure 2.1) serves three basic purposes:

- Date and time
- Network and battery status
- Notifications from a limited set of apps.

The lock screen contains a mix of Windows, user and app content.

- **Background image**: The image displayed as the lock screen background can be customized by the user through the Personalization page of PC settings. A light transparent is applied to the selected image to increase the visibility of lock screen text and icons.
- **Date and Time**: The date and time are always shown and cannot be customized.
- **Network status and battery life icons**: The network icon is always shown, but of course the battery icon is only shown for devices that have a battery.

Figure 2.1 Lock screen of Windows 10

Just click anywhere to go to the User Accounts Screen. This screen lets you choose which user you want to log in to from the lower-left corner. After choosing the right user, and entering a password if necessary, you will see the Windows Desktop (See Figure 2.2).

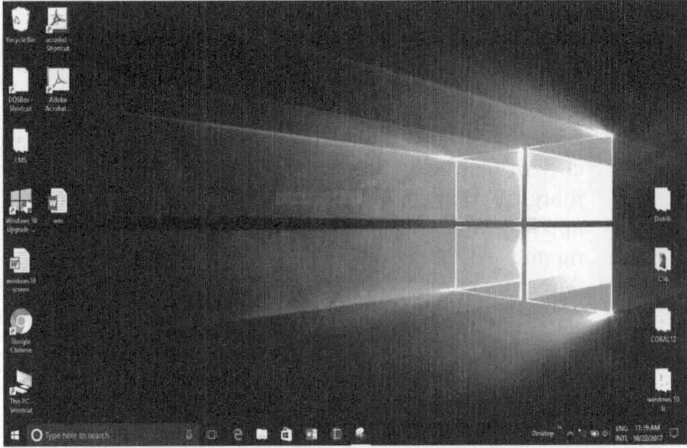

Figure 2.2 Desktop screen of Windows 10

☞ *Each time you start up your computer you will need to sign in. This is a security feature so that no one can gain unauthorized access to your account on your PC.*

2.2.1 View Account Commands

Up in the upper left is your picture and username. Click it to view commands related to your Microsoft account:

- Click the **Start** button.
- Click your user name.
- Select the desired command: Change account settings, Lock, Sign out.

Change account settings : Lets you to make changes to your Microsoft account, including your picture, password, and other options.

Lock: Locks your computer, requiring a password to use it again.

Sign out: Signs your account out of Windows, so another user can login.

The Windows Desktop is simply your operating system main screen. Here you have access to different tools like the Start Menu, Taskbar, and other icons. Windows 10 also introduces a search box in the Taskbar, which facilitates browsing both your computer and the Web.

2.3 THE DESKTOP AND TASKBAR

When you boot up Windows 10, it opens at the Desktop. This also displays the Taskbar at the bottom of the screen. Once you get to the Windows Desktop screen, here are some basic features you will see.

- Start Button
- Search Box / Cortana
- Task View Button
- Microsoft Edge
- File Explorer
- Store
- Notification Area

2.3.1 Start Button

Although Windows 8 replaced the old Start menu with the Start screen, the Start menu is back and better than before in Windows 10. The start button provides access to the apps on your Windows 10 PC and also to the enhanced Start Menu. When you click on the Start button the Start menu is displayed See Figure 2.3.

Figure 2.3 Start Menu of Windows 10

The left hand side of the Start menu contains links to frequently used apps, a list of quick links to items such as the Power button, and the alphabetic list of all the apps on the computer. The right hand side of Start menu is where apps can be pinned so that they are always available. This is displayed as a collection of large coloured tiles (square and rectangular-colored blocks called Tiles). When you clicked or tapped, it starts an app. The app will then perform a specific task such as sending and receiving email, viewing web pages, editing photographs or playing a game.
Some apps can be displayed as Live Tiles, which can show information from that app. For example, Mail messages will be summarized in the Mail app's tile, while the Weather app's tile will show your weather forecast
These tiles can be moved and dragged to different places by holding the mouse button. You can also configure them by right-clicking on them to see options to resize them or "unpin" them (remove them) from the Menu.

☞ *Other items can also be accessed from Start button by right clicking on it.*

2.3.2 Search Box/ Cortana

The "Search box" on the Taskbar will allow you to search within your documents and files or on the Web for anything you write. The initial results will appear within the Start Menu itself. The results will be grouped according to the closest match (or matches) labeled "Best match" at the top of the list. The remaining results will be grouped according to what they are or their location: Web results, Documents or folders, Apps, System settings.

Chatting with Cortana

You may notice an odd new box on the taskbar, just to the right of the Start button. That's Cortana, your new digital assistant bundled with Windows 10 See Figure 2.4. Cortana helps you find information, both on your computer and on the Internet. For example, type a few words from one of your files into the box, and Cortana should find the file and list its name, ready for you to open it with a click. Cortana should do the same if you type the name of a setting or program. Cortana also understands speech commands. Click the little microphone in the box and say your command.

Figure 2.4 Cortana in Windows 10

2.3.3 Task View

Another new feature in Windows 10 is Task View, which lets you have several desktops open. This allows you to have multiple desktop screens where you can keep open windows organized. A desktop is a set of apps that are saved on the same page. If you have a lot of apps that you're switching between, you can group them into a few different desktops and then switch between desktops instead of constantly minimizing one window.
To add a virtual desktop, follow these steps:

- Click **Task View** on the Taskbar
- Click the "**New desktop**" option on the lower-right corner. You can access or delete the new Desktop by clicking **Task View** again.

Whether you're running Windows on a PC, laptop, or tablet, you can bring any missing app to the forefront by following these two quick steps:

- Click or tap the **Task View** button. The screen clears, and Windows displays miniature views of your open apps and programs, shown in Figure 2.5.

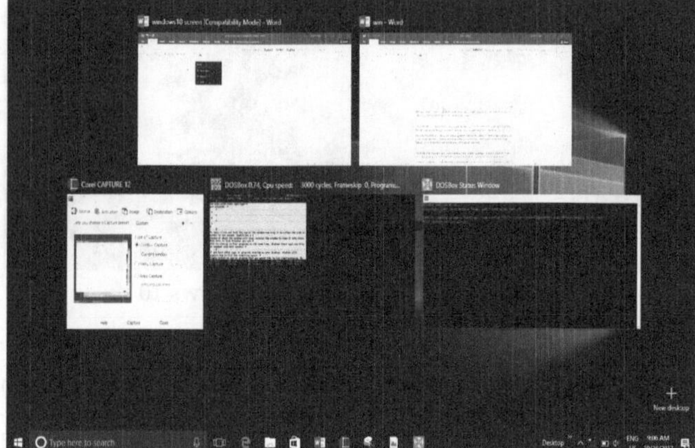

Figure 2.5 Taskview of Windows 10

- Tap or click any thumbnail to return the app or program to full size. Currently running apps and programs also appear as icons on the taskbar, the narrow strip along the bottom of the screen.
  a) To close an unwanted app shown in thumbnail view, click or tap the X in its upper right corner (shown in the margin). With a mouse, you can also right-click the app's thumbnail, and choose **Close** from the pop-up menu.
  b) After you close an app, the miniature views of the other running apps remain onscreen, letting you either switch to them or close them. Or, to leave the Task View mode, click or tap the desktop.

2.3.4 Microsoft Edge

Microsoft Edge - the new Windows 10 web browser (See Figure 2.6). By default, Edge can be accessed by clicking on the icon placed on the taskbar. When Edge opens, it presents a window similar to most browsers.
It features the following buttons:

- **Back** : Takes you to the previous web page.
- **Forward** : Takes you to the next web page.

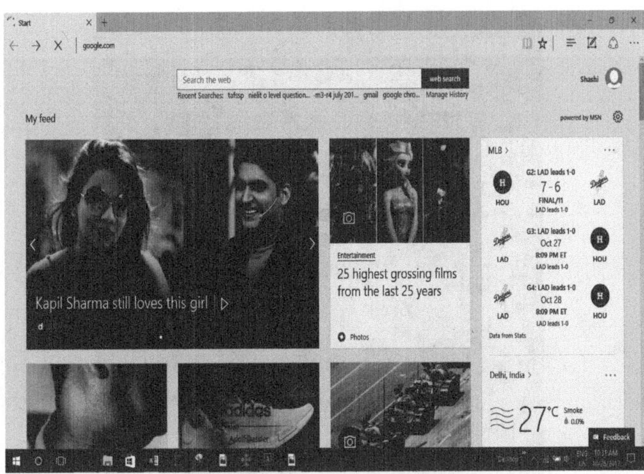

Figure 2.6 Microsoft Edge

- **Refresh** : Reloads the web page.
- **New tab** : Add another tab to see a different web page.
- **Hub (Favourites and History)** : See lists of favorite web pages and history of visited web pages.
- **Web Notes** : Make Web Notes on the web page.
- **Share** : Share the web page via e-mail or other methods.
- **More options** : See more options to configure the browser.

Use Add Favorite

Like most browsers, Edge allows you to store pages that you visit frequently as "Favourites".

To add webpage favourites do the following:

- Click the Star button.
- Specify a name and location for the webpage.
- Click Add. The webpage is added to your favourites.

You can then access your list of Favourite websites by clicking the "Hub" button on your browser. The same "Hub" button can also present you a list or "History" of web pages you have visited.

If you wish, you can clear the history by clicking on the "Clear all history" option in the menu.

Use Reading Mode

Edge also introduces a distraction-free reading mode, that takes an article and displays only the relevant text. To use Reading Mode do the following:

- Open a web page.
- Click the **Reading Mode** button to turn on Reading Mode. Now it will display no headers, sidebars, ads, or anything else to distract you from the article, just the text in a larger, easier-to-read font.
- Click the **Reading** Mode button again to turn off Reading Mode.

2.3.5 File Explorer

File Explorer - file browser (See Figure 2.7). Windows 10 adds a new feature to the File Explorer called Quick Access, that displays your frequently used folders and recent files. Quick Access replaces the favourite folders list in older versions of Windows.

File Explorer is the file management application used by Windows operating systems to browse folders and files. It provides a graphical interface for the user to navigate and access the files stored in the computer.

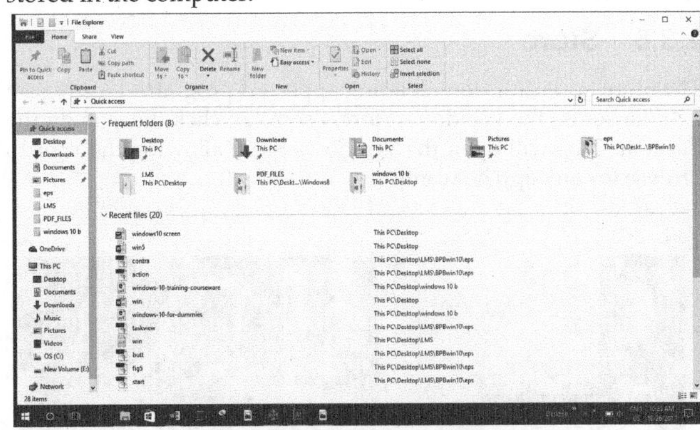

Figure 2.7 File Explorer

Let's take a look at Quick Access view:

- Click the **File Explorer Icon** on the taskbar or You can also click the **Start** button and choose **File Explorer.**

The initial File Explorer window is comprised of the following sections:

The File Explorer ribbon, which resembles the ribbon featured in Microsoft Office. The ribbon contains buttons for common tasks to perform with your files and folders.

The Navigation Pane gives you access to your libraries of documents and pictures, as well as your storage devices. It also features frequently used folders and network devices.

The Frequent folders section on the right features the folders you have worked with recently to allow for quick access to them.

The Recent files section in the lower part of the window features files and documents that you have opened recently.

In Windows 10, the File Explorer features a new ribbon toolbar, similar to the one featured in the recent versions of Microsoft Office. This ribbon contains buttons and commands for the most common tasks.

The Ribbon features four tabs, each with different commands. Among the tasks you can perform from the Home tab are:

- Copying and pasting files and folders from one place to another.
- Moving files and folders to another location.
- Copying files and folders to another location.
- Deleting a file or folder permanently or sending it to the Recycle Bin.
- Renaming a file or folder.
- Creating a new folder or other new items.
- Verifying or modifying the Properties of a document or folder.
- Opening a file or folder.
- Different options to select one or various files and folders.

You can easily pin folders to the Quick Access pane to the left. Find and select the folder you want to add to Quick Access. To pin folder to Quick Access do the following:

- Click the **Home** tab.
- Click the Pin to Quick Access button.

- The folder appears in the Quick Access group, with an icon indicating that it's been pinned.

To remove a pinned folder, right-click it and select **Unpin** from Quick Access.

2.3.6 Store

The Store app is for downloading apps and programs (See Figure 2.8). To access the Windows Store, users can click the icon on the Taskbar. This will open the Windows Store allowing the user to browse for any app he wants.

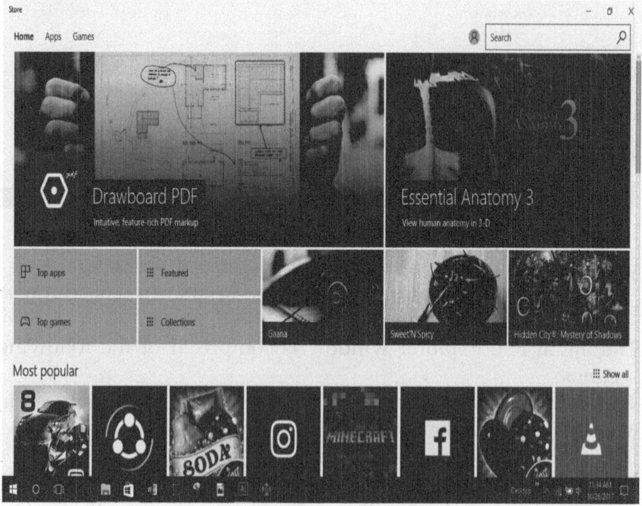

Figure 2.8 Store app

2.3.7. Notification Area

The Notification Area is located at the right side of the Taskbar. It shows different types of notifications from your computer like your Internet connection, or the volume level.

At first, the Notification Area shows a limited amount of icons. But you can click the upward arrow on its left-side to see other icons as well.

2.3.8 Opening the Action Center

The Action Center is a united place for all system notifications, such as incoming emails, and quick access to various system settings. The taskbar's right edge contains different icons. To open the Action Center

Click the **Action Center** icon, and then the Action Center pane appears, as shown in Figure 2.9.

The Action Center lists information about your latest e-mails, upcoming appointments, and other notifications. It also provides a list of four handy buttons along the bottom:

- **Tablet mode**: Click or tap this button to toggle Tablet mode. When it is colored, you're in Tablet mode, which works well only on touchscreens.
- **Connect**: This tells Windows to start searching for something you've connected, often wirelessly. Choose this after you turn on a wireless monitor or Bluetooth speaker.

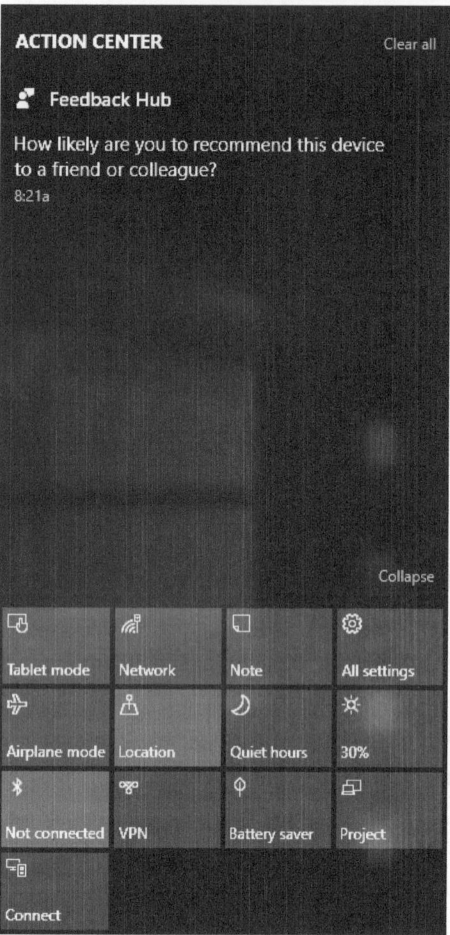

Figure 2.9 The Action Center pane

- **All Settings**: This brings up the new Windows 10 Settings app, a huge panel of organized switches, which replaces most of the Control Panel found in older Windows versions. You can also open the Settings app by clicking the Start button and clicking the word Settings.

Your Action Center may contain different buttons, based on your computer's configuration.

- **Tablet Mode** : Toggles between tablet and desktop mode.
- **Quiet Hours** : Temporarily disable notifications.
- **Battery Saver** : Turns on battery-saving features, at the cost of performance.
- **All Settings** : Opens the All Settings screen.
- **Connect** : Connect to a Bluetooth device
- **VPN** : Connect to a Virtual Private Network.
- **Bluetooth** : Manage Bluetooth devices.
- **Brightness** : Adjust your screen brightness.
- **Note** : Create a note in Microsoft OneNote.
- **WiFi** : Toggles WiFi.
- **Location** : Toggles location services on and off.
- **Airplane Mode** : Turns off WiFi and Bluetooth.

Navigation Pane

Windows gathers your PC's most frequently used items and places them in the Navigation Pane. Along the left edge of every folder, the Navigation Pane contains several main sections: Quick Access, OneDrive, and This PC. The detailed description of each part of the Navigation Pane is discussed below:

- **Quick Access**: Formerly called Favourites, these locations serve as clickable shortcuts to your most frequently accessed locations in Windows.
- **Desktop**: Your Windows desktop, is actually a folder which is always open across your screen. Clicking Desktop quickly shows you the content.
- **Downloads**: Click this shortcut to find the files which you have downloaded with Explorer while browsing the Internet.
- **Documents**: This folder stores most of your work: spreadsheets, reports, letters, and other things you have created.
- **Pictures**: This takes you to photos you shot yourself or saved from the Internet.
- **OneDrive**: This free online storage space was handed to you by Microsoft when you created a Microsoft account. Because it's password-protected and online, it's tempting to fill it with favorite files for access from any PC.
- **This PC**: This section lets you to browse through your PC's folders and hard drives.

Dismiss a Notification

You can also ignore notifications without opening them.

- Click the **Action Center** button on the taskbar.
- Click a notification's **Close** button in the upper right.

You can also click the **Clear All** button to clear all of your notifications at once.

2.3.9 Taskbar

The Windows 10 taskbar is at the bottom of the screen giving the user access to the Start Menu, as well as the icons of frequently used applications (See Figure 2.10). The icons in the middle of the Taskbar are "pinned" applications, which is a way to have a quick access to applications you use frequently. "Pinned" applications will stay in the Taskbar until you unpin them.

On the right-side, the Taskbar features the Notification Area which informs the user of different things like the state of the Internet connection or the charge of the laptop battery.

Figure 2.10 Windows 10 taskbar

2.3.10 Configure the taskbar

By default, you can move and resize the taskbar freely, but if you prefer you can lock the taskbar so that you don't accidentally drag the taskbar or its border. You can make changes to the taskbar only when it's unlocked.

When working with the taskbar, you can manage some of its features from the shortcut menu that appears when you right-click an empty area of the taskbar, some features from the Taskbar and Start Menu Properties dialog box, and some features in both places.

- To prevent or allow changes to the taskbar, On the taskbar shortcut menu, click **Lock the taskbar**. A check mark indicates that an option on the shortcut menu is active.

OR

➡ **To prevent or allow changes to the taskbar do the following:**

- Open the Taskbar and Start Menu Properties dialog box.
- On the **Taskbar** tab, select or clear the Lock the taskbar check box.
- Click **Apply** to implement the change or **OK** to implement the change & close the dialog box.

2.3.11 Move the Taskbar

➡ **To move the taskbar do one of the following:**

- Drag the taskbar to any edge of the screen.
- Right-click the taskbar, and then click **Properties**. On the Taskbar tab of the Properties dialog box, in the Taskbar location on screen list, click Left, Right, or Top (or click Bottom to return the taskbar to its default location).

2.3.12 Change the Taskbar height

➡ **To change the taskbar height, do the following:**

- Point to the inside edge of the taskbar.
- When the pointer changes to a double-headed arrow, drag the inside edge of the taskbar to change its height (or width, when vertical) to the size you want it. The height or width can be up to 50 percent of the screen height or width.

2.3.13 Pin an Application to the Taskbar

To attach or pin the application icon to your Windows Taskbar do the following:

- Search for the application you want to pin in the Start Menu.
- Right-click on the application.
- Select "**More**" option at the top of the menu.
- Select the "**Pin to taskbar**" option.

2.3.14 Unpin an Application from the Taskbar

To "unpin" it, just right-click the icon in the Taskbar and select **Unpin** from taskbar. You can pin it back again any time you want.

2.4 WORKING WITH APPS

In Windows 10 most programs are referred to as "apps". There are three clear types of apps within Windows 10. Windows 10 apps, Windows Classic apps, and windows Store apps.

- **Windows 10 apps** : Windows 10 apps are accessed from the brightly-coloured tiles on the Start menu such as communication, entertainment and information.
- **Windows classic apps** : The Windows classic apps are generally the ones that appeared as default with previous versions of Windows. The Windows classic apps can be accessed from the Start menu by using the alphabetic list, or searched from Search box of Taskbar.
- **Windows Store apps** : The Windows Store apps are accessed and downloaded from the online Windows Store.

2.4.1 Windows 10 Apps

The Windows 10 apps that are accessed from All apps list on the Start menu cover a range of communication, entertainment and information functions. The apps include :

- **Alarms & Clock**: This offers a world clock, timer, and stop-watch function. It lets you to set different wakeup times for every day of the week.
- **Calculator**: With a toggle between standard, scientific, and converter modes.
- **Calendar**: This app lets you to add your appointments and important dates.
- **Camera**: The Camera app lets you to snap photos with your computer's built-in camera or webcam.
- **Contact Support**: Click here to begin your journey through Microsoft's official technical support channels.
- **Cortana** : This is the Personal Digital Assistant for Windows 10 that can be used to search for variety of items.
- **Groove Music** : This can be used to access the online Music Store.
- **Mail**: The Mail app lets you to send and receive e-mail. You can use it to connect to email accounts.
- **Maps**: This provides online access to maps.
- **Messaging** : This is used to send text messages to other users, using a Microsoft Account.
- **Microsoft Edge**: Microsoft's new browser in Windows 10, replacing Internet Explorer.
- **Money**: This live tile opens with business headlines.
- **Movies & TV**: Microsoft's video storefront lets you to rent or buy movies and TV shows. The app also lets you watch videos you've taken with your camera or smartphone.
- **News**: This app provides real-time news, compiled from news services around the world.
- **OneDrive**: This is an online facility for storing and sharing content from your computer. You can access them from nearly any Internet-connected computer, phone, or tablet.
- **OneNote**: This popular note-taking app receives an entry on the Start menu in Windows 10.
- **People**: Windows 10's People app simply collects your friends' names and contact info.
- **Photos**: The Photos app displays photos stored in your computer, as well as on OneDrive, your Internet storage space.
- **Reader** : This can be used to open and view documents in different file formats such as PDF and TIFF.
- **Settings**: This takes you to the new Windows 10 Settings app, which contains almost all of the settings found in the Control Panel from earlier Windows versions.
- **Sport** : This app provide real-time sports news. You can add listings for your favorite sports teams.
- **Sticky Notes** : This is an app for creating short notes that can be stuck to the screen, so they are easily visible.
- **Store**: The Windows Store is the only way to add more apps on your Start menu. The Windows Store also carries some programs you can install on your Windows desktop.
- **Weather**: This weather station forecasts a week's worth of weather in your area.
- **Xbox**: Microsoft's Xbox One video game console, lets you track high scores ,chat with other gamers, view your achievements, and visit the Store app to buy more games.

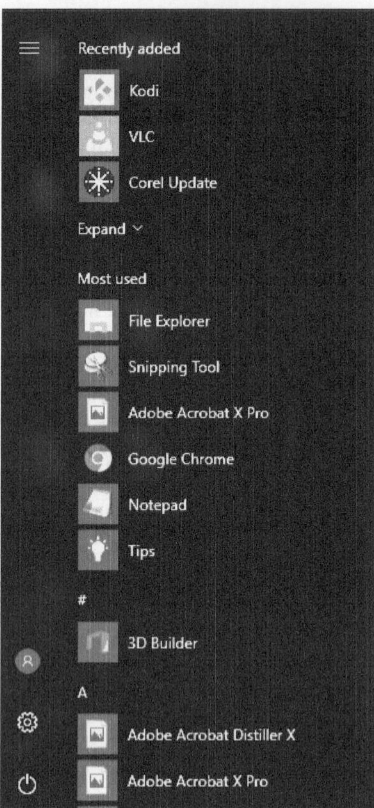

Figure 2.11 Different App list

Windows 10 offers you multiple ways to access your applications. Like discussed earlier, one of the most basic ways is to open the Search menu and click All Apps. This will present an alphabetical list of all the applications installed in your computer. If there is an application that was recently installed, it will be labeled as "New" in the menu.

The Start menu can also display different app lists (See Figure 2.11) as shown below:

- Most Used app list on a new Windows 10 installation, this list contains links to some standard Windows utilities, or to apps that were selected by the computer manufacturer. As you use Windows, the apps you use most often that aren't pinned to the Start screen appear in this list.
- Recently Added app list. This list displays apps for a short time after you install them. If no apps have been installed recently, the Start menu doesn't display the Recently Added list heading.
- Recently opened items When this setting is turned on, you can quickly access files that you've opened with apps that support this feature (such as Microsoft Office apps) from the Start menu or taskbar.

2.4.2 Manage Start screen tiles

The Start screen content is displayed in the form of tiles. Each tile is actually a shortcut to something else-usually an app, but tiles can also link to other things, such as folders in File Explorer or individual songs in your Groove Music library. You can add tiles to the Windows 10 Start screen by pinning shortcuts to it, including shortcuts to apps, files, folders, web links, contact cards, songs, movies, and pictures-almost anything you want to get to quickly.

Tiles are square or rectangular, and can be set to four different sizes: Small, Medium, Large, and Wide. All tiles support the Small and Medium sizes. App tiles also support the Wide and Large sizes, which are most appropriate for apps that display information (other than the app name and/or icon) on the tile that you want to see.

When you pin an item to the Start screen, the new app tile defaults to the Medium size and appears at the bottom or far right of the Start screen. Tiles for some Windows Store apps that provide access to frequently updated information (such as news, weather, traffic, stock market data, messages, social media network updates, and calendar events) can display and update content directly on the Start screen. These are called live tiles. Some apps even permit you to pin multiple live tiles that display different data to the Start screen. The content displayed on a live tile can come from an online source, such as a news service, or from a local source, such as your Pictures folder.

Configure the Start screen and Start menu

To display or hide app lists on the Start menu:

- Open the **Settings** window.
- Click **Personalization**, and then on the Personalization page, click **Start**.
  a) Click Show most used apps to turn off or on the Most Used list.
  b) Click Show recently added apps to turn off or on the Recently Added list.

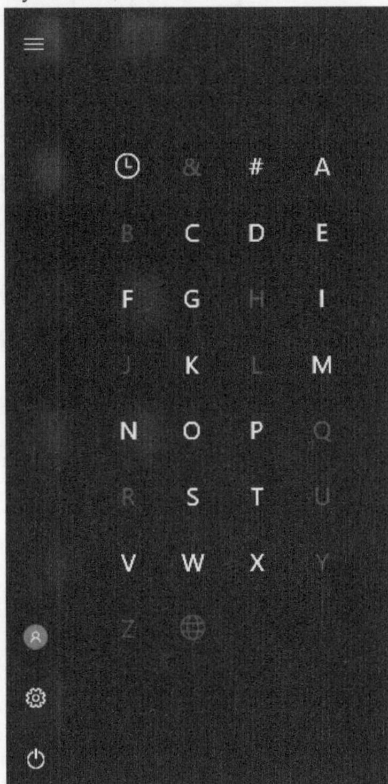

Figure 2.12 An alphabetic grid for finding apps

2.4.3 Uninstalling Applications

There are three ways in which you can remove an unwanted application:

- From the Start Menu
- From the Settings window
- From the Control Panel

To uninstall an Application from the Start Menu, do this:

- Open the **Start Menu** and click on **All Apps**.
- Find the application you want to uninstall on the list, and right-click on it.
- On the menu, choose **Uninstall**. After this, follow the steps needed to complete the process.

To uninstall an Application from the Settings window, do this:

- Open the **Start Menu** and click **Settings**.
- On the SETTINGS window, choose **System**.

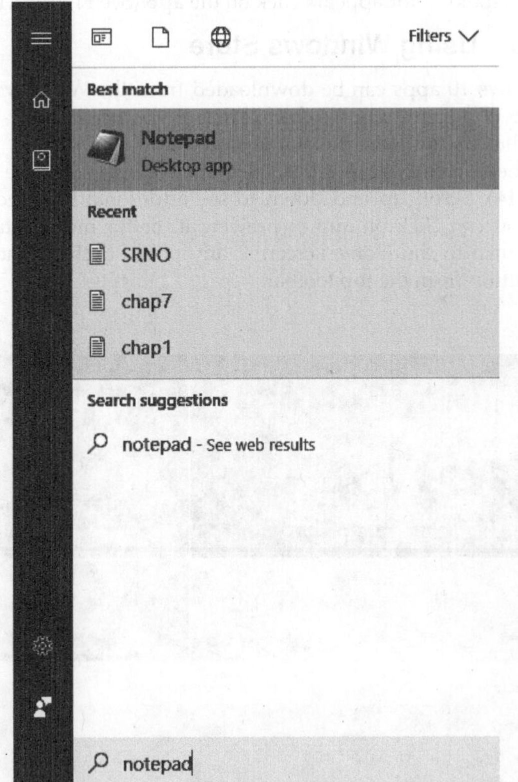

Figure 2.13 Relevant apps are displayed

- On the SYSTEM window, choose **Apps & features**.
- On the Apps & features window, search for the application you want to uninstall in the search box.
- From the displayed results, click on the application and choose **Uninstall**.

To Uninstall Applications from the Control Panel, do this:

- Open the **Control Panel** by searching for it in the Search bar.
- After the Control Panel is open, choose **Programs and Features**.
- The Programs and Features window will present a list of all the applications installed in your computer. To uninstall an application, just click on it and use the **Uninstall** button.

2.4.4 Viewing All Apps

To access all types of Apps, do the following:

- Click on the **Start** button.
- All of the apps are displayed. Use the scroll bar to move through all the apps which are used alphabetically.
- Click on the **letter heading** to view an alphabetic grid for finding apps. (See Figure 2.12) Click on a letter to move to that section.

2.4.5 Searching for Apps

To search any app by using search box of Windows 10, it lets us to search notepad through search box.

- Click in the **Search box** on the Taskbar.
- Enter a word in the search box say *Notepad*.
- As you type relevant apps are displayed. When the one you are looking for appears click on the **app** (See Figure 2.13).

2.4.6 Using Windows Store

Windows 10 apps can be downloaded from the Windows Store. To use Windows store, do the following

- Click on the **Store** tile on the **Start menu.**
- The currently featured apps will be displayed. (See Figure 2.14). Scroll up and down to see additional featured apps. You can click on app to preview it, or for more details. To return to the Home screen at any point, click on the home button from the top toolbar.

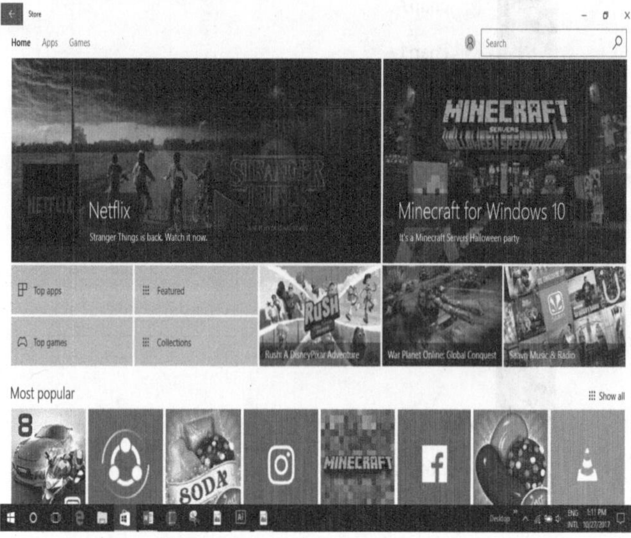

Figure 2.14 Currently featured apps are displayed

2.4.7 Closing Apps

There are several ways to close a Windows Apps, these are discussed below:

- Click on the **Close** button. Or
- Select **File -> Exit** from **File menu.** Or
- Press Alt + F4 keys Or
- Right click on the icon on the Taskbar and select **Close** Window.

If you have not saved your document warning message appears to save your associated file will be displayed.

2.4.8 Buying Apps

Required apps can be downloaded from the internet by paying some price for the app if there is a fee for an app, or downloaded free from the store. To download app do the following:

- Access the app and click on Free or Price button from the windows Store. The downloading message will be displayed.
- The app is added to the Start menu and has a New tag next to it. This disappears once the app has been opened.
- Click on the app to open and use.

2.4.9 Using Live Tiles

Before any of the Windows apps have been used, they are depicted on the Start menu with tiles of solid color. However, once you open an app it activates the Live Tile feature. The apps with Live Tile functionality include Mail, People, Calendar, photos, Groove Music, News, Spot and Money. This enables the tile to display real-time information from the app, even when it is not the app currently being used. This means that you can view information from your apps, directly from the Start menu.

➡ **To use Live Tiles, Do the following:**

- Right-click on the tile to select it. If it has Live Tile functionality, Click on **More -> Turn Live tile on** to activate this feature.
- Live Tiles display real-time text and images from the selected apps. These are updated automatically when there is any information available.
- To turn off the Live Tile, right click on the tile to select it and click on **More -> Turn live tile off**.

2.5 BASIC CONTROLS

2.5.1 Menus

Traditionally, Windows have a tabbed Menu bar near the top displaying the menu options relevant to that particular window. For app such as Notepad and Calculator, the Menu bar consist of tabbed drop-down menus. (See Figure 2.15).

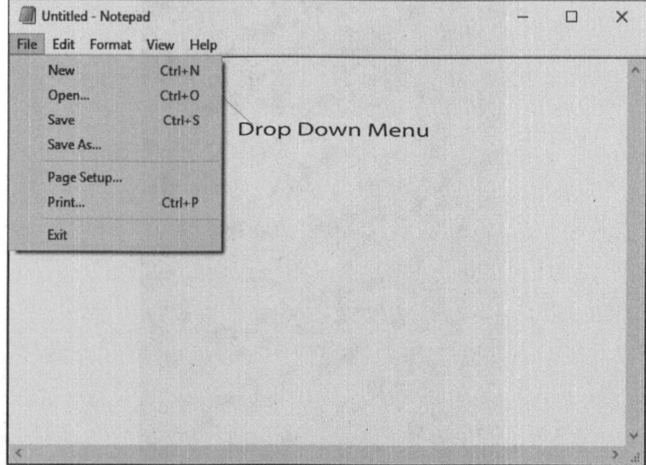

Figure 2.15 Tabbed drop-down menu of notepad

For Windows apps, such as Wordpad there is a ribbon called Scenic Ribbon at the top of window with Menu bar tabs (See Figure 2.16). If an option is grayed (dimmed-out), it is not available for use at this particular time. To maximize screen space, the ribbon automatically hides when it is not being used. However, you can click the arrow in the upper-right corner to keep the ribbon visible.

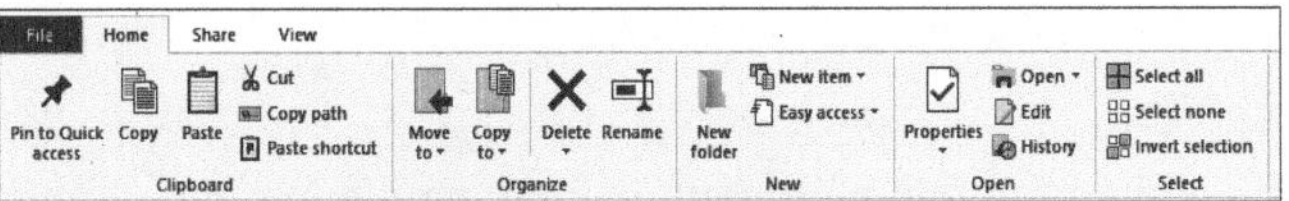

Figure 2.16 Scenic Ribbon

2.5.2 Dialog Boxes

A Dialog box will appear when you select a command with ellipsis(...) after it. Dialog boxes appear when Windows or its Application program needs more information to execute the command. Dialog boxes often have several sections in them. You can move between the sections in following ways:

- By clicking on the section you want to change.
- Using the keyboard, you can press the Tab key to move between sections and press the Spacebar to select them.

The dialog boxes have following types of sections where you need to enter information

- Tabs
- Check boxes
- Option buttons
- Command buttons
- List boxes
- Sliders
- Spinners

Tabs

Some dialog boxes are divided into two or more tabs (grouped options) Only one tab can be viewed at a time.

Check Boxes

Check boxes are small square boxes. Each check box is independent of all other check boxes in the dialog box. To select a check box item, click the box or anywhere in the text next to the box and similarly, to deselect repeat the same procedure. A check box when selected displays an (×) or (✔) within the box. Some check boxes have three states — *checked, unchecked,* and *partly checked*. A gray (in place of a black) check mark means that certain condition applies to it and some of the selections do not apply.

Option Buttons

Option buttons are also called *radio buttons* and present a set of mutually exclusive options. Option buttons are always present in groups of two or more and may either be round or diamond shaped. You may select any one option from the group, but not more than one. To select the option click the button or any where in the text next to the button.

Command Buttons

Command buttons are like option buttons and are used to execute a command immediately. They are rectangular and not square or circular in shape. An example of a command button is the OK button found on almost every dialog box.

List Boxes

A List box presents a list of options or items from which you can select. To make a selection from a list box, using the mouse, click on it or using the keyboard highlight the desired option and then press Enter to choose it.

Sliders

A slider works like a sliding control. Moving it in one direction increases some value, moving it in the other direction decreases the same value.

Spinners

A spinner is a pair of arrows used to increase or decrease the value in a text box. To increase the value in the text box, click the up arrow and to decrease the value click the down arrow.

2.5.3 Working with Multiple windows

To manage multiple open windows on the desktop is to size them so that you can see all of them at one time. Similarly, if two windows overlap each other and making it hard to read what is in other windows, in that case, you can also move the windows around or resize them. The window you choose appears in the foreground and becomes the active window.

Here, the most common ways to manage multiple open windows:

- **Minimize to the Taskbar**: You can minimize any maximized window to the taskbar. So it removes from the desktop. After it is removed (minimized), you can see the windows that were previously underneath it.
- **Shake the windows to keep**: To remove all but one window from the desktop and minimize the others to the taskbar, click, hold, and then shake the top of the window you would like to keep, the other windows will fall to the taskbar.
- **Resize a window**: You can resize a maximized window by dragging the window downward by the top-center part of the title bar. When it is in restore mode, you can drag from the corners of the window to control its size.
- **Snap a Window to Take up half the screen**: You can also double-click the title bar at the top of a window to have the window fill to the height of the screen without changing the width. You can also drag from the top part of most windows to the left or right of the screen to snap it into place so that it takes up half the screen.

If you have several windows open on your Desktop and you want automatically rearrange them neatly, rather than resize and move each one individually , use the Cascade or Tile options.

- Right click on the clear area of the Taskbar to display a context menu and select one of the arrangement options.
- Cascade windows overlaps all open windows revealing the Title bar areas and resizing the windows equally.
- Show window stacked resizes windows equally and displays them across the screen in rows.
- Show windows side by side resizes windows equally and displays them across the screen in columns.

Peek Function

When you have a number of windows open on the Desktop, you might wish to see what is hidden underneath. For this, Windows 10 offers Peek function. You can view your open windows on the taskbar by using Peek.

Right click on the Show desktop area and select Peek at desktop (See Figure 2.17). To see the thumbnail preview of the open window, do this:

- Move the mouse pointer to the Taskbar icon of the window you want to see the preview.
- A small picture of the window called thumbnail appears.
- Hover the mouse over the window in the thumbnail preview. A full-sized version of the window will appear.
- Click the X to close the window from Peek view.

Select the Show desktop option to show just the desktop when the cursor is moved over the Show desktop area.

☞ *The Show desktop area is on the Taskbar, next to the Notification center button.*

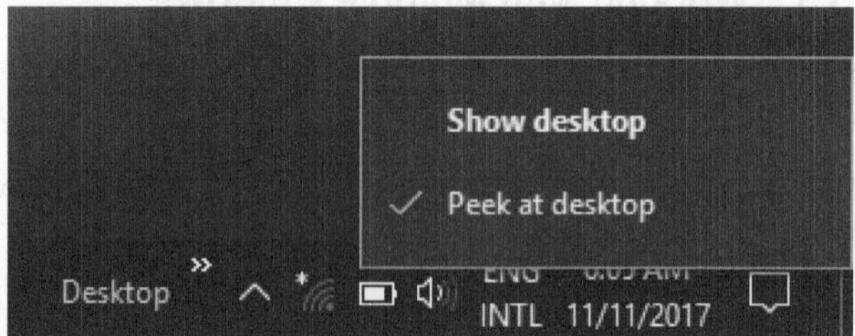

Figure 2.17 Peek at desktop option Selected

2.6 CUSTOMIZING WINDOWS

2.6.1 Using Themes

Desktop themes are the combinations of backgrounds plus sets of sounds, icons, and other elements that help in personalizing the desktop and the operating environment. The Personalization window is one of the most powerful and useful features of Windows 10. The settings which are related with computer or desktop is the personalize properties. These properties include desktop background, screen savers, window colors, font, etc. Personalize properties can be set through Personalization window.

Applying and Removing Themes

In Windows 10 several types of themes are available. Some themes are installed with the operating system. To apply a theme, do this:

- Open the Control Panel by right-click on the **Start** button and click on Control Panel from menu.
- Click on **Change the theme** underneath the Appearance and Personalization button. This will show the Personalization window on the screen as shown in Figure 2.18.
- Select the theme list you want to use.
- If you want to use a theme from the Microsoft website, click **Get More themes online** to open the Microsoft website in your default browser.
- To use an online theme, select it, and then click **Save theme**. When prompted, select a save location in your hard disk.
- The lower portion of the Personalization provides appearance for the selected theme. To change one of these items, click it.

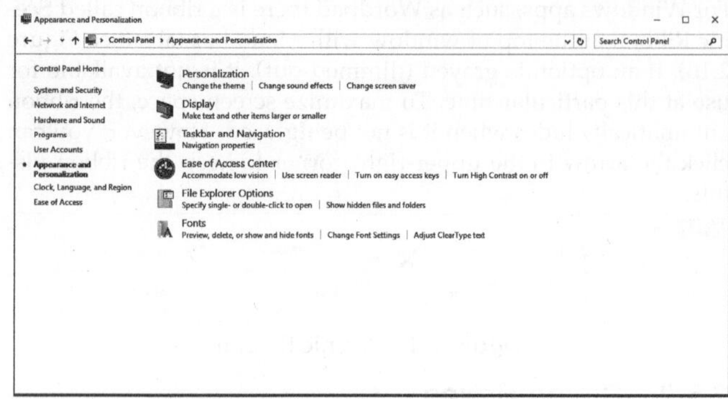

Figure 2.18 Personalization window

Changing Sound

To change sound effects do the following:

- Open the Control Panel by right-click on the **Start** button and click on Control Panel from menu.
- Select **Change sound effects** from Appearance and Personlization, to see the name of the sound theme which gets applied to events in Windows. (See Figure 2.19)
- Select a Program Event and Click the Test button to hear the associated sound. If you do not want to have sounds associated with Windows events, Select No Sounds from the options in the drop-down list.

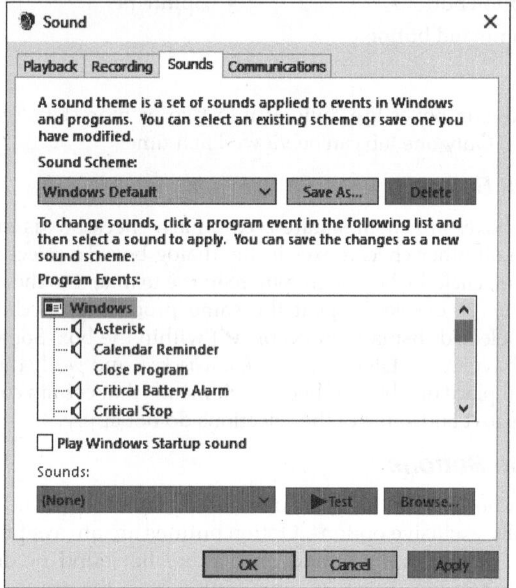

Figure 2.19 Sound Dialog box

Screen Saver

A screen saver is a picture or animation that covers your screen and appears after your computer has been idle for a specific amount of time that you set. You can configure your screen saver to require a password on waking up for extra security. To set the screen saver, do this:

- In Appearance and Personalization window, click on **Change Screen Saver.**

- Screen Saver Settings dialog box appears as seen in Figure 2.20.
- In this dialog box, select the desired screen saver from the drop down list of Screen Saver section.
- You can also set the time in Wait: spinner box under the Screen Saver section.
- To see the preview of the selected screen saver, click on **Preview** button.
- Click the On resume, display logon screen check box to ensure that anyone who interrupts the screen saver can see your work only if he/she know your password.
- To apply all the settings, click on the **Apply** button and then click on the **OK** button to close the dialog box.

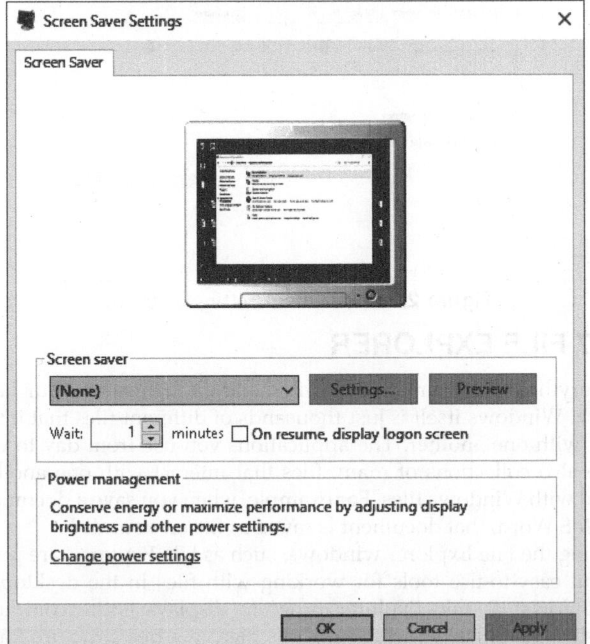

Figure 2.20 Screen Saver Setting dialog box

Desktop Icons

In Windows 10, by default, the Recycle Bin is added to the desktop. Double-clicking the Recycle Bin icon opens a window where you can view files and folders that you have marked for deletion. Other common desktop icons you can add to the desktop are as follows:

Computer: Double-clicking the Computer icon opens a window where you can access hard disk drives and devices with removable storage. Right-clicking the Computer icon and choose Manage to open the Computer Management window. Also clicking on Map Network Drive enables you to connect to shared network folders. Selecting Disconnect Network Drive enables you to remove a connection to a shared network folder.

Control Panel: Double-clicking the Control Panel icon opens Control Panel, which provides access to system configuration and management tools.

Network: Double-clicking the Network icon opens a window where you can access the computers and devices on your network.

User's Files: Double-clicking the User's Files icon opens your personal folder.

To choose which of the system icons appear, enter Desktop icons into the Control Panel Search box and click on the Show or hide common icons on the desktop link. See Figure 2.21.

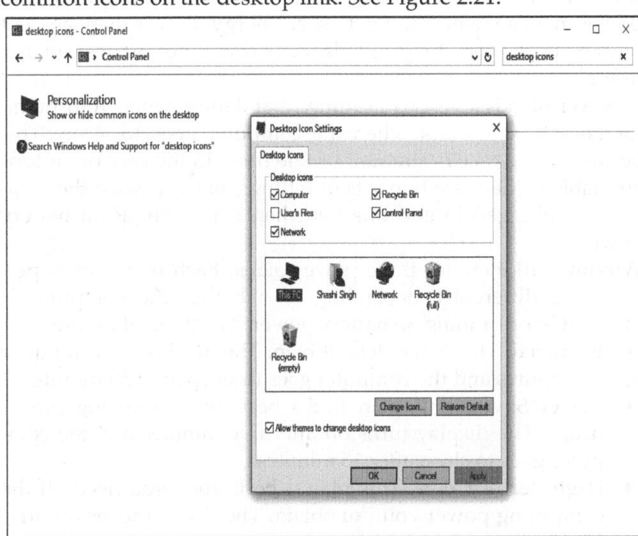

Figure 2.21 Desktop Icon Setting Dialog box

Select the check box for each (five system folders :Computer, User's Files, Network, Recycle Bin and Control Panel) that you want to add to the desktop, or clear the check box for each icon that you want to remove from the desktop. If check mark appears it means option is ON otherwise option is OFF.

- Select or clear the boxes to show or hide icons as required, then click Apply and OK to confirm the changes.

To control the display of icons on the Desktop, do the following:

- Right-click on the Desktop, click **View** and select **Show desktop icons**. A check mark is added. See Figure 2.22

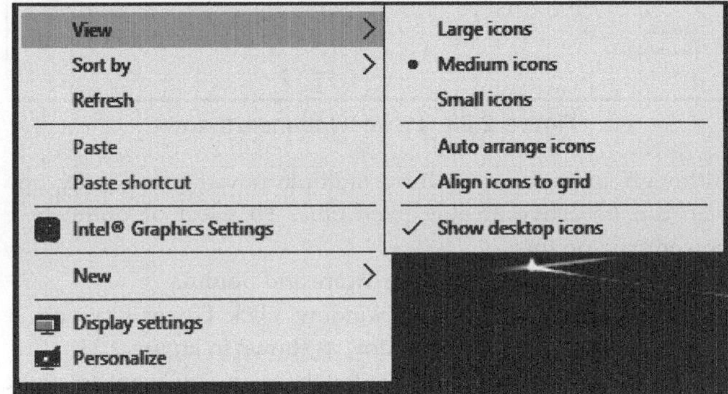

Figure 2.22 Show Desktop Icons View menu

- To resize the icons, display the **View** menu and click Large icons, Medium icons or Small icons.
- To remove the check mark and hide all the icons, display the **View** menu and select Show desktop icons again.

Configuring Power Management Settings

Power management settings control the behaviour of a computer in different power use situations, such as when it is plugged in or running on a battery. All computers should be configured with power management settings to save energy. Power management settings on laptops help to balance performance against energy usage.

A power plan is a group of settings that defines when your monitor goes to sleep and when the computer goes to sleep. This occurs after a specific amount of idle time. In the case of laptops and tablets, there are two sets of settings, one for when the computer is plugged in and one for when it is running on battery power.

Windows 10 includes three power plans. Each one adjusts performance differently depending on whether the computer is plugged in or running on battery power. The three plans are:

- **Balanced**: This is the default plan. The display turns off after 10 minutes and the computer goes to sleep after 30 minutes.
- **Power Saver**: This plan is the best for minimizing power usage. The display turns off after five minutes and the computer goes to sleep after 15 minutes.
- **High Performance**: This plan is best when you need all the computing power you can obtain. The display turns off after 15 minutes and the computer never goes to sleep.

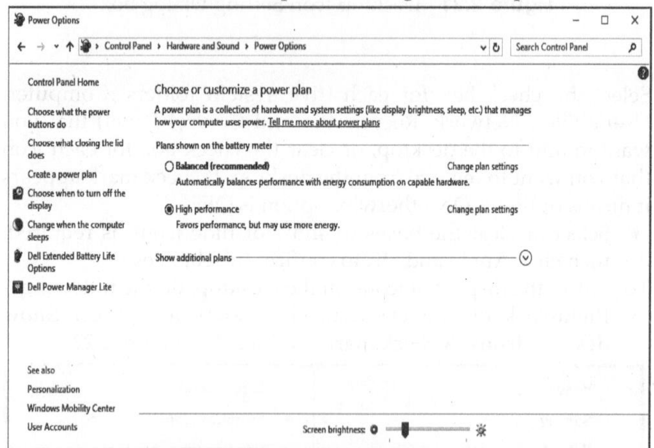

Figure 2.23 Power Options window

Although computers can have multiple power plans, only one plan can be active at any given time. To select or optimize a power plan, do this:

- In Control Panel, select **Hardware and Sound**.
- In Hardware and Sound window, click **Power** Options. It shows Power Options window as shown in Figure 2.23.
- Click **Change plan settings** for the plan you want to work with. It displays the Edit Plan Settings window as shown in Figure 2.24. Note that Laptop computing devices have separate On battery and Plugged in settings.
- Use the Turn off the display: list to specify whether or when the computer's display automatically turns off. Choose Never to disable this feature.
- Use the Put the computer to sleep: list to specify whether or when the computer automatically enters sleep mode. Choose Never to disable this feature.
- If you have made changes to Turn off display or Sleep, click Save Changes to save these changes.

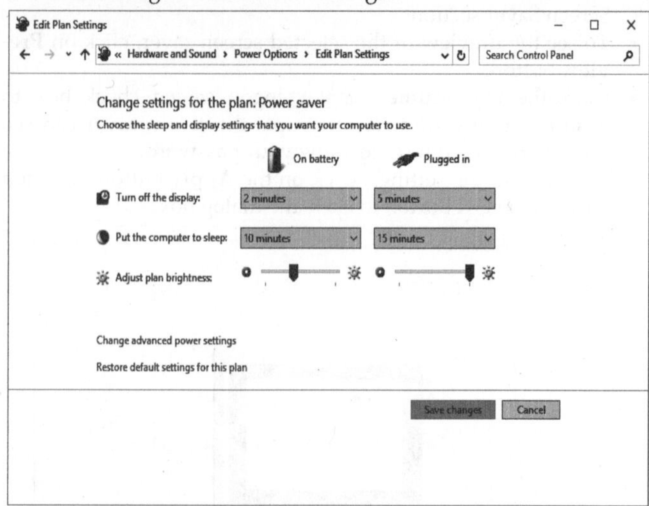

Figure 2.24 Edit Plan Settings window

2.7 FILE EXPLORER

Everything on your computer is made up of files on your hard disk. Windows itself is just thousands of different files that interact with one another. The applications you use from day to day are also collections of many files that interact with one another and with Windows files. For example, when you save a document in MS Word, that document is saved as file on your disk.

Using the File Explorer windows, such as File Explorer, are powerful easy-to-use tools for working with files in the desktop in Windows 10. File Explorer program displays entire computer system graphically including all its files, in a tree structure form. It includes a ribbon in place of the command bar. With Explorer, you can access every data inside computer hard disk.

To start File Explorer, do this:

- To open File Explorer, click the **File Explorer** icon on the taskbar. (It looks like a yellow folder.) See in Figure 2.25.

Figure 2.25 File Explorer icon on Taskbar

- File Explorer window will opened. Click on the **This PC** option to view the top level items on your hard drive and any removable devices that are connected. See in Figure 2.26.

2.7.1 Libraries

A library is a virtual folder that contains links to actual folders located on your system or on a network. When you view a library in File Explorer, the contents pane displays every file and folder contained in the locations that are a part of that library. You can browse your files the same way you would in a folder or you can view your files arranged by properties like date, type, and author. Different libraries are defined below:

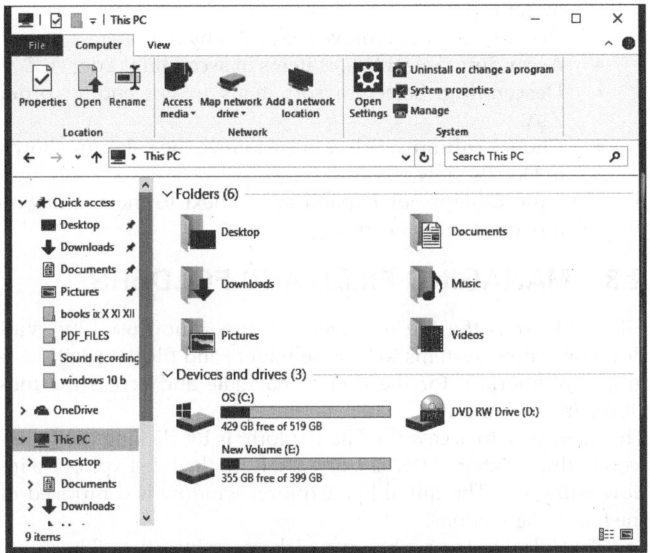

Figure 2.26 File Explorer window

- **Camera Roll** : This is the default folder for photos captures on your computer, if it has a camera attached.
- **Documents**: This library is used to organize and arrange default folders for files such as word processing documents, spreadsheets, presentations, and other text-related files.
- **Pictures**: This library is used to organize and arrange digital pictures.
- **Music**: This library is used to organize and arrange digital music whether it open from an audio CD or downloaded from the Internet.
- **Video**: This library is used to organize and arrange videos which are clips from digital camera, camcorder, or video files downloaded from the Internet.

☞ *In Windows 10 the Libraries are not visible by default. To show them, click on the Navigation pane button and click on the Show libraries button so that a tick appears.* (See Figure 2.27)

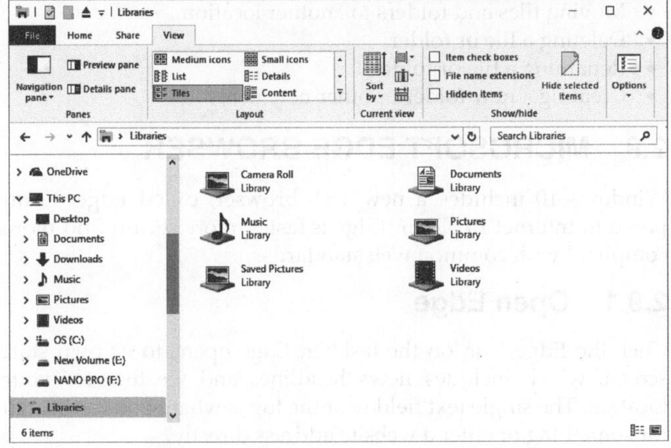

Figure 2.27 Navigation pane button

Elements of Folder or Library window

File Explorer give you more information and control how you work with your files. When you open a folder or library, you see it in a window. The various elements of this window are designed to help you navigate around Windows or work with files, folders, and libraries more easily. Each Explorer includes the following elements. These are:

Toolbar : Toolbar Use to access frequently used commands, such as the Quick Access Toolbar.

Scenic Ribbon : Use to access buttons or options organized in groups on tabs. The Scenic Ribbon is also referred to as just the Ribbon.

Address bar :Address bar is used to navigate to a different folder or library or to go back to a previous one. It also shows you where you are and helps you get where you want to go.

Back, Forward and Up buttons: Back, Forward and Up buttons are used to navigate to other folders or libraries you have already opened without closing the current window.

Navigation pane : Navigation pane appears at the left side of window. You can also use the navigation pane to access libraries, folders, saved searches, and even entire hard disks.

Search box : Type a word or phrase in the search box to look for an item in the current folder or library. The scope of search is restricted to the current location and displays search results immediately in the contents pane. The width of the search box can be adjusted by dragging its left edge in either direction.

Libraries : Use to access common folders, such as Camera Roll, Documents, Music, Pictures, Saved Pictures and Videos. A library is a collection of files and folders linked from different locations, including your PC computer

Status bar : Displays number of items and selected items in a folder, and Details and Icons view buttons.

This PC Folder

You can access the "This PC" Folder window from File Explorer. The Computer window displays several types of local, removable, and network drives. Drives and folders are represented by icons. Each drive is assigned a drive letter, denoted with parentheses and a colon, such as Local Disk (C:), to make it easier to identify. If your PC computer includes additional drives, your PC computer assigns them letters in alphabetical order. Once you open more than one drive or folder, you can use buttons on the Ribbon to help you to move quickly between folders.

To open and view This PC folder, do the following:

- Open File Explorer and select **This PC** in the Navigation pane.
- Select items and double-click to view their contents. Select the right-pointing arrow next to heading level, to expand that entry to the next level and select down-pointing arrow to collapse the entries to that heading level.

Navigation Panes

The normal view for File Explorer includes the Navigation pane. There is also a Preview pane and a Details pane available. You can choose different panes to display:

- Open File Explorer and click on **View** tab. This will open the Ribbon.

- The Pane options are located at the left-hand side of the Ribbon.
- Click on the **Navigation Pane** button to view this format. This appears down the left-hand side.
- Click on the arrow on the Navigation pane button and click here to show or hide the Navigation pane. There are also options for showing or hiding the libraries.
- Click on the **Preview pane** button to view a preview of the folder or file selected in the main window.
- Click on the Details pane button to view additional information about the folder of file selected in main window.

2.7.2 Sorting and Grouping Files

In Explorer windows, files and folders appear sorted or grouped by different attributes, such as name or type, in the different views. You can select the attributes you want to use and then select whether to display the files and folders in ascending or descending order. You can use the Sort by or Group by buttons on the View tab to specify the options you want to apply to the current folder. To sort files and folders, do this:

1. In the desktop, click the **File Explorer** button on the taskbar.
2. Open the folder that contains the files you want to sort.
3. Click the Sort by drop-down arrow button on the View tab as shown in Figure 2.28.

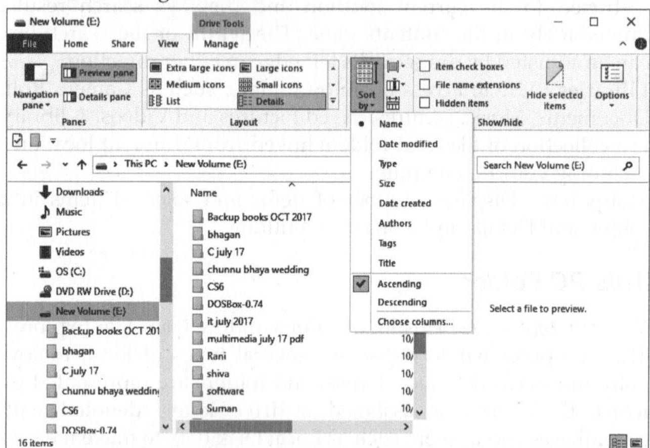

Figure 2.28 Selecting Sort options from the view tab

4. Select a desired Sort by option on the drop-down menu.
   - **Options**: Select an option, such as Name, Date, Size, Type, Date modified, and Date created.
     The available options vary depending on the selected folder type.
   - **Ascending**: Select to sort items in ascending order A-Z.
   - **Descending**: Select to sort items in descending order Z-A.
   - **Choose columns**: Select to customize the columns shown in Details view.

➡ **To group files and folders, do this:**

1. In the desktop, click or tap the **File Explorer** button on the taskbar.
2. Open the folder that contains the files you want to group.
3. Click the Group by drop-down arrow button on the **View** tab.
4. Select a desired Group by option on the drop-down menu.
   - **Options**: Select an option, such as Name, Date, Size, Type, Date modified, and Date created.
   - The available options vary depending on the selected folder type.
   - **(None)**: Select to remove the group by option.
   - **Ascending**: Select to sort items in ascending order A-Z.
   - **Descending**: Select to sort items in descending order Z-A.
   - **Choose columns**: Select to customize the columns shown in Details view.
5. Click the Collapse or Expand arrow next to the heading to collapse or expand the grouping.

2.8 MANAGING FILES AND FOLDERS

File Explorer is the file management application used by Windows operating systems to browse folders and files. It provides a graphical interface for the user to navigate and access the files stored in the computer.

The main way to access the File Explorer is by clicking the folder icon in the Taskbar. After clicking the icon, the File Explorer window will open. The initial File Explorer window is comprised of the following sections:

- The File Explorer ribbon, which resembles the ribbon featured in Microsoft Office. The ribbon contains buttons for common tasks to perform with your files and folders.
- The Navigation Pane gives you access to your libraries of documents and pictures, as well as your storage devices. It also features frequently used folders and network devices.
- The Frequent folders section on the right features the folders you have worked with recently to allow for quick access to them.

2.8.1 The File Explorer Ribbon

In Windows 10, the File Explorer features a new ribbon toolbar, similar to the one featured in the recent versions of Microsoft Office. This ribbon contains buttons and commands for the most common tasks. The Ribbon features four tabs, each with different commands. Among the tasks you can perform from the Home tab are:

- Copying and pasting files and folders from one place to another.
- Moving files and folders to another location.
- Deleting a file or folder
- Renaming a file or folder
- Creating a new folder or other new items

2.9 MICROSOFT EDGE BROWSER

Windows 10 includes a new web browser, called Edge. Compared to Internet Explorer, Edge is faster, more secure, and more compliant with common web standards.

2.9.1 Open Edge

Click the Edge Icon on the taskbar. Edge opens to its own start screen, which includes news headlines and weather for your location. The single text field near the top is where you can search for something or enter a website address directly.

2.9.2 View Favourites

Click the **Hub** button. Click the **favorites** tab. Your favorites appear on the first tab of this menu. Click the favorite site you want to open.

2.9.3. Add a Webpage Favorites

It's easy to add sites to your Favorites. Go to the site you want to add. Click the **Start** button. Specify a name and location for the webpage. Click **Add**.

2.9.4 Use Reading Mode

Edge also introduces a distraction-free reading mode, that takes an article and displays only the relevant text.
To use Reading Mode - Open a web page. Click the **Reading Mode** button to turn on Reading Mode. Now there are no headers, sidebars, ads, or anything else to distract you from the article, just the text in a larger, easier-to-read font (See Figure 2.29). Click the **Reading Mode** button again to turn off Reading Mode.

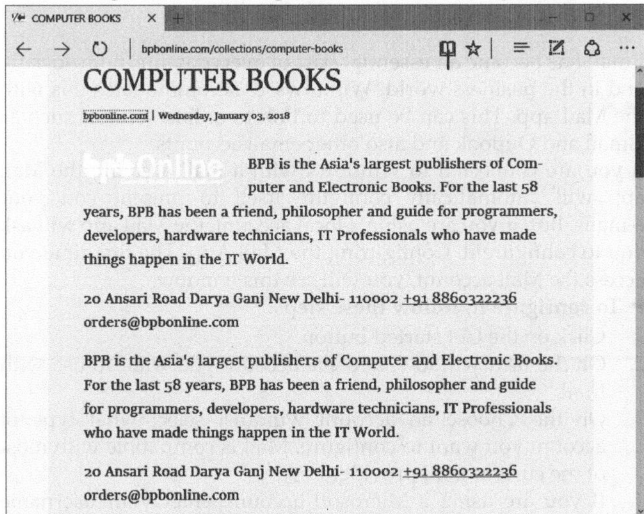

Figure 2.29 Reading Mode

2.9.5 Microsoft Edge's secret history

Microsoft Edge's secret history of your web visits Microsoft Edge keeps a record of every website you visit.
To keep tabs on what Microsoft Edge is recording, click your Hub button and click the History icon "it looks like a clock" from the drop-down menu's top. Microsoft Edge lists every website you have visited in the past few weeks, sorted by date. (Your latest visits appear at the list's top.) By presenting the sites in the order you viewed them, Microsoft Edge makes it easy to jump back to that site you found interesting this morning or last week. To delete a single entry from the history, right click it and choose Delete from the pop-up menu. To delete the entire list, click the words Clear All History at the list's top.

2.10 DIGITAL LIFE STYLE

Cloud computing involves saving content to an online server connected to the service that you are using. Cloud computing consists of hardware and software resources made available on the Internet as managed third-party services. These services rely on advanced software applications and high-end networks of server computers. Service providers create cloud computing systems to serve common business or research needs.

2.10.1 Using OneDrive

Cloud computing is now a mainstream part of our online experience. This involves saving content to an online server connected to the service that you are using through your Microsoft Account. You can then access this content from any computer, using your account login details, and also share it with other people by giving your account login details, and also share it with other people by giving them access to your Cloud service. The Cloud service with Windows 10 is known as OneDrive, and you can use it providing that you have a Microsoft Account.
OneDrive is installed by default on most Windows 10 machines. OneDrive allows users to save files locally, upload them to the cloud, and share view links by default. That means you can upload, delete, edit, and download a variety of files and formats using OneDrive cloud storage. This saves precious local storage space and provides you peace of mind concerning the storage of your most important documents. Windows 10 which comes with OneDrive built right into the operating system.

1. Open the **Start** Menu and search for OneDrive and follow the Wizard to sign-in to OneDrive. (See Figure 2.30 and 2.31).
2. Open File Explorer and click on the **OneDrive** folder to view its contents.

Figure 2.30 OneDrive setup screen

Adding Files to OneDrive

OneDrive is built into the file structure of Windows 10 and as well as adding files from OneDrive itself, it is also possible to add them to the OneDrive folder from your computer (See Figure 2.32). To add files from File Explorer do the following:

1. In File Explorer, the **OneDrive** folder is located underneath Quick access.
2. Click on the OneDrive folder to view its contents.
3. Add files to the OneDrive folder by dragging and dropping them from another folder or by using Copy and Paste.
4. The new content is available from the OneDrive app and also online from your OneDrive account.

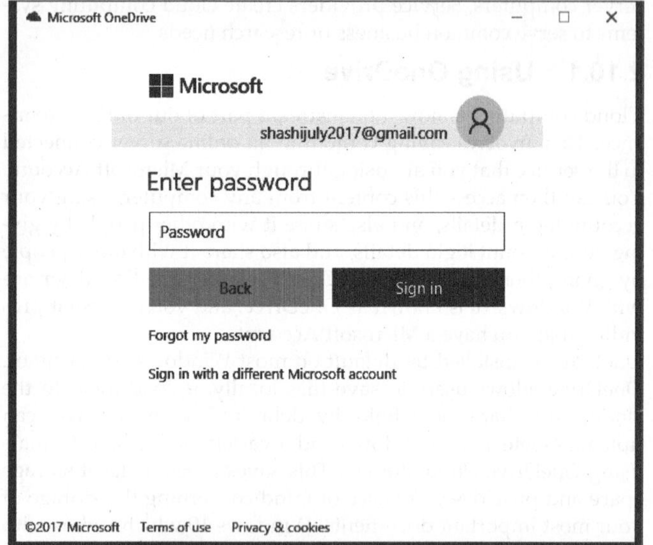

Figure 2.31 OneDrive sign-in screen

Figure 2.32 OneDrive folder for adding files

Saving Files to OneDrive

Files can also be saved directly to OneDrive when they are created. To do this follow the following steps:

1. Open a new file in any app and create the required content.
2. Click on **File** > **Save** from the menu bar and select a OneDrive folder into which you want to save the file.
3. Click on **Save** button.

2.11 MEDIA MANAGEMENT

Windows 10 offers multiple ways to work with your media files (music and videos). Some of the features needed to handle these files have been integrated into Windows to facilitate the way you access them.

Media Applications Although you can have multiple media programs in your computer, Windows 10 includes several options for you to use. For music files, Windows includes the traditional Windows Media Player. However, new Windows versions also include the Groove Music app (previously known as Xbox Music). The Groove Music app is used to access music that you have added to your computer and also the Music section of the Windows Store, where you can preview, buy and download more music. For video files, Windows also uses Windows Media Player, but now also includes the Movies & TV app. Windows 10 also includes the Windows DVD Player app for playing DVD's in your computer. You can also choose which application you want to use to open your media file by following these steps:

1. Right-click any media file (music or video).
2. Select the **Open with** option.
3. Choose what application you want to use to open the media file.

2.12 KEEPING IN TOUCH

Email has become an essential part of everyday life, both socially and in the business world. Windows 10 accommodates this with the Mail app. This can be used to link to online services such as Gmail and Outlook and also other email accounts.

If you are connected to Windows with a mail account, the Mail app will automatically configure itself to present you your e-mails. But, if you are using a local account, the Mail app will ask you to configure it. Configuring the Mail App. The first time you access the Mail account, you will see this window

➡ **To configure it, follow these steps:**

1. Click on the Get started button.
2. On the next window, add the account you want to use with Mail.
3. On the Choose an account window, select what type of account you want to configure. Mail is compatible with most of the current mail providers.
4. If you are using a Microsoft account, enter your username and password.
5. After a while, the Mail app will start loading your emails. The list of emails appears in the main window. Double -click on an email to view it at full size.

2.12.1 Working with Mail

Once you have set up an account in the Mail app you can then start creating and managing your emails with it.

1. On the Inbox page, open an email and click on the Reply, Reply all or Forward buttons to respond. (See Figure 2.33).
2. Open an email and click on delete button to delete the mail.

Figure 2.33 Inbox with different buttons to respond

2.12.2 Composing email

You can use the Compose pane to write and send an email message from the Mail app. From here, you can add the email address of the recipient(s), the subject, and the body of the email.

➡ To compose a New Message, do the following:

1. Click on (+) **New mail** button to create a new message.
2. Type email address in the To: box. If you want to add more than one email addresses, separate it by commas.
3. Click on the Cc & Bcc link to access options for blind copying.
4. Type the subject heading and body text to the email.
5. Click on the Insert button on the top toolbar in the new email window and select one of the options, such as Pictures.
6. Click on a folder from which you want to attach the file, and click on the Insert button. The file will be shown in the body of the email. (See Figure 2.34).
7. Select an item of text and select the text formatting options from the top toolbar.
8. After you completed, click the **Send** button to send the email.

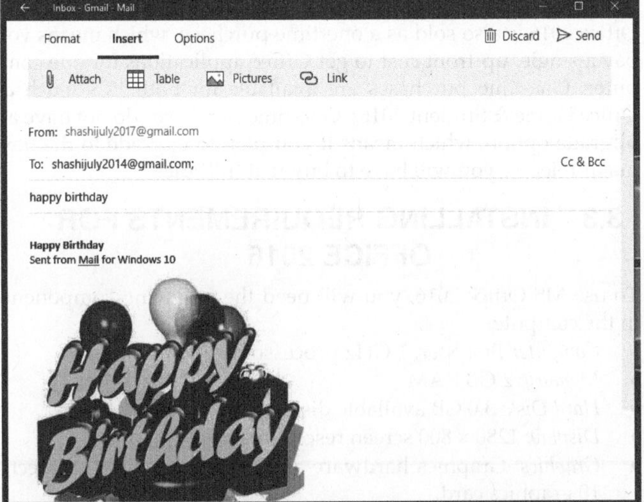

Figure 2.34 Compose a New Message box

2.12.3 Reading and Replying to Messages

By default, any email you receive will go to your Inbox. Unread emails are always appear in bold.

1. From the Mail app, select the message you want to read.
2. The message will appear on the right-side of the screen in the Message pane.
3. To reply to the message, click the Reply option from the top of the screen.
4. The Compose pane will appear showing RE: in subject section. Type your message. After you completed, click the Send button to send your message.

2.12.4 Finding People

An electronic address book is always a good feature to have on a computer, and with Windows 10 this function is provided by the People app. The People app is much more than an address book. The People app displays all the contacts you have for all the email accounts and services you have added in the Mail app and, through your Microsoft account (also known as Windows Live ID). It can also access social networking services such as Facebook, Twitter, and LinkedIn after you authorize your Microsoft account to access these services.

When you open the People app, you are presented with a lot of information. A column on the left is for accessing your own updates, viewing notifications, and accessing what is new. On the right, your contacts are listed in alphabetical order. The top-right corner displays Connected To, followed by a list of icons that represent the accounts to which the People app is connected. The People app will download all your friends and contacts and share their latest updates.

☞ *The People app displays all your friends and contacts and share their latest updates.*

To add your account to the People app, do this:

1. Click the **People apps** on the **Start** menu. Make sure you are connected to the Internet before opening the People app.
2. The current contacts are displayed. By default, these will be linked to your Microsoft Account, if you have created one.
3. Click on **Settings** button to add new accounts from which you want to import contacts.
4. Select the desired app to access your accounts.
5. Enter your sign in details for the selected account and click on the Sign in button.
6. A confirmation window informs you that the account has been set up and linked to the People app. Click on the Done button.
7. The contacts from the linked account are imported and added under the Contacts heading.
8. Click on a contact to view its details.

2.12.5 Chatting with Skype

Skype is one of the premier services for free voice calls and instant messaging for text messages. It can now be incorporated into your Windows experience and used to keep in touch with family, friends and colleagues. To work with Skype, do the following:

1. Click on the **Skype Preview** button on the **Start** menu. If the Skype button is not available on the Start menu, the app can be downloaded from the Windows Store.
2. If you have already have a Skype account you can sign in with these details, or with your Microsoft Account details. Click on **Create a new account** to create a new Skype account.
3. Once you have entered your Skype sign in details you can check your speakers, microphone and webcam, for voice and video calls. Click on **Sign In** button.
4. Recent conversations are listed in the left-hand panel, or contacts can be selected to start a new conversation.
5. Click on the button to view your Skype contacts. Tap on one to start a voice or video call, or a text message.
6. Click in the Search Skype directory box to look for other Skype contacts.
7. Select a contact and click in the in Type in massage box to start a text conversation.
8. Select a contact and click on the phone button to make a voice call, or the video button to make a video call.

CHAPTER 3

Introduction to Office 2016

3.1 INTRODUCTION

MS Word is the most popular word processing software used today. A Word processor is essentially a computerized version of the standard typewriter. However, the features of having like spell check, the ability to save and store documents, copy and past functions, the ability to add images and shapes to documents and many more. When attached to an electronic documents created by MS Word can be delivered in seconds. The benefit is that it helps the user to type faster and accurate.

3.2 OFFICE 2016

MS Office 2016 is a suite of productivity applications that share common features. There have been many versions, but the latest version Office 2016, released in September 2015.

Office Home & Student 2016 Includes:

It is designed to help you to create and organize faster with time-saving features, a new modern look and built-in collaboration tools. The easy way to type what help you get from the new Tell Me box on the ribbon and it will tell you how to do it.

- *Word 2016*–Create and share professional-looking documents with state of the art editing, reviewing and sharing tools.
- *Excel*–Analyze and visualise your data in new and intuitive ways with a fresh user interface and keyboard shortcuts.
- *PowerPoint*–Create, collaborate and effectively present your ideas with new slide transitions and an improved animations task pane.
- *OneNote*–It is your very own digital notebook, so you can keep notes, ideas, web pages, photos, audio and video all in one place. Whether you are at home, or in the office or on the move, you can take it all with you wherever you go while sharing and collaborating with others.

Office Home & Student 2016 Includes:

Office Home & Business 2016 edition contains all of the apps in the Home & Student edition, plus such as

- *Outlook*–Easily manage your email, calendar, contact and tasks. E-mail keeps your inbox up to date.

Office Professional 2016 Includes:

Office Professional editions contains all applications found in the Home & Business edition, plus two additional apps such as

- *Access*–It is easy-to-use tool for quickly creating database applications that your data is automatically stored in a SQL database.
- *Publisher*–Easily create, personalize, and share a wide range of professional-quality publications.

Difference between Office 365 and Office 2016

Office 365 is a subscription service that ensures you always have the most up-to-date tools from MS Office. There are Office 365 plans for home and personal use, as well as for small and businesses enterprises.

All Office 365 plan for home and personal use include Office 2016 with the fully installed Office applications that you are familiar with, like Word, PowerPoint and Excel plus extra online storage. You can choose to pay for your subscription on a monthly or year basis, and the Office 365 Home plan lets you share your subscription with up to four members of your household.

Office 2016 is also sold as a one-time purchase, which means you pay a single, up-front cost to get Office applications for one computer. One-time purchases are available for both PCs (such as Office Home & Student 2016). One-time purchases do not have an upgrade option, which means if you plan to upgrade to the next major releaser you will have to buy it at full price.

3.3 INSTALLING REQUIREMENTS FOR OFFICE 2016

To use MS Office 2016, you will need the following components in the computer:

- *Computer Processor:* 1 GHz processor (32-bit or 64-bit)
- *Memory:* 2 GB RAM
- *Hard Disk:* 3.0 GB available disk space
- *Display:* 1280 × 800 screen resolution
- *Graphics:* Graphics hardware acceleration requires a DirectX 10 graphics card.
- *Operating system:* Windows 10, 8.1, 8 and Windows 7 with Service Pack 1, Windows server 2013 R2, 2008 R2.
- *Browser:* The current version of Internet Explorer, Safari, Chrome or Firefox.
- *.NET version:* .NET 3.5 required. Some features may require .NET 4.0, 4.5, or 4.6.
- Some functions will have additional requirements, for example:
- A touch-enabled device is require to use any multi-touch functionality.
- Internet connection for online help.
- CD-ROM or DVD drive for install, backup and data storage.

3.4 START AN APPLICATION

The way that you start Word 2016 is dependent on the operating system you are running on your computer. For example:

- In Windows 10, you can start Word from the **Start** menu, the **All Apps** menu, the **Start** screen, or the taskbar search box.
- In Windows 8, you can start Word from the **Apps** screen or **Start** screen search results.

- In Windows 7, you can start Word from the **Start** menu, **All Programs** menu, or **Start** menu search results.

Here, we have started in Word in Windows 7

➡ **To start Word:**

1. Click **Start** button as shown in Figure 3.1.

Figure 3.1 Starting MS Word 2010

2. Highlight **All Programs.**
3. Select **Word 2016.**

Word opens the screen Recent documents that are created in previous version in the left pane. At the right side you can see the Blank document and templates (See Figure 3.2).

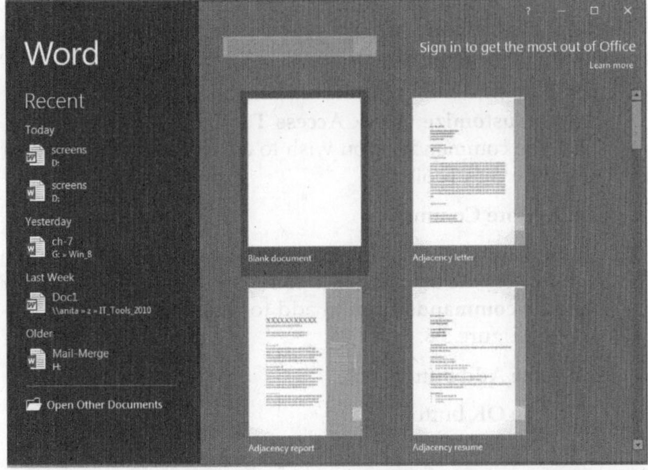

Figure 3.2 Recent document

3.4.1 The Application Window

When you start an Office application such as Word, Excel, PowerPoint the program window is displayed with a blank document with default name such as Book1, Presentation1 or Document1 respectively. For example, using Word the application window screen are explained in detail as given below (See Figure 3.3).

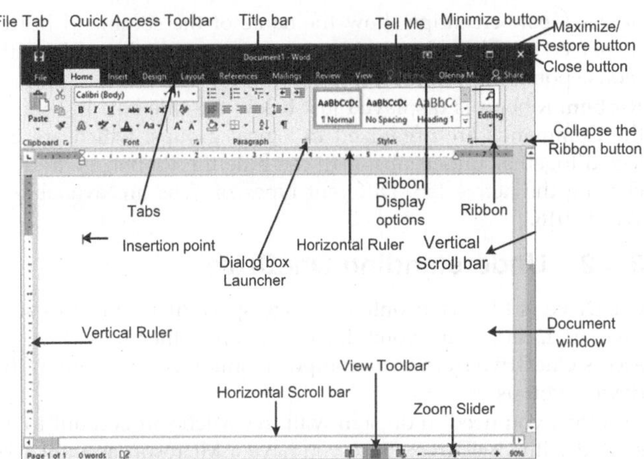

Figure 3.3 Application window

File tab: This button is located in the upper-left corner of Word 2016 window. The command related to managing Word 2010 and its documents are put together on a menu.

Quick Access Toolbar: This toolbar is located by default at the top of Word 2016 window. This toolbar displays the New, Open, Save, Quick Print, Email, Touchscreen device, Undo and Redo etc.

Dialog box Launchers: The dialog box launchers are small icons that appear in some groups. Clicking a Dialog Box Launcher opens a related dialog box or task pane, providing more options related to that group.

Document window: You create a document in the document window. When more than one document is opened, each document has its own window.

Title bar: It is displayed at the top of the application window. It also displays the name of the active file, identifies the app, and provides tools for managing the app window, ribbon, and content.

Minimize button: An underscore (_) at the right of a title bar which stores an application programme at the bottom of the screen

Maximize button: A box at the right of a title bar that fills available space with the document or application.

Close button: A box at the right of a title bar (X) that closes the window or dialog box.

Restore button: A double box at the right of a title bar that restores an application or document into a sizeable window.

Tell Me: Entering a term in the Tell Me What You Want To Do box located to the right of the ribbon tabs displays a list of related commands and links to additional resources online.

Status bar: At the bottom of the window, the status bar gives you information about the current document. You can turn off the display of an item of information by right-clicking the status bar and then clicking that item.

View toolbar: At the right end of the status bar is the view toolbar. It provides tools for adjusting the size of document.

Mouse pointer: On-screen arrow, I-beam, or drawing button indicates the current location affected by your mouse actions.

Ruler: A bar containing a scale that indicates tabs, paragraph indents, and margins in the paragraph where the insertion point (cursor) is located.

ScreenTips: Screentips show the name of the command button displayed in ribbon. Screentips appear as soon as you position the mouse pointer on the toolbar button.

Ribbon: Ribbon is displayed just below the title bar. In Ribbon, the Commands are organized in logical groups, which are collected together under tabs. You can hide the Ribbon by double-clicking the active tab. Different types of Tabs are available in Word 2016.

3.4.2 Understanding OneDrive

OneDrive is Microsoft online storage space that you can use to save, edit, and share your documents and other files. You can access OneDrive from your computer, smartphone, or any of the devices you use.

Before, you need to do sign with free Microsoft account to get started with OneDrive. Once you have a Microsoft account, you will be able to Sign-in in the upper-right corner of the Word window (See Figure 3.4).

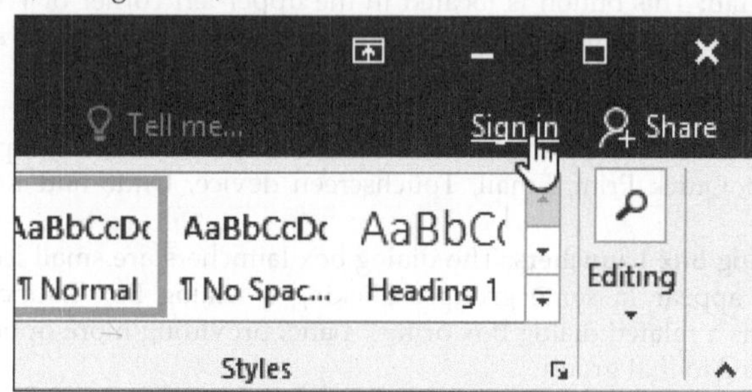

Figure 3.4 Select Sing in

Benefits of OneDrive

- **Access your files anywhere:** When you save your files to OneDrive, you will be able to access them from any computer, tablet, or smartphone that has an Internet connection. You will also be able to create new documents from OneDrive.
- **Back up your files:** Saving files to OneDrive gives them an extra layer of protection. Even if something happens to your computer, OneDrive will keep your files safe and accessible.
- **Share files:** It is easy to share your OneDrive files with friends and co-workers. You can choose whether they can edit or simply read files. This option is great for collaboration because multiple people can edit a document at the same time.

3.4.3 Working with Ribbon

Ribbon is displayed just below the title bar. In Ribbon, Commands are organized in logical groups, which are collected together under tabs. You can hide the Ribbon by double-clicking the active tab. Each tab is further divided into groups such as the Font and Paragraphs (as shown in Figure 3.5).

At the bottom right-hand corner of some groups, there is a diagonal arrow called a Dialog Box Launcher (See Figure 3.6).

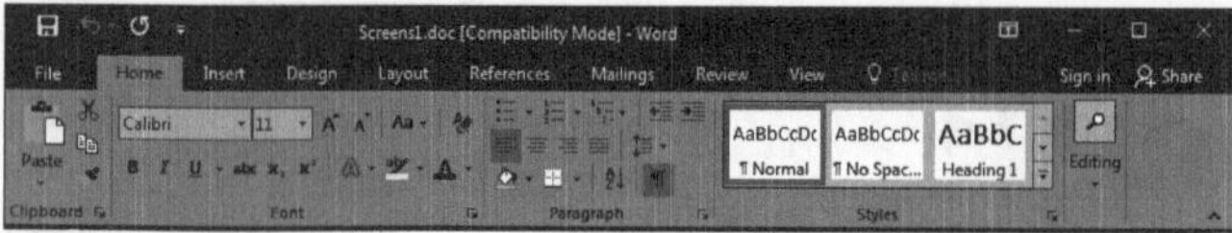

Figure 3.5 Ribbon

Clicking this button opens a dialog box for that group containing further option selections for the group.

Figure 3.6 Dialog box Launcher

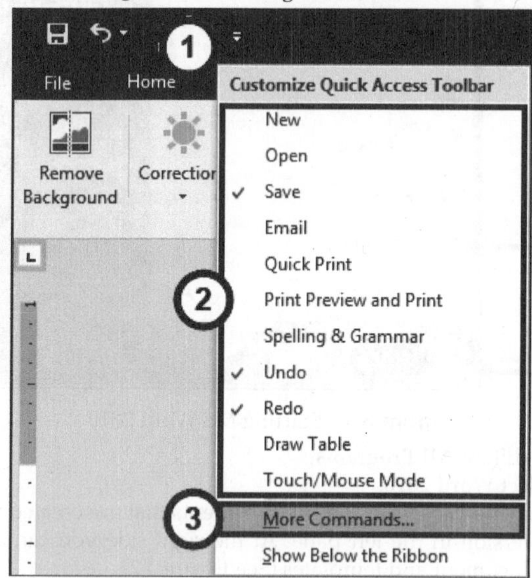

Figure 3.7 Customize Quick Access Toolbar

1. Click the drop-down arrow in the Quick Access Toolbar See Figure 3.7.
2. In the **Customize Quick Access Toolbar** drop-down menu, click the command(s) you wish to add or remove from your Quick Access Toolbar.
3. Click **More Commands**.
4. In the **Customize Quick Access Toolbar** window, from the column on the left, select a command from the list under **Choose commands from** to add to your Quick Access Toolbar See Figure 3.8.
5. Click the **Add** button.
6. Click the **OK** button.

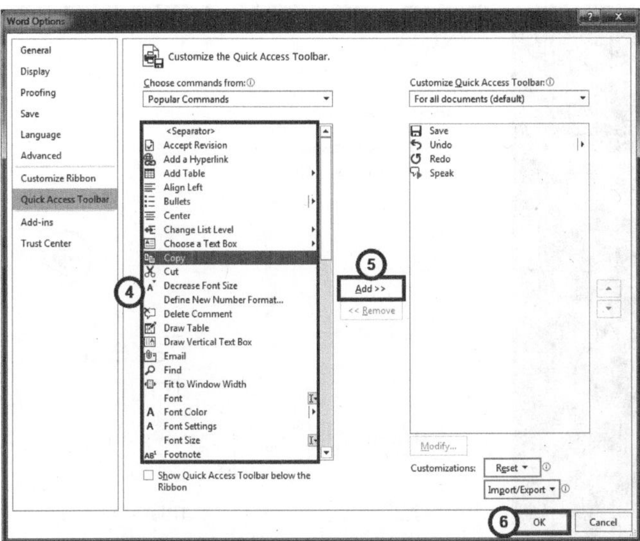

Figure 3.8 Word Options dialog box

3.4.4 File Extension

To see the file extensions that are associated with the various document types:

1. Click the **Windows Explorer** window, select the **Tools** menu and choose **Folder options...** .
2. The **Folder** dialog box appears as shown in Figure 3.9, click the **View** tab.

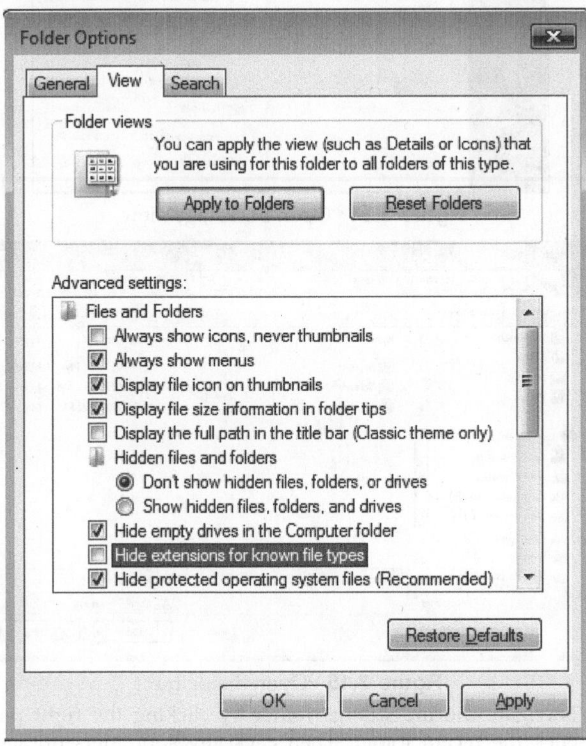

Figure 3.9 Folder options

3. Click the Files and Folders options in the **Advanced settings:** list box.
4. Uncheck the **Hide extensions for known file types.**
5. The file type will be shown, along with the file name extension, whichever folder view you choose.

3.4.5 Office Document Types

The files you are creating in Office applications are various types. Each item will be a separate file. You can be saved in your OneDrive documents folder or on your local computer.

1. To review the files, open window explorer and select your OneDrive or local document folder.
2. It change the view of files in large icons. Click the **View** tab and select **Details** option to show the file information such as date modified, size and type.

3.4.6 Compatibility Mode

Sometimes you may need to work with documents that were created in earlier versions of Microsoft Word, such as Word 2010 or Word 2007. When you open these types of documents, they will appear in Compatibility Mode.

Compatibility Mode disables certain features, so you will only be able to access commands found in the program that was used to create the document. For example, if you open a document created in Word 2007 you can only use tabs and commands found in Word 2007.

In the Figure 3.10, the document on the left is in Compatibility Mode, you can see the affect which commands are available and it only shows commands that were available in Word 2016.

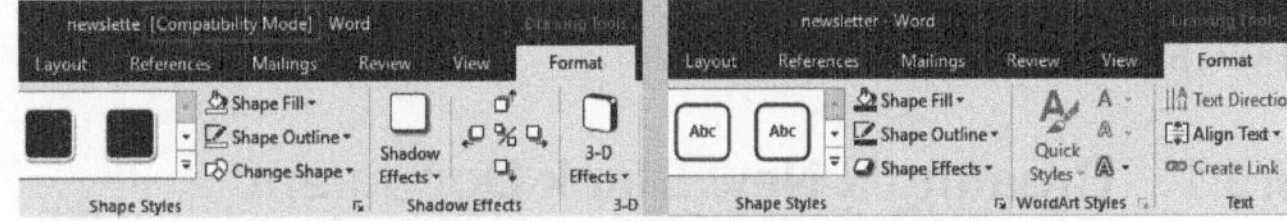

Figure 3.10 Compatibility Mode

3.4.7 Convert a Document

If you want access to all Word 2016 features, you can convert the document to the 2016 file format.

1. Click the **File** tab to access **Backstage** view.
2. On the **Info** page of the backstage view, click the **convert** button as shown in Figure 3.11.

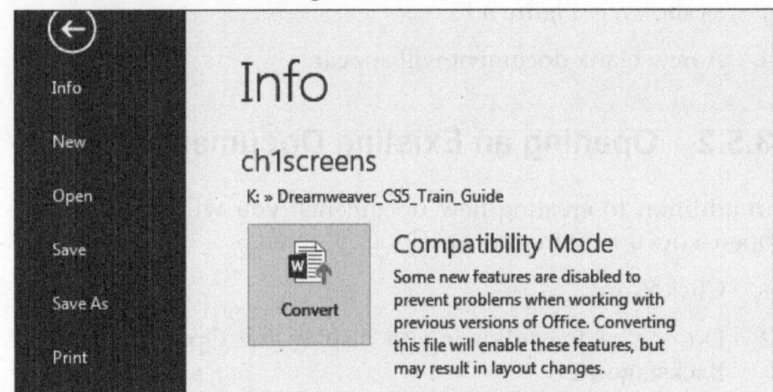

Figure 3.11 Info backstage view

3. A dialog box will appear as shown in Figure 3.12. Click OK to confirm the file upgrade.

4. The document will be converted to the upgraded newest file type. Converting a file may cause some changes to the original layout of the document (See Figure 3.12).

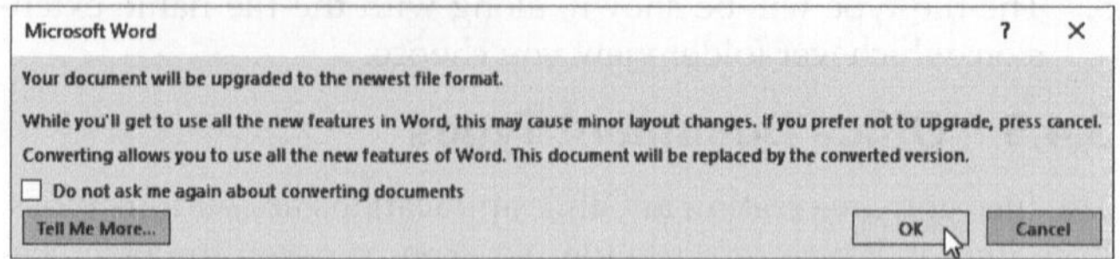

Figure 3.12 Confirm the file upgrade dialog box

3.4.8 Quick Access Toolbar

This toolbar is located by default at the top of Word 2016 window. By default, this toolbar displays the Save, Undo and Repeat buttons.

3.4.9 Dialog Box Launchers

Dialog box launchers are small icons that appear in some groups. Clicking a Dialog Box Launcher opens a related dialog box or task pane, providing more options related to that group.

3.5 CREATING WORD DOCUMENTS

Word files are called documents. Whenever you start a new project in Word, you will need to create a new document, which can either be blank or from a template. You will also need to know how to open an existing document.

3.5.1 Creating a New Blank Document

To create a document in Word, then click the Blank document in the New backstage area options.

1. Click the **File** tab to display the Backstage view.
2. In the left pane of the backstage view, click **New** to display the **New backstage** page.
3. On the right side pane, click the **Blank document** thumbnail as shown in Figure 3.13.
4. A new blank document will appear.

3.5.2 Opening an Existing Document

In addition to creating new documents, you will often need to open a document that was previously saved.

1. Click Word.
2. Do one of the following to display the Open page of the Backstage view:
    - On the Start screen, at the bottom of the left pane, click Open Other Documents.
    - It displays the Backstage view, then click **Open**.

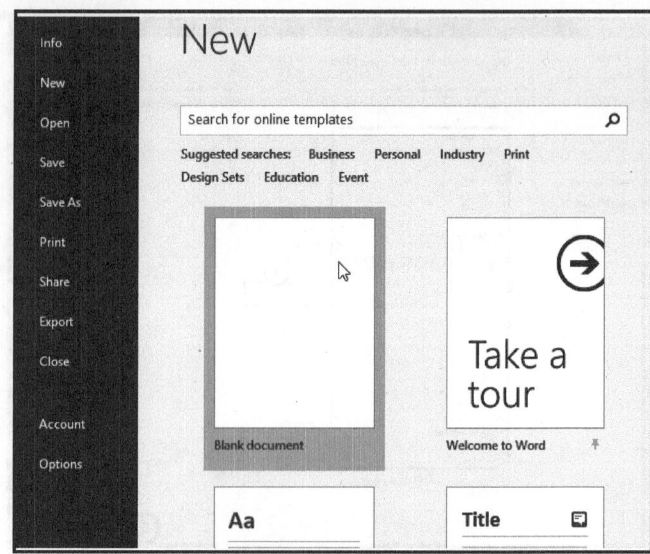

Figure 3.13 New Backstage view

3. Under the **Recent** list, click the local or network storage location (This PC, Browser or OneDrive) where the file is stored (See Figure 3.14).

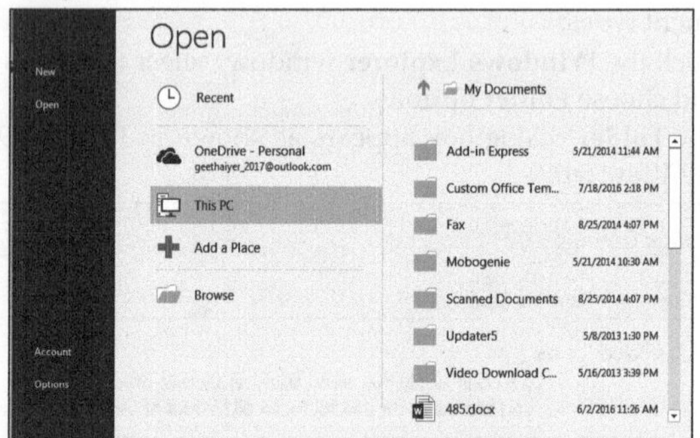

Figure 3.14 Open Backstage view

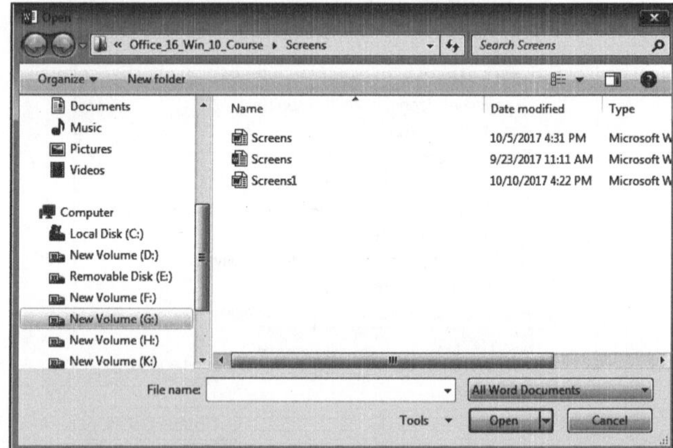

Figure 3.15 Open dialog box

4. Navigate the file storage folder by clicking the right pane, click the recent folder. Then click any subfolders until you reach the folder you want. Or

5. In the left pane, click **Browser** to open the **Open** dialog box as shown in Figure 3.15.
6. Locate and select the document, then click open.
7. The selected document will appear.

3.5.3 Saving a Document

It is important to save your document whenever you start a new document or make changes to an existing one. Saving can prevent your work from being lost. You need to know where you save the document so it will too easy to find later. You can also save your work to share the file with others.

To save a document for the first time, you need to specify three items:

a. The drive and folder to store your file.
b. The name of your file.
c. The format to save your file.

1. Click the **File** tab. Alternatively, choose the **Save** button on the **Quick Access** toolbar.
2. **Save As** Backstage view appear as shown in Figure 3.16.

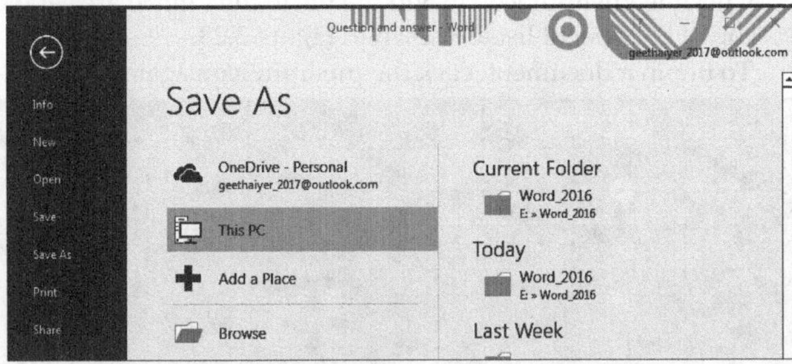

Figure 3.16 Save Backstage view

3. In the Left pane of the backstage view, click **Save As**.
4. Click the **Browser** or **This PC** option to save the document.
5. The **Save As** dialog box appear 3.17, select the location where you want to save the document in the address bar.

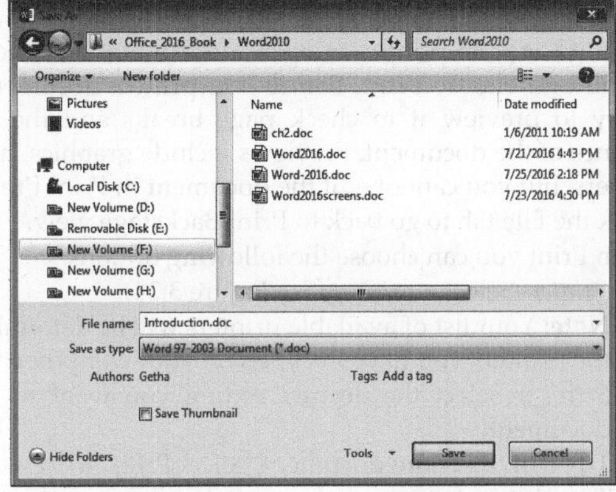

Figure 3.17 Save As dialog box

6. In the **File name:** text box and type a name for your file.
7. Choose the file format you want to save in the **Save as** type drop-down list.
8. Click the **Save** button.
9. The document gets saved. You can click the save command again to save your changes as you modify the document.

3.5.4 Saving and Opening Files in OneDrive

When you are signed in to your Microsoft account, OneDrive will appear as an option whenever you save or open a file. However, saving files to your OneDrive allows you to access them from any other computer, and it also allows you to share files with friends and co-workers.

1. Click a file that you want to save to an **OneDrive** folder.
2. Click the **File** tab to access the Backstage view.
3. The **Save As** Backstage view appears as shown in Figure 3.18.

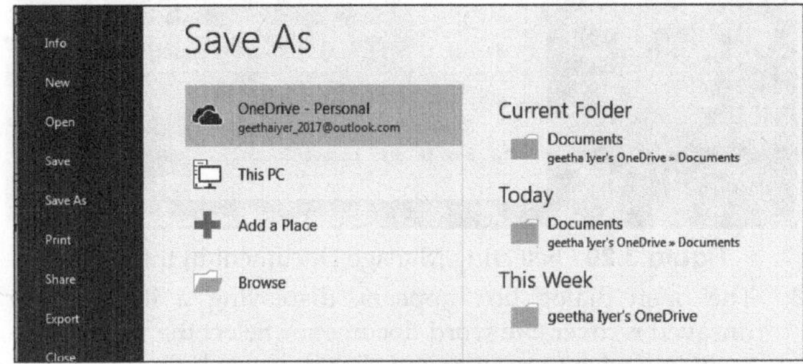

Figure 3.18 Save As Backstage view

4. Select **OneDrive**. The **Save As** dialog box appears 3.19.

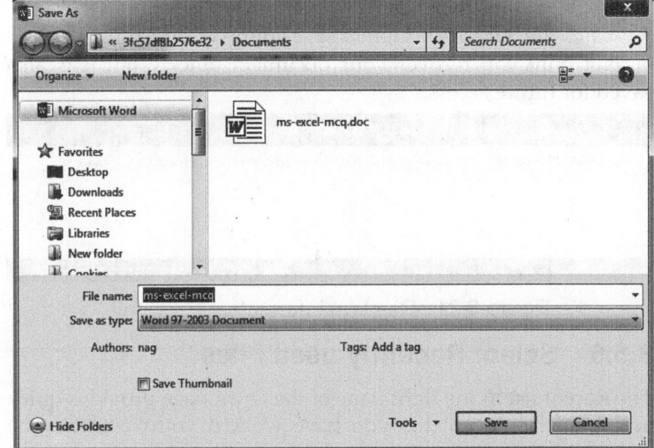

Figure 3.19 Save As dialog box

5. In the **Save As** dialog box, notice the path to the **OneDrive** folder where the file will be saved.
6. Click **Save** button.
7. You can look at the **Save** button on the Quick Access toolbar after you save your file. It looks a little different from the conventional Save button. The circular lines on the Save button tell you that the file is stored at OneDrive. When you click the Save button, you save your work and also refresh the file with work done by people who share the file with you.

3.5.5 AutoRecover

Word automatically saves your documents to a temporary folder while you are working on them. If you forget to save your changes or if Word crashes, you can restore the file using AutoRecover.

1. Click the **File** menu and choose **Info** option from the left pane.

2. Click the **Manage Document** drop-down list, click **Recover Unsaved Documents** as shown in Figure 3.20.

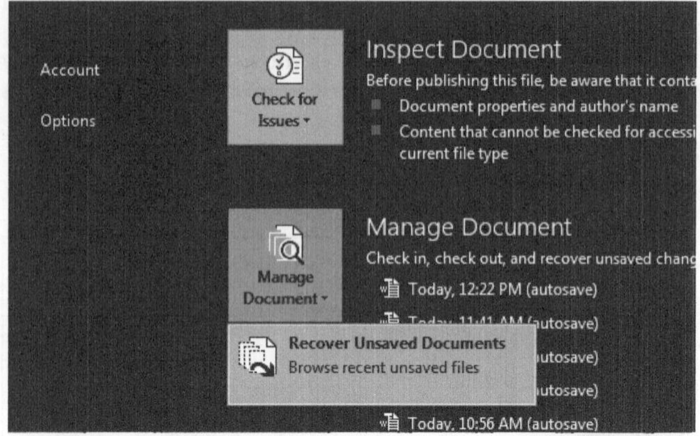

Figure 3.20 Selecting Manage Document in Info tab

3. The open dialog box appears, displaying a list of your unsaved recoverable word documents. Select the word document you wish to recover and click the open button.
4. The recover word document is opened and displays information banner across the top recommending that you save the file as shown in Figure 3.21.
5. Click the **Save As** button to save your word document.

Not only you recover your document quickly but it is also saved for future access.

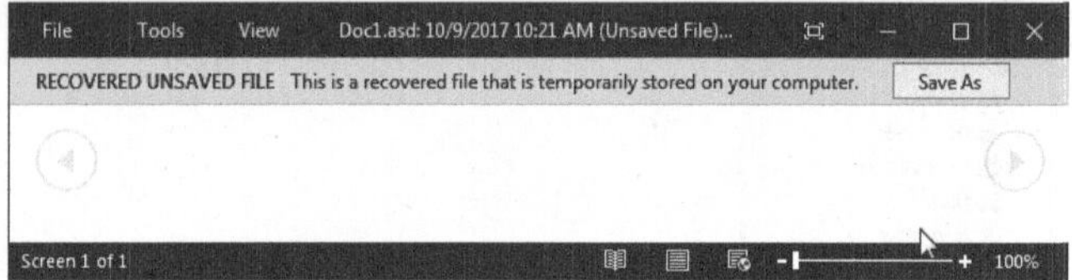

Figure 3.21 Displays information at the top

3.5.6 Select Recently used Files

The Recent list in the right pane of the Open page provides quick access to the documents you have worked with recently. The Recent list includes locally stored documents and documents that you have worked with while signed in with your current account on any computer, tablet, or other device, if the documents are stored in a shared location.

➡ **To open a recent document:**

1. Start Word.
2. On the **Start** screen, in the **Recent** list, click the file name you want to open. Or
3. With Word running, click the **File** tab to display the Backstage view.
4. In the left pane of the Backstage view, click **Open** to display the **Open** page.
5. With Recent selected at the top of the left pane of the Open page, scroll the file list in the right pane to select the file name you want to open (See Figure 3.22).

Pin a Document

To pin a document to the Recent file list.

1. Display the **Recent** list on the **Open** page of the Backstage view.
2. Point to the file name, and then click the **Pin** button that appears at the right of the file name.

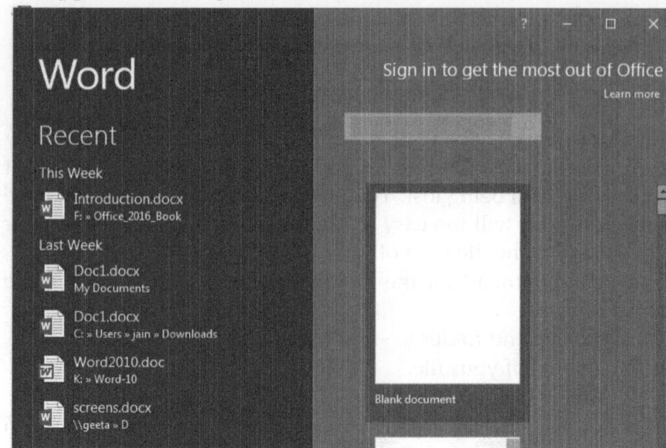

Figure 3.22 Open Recent document

3. Click the **Pushpin** icon to add the file to the Pinned area at the top of the **Recent** list as shown in Figure 3.23.
4. To unpin a document, click the **pushpin** icon again.

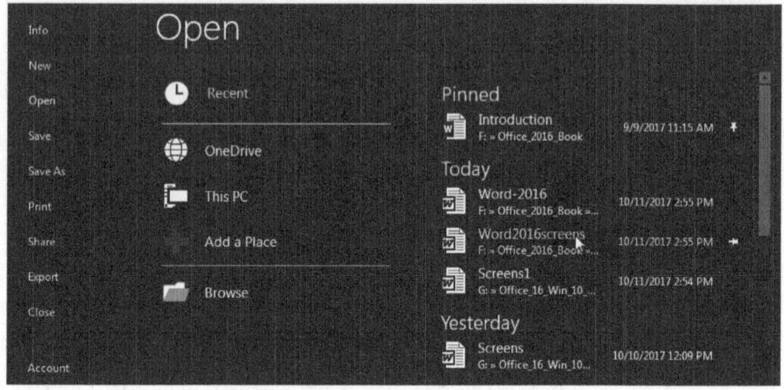

Figure 3.23 Pin a document

3.5.7 Print and Previewing a Document

The simplest way to print is to open a document and then click File menu and choose Print. Before you print a document, it is necessary to preview it to check page breaks and the overall appearance of the document. Previews include graphics, headers, and footers, but you cannot edit the document in Print Preview.

1. Click the File tab to go back to Print Backstage view.
2. From Print you can choose the following options:
   a. *Printer*–Select a printer (See Figure 3.24).
      Note: Your list of available printers will be determined by the printers you have installed on your computer.
   b. *Settings*–Select the desired setting you want to print a document.
   c. To print the entire document, select *Print All pages*.
   d. To print just one page in your document currently containing the insertion point, click on the **Print Current Page** button.
   e. If you choose **Custom** print. Enter specific pages to print for example says 1-4 in a document, type the first page number and the last desired page number in the **Pages:** text box. Separate the numbers with the hyphens like 1-4.
   f. *Copies*–Set the number of copies you want to print.

3. Click the **Print** button.

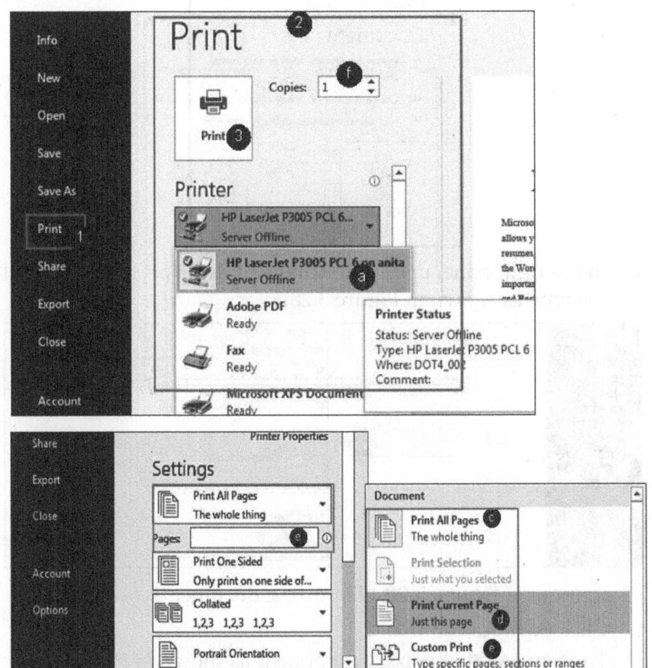

Figure 3.24 Print backstage view

3.5.8 To Preview Design Template

1. Display the New page of the Backstage view.
2. On the New page, scroll the pane to view the design templates that were installed with Word.
3. Click any thumbnail to open a preview window that displays a sample document page.
4. Do any of the following options:
   - To create a document based on the template that is active in the preview window, click the Create button.
   - To view the next template, click the arrow to the right of the preview window,
   - To close the preview window without creating a document, click the Close button in the upper-right corner of the preview window.

3.5.9 To Create a New document from a Template

Word includes a number of in-built pre-designed document templates that you can use to create a new document by quickly. You can easily create a variety of documents, such as letters and reports with specialized formatting.

1. Click the **File** tab to access Backstage view, then select **New**.
2. The **New** backstage view there are several templates will appear as shown in Figure 3.25.
3. In the **Search** box at the top of the page, enter a term related to the template content. In our example, we will search for an education template.
4. Word displays templates matching the category, click the desire template to preview it.

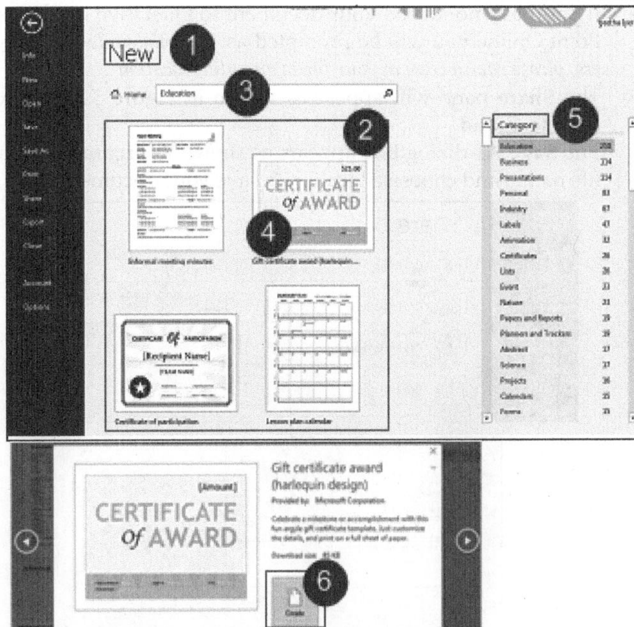

Figure 3.25 Create a new document from template

5. In the **Category** list, click any categories to further filter the templates. Active category filters are indicated by colored bars at the top of the Category list.
6. A **Preview** of the template will appear. Click **Create** to use the selected template (See Figure 3.25). Or
7. Double-click any thumbnail to create a file based on the template.
8. A new document will appear with the selected template.

3.5.10 Closing and Quitting Word

1. If you want to close the open document, click **File** tab and then select **Close** (See Figure 3.26).
2. To quit Word 2010, click **File** tab and choose **Exit** button.

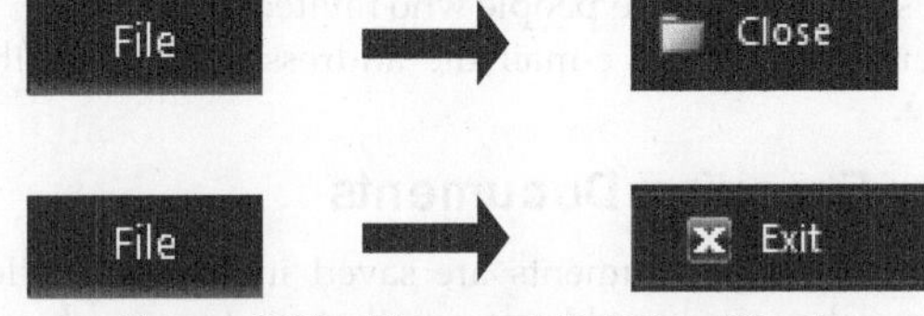

Figure 3.26 Close and Quitting Word

3.5.11 Sharing Documents

In Word 2016 for Windows, it's easier than ever to share your documents. When you share your files by using OneDrive. You can invite people to the document directly from within Word, or Word file as an email attachment.

1. To share a document, you must first be saved it to your OneDrive.
2. Click the **File** tab to access Backstage view, then click **Share**. Or
3. Open your Word document, and choose the **Share** tab on the right side of the tab.

4. If you have not saved your document to OneDrive or SharePoint Online you will be prompted as "*To collaborate with others, please save a copy of your file to an online location*".
5. The **Share** pane will appear as shown in Figure 3.27. Click **Save to Cloud**.
6. The **Save As** dialog box appears as shown in Figure. Enter a file name, and choose a location to save your document.

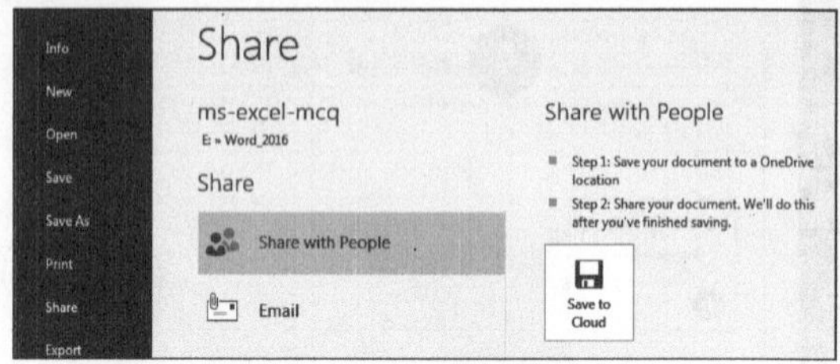

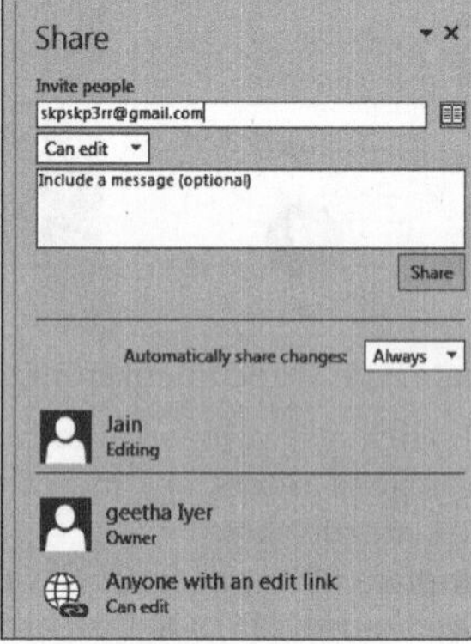

Figure 3.27 Sharing Documents

7. Once your document is saved to a shared location, you can invite others to work on it.
8. In the **Share** task pane, enter the email address of the person you would like to share it in the **Invite people** box.
9. Click **Share** button. If you already have the person's contact stored, you can just enter the name.
10. The processing job message appears with "sending emails and sharing with the people who invited".
11. After you send an e-mail the address appears in the task pane.

3.5.12 Exporting Documents

By default, Word documents are saved in the .docx file type. However, when you need to use another file type, such as a PDF or Word 97-2003 document. It is easy to export your document from Word to other file types.

1. To export a document as a PDF file.
2. Click the **File** tab to access the **Backstage** view.
3. Select **Create PDF/XPS**.
4. The **Publish as PDF or XPS** dialog box will appear. Select the location where you want to export the document, enter a file name, and then click Publish.

- **To export a document to other file types:**

1. Click **File** tab to access backstage view, select **Export**.
2. Then select **Change File Type**.

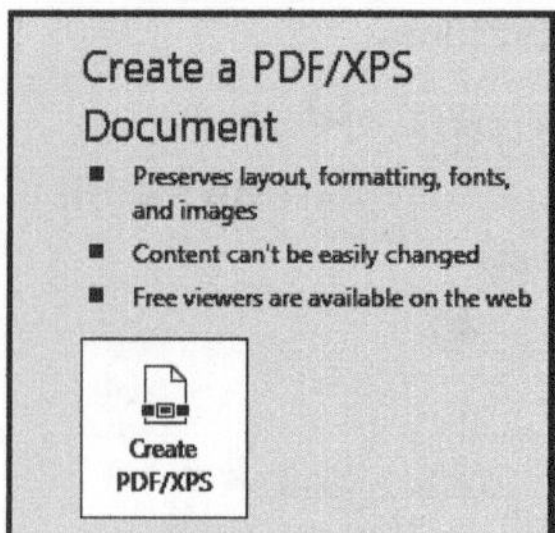

3. In the right pane, under the **Change File Type**, select desired file type as shown in Figure 3.28.

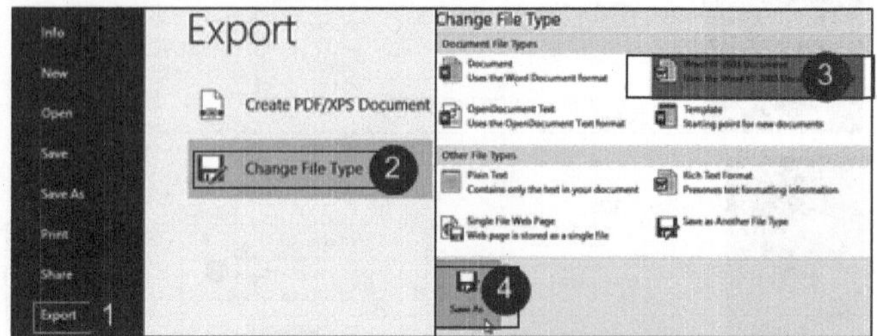

Figure 3.28 Exporting documents

4. Click **Save As** command.
5. The **Save As** dialog box will appear as shown in Figure 3.29.

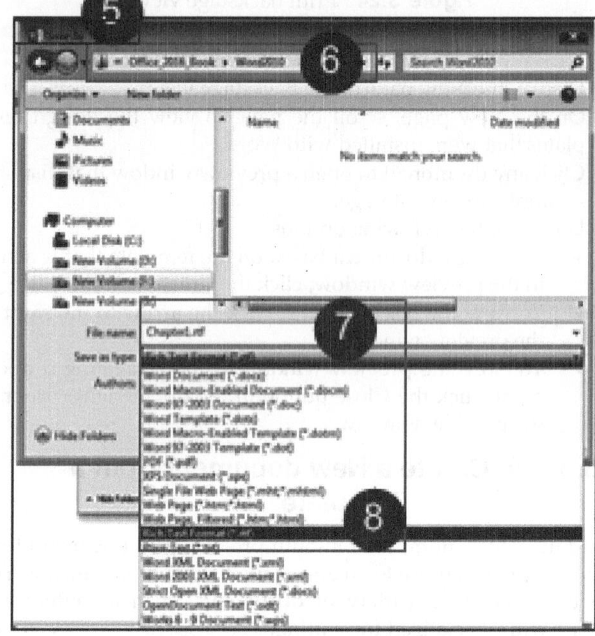

Figure 3.29 Save As dialog box

6. Select the location where you want to export the document.
7. Enter the file name in the **File name:** list box.
8. You can also use the **Save as type:** drop-down menu, to save the document to a variety of file types.
9. Then click **Save** button.

3.5.13 Different Views in Documents

You can display a document in different views that provide different types of information and make it easier to interact with specific document elements. Word 2016 has five views in which you can create, organize, and preview documents. Each view is suited to a specific purpose. The views are:

Print Layout View

This is the default view. Print Layout view is used to see how text, graphics and other elements such as header, footer, etc. will look on the printed output. This view is useful for editing headers and footers, for adjusting margins and for working with columns and drawing objects (See Figure 3.30).

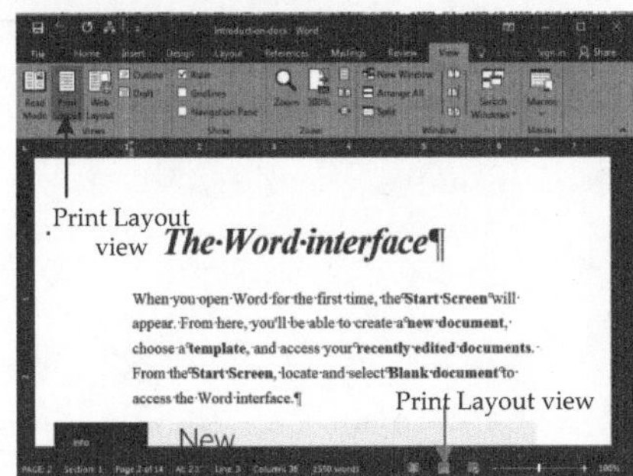

Figure 3.30 Print Layout view

1. Click the **View** tab, in the views group and click **Print Layout** command. Alternatively, click on the status bar icon.

Read Mode View

This view display as much of the typed area of the document as will fit on the screen at a size that is comfortable for reading. In this view, the Ribbon is replaced by a single toolbar at the top of the screen with button for searching and navigating in the document. You can display comments, but you cannot edit the document in this view.

- To Navigate the page in Read Mode

Press this key	Action
Page Down or spacebar	Move to next page
Page Up or Backspace key	Move to previous page
Right Arrow	Move to next page
Left Arrow	Move to previous page
Home	Move to first page in document
End	Move to last page in document
Esc	Return to previous view

Zooming In an Object in Read Mode

If your document contains an object as an image, Shape, SmartArt, or table, you can zoom in the object in Read Mode by double-clicking the object. The object appears larger on the screen and a button displays outside the upper right corner of it. Click this button to zoom in. Click once outside the object to return it to its original size.

Web Layout View

This view displays the document the way it will look when viewed in a web browser, so that you can review the text wraps to fit the window and the positioning of graphics. Web Layout view also displays page backgrounds and effects (See Figure 3.31).

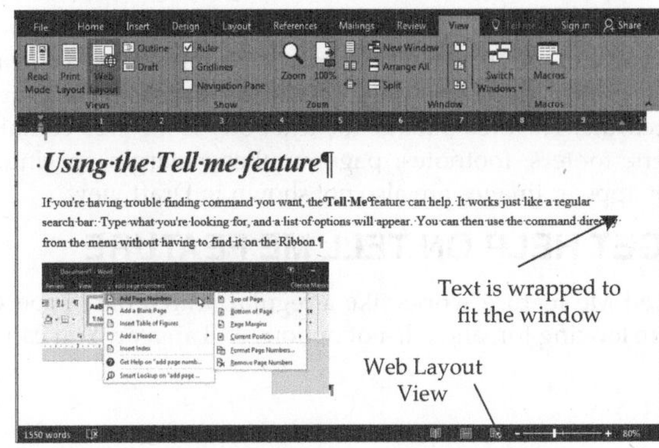

Figure 3.31 Web Layout view

1. Click the **View** tab, in the **Views** group and click **Web Layout** view command. Alternatively click from the status bar icons.

Outline View

In the Outline View, you can collapse a document to see only the main headings or expand it to see the entire document. In this view it is easy to scroll or move text to a longer distance or to change the hierarchy of topics (See Figure 3.32).

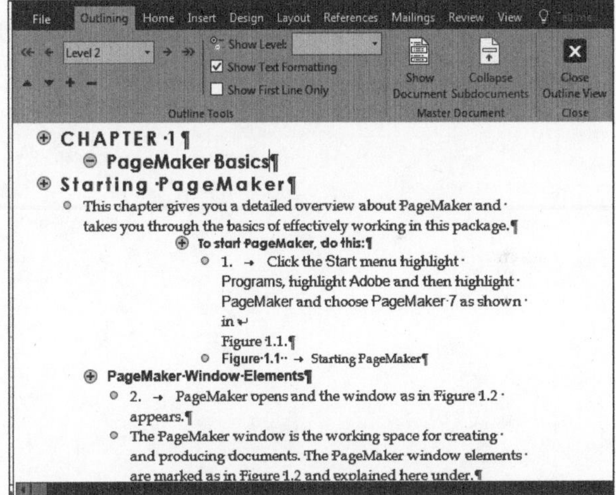

Figure 3.32 Outline view

1. Click the **View** tab, in the Views group and click **Outline** view command. It automatically generates an outline and opens the Outlining tools group.
2. Click the **Outline** level box to change the headings level you want. Alternatively, you can press **Alt+Shift+Left** arrow to change higher level.
3. To change the heading the lower level click the **Alt+Shift+-Right** arrow.
4. Select the text or heading to move text or heading up and down click up or down arrows.

5. Select the heading and click the (+) or (-) sign symbols to expand or collapse text.
6. Click the X on the **Close** Outline view button to the close Outline view.

Draft View

It is the best view for most of your typing and editing. In this view, you can see character and paragraph formatting as the page will be printed. Line and page breaks, tab stops and alignments are accurate. The area outside the text body is the area containing headers, footers, footnotes, page numbers, margin spacing, etc. do not appear. Images are also not shown in Draft view.

3.6 GET HELP ON TELL ME FEATURE

The Tell Me feature works like a regular search bar. Type what you are looking for, and a list of options will appear. You can then use the command directly from the menu without having to find it on the Ribbon (See Figure 3.33).

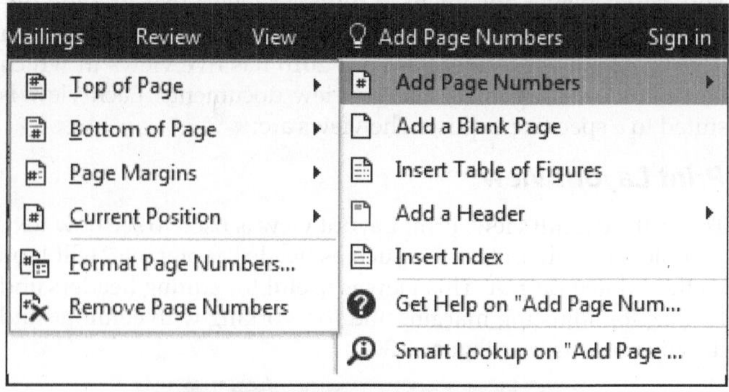

Figure 3.33 Get help on tell me box

CHAPTER 4

Word 2016

4.1 TEXT BASICS

It is important to know how to perform basic tasks with text when working in a word processing application. The basics of working with text includes how to insert, delete, select copy, cut, paste and drag and drop text.

4.1.1 Enter Text

Entering new text in a document is easy. A blinking cursor shows where the next character you enter will appear as shown in Figure 4.1. When you begin entering text, any existing text to the right of the cursor moves to make room for the new text. When the cursor reaches the right margin, the word you are entering moves to the next line.

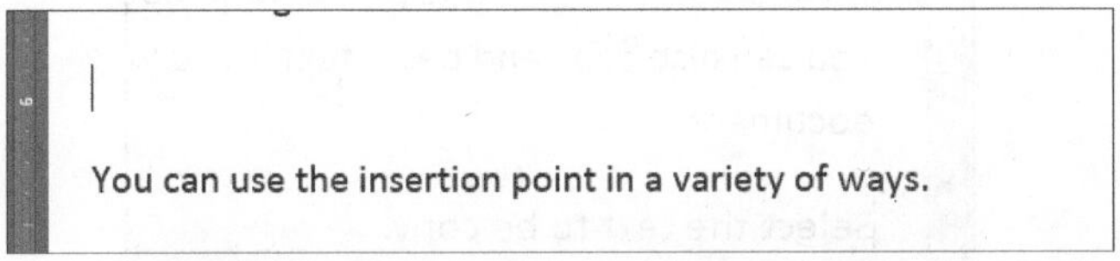

You can use the insertion point in a variety of ways.

Figure 4.1 Showing insertion point to enter text

You can use the insertion point in a variety of ways.

- *Blank document:* When a new blank document opens, the insertion point will appear in the top-left corner of the page.
- *Adding spaces:* Press the spacebar to add spaces after a word or in between text.
- *New paragraph line:* Press Enter on your keyboard to move the insertion point to the next paragraph line.
- *Manual placement:* Once you begin typing, you can use the mouse to move the insertion point to a specific place in your document. Simply click the location in the text where you want to place it.

➡ **To enter text:**

1. Click to position the cursor where you want to add your text, and begin typing.

4.1.2 Select Text

Before you can move or format text, you will need to select it.

➡ **To select text:**

1. Place the insertion point next to the text you wish to select.
2. Click the mouse, and while holding it down, drag your mouse over the text to select it.
3. Release the mouse button. You have selected the text. A highlighted box will appear over the selected text as shown in Figure 4.2.

➡ **To select multiple lines of text:**

1. Move the mouse pointer to the left of any line so it becomes a right slanted arrow. Click the mouse. The line will be selected.
2. To select multiple lines, click and drag the mouse up or down (See Figure 4.3).

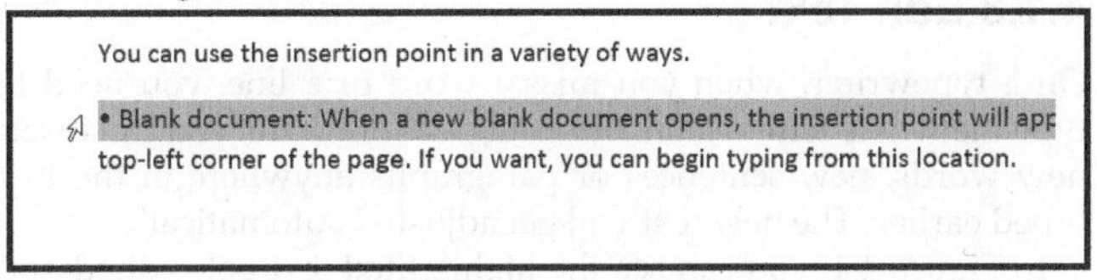

You can use the insertion point in a variety of ways.

• Blank document: When a new blank document opens, the insertion point will app top-left corner of the page. If you want, you can begin typing from this location.

Figure 4.2 Select the text

New paragraph line: Press Enter on your keyboard to move the insertion point to the next paragraph line.

Manual placement: Once you begin typing, you can use the mouse to move the insertion point to a specific place in your document. Simply click the location in the text where you want to place it.

Arrow keys: You can also use the arrow keys on your keyboard to move the insertion point. The left and right arrow keys will move between adjacent characters on the same line, while the up and down arrows will move between paragraph lines. You can also press Ctrl+Left or Ctrl+Right to quickly move between entire words.

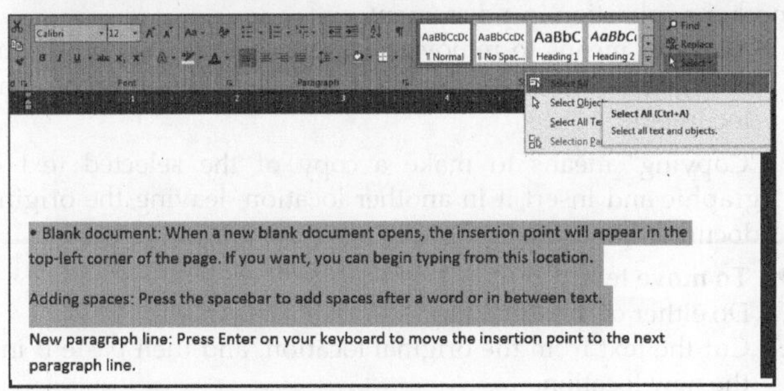

Figure 4.3 Select Multiple lines of text

3. To select all of the text in your document, choose the Select command on the Home tab, then click Select All. Alternatively, you can press Ctrl + A on your keyboard (See Figure 4.3).
4. To select a sentence, hold down the **Ctrl** key and click anywhere in the sentence.
5. To select adjacent words, lines, or paragraphs, drag through the text.
6. Position the cursor at the beginning of the text you want to select, and then do any of the following:
   - To select one character at a time, hold down the **Shift** key and then press the **Left Arrow** or **Right Arrow** key.
   - To select one word at a time, hold down the **Shift** and **Ctrl** keys and then press the **Left Arrow** or **Right Arrow** key.
   - To select one line at a time, hold down the **Shift** key and then press the **Up Arrow** or **Down Arrow** key.

- To select any amount of adjacent content, hold down the Shift key and then click at the end of the content that you want to select.
- To select a word, double-click anywhere in the word. Word selects the word and the space immediately after the word, but not any punctuation after the word.

7. Other shortcuts include double-clicking to select a word and triple-clicking to select an entire sentence or paragraph.

➡ **To release a selection:**

1. Click anywhere in the window other than the selection area.

4.1.3 Edit Text

On a typewriter, when you miss a word or a line, you need to type the whole letter again. But using a Word 2016, you can insert new words, new sentences or paragraphs anywhere in the text typed earlier. The new text will get adjusted automatically.

In Figure 4.4, you can see the highlighted text gets edited and rest of the sentence gets deleted.

When you edit text, you change it, format it, move it from one place in the document to another, or cut chunks out of the document completely.

When you edit text, you change it, move it from one place to another in the document .

Figure 4.4 Editing text in a document

4.1.4 Copying and Moving Text

You can move or copy *text*, a *graphic*, or an item you inserted from another application in a document.

- "Moving" means to remove (cut) the selected text or graphic from one location and insert it in another location in the same document.
- "Copying" means to make a copy of the selected text or graphic and insert it in another location, leaving the original document unchanged.

➡ **To move text:**

1. Do either of the following:
2. Cut the text from the original location, and then paste it into the new location.
3. Drag the text from the original location to the new location.

4.1.5 Cut, Copy and Past Text

To remove text from one place in the document and put it in another you cut and paste the text. You can also copy and paste text if you want to add copies of your selection elsewhere in your document.

➡ **To Copy and Past text:**

1. Select the text you want to copy.
2. On the **Home** tab, in the **Clipboard** group, click the copy button. You can also right-click your document and select **Copy** (See Figure 4.5).
3. Place the insertion point where you want the text to appear.
4. Click the **Paste** command on the **Home** tab. The text will appear as shown in Figure 4.6.

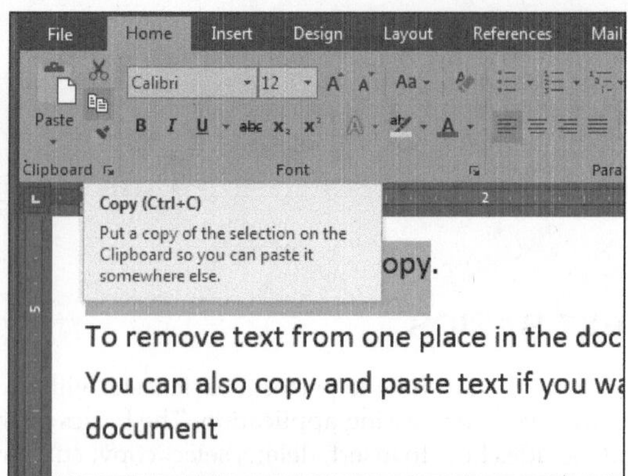

Figure 4.5 Copy text

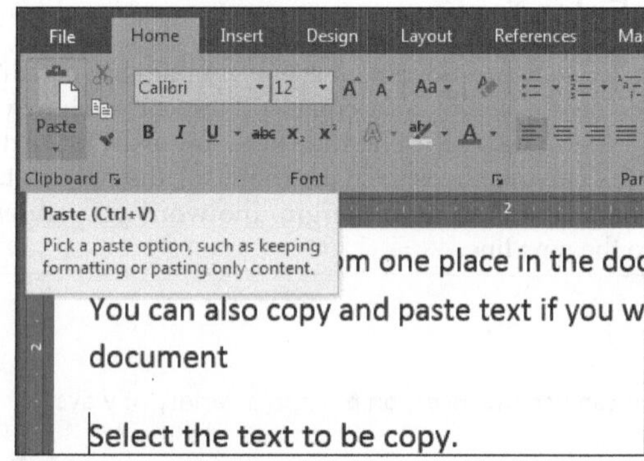

Figure 4.6 Paste text

➡ **To Cut and Paste Text:**

1. Select the text you want to copy.
2. On the **Home** tab, in the **Clipboard** group, click the **Cut** button. You can also right-click your document and select **Cut** (See Figure 4.7).

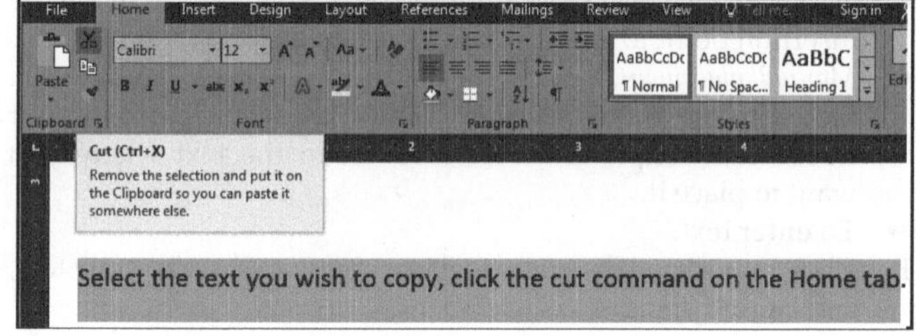

Figure 4.7 Cut the text

3. Place the insertion point where you want the text to appear.
4. On the **Home** tab of **Clipboard** group, click the **Paste** button. The text will appear as shown in Figure 4.8.

4.1.6 Drag and Drop Text

1. Select the text you want to move.
2. Click and drag the text to the location you want it to appear. The cursor will have a rectangle under it to indicate that you are moving text (See Figure 4.9).

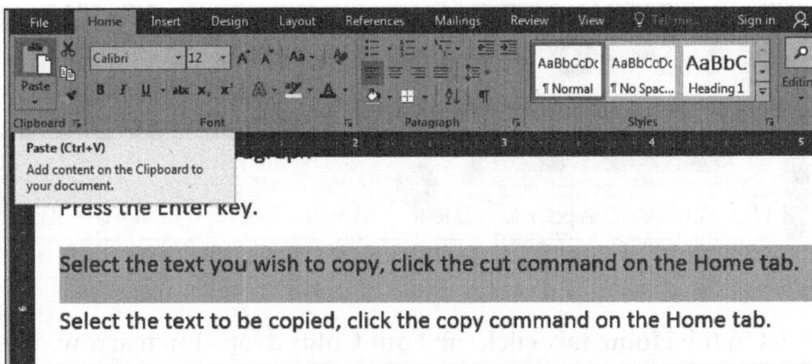

Figure 4.8 Paste the text

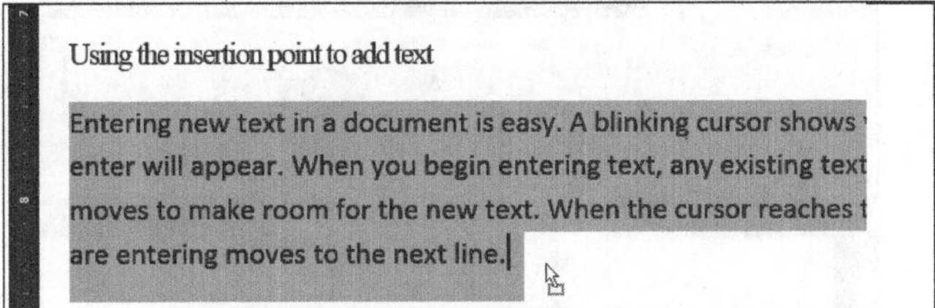

Figure 4.9 Dragging and Dropping text

3. Release the mouse button and the text will appear.
4. If text does not appear in the exact location you wish, you can click the Enter key on your keyboard to move the text to a new line.

4.1.7 Undo and Redo

When you are working in a document, by accidentally delete some text. Fortunately, you would not have to retype again you just deleted. Word allows you to undo your most recent action when you make a mistake.

➡ **To undo the action:**

1. Select the **Undo** command on the **Quick Access Toolbar** (See Figure 4.10). Alternatively, you can press **Ctrl+Z** on your keyboard.

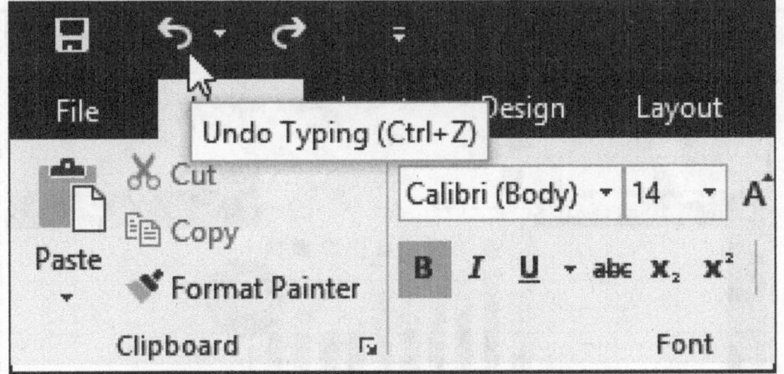

Figure 4.10 Selecting Undo command

You can continue using this command to undo multiple changes in a row.

2. By contrast, the **Redo** command allows you to reverse the last undo. You can also access this command by pressing **Ctrl+Y** on your keyboard (See Figure 4.11).

4.1.8 Zooming In or Out a Document

To zoom in or out, click and drag the zoom control slider in the bottom-right corner of the window. You can also select the + or -

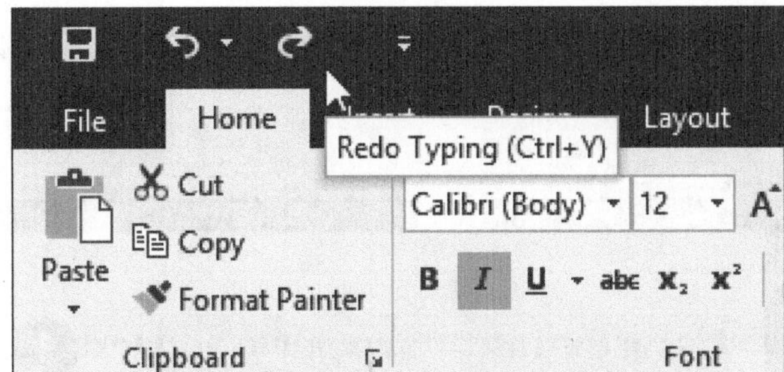

Figure 4.11 Selecting Redo command

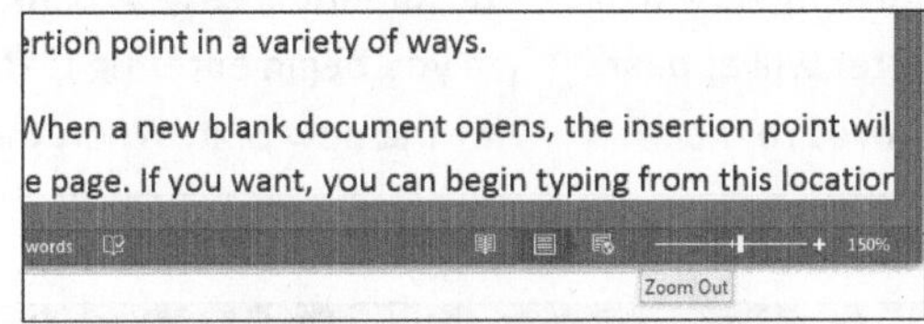

Figure 4.12 Selecting Zoom controls

commands to zoom in or out by smaller increments. The number next to the slider displays the current zoom percentage, also called the zoom level (See Figure 4.12).

➡ **In the zoom controls at the right end of the status bar, do any of the following:**

1. Drag the slider to the left to decrease the magnification or to the right to increase the magnification.
2. At the left end of the slider, click the Zoom Out button to decrease the magnification in 10-percent increments.
3. At the right end of the slider, click the Zoom In button to increase the magnification in 10-percent increments.

4.2 FORMATTING TEXT

Character and paragraph formatting commands are found on the Home tab of the Ribbon. To apply any of the formatting options, first select the text and then click the button or check box for the option(s) that you want to apply. In Word, you have several options for adjusting text, including font, size, and color. You can also adjust the alignment of the text to change how it is displayed on the page.

4.2.1 Change Font and Font Size

➡ **To change the font size:**

1. Select the text size you want to change.
2. On the **Home** tab, click the **Font** size drop-down arrow. Select a font size from the menu as shown in Figure 4.13. If the font size is not available in the menu, you can click the Font size box and type the desired font size, then press Enter.
3. The font size will change in the document (See Figure 4.14).
4. You can also use the Grow Font and Shrink Font commands to change the font size.
   - To increase the font size in set increments, click the **Increase Font Size** button, or press **Ctrl + >**.
   - To decrease the font size in set increments, click the **Decrease Font Size** button, or press **Ctrl + <**.

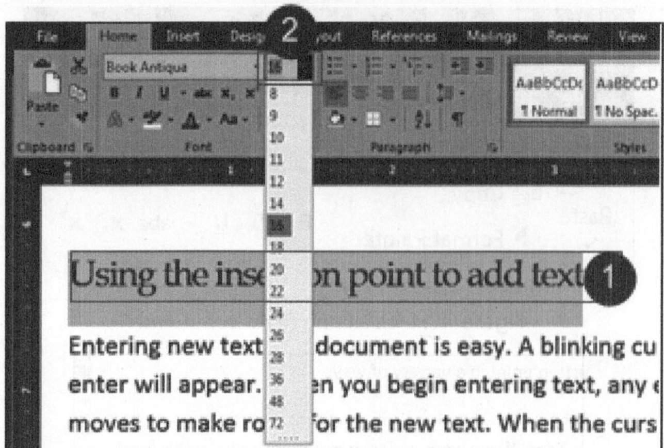

Figure 4.13 Selecting font size

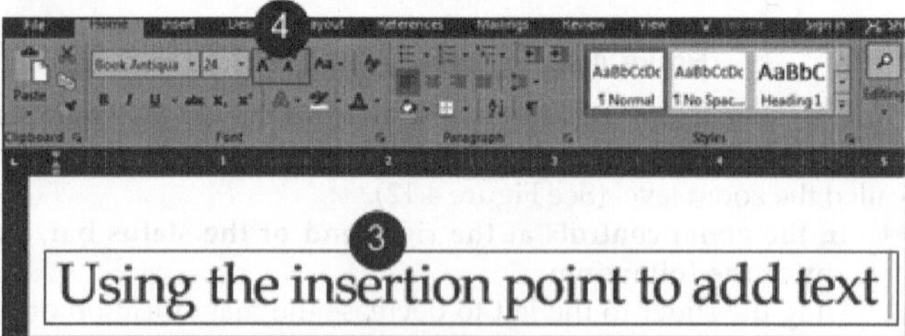

Figure 4.14 Applied font size in the document

➡ **To change the font:**

By default, the font of each new document is set to Calibri. However, Word provides many other fonts you can use to customize text. When creating a professional document or a document that contains multiple paragraphs, you will want to select a font that is easy to read.

1. Select the text you want to change.
2. On the **Home** tab, click the drop-down arrow next to the Font box. A menu of font styles will appear as shown in Figure 4.15. Or On Right clicking the mouse button a Mini Toolbar appear select the font from the font drop-down list. Alternatively **Ctrl+Shift+F**.

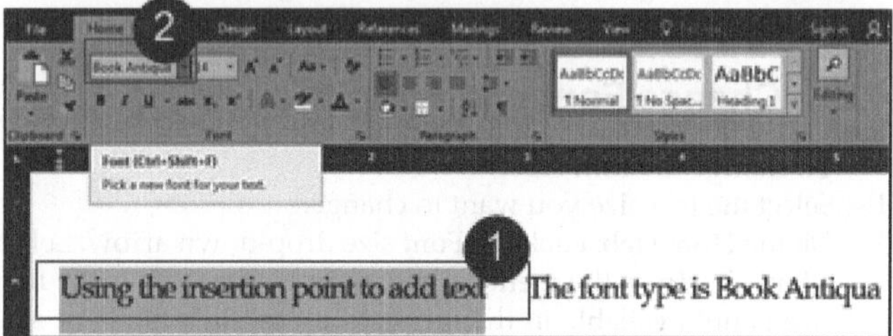

Figure 4.15 Selecting font type

3. Select the font style you want to use.
4. The font will change in the document (See Figure 4.16).

4.2.2 Change Color

➡ **To change the font color:**

1. Select the text which you want to change the font color.

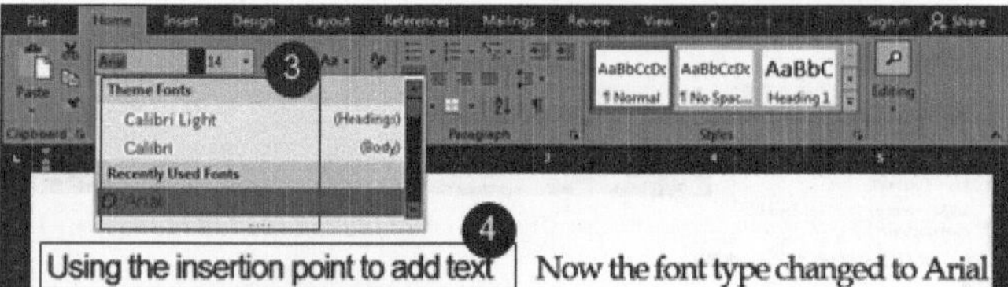

Figure 4.16 Applied font type

2. On the **Home** tab, click the **Font Color** drop-down arrow. The **Font Color** menu appears as shown in Figure 4.17.

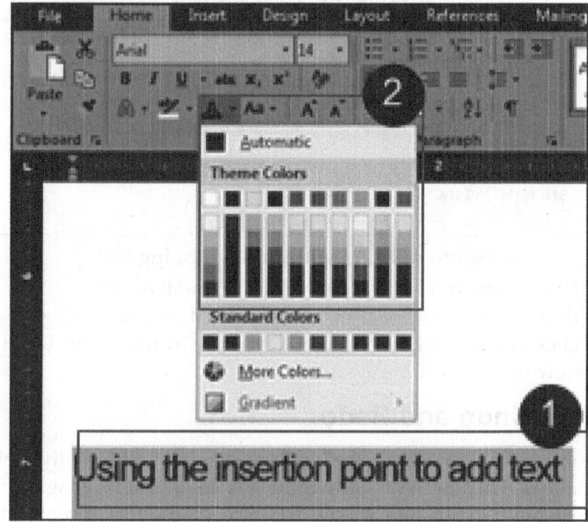

Figure 4.17 Selecting font color

3. Select the font color you want to use.
4. The font color will change in the document as shown in Figure 4.18.

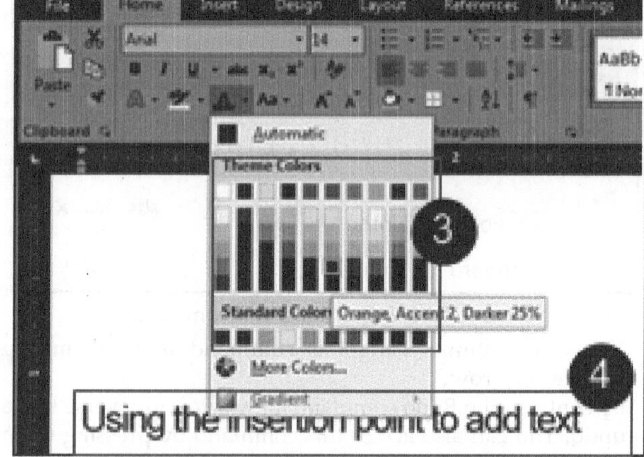

Figure 4.18 Applied font color in the document

5. Select **More Colors** at the bottom of the menu to access the Colors dialog box. Choose the color you want, then click OK.

4.2.3 Use the Bold, Italic, and Underline Commands

The Bold, Italic, and Underline commands can be used to help draw attention to important words or phrases.

➡ **To format selected text as bold, italic, or underlined button:**

1. Select the text which you want to change the style.
2. On the Home tab, click the Bold (B), Italic (I), or Underline (U) command in the Font group. In our example, we will click Bold and underline. (See Figure 4.19)
3. The selected text will be modified in the document.

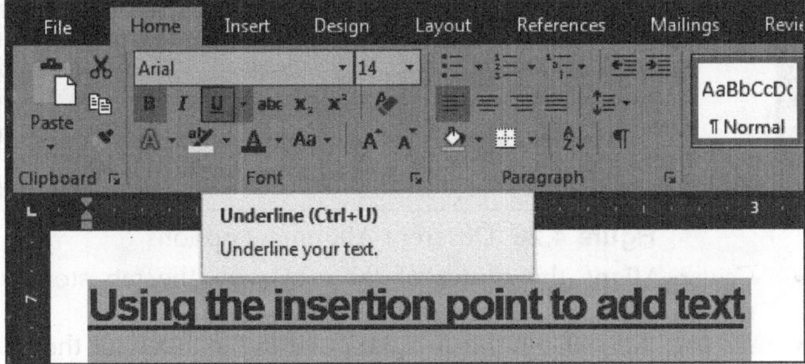

Figure 4.19 Selecting text format Bold and Underline

4.2.4 Change Text Case

When you need to quickly change text case, you can use the Change Case command instead of deleting and retyping text.

➡ **To change text case:**

1. Select the text of which you want to change the text case.
2. On the Home tab, click the Change Case command in the Font group.
3. A drop-down menu will appear as shown in Figure 4.20. Select the desired case option from the menu.
4. The text case will be changed in the document.

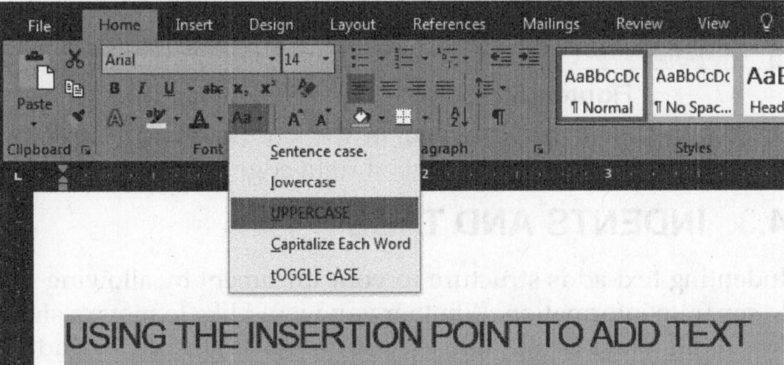

Figure 4.20 Selecting Change Case command in the Font group

Apply Style

A style is a pre-defined combination of font style, color, and size that can be applied to any text in your document. Styles can help your documents to achieve a more professional look. You can also use styles to quickly change several styles in the document at the same time.

➡ **To apply a style**

1. Select the text you want to apply style. Place your cursor at the beginning of the line.
2. In the Styles group on the Home tab, click the More drop-down arrow as shown in Figure 4.21.

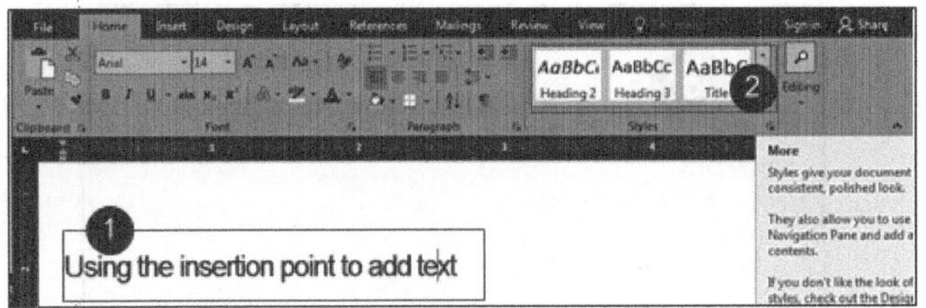

Figure 4.21 Selecting Style from the home tab

3. Select the desired style from the drop-down menu.
4. The selected style will appear in the text as shown in Figure 4.22.

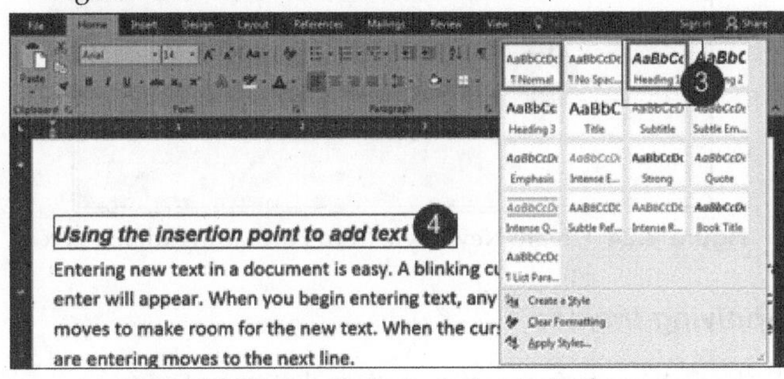

Figure 4.22 Applied selected style in the text

➡ **To create a new style:**

1. On the **Home** tab, click the arrow in the bottom-right corner of the **Styles** group.
2. The **Styles** task pane will appear as shown in Figure 4.23. Select the **New Style** button at the bottom of the task pane.

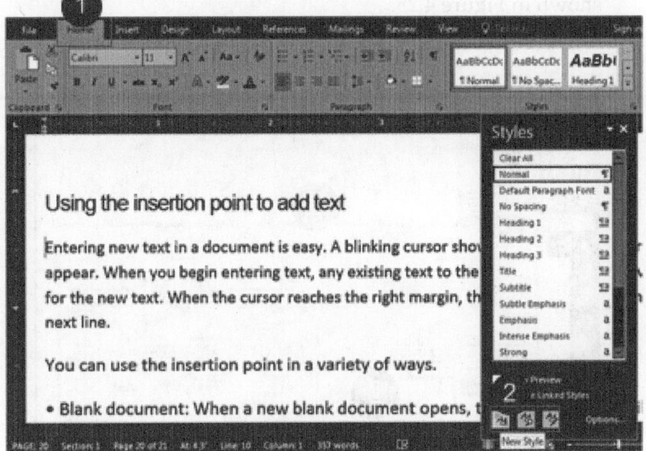

Figure 4.23 Selecting Style task pane in the home tab

3. Create **New Style from Formatting** dialog box will appear as shown in Figure 4.24. Enter a name for the style, for example, we have typed BodyText, choose the desired text formatting such as choose font type, font size and Alignment under the formatting section.
4. Click the **Add to the Styles** gallery check box. Then click OK.
5. The new style applied in the **Styles** group.

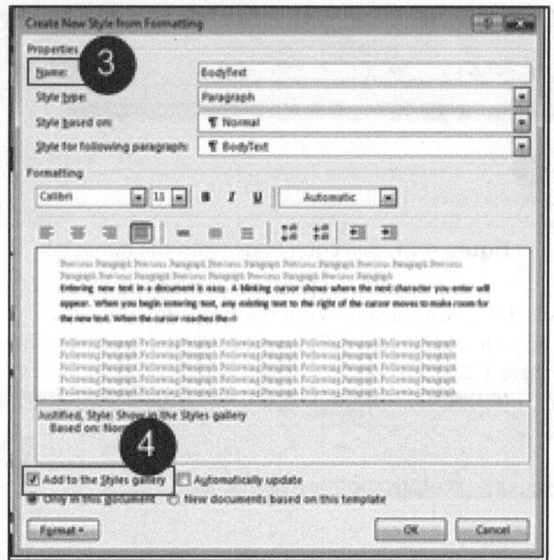

Figure 4.24 Create New Style from Formatting dialog box

Applying themes

A Theme is a set of formatting options that is applied to an entire document. A theme includes a set of colors, fonts and effects. Using themes shortens formatting time and provides a unified, professional appearance.

➡ **To apply a style set:**

1. From the **Design** tab, click the **More** drop-down arrow in the **Document Formatting** group.
2. Choose the desired style set from the drop-down menu as shown in Figure 4.25.
3. The selected style set will be applied to the entire document.

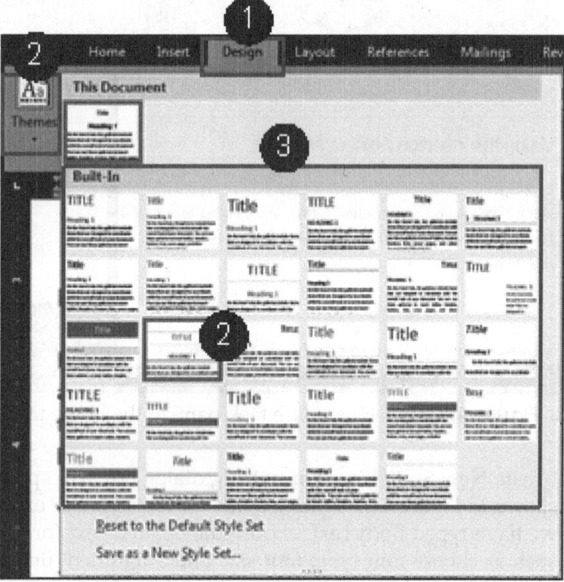

Figure 4.25 Applied Theme

4.2.5 Text Alignment

By default, Word aligns text to the left margin in new documents. The alignment settings control the horizontal position of the paragraph text between the page margins. There are four alignment options (See Figure 4.26):

- *Align Left*–This is the default paragraph alignment. Aligns the left end of the text with the tap stop. It results in a straight left edge and a ragged right edge.
- *Align Right*–Aligns the right end of the text with the tab stop. It results in a straight right edge and a ragged left edge.

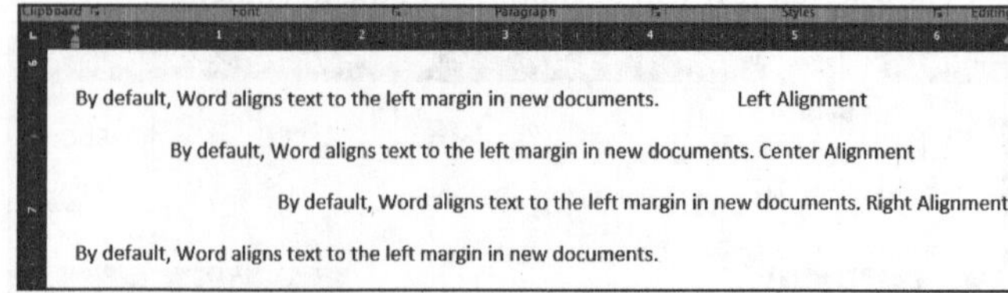

Figure 4.26 Different Alignment options

- *Center*–Aligns the center of the text with the tab stop. It results in ragged left and right edges.
- *Decimal Tab*–Aligns the decimal point in the text with the tab stop.
- *Bar Tab*–Draw a vertical line at the position of the tab stop.

➡ **To change text alignment:**

1. Select the text which you want to change.
2. On the Home tab, select one of the four alignment options from the Paragraph group. In our example, we have selected Left Alignment as shown in Figure 4.27.

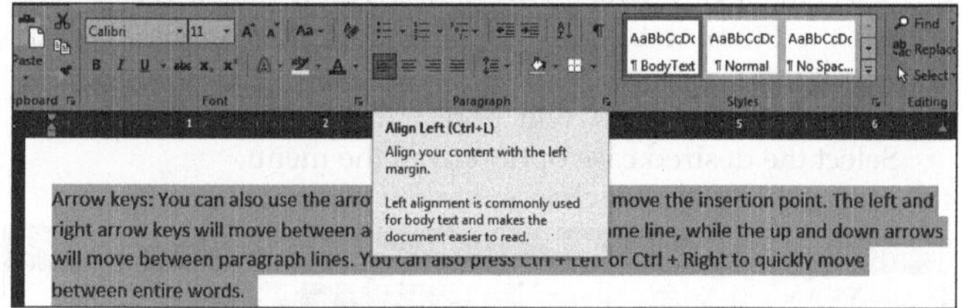

Figure 4.27 Select Align Left command

3. The text will be realigned in the document. If text shows straight left edge and a ragged right edge.

4.3. INDENTS AND TABS

Indenting text adds structure to your document by allowing you to separate information. Whether you would like to move a single line or an entire paragraph, you can use the tab selector and the horizontal ruler to set tabs and indents.

4.3.1 Indenting text

In many types of documents, you may want to indent only the first line of each paragraph. This helps to visually separate paragraphs from one another. A quick way to indent is to use the Tab key. This will create a first-line indent of 1/2 inch.

➡ **To indent using the Tab key:**

1. Place the insertion point at the very beginning of the paragraph you want to indent.
2. Press the **Tab** key. On the Ruler, you should see the first-line indent marker move to the right by 1/2 inch.

3. The first line of the paragraph will be indented as shown in Figure 4.28.

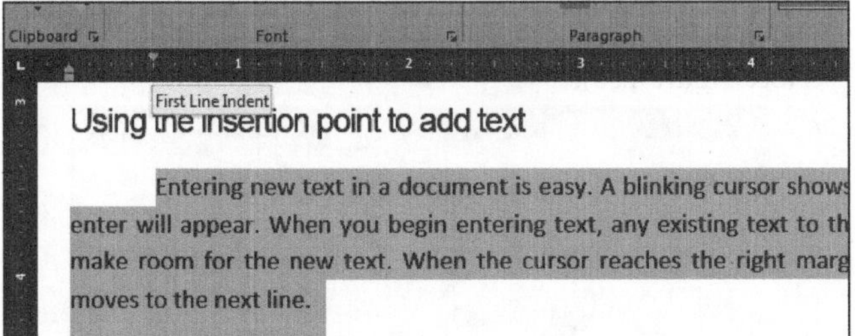

Figure 4.28 Using Tab key to indent text

4.3.2 Indent Markers

A Paragraph indent is the space from the page margin to the text. Word provides indent markers that allow you to indent paragraphs to the location you want. You can change the left indent by clicking buttons on the Home tab, or you can set the indents directly on the ruler.

The indent markers are located to the left of the horizontal ruler, and they provide several indenting options:

- *First-line indent marker*–adjusts the first-line indent
- *Hanging indent marker*–adjusts the hanging indent
- *Left indent marker*–moves both the first-line indent and hanging indent markers at the same time.

➡ **To indent using the indent markers:**

1. Place the insertion point anywhere in the paragraph you want to indent, or select one or more paragraphs as shown in Figure 4.29.

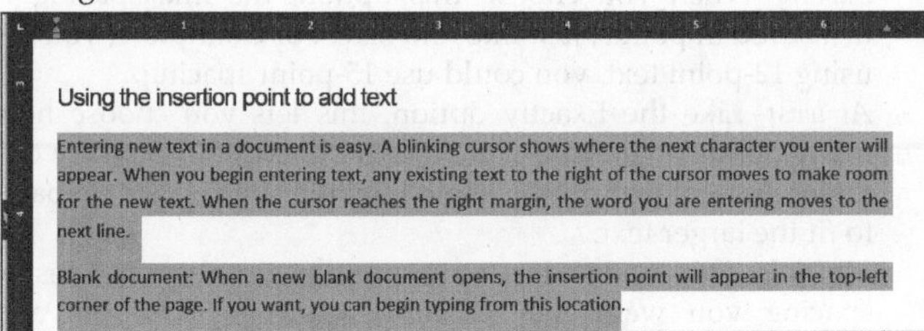

Figure 4.29 Select Paragraphs

2. Click and drag the desired indent marker. In our example, we have click and drag the left indent marker.
3. Release the mouse. The paragraphs will be indented as shown in Figure 4.30.

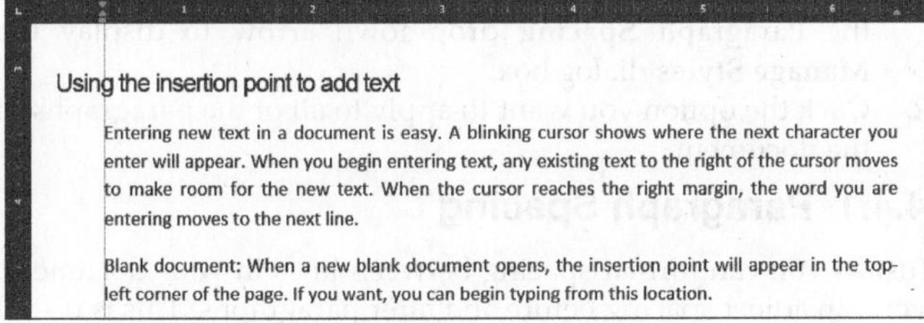

Figure 4.30 The paragraphs get Left indent indented

4.3.3 Indent Commands

If you want to indent multiple lines of text or all lines of a paragraph, you can use the Indent commands. The Indent commands will adjust the indent by 1/2-inch increments.

➡ **To indent using the Indent commands:**

1. Select the text you want to indent.
2. On the Home tab, click the Increase Indent or Decrease Indent command.
3. The text will indent as shown in Figure 4.31.

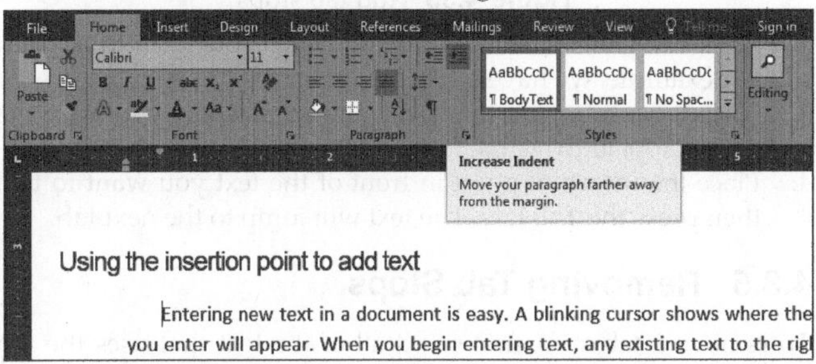

Figure 4.31 Indent commands on the Home tab

4. You can also customize the indent amounts, select the Layout tab near the desired values in the boxes under Indent.

4.3.4 Tabs and Tab Selector

Using tabs gives you more control over the placement of text. By default, every time you press the Tab key, the insertion point will move 1/2 inch to the right. At the far left of the horizontal ruler is the tab selector that lets you choose from different types of tab stops. The most commonly used tab stop is a Left Tab and more can be selected by clicking the tab selector.

Figure 4.32 shows different tab stops with explanation:

- *Left Tab*–Left aligns text to the left of the tab stop.
- *Center Tab*–Centers the text on the tab stop.
- *Right Tab*–Right aligns the text to the right of the tab stop.
- *Decimal Tab*–Aligns decimal numbers by their decimal point.
- *Bar Tab*–Draws a vertical line on the document.
- *First Line Indent*–Inserts the indent marker on the ruler and indents the first line of text in a paragraph.
- *Hanging Indent*–Inserts the hanging indent marker and indents all lines other than the first line.

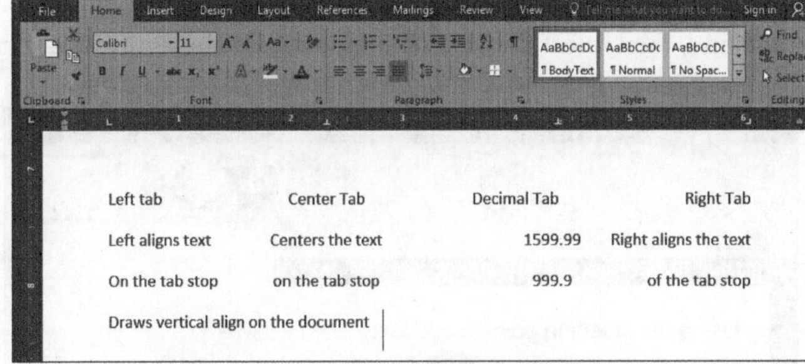

Figure 4.32 Set different tab stops

➡ **To add tab stops:**

1. Select any portion of one or more paragraphs that you want to set the tab stop for (See Figure 4.33).

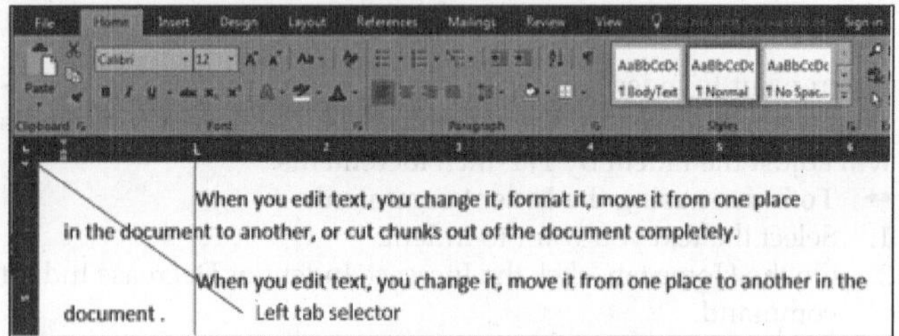

Figure 4.33 Add tab stops

2. Click the tab selector until the tab stop you want to appear. For example, we have selected Left tab.
3. Click the location on the horizontal ruler where you want the text to appear to set the tab.
4. Place the insertion point in front of the text you want to tab, then press the Tab key. The text will jump to the next tab.

4.3.5 Removing Tab Stops

To remove a tab stop, first select all of the text that uses the tab stop. Then click and drag it off of the Ruler. You can also display hidden formatting symbols such as spaces, paragraph marks, and tabs to help you to see the formatting in your document. To show hidden formatting symbols, select the Home tab, then click the Show/Hide command.

4.4 LINE AND PARAGRAPH SPACING

The default line spacing for documents created in Word 2016 is 1.08 lines which is slightly larger than single spaced. Changing the line spacing changes the appearance and readability of the text in the paragraph. Paragraphs have two types of vertical spacing:

Paragraph spacing–The space between paragraphs, defined by setting the space before and after each paragraph. This space is usually measured in points.

Line spacing–The space between the lines of the paragraph, defined by setting the height of the lines either in relation to the height of the text (Single,Double, or a specific number of lines) or by specifying a minimum or exact point measurement.

➡ **To format line spacing:**

1. Select the text you want to format.
2. On the Home tab, click the Line and Paragraph Spacing command, then select the desired line spacing (See Figure 4.34).

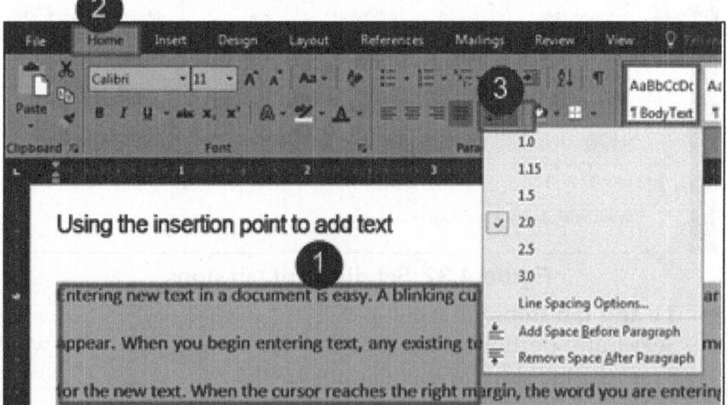

Figure 4.34 Select Line spacing

3. The line spacing will change in the document. Alternatively, you can also choose the paragraph dialog box Launcher.
4. The following options describes the effect of each Paragraph Spacing option on the paragraph and line spacing settings (See Figure 4.35).

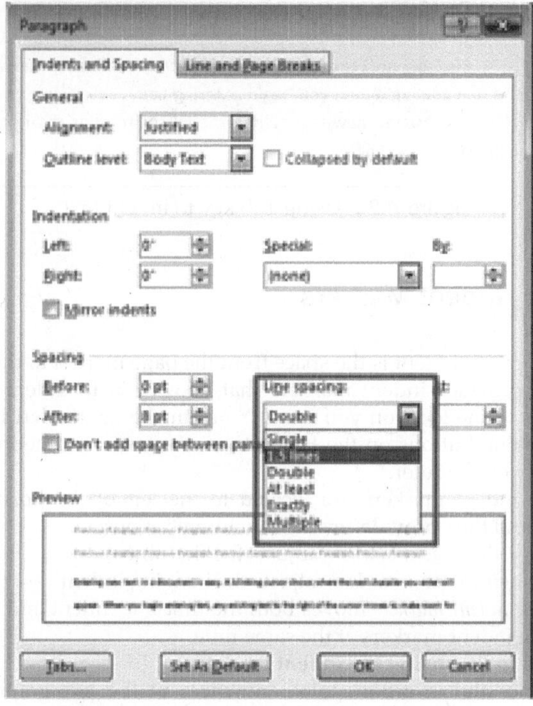

Figure 4.35 Paragraph Spacing dialog box

Exactly–When you choose this option, the line spacing is measured in points, just like font size. For example, if you are using 12-point text, you could use 15-point spacing.

At least–Like the Exactly option, this lets you choose how many points of spacing you want. However, if you have different sizes of text on the same line, the spacing will expand to fit the larger text.

Multiple–This option lets you type the number of lines of spacing you want. For example, choosing Multiple and changing the spacing to 1.2 will make the text slightly more spread out than single-spaced text. You can also choose a smaller value, like 0.9 to be closer together between the paragraph.

➡ **To quickly adjust the vertical spacing before, after, and within all paragraphs in a document**

1. On the **Design** tab, in the **Document Formatting** group, click the **Paragraph Spacing** drop-down arrow to display the **Manage Styles** dialog box.
2. Click the option you want to apply to all of the paragraphs in the document.

4.4.1 Paragraph Spacing

Just as you can format spacing between lines in your document, you can adjust spacing before and after paragraphs. This is useful for separating paragraphs, headings, and subheadings.

➡ **To format paragraph spacing:**

1. Select the paragraph or paragraphs you want to format.

2. Select all the paragraphs you want to adjust.
3. On the **Layout** tab, in the **Paragraph** group, adjust the **Spacing Before** and **Spacing After** settings (See Figure 4.36). Or

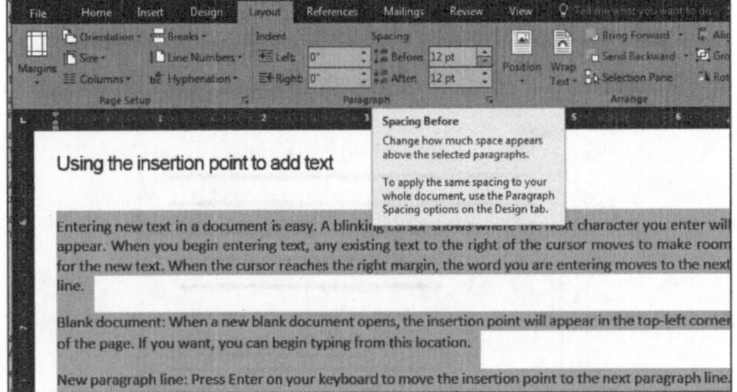

Figure 4.36 Selecting Paragraph spacing

4. From the drop-down menu, you can also select **Line Spacing Options** to open the **Paragraph** dialog box. From here, you can control how much space there is before and after the paragraph.
5. The paragraph spacing will change in the document.

4.4.2 Working with Lists

Bulleted and numbered lists can be used in the documents to outline, arrange, and emphasize text. You can also learn how to insert new bulleted and numbered lists, select symbols as bullets, and format multilevel lists.

4.4.3 Create Bullets Lists

➡ **To create a bulleted list:**

1. Select the text you want to format as a list.
2. On the **Home** tab, click the drop-down arrow next to the **Bullets** command. A menu of bullet styles will appear as shown in Figure 4.37.
3. Move the mouse over the various bullet styles. A live preview of the bullet style will appear in the document. Select the bullet style you want to use.

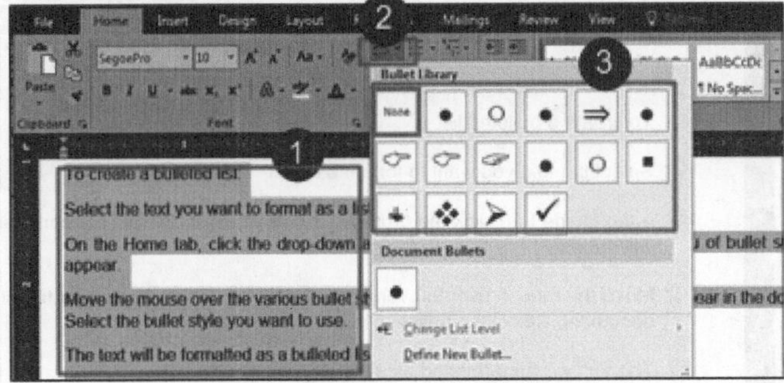

Figure 4.37 Selecting Bullet style

4. The selected bullet style formatted in the text as shown in Figure 4.38.

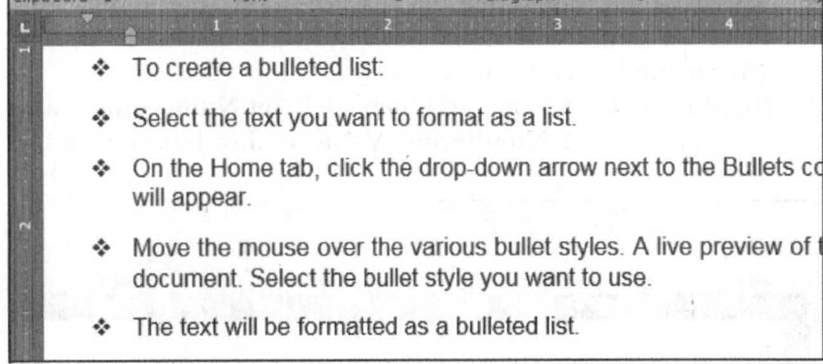

Figure 4.38 Applied Bullet style in the document

4.4.4 Create Number Lists

When you need to organise text into a numbered list, Word offers several numbering options. You can format your list with numbers, letters, or Roman numerals.

1. Select the text which you want to format as a list.
2. On the **Home** tab, click the drop-down arrow next to the **Numbering** command. A menu of numbering styles will appear as shown in Figure 4.39.

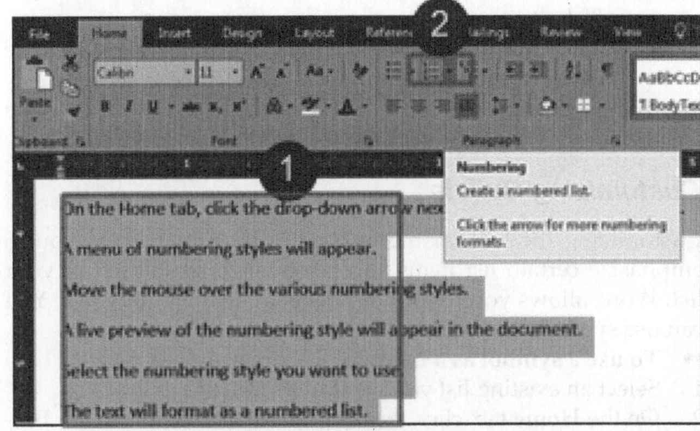

Figure 4.39 Selecting Number style

3. Move the mouse over the various numbering styles. A live preview of the numbering style will appear in the document. Select the numbering style you want to use.
4. The text will format as a numbered list (See Figure 4.40).

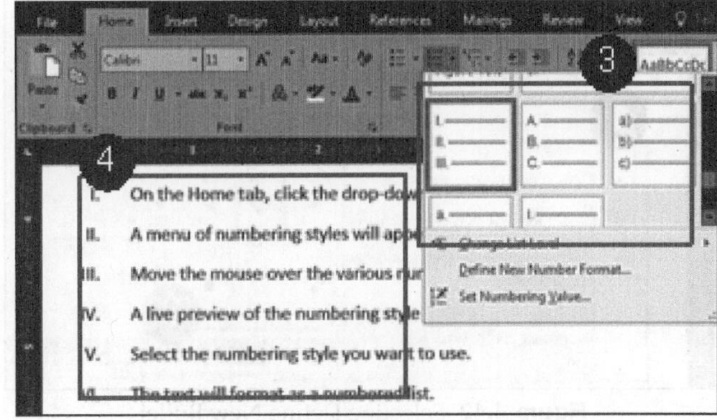

Figure 4.40 Applied Number style in the document

➡ **To start a list or part of a list at a pre-defined number**

1. Place the cursor within an existing list, in the list paragraph whose number you want to set.
2. Right-click the list item and then click **Set Numbering Value** to open the **Set Numbering Value** dialog box appears as shown in Figure 4.41.

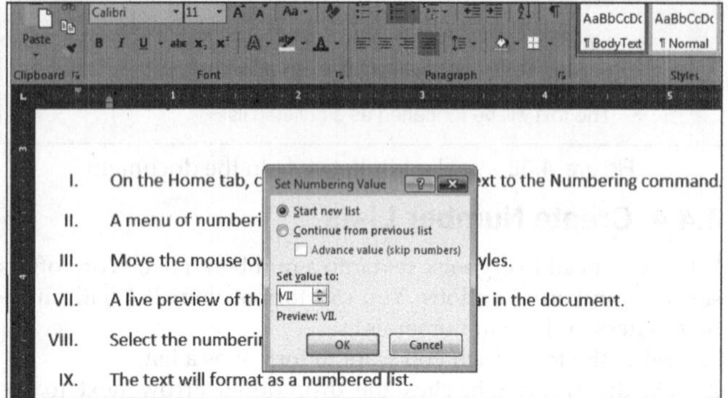

Figure 4.41 Set Numbering value dialog box

3. Do either one of the following to choose custom numbering:
   - Click **Start** new list.
   - Click **Continue from previous** list, and then select the **Advance value** (skip numbers) check box.
4. In the **Set value to** box, enter the number you want to assign to the list item. Then click OK.

Customizing Bullets

Customizing the look of the bullets in the list can help you to emphasize certain list items and personalize the design of your list. Word allows you to format bullets in a variety of ways. You can use symbols as a bullet.

➡ **To use a symbol as a bullet:**

1. Select an existing list you want to format.
2. On the **Home** tab, click the drop-down arrow next to the **Bullets** command. Select **Define New Bullet** from the drop-down menu as shown in Figure 4.42.

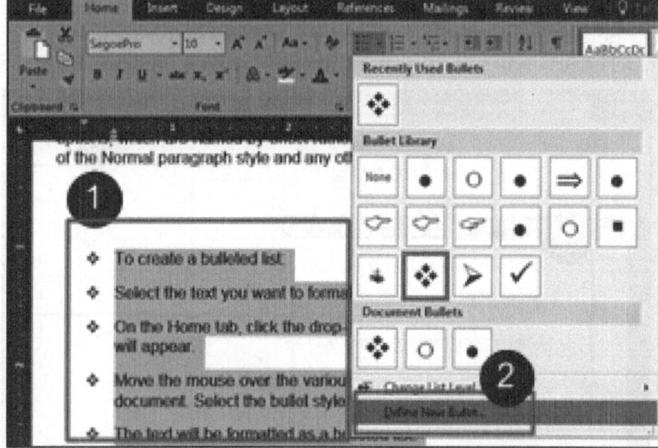

Figure 4.42 Selecting Define New Bullet

3. The **Define New Bullet** dialog box will appear as shown in Figure 4.43. Click the **Symbol** button.
4. The **Symbol** dialog box will appear as shown in Figure 4.44.

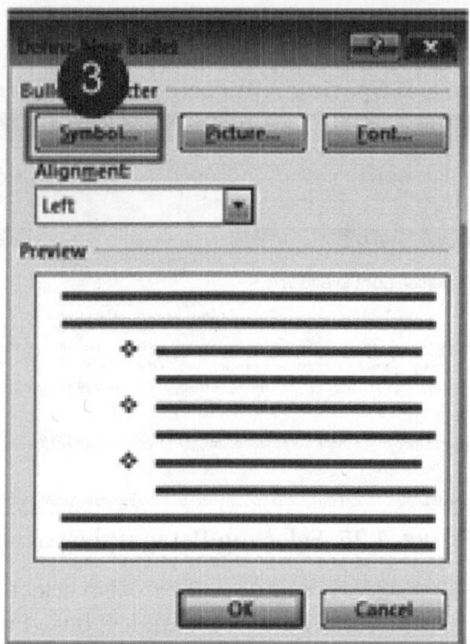

Figure 4.43 Define New Bullet dialog box

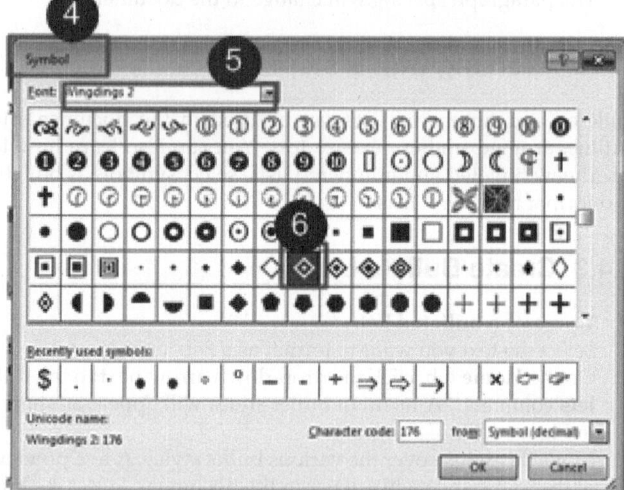

Figure 4.44 Symbol dialog box

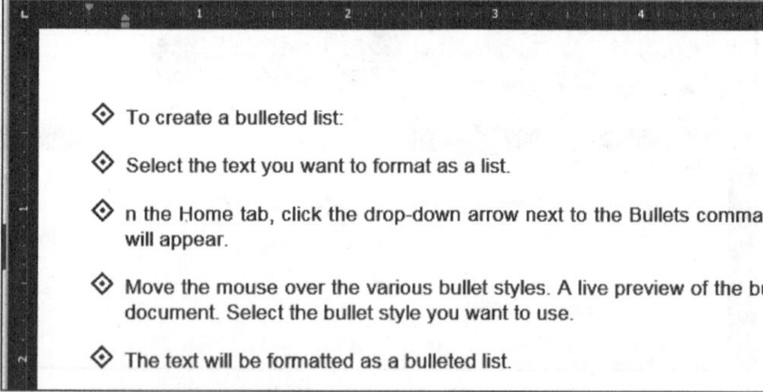

Figure 4.45 The selected symbol style in the document

5. Click the **Font:** drop-down box and select a font. The **Wingdings** and **Symbol** fonts are good choices because they have many useful symbols.
6. Select the desired symbol, then click OK.

7. The symbol will appear in the **Preview** section of the **Define New Bullet** dialog box. Click OK.
8. The selected symbol style appears in the text document as shown in Figure 4.45 and also appears in the bullet list.

Multilevel lists

Multilevel lists allow you to create an outline with multiple levels. Any bulleted or numbered list can be turned into a multilevel list by using the Tab key.

- **To create a multilevel list:**

1. Place the insertion point at the beginning of the line you want to move.

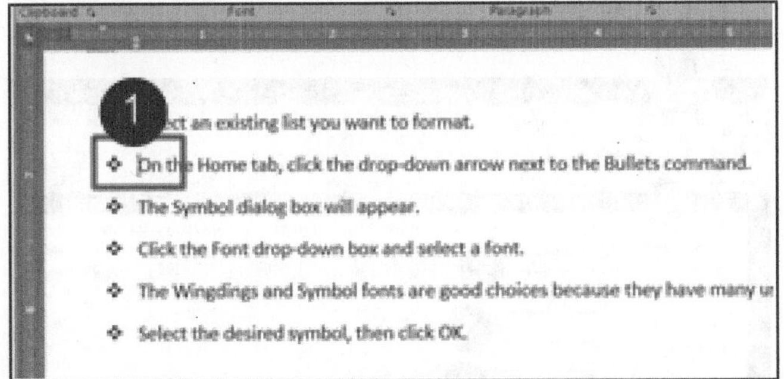

2. Press the **Tab** key to increase the indent level of the line. The line will move to the right and insert default bullet.

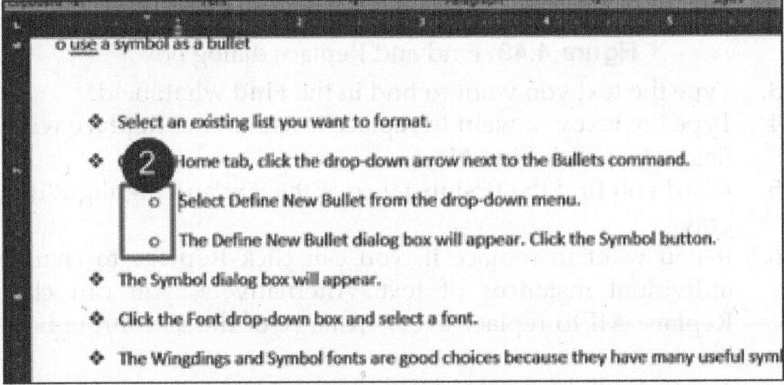

Increase or Decrease an indent level

You can make adjustments to the organization of a multilevel list by increasing or decreasing the indent levels. There are several ways to change the indent level.

- To increase the indent by more than one level, place the insertion point at the beginning of the line, then press the **Tab** key until the desired level is reached.

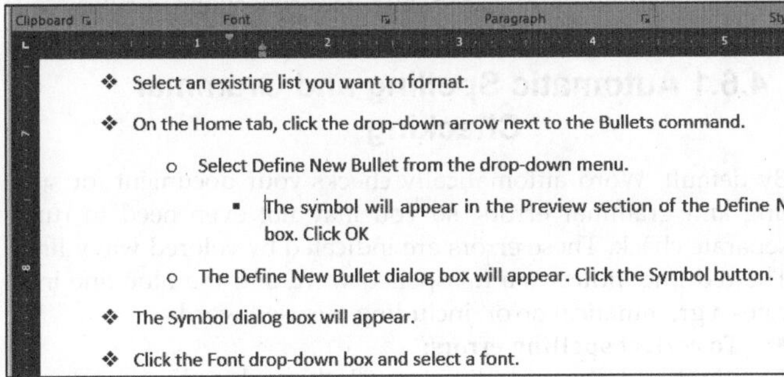

- To decrease the indent level, place the insertion point at the beginning of the line, then hold the **Shift** key and press the **Tab** key.

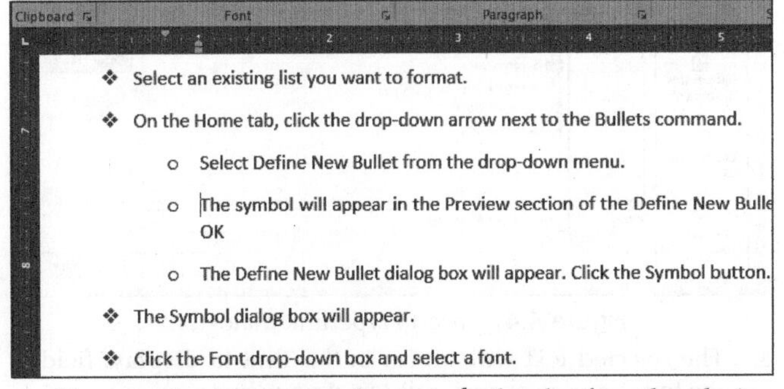

- You can also increase or decrease the levels of text by placing the insertion point anywhere in the line and clicking the **Increase Indent** or **Decrease Indent** commands.

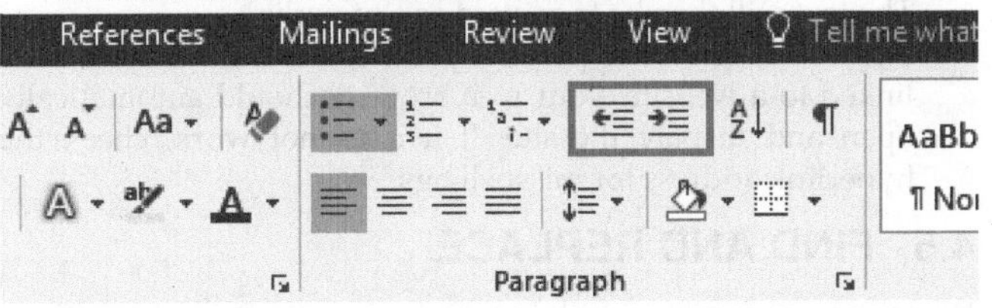

4.4.5 Understanding hyperlinks in Word

Hyperlinks have two basic parts: the address (URL) of the webpage and the display text. For example, the address could be http://www.bpbonline.com, and the display text could be Popular Book Store. When you create a hyperlink in Word, you will be able to choose both the address and the display text.

Word often recognizes email and web addresses as you type and will automatically format them as hyperlinks after you press Enter or the spacebar.

➡ **To format text with a hyperlink:**

1. Select the text you want to format as a hyperlink.
2. Select the **Insert** tab, then click the **Hyperlink** command as shown in Figure 4.46.

   Alternatively, you can open the **Insert Hyperlink** dialog box by right-clicking the selected text and selecting **Hyperlink...** from the menu that appears.

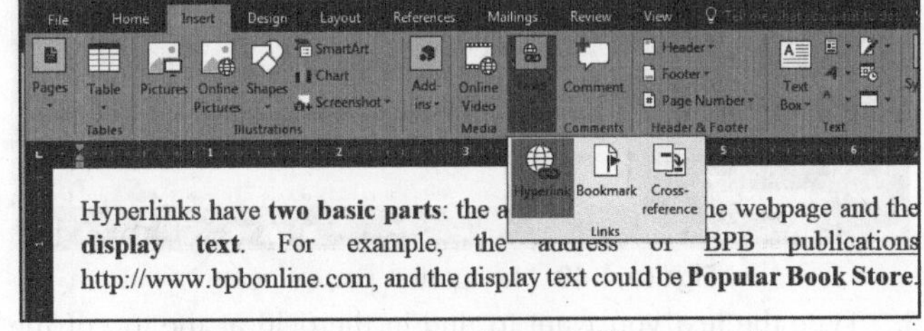

Figure 4.46 Selecting hyperlink command

3. The **Insert Hyperlink** dialog box will appear as shown in Figure 4.47.

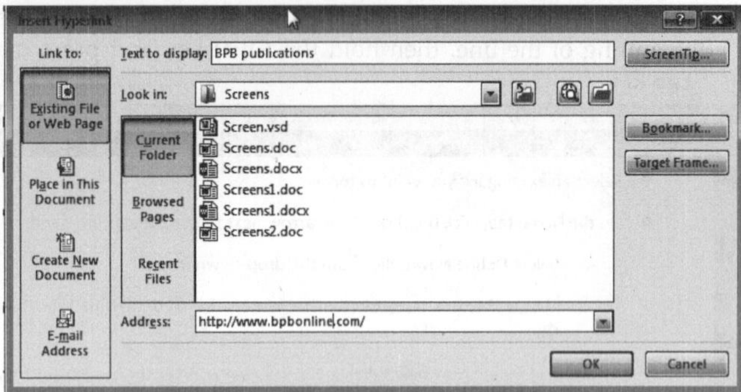

Figure 4.47 Insert Hyperlink dialog box

4. The selected text will appear in the **Text to display:** field at the top. You can change this text if you want.
5. In the **Address:** field, type the address you want to link to, then click OK.
6. The text will then be formatted as a hyperlink.

   After you create a hyperlink, you should test it. If you have linked to a website, your web browser should automatically open and display the site. If it does not work, check the hyperlink address for misspellings.

4.5 FIND AND REPLACE

When you are working with longer documents, it can be difficult and time consuming to locate a specific word or phrase. Word can automatically search your document using the Find feature, and it even allows you to change words or phrases using Replace.

4.5.1 Finding Text

- **To find text:**

1. From the **Home** tab, click the **Find** command. Alternatively, you can press **Ctrl+F** on your keyboard.
2. The **navigation** pane will appear on the left side of the screen as shown in Figure 4.48.

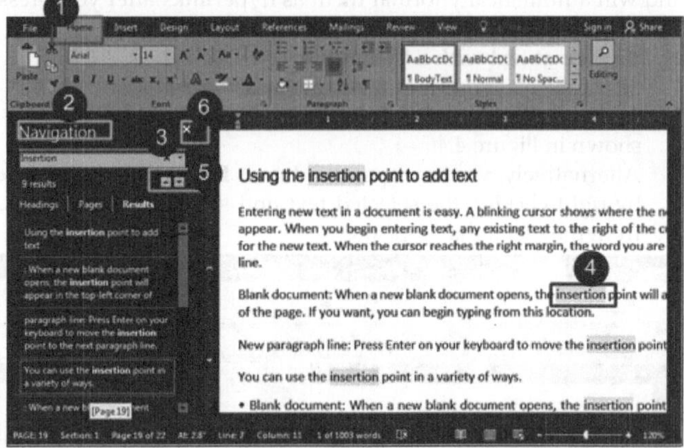

Figure 4.48 Navigation pane screen

3. Type the text you want to find in the field at the top of the navigation pane. In our example, we have type the word i.e. insertion.
4. If the text is found in the document, it will be highlighted in yellow and a preview of the results will appear in the navigation pane.
5. If the text appears more than once, you can click the arrows on the Navigation pane to step through the results. You can also click the result previews on the Navigation pane to jump to the location of a result in your document.
6. When you are finished, click the X to close the navigation pane. The highlight will disappear.

4.5.2 Replacing Text

- **To Replace Text:**

1. From the **Home** tab, click the **Replace** command. Alternatively, you can press **Ctrl+H** on your keyboard.
2. The **Find and Replace** dialog box will appear as shown in Figure 4.49.

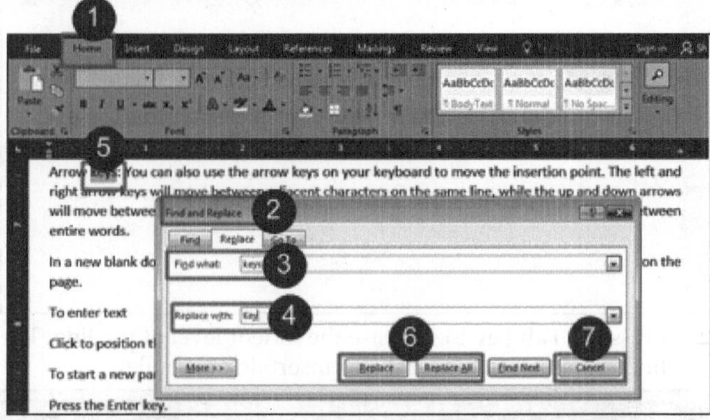

Figure 4.49 Find and Replace dialog box

3. Type the text you want to find in the **Find what:** field.
4. Type the text you want to replace it with in the **Replace with:** field. Then click **Find Next.**
5. Word will find the first instance of the text and highlight it in gray.
6. If you want to replace it, you can click **Replace** to change individual instances of text. Alternatively, you can click **Replace All** to replace every instance of the text throughout the document.
7. The text will be replaced. When you are done, click **Close** or **Cancel** to close the dialog box.

4.6 CHECKING SPELLING AND GRAMMAR

Spelling checker is a flexible and powerful tool that will automatically check spelling in a paragraph or the entire document. It finds and corrects the spelling errors but does not consider the context of words. While grammar checker evaluates a document for grammatical errors. Word 2016 uses collections of rules while reading a document.

4.6.1 Automatic Spelling and Grammar Checking

By default, Word automatically checks your document for spelling and grammar errors, so you may not even need to run a separate check. These errors are indicated by colored wavy lines. The red line indicates a misspelled word and the blue line indicates a grammatical error, including misused words.

➡ **To correct spelling errors:**

1. Right-click the underlined word, then select the correct spelling from the list of suggestions as shown in Figure 4.50.

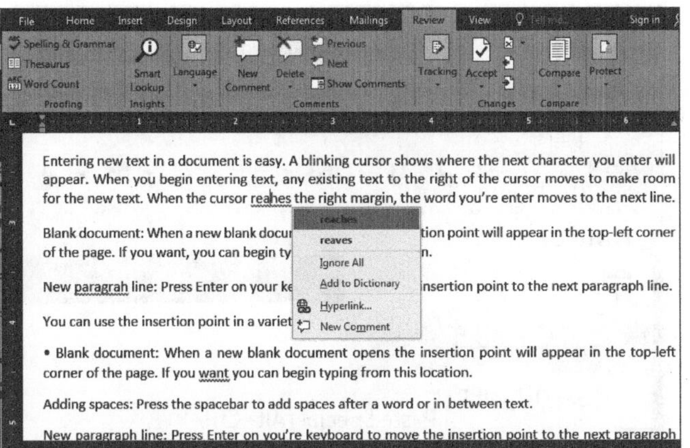

Figure 4.50 Spelling error in the document

2. The corrected word will appear in the document.
3. You can also choose to Ignore All instances of an underlined word or add it to the dictionary.

➡ **To correct grammar errors:**

1. Right-click the underlined word or phrase, then select the correct spelling or phrase from the list of suggestions as shown in Figure 4.51.
2. The corrected phrase will appear in the document.

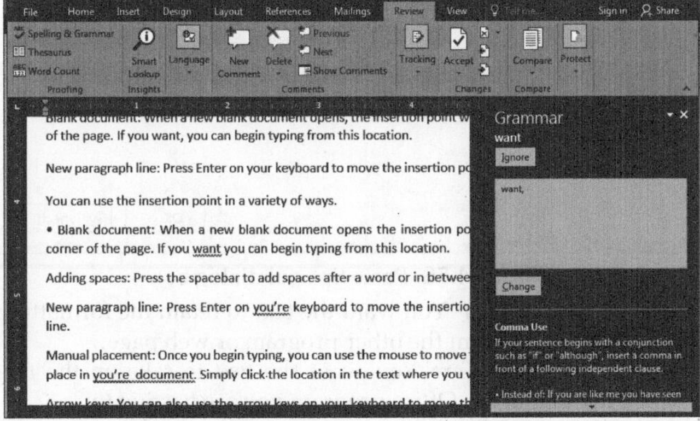

Figure 4.51 Grammar navigation pane

4.6.2 Hide Spelling and Errors in a document

If you are sharing a document like a resume with someone, you might not want that person to see the red and blue lines. Turning off the automatic spelling and grammar checks only applies to your computer, so the lines may still show up when someone else views your document. Fortunately, Word allows you to hide spelling and grammar errors so the lines will not show up on any computer.

➡ **To hide spelling and grammar errors in a document:**

1. Click the **File** tab to go to **Backstage** view, then click **Options**.
2. A dialog box will appear. Select **Proofing**, then check the box next to *Hide spelling errors in this document only* and *Hide grammar errors in this document only*, then click OK (see below).
3. The lines in the document will be hidden.

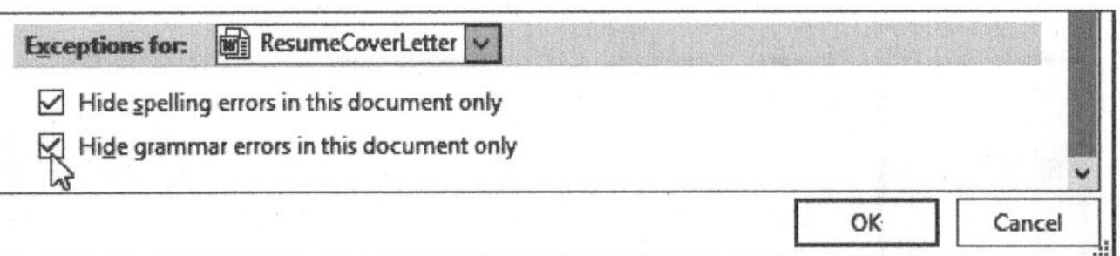

4.6.3 Correct Proofing Errors

To check the spelling or grammar of the entire document, click the **Spelling & Grammar** button in the **Proofing** group on the **Review** tab. Word then works its way through the selection or the document and displays the Spelling pane or Grammar pane if it encounters a potential error.

➡ **To correct proofing errors:**

1. If you want to begin checking error from the beginning of the document, press **Ctrl+Home** keys together.
2. On the **Review** tab, in the **Proofing** group, click the **Spelling & Grammar** button to begin the review. The **Spelling** pane opens and displays the first possible error. The corresponding location in the document is highlighted. (See Figure 4.52)

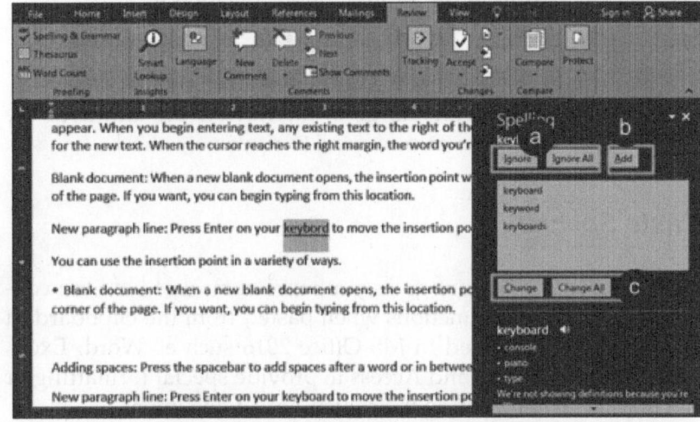

Figure 4.52 Spelling navigation pane

3. If the selection is identified as a possible spelling error, do any of the following:
   a. Click **Ignore** to continue the review without changing the highlighted word or **Ignore All** to continue and to ignore other instances of the word in the current document.
   b. Click **Add** to add the word to the **Spelling Checker** dictionary on your computer.
   c. Select the correct spelling of the word in the suggestions list, and then click **Change** to change only this instance of the word or **Change All** to change all instances of this word in the document.
4. Click the **Change** button to change the correct spelling word in the suggestion list.

4.6.4 Change Proofing Settings

1. Click the **File** tab to access **Backstage** view, then click **Options.**
2. **Word Options** dialog box will appear as shown in Figure 4.53. On the left side of the dialog box, select **Proofing.** For example, if you do not want Word to mark spelling errors, grammar errors, or frequently confused words automatically, Ignore words in UPPERCASE simply uncheck the desired option.

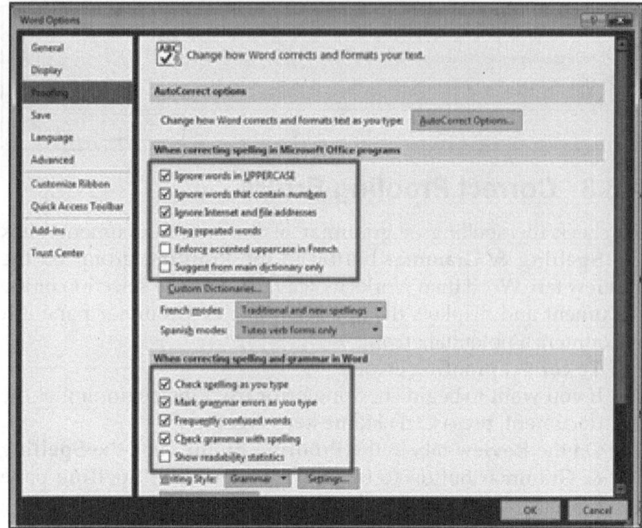

Figure 4.53 Word Options dialog box

3. Some options are specific to the document being worked on.
4. If you have turned off the automatic spelling and/or grammar checks, you can still go to the Review tab and click the **Spelling & Grammar** command to run a new check.

Paste Special

Paste Special is a feature gives you more control of how the content is displayed or functions when pasted from the clipboard. It is very commonly used in MS Office 2016 such as Word, Excel, PowerPoint, Outlook and Access to provide special formatting or calculations when pasting the content into a document.

1. Select the text you want to **Cut**, **Copy** or object that you want to paste. For example, we have selected some portion of text contain formatting as shown in Figure 4.54.

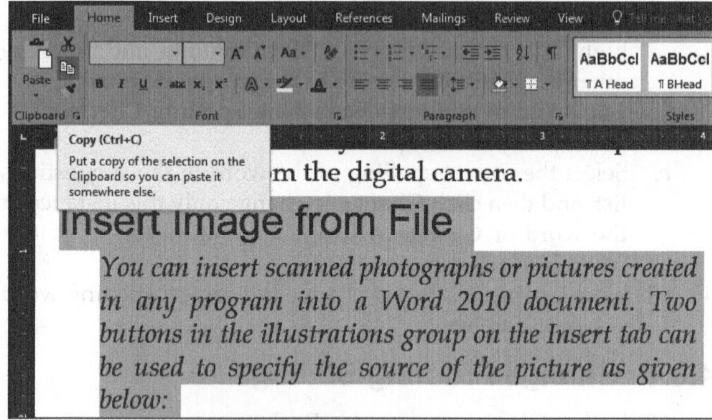

Figure 4.54 Text to be Copied

2. On the **Home** tab, in the **Clipboard** group, click the arrow under **Paste**, Click **Paste Special** as shown in Figure 4.55.

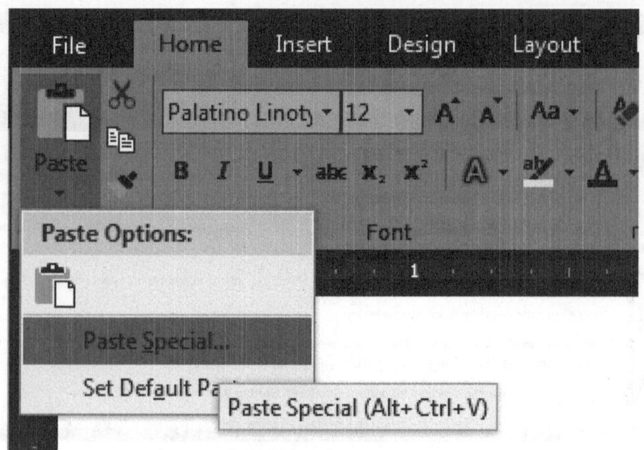

Figure 4.55 Selecting Paste Special

3. The **Paste Special** dialog box appears as shown in Figure 4.56 and then choose one of the options below:

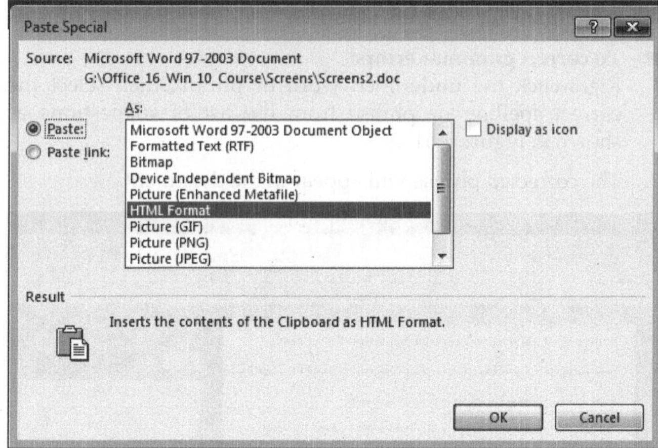

Figure 4.56 Paste Special dialog box

- *Formatted Text*–You want the text to retain the formatting of the text from the other program or web page.
- *Unformatted Text*–You want the text to take on the formatting of the Office program you are pasting to.
- *Microsoft Office Drawing Object*–You want the contents of the Clipboard to appear as a Microsoft Office drawing object.
- *Picture (Enhanced Metafile)*–You want the contents of the Clipboard to appear as an Enhanced Metafile (EMF) format.
- *Picture such as (GIF, JPEG and PNG)*–If you want the contents of the Clipboard to appear as PNG, GIF and JPEG format.
- *Device Independent Bitmap*–A DIB is a representation (that consists of rows and columns of dots) of a graphic image in computer memory. The value of each dot is stored in one or more bits of data.

4. Select the desired format and click OK.

Using Paste Options

Right-click anywhere on your Word document after copying something to reveal Word's **Paste Options** as shown in Figure 4.57. You can also find the Paste options by clicking the **Paste** button under the **Home** menu or by clicking the **Ctrl** button that appears after pasting text using Ctrl+V. Here are the choices:

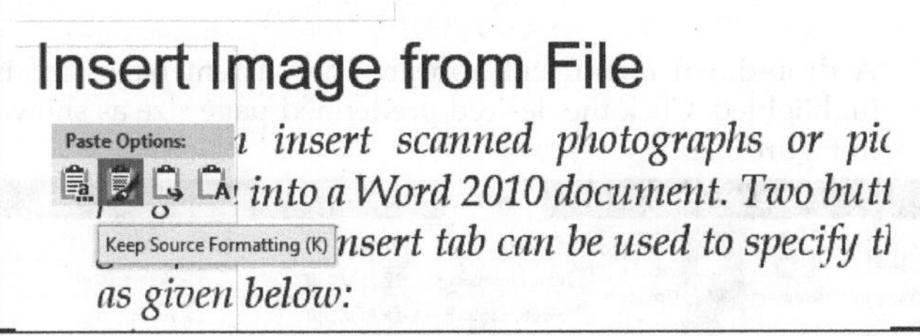

Figure 4.57 Paste Options

- *Keep Source Formatting*–The text or object retains its look from its original location.
- *Match Destination Formatting*–The object or text is stripped of any previous formatting and the formatting of the new location is applied.
- *Keep Text Only*–The object is stripped of any previous formatting and remains stripped in the new location.

4.6.5 Word Count

The **Word Count** command totals the number of *pages, words, characters paragraphs* and *lines* in a document (Figure 4.58). You can even choose to include footnotes and endnotes in the total. You can also find the word count in the status bar at the bottom of the window.

➡ **To use the word count feature:**

1. Click the **Review** tab and choose **Word Count** command in the **Proofing** group.

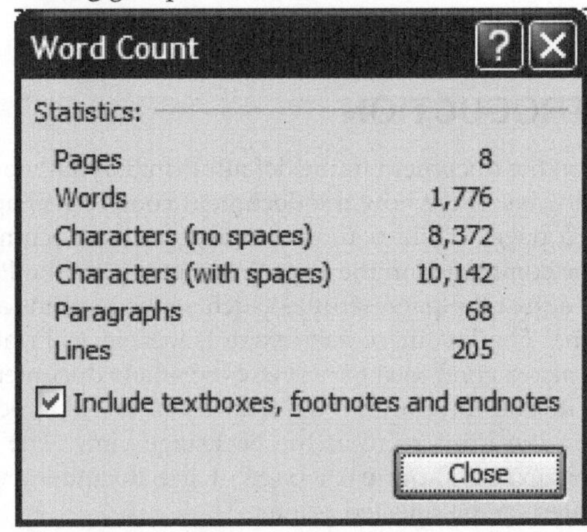

Figure 4.58 Word Count dialog Box

2. The **Word Count** dialog box appears (Figure 4.58). Word 2016 would then perform the totalling and show the results.
3. Choose Include footnotes and endnotes if you wish them to be included. Word 2016 would do the total again and show the result.
4. Click the **Close** button.

CHAPTER 5

Layout and Printing

5.1 INTRODUCTION

Working on the document in the default Print Layout view means that you always know how the document content will appear on the printed page. While you are working in the document, you can use the commands in the Page Setup group on the Page Layout tab to adjust the page settings (such as the margins and page orientation). The layout of each page is visible in Print Layout view, it is also a good idea to preview the whole document before you print it. You can preview a document as it will appear when printed, on the Print page of the backstage view. The preview area shows exactly how each page of the document will look when printed on the selected printer.

5.1.1 Page Orientation

Word offers two page orientation options: landscape and portrait. The default orientation is Portrait, in which the page is taller than it is wide. You can set the orientation to Landscape, in which the page is wider than it is tall. You can customize the page orientation, paper size, and page margins depending on how you want your document to appear.

- Landscape means the page is oriented horizontally.
- ∂ Portrait means the page is oriented vertically.

➡ **To change page orientation:**

1. Select the **Layout** tab.
2. Click the **Orientation** command in the **Page Setup** group.
3. A drop-down menu will appear. Click either **Portrait** or **Landscape** to change the page orientation as shown in Figure 5.1.

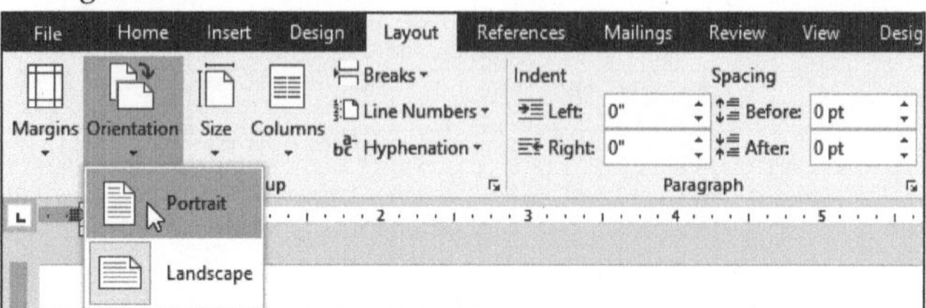

Figure 5.1 Selecting Page Orientation

4. The page orientation of the document will be changed.

5.1.2 Page Size and Margins

Page size

By default, the page size of a new document is 8.5 inches by 11 inches. Depending on your project, you may need to adjust your document's page size. It has a variety of predefined page sizes in Word.

➡ **To change the page size:**

1. Select the **Layout** tab, then click the **Size** command.
2. A drop-down menu will appear. The current page size is highlighted. Click the desired predefined page size as shown in Figure 5.2.

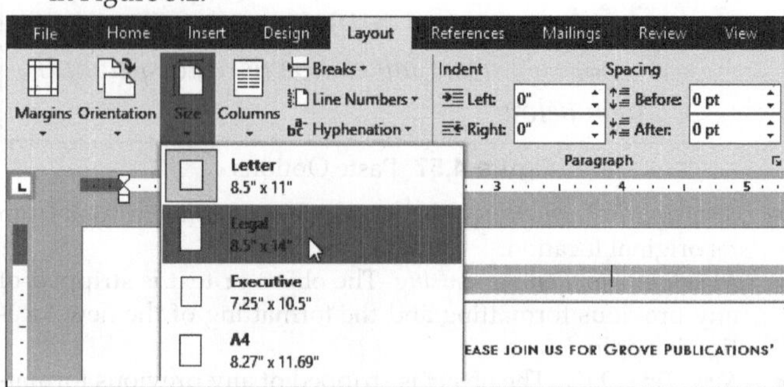

Figure 5.2 Selecting Page Size

3. The page size of the document will be changed.

➡ **To use a custom page size:**

1. From the **Layout** tab, click **Size**. Select **More Paper Sizes...** from the drop-down menu as shown in Figure 5.3.

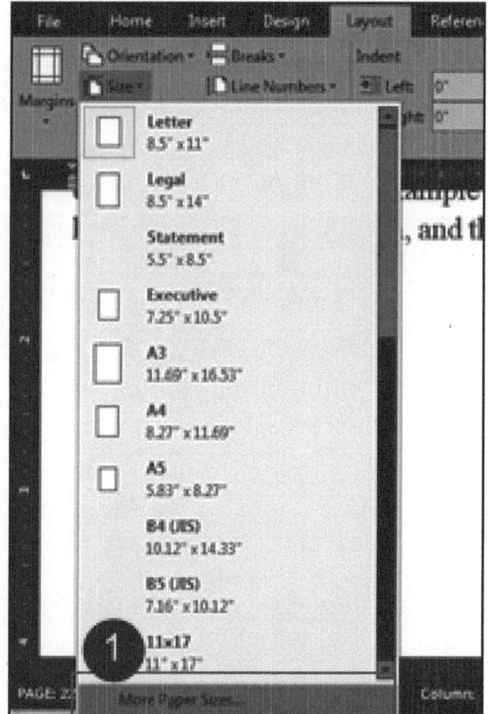

Figure 5.3 Selecting More paper sizes

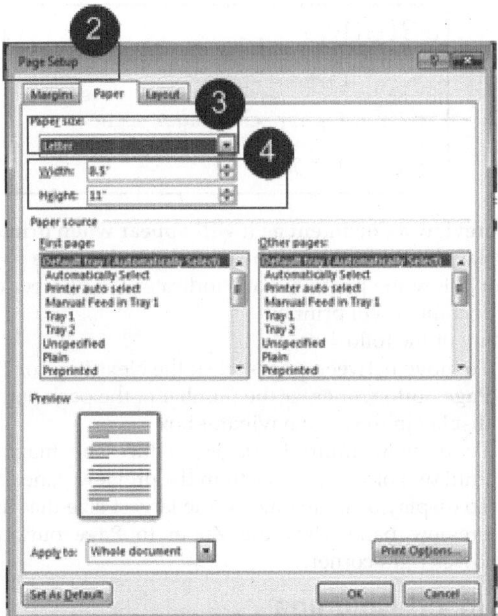

Figure 5.4 Page Setup dialog box

2. The **Page Setup** dialog box will appear as shown in Figure 5.4.
3. Select the **paper** tab under the **paper size:** drop-down list.
4. Adjust the values for **Width:** and **Height:**, then click OK.
5. The page size of the document will be changed.

Page Margins

A margin is the space between the text and the edge of your document. By default, a new document's margins are set to Normal, which means it has a one-inch space between the text and each edge. Depending on your needs, Word allows you to change your document's margin size.

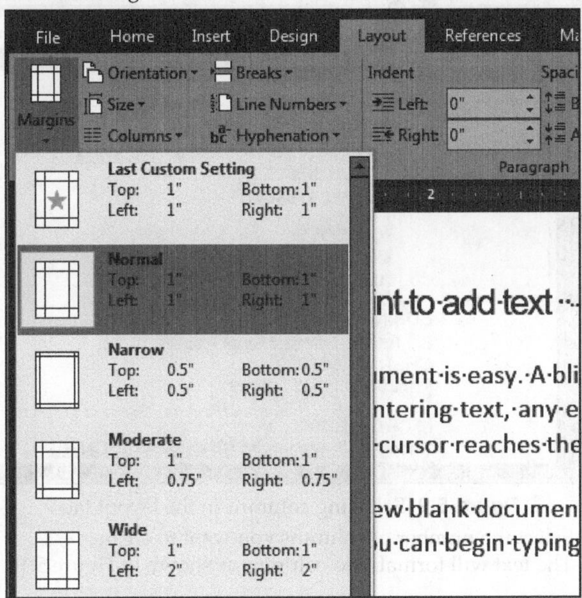

Figure 5.5 Selecting predefined margin size

➡ **To format page margins:**

1. Select the **Layout** tab, then click the **Margins** command.
2. A drop-down menu will appear as shown in Figure 5.5. Click the predefined margin size you want.
3. The margins of the document will be changed.

➡ **To use custom margins:**

1. From the **Layout** tab, click **Margins**. Select **Custom Margins** from the drop-down menu as shown in Figure 5.6.

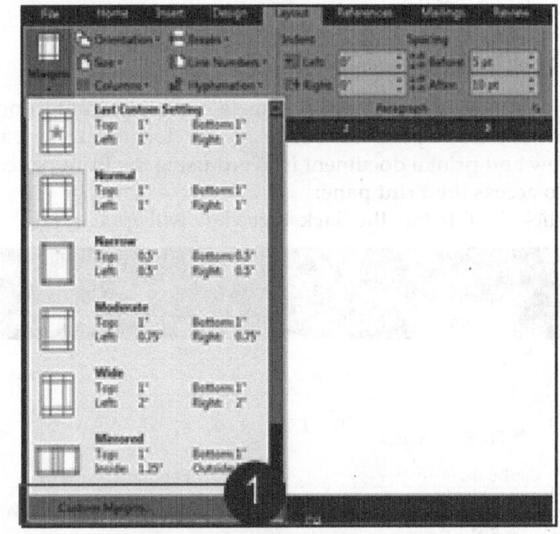

Figure 5.6 Select Custom margins

2. The **Page Setup** dialog box will appear as shown in Figure 5.7.

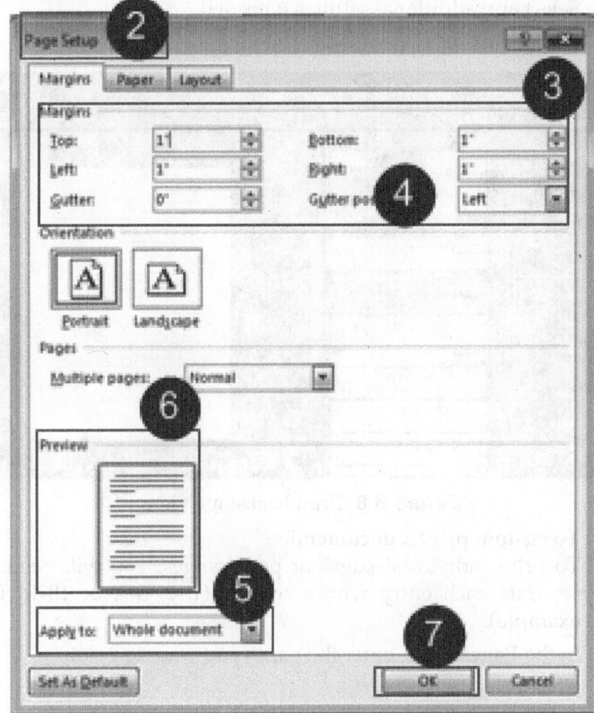

Figure 5.7 Page Setup with Margins tab selected

3. Click the **Margins** tab, select or type out the desired margin height from the **Top:** or **Bottom:** of the page.
4. Select or type out the desired margin width from the **Left:** and **Right:** of the page edge.
5. In the **Apply to:** choose the portion of the document from where you want to apply the new settings.
6. The **Preview** box displays the effect of the settings you select.
7. Click OK.

5.1.3 Printing Documents

Once you have created your document, you may want to print it to view and share your work and save the document. It is easy to preview and print a document in Word using the Print pane.

➡ **To access the Print pane:**

1. Click the **File** tab, the **Backstage** view will appear.

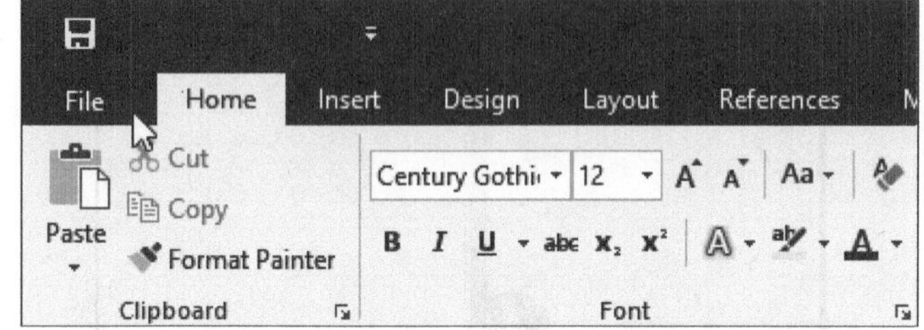

2. Select **Print**. The **Print** pane will appear as shown in Figure 5.8.
3. Click the drop-down arrow to navigate Printer and select the desired printer settings.
4. Enter the number of copies you want to print.
5. Select any additional settings if needed.
6. Click **Print**.

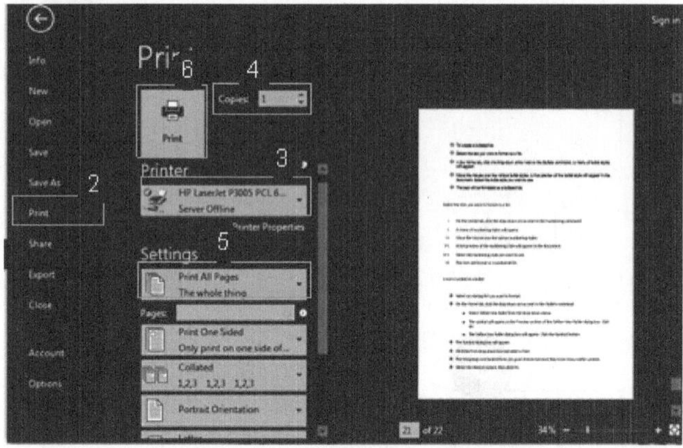

Figure 5.8 Print backstage view

➡ **To custom print a document:**

1. To print individual pages or page ranges, you will need to separate each entry with a comma (1, 3, 5-7, or 10-14 for example).
2. In the **Pages:** field, enter the pages you want to print.
3. Click **Print**.

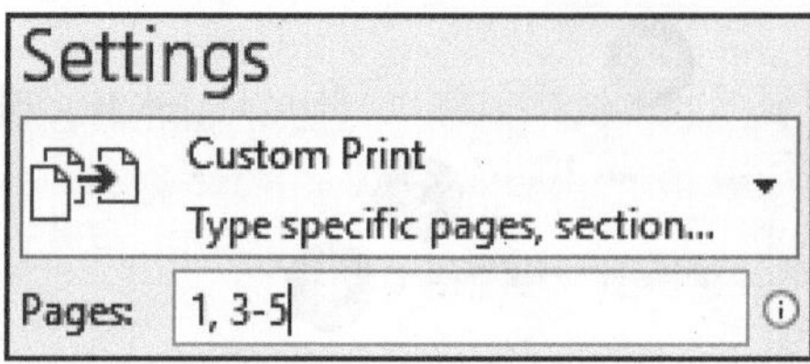

➡ **To preview a document as it will appear when printed:**

1. Display the Print page of the Backstage view. The page navigator below the preview pane indicates the number of pages the document will print on.
2. Do any of the following:
   - To move between pages, click the **Next Page** or **Previous Page** button, or enter the number of the page you want to display in the page navigator box.
   - To preview multiple pages, reduce the magnification until two or more pages fit in the preview pane.
   - To display a single page at the largest size that fits in the preview pane, click the **Zoom to Page** button in the lower-right corner.

5.1.4 Insert Columns

By default, Word displays text in one column that spans the width of the page between the left and right margins. You can specify that text be displayed in two, three, or more columns to create layouts like those used in newspapers and magazines.

➡ **To add columns to a document:**

1. Select the text you want to format.
2. Select the **Layout** tab, then click the **Columns** command. A drop-down menu will appear as shown in Figure 5.9.

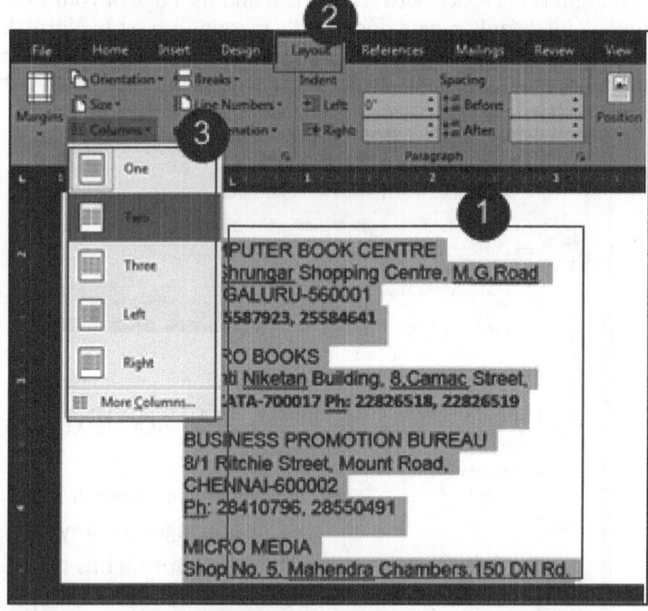

Figure 5.9 Selecting columns in the layout tab

3. Select the number of columns you want to create.
4. The text will format into columns as shown in Figure 5.10.

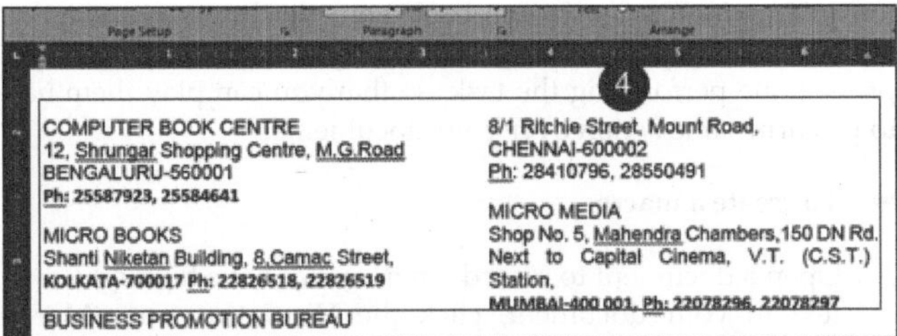

Figure 5.10 Text get formatted in to columns

Select **More Columns** at the bottom of the menu to access the **Columns** dialog box. Click the arrows next to **Number of columns:** to adjust the number of columns.

➡ **To remove columns:**

1. To remove column formatting, place the insertion point anywhere in the columns, then click the **Columns** command on the **Layout** tab. Select One from the drop-down menu that appears.

5.1.5 Headers and Footers

The header is a section of the document that appears in the top margin, while the footer is a section of the document that appears in the bottom margin. Headers and footers generally contain additional information such as page numbers, dates, an author's name, and footnotes, which can help keep longer documents organized and make them easier to read. Text entered in the header or footer will appear on each page of the document.

➡ **To insert a preset header or footer:**

1. Select the **Insert** tab, then click the **Header or Footer** command. In our example, we have click the **Header** command.
2. In the menu that appears as shown in Figure 5.11, select the desired preset header or footer list.

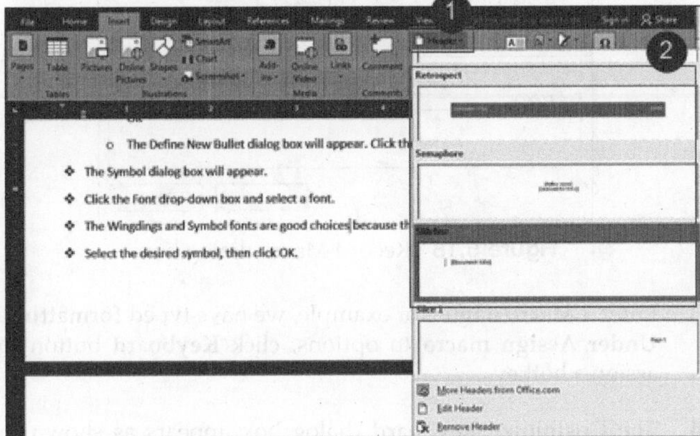

Figure 5.11 Selecting header in the preset list

The header appear in the document. Many preset headers and footers contain text placeholders called **Content Control fields.** These fields are good for adding information like the document title, author's name, date, and page number.

3. To edit a **Content Control field,** click it and type the desired information. For example, we have typed Document title as Introduction to chapter 1 as shown in Figure 5.12.

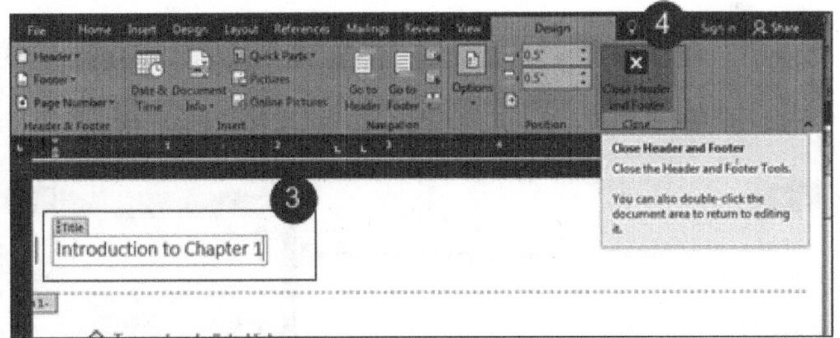

Figure 5.12 Type the text to display in the document

4. When you are finished, click **Close Header and Footer**. Alternatively, you can press the **Esc** key.
5. If you want to delete a Content Control field, right-click it and select **Remove Content Control** from the menu that appears as shown in Figure 5.13. Or In the **Header** Gallery drop-down menu, click **Remove Header.**

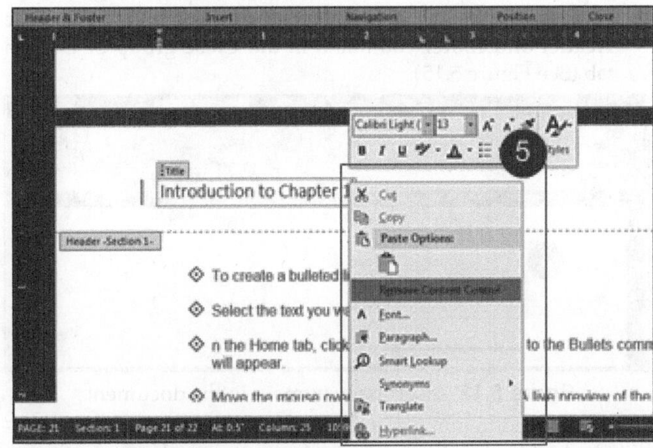

Figure 5.13 Remove header content control

Editing headers and footers

After you close the header or footer, it will still be visible, but it will be locked.

1. Click the **Insert** tab and then click **Header**.
2. In the **Header Gallery** drop-down menu, click **Edit header**.
3. The **Header and Footer** Tools – **Design** tab will open. You will be able to make your edit to the header or footer.

5.1.6 Page Numbers

Word can automatically label each page with a page number and place it in a header, footer, or side margin. If you have an existing header or footer, it will be removed and replaced with the page number.

➡ **To add page numbers:**

1. On the **Insert** tab, click the **Page Number** command in the **Header & Footer** group.
2. Select the desired options where you want appear page number to be positioned in the document. Select the desired style of header. For example, we have selected **Bottom of Page** as shown in Figure 5.14.

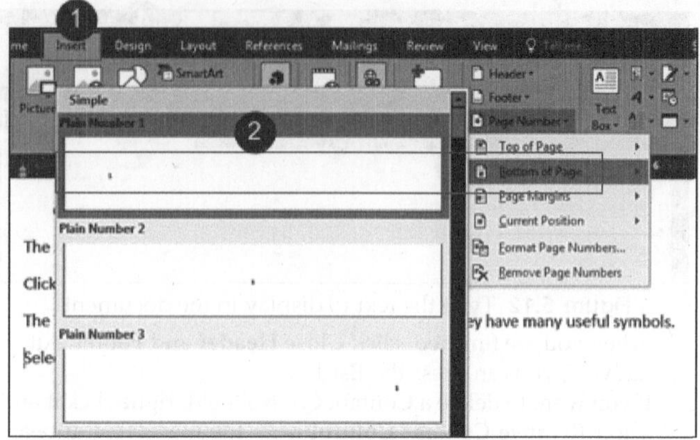

Figure 5.14 Selecting Page number

3. Page number appears at the bottom of the page.
4. Press the **Esc** key to lock the header and footer. Or click **Close Header and footer** command in the **Close group** of **Design** tab (See Figure 5.15).

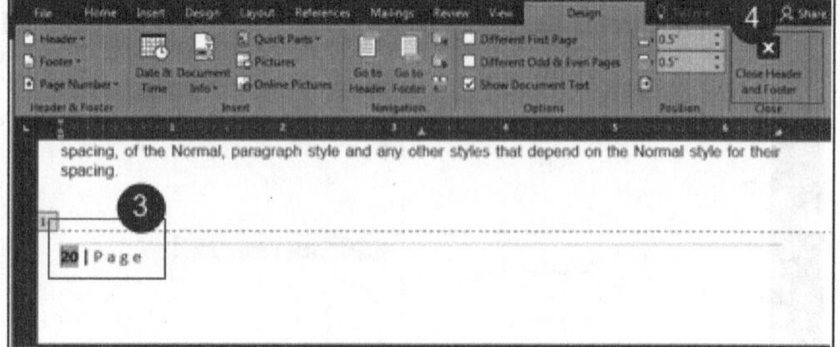

Figure 5.15 Insert page number in the document

5. If you need to make any changes to your page numbers, simply double-click the header or footer to unlock it.

➡ **To hide the page number on the first page:**

1. Double-click the header or footer to unlock it.
2. From the **Design** tab, place a check mark next to **Different First Page**. The header and footer will disappear from the first

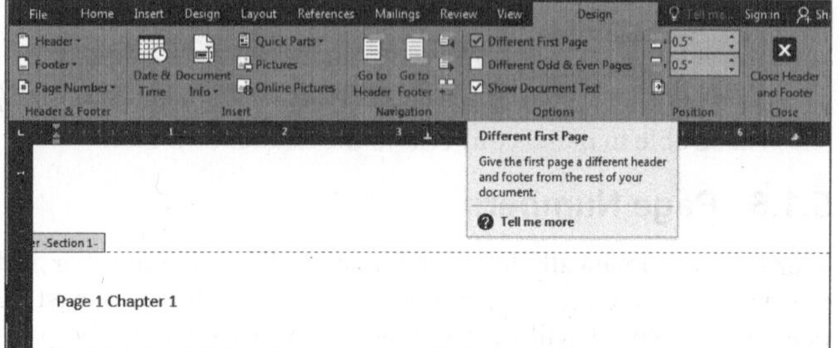

Figure 5.16 Different First page

page. If you want, you can type something new in the header or footer, and it will only affect the first page (See Figure 5.16).

5.1.7 Macros

A macro is simply a recording of a repetitive task. Through Macros, you do not need to perform same action, i.e. change formatting, font style, size, and color over and over again in document. It actually records each and every click and keystroke you press while performing the task, so that you can play them back to perform same action over your documents.

➡ **To create a macro:**

1. Open a document to record a macro. We have highlight some text in your document, click the **View** tab, from **Macros** group, click **Record Macro** as shown in Figure 5.17.

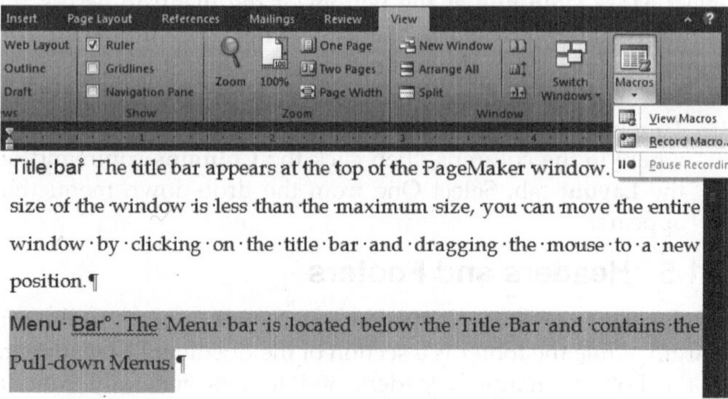

Figure 5.17

2. **Record Macro** dialog box appears as shown in Figure 5.18.

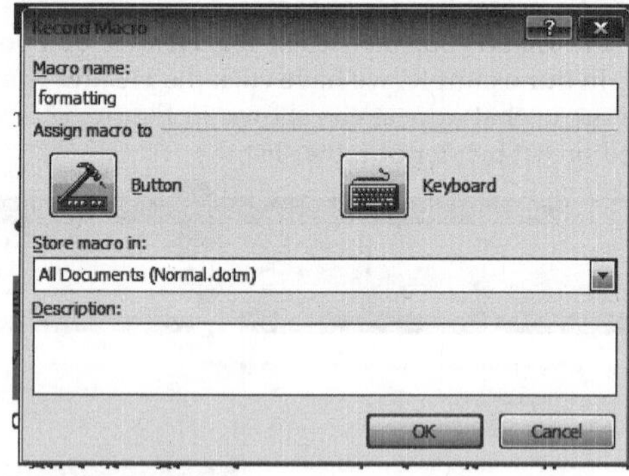

Figure 5.18 Record Macro dialog box

3. Enter a **Macro name:** for example, we have typed **formatting**. **Under Assign macro to** options, click **Keyboard** button to assign a hotkey.
4. The **Customize keyboard** dialog box appears as shown in Figure 5.19.
5. Now place insert cursor in **Press new shortcut key:** box, and assign a hotkey by pressing keys combination like **Ctrl+Shift+M**. Click **Assign** to assign hotkey to macro, and then click close button (See Figure 5.19).
6. You will see recorder-like image with pointer, indicating that macro is being recorded. Here, we will do some formatting over the text such as (See Figure 5.20).

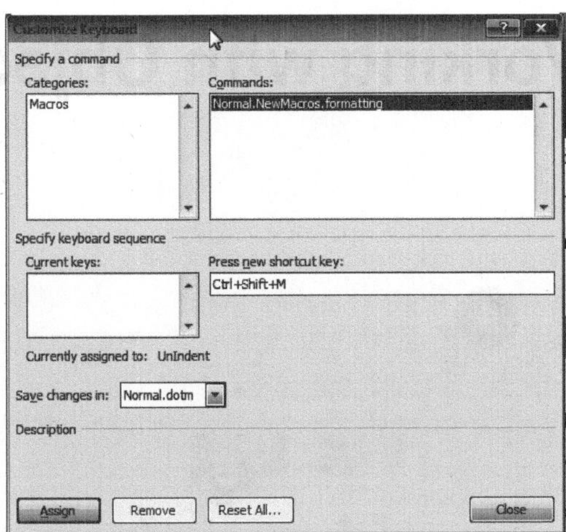

Figure 5.19 Customize keyboard dialog box

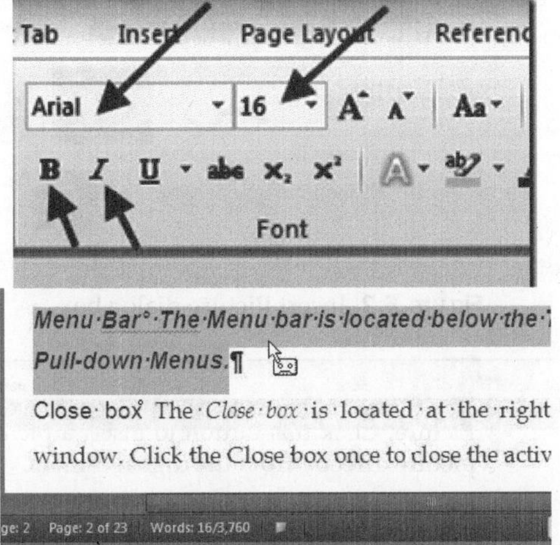

Figure 5.20 Selecting the style you want to record

- Click on the **Current Font box** and select **Ariel**.
- Click on the **Font Size** box and select **16**.
- Click on the **Bold** and *Italics* icons.

7. After selecting above formatting options, to make it stop recording, again click on the **View** tab from **Macros** group, and then **Stop recording** (See Figure 5.21).

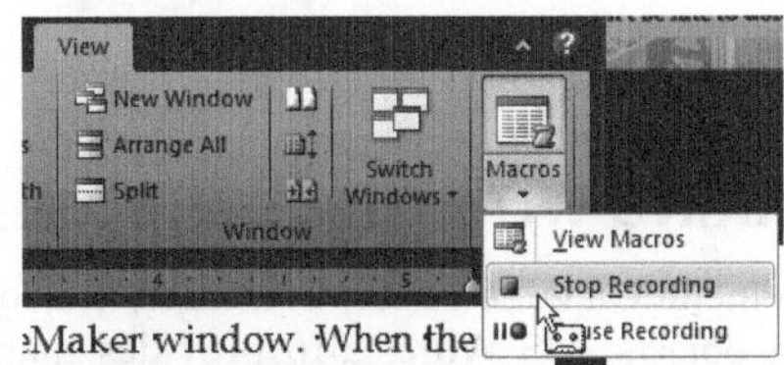

Figure 5.21 Selecting stop recording

8. Run the macro by pressing the specified hotkey. In our case, it is **Ctrl+Shift+M**. It will immediately apply recorded formatting style to the new paragraph.
9. For saving a macro-enabled document, on **File** menu, click **Save As** from **Save As** dialog, under **Save as type options**, click Word Macro-Enabled Template (*dotm) (See Figure 5.22).
10. Enter an appropriate name of document and click save.

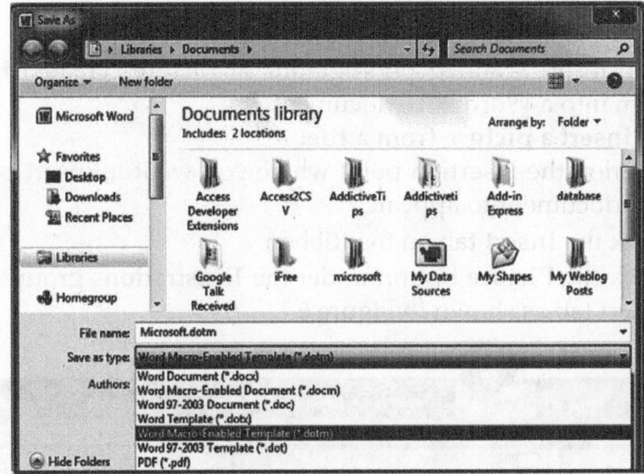

Figure 5.22 Save As dialog box

CHAPTER 6

Working with Objects

6.1 WORKING WITH GRAPHICS

Graphics can include a wide variety of images, including pictures and drawing objects. MS Word 2016 provides many graphical tools such as Smart-Art, Shape and Online Pictures. This helps a user to make the document impressive. It also allows you to edit the graphics and pictures in the document. For instance, to resize or crop the picture in the document, you can use related option provided in Word 2016.

Further, You will also learn how to edit graphic objects such as aligning, arranging and grouping multiple pictures in the document. Finally, you will learn how to insert a table in a document, modify the table by adding, deleting rows and columns, split and merging cells in a table.

6.1.1 Inserting a Picture

You can insert scanned photographs or pictures created in any program into a Word 2016 document.

➡ **To insert a picture from a file:**

1. Position the insertion point where you want to insert picture in a document to appear.
2. Click the **Insert** tab on the Ribbon.
3. Click the **Picture** button under the **Illustrations** group of the **Insert** tab as shown in Figure 6.1.

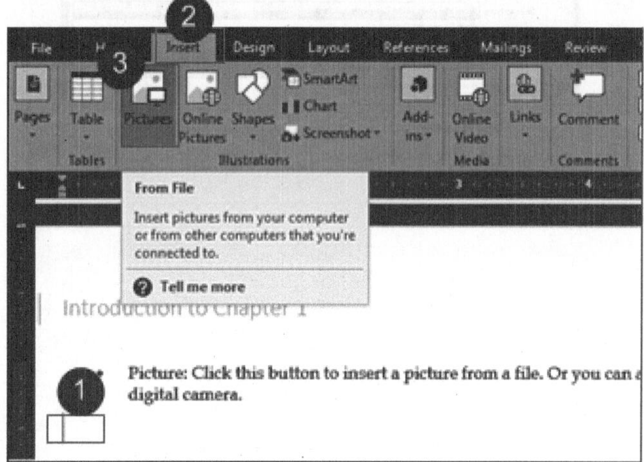

Figure 6.1 Selecting Picture command

4. The **Insert Picture** dialog box appears as shown in Figure 6.2.
5. Select the picture saved locally in your computer.
6. Click the **Insert** button in the **Insert Picture** dialog box to insert the picture in the document.
7. The picture is inserted in the document as shown in Figure 6.3.

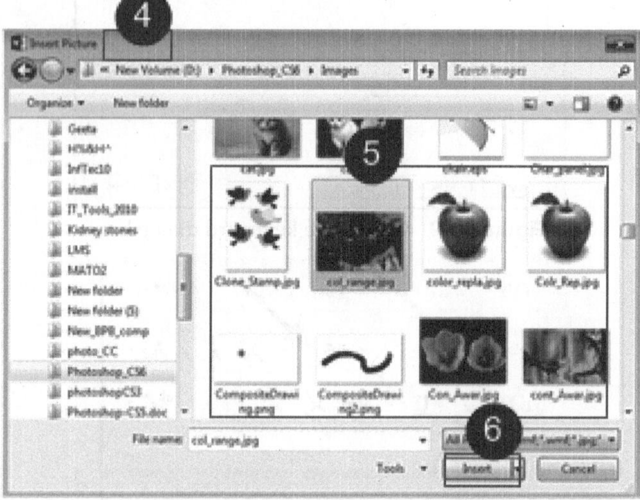

Figure 6.2 Insert Picture dialog box

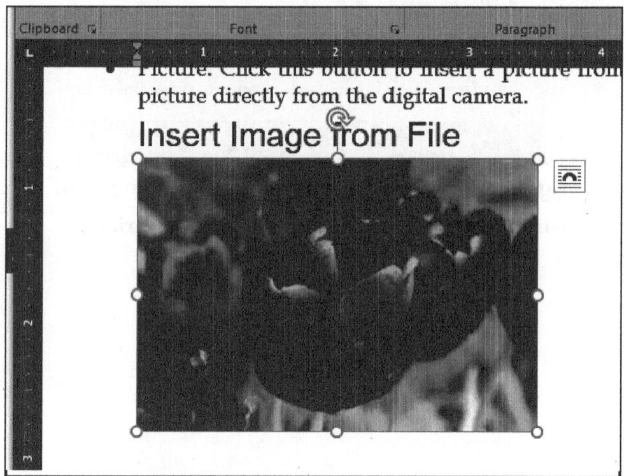

Figure 6.3 Picture inserted in the document

➡ **To resize the Picture:**

1. Select the picture which you want to resize. The picture is surrounded by a box containing eight handles, click and drag one of the corner sizing handles as shown in Figure 6.4.

2. The image will change size while keeping the same proportions. If you want to stretch it horizontally or vertically, you can use the side sizing handles.

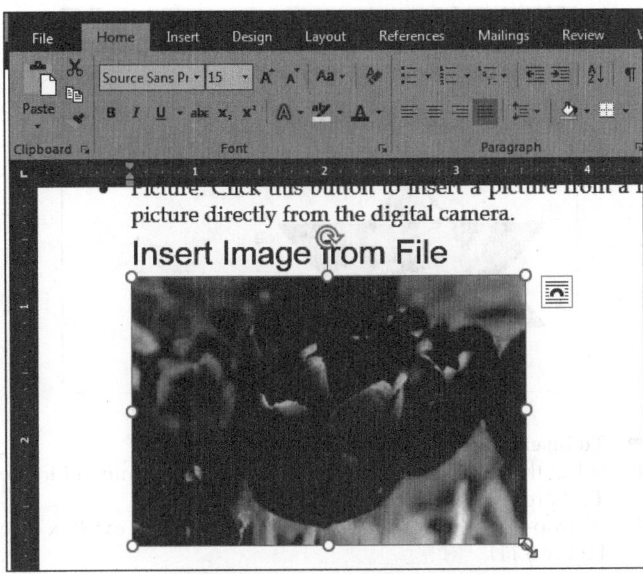

Figure 6.4 Resize the picture

6.1.2 Text Wrapping

When you insert a picture from a file, you may notice that it is difficult to move it exactly where you want. This is because the text wrapping for the image is set to In Line with Text. You will need to change the text wrapping setting if you want to move the image freely, or if you just want the text to wrap around the image in a more natural way.

➡ **To wrap text around an image:**

1. Select the image you want to wrap text around. The **Format** tab will appear on the right side of the Ribbon.
2. On the **Format** tab, click the **Wrap Text** command in the **Arrange** group.
3. Select the desired options from drop-down list. For example, we have selected **Square Text wrapping** so we can freely move it without affecting the text (See Figure 6.5).

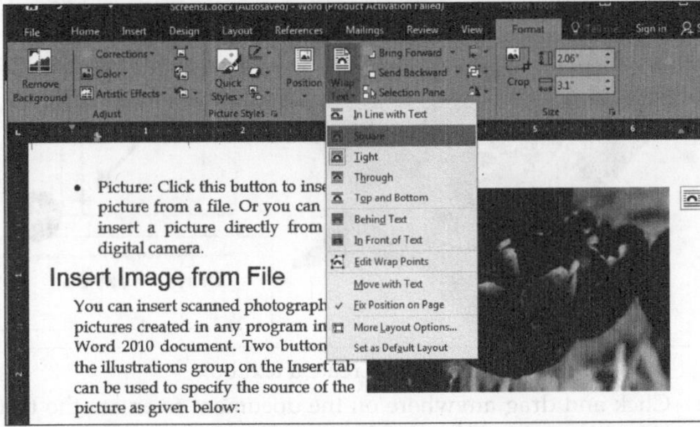

Figure 6.5 Wrap Text

6.1.3 Formatting Pictures

There are many ways to format pictures in Word. For instance, you can change the size or shape of an image to better suit your document. You can also enhance its appearance using Word's image adjustment tools.

Cropping an Picture

When you crop an image, part of the picture is removed. Cropping can be useful if you are working with an image that is too big and you want to focus on only part of it.

➡ **To crop an image:**

1. Select the image you want to crop. The **Format** tab will appear.
2. From the **Format** tab, click the **Crop** command under the **Size** group (See Figure 6.6).
3. The cropping handle appears around on the sides and corners of the image as shown in Figure 6.7.

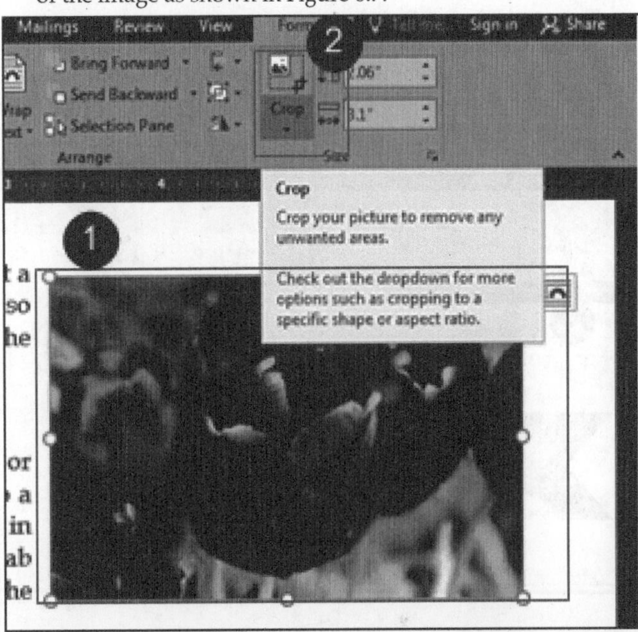

Figure 6.6 Selecting Crop command

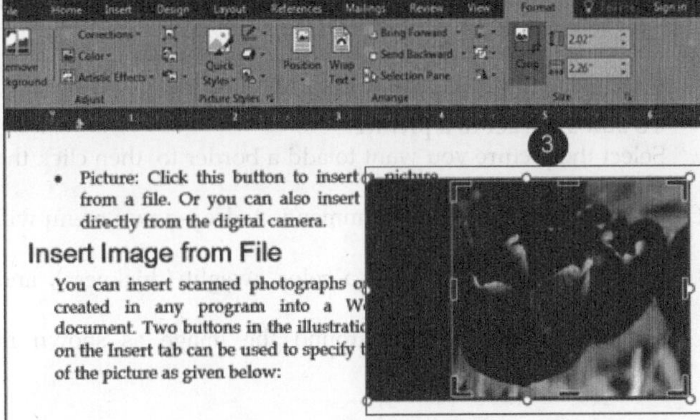

Figure 6.7 Cropping handles appear

4. Click and drag any handles to crop the image.
5. To confirm, click the **Crop** command again. The image get cropped within the specified area as shown in Figure 6.8.

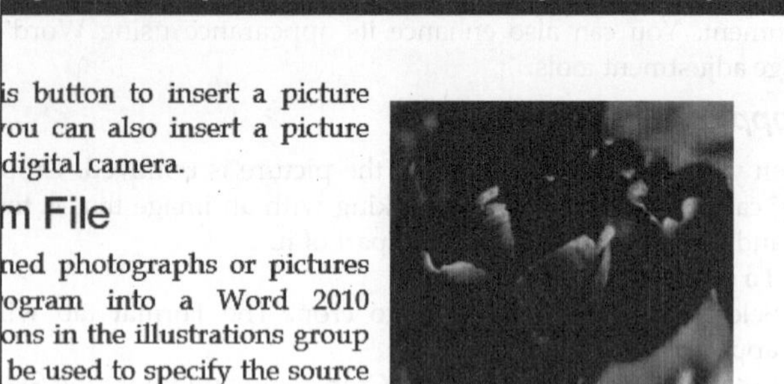

Figure 6.8 Image get cropped

➡ **To crop an image to a shape:**

1. Select the image you want to crop, then click the **Format** tab.
2. Click the **Crop** drop-down arrow. Hover over **Crop to Shape**, then select the desired shape from the drop-down menu as shown in Figure 6.9.

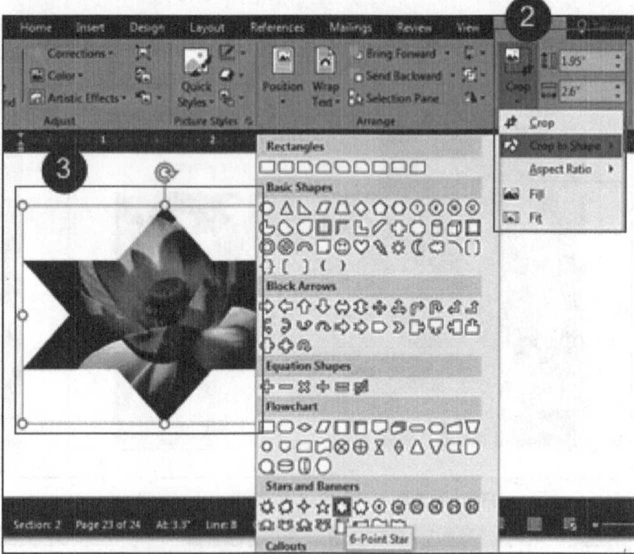

Figure 6.9 Crop an image to a shape

3. The image will be cropped to the chosen shape.

➡ **To add a border to a picture:**

1. Select the picture you want to add a border to, then click the **Format** tab.
2. Click the **Picture Border** command. A drop-down menu will appear.
3. From here, you can select a color, weight (thickness), and whether the line is dashed.
4. The border will appear around the image as shown in Figure 6.10.

6.1.4 Creating Text Boxes

Text boxes can be useful for drawing attention to specific text. Word allows you to format text boxes and the text within them with a variety of styles and effects.

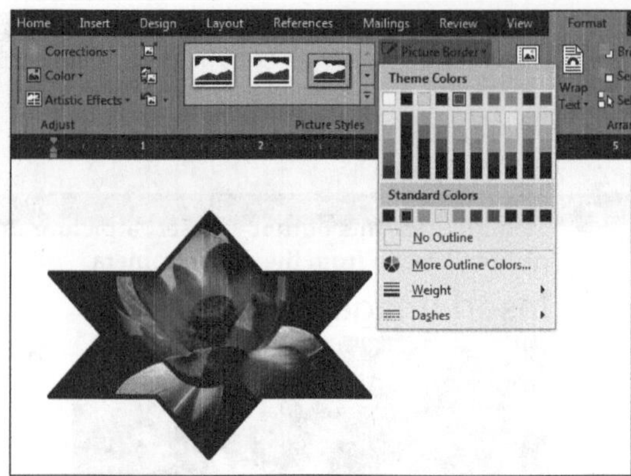

Figure 6.10 Add a border to an image

➡ **To insert a text box:**

1. Select the **Insert** tab, then click the **Text Box** command in the **Text** group.
2. A drop-down menu will appear, select **Draw Text Box** (See Figure 6.11).

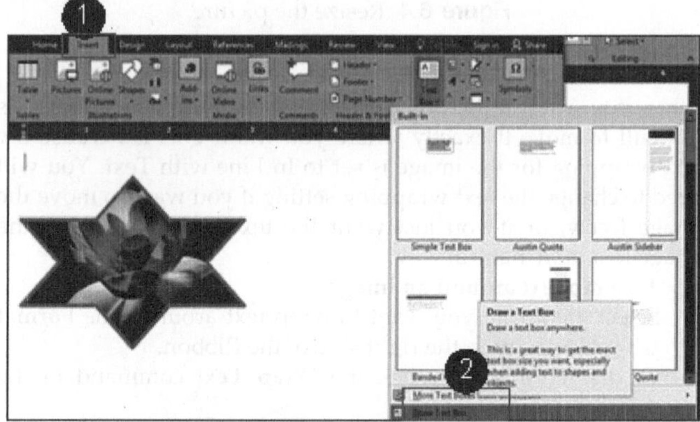

Figure 6.11 Selecting Draw Text box

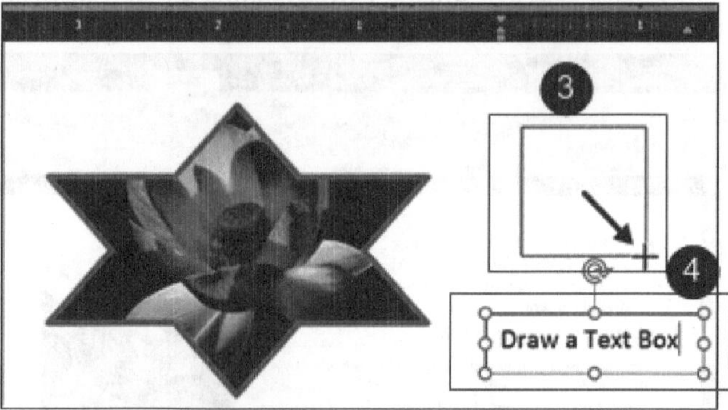

Figure 6.12 Create a text box

3. Click and drag anywhere on the document to create the text box as shown in Figure 6.12.
4. The insertion point will appear inside the text box. You can now type inside the text box.
5. If you want, you can select the text and then change the font, color, and size by using the commands on the **Format** and **Home** tabs.

6. Click anywhere outside the text box to return to your document.

➡ **To move a text box:**

1. Click the text box you want to move.
2. Hover the mouse over one of the edges of the text box. The mouse will change into a cross with arrows.
3. Click and drag the text box to the desired location.

➡ **To resize a text box:**

1. Click the text box you want to resize.
2. Click and drag any of the sizing handles on the corners or sides of the text box until it is the desired size.

Modifying Text Boxes

Word offers several options for changing the way text boxes appear in your document. You can change the shape, style, and color of text boxes or add various effects.

➡ **To change the shape style:**

1. Select the text box you want to change.
2. On the **Format** tab, click the **More** drop-down arrow in the **Shape Styles** group.

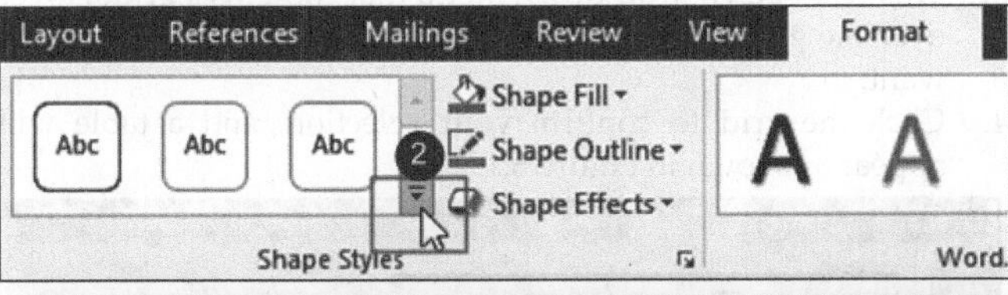

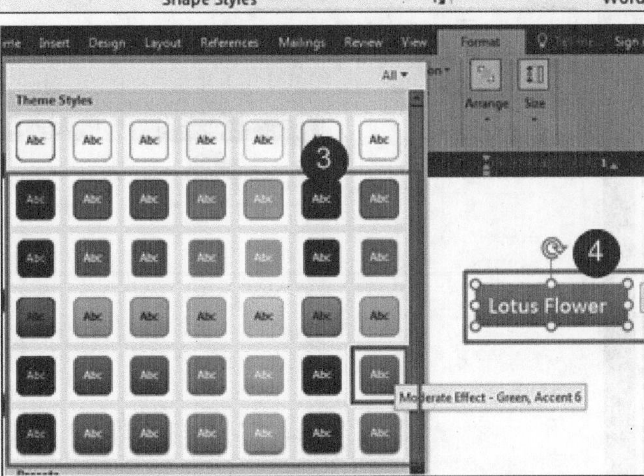

Figure 6.13

3. A drop-down menu of styles will appear, select the style you want to use as shown in Figure 6.13.
4. The text box will appear in the selected style.

6.1.5 Aligning, and Grouping Objects

Aligning Objects

When your documents have multiple objects, such as pictures, shapes, and text boxes. You can arrange the objects any way you want by aligning, grouping them in various ways.

➡ **To align two or more objects:**

1. Select the shape that you want to align. For example, we have selected the shapes objects such as teardrop and plaque.
2. Hold the Shift (or **Ctrl**) key and click the objects you want to align. In our example, we have select the three shapes on the right.
3. From the **Format** tab, click the **Align** command, then select one of the alignment options. In our example, we have choose **Align Right** (See Figure 6.14).
4. The objects will be aligned based on the selected option. The shapes are now aligned with each other as shown in Figure 6.15.

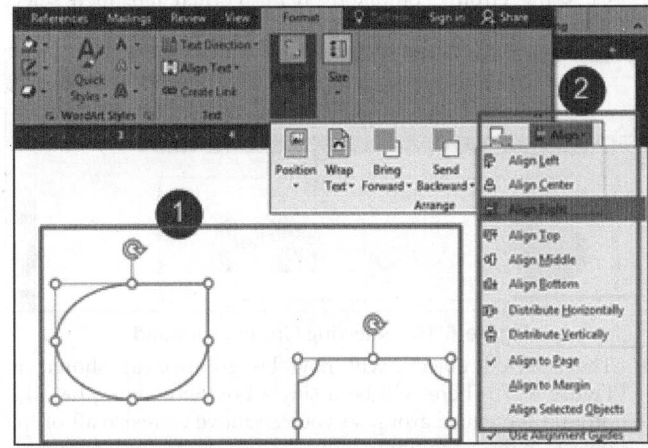

Figure 6.14 Selecting Align command

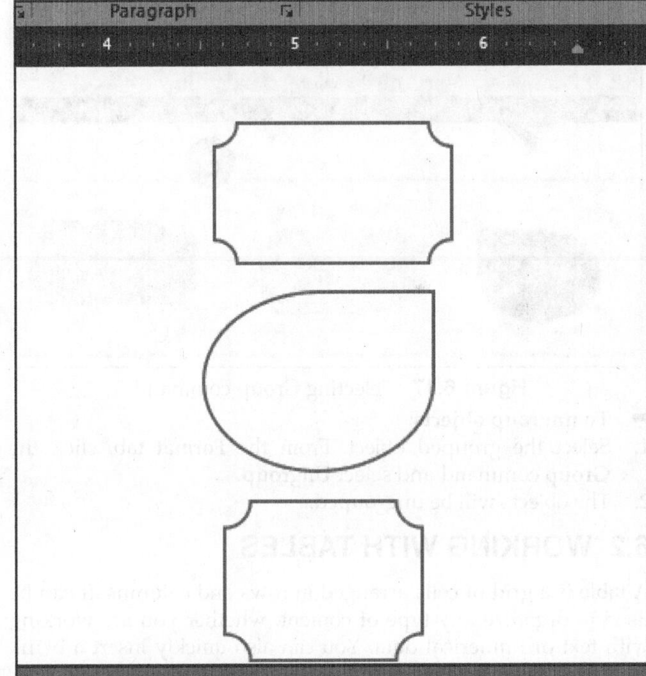

Figure 6.15 Selected object aligned Right

Note that the **Align Selected Objects** option is selected by default, which allows you to align objects without moving them to a different part of the page. However, if you want to move the objects the top or bottom of the page, select **Align to Page** or **Align to Margin** before choosing an alignment option.

Grouping objects

You may want to group multiple objects into one object so they will stay together. This is usually easier than selecting them individually, and it also allows you to resize and move all of the objects at the same time.

➡ **To align two or more objects:**

1. Hold the **Shift** (or **Ctrl**) key and click the objects you want to group.
2. Click the **Group** command on the **Format** tab, then select **Group** as shown in Figure 6.16.

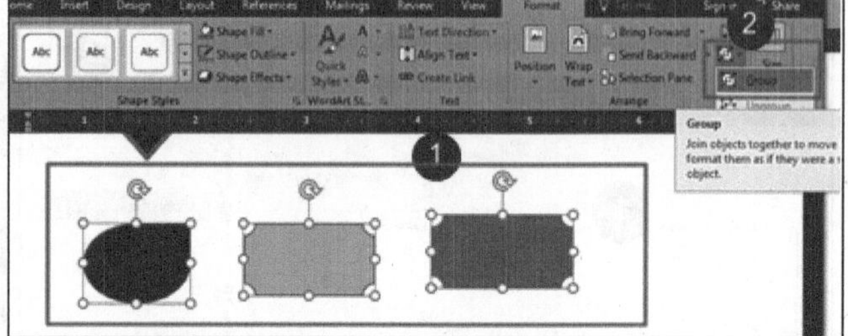

Figure 6.16 Selecting Group command

3. The selected objects will now be grouped as shown in Figure 6.17. There will be a single box with sizing handles around the entire group so you can move or resize all of the objects at the same time.

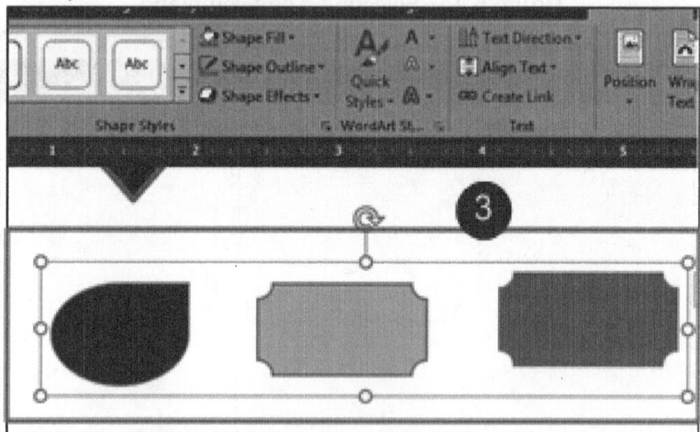

Figure 6.17 Selecting Group command

➡ **To ungroup objects:**

1. Select the grouped object. From the **Format** tab, click the **Group** command and select **Ungroup**.
2. The objects will be ungrouped.

6.2 WORKING WITH TABLES

A table is a grid of cells arranged in rows and columns. It can be used to organize any type of content, whether you are working with text or numerical data. You can also quickly insert a blank table or convert existing text to a table. And also customize your table using different styles and layouts.

6.2.1 Inserting a Table

➡ **To insert a blank table:**

1. Place the insertion point where you want the table to appear.
2. Click the **Insert** tab, then click the **Table** command in the **Tables** group as shown in Figure 6.18.

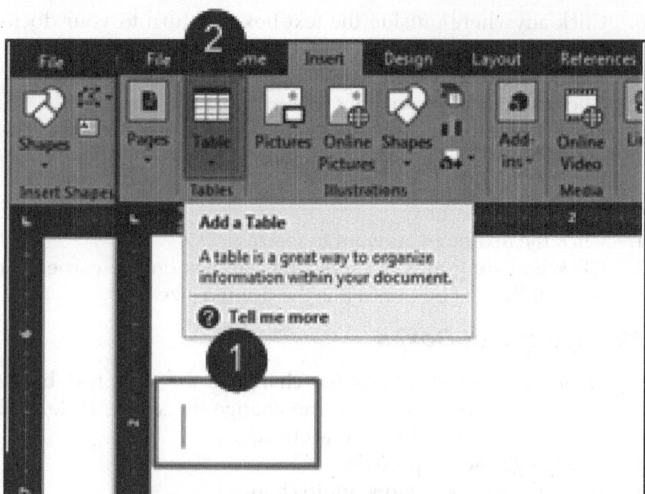

Figure 6.18 Selecting Table command

3. This will open a drop-down menu that contains a grid. Hover over the grid to select the number of columns and rows you want.
4. Click the grid to confirm your selection, and a table will appear as shown in Figure 6.19.

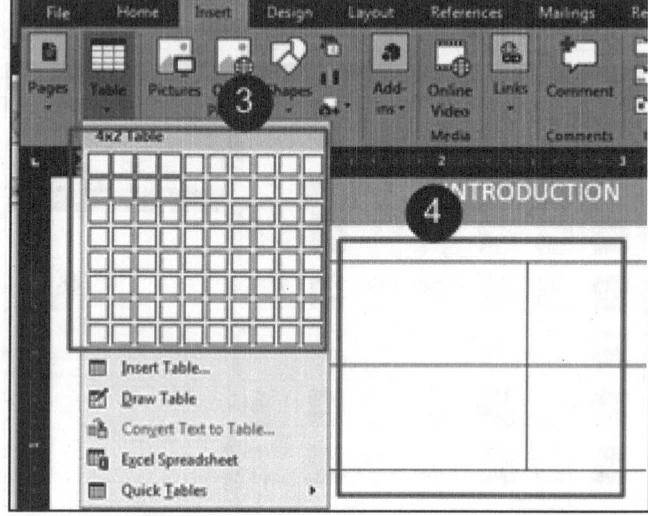

Figure 6.19 Grid selecting appear in the document

5. To enter text, place the insertion point in any cell, then begin typing as shown in Figure 6.20.

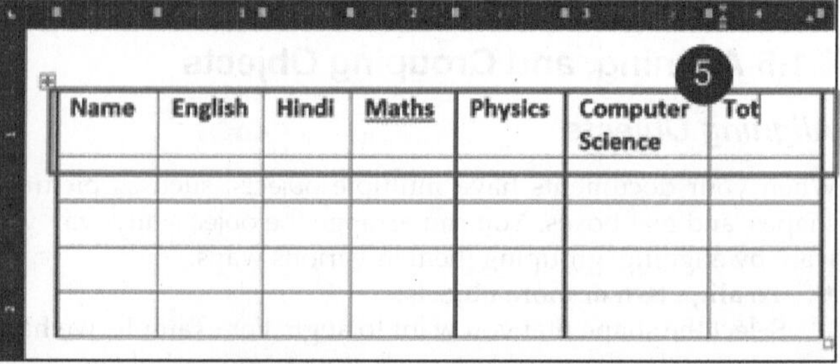

Figure 6.20 Enter text in a cell

To navigate between cells, use the **Tab** key or arrow keys on your keyboard. If the insertion point is in the last cell, pressing the **Tab** key will automatically create a new row.

6.2.2 Modifying Tables

You can easily change the appearance of your table once you have added one to your document. There are several options for customization, including adding rows or columns and changing the table style.

➡ **To add a row or column:**

1. Hover outside the table where you want to add a row or column. Click the plus sign that appears. You can also hover inside the table to insert row or column.
2. A new row or column will be added to the table as shown in Figure 6.21.

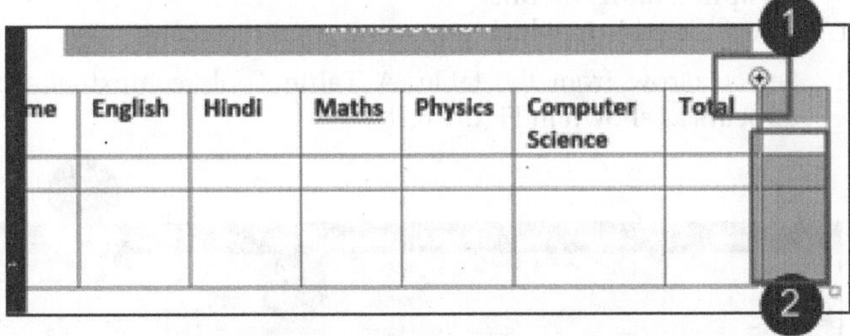

Figure 6.21 Add a Row in a table

3. Alternatively, you can right-click the table, then hover over Insert to see various row and column options.

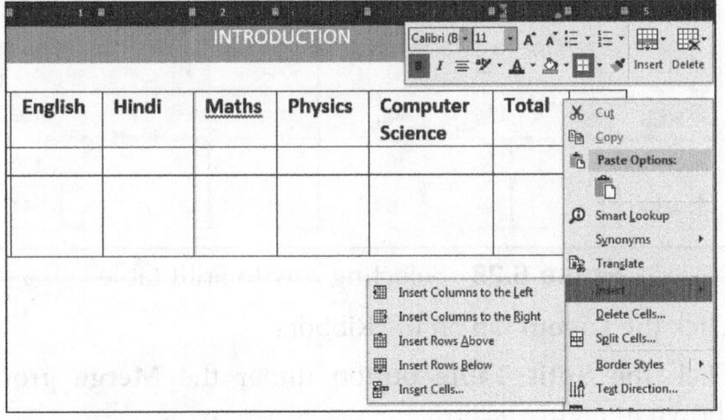

➡ **To delete a row or column:**

1. Place the insertion point in the row or column you want to delete.

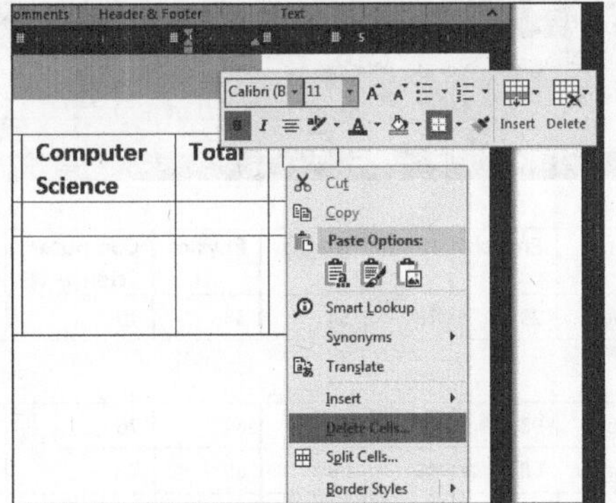

Figure 6.22 Delete cells from the right click mouse options

2. Right-click, then select **Delete Cells** from the menu as shown in Figure 6.22.
3. A **Delete Cells** dialog box will appear as shown in Figure 6.23. Choose **Delete entire row** or **Delete entire column**, then click OK.

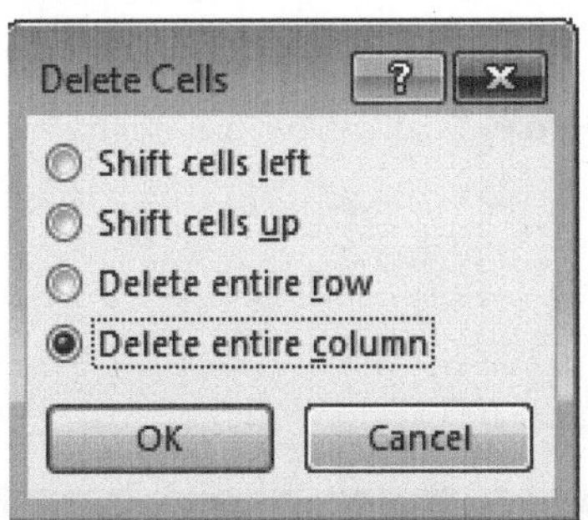

Figure 6.23 Delete cells dialog box

4. The row or column will be deleted.

6.2.3 Merging and Splitting Cells

Cells can be merged by combining two or more cells into one cell. Splitting cells means to divide a cell into two or more cells.

➡ **To merge the cells in a table:**

1. Select the cells that you want to merge from the table. A **Table Tools** contextual tab appears as shown in Figure 6.24.

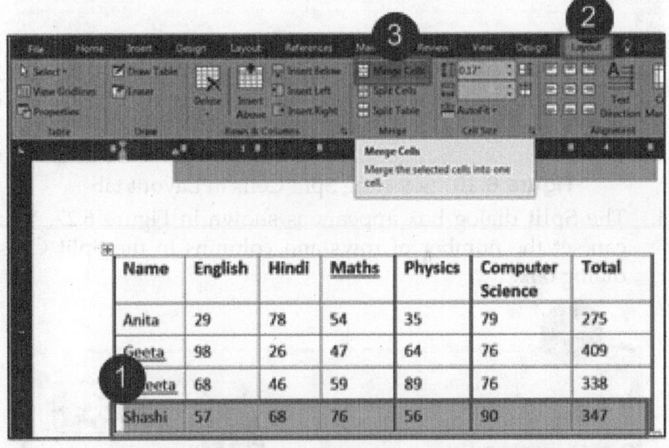

Name	English	Hindi	Maths	Physics	Computer Science	Total
Anita	29	78	54	35	79	275
Geeta	98	26	47	64	76	409
Neeta	68	46	59	89	76	338
Shashi	57	68	76	56	90	347

Figure 6.24 Selecting Merge cells

2. Click the **Layout** tab on the Ribbon.
3. Click the **Merge Cells** button under the **Merge** group as shown in Figure 6.25.
4. The selected cells of the table are merged, as shown in Figure 6.26.

➡ **To split a cell in a table, do this:**

1. Select the cell that you want to split in the table. A **Table Tools** contextual tab appears.
2. Click the **Layout** tab on the **Ribbon.**
3. Click the **Split Cells** button under the **Merge** group as shown in Figure 6.26.

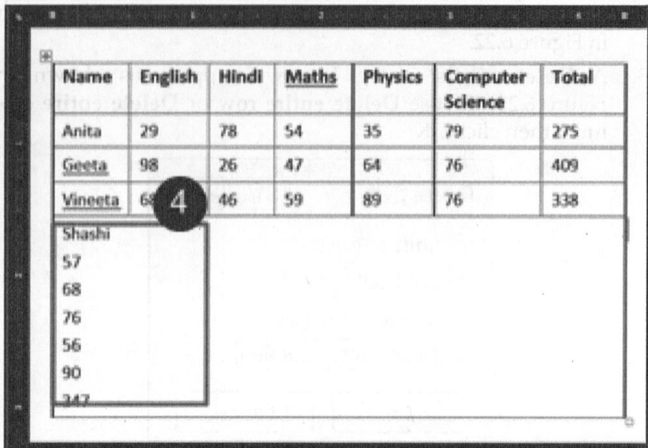

Figure 6.25 The selected cells get merged

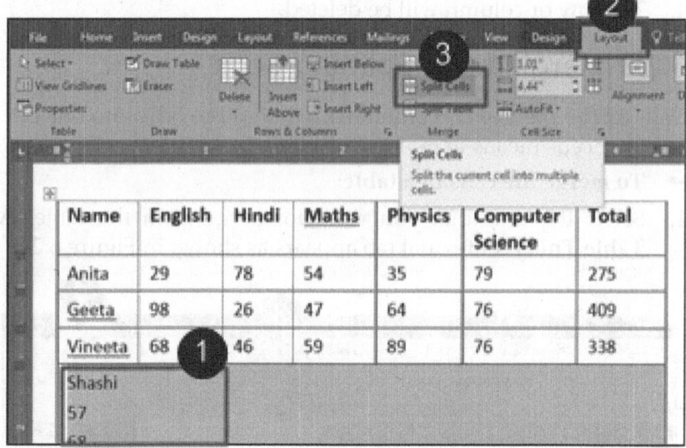

Figure 6.26 Selecting Split Cells in Layout tab

4. The **Split** dialog box appears as shown in Figure 6.27. You can set the number of rows and columns in the Split Cells dialog box.

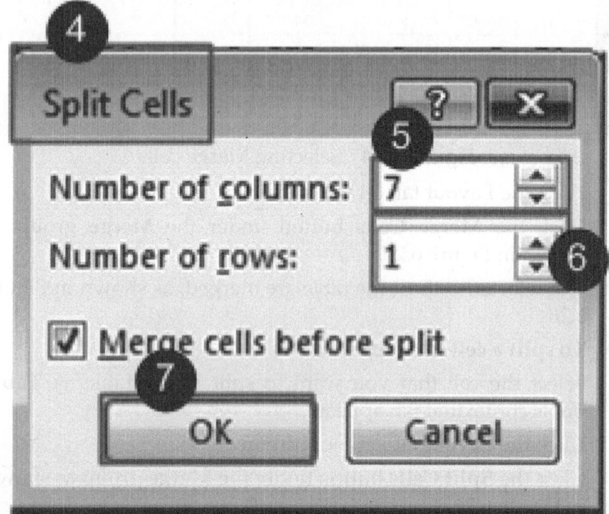

Figure 6.27 Split Cells dialog box

5. Specify the number of columns in the **Number of columns:** spin box. For example, we have selected 7 as shown in Figure 6.27.
6. Specify the number of rows in the **Number of rows:** spin box. For example, we have selected 1 as shown in Figure 6.27.
7. Click the OK button in the **Split Cells** dialog box as shown in Figure 6.27.
8. The selected cell is split according to the number set in the number of columns and rows in the **Split** dialog box.

Splitting a Table

Splitting a table means divide the rows and columns into separate table so that they could be arranged with ease and comfort.

➡ **To split a table, do this:**

1. Select the table in which you want to split a table.
2. Select a row from the table. A **Table** Tools contextual tab appears as shown in Figure 6.28.

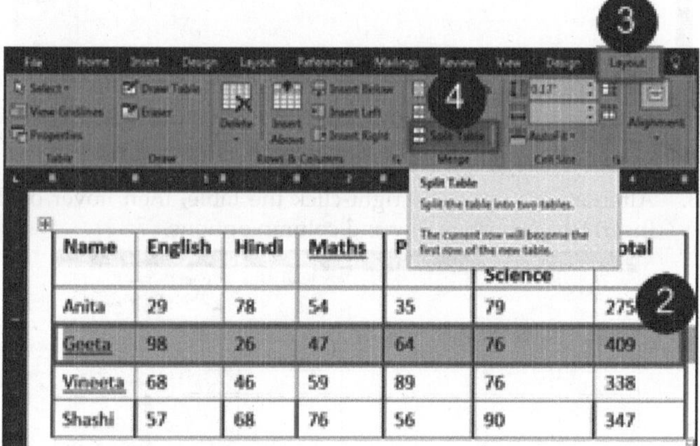

Figure 6.28 Selecting row to Split table

3. Click the **Layout** tab on the Ribbon.
4. Click the **Split Table** button under the **Merge** group as shown in Figure 6.28.
5. The selected table is split into two tables are shown in Figure 6.29.

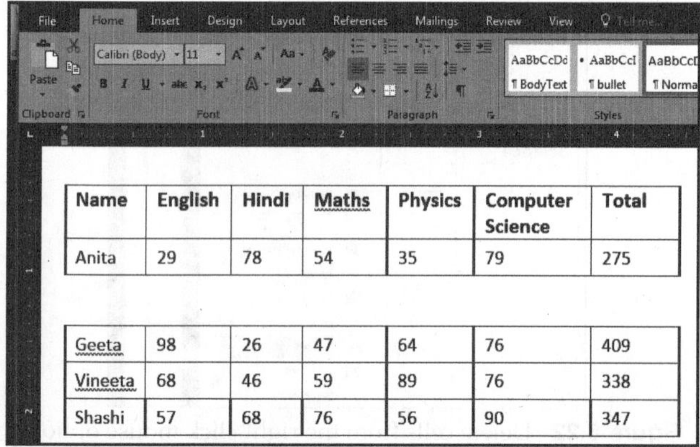

Figure 6.29 The table split int two

6.2.4 Aligning Text in a Table Cell

You can align text in a table cell in nine different ways: Top Left (the default alignment), Top center, Top Right, Center Left, Center Right, Bottom Left, Bottom Center, and Bottom Right as shown in Figure 6.30.

➡ **To align one or more cells:**

1. Click the cell that contains text that you want to align.
2. Click **Layout** contextual tab, click **Alignment** icons and then choose the text direction options you want in the cells.
3. Select the desired option you want the text to be **Top Right**, choose Align text to the top right corner of the cell in the **Alignment** group options.
4. For example, we have selected center alignment. The selected cell aligned center as shown in Figure 6.30.

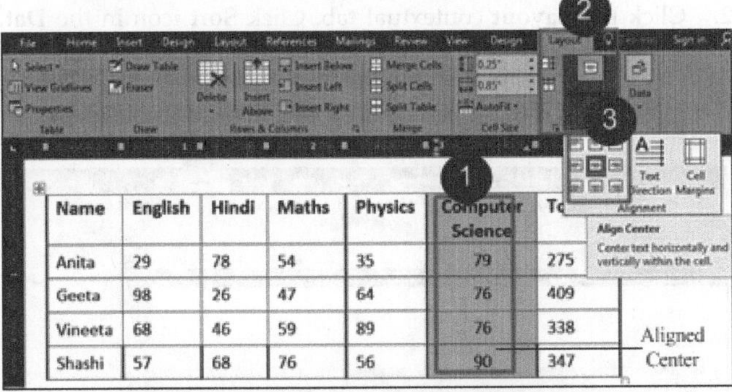

Figure 6.30 Text aligned center in a Cell

6.2.5 Convert Text to a Table

If you have an existing text that you would like to turn into a table, you need to first separate text into block. So Word 2016 knows how to place the text into individual cells in a table. You can change the delimiter character to commas, tabs, or any other character, such as # or *.

➡ **To convert text to a table, do this:**

1. Select the table that you want to convert into a text.
2. Click **Insert** tab, click **Table**, drop-down menu appears as shown in Figure 6.31.

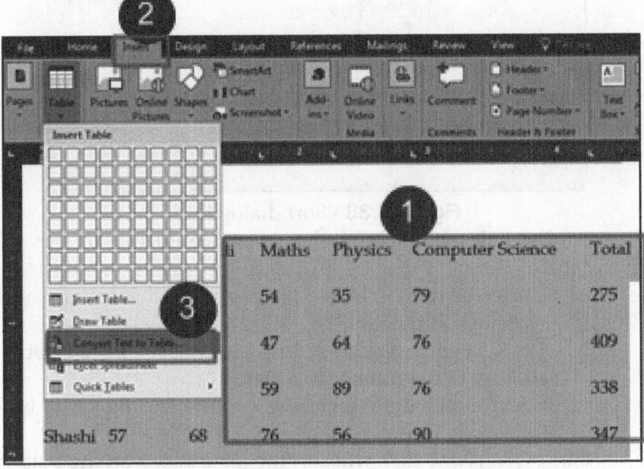

Figure 6.31 Selecting Convert text to table option

3. Click the **Convert Table to Text...** command.
   The **Convert Table to Text** dialog box appears as shown in Figure 6.32.
4. In **Convert Table to Text** dialog box, in the *Separate text at* section, select the radio button such as Paragraphs, Tabs or Commas.
   You must choose the option that corresponds to the way you divided your text. For example, if you divided your text by tabs, you would click the Tabs radio button. (Figure 6.32)

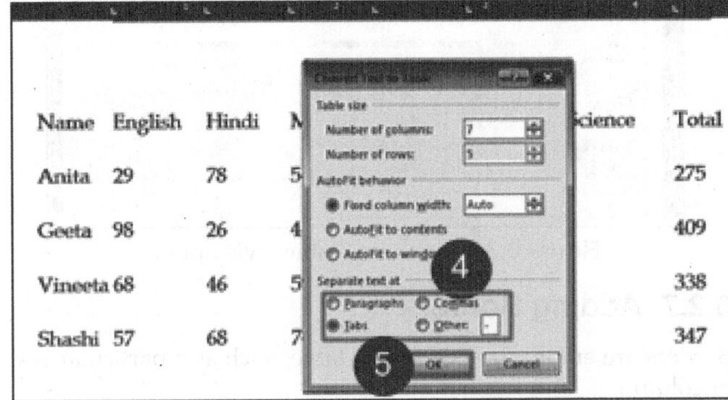

Figure 6.32 Convert Table to Text dialog box

5. Click OK. Word 2016 converts your text into a table as shown in Figure 6.33.

Name	English	Hindi	Maths	Physics	Computer Science	Total
Anita	29	78	54	35	79	275
Geeta	98	26	47	64	76	409
Vineeta	68	46	59	89	76	338
Shashi	57	68	76	56	90	347

Figure 6.33 Text converted to Table

6.2.6 Formatting Table Styles

Table styles let you change the look and feel of your table instantly. They control several design elements, including color, borders, and fonts.

➡ **To format a table style:**

1. Select the entire table by pressing at the top corner of the arrow in the table or press Alt+5 on the numeric keypad with Numlock off.
2. Click **Design** contextual tab. In the **Table Style Options** group, click the check boxes, such as *Header Row* or *Banded Columns* to modify the options in the table.
   Click the **More** button on the **Table Styles** group.
3. A pull down menu of all available styles appears, as seen in Figure 7.33. As you move the mouse pointer over a table style, Word 2016 displays a live preview of how your table will look.
4. Click a table desired style. Word 2016 format your table according to the style you select as shown in Figure 6.34.

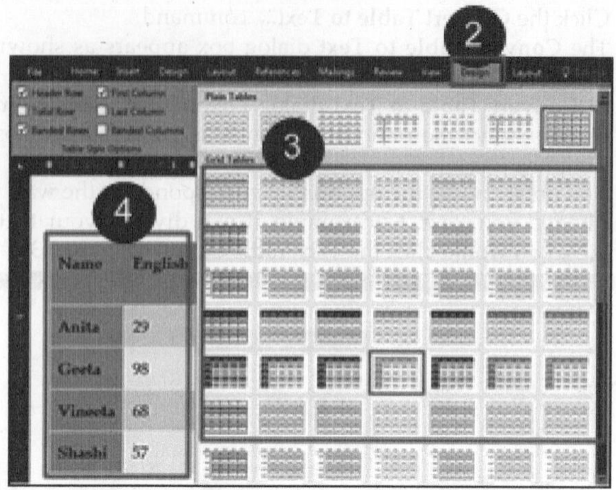

Figure 6.34 Selecting Table style options

6.2.7 Adding Borders

Borders are emphasize parts your table, such as a particular row or column.

➡ **To apply borders to a table:**

1. Select the table you want to apply a border.
2. Click the **Design** tab choose the desired **Line Style**, **Line Weight**, and **Pen Color** as shown in Figure 6.35.

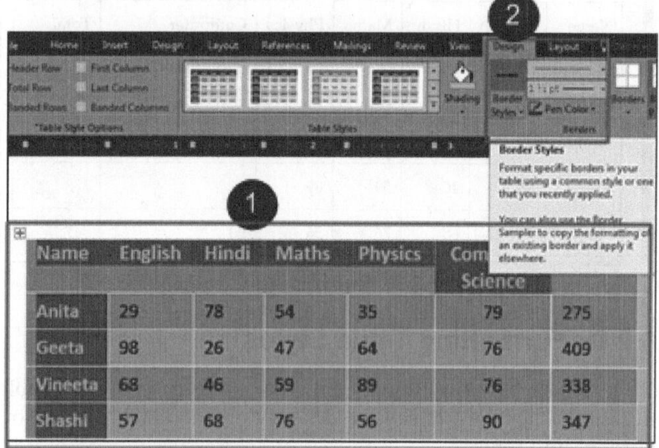

Figure 6.35 Selecting border style

3. Click the drop-down arrow below the **Borders** command as shown in Figure 6.36.
4. Choose a border type from the menu.
5. The border will be applied to the selected cells.

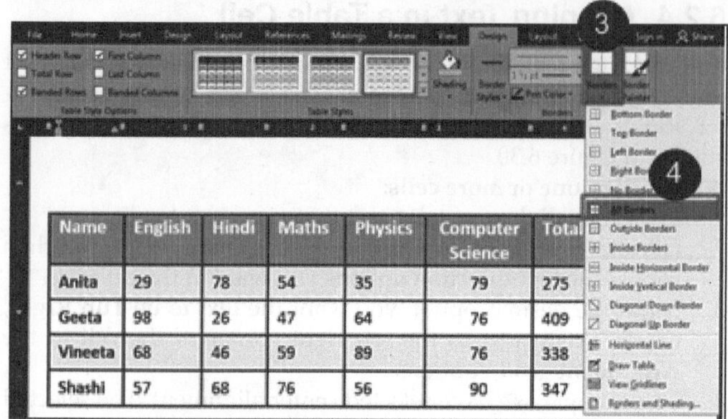

Figure 6.36 Applying borders

6.2.8 Sorting the Contents of a Table

Tables can not only organize data, but they can also arrange your data alphabetically. The **Sort** command can be used to arrange the rows in a specific order *ascending*, *descending*, etc. Word 2016 can sort lines of tabular text, items you have entered in tables, or even paragraphs in a document. (Figure 6.37)

➡ **To sort a table:**

1. Position the insertion point in the table you wish to sort. *Alternatively*, select the cells you want to sort.
2. Click the **Layout** contextual tab. Click **Sort** icon in the **Data** group as shown in Figure 6.37.
3. Click **Sort** command. The **Sort** dialog box appears, as shown in Figure 6.38.

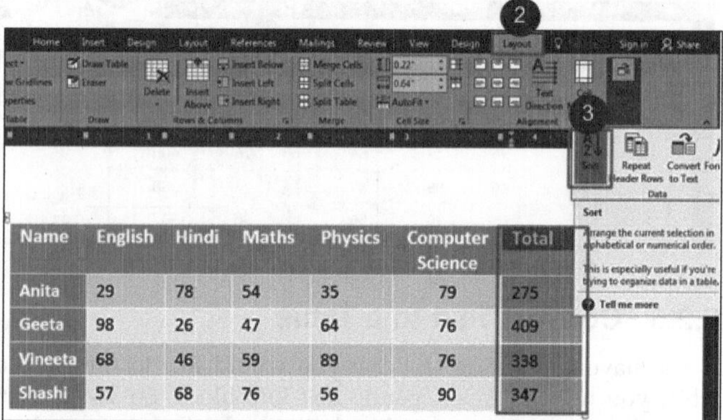

Figure 6.37 Select Sort command in the Layout tab

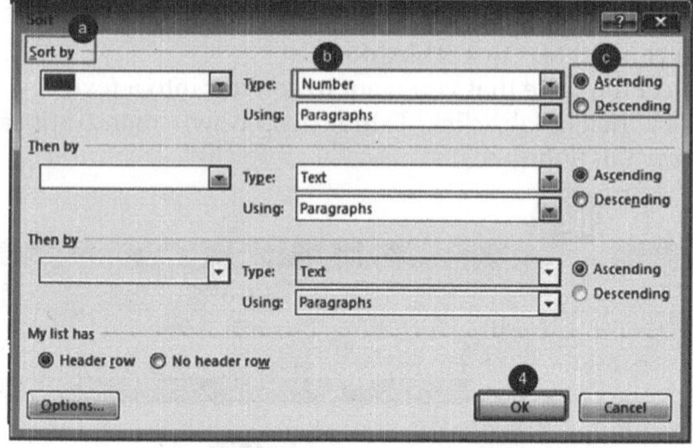

Figure 6.38 Sort dialog box

4. In the dialog box, choose how you would like to sort the table.
   a. Under **Sort by**, choose the name of the column you want to sort the table by.
   b. Click **Type:** drop-down arrow to choose desired option such as Text, Number or a Date.
   c. Select either the **Ascending** or **Descending** radio button.
5. Click OK. Word 2016 will sort the table based on the data in the column you selected.

CHAPTER 7

Creating Mail Merge

7.1 USING MAIL MERGE

Mail Merge is a useful tool that allows you to produce multiple letters, labels, envelopes, name tags, and more by using information stored in a list, database, or spreadsheet. The process for creating a mail merge document is quite straight forward and logical. All the tools for performing mail merge operations are available from the Mailings tab. From this tab, you can run the wizard or perform individual steps of the mail merge process on your own.

7.1.1 Creating a Mail Merge Letter

The best way to learn how to create and print a merged document is to consider a practical example. This is described in the following sections.

Creating a Document for Mail-Merge

For mail-merge, you need to do the following:

- Create a data source
- Create main document
- Insert fields into the main document
- Check for design and data entry errors
- Merge the data source document and the main document and finally, print merged documents

7.1.2 Starting Mail Merge

Word 2016 has a step-by-step Mail Merge Wizard that guides you through the steps for creating merged documents.

➡ **To use the mail merge:**

1. Open an existing Word document, or create a new one.
2. Click the **Mailings** tab in the **Start Mail Merge** group and click on the down pointing arrow and select **Step by Step Mail Merge Wizard...** as shown in Figure 7.1.

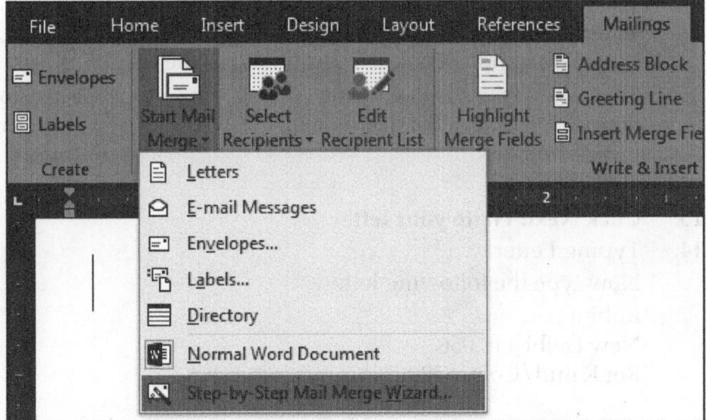

Figure 7.1 Select step-by-step Mail Merge Wizard

Figure 7.2 Step 1 of Mail Merge task pane

3. On the right hand side the Mail Merge task pane box appears as shown in Figure 7.2 showing Step 1 of the Wizard's six steps. The following example demonstrates how to create a form letter and merge the letter with a recipient list.
4. Under the **Select document type**, click Letters radio button.
5. Click **Next: Starting document.**
   - The wizard guides you through the rest of the mail process. The following are more details, listed in step-by-step order.
   - There are three options under **select starting document**, click **use the current document** radio button, which specifies *how do you want to set up your letters?* (See Figure 7.3).

Figure 7.3 Step 2 of Mail Merge task pane

6. Click **Next: Select recipients.**
   - Under **Select recipients**, click **Type a new list** radio button (Figure 7.4).

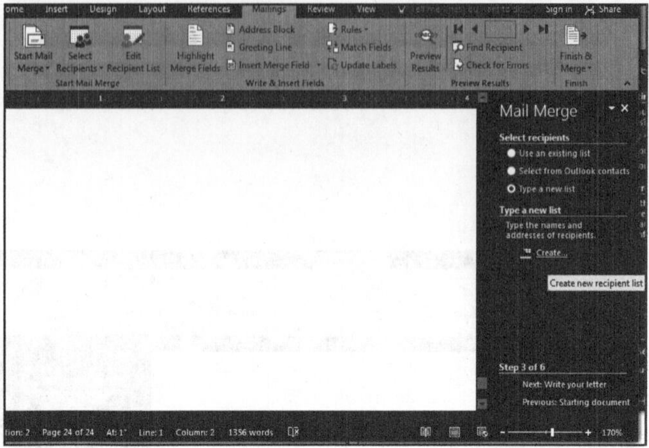

Figure 7.4 Step 3 of Mail Merge task pane

- Click **Create...** under Type a new list section.

6. A **New Address List** dialog box appears as shown in Figure 7.5. Type the information you want to include for the data source.

As you may not require all the field names in the **New Address List** dialog box, so for each of the following field names, first select the field and then click the **Customize Columns...** button. The **Customize Address** list dialog box appears as shown in Figure 7.6.

7. Select the Field names order appears in the **Customize Address list** dialog box, If you don't want any field, select the field and then click delete button.
8. The Selected Field names are: *Title, First Name, Last Name, Address Line 1, City, Zip Code.*

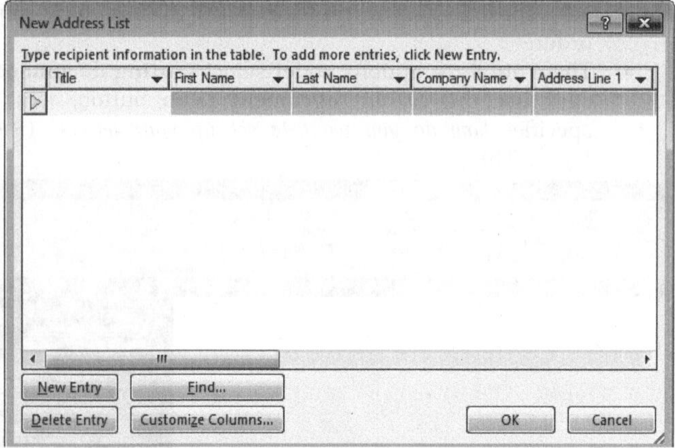

Figure 7.5 New Address List dialog box

9. Under Field names: type (use tab key to go next field)
   `Title: Mr.`
   `First Name: Sanjay`
   `Last Name: Sharma`
   `Address Line 1: 120-A, Vikaspuri`
   `City: New Delhi`
   `Zip Code: 110 018`
   After completing the First entry, click New Entry to enter another data records.

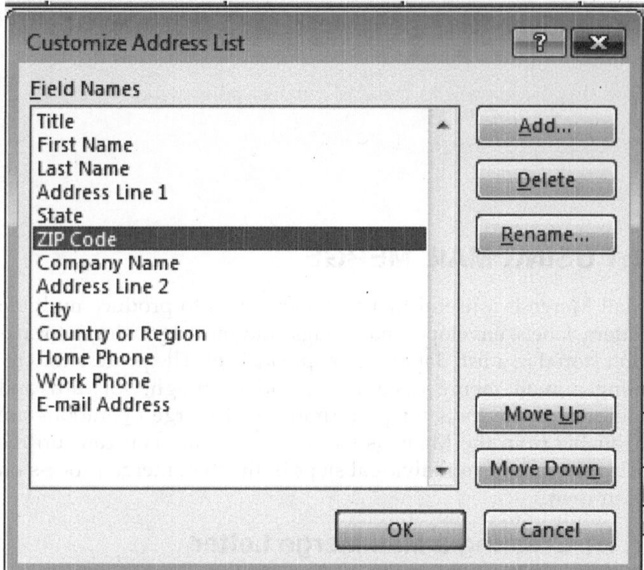

Figure 7.6 Customize Address list dialog box

When you have finished adding fields, click **OK** to save your data source in the **New Address List** dialog box as shown in Figure 7.7.

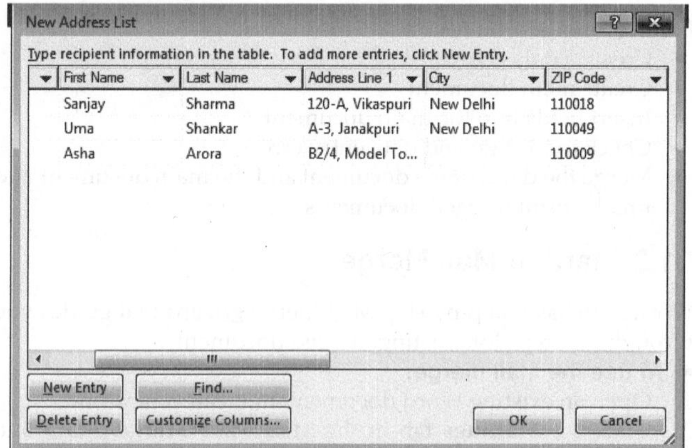

Figure 7.7 Adding fields in the Address list dialog box

10. The **Save Address List** dialog box appears as in Figure 7.8. Enter a name and location for your data source file, say, **`Data.doc`** and click Save button to save the file.
11. The Mail Merge Recipients dialog box appears as in Figure 7.9. Select the recipients that will be used in your merge process.
12. Click OK.
13. Click **Next: Write your letter.**
14. Typing Letter
    Now type the following letter.
    Rohini
    New Delhi-110 056
    Ref.Rahul/Comm/20

Dated: 3rd April, 2018

To

<<Title>> <<First_Name>>

<<Last_Name>>

<<Address_Line_1>>

<<City>>-<<ZIP_Code>>

Dear <<Title>> <<Last_Name>>

I have to inform you that the meeting of the club committee will be held at the Subroto Park Auditorium on Tuesday 25th June, 2018 at 8.00 A.M. I hope you will make it convenient to attend the conference.

The agenda for the conference is as under:

1. Confirmation of the minutes of the last meeting (enclosed).
2. Accounts and Internal Auditors Report for the months of Feb and March 2018 (enclosed).
3. Election of new members.
4. List of outstanding.
5. Any other matter with the permission of the Chairman.

Yours faithfully,

P.K. Verma

(Secretary)

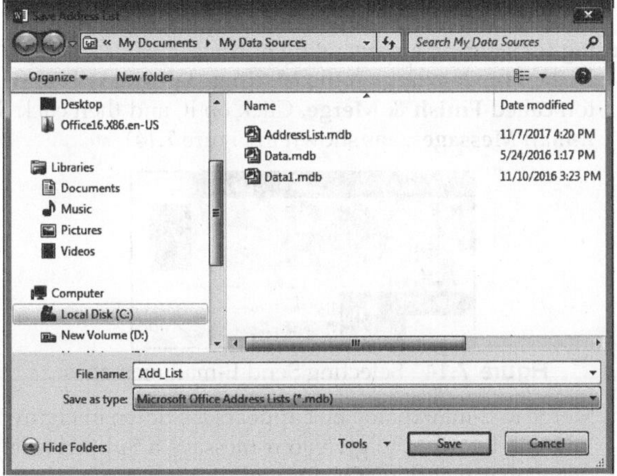

Figure 7.8 Save Address List dialog box

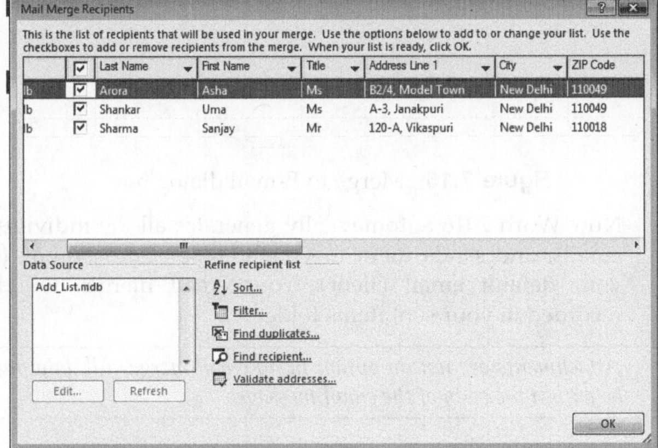

Figure 7.9 Mail Merge Recipients dialog box

➡ **To insert a field:**

1. In the **Mailing** tab, click **Insert Merge Field** in the **Write & Insert Fields** group. Click the down pointing arrow and choose the field names that you can insert in your master document appears. You can also select the field names from this list (See Figure 7.10).
2. Click the Title from merge field name to insert it into the document.
3. Press the Spacebar key to insert a blank space between the Title and the FirstName.
4. Click the **Insert Merge Field** button to insert the next field name and select FirstName.
5. Press the Spacebar key to insert a blank space between the fields FirstName and LastName.

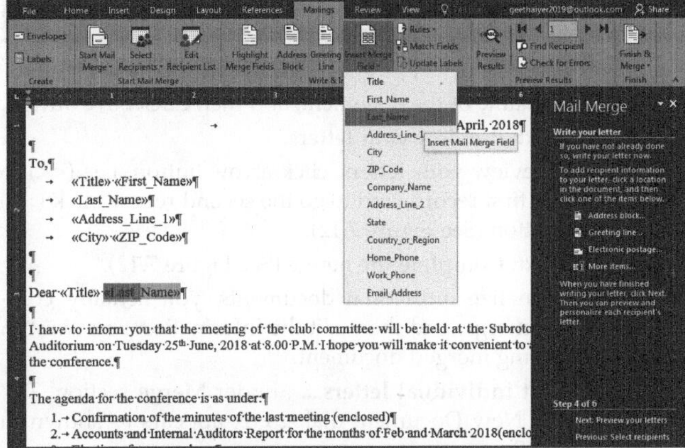

Figure 7.10 Step 4 of Mail Merge task pane

6. Click the **Insert Merge Field** button and select **LastName**.
7. Press the Enter key to move to the next line.
8. Place the cursor below the **<<Title>>**. Click the **Insert Merge Field** button. Select **<<Address1>>** and press the Enter key.
9. Again place the cursor below **<<Address1>>**. Click the **Insert Merge Field** button. Select **<<City>>** type a hyphen and select **<<Pin>>** from the merge field button and press Enter key.
10. Press the Enter key twice to leave a blank line.
11. Type *Dear* and press the Spacebar key.
12. Click the **Insert Merge Field** button and select **<<Title>>**.
13. Press the Spacebar to leave a space between the Title and the LastName.
14. Click the **Insert Merge Field** button and select **<<Last-Name>>**.
15. Type a comma, and then press the Enter key twice to leave a blank line.
16. After completing the above steps, your screen will be as shown in Figure 7.11.
17. Now type the remaining part of the letter.

7.1.3 Saving the Master Document

18. After you have completed the main document and inserted all of the merge fields, click Save As on the Office button.

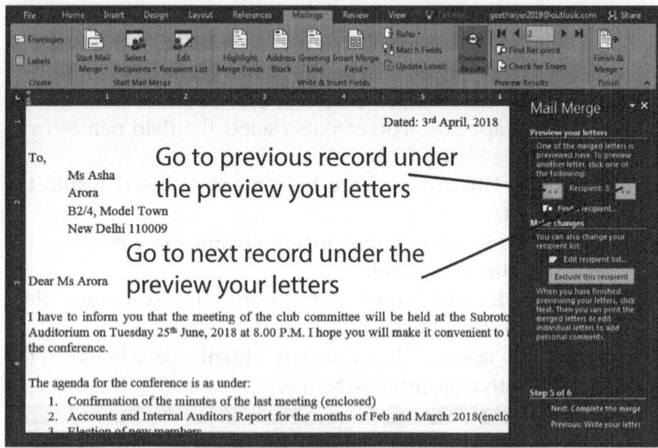

Figure 7.11 Step 5 of partially completed screen

19. Give the name of the document, and then Click Save button.
20. Click **Next: Preview your letters.**
21. In the Preview your letters, click arrow button, i.e., (<<) to show the first record, and to go the second record click (>>) arrow button (See Figure 7.12).
22. Click **Next: Complete the merge** (See Figure 7.12).
23. To personalize individual documents, you actually complete the merge, and then edit the information you want in the resulting merged document.
24. Click **Edit individual letters....** . under **Merge** section. The Merge to New Document dialog box appears as shown in Figure 7.12.
25. In the Merge records area, select the records you want to merge.

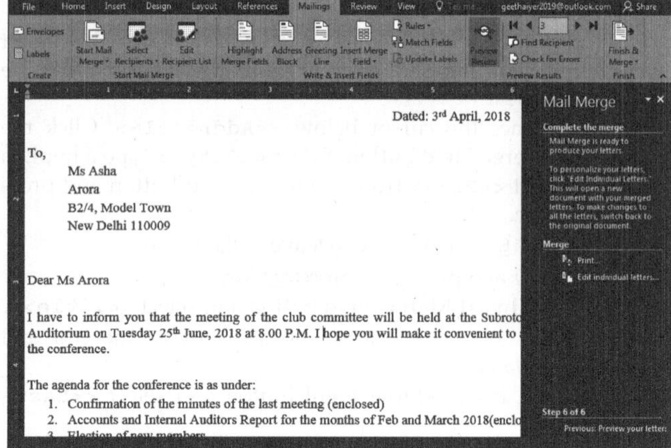

Figure 7.12 Step 6 of partially completed screen

26. Click All radio button and then click OK.

    Word 2016 creates and opens a new merged document. Your main document also remains open. You can switch back to it if you want to make a change to all the documents and then save all the merged documents. Click Office button and Save the file.

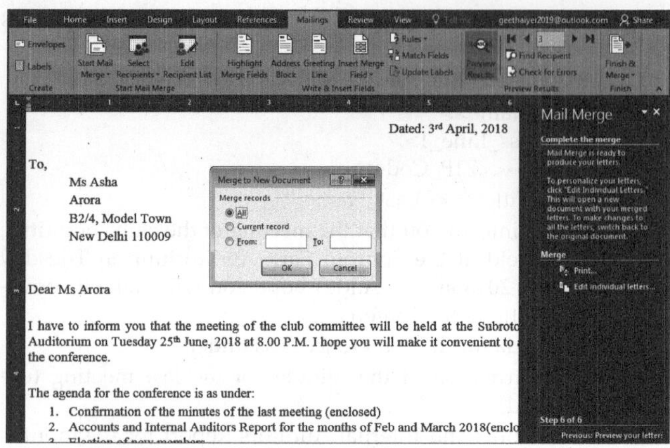

Figure 7.13 Merge to New Document dialog box

7.1.4 Printing the Merged Letters

If you want to print the letters, make sure that the printer is switched on and is in ready to print. Then click **Finish & Merge** in **Finish** group. Click down pointing arrow and choose **Print Documents...** . The **Merge to Printer** dialog box appears. Select the records and click OK.

Merging for sending emails using outlook

27. In the **Finish** group on the **Mailings** tab you will see a button called **Finish & Merge**. Click on it, and then click **Send E-mail Messages...** as shown in Figure 7.14)

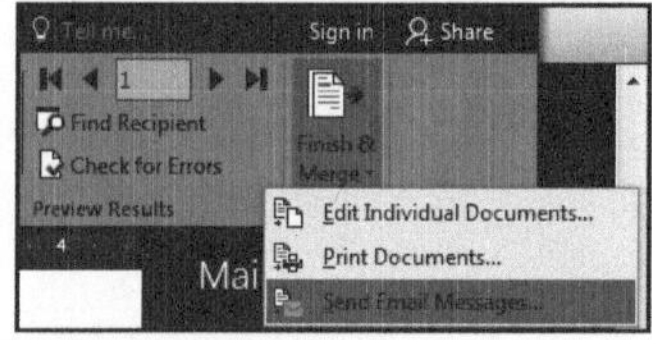

Figure 7.14 Selecting Send E-mail messages

28. Merge to E-mail dialog box appears as shown in Figure 7.15. You will be asked to give your message a **Subject line:** and then you can click on OK to send the messages.

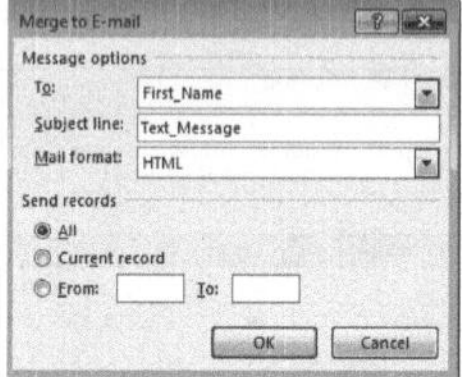

Figure 7.15 Merge to E-mail dialog box

29. Now Word 2016 automatically generates all the individual emails, and sends them to your Outlook 2010 outbox (or your default email client). Your email merges will be recorded in your sent items folder.

☞ *Attachments are not an option in an email merge. All data must be within the body of the email message.*

CHAPTER 8

Complex Documents

8.1 START A BOOKLET

A brochure is a paper document or a booklet that gives information about an event. Word allows you to create basic booklets that look both, professional and impressive. Word features pre-built page settings for booklets that enable you to create a booklet.

8.1.1 Create a Booklet

Before you can start entering content into your document, you need to page setup document settings in Word.

1. Select the document that you want to create a booklet.

8.1.2 Choose Page Arrangement

Specify the paper size, the margins and the page style.

1. Click the **Layout** tab at the bottom-right corner of the **Page setup** group to open the **Page Setup** dialog box as shown in Figure 8.1.

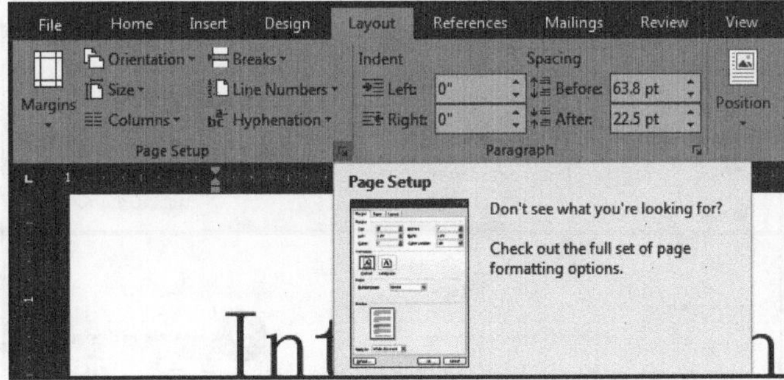

Figure 8.1 Selecting Page setup in the Layout tab

2. In the Pages section, click the **Multiple pages** drop-down arrow to select **Book fold** option. The orientation automatically changes to **Landscape** (See Figure 8.2).
3. Select the number of pages you would want to be printed per booklet in the **Sheets per booklet:** to select the desired option. For example, we have select 4 drop-down menu.
4. Select the **Gutter:** drop-down list to increase the space on the inside fold for binding.
5. Select the **Paper size:** drop-down list to select the size for the Booklet. Make sure the margins are set appropriately for your document (See Figure 8.3).
6. Type the Contents of your booklet. For example, put a title on the first page of the booklet and use the **Style** and **Font** options under the **Home** tab to format the text (See Figure 8.4). For example, we have type **Word 2016 Training Guide**.

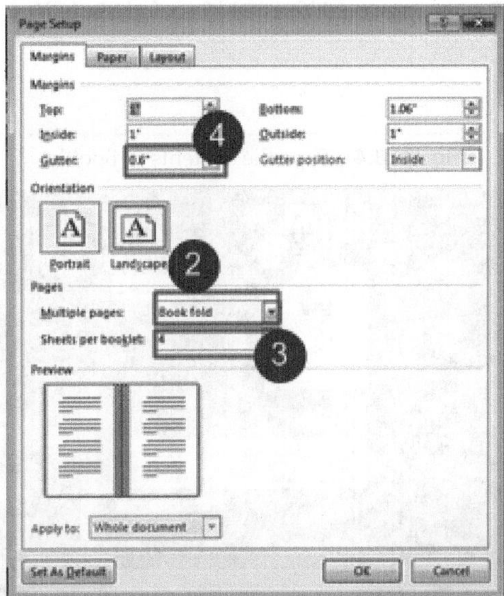

Figure 8.2 Selecting Book fold option

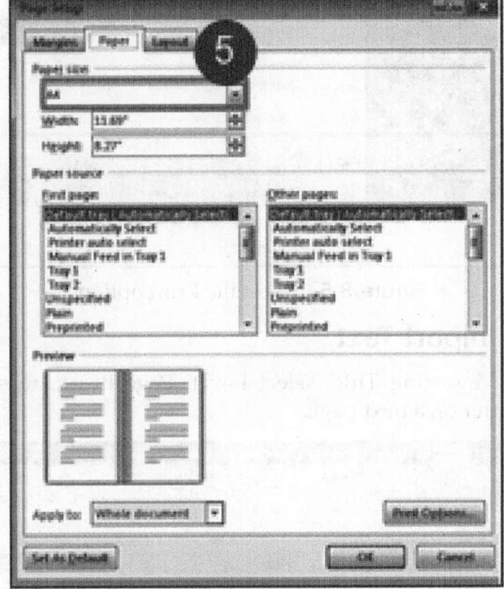

Figure 8.3

Click the **Save** icon to save the booklet.

7. If your printer supports double-side printing, click on **Both sides** option that has the correct paper-flipping edge-quite likely the short edge (See Figure 8.5).
8. Click the **Print** button to print.

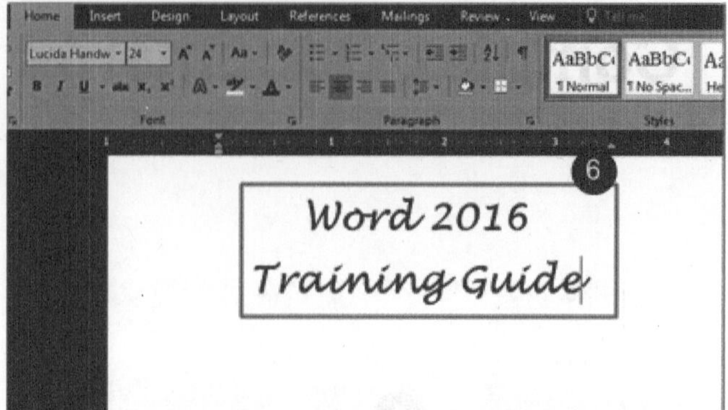

Figure 8.4 Type the contents of Booklet

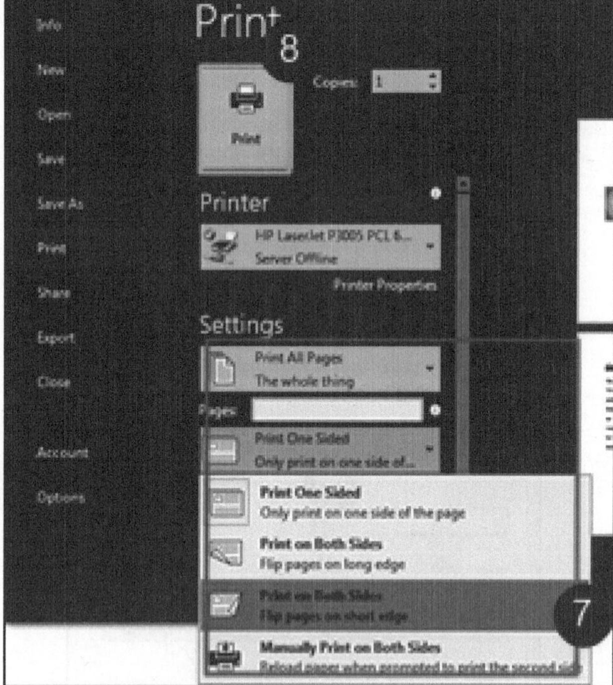

Figure 8.5 Select the Print option

8.1.3 Import Text

1. After inserting Title, select Insert, Page Break, to start the Chapter on a next page.

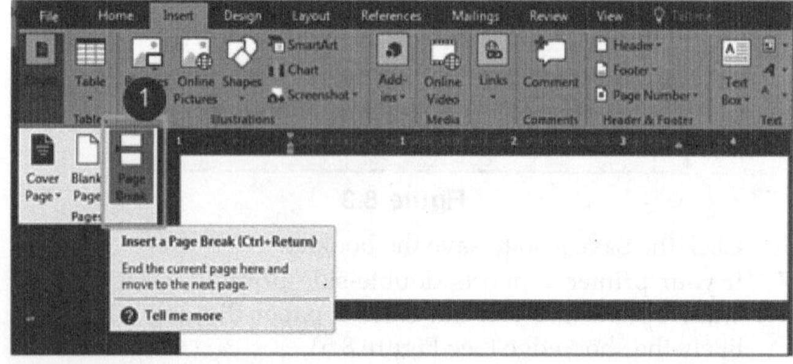

2. Position the insertion point to insert the text.

3. On the **Insert** tab, in the **Text** group, click the **Object** arrow. Then click **Text from File** as shown in Figure 8.6.

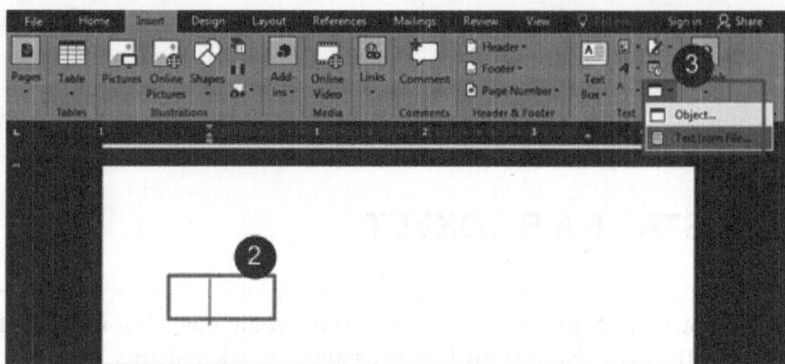

Figure 8.6 Select the Text from file in Text group

4. The **Insert File** dialog box appears as shown in Figure 9.7. Browse to the file that contains the text you want to insert in the Address bar.

5. Select the file, and then click the **Insert** button to import the text into your document as shown in Figure 8.7.

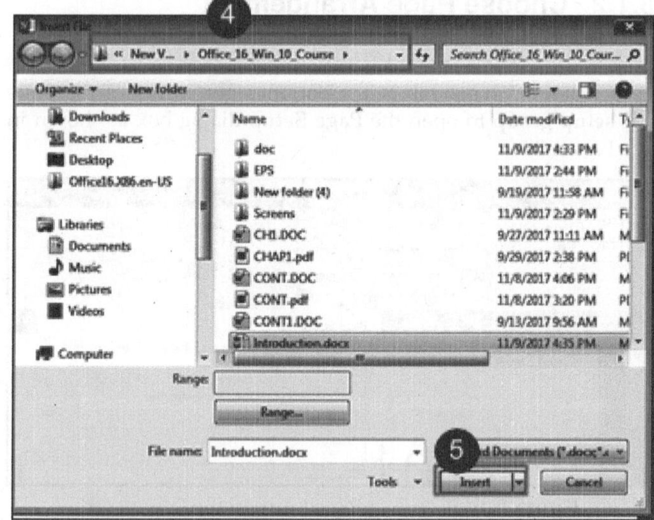

Figure 8.7 Insert file dialog box

6. The text will be inserted in the document at the selected location.

➡ **To adjust the style for the inserted text:**

1. On the **Home** tab in the **Editing** group, click **Select** drop-down arrow to **Select Text with similar Formatting** option as shown below.

   The inserted text may not have be formatted, but you can change all the inserted text in a single operation to a style that you prefer.

2. The text will be selected, you can change the style such as align the text to **justify**, **Spacing** and **Font** type in the **Home** tab. Or

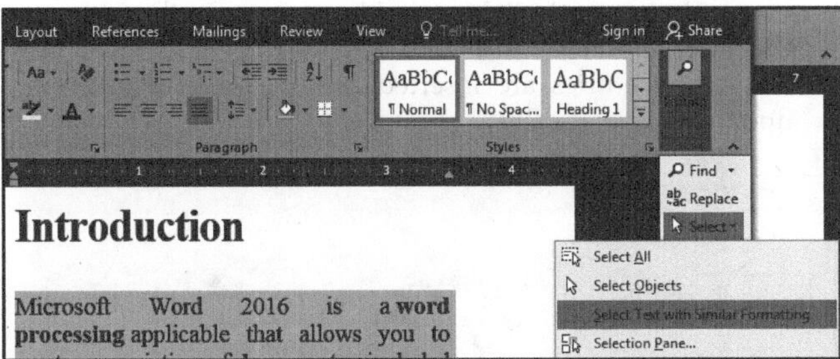

3. You can click the in-built style in the **Style** group in **Home** tab as shown below.

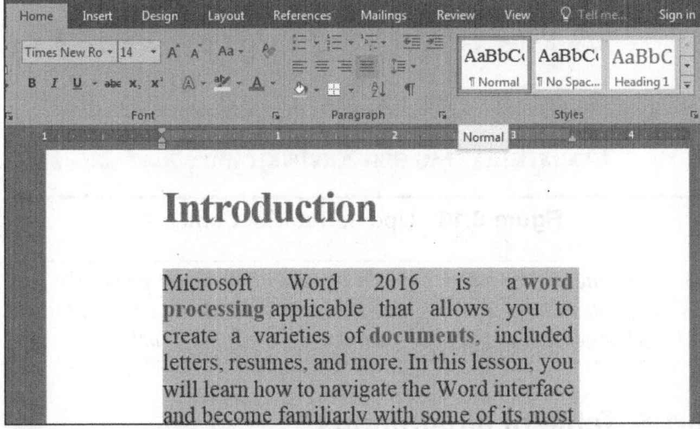

8.1.4 Insert Illustrations

1. Position the insertion point to insert the picture. Or Click the **Find** command on the **Home** tab to enter a search term, as shown in Figure 8.8.

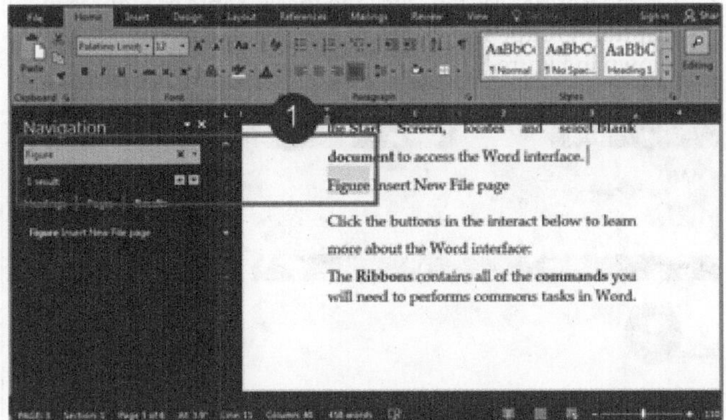

Figure 8.8 Search an item in the Navigation pane

2. Select the placeholder text describing the illustrations, then choose the **Insert** tab and click **Pictures**.
   The **Insert Picture** dialog box appears.
3. Navigate the folder containing file location in the Address bar as shown in Figure 8.9.
4. Select the required file to insert the picture in the document.
5. Click **Insert** button. Adjust its size and position of the picture as required.

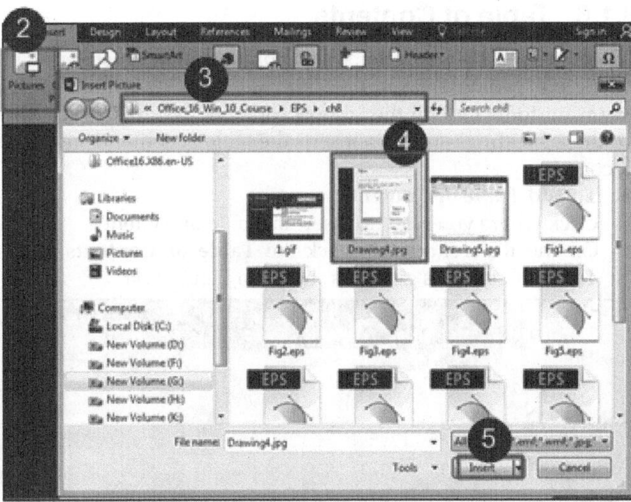

Figure 8.9 Insert Picture dialog box

8.1.5 Add Captions

To add Figure captions in the document to reference of the picture contained.

➡ **To add captions for figures:**

1. On the **References** tab, select **Insert Caption** command on the **Captions** group.
2. The **Caption** dialog box appears as shown in Figure 8.10. Type the text for the picture title to follow the figure number in the **Caption:** text box.

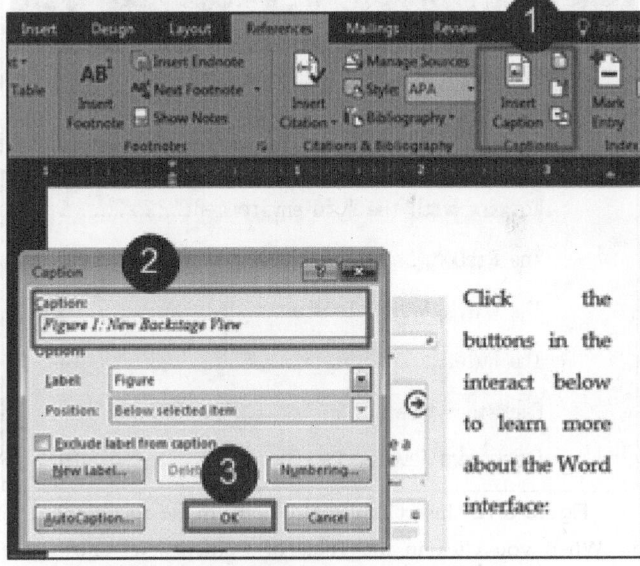

Figure 8.10 Caption dialog to insert caption

3. Click OK to accept the automatic number. The figure caption will appear in the document.
4. Repeat this above steps for each of the picture in the document, until you have all the figures and captions.

8.1.6 Table of Contents

To create a table of contents by applying heading styles – for example, Heading 1, Heading 2, and Heading 3 – to the text that you want to include in the table of contents. Word 2016 searches for those headings and then inserts the table of contents into your document.

➡ **To add Table of Contents:**

1. Click where you want to insert the table of contents.
2. On the **References** tab, click the **Table of Contents** in the **Table of contents** group as shown in Figure 8.11.

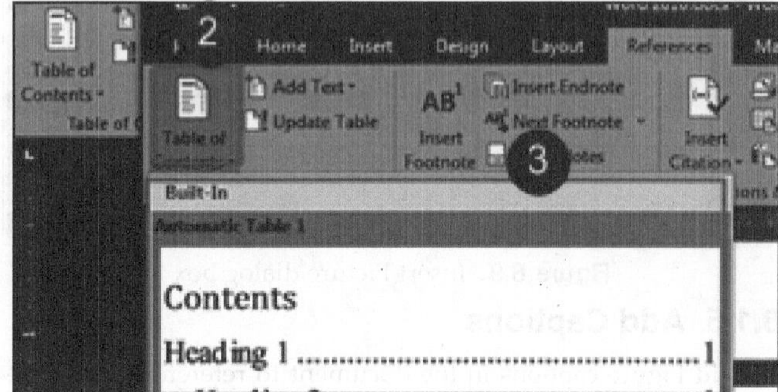

Figure 8.11 Selecting Table of Contents in Built-in styles

3. A List of Built-in Styles appear as shown in Figure 8.11, choose the type of table that you want. For example, we have select **Automatic Table 1**.
4. The Table of Contents is inserted in the document as shown in Figure 8.12.

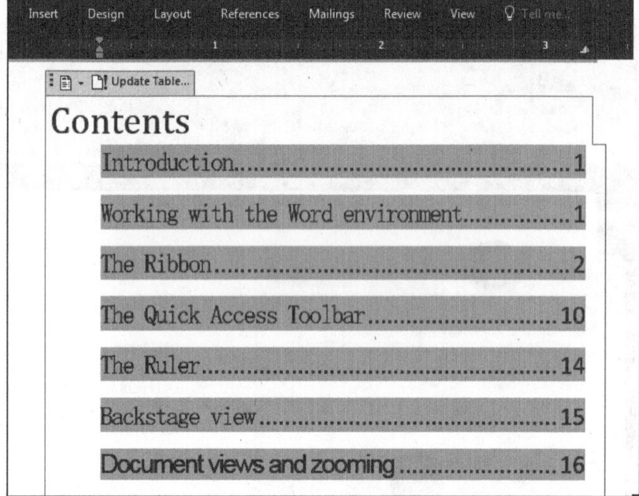

Figure 8.12 Insert Table of Contents in the document

5. When you click in the Table of Contents, its entries are grayed, to indicate they are field codes. Ctrl+Click to links the contents of Headings.

8.1.7 Update Table of Contents

If you added or removed headings or other table of contents entries in your document, you can quickly update the table of contents.

1. Click **Update Table** at the top of the table.
2. Check **Update entire table** to add new items in the table.
3. Click OK button.
4. Now, new entries are inserted and the page numbers are updated automatically as shown in Figure 8.13.

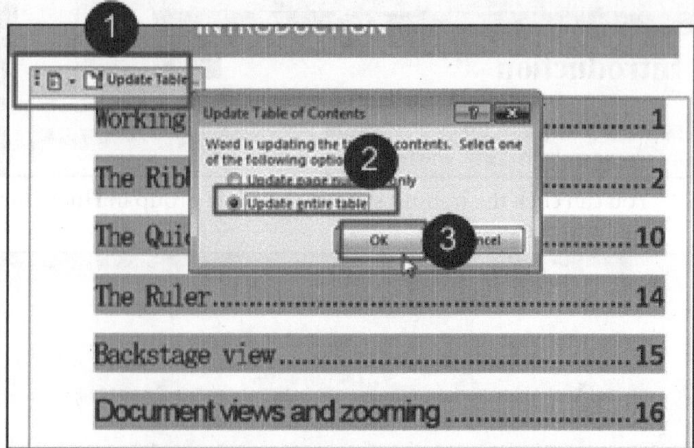

Figure 8.13 Update Table of Contents

☞ *Whenever you add text to the document, or insert pages, the page numbers for the entries in the Table of Contents change, but the changes will not appear until you select Update Table.*

8.1.8 Table of Illustrations

1. Insert Page break to insert the new page in the document.
2. Position the insertion point to insert a list of illustrations in the document.
3. On the **References** tab, click the **Insert Table of Figures** in the **Caption** group. The **Table of Figures** dialog box appears as shown in Figure 8.14.

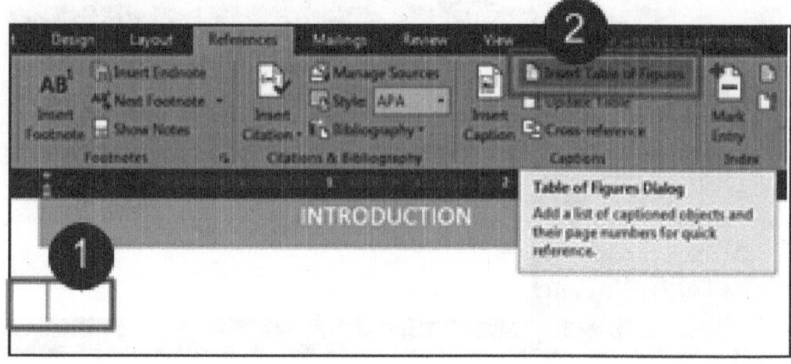

4. Under the **General** section, select the formats of illustration in the **Formats:** drop-down list.
5. Select Figure in the **Caption label:** drop-down list.
6. Click the check box to **Include label and number** options in the document.
7. Click OK to insert the **Table of Figures** as shown in Figure 8.14.
8. The layout for the **Table of Figures** appears in the document you just now created previously the **Table of Contents** as shown in Figure 8.15.

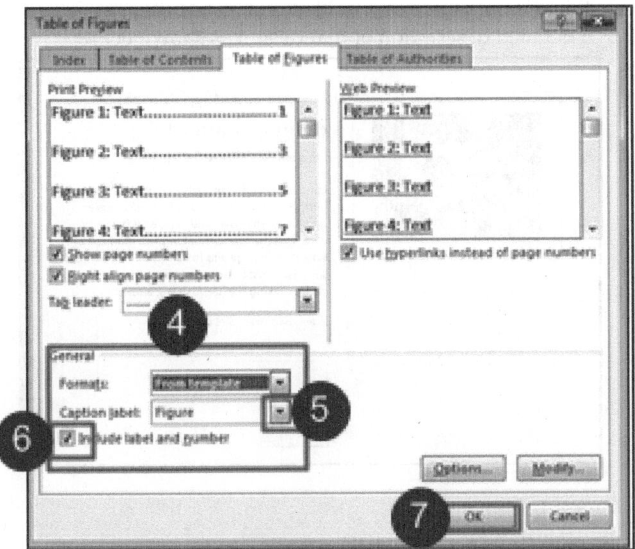

Figure 8.14 Table of Figures dialog box

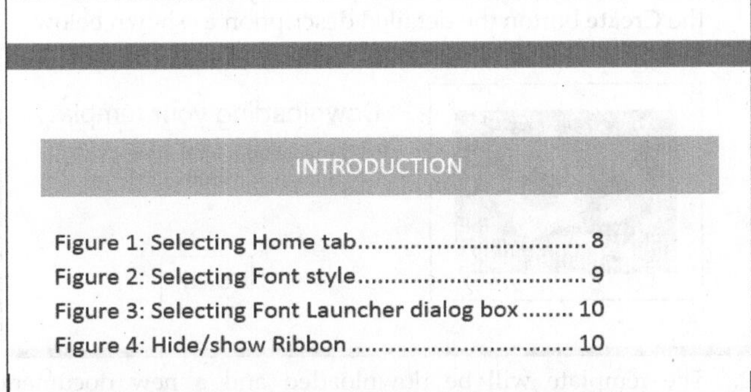

INTRODUCTION

Figure 1: Selecting Home tab........ 8
Figure 2: Selecting Font style........ 9
Figure 3: Selecting Font Launcher dialog box........ 10
Figure 4: Hide/show Ribbon........ 10

Figure 8.15 Table of Figures appears in the document

7. Click the table to see the grayed entries indicating that there are field codes and links to the figures. For example, you can hold down the Ctrl key and click on a heading in a table of figures to access the corresponding section in the text.

8.1.9 Insert Preface

1. You can insert a blank page for the book Preface.
2. On the new page, type Preface, select the Home tab then apply the desired styles in the **Styles** group button, for example, choose **Heading 2.**
3. On the **Insert** tab, in the **Text** group, click the **Object** arrow. Then click **Text from File** as shown in Figure 8.6.
4. Adjust the formatting and alignment of the text as desired, for example, selecting Justify for the selected paragraph.
5. Click the **Save** button to save the preface.

8.1.10 Decorate the Page

You can enhance the formatting of the title page using WordArt or Styles.

1. Select the text, click the Styles to expand, and move the mouse over the options present to preview the styles as shown below.

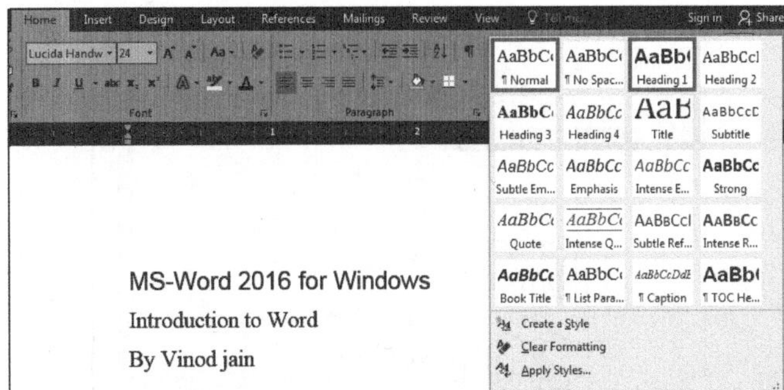

2. Select desired style to apply that format to the selected text. For example, we have select the book title and choose the Title style. For other selections of text, we select a style such as **Subtitle** and **Intense Quote** (See Figure 8.16).

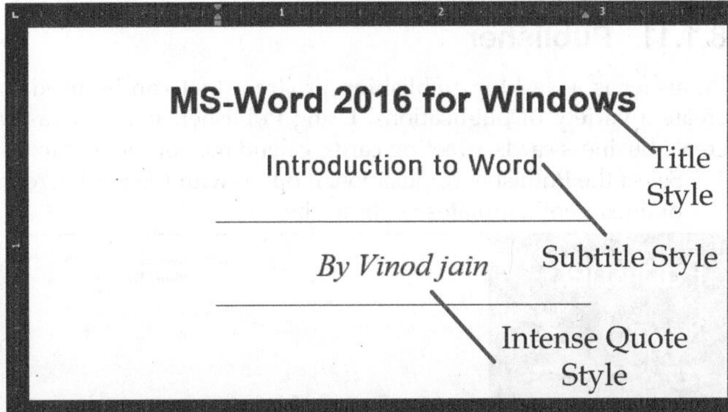

Figure 8.16 Table of Figures appears in the document

3. Now, align the Title, Subtitle and Intense Quote to be centered.
4. If you want more impact, then select the text and choose **WordArt** from the **Text** group on the **Insert** tab as shown in Figure 8.17.

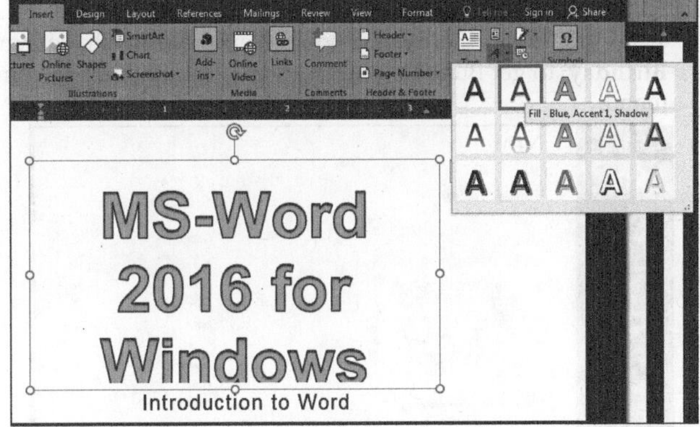

Figure 8.17 Select the WordArt Style

5. A list of WordArt styles appears. Select the desired style you want to apply. The text effects is displayed in the selected style.
6. Now, the text appears around the textbox, you can WordArt Styles of **Text Fill**, **Text Outline** and **Text Effects**. For example, we have applied Text Effects such as Inside Top option as shown in Figure 8.18.

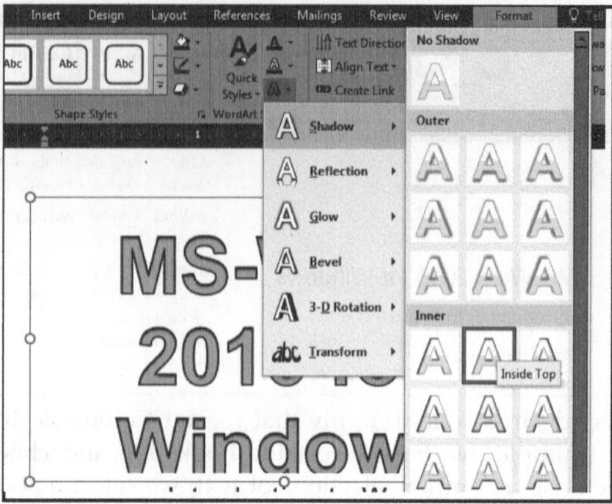

Figure 8.18 Applied WordArt styles effects

8.1.11 Publisher

Publisher is a desktop publishing program that can be used to create a variety of publications. Using Publisher, you can easily create business cards, greeting cards, calendars, newsletter etc.

1. Select the Publisher application, it opens with the Start Screen of document templates as shown below.

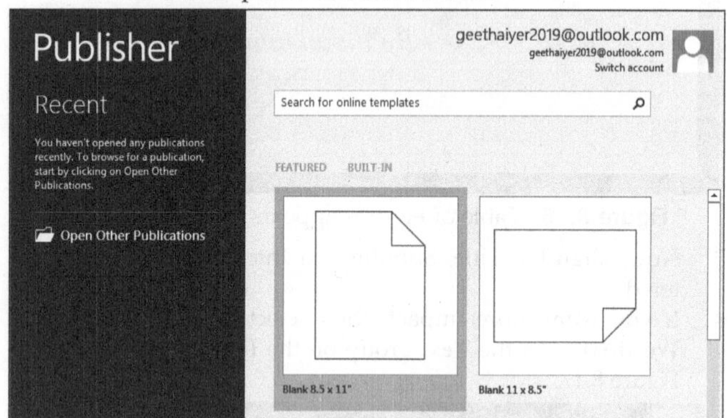

2. Type the text in the **Search** box for example, we have type **Birthday**, to get Built-In templates. Or click the Built-in command.

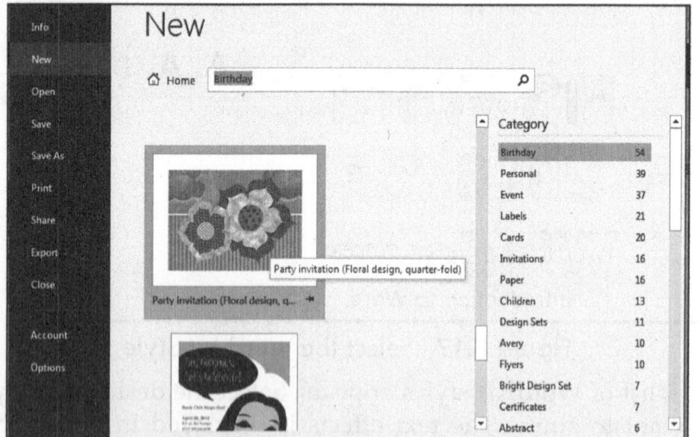

3. The Birthday selection templates appears in the contents pane. Click the desired templates. For example, we have selected Birthday selection.

4. Review the selection provided, and select the template to see a detailed description of that design as shown below

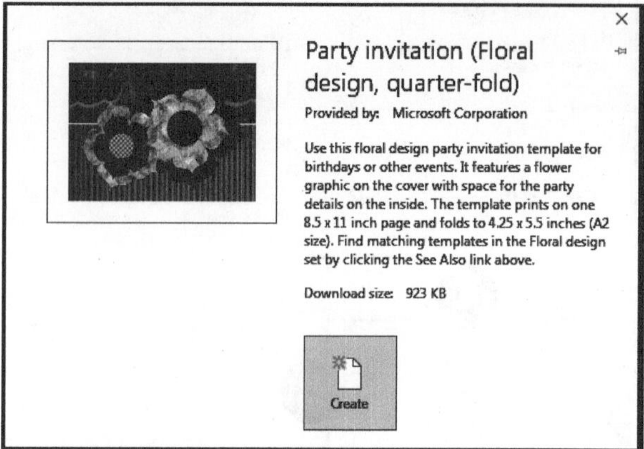

8.1.12 Create a Publication

1. Choose a template, for example, **Party invitation** and click the **Create** button the detailed description as shown below.

2. The template will be downloaded and a new document opens, based upon that template as shown below.
3. To modify the selected card click the middle part of the card i.e. section labelled 2 & 3. Enter the title, description and details of the text frame, and click save command to save the document.

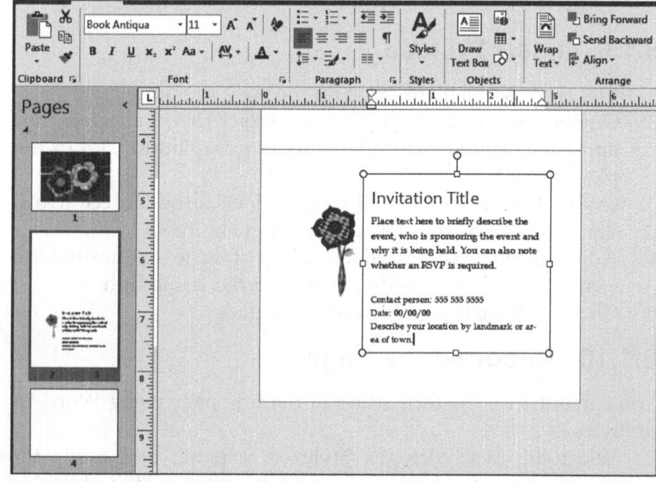

8.1.13 Print the Publication

1. Select pages 2,3 and 4 to add the required text and images to those section, then save the final document as shown below.

2. Select **File** menu and choose **Print**, to preview the document as it appears on paper – a single sheet, with sections 2,3 and 4 inverted.

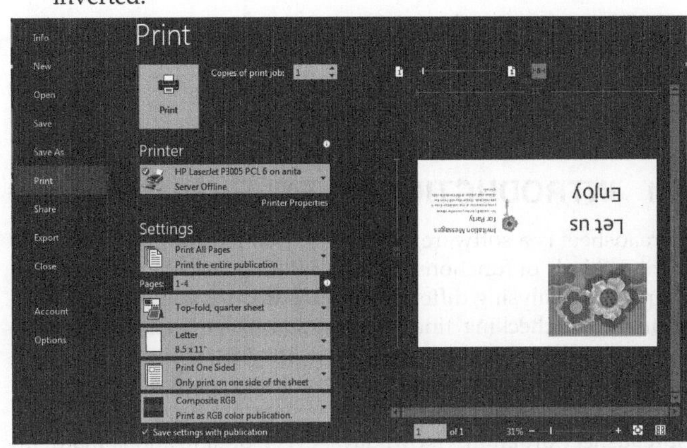

3. Select the printer that you wish to use and then click **Print** button.

CHAPTER 9

Excel 2016

9.1 INTRODUCTION TO EXCEL 2016

Spreadsheet is a software application that allows you to perform various kinds of functions, such as entering, calculating, manipulating and analysing different sets of data. It is used for planning a project or checking financial position of an organization. The term spreadsheet and worksheet are often used interchangeably. Spreadsheet usually refers to a computer program, where as worksheet refers to the actual document you create by using the spreadsheet program. Nowadays, every organizations maintain their data using spreadsheet applications that have simplified data management.

9.2 BASIC EXCEL CONCEPTS

9.2.1 Electronic Spreadsheet

A spreadsheet (or spreadsheet program) is software that permits numerical data to be used and to perform automatic calculations on numbers contained in a table. It is also possible to automate complex calculations by using a large number of parameters and by creating tables called worksheets.

9.2.2 Excel 2016 Terminology

When you are working with a spreadsheet package you have to know some spreadsheet terminologies. Some such terms are as discuss below

- **Workbook**–A workbook is a collection of many worksheets. In a single workbook, you can store information in an organized manner. By default, a workbook opens with three worksheets and it can contain a maximum of 255 worksheets. The workbook store all of the data that you have entered and allows you to sort or calculate the results. A workbook that is available to be viewed and edited by multiple users on a network is known as a Shared Workbook.
- **Worksheet**–A worksheet is a sheet made up of rows and columns. A worksheet begins with row number one and column A. Each cell can contain a number, text or formula. A cell can also reference another cell in the same worksheet, the same workbook or a different workbook. A worksheet is always stored in a workbook.
- **Chartsheet**–Chartsheet is a separate sheet in a workbook that contains only graphs or charts. It is useful when you want to see a chart or tabular data separated from other type of data.
- **Row**–A row is a horizontal block of cells that runs through the entire width of the worksheet. The rows are numbered from top to bottom along the left edge of the worksheet. The first row is numbered 1, the second 2, and so on. There can be a maximum of 1,048,576 rows in an Excel 2010 worksheet.
- **Column**–A column is a vertical block of cells that runs through the entire worksheet. A worksheet contains 16,384 (A to XFD) columns. The first column is **A**, the second is **B** and so on until you reach **Z**. Then comes column **AA** through **XFD**. The last (or rightmost) column of the worksheet, **XFD** is the 16,384th column.
- **Cell**–A cell is the intersection of a row and a column. For example, the uppermost cell is A1 (column A, row 1). Cell G9 is the intersection of column G, row 9. When you select a cell by clicking it with the mouse, or moving to it using the keyboard, it becomes the active cell.
- **Formula**–Formulas are equations that perform calculations on values in your worksheet. It is an order of values, names, cell references, functions and operators in a cell that together give a new values. A formula always begins with = (equal) sign.
- **Function**–*Functions* are pre-defined formulas or programs that perform calculations in Excel on specific values, called arguments. Each function takes specific types of arguments such as numbers, references, text, or logical values.

9.2.3 Working with Excel 2016

In Excel 2016, each workbook can contain many worksheets. These sheets may also contain *charts*, *macros*, etc. Sheets may contain different types of information but all data or information is related to each other.

Each worksheet contains 16,384 columns and 1,048,576 rows. The intersection of a row and a column forms a cell in which you can enter data or a formula. Column headings start at **A** and as they reach the letter **Z** column, headings restart with **AA**, **AB**, and so on till **XFD**. Row headings, down the left side of a sheet, go from **1** to **1,048,576**. It is equally easy for formulas to refer to information in another worksheet of the same workbook as it is in the same worksheet.

9.3 STARTING EXCEL2016

MS Excel 2016 needs Windows 8 & 10 as operating system to run on an PC. However, Excel 2016 can also be run on *Windows 7* operating system, if *service pack 3* is installed on *Windows 7*.

➡ **To start Excel:**

1. Click **Start** button.
2. Highlight **All Programs**.
3. Select **Excel 2016** as shown in Figure 9.1.

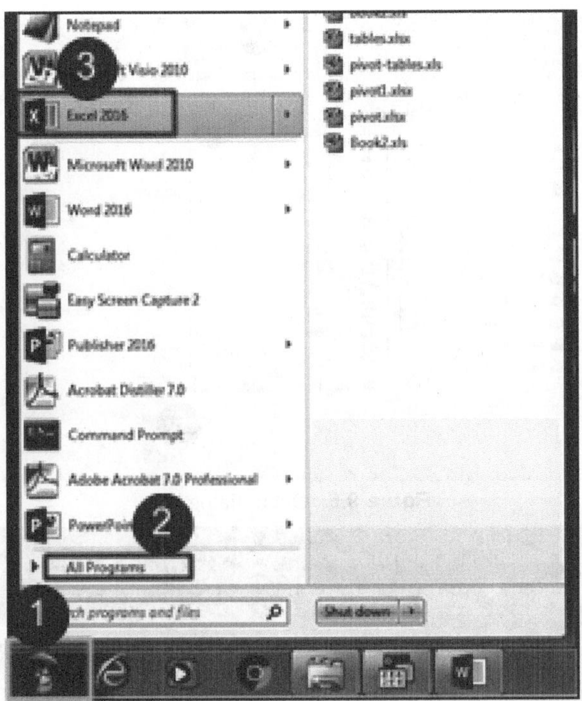

Figure 9.1 Starting Excel 2016

9.4 EXCEL2016 INTERFACE

Excel 2016 includes the MS Office Fluent interface, which consists of a customizable visual system of tools and commands. Figure 9.2 shows the elements of Excel 2016 application window and an open Excel 2016 workbook in detail.

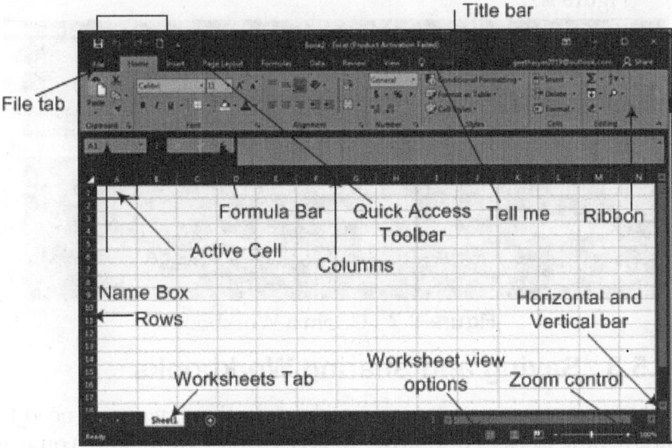

Figure 9.2 Elements of Excel 2016 window

Title Bar–At the top of an Excel 2016 window, there is the title bar. The left edge of this bar has the Office button next to which the name of the open document is displayed. On the right edge of the title bar, the *minimize, restore/maximize* and *close* button are placed (Figure 9.2).

Quick Access Toolbar–The Quick Access Toolbar lets you access common commands no matter which tab is selected. You can customize the commands depending on your preference. This toolbar is located by default at the top of Excel 2016 window. It provides tools that you use frequently such as Save, Undo and Repeat buttons (See Figure 9.2). You can customize the Quick Access Toolbar by adding commands to it.

Workbook Window–A window within the Excel 2010 application window in which a worksheet, chart, or dialog box is shown.

File Tab–File tab is the colored tab which is located in the upper-left corner of MS Office 2016 programs and below the Quick Access Toolbar (See Figure 9.2). When you click the File tab, you can see the Backstage view.

Ribbon–Ribbon is displayed just below the title bar (See Figure 9.2). In Ribbon, *Commands* are organized in logical *groups*, which are collected together under *tabs*. You can hide the Ribbon by double-clicking the active tab. Different types of Tabs described here, which are available in the Ribbon of Excel 2016.

Worksheets Tab–A tab is near to the bottom of a workbook window that displays the name of a sheet. Click the sheet tab to move to the next sheet. To display the shortcut menu, right click the sheet tab. To scroll through the sheet tabs, use the tab scrolling button.

Name Box–The *name box* is at the left end of the formula bar (Figure 9.2). It displays the location, or name, of a selected cell.

Formula Bar–The *formula bar* displays the constant value or formula used in the active cell. The formula bar is also used for editing the cell contents (Figure 9.2).

Status Bar–Status bar appears at the bottom of the Excel 2016 window. It displays information regarding a selected command or an operation in progress. Note that the right side of the status bar shows zoom slider, different views tool such as Normal, Page Layout and Page Break view.

Tell me–The Tell me box works like a search bar to help you quickly find tools or commands you want to use.

Cell–Each rectangle in a workbook is called a cell. A cell is the intersection of a row and a column. Simply click to select a cell.

Worksheet View Options–There are three ways to view a worksheet. Simply click a command to select the desired view.

Zoom Control–Click and drag the slider to use the zoom control. The number to the right of the slider reflects the zoom percentage.

Vertical and Horizontal Scroll Bars–The scroll bars allow you to scroll up and down or side to side. To do this, click and drag the vertical or horizontal scroll bar.

9.5 CREATING AND OPENING WORKBOOK

Whenever you start a new project in Excel, you will need to create a new workbook. There are several ways to start working with a workbook in Excel. You can choose to create a new workbook – either with a blank workbook or a predesigned template–or open an existing workbook.

9.5.1 Creating a new Workbook

➡ **To create a new workbook, do this:**

1. Click the **File** Tab as shown in Figure 9.3. Here, Select **New**. Under **Available Templates**, click **Blank Workbook**. *Alternatively*, press Ctrl + N keys together.

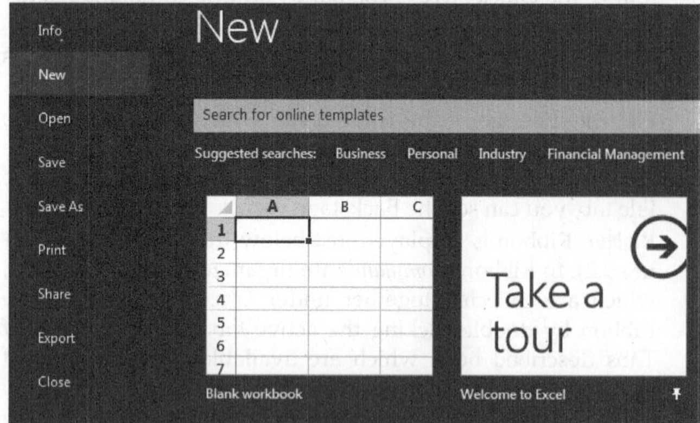

Figure 9.3 Selecting Blank Workbook

2. A new blank workbook will appear as shown in Figure 9.1.

9.5.2 Opening an Existing Workbook

In addition to creating new workbooks, you will often need to open a workbook that was previously saved.

➡ **To open an existing workbook:**

1. Click the **File** tab to open **Backstage** view, then click **Open**.
2. Click **Browse** button. Alternatively, you can choose **OneDrive** to open files stored on your OneDrive as shown in Figure 9.4.

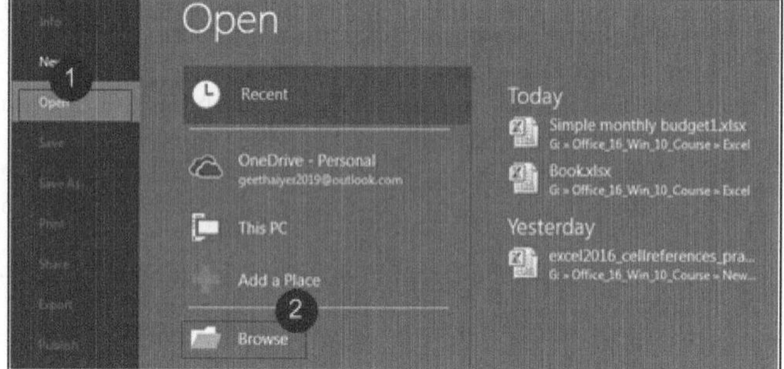

Figure 9.4 Selecting Open backstage view

3. The **Open** dialog box will appear as shown in Figure 9.5. Locate the file or folder in the Address bar
4. Select the file in the contents pane.
5. Then click **Open** button.

   If you have opened the desired workbook recently, you can browse your Recent Workbooks rather than search for the file.

➡ **To pin a workbook:**

1. If you frequently work with the same workbook, you can pin it to Backstage view to access the file.
2. Navigate to Backstage view, then click **Open**. Your recently edited workbooks will appear as shown in Figure 9.6.

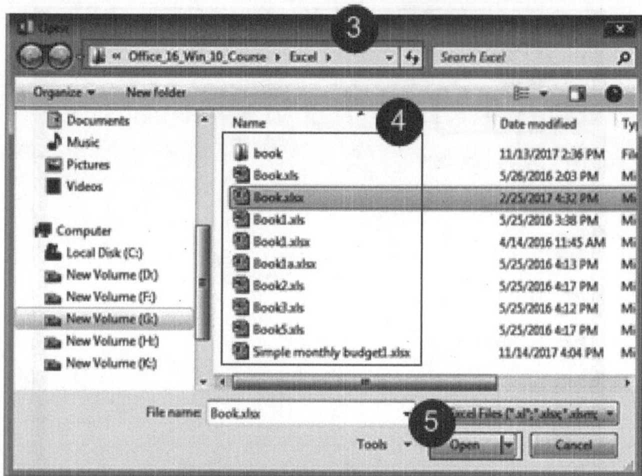

Figure 9.5 Open dialog box

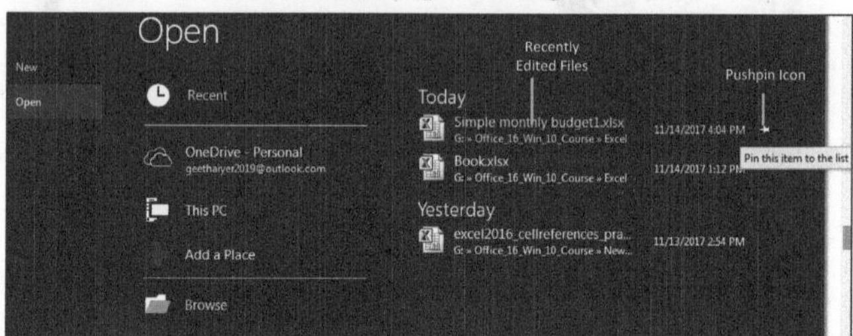

Figure 9.6 Recently edited files

3. Hover the mouse over the workbook you want to pin. A pushpin icon will appear next to the workbook. Click the **pushpin** icon.
4. The workbook will stay in Recent Workbooks. To unpin a workbook, simply click the pushpin icon again as shown in Figure 9.7.

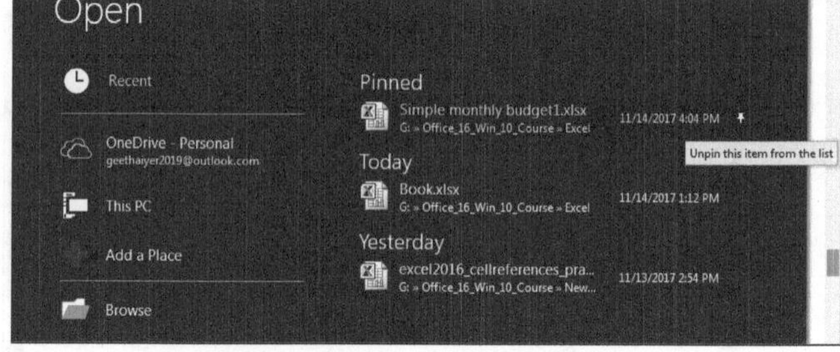

Figure 9.7 Unpin a Workbook

9.5.3 Saving and Sharing Workbooks

Whenever you create a new workbook in Excel, you will need to know how to save it in order to access and edit it later. You can save a workbook to the cloud using OneDrive.

Excel offers two ways to save a file: **Save** and **Save As**. These options work in similar ways, with a few important differences:

- *Save:* When you create or edit a workbook, you will use the **Save** command to save your changes. When you save a file, for the first time you will need to choose a file name and location. After that, you can just click the Save command to save it with the same name and location.

- *Save As:* You will use this command to create a copy of a workbook while keeping the original. When you use Save As, you will need to choose a different name and/or location for the copied version.

Saving Workbook

It is important to save your workbook whenever you start a new project or make changes to an existing one. Saving early and often can prevent your work from being lost.

➡ **To save a workbook:**

1. If you are saving the file for the first time, click the **File** tab to open the Backstage view.
2. Click **Save As**. The **Save As** pane will appear in Backstage view as shown in Figure 9.8. You can also access the **Save** command by pressing **Ctrl+S** on the keyboard.

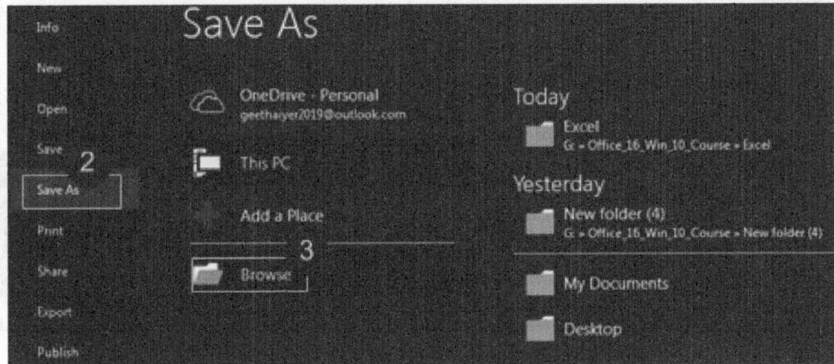

Figure 9.8 Save As Backstage view

3. Click **Browse**. Alternatively, you can click **OneDrive** to save the file to your OneDrive.

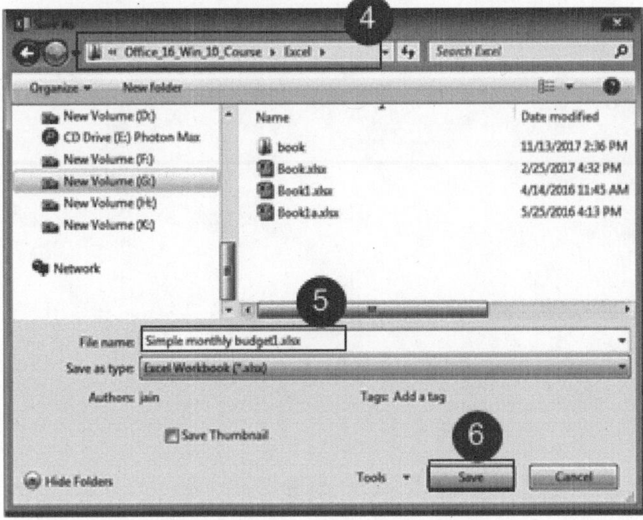

Figure 9.9 Save As dialog box

The **Save As** dialog box will appear as shown in Figure 9.9.

4. Select the location where you want to save the workbook in the Address bar.
5. In the File name: box give the name of the file.
6. Click Save button.

☞ *Excel 2010 worksheet is saved with .xlsx extension indicating that it uses the XML-based file format.*

Sharing Workbooks

Excel makes it easy to share and collaborate on workbooks using OneDrive. In the past, if you wanted to share a file with someone you could send it as an email attachment. When share a workbook, you are actually giving others access to the exact same file. This lets you and the people you share to edit the same workbook without having to keep track of multiple versions. In order to share a workbook, it must first be **saved to your OneDrive.**

➡ **To share a workbook:**

1. Click the **File** tab to access Backstage view, then click **Share.**
2. The **Share** pane will appear. If you have not already done so, you will be prompted to save your document to **OneDrive.** (i.e. Save to Cloud) as shown below.

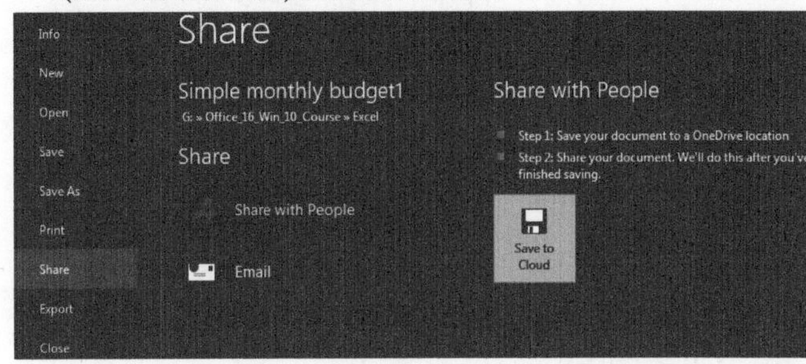

After you save a file in OneDrive, you may need to navigate back to the Share pane after saving.

3. On the Share pane, if your document is saved to **OneDrive,** click the **Share with People button.**

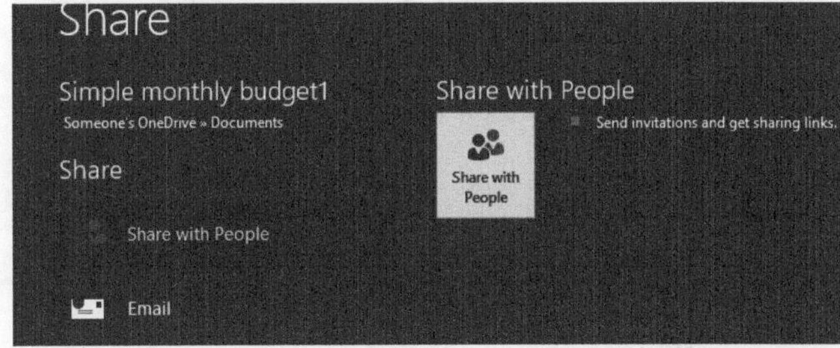

4. Excel will return to Normal view and open the Share panel on the right side of the window.
5. Type email addresses in the **Invite** people box to share your document. You can see a list of who has access to the document, and set whether they can edit or only view the document (See Figure 9.10).

Figure 9.10 Save As dialog box

9.5.4 Closing a Workbook Window

When you finish using worksheet or chart, you close its window. If you have made any changes since the last time you saved the workbook, Excel 2016 displays an alert dialog box, as shown in Figure 9.11, asking whether you want to save your work before closing.

➡ **To close a file in a workbook:**

1. Click on the **File** Tab and choose **Close**. The window closes provided no change has been made to the workbook since it was saved last. Alternatively, press Ctrl+W key together to close the workbook.
2. If you have made changes to the workbook since the last save, the Alert dialog box appears. In the dialog box, choose *Don't Save* if you do not want to save a changed version of the file, or choose *Save* if you do want to save changes. Type a new file name and choose **Save** button.

9.6 QUITTING EXCEL2016

➡ **To quit Excel 2016:**

1. Click the Close button (x) in the top-right corner or press Alt+F4 or double-click the Control icon at the left of the title bar.
2. When all workbooks are closed, Excel 2016 window closes, and the application is terminated.

9.7 GETTING HELP ON TELLME

Excel 2016 new features is the Tell me help features what you want to do. This is a text field where you can enter words and phrase about what you want to do next and quickly get to features you want to use or actions you want to perform. You can also use Tell me to find help about what you are looking for to define the term you entered.

➡ **To get help on Tell me:**

1. As you enter a help topic into this text box, Excel displays a list of related Excel commands in a drop-down list.
2. For example if you type Insert Table into the Tell Me what you want to do with text box, Excel display a list with the following Items as shown in Figure 9.11.

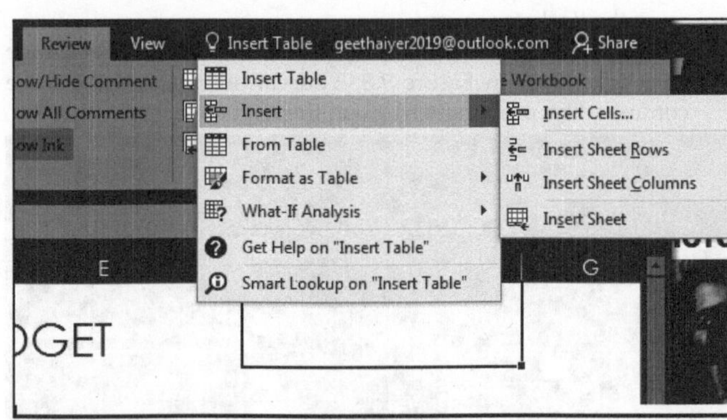

Figure 9.11 Get Help on Tell me text box

3. If you select **Insert Sheet Columns**, it Insert the sheet columns in the worksheet.

Working with Cells and Sheets

10.1 CELL BASICS

Whenever you work with Excel, you will enter information –or content –into cells. Cells are the basic building blocks of a worksheet. You will need to learn the basics of cells and cell content to calculate, analyze, and organize data in Excel.

10.1.1 Understanding Cells

A spreadsheet consists of rows and columns which combine to form cells. A cell is a box where you can enter data. Columns form the vertical lines of cells while rows form the horizontal lines of cells. Cell is an intersection of rows and columns. To describe the location or address of a cell, we have to write the names of the column and the row whose intersection has created this cell. Figure 10.1, shows the intersection of the Column C and the Row 3 is C3. Here C3 is called as a cell and C3 in its address.

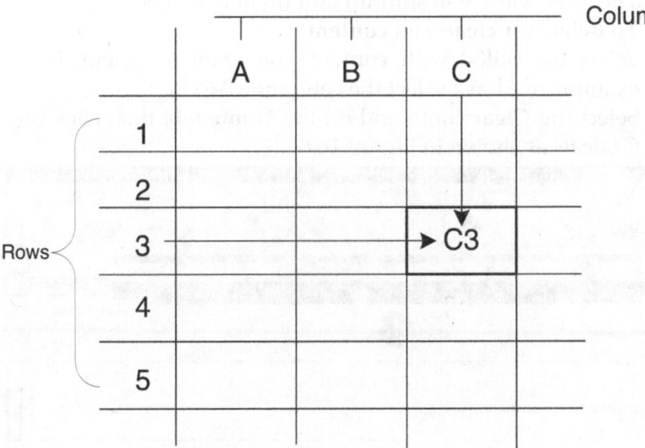

Figure 10.1 Addressing of cells

Cells can have two types of data in a worksheet.

Constant value: A constant value is data that you type directly into a cell. It can be a number, a date, time, currency, percentage, fraction or text. Constant values do not change unless we edit them.

Formula: A formula is a sequence of values, cell references, names, functions or operators that produce a new value from the existing values. Formulas always start with the equal sign (=). A value that is produced as the result of the formula changes automatically when other values involved in the formula in the worksheet change.

MS Excel helps you to perform calculations on numerical data. For example, you need to find the sum of some data or calculate through a complex set of formulas and Excel can quickly provide the answer. By using formulas, you can efficiently keep track of your business or personal finances.

To find the sum of numbers from cell address A1 to A10 the formula would be as follows:

= +Al+A2+A3+A4+A5+A6+A7+A8+A9+A10

A function is a shortcut for a formula. For example, to calculate the sum of numbers from cell address Al to A10, the function used would be as follows:

= Sum(A1:A10)

Colon (:) Symbol indicates a group of cell addresses. It is easier to write a function as compared to a formula.

➡ **To select a cell:**

1. To input or edit cell content, you must first need to select the cell.
2. Click a cell to select it. In our example, we have selected cell D25. A border will appear around the selected cell, and the column heading and row heading will be highlighted. The cell will remain selected until you click another cell in the worksheet as shown in Figure 10.2.

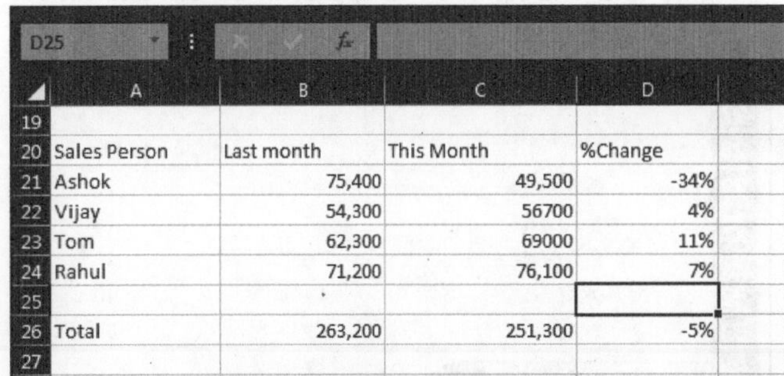

D25

	A	B	C	D
19				
20	Sales Person	Last month	This Month	%Change
21	Ashok	75,400	49,500	-34%
22	Vijay	54,300	56700	4%
23	Tom	62,300	69000	11%
24	Rahul	71,200	76,100	7%
25				
26	Total	263,200	251,300	-5%
27				

Figure 10.2 Selecting the cell

B21 75400

	A	B	C	D
19				
20	Sales Person	Last month	This Month	%Change
21	Ashok	75,400	49,500	-34%
22	Vijay	54,300	56700	4%
23	Tom	62,300	69000	11%
24	Rahul	71,200	76,100	7%
25				
26	Total	263,200	251,300	-5%
27				

Figure 10.3 Selecting the cell range

3. You can also select cells using the arrow keys on your keyboard.

➡ **To select a cell range:**

1. Sometimes you may want to select a larger group of cells, or a cell range.

2. Click and drag the mouse until all of the adjoining cells you want to select are highlighted. In our example, we have selected the cell range B21:C24 as shown in Figure 10.3.
3. Release the mouse to select the desired cell range. The cells will remain selected until you click another cell in the worksheet.

10.1.2 Cell Content

Any information you enter into a spreadsheet will be stored in a cell. Each cell can contain different types of content, including text, formatting, formulas, and functions.

- *Text:* Cells can contain text, such as letters, numbers, and dates.
- *Formatting attributes:* Cells can contain formatting attributes that change the way letters, numbers, and dates are displayed. For example, percentages can appear as 0.15 or 15%. You can also change a cell's text or background color.
- *Formulas and functions:* Cells can contain formulas and functions that calculate cell values. In our example, SUM(B2:B8) adds the value of each cell in the cell range B2:B8 and displays the total in cell B9.

➡ **To insert content:**

1. Click a cell to select it. In our example, we will select cell A35.
2. Type something into the selected cell, for example, we have type **Total** then press Enter on your keyboard as shown in Figure 10.4. The content will appear in the cell and the formula bar. You can also input and edit cell content in the formula bar.

27			
28	Date	Sales	Percentage of Total
29	4-Apr-16	93	22%
30	5-Apr-16	85	18%
31	6-Apr-16	76	18%
32	7-Apr-16	43	10%
33	8-Apr-16	89	21%
34	9-Apr-16	32	8%
35		418	
36			

27			
28	Date	Sales	Percentage of Total
29	4-Apr-16	93	22%
30	5-Apr-16	85	18%
31	6-Apr-16	76	18%
32	7-Apr-16	43	10%
33	8-Apr-16	89	21%
34	9-Apr-16	32	8%
35	Total	418	
36			

Figure 10.4 Insert content in a cell

Delete Cells

There is an important difference between deleting the content of a cell and deleting the cell itself. If you delete the entire cell, the cells below it will shift to fill in the gaps and replace the deleted cells.

➡ **To delete cells:**

1. Select the cell(s) you want to delete. In our example, we have selected A7:C7.
2. Select the **Delete** command from the **Home** tab on the **Ribbon** as shown in Figure 10.5.

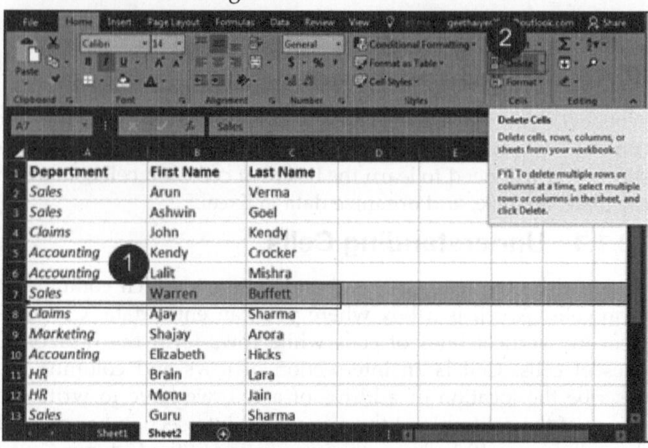

Figure 10.5 Delete command from the Home tab

3. The cells below will shift up and fill in the gaps.

➡ **To delete (or clear) cell content:**

1. Select the cell(s) with content you want to delete. In our example, we have select the cell range A6:C6.
2. Select the **Clear** command on the **Home** tab, then click *Clear Contents* as shown in Figure 10.6.

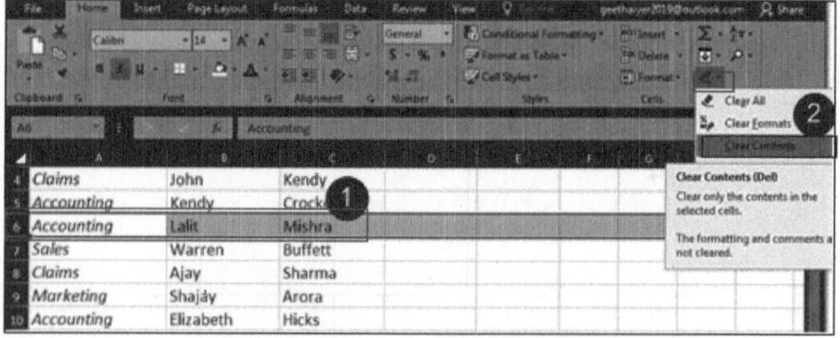

Figure 10.6 Clear cell contents

3. The cell contents will be deleted as shown in Figure 10.7.

	A	B	C
1	Department	First Name	Last Name
2	Sales	Arun	Verma
3	Sales	Ashwin	Goel
4	Claims	John	Kendy
5	~~Accounting~~	~~Kendy~~	~~Crocker~~
6			
7	Sales	Warren	Buffett

Figure 10.7 Cell contents get deleted

You can also use the **Delete** key on the keyboard to delete content from multiple cells at once. The **Backspace** key will only delete content from one cell at a time.

10.1.3 Copy and Paste Cell Content

To copy content that is already entered into the spreadsheet and paste that content to other cells, which can save you time and effort.

➡ **To copy and paste cell content:**

1. Select the cell(s) you want to copy. In our example, we have select **D4:D6**.
2. Click the **Copy** command on the **Home** tab, or press **Ctrl+C** on the keyboard as shown in Figure 10.8.

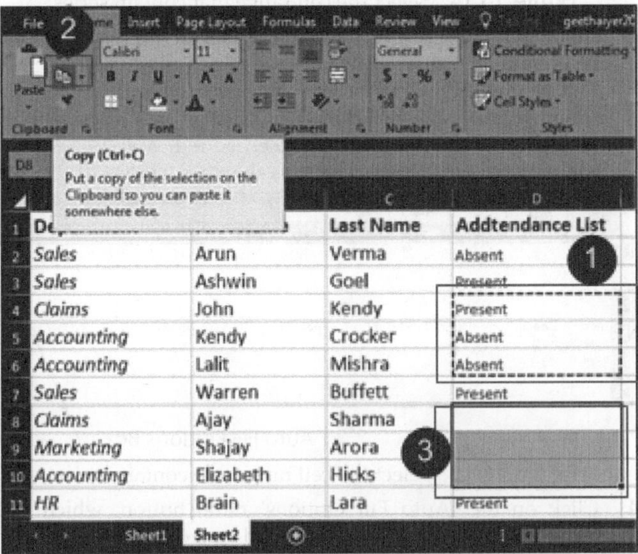

Figure 10.8 Select the content to Copy

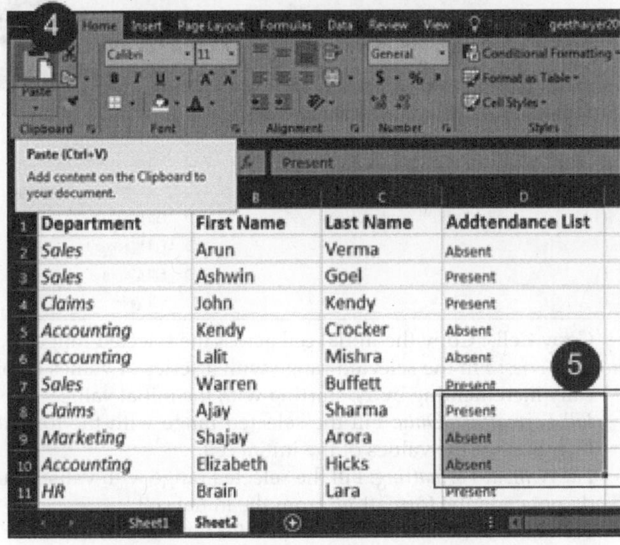

Figure 10.9 Selected content get pasted

3. Select the cell(s) where you want to paste the content. In our example, we have selected **D8:D10**. The copied cell(s) will have a dashed box around them.
4. click the **Paste** command on the **Home** tab, or press **Ctrl+V** on your keyboard.
5. The content will be pasted into the selected cells as shown in Figure 10.9.

➡ **To cut and paste cell content:**

Unlike copying and pasting, which duplicates cell content, cutting allows you to move content between cells.

1. Select the cell(s) you want to cut. In our example, we have selected D9:D10.
2. Right-click the mouse and select the **Cut** command. Alternatively, you can use the command on the **Home** tab, or press **Ctrl+X** on your keyboard as shown in Figure 10.10.

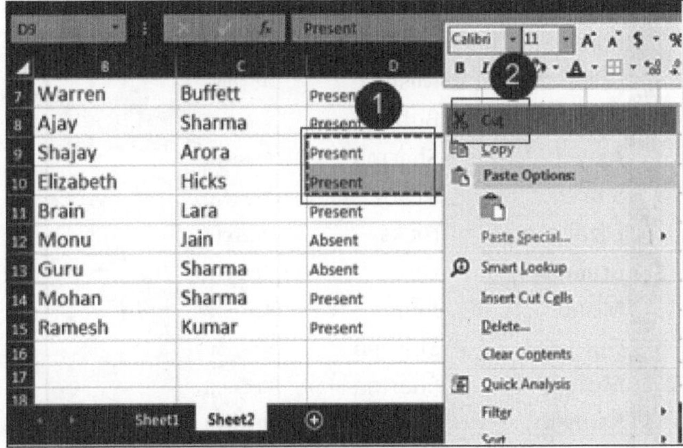

Figure 10.10 Select the content to Cut

3. Select the cells where you want to paste the content. In our example, we have selected E9:E10. The cut cells will now have a dashed box around them.
4. The cut content will be removed from the original cells and pasted into the selected cells as shown in Figure 10.11.

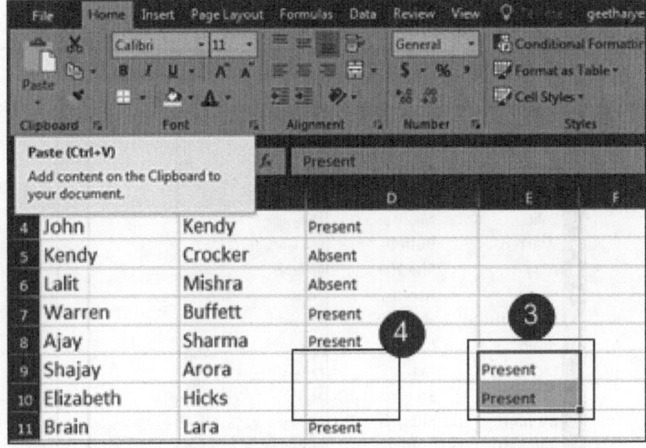

Figure 10.11 Cut and Paste the content to new selected cell

10.1.4 Drag and Drop Cells

Instead of cutting, copying, and pasting, you can drag and drop cells to move their contents.

➡ **To drag and drop cells:**

1. Click and drag the cells to the desired location. In our example, we'll move them to D1:D15.

2. Hover the mouse over the border of the selected cell(s) until the mouse changes to a **pointer with four arrows** as shown in Figure 10.12.

	B	C	D
1	First Name	Last Name	Addtendance List
2	Arun	Verma	Absent
3	Ashwin	Goel	Present
4	John	Kendy	Present
5	Kendy	Crocker	Absent
6	Lalit	Mishra	Absent
7	Warren	Buffett	Present
8	Ajay	Sharma	Present
9	Shajay	Arora	Present
10	Elizabeth	Hicks	Present
11	Brain	Lara	Present
12	Monu	Jain	Absent
13	Guru	Sharma	Absent
14	Mohan	Sharma	Present
15	Ramesh	Kumar	Present
16			

Figure 10.12 Selecting to Drag the Cells

3. Click and drag the cells to the desired location. In our example, we have move them to E1:E15.
4. Release the mouse. The cells will be dropped in the selected location as shown in Figure 10.13.

	B	C	D	E
1	First Name	Last Name	Addtendance List	
2	Arun	Verma	Absent	
3	Ashwin	Goel	Present	
4	John	Kendy	Present	
5	Kendy	Crocker	Absent	
6	Lalit	Mishra	Absent	
7	Warren	Buffett	Present	
8	Ajay	Sharma	Present	
9	Shajay	Arora	Present	
10	Elizabeth	Hicks	Present	
11	Brain	Lara	Present	
12	Monu	Jain	Absent	
13	Guru	Sharma	Absent	
14	Mohan	Sharma	Present	
15	Ramesh	Kumar	Present	
16				E1:E15

Figure 10.13 Drop the desired location

10.1.5 Quick Fill

The quick fill handle can also be used to continue a series. Whenever the content of a row or column follows a sequential order, like numbers (1, 2, 3) or days (Monday, Tuesday, Wednesday), the fill handle can guess what should come next in the series.

➡ **To Quick Fill:**

1. Select the cell range that contains the series you want to continue. In our example, we have selected C21:H21 as shown in Figure 10.14.

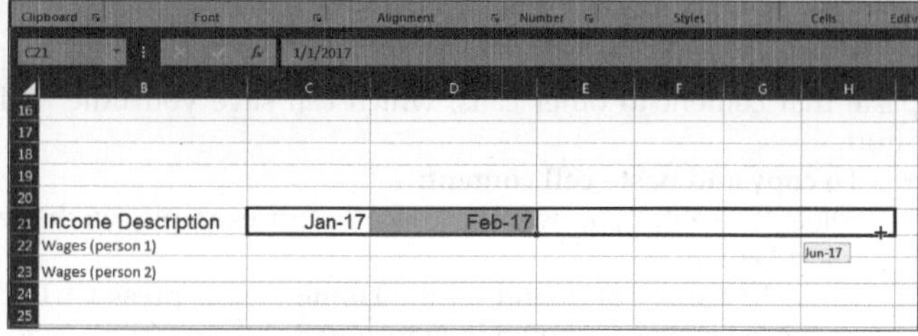

Figure 10.14 Select the cell range that contain series

2. Click and drag the fill handle to continue the series i.e. the mouse pointer over the left
3. Release the mouse button. If Excel understood the series, the month name is detected and succeeding month names are inserted. In our example, Excel added Mar-17, Apr-17, May-17 and Jun-17 to E21:H21 as shown in Figure 10.15.

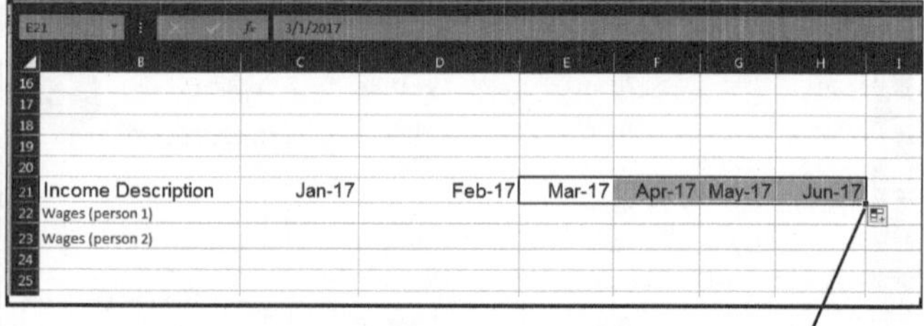

Figure 10.15 Select the cell range that contain series

4. Click on the 'Auto Fill Options' radio button, which will appear at the end of your selected range of cells as shown below. This will give you the following different options:

Feb-17	Mar-17	Apr-17	May-17	Jun-17

- Copy Cells
- Fill Series
- Fill Formatting Only
- Fill Without Formatting
- Fill Days
- Fill Weekdays
- Fill Months
- Fill Years

Copy Cells: Copy the initial cell across the selected range.
Fill Series: Fill the selected range with a series of values (typically incrementing by 1), starting with the initial value.
Fill Formatting Only: Fill the selected range with the formatting, but not the values of the initial cell.
Fill Without Formatting: Fill the selected range with values, but do not copy the formatting from the initial cell.

5. Select the option that you required for the filled cells.

10.1.6 Workbook Views

Excel 2016 has a variety of viewing options that change how your workbook is displayed. These views can be useful for various tasks, especially if you are planning to print the spreadsheet. To change worksheet views, locate the commands in the bottom-right corner of the Excel window and select **Normal** view, **Page Layout** view, or **Page Break** view.

Normal view is the default view for all worksheets in Excel.

Page Layout view displays how your worksheets will appear when printed. You can also add headers and footers in this view.

Page Break view allows you to change the location of page breaks, which is especially helpful when printing a lot of data from Excel.

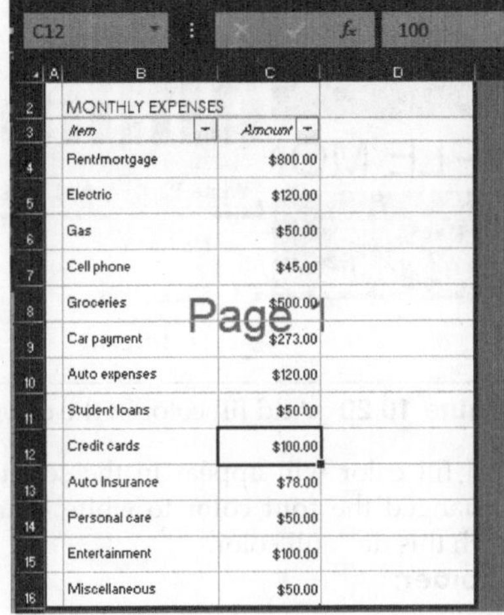

Item	Amount
MONTHLY EXPENSES	
Rent/mortgage	$800.00
Electric	$120.00
Gas	$50.00
Cell phone	$45.00
Groceries	$500.00
Car payment	$273.00
Auto expenses	$120.00
Student loans	$50.00
Credit cards	$100.00
Auto Insurance	$78.00
Personal care	$50.00
Entertainment	$100.00
Miscellaneous	$50.00

10.1.7 Controlling the Display of Sheet Tabs

Excel 2010 gives you the flexibility to control the display of the sheet tabs at the bottom of the workbook. You can edit or choose the option to display the names of the sheet or turn off the display as per your convenience.

➡ **To control the display of sheet tabs:**

1. Click the **File** Tab and then click **Options**. In this dialog box, click on **Advanced** button on the left side. **Excel Options** dialog box appears with **Advanced** properties as shown in Figure 10.16.

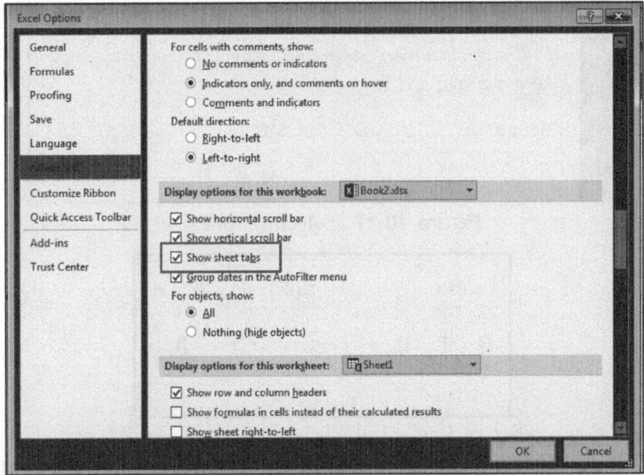

Figure 10.16 Controlling the display of sheet tabs in a worksheet

2. Click on the Show sheet tabs check box under the **Display options for this workbook:** group.
3. Then click **OK** button.

10.2 FORMATTING CELLS

Basic formatting can customize the look and feel of your workbook, allowing you to draw attention to specific sections and making your content easier to view and understand.

10.2.1 Change Font and Font Size and Color

➡ **To change the font size:**

1. Select the cell(s) of which you want to change the font size.
2. On the **Home** tab, click the drop-down arrow next to the **Font Size** command, then select the desired font size. In our example, we have selected 22 to make the text larger. Hover the mouse pointer over the font size to see the text font size change as shown in Figure 10.17.
3. The text will change to the selected font size.
4. You can also use the **Increase Font Size** and **Decrease Font Size** commands or enter a custom font size using your keyboard.

➡ **To change the font:**

By default, the font of each new workbook is set to Calibri. However, Excel provides many other fonts you can use to customize your cell text.

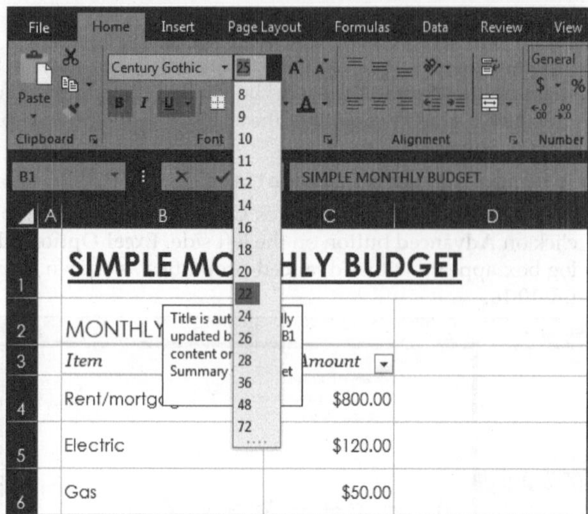

Figure 10.17 Selecting font size

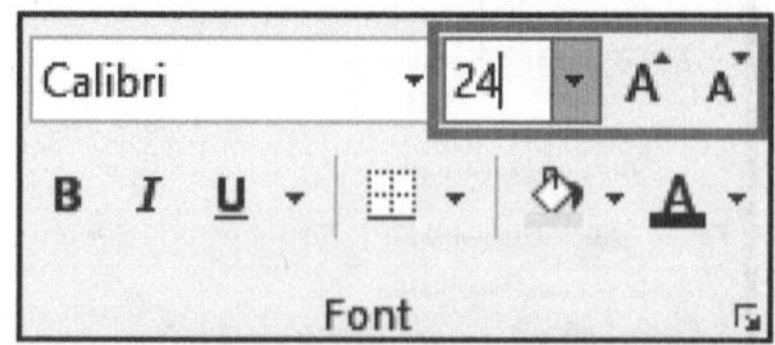

1. Select the cell(s) of which you want to change the font.
2. On the **Home** tab, click the drop-down arrow next to the **Font** command, then select the desired font. In our example, we have choose **Arial** font type as shown in Figure 10.18.

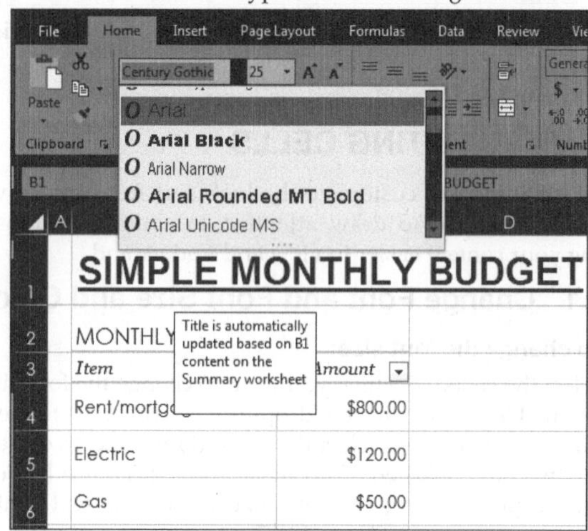

Figure 10.18 Selecting font type

3. The text will change to the selected font.

➡ **To change the font color:**

1. Select the cell(s) which you want to change font color.
2. On the **Home** tab, click the drop-down arrow next to the **Font Color** command, then select the desired font color. In our example, we have selected **Red** color.
3. The text will change to the selected font color as shown in Figure 10.19.

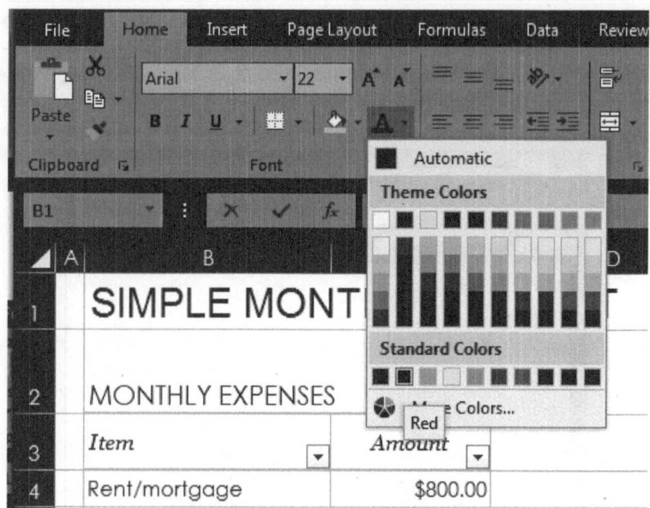

Figure 10.19 Selecting font color

10.2.2 Cell Borders and Fill Colors

Cell borders and fill colors allow you to create clear and defined boundaries for different sections of the worksheet. To add cell borders and fill color to our header cells to help distinguish them from the rest of the worksheet.

➡ **To add a fill color:**

1. Select the cell(s) which you want to add a fill color.
2. On the **Home** tab, click the drop-down arrow next to the **Fill Color** command, then select the fill color you want to use. In our example, we have selected a dark gray as shown in Figure 10.20.

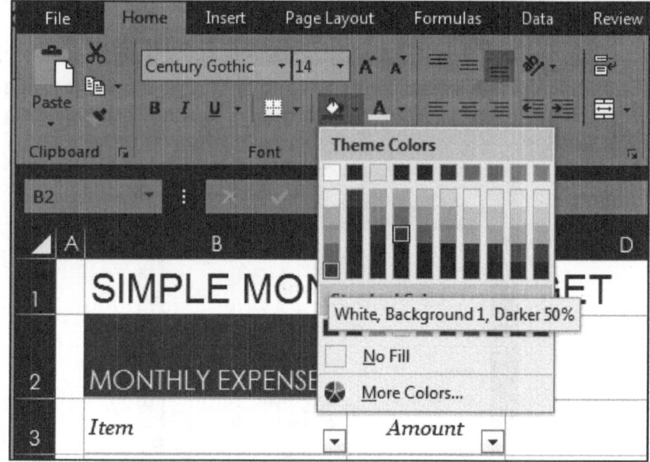

Figure 10.20 Add fill color in the cell

3. The selected fill color will appear in the selected cells. We have also changed the **font color** to white to make it more readable with this dark fill color.

➡ **To add a border:**

1. Select the cell(s) which you want to add a border.

2. On the **Home** tab, click the drop-down arrow next to the **Borders** command, then select the border style you want to use. In our example, we have selected to display **All Borders** as shown in Figure 10.21.

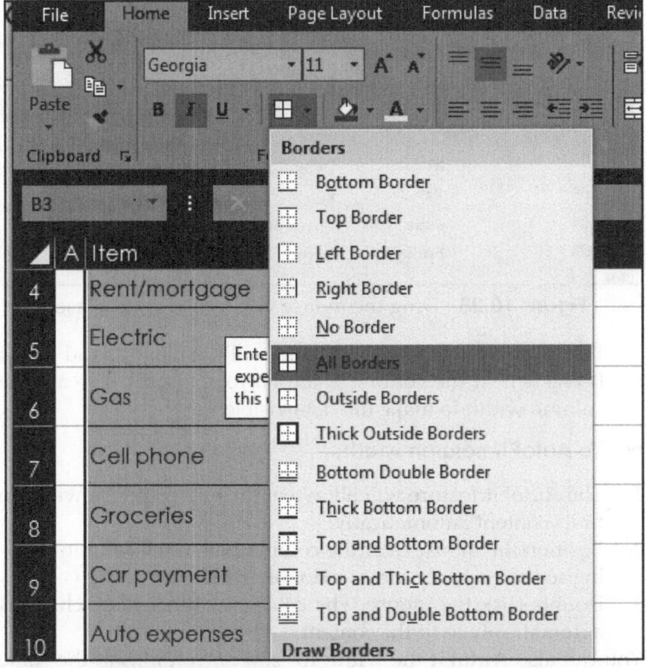

Figure 10.21 Add Border to the selected cell

3. The selected border style will appear as shown in Figure 10.22.

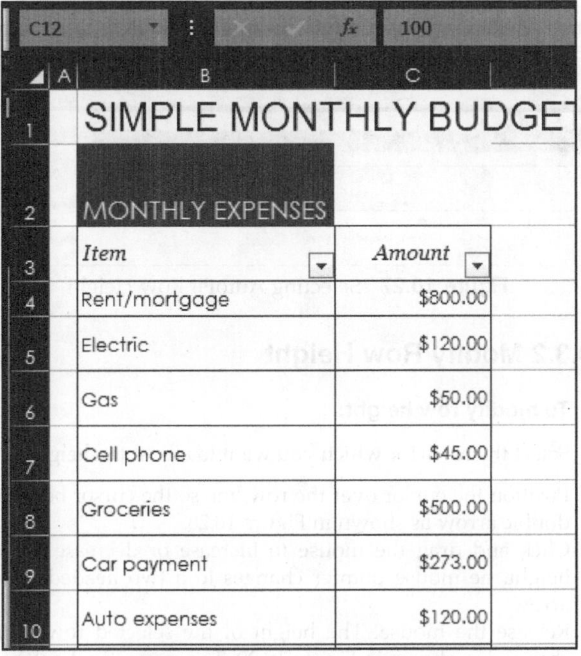

Figure 10.22 Applied Border

4. You can draw borders and change the line style and color of borders with the Draw Borders tools at the bottom of the Borders drop-down menu.

10.2.3 Cell Styles

Instead of formatting cells manually, you can use Excel's predesigned cell styles. Cell styles are a quick way to include professional formatting for different parts of your workbook, such as titles and headers.

➡ **To apply a cell style:**

1. Select the cell(s) of which you want to apply cell style.
2. Click the **Cell Styles** command on the **Home** tab in the **Styles** group, then choose the desired style from the drop-down menu as shown in Figure 10.23.

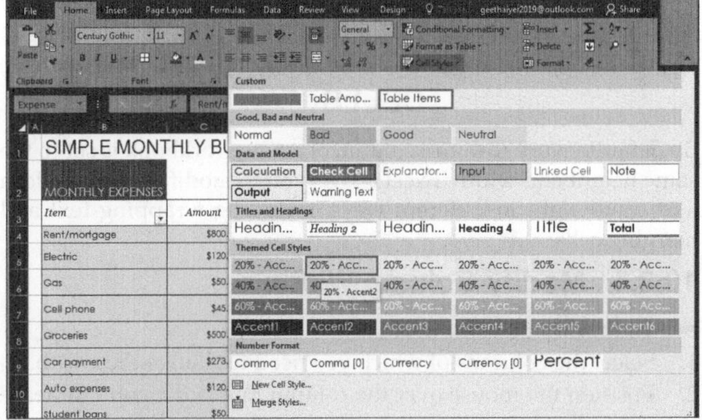

Figure 10.23 Selecting in-built style in the Styles group

3. The selected cell style will appear.
4. Applying a cell style will replace any existing cell formatting except for text alignment.

10.2.4 Text Alignment

By default, any text entered into your worksheet will be aligned to the bottom-left of a cell, while any numbers will be aligned to the bottom-right. Changing the alignment of your cell content allows you to choose how the content is displayed in any cell, which can make your cell content easier to read.

➡ **To align text alignment using Ribbon Command:**

1. Select the cell or range of cells containing the contents you want to align.
2. To horizontal alignment, click the **Left**, **Center**, or **Right Align** button from the **Alignment** group under the **Home** Tab. In our example, we have select **Center horizontal** align as shown in Figure 10.24.
3. To vertical alignment, click the **Top align**, **Middle align** or **Bottom align** button from the **Alignment** group under the **Home** Tab. In our example, we have select **Middle vertical align**.
4. To indent the cell contents, click the **Increase Indent** button. To decrease indent, click **Decrease Indent** button.

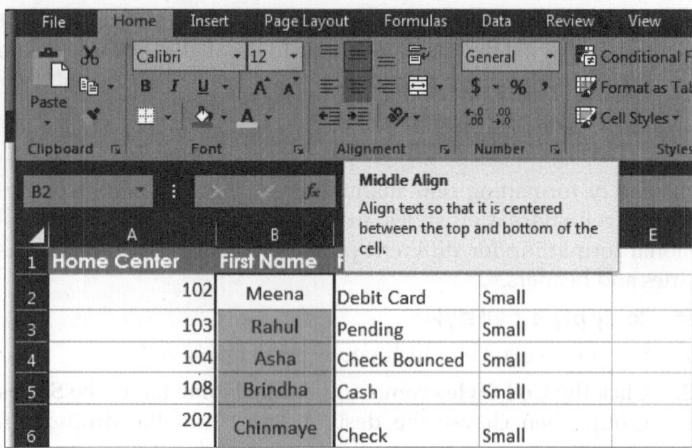

Figure 10.24 The selected cell aligned in horizontal and Vertical using ribbon command

10.3 MODIFYING COLUMNS, ROWS AND CELLS

By default, every row and column of a new workbook is set to the same height and width. Excel allows you to modify column width and row height in different ways, including wrapping text and merging cells.

10.3.1 Modify Column Width

➡ **To modify column width:**

1. Select the columns of which you need to change the width.
2. Position the mouse over the column line in the column heading so the cursor becomes a double arrow as shown in Figure 10.25. Pointer changes to a two-headed, horizontal arrow.

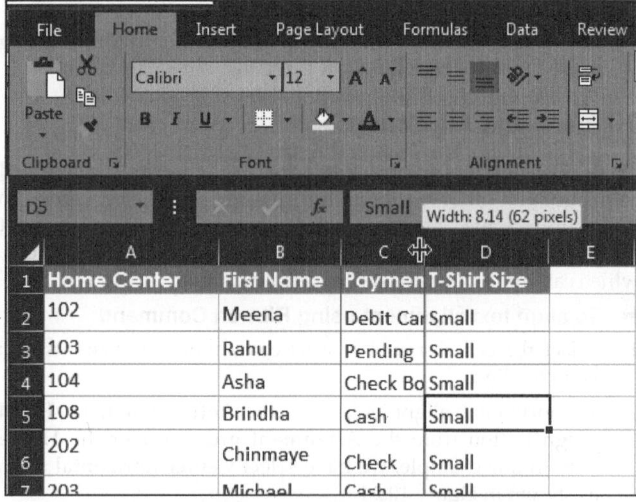

Figure 10.25 Select the column heading

3. Click and drag the mouse to **increase** or **decrease** the column width.
4. Release the mouse. The column width will be changed as shown in Figure 10.26. The Width box that appears as you drag the column, displaying the numeric value for the column width.

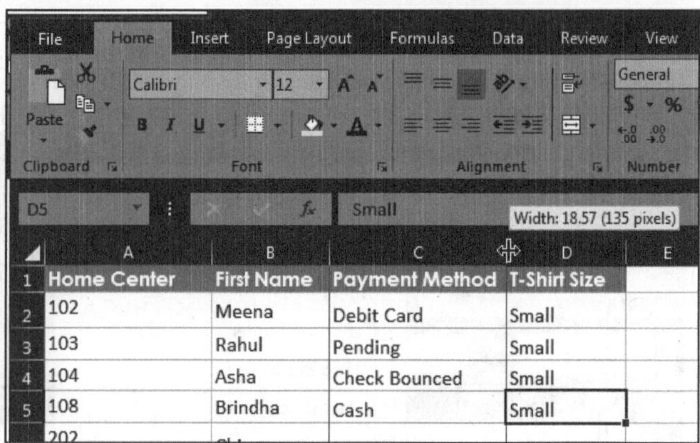

Figure 10.26 Drag the mouse to increase or decrease

With numerical data, the cell will display pound signs (#######) if the column is too narrow. Simply increase the column width to make the data visible.

➡ **To AutoFit column width:**

1. The AutoFit feature will allow you to set a column's width to fit its content automatically.
2. Position the mouse over the column line in the column heading so the cursor becomes a double arrow.
3. Double-click the mouse. The column width will be changed automatically to fit the content.

You can also **AutoFit** the width for several columns at the same time. Simply select the columns you want to AutoFit, then select the **AutoFit Row Height** command from the **Format** drop-down menu on the **Home** tab. This method can also be used for row height as shown in Figure 10.27.

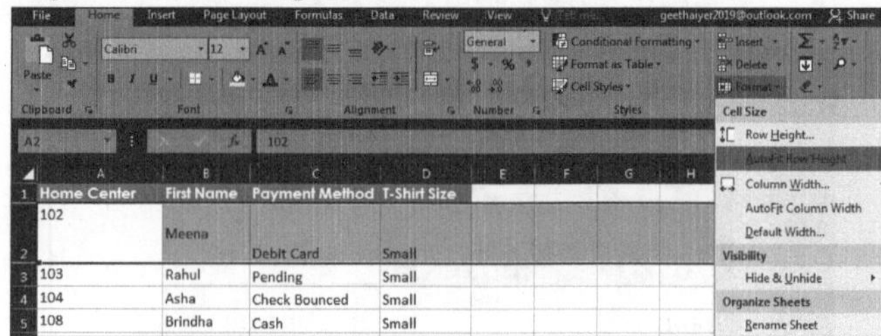

Figure 10.27 Selecting AutoFit Row Height

10.3.2 Modify Row Height

➡ **To modify row height:**

1. Select the rows for which you want to adjust the height.
2. Position the cursor over the row line so the cursor becomes a double arrow as shown in Figure 10.28.
3. Click and drag the mouse to increase or decrease the row height. he mouse pointer changes to a two headed vertical arrow
4. Release the mouse. The height of the selected row will be changed as shown in Figure 10.29. The screen tip displays the numeric value for the row height.

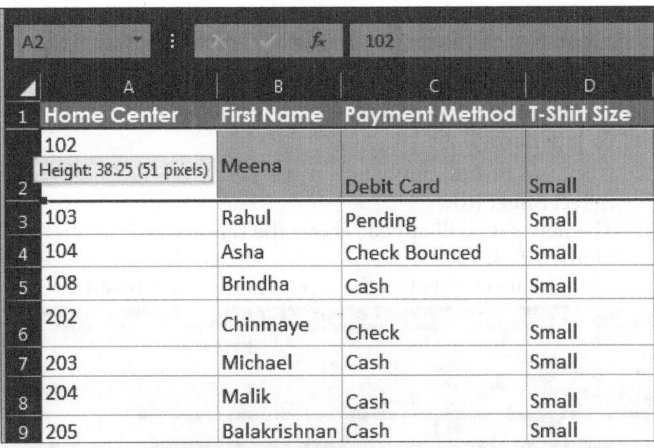

Figure 10.28 Modify Row height

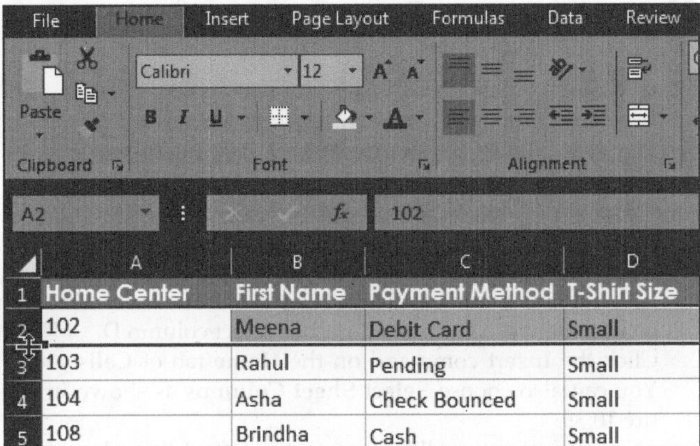

Figure 10.29 The selected Row height changed

10.3.3 Modify All Rows or Columns

Instead of resizing rows and columns individually, you can modify the height and width of every row and column at the same time. This method allows you to set a uniform size for every row and column in your worksheet. In our example, we will set a uniform row height.

➡ **To modify all rows or columns:**

1. Locate and click the **Select All** button just below the name box to select every cell in the worksheet.
2. Position the mouse over a row line so the cursor becomes a double arrow as shown in Figure 10.30.
3. Click and drag the mouse to increase or decrease the row height, then release the mouse when you are satisfied. The row height will be changed for the entire worksheet as shown in Figure 10.31.

10.3.4 Inserting Cells, Rows and Columns

Sometimes you may need to insert cells, rows, or columns to make place for new formulas or data. You can insert cells, rows, or columns as easily as you can delete them.

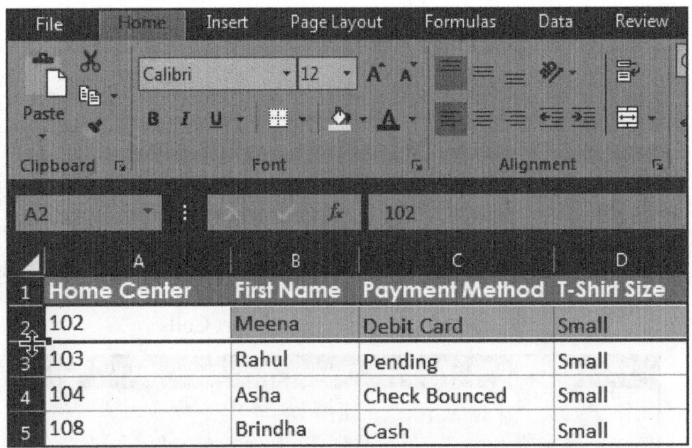

Figure 10.30 Selecting Rows and Columns

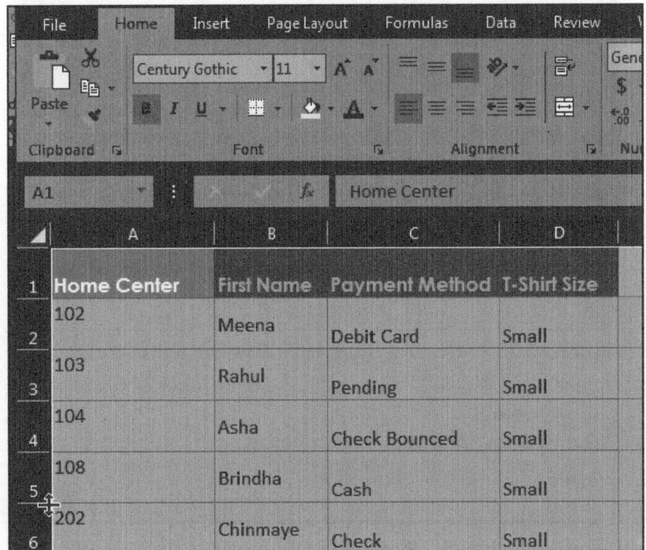

Figure 10.31 Select the entire worksheet to change row and height

Inserting Cells

➡ **To insert cells:**

1. Select a cell or range of cells where you need new cells to insert. Or, select cells in the rows or columns where you want to insert new rows or columns.
2. Select **Insert Cells...** option from **Insert** drop down list of the **Cells** group of the **Home** Tab. *Alternatively,* press Ctrl+Shift+= (equal) keys or click the right mouse button and select Insert... . The **Insert** dialog box appears as shown in Figure 10.32.
3. To insert cells, select the direction you want selected cells to be inserted. For example, we have selected **Shift cells down** option as shown in Figure 10.33.

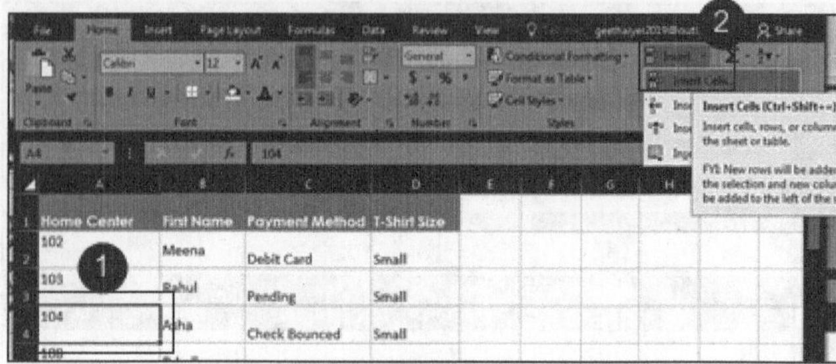

Figure 10.32 Selecting Insert Cells

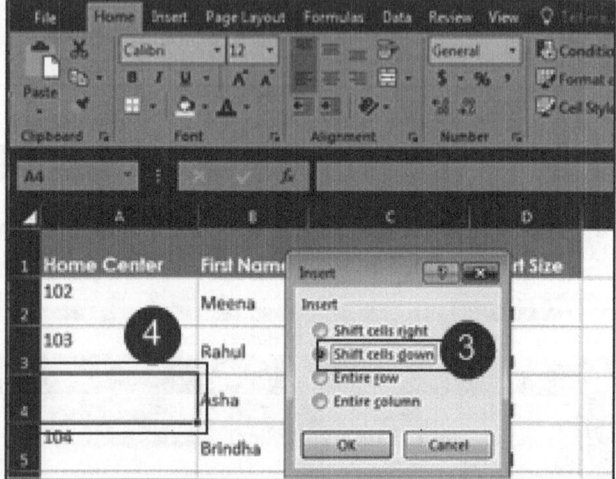

Figure 10.33 Selecting Insert cells down in insert dialog box

4. Click OK. The new cells will appear above the selected row above rows 5.

The various options to insert cells are:

Option	Function
Shift cells right	Selected cells move right.
Shift cells down	Selected cells move down.
Entire row	Insert a row at each selected cell.
Entire column	Insert a column at each selected cell.

When inserting new rows, columns, or cells, you will see a paintbrush icon next to the inserted cells. This button allows you to choose how Excel formats these cells. By default, Excel formats inserted rows with the same formatting as the cells in the row above. To access more options, hover your mouse over the icon, then click the drop-down arrow as shown below.

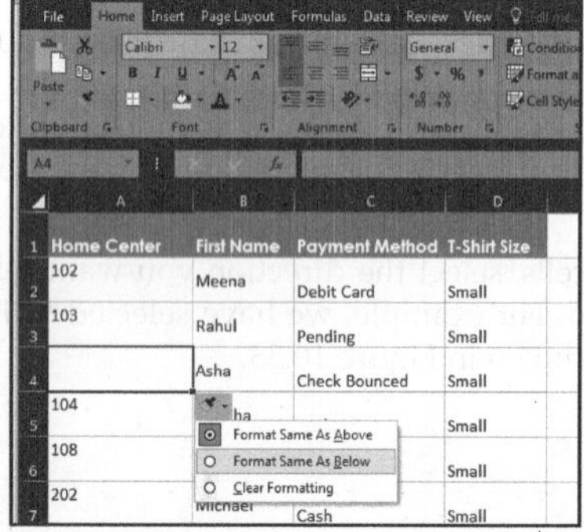

Inserting Rows

Select the row heading below where you want the new row to appear. In this example, we want to insert a row between rows 7 and 8. So we have selecte row 8.

➡ **To insert row:**

1. Click the **Insert** command on the **Home** tab of **Cells** group. **Select Sheet Rows.**
2. The new row will appear above the selected row as shown in Figure 10.34.
3. You can also right click the mouse and choose **Insert**.

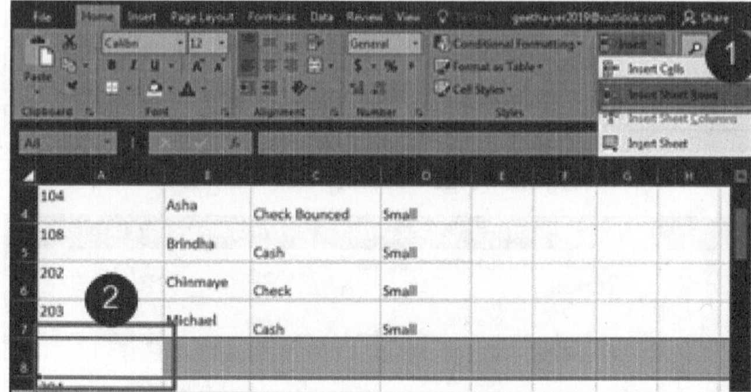

Figure 10.34 Selecting insert sheet row

➡ **To insert column:**

1. Select the column heading to the right of where you want the new column to appear. For example, if you want to insert a column between columns C and D, select column D.
2. Click the **Insert** command on the **Home** tab of **Cells** group. You can also choose **Select Sheet Columns** as shown in Figure 10.35.
3. The new column will appear to the left of the selected column. Alternatively, right click the mouse and choose **Insert** command.

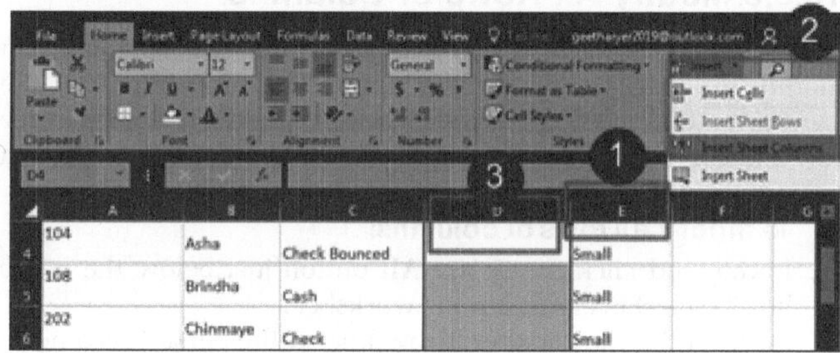

Figure 10.35 Selecting insert sheet row

When inserting rows and columns, make sure you select the entire row or column by clicking the heading. If you select only a cell in the row or column, the **Insert** command will only insert a new cell.

10.3.5 Deleting Cells, Rows and Columns

It is easy to delete a row or column that you no longer need. In our example, we will delete a row, but you can delete a column the same way.

➡ **To Delete rows:**

1. Select the row you want to delete. In our example, we have selected row 15.

2. Click the **Delete** command on the **Home** tab of **Cells** group. Select **Delete Sheet Rows** as shown in Figure 10.36. Right click the mouse and choose **Delete** command.

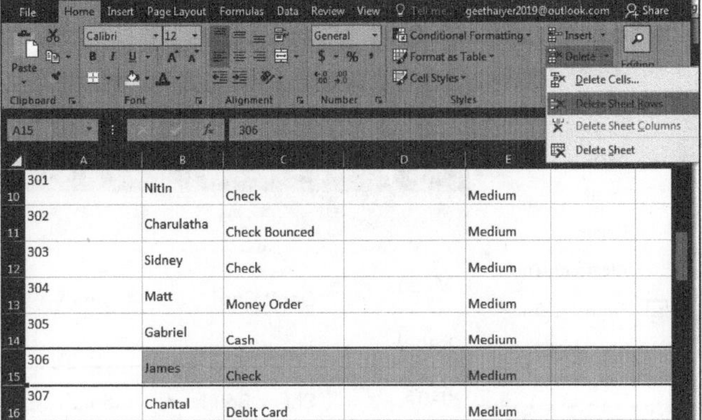

Figure 10.36 Select delete sheet rows

3. The selected row will be deleted. Now, row 16 has moved up, and it is now row 15.

➡ **To Delete columns:**

1. Select the column you want to delete. In our example, we have selected column D.
2. Click the **Delete** command on the **Home** tab of **Cells** group. Select **Delete Sheet Columns** as shown in Figure 10.37. Right click the mouse and choose **Delete** command.

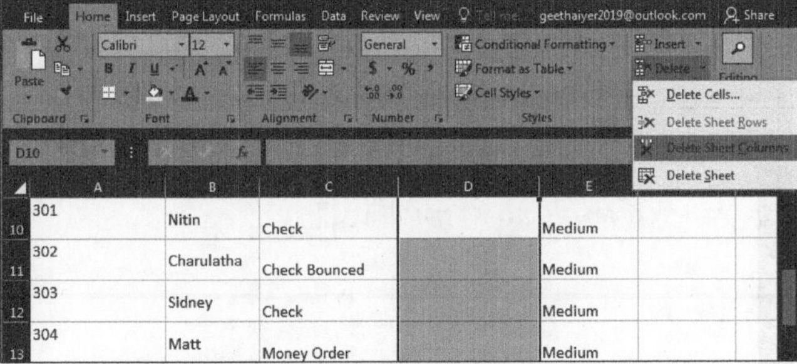

Figure 10.37 Select delete sheet columns

➡ **To Delete cells:**

1. Select the cells you want to delete. In our example, we have selected C5 cell.
2. Click the **Delete** command on the **Home** tab of Cells group. Select **Delete Cells...** as shown in Figure 10.38. Alternatively, press **Ctrl** + - (minus) keys together.

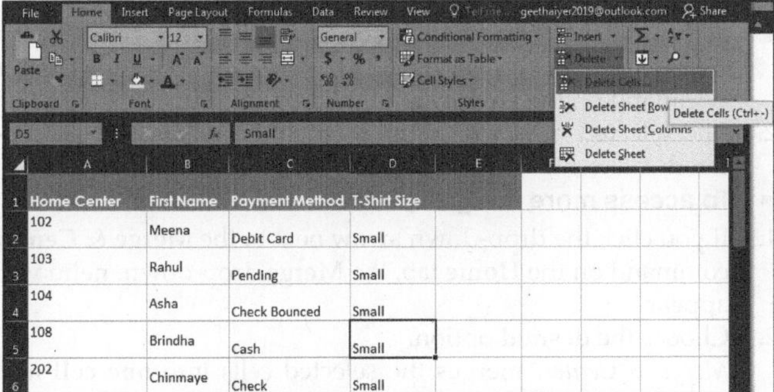

Figure 10.38 Select Delete Cells

3. The **Delete** dialog box appears, select the **Shift Cells up** or **left**.

10.3.6 Clearing Cells Contents

It is important to understand the difference between deleting a row or column and simply clearing its contents. If you want to remove the content from a row or column without causing rows to shift, right-click a heading, then select **Clear Contents** from the drop-down menu.

➡ **To Clear Cell Contents:**

1. Select the cell or range of cells you want to clear.
2. Click on the **Home** Tab and then click arrow next to **Clear** button under the **Editing** group and then select the option that you want (Figure 10.39).

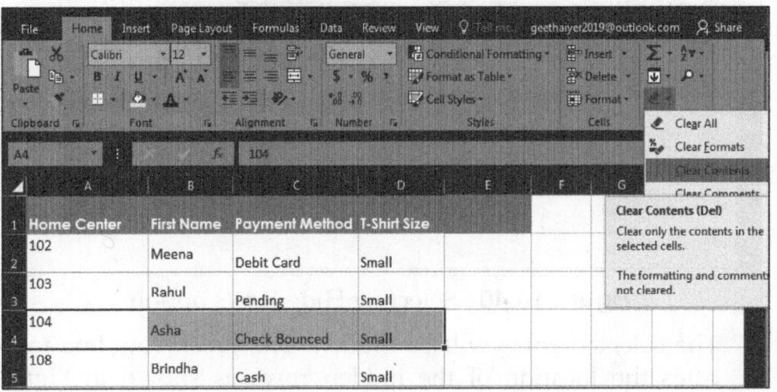

Figure 10.39 Select Clear Cell Contents

3. Select the command from the following table, that describes what you want to be cleared:

Command	Description
All	Clears cell contents and notes; returns the format to General format.
Formats	Returns the format to General format.
Contents	Clears contents but does not change formats or notes.
Comments	Clears comments but does not change contents or formats.
Hyperlink	Clears hyperlinks but does not change contents or formats.
Remove Hyperlinks	Clears hyperlinks and formatting.

- To clear the contents of a cell or range of cells, select the cell(s), click the right mouse button and choose **Clear Contents**.

10.3.7 Hide and Unhide Columns in a Worksheet

Excel allows you to hide rows and columns as needed. There are two ways to hide columns and rows in a worksheet.

- *Using the mouse*: Move the mouse pointer over the column separator line that is on the right of the column you want to hide. The mouse pointer changes to a two-headed pointer. Drag the column separator left until crosses the separator on its left.

- *Using the Ribbon*: Select the cells (or columns). Under **Home** Tab, click **Cells** group and then click arrow next to **Format**. Here, select **Hide** & **Unhide** from the **Visibility** Section. It pops up menu as shown in Figure 10.40. Here, select the desired option from the pop-up menu.

➡ **To hide and unhide a row or column:**

1. Select the row which you want to hide, right-click the mouse, then select Hide from the formatting menu. Or
2. On the **Home** tab click **Format** drop-down arrow, in **Visibility** section, select **Hide & Unhide** option. In our example, we have selected 5 and 6th Row and select **Hide Rows** option as shown in Figure 10.40.

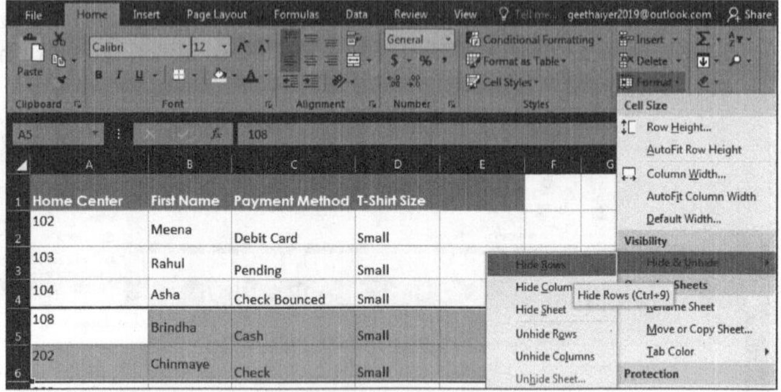

Figure 10.40 Selecting Hide Rows option

3. The selected rows will be hidden. The green row line indicates the location of the hidden rows as shown in Figure 10.41.

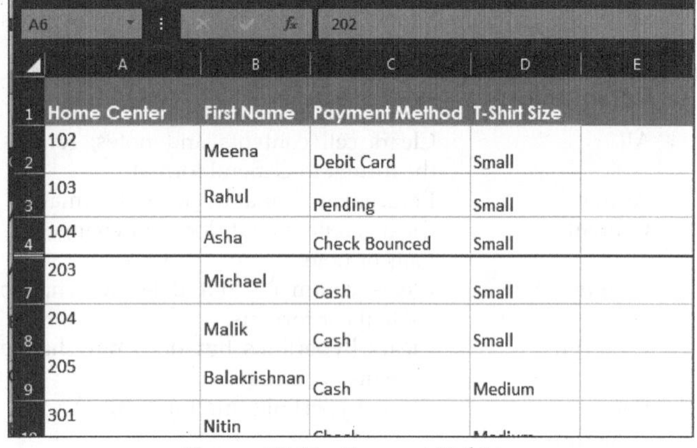

Figure 10.41 Row get Unhide

4. To unhide the rows, select the rows on both sides of the hidden rows. In our example, we have select rows 4 and 7. Then right-click the mouse and select **Unhide** from the formatting menu as shown in Figure 10.42.
5. The hidden rows will reappeared.

10.3.8 Wrapping Text and Merging Cells

Whenever you have too much cell content to be displayed in a single cell, you may decide to wrap the text or merge the cell rather than resize a column. Wrapping the text will automatically modify a cell's row height, allowing cell contents to be displayed on multiple lines. Merging allows you to combine a cell with adjacent empty cells to create one large cell.

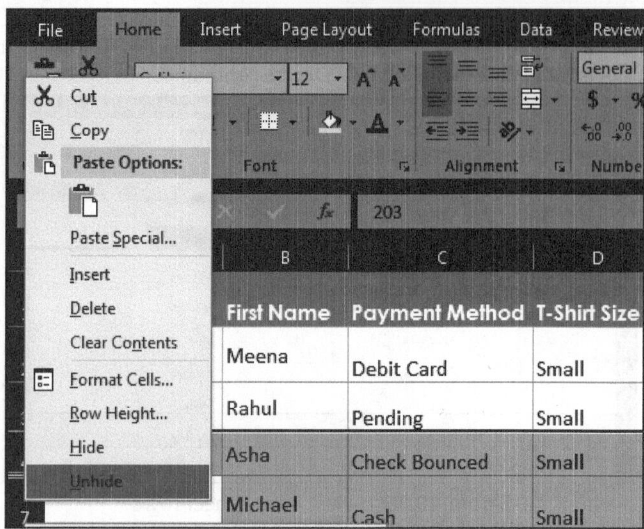

Figure 10.42 Selecting Unhide option

➡ **To wrap text in cells:**

1. Select the cells you want to wrap. In this example, we have select the cells in column C.
2. Click the **Wrap Text** command on the **Home** tab on the **Alignment** group as shown in Figure 10.43.

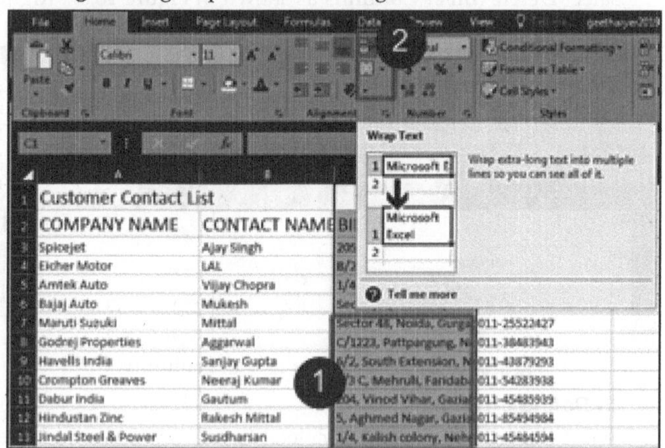

Figure 10.43 Selecting Wrap Text option

3. The text in the selected cells will be wrapped as shown in Figure 10.44.

➡ **To merge cells using the Merge & Center command:**

1. Select the cell range which you want to merge cells. In our example, we have selected **A2:D2**. Click the **Merge & Center** command on the **Home** tab of **Alignment** group.
2. The selected cells will be merged, and the text will be centered.

➡ **To access more merge options:**

1. If you click the drop-down arrow next to the **Merge & Center** command on the **Home** tab, the **Merge** drop-down menu will appear.
2. Choose the desired option:
   Merge & Center: merges the selected cells into **one cell** and **centers** the text.

Figure 10.44 Text get wrapped

Merge Across: merges the selected cells into larger cells while keeping each row separate.

Merge Cells: merges the selected cells into one cell but does not center the text.

Unmerge Cells: unmerges selected cells.

You will be careful while using this feature. If you merge multiple cells that all contain data, Excel will keep only the contents of the upper-left cell and discard everything else.

➡ **To merge cell to center across selection:**

1. Select the range of cells you want to merge to center across selection. In our example, we have selected A2:D2.
2. Under **Home** Tab, click **Cells** group and then click arrow next to **Format**. Here, select Format Cells... *alternatively,* press Ctrl+1 and then click on the **Alignment** Tab as shown in Figure 10.45 *or* click on the **Home** tab in the **Alignment** group, click the **Dialog Box Launcher.**

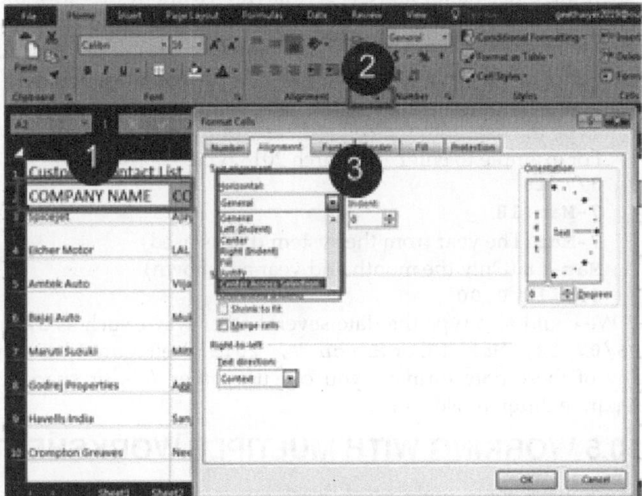

Figure 10.45 Selecting center across selection from Format cells dialog box

3. The **Format Cells** dialog box appears as shown in Figure 10.45. Locate and select the **Horizontal:** drop-down menu, select **Center Across Selection,** then click **OK.**
4. The content will be centered across the selected cell range.

10.4 UNDERSTANDING NUMBER FORMATS

Number formats tell your spreadsheet exactly what type of data you are using, like Number, percentages (%), currency ($), times, dates, and so on.

10.4.1 Why use number formats?

When you apply a number format, you are telling your spreadsheet exactly what types of values are stored in a cell. For example, the date format tells the spreadsheet that you are entering specific calendar dates. This allows the spreadsheet to better understand your data, which can help ensure that your data remains consistent and that your formulas are calculated correctly.

If you do not need to use a specific number format, the spreadsheet will usually apply the general number format by default. However, the general format may apply some small formatting changes to your data.

10.4.2 Enter Number Formats Correctly

There's more to number formatting than selecting cells and applying a format. Spreadsheets can actually apply a lot of number formatting automatically based on the way you enter data. This means you will need to enter data in a way the program can understand, and then ensure that those cells are using the proper number format. For example, the entries listed in Table 10.1 shows how to use different number formats correctly for dates, percentages, and times, fraction etc. The entries of the Table 10.1 are displayed in Figure 10.46, as entry would appear in an Excel 2016 worksheet.

Table 10.1 Excel's Number Formats

Typed Entry	Chosen Format	Result
897	Number, General	897
7999 Mg Rd.	Text, left aligned	7999 Mg Rd
450.09	Number, dollar format	$450.09
54.6%	Number, percent format	5460.00%
(678)	Number, negative	-678
2 3/4	Number, fraction	2 3/4
45600	Number, comma format	45,600.00
-678	Number, negative, decimal	-678.00
1/5/17	Date, m/d/yyyy	01/05/2017
4/5	Date, m/d/yy (current year assumed)	05-Apr

➡ **To enter number format correctly:**

1. Select the cells to which you want to apply the format.
2. On the **Home** tab, in the **Number** group, click the **Number Format** dialog box Launcher, and then click **More Number Formats.**
3. In the **Format Cells** dialog box appears as shown in Figure 10.47. Select **Number** tab.

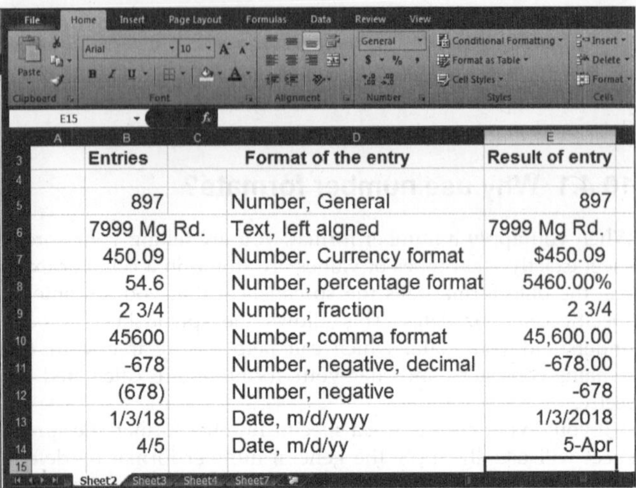

Entries	Format of the entry	Result of entry
897	Number, General	897
7999 Mg Rd.	Text, left algned	7999 Mg Rd.
450.09	Number. Currency format	$450.09
54.6	Number, percentage format	5460.00%
2 3/4	Number, fraction	2 3/4
45600	Number, comma format	45,600.00
-678	Number, negative, decimal	-678.00
(678)	Number, negative	-678
1/3/18	Date, m/d/yyyy	1/3/2018
4/5	Date, m/d/yy	5-Apr

Figure 10.46 Different Number formats done for data given in Table 10.1

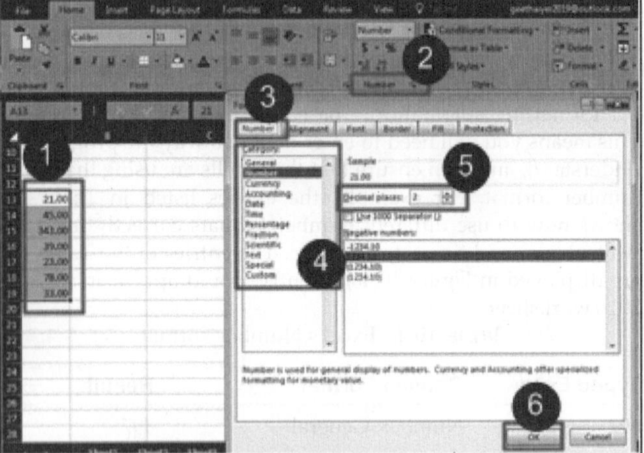

Figure 10.47 Format Cells showing Number tab

4. In the **Category:** list, select the format you want to apply. For example, here we select **Number** format.
5. Enter the decimal places in the **Decimal places:** in the spinner box.
6. Click OK.

   If you select any cells with number formatting, you can see the actual value of the cell in the formula bar. The spreadsheet will use this value for formulas and other calculations.

10.4.3 Entering Date and Time in a Worksheet

Whenever you are working with dates, you want to use a date format to tell the spreadsheet that you are referring to specific calendar dates, such as March 17, 2018. Date formats also allow you to work with a powerful set of date functions that use time and date information to calculate an answer.

Spreadsheets do not understand information the same way a person would type October into a cell, the spreadsheet would not know you are entering a date so it will treat it like text. Instead, when you enter a date, you will need to use a specific format your spreadsheet understands, such as month/day/year (or day/month/year depending on which country you are in). In the example below, we will type 02/03/2018 for March 2, 2018. Our spreadsheet will then automatically apply the date number format for the cell.

Now, we have enter data format correctly, and we can do many different things with this data. For example, we could use the fill handle to continue the dates through the column, so a different day appears in each cell as shown below:

If the date formatting is not applied automatically, it means the spreadsheet did not understand the data you entered. In the example below, we have typed March 15th. The spreadsheet did not understand that we were referring to a date, so this cell is still using the general number format.

	E	F	G	H	I
14					
15					
16			2-3-18		
17			3-3-18		
18			4-3-18		March 15th
19			5-3-18		
20			6-3-18		
21			7-3-18		
22			8-3-18		
23			9-3-18		
24			10-3-18		
25			11-3-18		
26				11-3-18	
27					

On the other hand, if we type March 7 (without the "th"), the spreadsheet will recognize it as a date. Because it doesn't include a year, the spreadsheet will automatically add the current year so the date will have all of the necessary information.

1. Select the cell in which you want to enter the date.
2. Type the date into the cell with any of the following formats. For example to enter 7th March 2018 type:

   `3/7/18`

   `7-Mar-18`

   `7-Mar` (The year from the system date is used)

   `Mar-18` (Only the month and year are shown)

   `3/7/18 0:00`

We could also type the date several other ways, such as `3/7`, `03/07/18`, `Mar-18`, or `March 7, 2018` (See Figure 10.48). In any of these date formats, you can use either /, -, or space to separate different elements.

10.5 WORKING WITH MULTIPLE WORKSHEETS

Every workbook contains at least one worksheet by default. When working with a large amount of data, you can create multiple worksheets to help organize your workbook and make it easier to find content. You can also group worksheets to quickly add information to multiple worksheets at the same time.

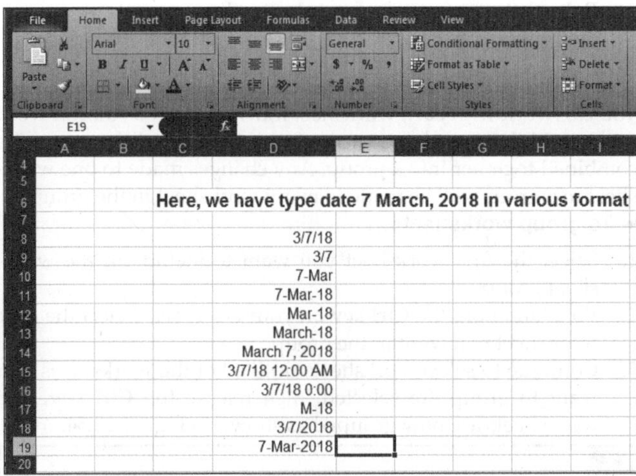

Figure 10.48 Various ways to enter date in a worksheet

10.5.1 Inserting and Deleting Sheets

➡ **To insert a new worksheet:**

1. Click the **New sheet** button near the bottom-right corner of the Excel window.
2. A new blank worksheet will appear as shown in Figure 10.49. Alternatively, you can also:
3. Select **Insert Sheet** option from **Insert** drop down list of the **Cells** group of the **Home** Tab (See Figure 10.49). *Alternatively,* position the mouse pointer on the tab of any sheet, click the right mouse button and then choose Insert... . A dialog box appears. In this dialog box, click **Worksheet** and then click OK button. *Or,* using keyboard press Shift+F11 keys together to insert a new worksheet.

☞ *You can also insert a new sheet in the workbook at any location you desire.*

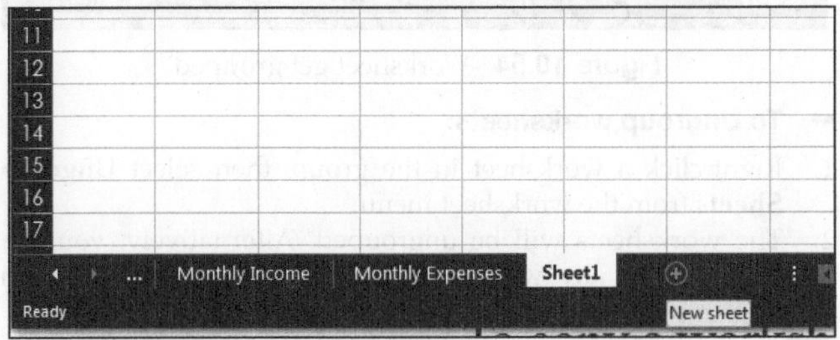

Figure 10.49 Click the +(plus) sign at bottom to insert new worksheet

4. By default, any new workbook you create in Excel will contain one worksheet, called **Sheet1**. To change the default number of worksheets, navigate to Backstage view, click Options, then choose the desired number of worksheets to include in each new workbook.

➡ **To delete a worksheet:**

1. Right-click the worksheet you want to delete, then select **Delete** from the worksheet menu.
2. The worksheet will be deleted from your workbook.
3. Click on the **Home** tab, in the **Cells** group. Select **Delete Sheet** from the **Delete** drop-down list (See Figure 10.50). *Alternatively,* position the mouse pointer on the tab of the sheet to be deleted, click the right mouse button and then choose Delete.

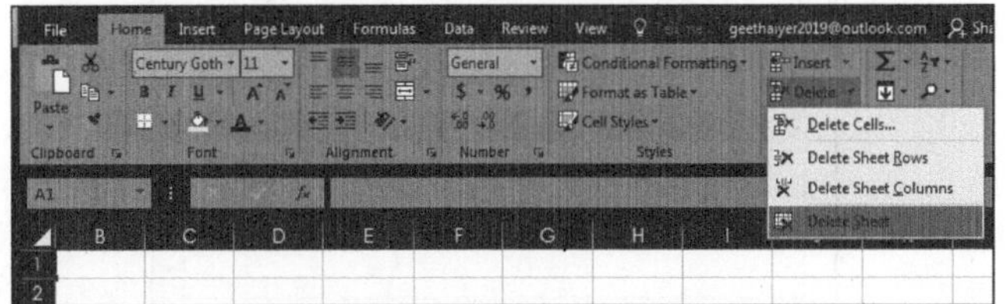

Figure 10.50 Deleting a worksheet

☞ *You cannot undo or get back a worksheet after deletion. Therefore, you should be very careful before you delete a worksheet.*

10.5.2 Copying and Moving Worksheets

Suppose that you use a budget worksheet in one workbook and the same worksheet is also required for another workbook. You could re-create the worksheet in the new workbook or copy the data from one workbook to another, but it would be much easier if you just copy the entire worksheet of other workbook.

➡ **To copy/ move a worksheet:**

1. Select the sheet you want to ***copy*** or ***move*** as shown in Figure 10.51.
2. The **Move or Copy** dialog box will appear as shown in Figure 10.52. Choose where the sheet will appear in the **Before sheet:** field.

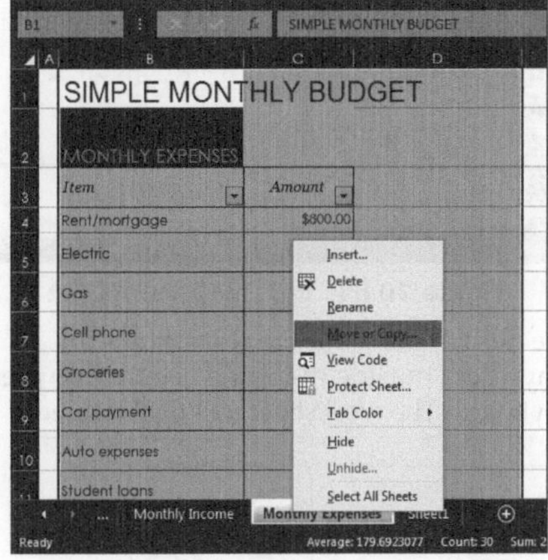

Figure 10.51 Selecting the data to copy

3. The worksheet will be copied. It will have the same title as the original worksheet. In our example, we copied the **Monthly Expenses** worksheet, so our new worksheet is named Monthly Expenses (2). All content from that worksheet has also been copied to the new worksheet.
4. You can also copy a worksheet to an entirely different workbook. You can select any workbook that is currently open from the **To book:** drop-down menu.

Figure 10.52 Move or copy dialog box

10.5.3 Renaming a Worksheet

➡ **To rename a worksheet:**

1. Right-click the worksheet you want to rename, then select **Rename** from the worksheet menu as shown in Figure 10.53.

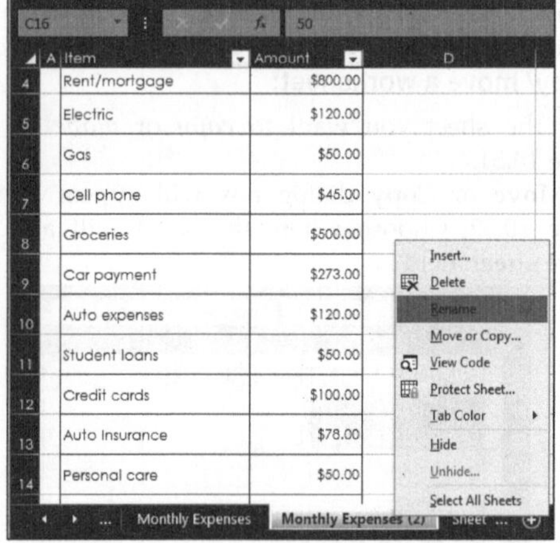

Figure 10.53 Rename a worksheet

2. Type the desired name for the worksheet.
3. Click anywhere outside the worksheet tab, or press Enter on your keyboard. The worksheet will be **renamed**.

10	Auto expenses	$120.00	
11	Student loans	$50.00	
12	Credit cards	$100.00	
13	Auto Insurance	$78.00	
14	Personal care	$50.00	

... Monthly Expenses | Yearly Expenses | Sheet1

➡ **To move a worksheet:**

1. Click and drag the worksheet you want to move until a small black arrow appears above the desired location.
2. Release the mouse. The worksheet will be moved.

10.5.4 Grouping and Ungrouping Worksheets

You can work with each worksheet individually, or you can work with multiple worksheets at the same time. Worksheets can be combined together into a group. Any changes made to one worksheet in a group will be made to every worksheet in the group.

➡ **To group worksheets:**

1. Select the first worksheet you want to include in the worksheet group.
2. Press and hold the **Ctrl** key on your keyboard. Select the next worksheet you want in the group.
3. Continue to select worksheets until all of the worksheets you want to group are selected, then release the **Ctrl** key. The worksheets are now grouped as shown in Figure 10.54.

7					
8	Subject	Sem-I	Sem-II	Sem-III	Total
9					
10	**Maths**	69	78	76	223
11	**Physics**	56	76	74	200
12	**Comp. Sc.**	78	67	65	200
13	**Chemistry**	98	71	78	200
14	**English**	65	72	67	204
15				**Total**	**1027**
16					
17					
18					
19					
20	Now the Worksheet are grouped				
21					

Sheet2 | Sheet1 | Chart1 | Sheet3

Ready

Figure 10.54 Worksheet get grouped

➡ **To Ungroup worksheets:**

1. Right-click a worksheet in the group, then select **Ungroup Sheets** from the worksheet menu.
2. The worksheets will be ungrouped. Alternatively, you can simply click any worksheet not included in the group to ungroup all worksheets as shown in Figure 10.55.

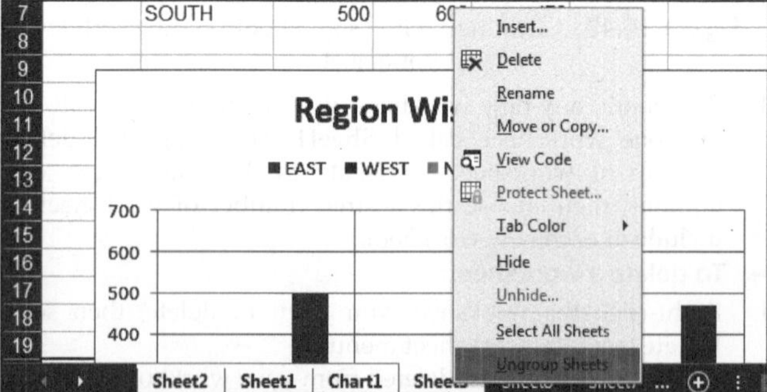

Figure 10.55 Ungroup worksheet

10.6 USING FIND AND REPLACE FEATURE

Find feature enables you to find *text, numbers,* or *formula* that are anywhere in the worksheet. ***Replace*** enables you to find and replace in a worksheet.

10.6.1 Find Command

You can easily search your workbook using the **Find** feature, which also allows you to modify content using the **Replace** feature.

➡ **To find text:**

1. Select the cells in which you want to search or select a single cell to search the entire worksheet.
2. Click on **Home** Tab and then in **Editing** group, click on the arrow next to **Find & Select** command (Figure 10.56). Then choose **Find...** or press Ctrl+F keys or press Shift+F5 keys to display the **Find** tab dialog box (Figure 10.57).

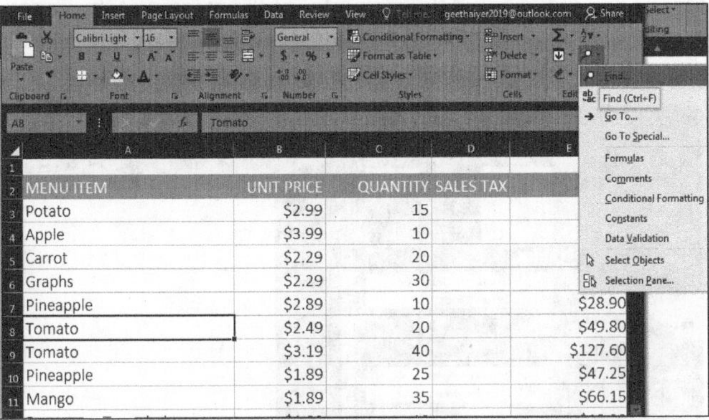

Figure 10.56 Find & Select Command Options

3. In the Find what: box enter the content you want to find. For example, we have type the **Menu Item** name i.e. Tomato

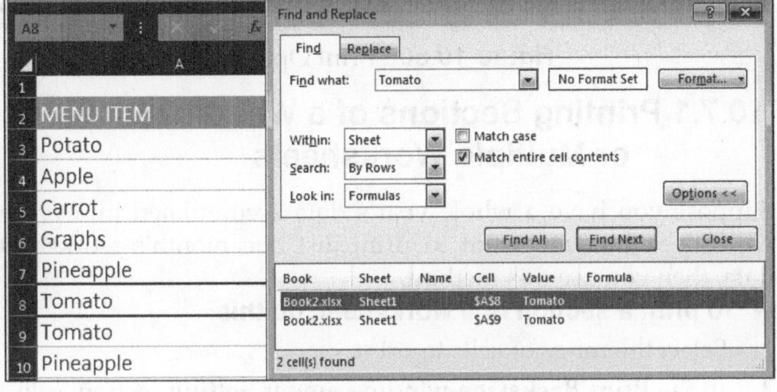

Figure 10.57 Find dialog box

4. Click **Find Next.** If the content is found, the cell containing that content will be selected.
5. In the Look in: drop-down list box, select the name of the items you want to search through. The items are as under:

Item	Function
Formulas	Search through formulas in the cells indicated.
Values	Search through values in the cells indicated.
Comments	Search through comments attached to the cells indicated.

(Contd...)

6. Match entire cells contents. Select this check box if you want to find matches where only the entire cell contents match the contents in the Find what: text box. This option is to be selected, otherwise, you will also find matches where only part of the cell contents match.
7. In the Search: drop-down list box, select the option that describes the direction in which you want the search to proceed.

Item	Function
By Rows	Searches across rows starting at the current cell.
By Columns	Searches down columns starting at the current cell.

8. In the Within: drop-down list box, select the option that describes the area in which you want the search to proceed.

Item	Function
Sheet	Search within the worksheet.
Workbook	Search in full workbook.

9. Match case select this check box if you want to exactly match *upper* or *lowercase.*

   Click on Format... button if you perform search on the particular format.
10. Click Find Next button to find next instances, or Find All to see the every instances of the search item.
11. When you are finished, click **Close** to eixt the Find and Replace dialog box.

10.6.2 Replace Text

If you have repeatedly made a mistake throughout your workbook (such as misspelling someone's name) or that you need to exchange a particular word or phrase for another. You can use Excel's Find and Replace feature to make quick revisions.

➡ **To Replace text:**

1. Select the cells in which you want to replace the text.
2. Click on **Home** Tab and then in **Editing** group, click on the arrow next to **Find & Select** command (Figure 11.56). Then choose **Replace...** or press Ctrl+H keys to display the **Replace** tab dialog box (Figure 10.58).
3. The **Find and Replace** dialog box will appear. Type the text you want to find in the **Find what:** field. For example, we have correct a list of Menu items i.e. Beetroot.
4. Type the text you want to replace it with in the **Replace with:** field, then click **Find Next.**
5. If the content is found, the cell containing that content will be selected. Review the text to make sure you want to replace it.
6. If you want to replace it, select **Replace** options. Choosing **Replace** will replace individual instances, while **Replace All** will replace every instance of the text throughout the workbook.
7. The selected cell content will be replaced.

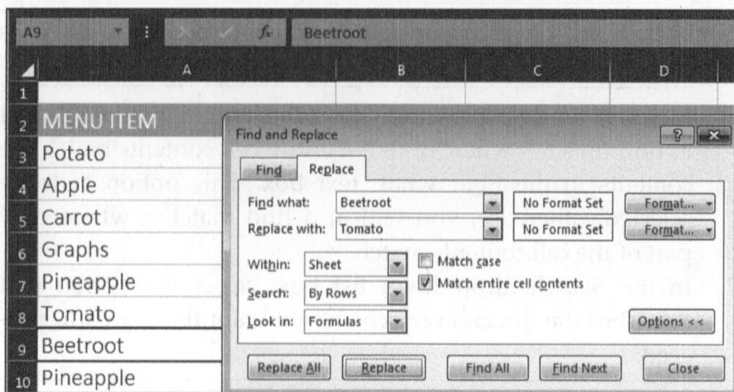

Figure 10.58 Replace tab

8. When you are finished, click **Close** to exit the **Find and Replace** dialog box.

10.7 PAGE LAYOUT AND PRINTING

You can set *margins* and *fonts* and include *headers/footers* as well as *titles* while printing a worksheet in Excel 2016. You can preview a worksheet to see how it will look when you print it.

➡ **To print a worksheet:**

1. Open the worksheet that you want to print.
2. Click the **File** tab and then choose **Print** command (See Figure 10.59) or *alternatively*, press Ctrl+Shift+F12 keys together.

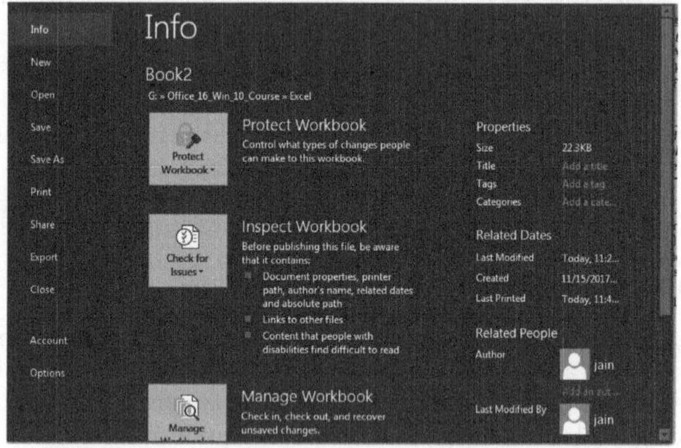

Figure 10.59 Print command in Backstage view

3. The Print Backstage view appears. Here, click **Print** icon.
4. The Print Backstage view closes and in the status bar displays the process of the print job.

Backstage Print Options shown in Figure 10.60, are described as follows:

Option	Function
Print Section:	
Copies	Specify the number of copies to be printed.
Printer Section:	This section shows selected printer from a drop-down list. Select the desired printer from the Printer drop-down list.
Settings:	This section shows the Page Setup options, such as page orientation, paper size, and page margins. These options are described below:
Print what option:	
Print Active Sheets	Prints only selected worksheet.
Print Entire Workbook	Prints currently open workbook.
Print Selection	Prints selected cells.
Ignore Print Area	Select this option if you want to ignore the print area you have selected.
Page(s) From:/To:	Select this option to print pages you wish to print.
Collate	Select this option to collate multiple copies.
Page Orientation	Allows you to change the page orientation, i.e., portrait (vertically) or landscape (horizontally).
Page Size	Allows you to select the paper size.
Margin	Allows you to set the margin of the pages.
Scaling	Allows you to adjust the size of the worksheet.

(*Contd...*)

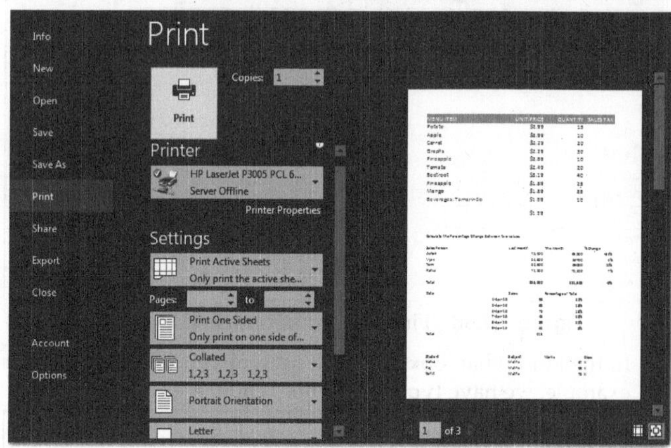

Figure 10.60 Print Options

10.7.1 Printing Sections of a Worksheet or Multiple Worksheets

Suppose you have a whole year's data accumulated in a given worksheet, but you want to print just one month's worksheet data, then you use this method.

➡ **To print a section of a worksheet, do this:**

1. Select the range of cells to print.
2. In the **Print Backstage** window, under **Setting** section, select **Print Selection** to print the selected cells (See Figure 10.60). Excel 2016 ignores any Print Area that has been set and prints the selected range.

➡ **To print several worksheets with one command, do this:**

1. Select all the sheets (the worksheets must be within the same workbook) you want to print.
2. In the **Print Backstage** window, under **Setting** section, in the **Print what** drop-down list, select **Print Active Sheets**.

10.7.2 Adjusting Content

On occasion, you may need to make small adjustments from the Print pane to fit your workbook content neatly onto a printed page. The Print pane includes several tools to help fit and scale your content, such as scaling and page margins.

➡ **To change page orientation:**

1. In **Print** pane under **Settings** select Orientation.
2. Excel offers two page orientation options: landscape and portrait. Landscape orients the page horizontally, while portrait orients the page vertically. For example, we have select to set the page orientation to landscape as shown in Figure 10.61.

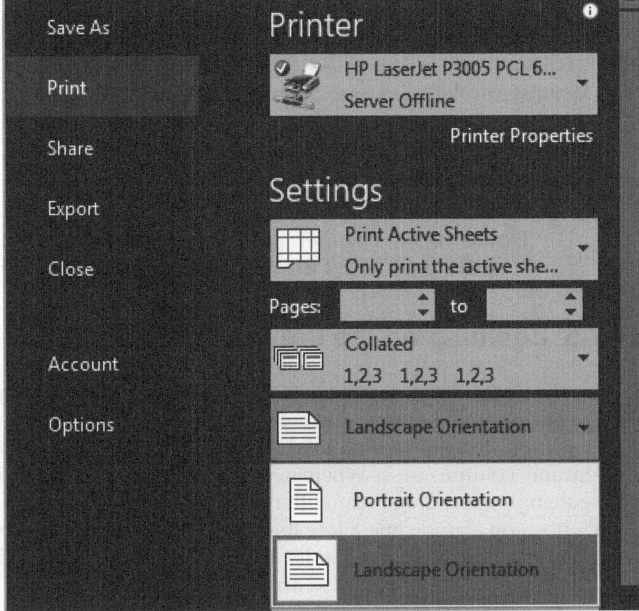

Figure 10.61 Selecting Page Orientation

3. The new page orientation will be displayed in the Preview pane.

➡ **To fit content before printing:**

1. If some of your content is being cut off by the printer, you can use scaling to fit your workbook to the page.
2. Select the desired option from the **Scaling** drop-down menu. Here, we select **Fit All Columns on One Page** as shown in Figure 10.62.

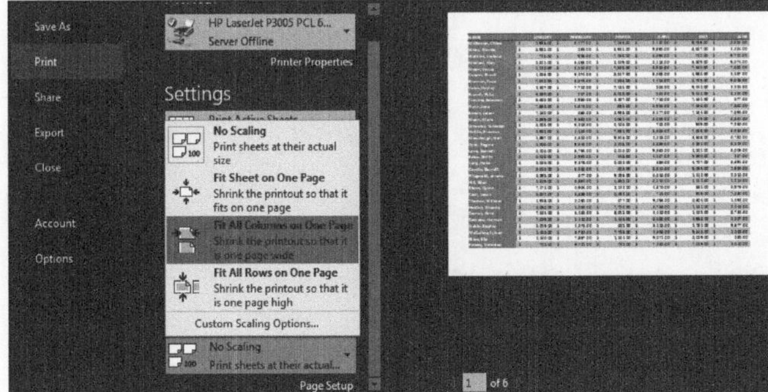

Figure 10.62 Selecting Fit content before printing

3. The worksheet will be condensed to fit onto a single page.

☞ *Keep in mind that worksheets will become more difficult to read as they are scaled down. So you may not want to use this option when printing a worksheet with a lot of information in one page.*

10.7.3 Print Tiles

It is important to include these headings on each page of your printed worksheet. The Print Titles command allows you to select specific rows and columns to appear on each page.

➡ **To include Print Tiles:**

1. Click the **Page Layout** tab on the Ribbon, then select the **Print Titles** command as shown below.

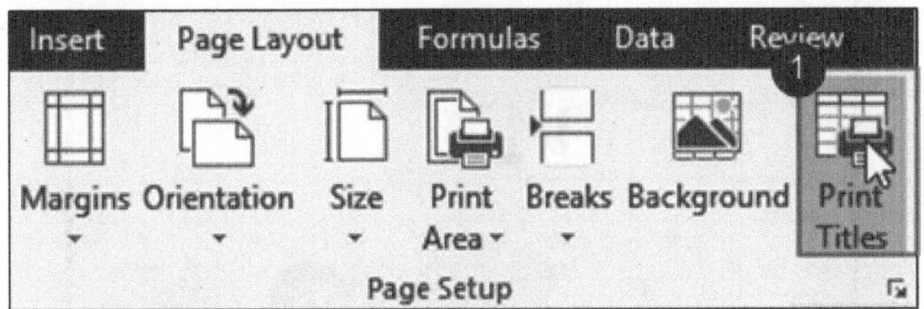

2. The **Page Setup** dialog box will appear as shown in Figure 10.63. Select the **rows** to repeat at top: or **columns** to repeat at left on each page. For example, we have select rows to repeat at top.

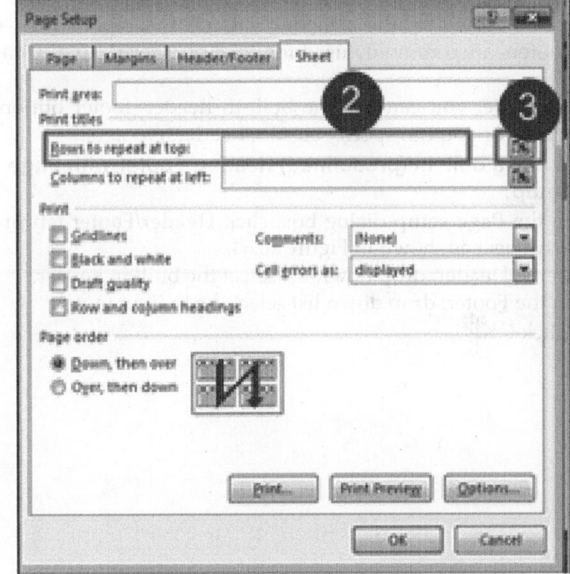

Figure 10.63 Page Setup dialog box

3. Click the **Collapse Dialog** button next to the **Rows to repeat at top:** field.
4. The cursor will become a small **selection arrow**, and the **Page Setup** dialog box will be collapsed. Select the row(s) you want to repeat at the top of each printed page. In our example, we have selected row 2 as shown below.

5. Row 2 will be added to the Rows to repeat at top: field. Click the Collapse Dialog button again.
   The **Page Setup** dialog box will expand . To repeat a column as well, use the same process shown in steps 4 and 5.
6. After you have finished with your selections, click OK button in the Page Setup dialog box as shown below.

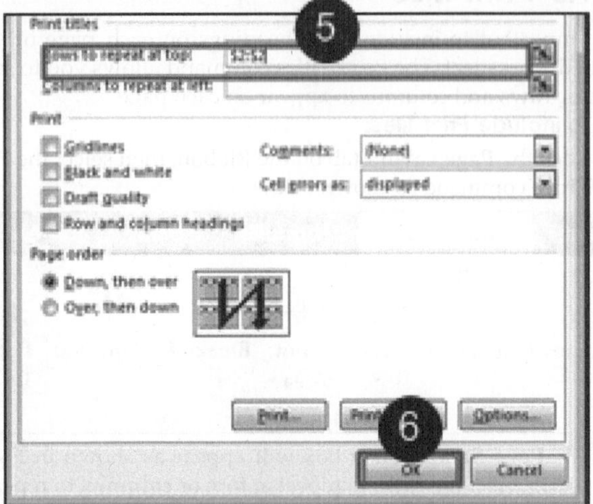

10.7.4 Headers and Footers

You use headers for the company's name and report titles, etc. The footers are commonly used for page numbering and printing date/time.

If need be, you can use the built-in header/footer option in Excel 2016 or you can specify custom headers/footers.

➡ **To use a built in (predefined) Header/ Footer with Page Setup:**

1. In the **Page setup** dialog box, click **Header/Footer** tab property sheet as shown in Figure 10.64.
   In the Header: drop down list select the built in header.
   In the Footer: drop down list select the built in footer.
2. Click OK.

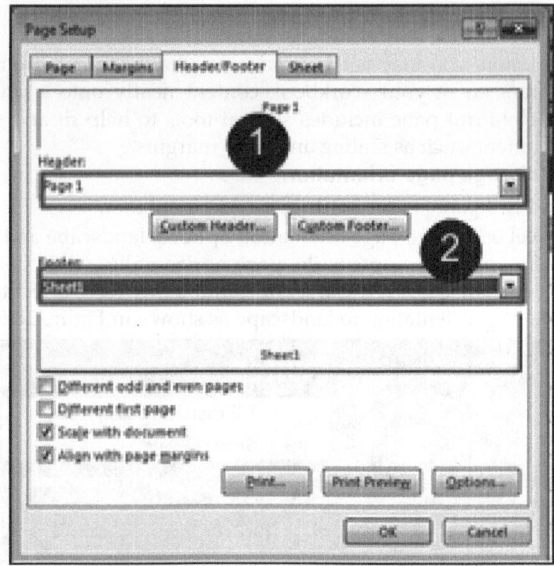

Figure 10.64 Page Setup dialog box with Header/Footer Tab Property sheet

10.7.5 Zooming on the Previewed Worksheet

To zoom in and out view of the worksheet, you can use the **Zoom to Page** button from bottom right corner of the preview window.

In addition, the Show Margins buttons toggle the display of margin and column lines. When margin and column lines are visible then you can drag them with the mouse to a new position.

To reposition a guide line, place the mouse pointer on a margin line, a column gridline, or a handle at the edge of the page, and drag the line with the two-headed arrow.

The inner horizontal margins are text margins (i.e., they define the worksheet). The outer horizontal margins are header/footer margins. The extra handles along the top of the page refers to column lines.

Formulas and Functions

11.1 INTRODUCTION

Functions are the predefined formulas or programs that perform calculations in Excel on specific values, called arguments. Each function takes specific types of arguments, such as *numbers*, *references*, *text* or *logical values*. You can enter the arguments, enclosing them in parentheses i.e. ( ), after the function name. Functions use these arguments in the same way that algebraic equations use variables. For example, the SUM function adds values or range of values, and the PMT function calculates the loan payments based on an interest rate, the period of loan, and the principal amount of loan.

11.1.1 Creating Formula

A formula is entered into a cell. It performs calculations of some type or returns a result, which is displayed in the cell. Formulas in Excel always begin with an equal sign (=) and can include following types of data items:

- *numeric* and text values (constants)
- arithmetic operator, comparison operators (<,=>) text operators (&), functions (SUM), parentheses
- cell references, and names

By combining these components, you can calculate the result you want by using the information in the worksheet. Excel also gives you the option to display formulas on worksheet, or the results of the formulas.

➡ **To create a formula:**

1. Select the cell that will contain the formula. In our example, we have select cell B7.
2. Type the equals sign (=). Notice how it appears in both the cell and the formula bar as shown in Figure 11.1.

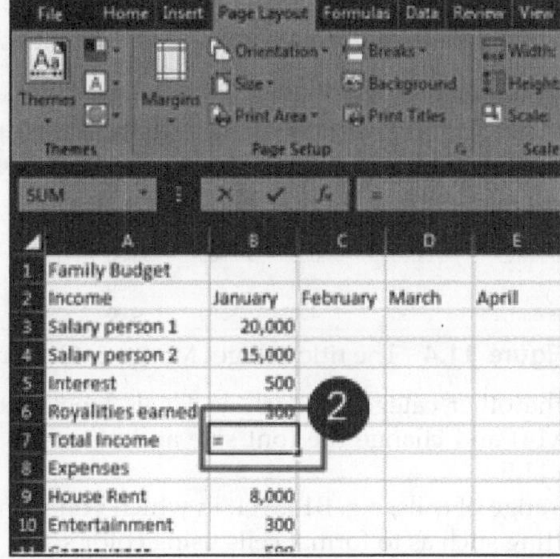

Figure 11.1 Type the equal sign in the cell

3. Type the cell address of the cell you want to reference first in the formula: cell B3 in our example. A blue border will appear around the referenced cell as shown in Figure 11.2.
   Type the mathematical operator you want to use. In our example, we have type the addition sign (+) as shown in Figure 11.2.

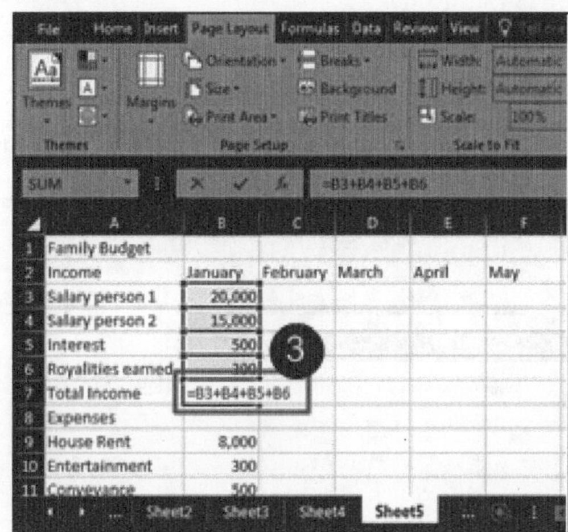

Figure 11.2 Type the addition sign

Type the cell address of the cell you want to reference second in the formula: cell B4 in our example. A red border will appear around the referenced cell.

4. Press **Enter** on your keyboard. The formula will be calculated, and the value will be displayed in the cell. If you select the cell again, notice that the cell displays the result, while the formula bar displays the formula as shown in Figure 11.3.

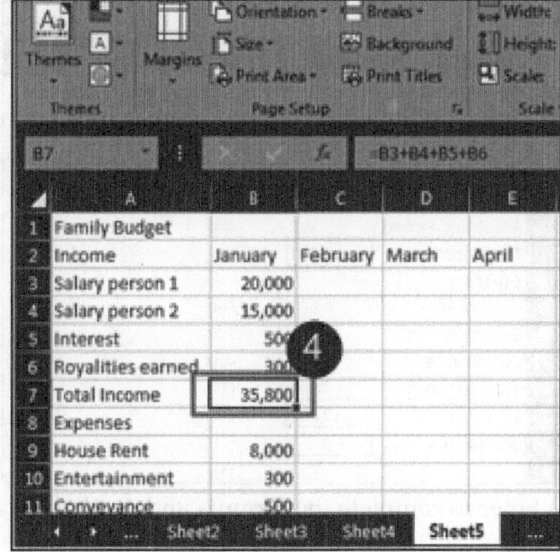

Figure 11.3 The formula will be calculated

11.1.2 Sum and Differences

To sum several ranges, simply refer to each of them, separated by a comma, using the SUM function. We explained how to create the formula and show the (total income for January) values.

➡ **To sum several ranges:**

1. Click Cell C7 (total income for February), then select the **Home** tab, click **Editing** group, click **AutoSum** to sum adjacent values.

	A	B	C	D	E
1	Family Budget				
2	Income	January	February	March	April
3	Salary person 1	20,000	20,000	20,000	20,000
4	Salary person 2	15,000	15,000	15,000	15,000
5	Interest	500	200	150	300
6	Royalities earned	300	400	500	200
7	Total Income	35,800	=SUM(C3:C6)		

2. Press **Enter** to show the total, then repeat the procedure for cell B14 (total expenses for February)

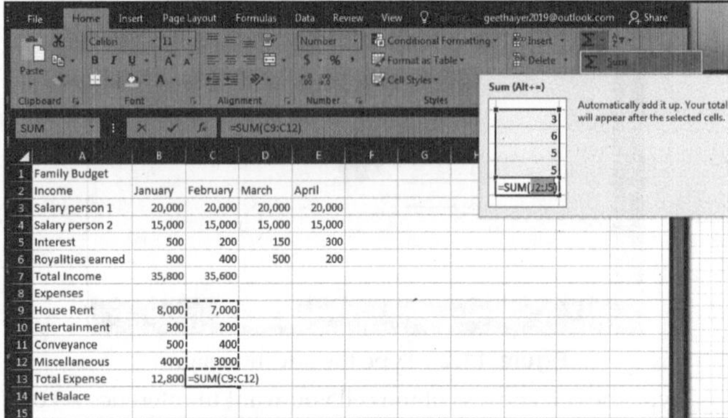

	A	B	C	D	E
1	Family Budget				
2	Income	January	February	March	April
3	Salary person 1	20,000	20,000	20,000	20,000
4	Salary person 2	15,000	15,000	15,000	15,000
5	Interest	500	200	150	300
6	Royalities earned	300	400	500	200
7	Total Income	35,800	35,600		
8	Expenses				
9	House Rent	8,000	7,000		
10	Entertainment	300	200		
11	Conveyance	500	400		
12	Miscellaneous	4000	3000		
13	Total Expense	12,800	=SUM(C9:C12)		
14	Net Balace				

3. Now, calculate the Difference between the month of January of Net Balance in the Cell B14
4. Type =, click B7, type - (minus), then click B13 (to calculate total income minus total expenses for the month of January) as shown below.

B13 =B7-B13

	A	B	C	D	E
1	Family Budget				
2	Income	January	February	March	April
3	Salary person 1	20,000	20,000	20,000	20,000
4	Salary person 2	15,000	15,000	15,000	15,000
5	Interest	500	200	150	300
6	Royalities earned	300	400	500	200
7	Total Income	35,800	35,600		
8	Expenses				
9	House Rent	8,000	7,000		
10	Entertainment	300	200		
11	Conveyance	500	400		
12	Miscellaneous	4000	3000		
13	Total Expense	12,800	10,600		
14	Net Balance	=B7-B13			
15					

5. Press Enter to complete the formula and display the result of the sum.
6. Select Cell C7 and use the Fill handle to replicate the formula for the other months (March and April), and repeat this process for cells C14 and E14 as shown below.

B14 =B7-B13

	A	B	C	D	E
1	Family Budget				
2	Income	January	February	March	April
3	Salary person 1	20,000	20,000	20,000	20,000
4	Salary person 2	15,000	15,000	15,000	15,000
5	Interest	500	200	150	300
6	Royalities earned	300	400	500	200
7	Total Income	35,800	35,600	35,650	35,500
8	Expenses				
9	House Rent	8,000	8,000	8,000	8,000
10	Entertainment	300	200	100	300
11	Conveyance	500	400	200	400
12	Miscellaneous	4000	3000	2000	3000
13	Total Expense	12,800	11,600	10,300	11,700
14	Net Balance	23,000	24,000	25,350	23,800
15					

Format Cells using Color Scale

Color scales in Excel 2016 are visual guides that help you understand data distribution and variation. A color scale helps you to compare a range of cells by using a gradation of two or three colours. The shade of the colour represents higher, middle or lower values.

➡ **To format cells:**

1. Click the title cell i.e. A1, then select the **Home** tab, choose a font and font size and font effect to format a cell.
2. Press **Shift**, and then click E1 to highlight the row across the data, then click the **Merge & Center** button in the **Alignment** group as shown in Figure 11.4.

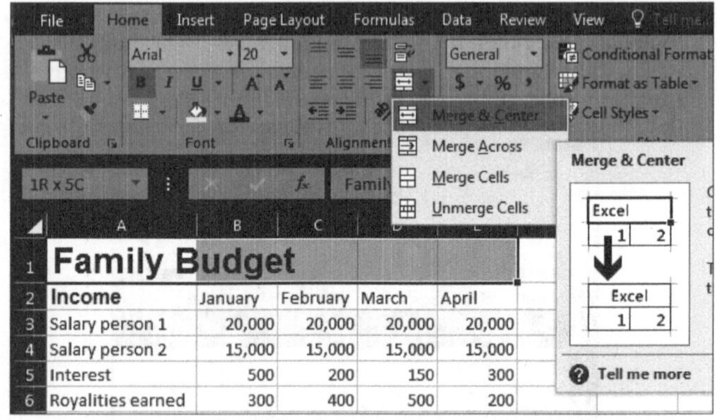

Figure 11.4 The title cell get Merge & Center

3. Click the other categories such as Totals labels (i.e. A7, A8, A13, A14) and change the font size and effects as shown in Figure 11.5.
   Select range of cells, e.g. B14:E14, in which you want to apply formatting such as to format cells using color scale.

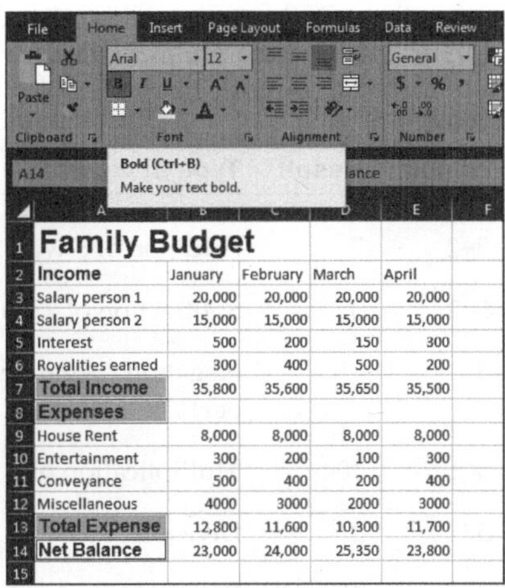

	A	B	C	D	E
1	Family Budget				
2	Income	January	February	March	April
3	Salary person 1	20,000	20,000	20,000	20,000
4	Salary person 2	15,000	15,000	15,000	15,000
5	Interest	500	200	150	300
6	Royalities earned	300	400	500	200
7	Total Income	35,800	35,600	35,650	35,500
8	Expenses				
9	House Rent	8,000	8,000	8,000	8,000
10	Entertainment	300	200	100	300
11	Conveyance	500	400	200	400
12	Miscellaneous	4000	3000	2000	3000
13	Total Expense	12,800	11,600	10,300	11,700
14	Net Balance	23,000	24,000	25,350	23,800

Figure 11.5 Change other categories to change effects

4. In the **Home** Tab, under the **Styles** group, click arrow next to **Conditional Formatting** and then click on **Color Scales** as shown in Figure 11.6.

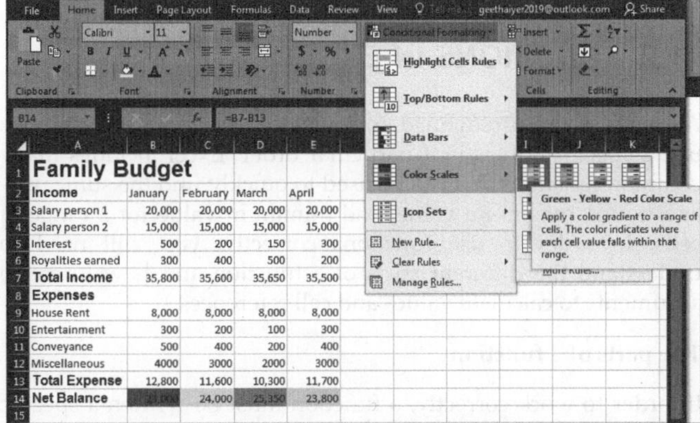

Figure 11.6 Selecting color scales to add shaded the value

5. Select the desired color scales and the cells are colored and shaded appropriately for the values that they contain.

☞ *Positive balances are green – the larger the balance, the deeper the shade. Modest balances are yellow, and shades of red are applied to negative balances.*

11.1.3 Entering Cell References

Relative Cell References

By default, all cell references are relative references. When copied across multiple cells, they change based on the relative position of rows and columns. For example, if you copy the formula =A1+B1 from row 1 to row 2, the formula will become =A2+B2. Relative references are especially convenient whenever you need to repeat the same calculation across multiple rows or columns.

We want to create a formula that will multiply each item's price by the quantity. Instead of creating a new formula for each row, we can create a single formula in cell D2 and then copy it to the other rows. We will use relative references so the formula calculates the total for each item correctly.

➡ **To create and copy a formula using relative references:**

1. Select the cell that will contain the formula. In our example, we have select cell D4.
2. Enter the formula to calculate the desired value. Type **=B4*C4** as shown in Figure 11.7.

	A	B	C	D
3	MENU ITEM	UNIT PRICE	QUANTITY	LINE TOTAL
4	PineApple	₹ 2.99	15	₹ 44.85
5	Orange	₹ 3.99	10	
6	Papaya	₹ 2.29	20	
7	Orange	₹ 2.29	30	
8	Grapes	₹ 2.89	10	
9	Apple	₹ 2.49	20	
10	Banana	₹ 3.19	40	
11	Mango	₹ 1.89	25	
12	Fruit juice	₹ 1.89	35	
13	Jackfruit	₹ 1.89	10	

Figure 11.7 Enter the formula in the cell

3. Press **Enter** on your keyboard. The formula will be calculated, and the result will be displayed in the cell.
4. Click and drag the fill handle over the cells you want to fill. In our example, we have select cells D5:D13 as shown in Figure 11.8.

D13 =B13*C13

	A	B	C	D
3	MENU ITEM	UNIT PRICE	QUANTITY	LINE TOTAL
4	PineApple	₹ 2.99	15	₹ 44.85
5	Orange	₹ 3.99	10	₹ 39.90
6	Papaya	₹ 2.29	20	₹ 45.80
7	Orange	₹ 2.29	30	₹ 68.70
8	Grapes	₹ 2.89	10	₹ 28.90
9	Apple	₹ 2.49	20	₹ 49.80
10	Banana	₹ 3.19	40	₹ 127.60
11	Mango	₹ 1.89	25	₹ 47.25
12	Fruit juice	₹ 1.89	35	₹ 66.15
13	Jackfruit	₹ 1.89	10	₹ 18.90

Figure 11.8 Drag the fill handle displayed the result in each cell

5. Release the mouse. The formula will be copied to the selected cells with relative references, displaying the result in each cell.

   You can double-click the filled cells to check their formulas the relative cell references should be different for each cell, depending on their rows.

11.1.4 Using Operators in Formulas

Operators are used in formulas to execute operations on the values taken by formulas. Excel uses four types of operations. These are given below:

Operators	Signs
Arithmetic	+, –, *, /, %, ^
Text	& (ampersand)
Comparative	=, <, <=, >, >=, <>
Reference	Colon (:), comma(,), space ()

All formulas in Excel must begin with an equal signs (=). This is because the cell contains, or is equal to, the formula and the value it calculates.

Understanding Cell References

While you can create simple formulas in Excel using numbers (for example, =4+4 or =7*7), most of the time you will use cell addresses to create a formula. This is known as making a cell reference. Using cell references will ensure that your formulas are always accurate because you can change the value of referenced cells without having to rewrite the formula.

In the formula below, cell A3 adds the values of cells A1 and A2 by making cell references:

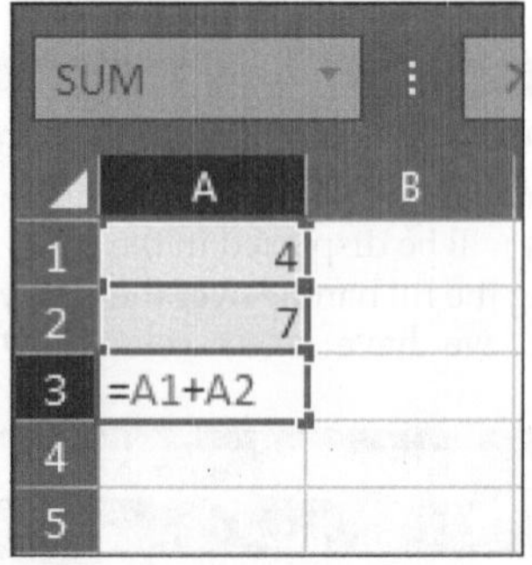

When you press Enter, the formula calculates and displays the answer in cell A3:

If the values in the referenced cells change, the formula automatically recalculates.

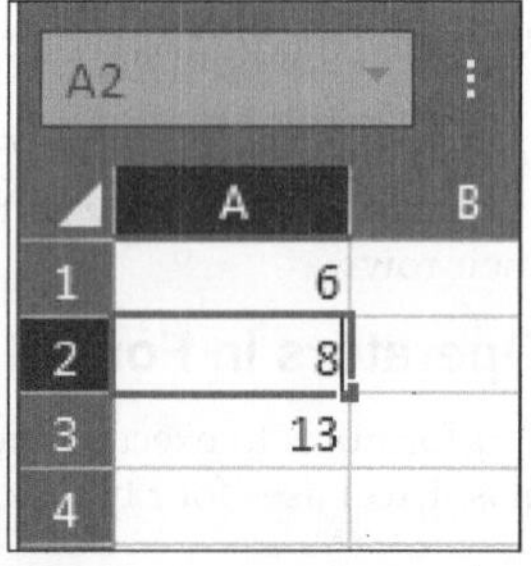

By combining a mathematical operator with cell references, you can create a variety of simple formulas in Excel. Formulas can also include a combination of cell references and numbers, as in the examples below:

Operator	Formula	Result	Type of Operation
+	=5+2	7	Addition of 5 with 2
–	=5–2	3	Subtraction of 2 from 5
–	-5	–5	Negation (negative of the number)
*	=5*2	10	Multiplication of 5 with 2
/	=5/2	2.5	Division of 5 by 2
%	5%	.05	Percentage
^	=5^2	25	Exponentiation (to the power of)

11.2 FUNCTIONS IN EXCEL 2016

A function is a predefined formula that performs calculations using specific values in a particular order. Excel includes many common functions that can be used to quickly find the sum, average, count, maximum value, and minimum value for a range of cells. In order to use functions correctly, you will need to understand the different parts of a function and how to create arguments to calculate values and cell references.

The parts of a function

In order to work correctly, a function must be written a specific way, which is called the syntax. The basic syntax for a function is the equals sign (=), the function name (SUM, for example), and one or more arguments. Arguments contain the information you want to calculate. The function in the example below would add the values of the cell range A1:A20.

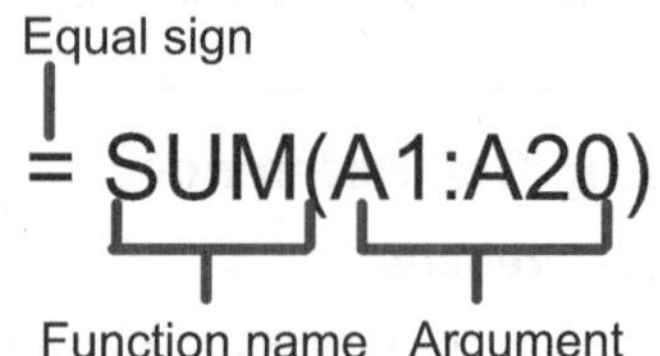

Working with arguments

Arguments can refer to both individual cells and cell ranges and must be enclosed within parentheses. You can include one argument or multiple arguments, depending on the syntax required for the function.

For example, the function =AVERAGE(D16:D23) would calculate the average of the values in the cell range D16:D23. This function contains only one argument as shown below:

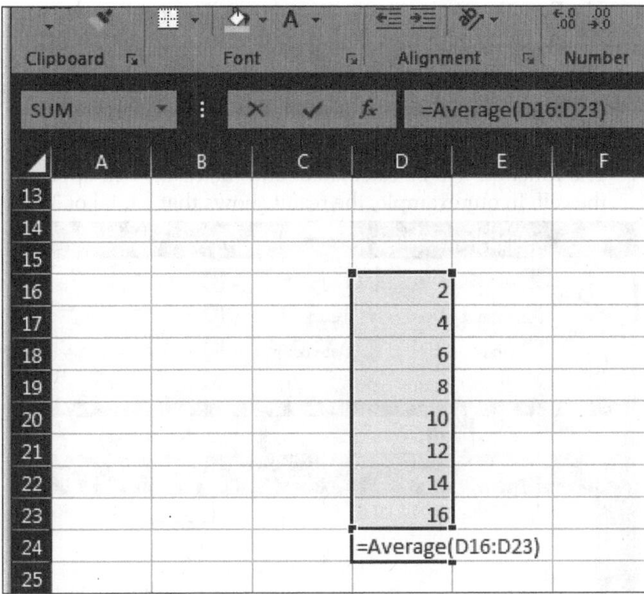

Multiple arguments must be separated by a comma. For example, the function =SUM(H20:H23, J20:J23, L20) will add the values of all of the cells in the three arguments.

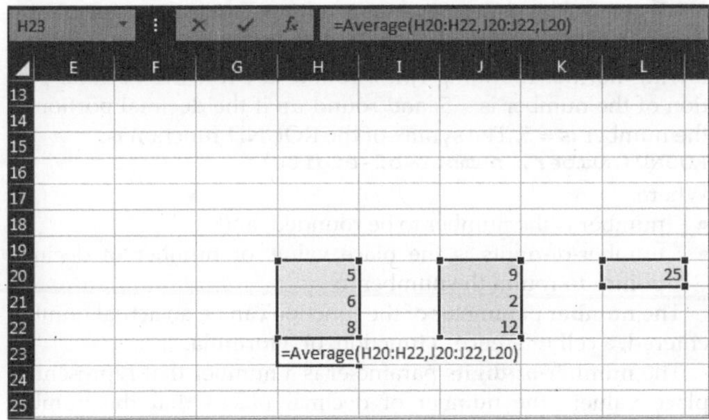

11.2.1 Creating a Function in a Worksheet

There are a variety of functions available in Excel. Here some of the common functions are:

Average–This function determines the average of the values included in the argument. It calculates the sum of the cells and then divides that values by the number of cells in the argument. Here, we use the AVERAGE function to calculate the average marks of maths subject of three semester.

- **To create a function using the Average command:**

1. Select the cell that will contain the function. In our example, we have select cell G10 as shown in Figure 11.9.
2. Type the equals sign (=), and enter the desired function name. You can also select the desired function from the list of suggested functions that appears below the cell as you type. For example type **=AVERAGE** as shown in Figure 11.10.

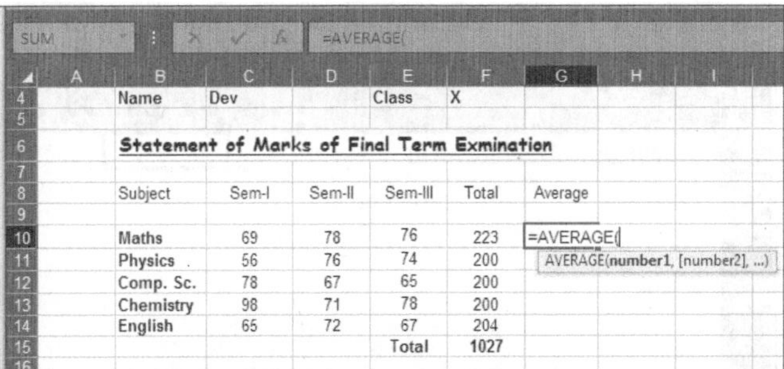

Name	Dev		Class	X	
Statement of Marks of Final Term Exmination					
Subject	Sem-I	Sem-II	Sem-III	Total	Average
Maths	69	78	76	223	=AVERAGE(
Physics	56	76	74	200	AVERAGE(number1, [number2], ...)
Comp. Sc.	78	67	65	200	
Chemistry	98	71	78	200	
English	65	72	67	204	
			Total	1027	

Figure 11.9 Type function name

Name	Dev		Class	X	
Statement of Marks of Final Term Exmination					
Subject	Sem-I	Sem-II	Sem-III	Total	Average
Maths	69	78	76	223	=AVERAGE(C10:E10)
Physics	56	76	74	200	
Comp. Sc.	78	67	65	200	
Chemistry	98	71	78	200	
English	65	72	67	204	
			Total	1027	

Figure 11.10 Select the cell range

3. Enter the cell range for the argument inside parentheses. Type (C10:E10). This formula will add the values of cells C10:E10, then divide that value by the marks obtained in three semester.
4. Press **Enter** on your keyboard. The function will be calculated, and the result will appear in the cell. In our example, the average number of marks in three semester as shown in Figure 11.11.

Name	Dev		Class	X	
Statement of Marks of Final Term Exmination					
Subject	Sem-I	Sem-II	Sem-III	Total	Average
Maths	69	78	76	223	74.33333
Physics	56	76	74	200	
Comp. Sc.	78	67	65	200	
Chemistry	98	71	78	200	
English	65	72	67	204	
			Total	1027	

Figure 11.11 The function will be calculated

COUNT–The COUNT function counts the number of cells that contain numbers, and counts numbers within the list of arguments, Use the COUNT function to get the number of entries in a number field that is in a range or array of numbers.

- **To use the COUNT function**

1. Select the cell that contain the function. In our example, we have selected cell **C1** as shown in Figure 11.12.
2. Click the **Formula** tab on the Ribbon to access the **Function Library**.

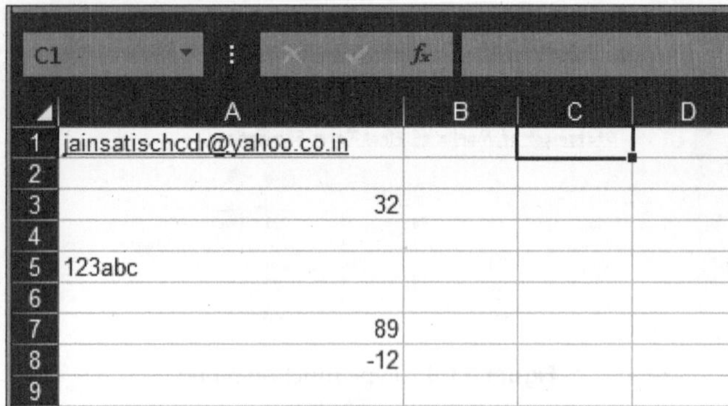

Figure 11.12 Select the cell

3. From the **Function Library** group, click **More Functions** drop-down list, then hover the mouse over **Statistical** command. A sub menu appears as shown in Figure 11.13.

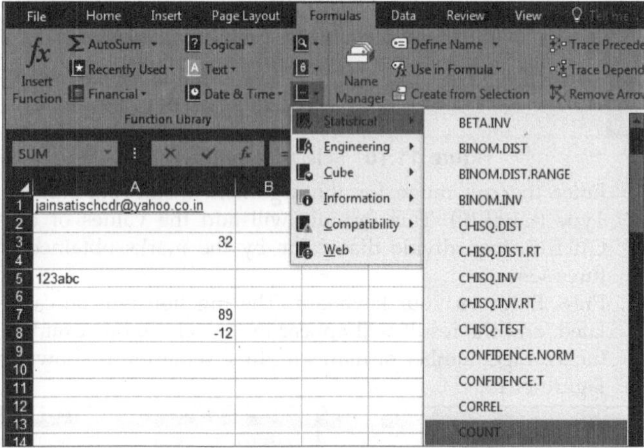

Figure 11.13 Select COUNT function in More Functions drop-down list

4. Select the desired function form the drop-down menu. Here, we have select the COUNT function, which will count the number of cells in the column.

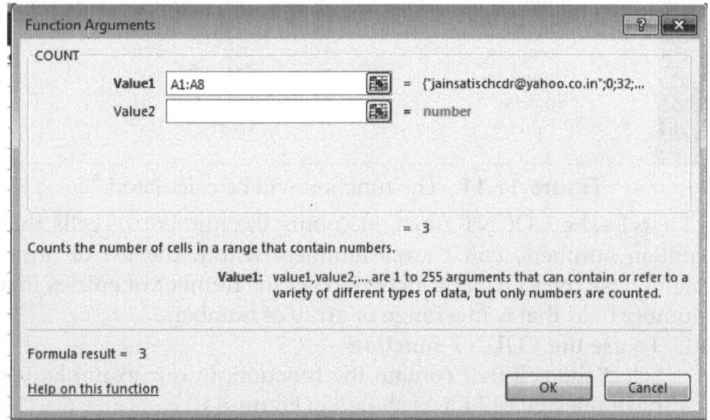

Figure 11.14 Function Arguments dialog box

5. The **Function Arguments** dialog box will appear as shown in Figure 11.14. Select the **Value1** field, then enter or select the desired cells. In our example, we have enter the cell range A1:A8, we only want to count the number of cells in the cell range A1:A8.
6. When you are satisfied, click OK.
7. The function will be calculated, and the result will appear in the cell. In our example, the result shows that a total of 3.

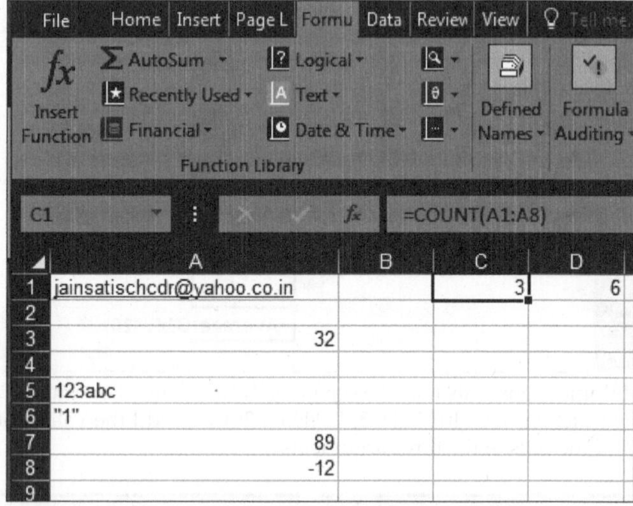

ROUND–The ROUND function rounds the value in a cell following normal rounding rules: round down if the decimal portion of the number is < 5, and round up if the decimal portion of the number is = 5. The syntax of the ROUND function is:

```
ROUND(number, number-of-digits)
```

Where:

- number is the number to be rounded, and
- number-of-digits is the place value, or number of decimal points, to round the number to

The **number** parameter of the function can be an actual number entered, a cell reference, a function, or a formula.

The **number-of-digits** parameter is a number that represents a place value: the number of decimal places that the number should be rounded to. Negative numbers are used to specify place values to the left of the decimal point.

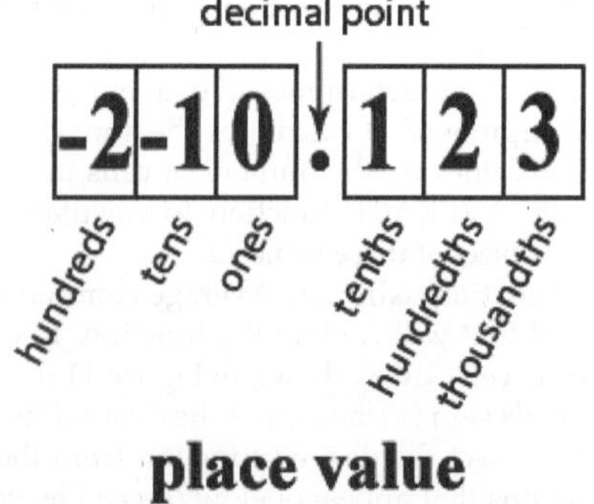

How to Determine Number-of-Digits

Excel has a number system to specify the place value in a ROUND function. The numbers in the image below show what "number-of-digits" to specify for the corresponding place values.

Rounding to shorten the decimal portion of a number

When rounding to a place value in the decimal range, use a positive number starting with 1 in the tenths position. The number-of-digits will equal the number of digits to the right of the decimal point in the rounded number (See Figure 11.15).

Example: =ROUND(1.6666,2) = 1.67

Rounding to an integer place value to simplify numbers

When rounding to the left of the decimal point, the number-of-digits to use is either zero (ones place value) or a negative number (See Figure 11.15).

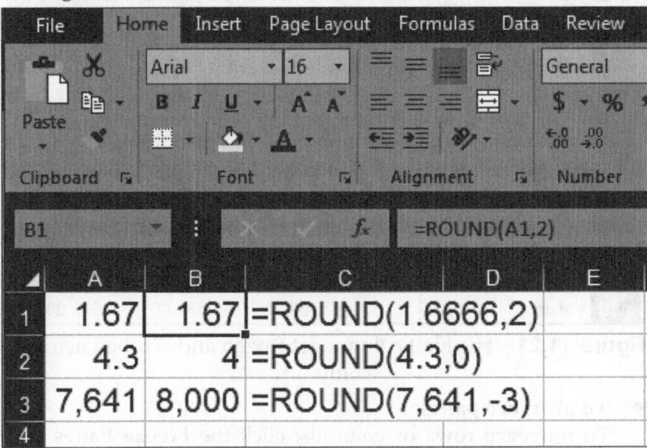

Figure 11.15 ROUND function

Example: =ROUND(4.3,0) = 4

HINT: When rounding to the left of the decimal point, the number-of-digits will always equal number of zeros that will exist in the number after it has been rounded. Example: =ROUND(7,641,-3) = 8,000.

11.2.2 Using the Insert Function

PMT()–The Excel PMT function is a financial function that returns the periodic payment for a loan. You can use the NPER function to figure out payments for a loan, given the loan amount, number of periods, and interest rate.

Syntax

```
=PMT (rate, nper, pv, [fv], [type])
```

To calculate a loan payment amount, given an interest rate, the loan term, and the loan amount, you can use the PMT function. The arguments required by the function are as follows:

- *Rate*–The interest rate per period. We divide the value in D9 by 12 since 12% represents annual interest, and we need the periodic interest.
- *nper*–the number of periods comes from cell D10; 60 monthly periods for a 5 year loan.
- *pv*–the loan amount comes from D8.
- *Fv*–Is the future value, or a cash balance you want to attain after the last payment is made. If Fv is omitted, it is assumed to be 0 (zero), that is, the future value of a loan is 0.
- *Type*–Is the number 0 (zero) or 1 and indicated when payments are due.

For this example, we want to find the payment for a 50,000 loan with a 12% interest rate, and a term of 60 months. To do this, we configure the PMT function as follows:

1. Select the cell.
2. Under the **Formulas** tab, click on the **Insert Function**. *Alternatively*, click on the **Insert Function** button on the center of the formula bar, i.e., *fx* or press Shift+F3 keys together. It will display the Insert Function Dialog box as shown in Figure 11.16.

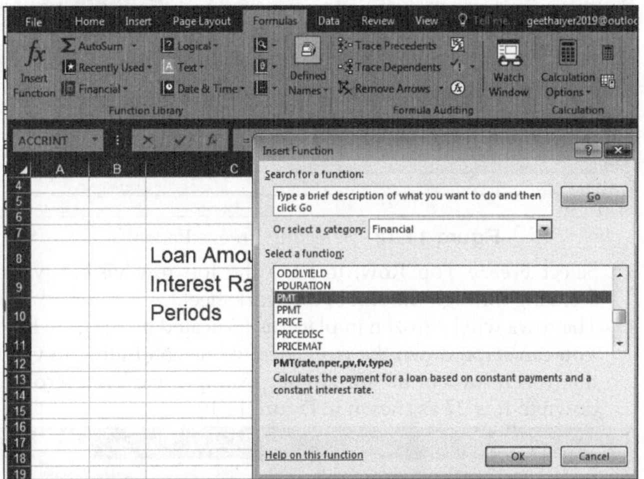

Figure 11.16 Insert Function dialog box

3. Select a Financial category from the select a category: drop-down list.
4. Click on PMT Function from the Select a function: list box.
5. Click OK. It will display a Function Arguments dialog box as shown in Figure 11.17, and the result applied in the selected cell.

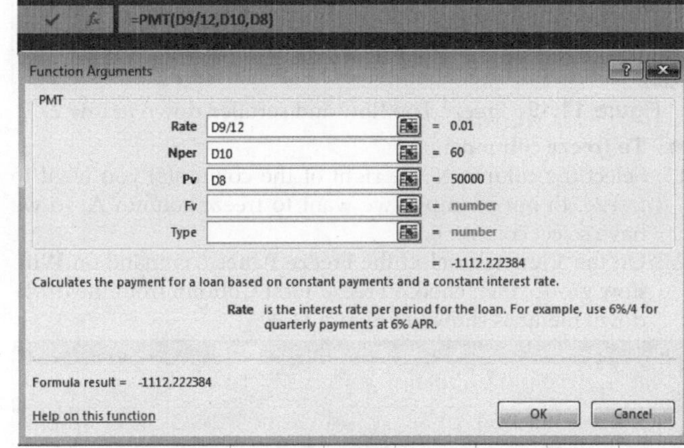

Figure 11.17 Insert Arguments dialog box

11.2.3 Freezing Rows and Columns

Whenever you are working with a lot of data, it can be difficult to compare information in the workbook. Fortunately, Excel includes several tools that make it easier to view content from different parts of the workbook at the same time, including the ability to freeze panes and split your worksheet.

➡ **To freeze rows:**

1. Select the row below the row(s) you want to freeze. In our example, we want to freeze rows 1 and 2, so we have select row 3.
2. On the **View** tab, select the **Freeze Panes** command on **Window** group, then choose **Freeze Panes** from the drop-down menu as shown in Figure 11.18.

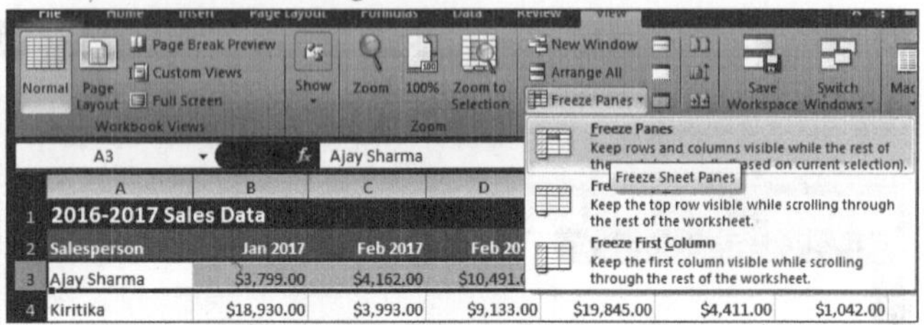

Figure 11.18 Selecting Freeze Panes

3. Select **Freeze Top Row**, to keep the top row visible while scrolling through the rest of the worksheet.
4. The rows will be frozen in place, as indicated by the gray line. You can scroll down the worksheet while continuing to view the frozen rows at the top. In our example, we have scrolled down to row 27 as shown in Figure 11.19.

	A	B	C	D	E
1	2016-2017 Sales Data				
2	Salesperson	Jan 2017	Feb 2017	Feb 2017	Feb 2017
24	Hena	$14,226.00	$2,651.00	$10,663.00	$15,453.00
25	Rajendran	$18,252.00	$11,534.00	$16,895.00	$4,554.00
26	Balaram	$8,548.00	$7,020.00	$11,442.00	$18,930.00
27	Sreeja	$9,945.00	$5,296.00	$6,821.00	$13,982.00
33					

Figure 11.19 Freeze Top Row and scrolled down to row 27

➡ **To freeze columns:**

1. Select the column to the right of the column(s) you want to freeze. In our example, we want to freeze column A, so we have select column B.
2. On the **View** tab, select the **Freeze Panes** command on **Window** group, then choose **Freeze First Column** from the drop-down menu as shown in Figure 11.20.

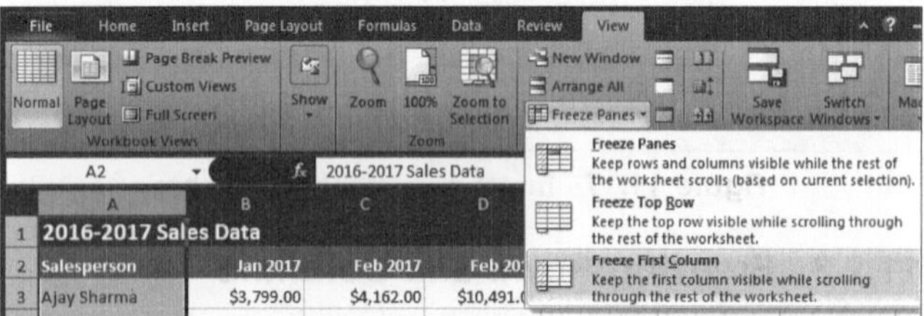

Figure 11.20 Selecting Freeze First column

3. The column will be frozen in place, as indicated by the gray line. You can scroll across the worksheet while continuing to view the frozen column on the left. In our example, we have scrolled across to column K as shown in Figure 11.21.

	A	K	L	M
1	2016-2017 Sal			
2	Salesperson	Oct 2017	Nov 2017	Dec 2017
3	Ajay Sharma	$8,690.00	$10,776.00	$16,904.00
4	Kiritika	$18,749.00	$1,144.00	$9,777.00
5	Ashok	$8,046.00	$12,686.00	$8,065.00
6	David	$20,114.00	$18,400.00	$18,373.00
7	Rahul	$10,733.00	$6,394.00	$6,272.00
8	Watson	$18,524.00	$6,063.00	$7,361.00
9	Robinson	$13,953.00	$17,950.00	$10,806.00
10	Varun	$15,275.00	$3,639.00	$12,801.00

Figure 11.21 The First column get frozen and scrolled across to column K

➡ **To unfreeze panes:**

1. To **unfreeze** rows or columns, click the **Freeze Panes** command, then select **Unfreeze Panes** from the drop-down menu.

11.3 GOAL SEEKING

Goal Seek is a part of a suite of commands sometimes called what-if analysis i.e. process of changing the values in cells to see how those changes affect the outcome of formulas on the worksheet. With Goal seek, you can specify the value you want in a formula to calculate, and then Excel 2016 changes the data in the formulas cell reference to tell you what values you need to achieve that goal.

For example, your business has a modest profit of 25,000. You have set yourself a new profit Goal of 35,000. At the moment, you are selling 1000 items at 25 each. Assume that you will still sell 1000 items. To hit your new profit of 35,000 by how much do you have to raise your prices?

- In our example, we have create **Current sales** and **Future sales** of item sold. We will be changing the Future Sales with Goal Seek. But for now, enter the same values for both sections. The formula to enter for B4 is:

  = B2* B3

  And the formula to enter for E4 is:

  = E2* E3

  The current price per item is Rs 25. We want to change this with Goal Seek, because our prices will be going up to hit our new profits of Rs 35,000.

➡ **To use the goal seek feature:**

1. Under the **Data** tab, in the **Forecast** group, click arrow next to **What-If Analysis** and then click on the **Goal Seek...** to display the **Goal Seek** dialog box (Figure 11.22).

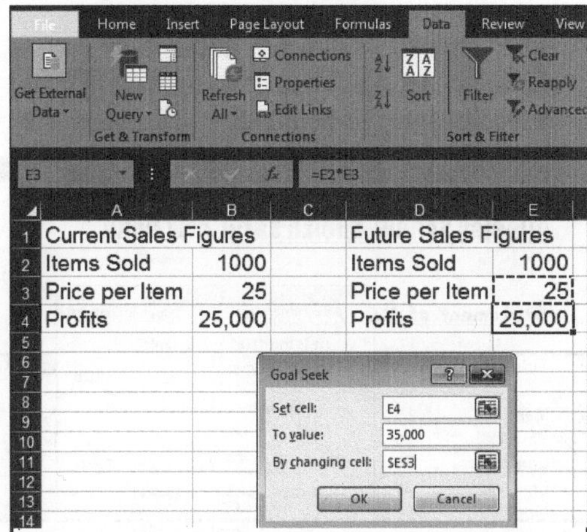

Figure 11.22 Goal Seek dialog box

2. In Set cell: box, enter the reference for the cell (i.e. E4) that contains the formula.
3. In To value: box, type the new value we want to our new profit to be. For example, type 35,000.
4. In By changing cell: box, enter the reference for the cell whose value you want to adjust. We are not sure of, this was the price each item needs to be increased by. This was coming from cell E3 on the spreadsheet.
5. Enter E3 in the **By Changing cell** box. Your Goal Seek dialog box as shown in Figure 11.22.
6. Click OK button. The new price per item is 35 and Excel has also changed the Profits cell to 35,000 as shown in Figure 11.23.

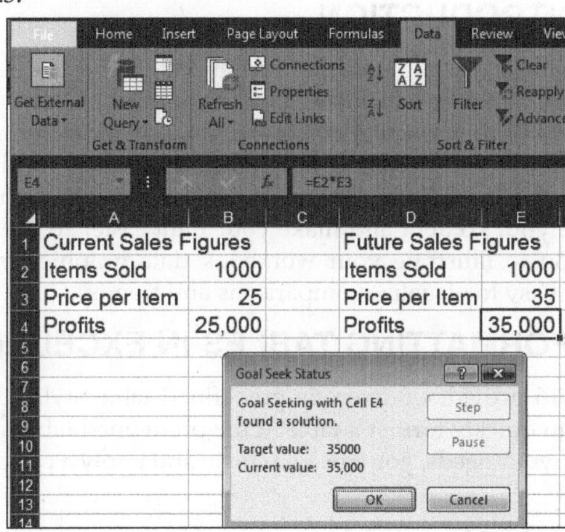

Figure 11.23 Goal seek status dialog box

CHAPTER 12

Tables and Charts in Excel 2016

12.1 INTRODUCTION

Excel includes several tools and predefined table styles, allowing you to create tables quickly and easily. Once you have entered information into your worksheet, you may want to format your data as a table. Just like regular formatting, tables can improve the look and feel of your workbook, and they will also help you organize your content and make your data easier to use. Charts allow you to illustrate your workbook data graphically, which makes it easy to visualize comparisons and trends.

12.2 FORMATTING TABLES IN EXCEL 2016

Excel 2016 provides numerous predefined table styles that you can use to quickly format a table. If the predefined table styles do not meet your needs, you can also create and apply a custom table style.

12.2.1 Create a Table

Excel can also create an Excel table from an existing cell range as long as the range has no blank rows and columns within the data and there is no extraneous data in cells immediately below or next to the list.

➡ **To create a table:**

1. Select the data range you want to make into an Excel table as shown in Figure 12.1.

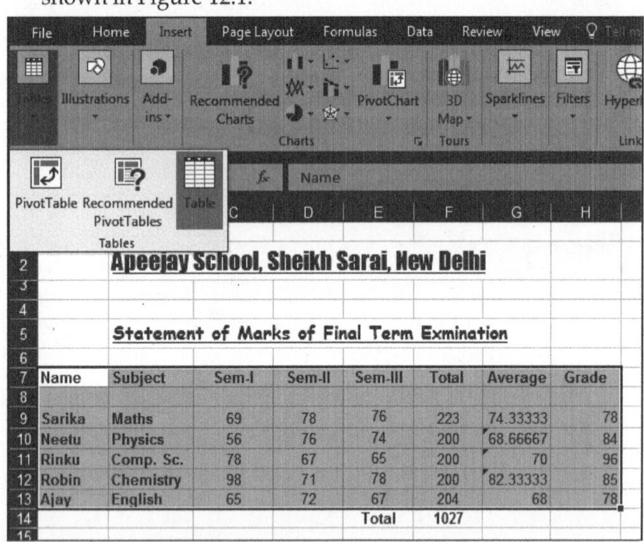

Figure 12.1 Select the data range

2. Click **Insert** tab and select **Table** command in the **Tables** group.
3. The **Create Table** dialog box appears as shown in Figure 12.2.
4. The highlighted cell reference appears in the list box.

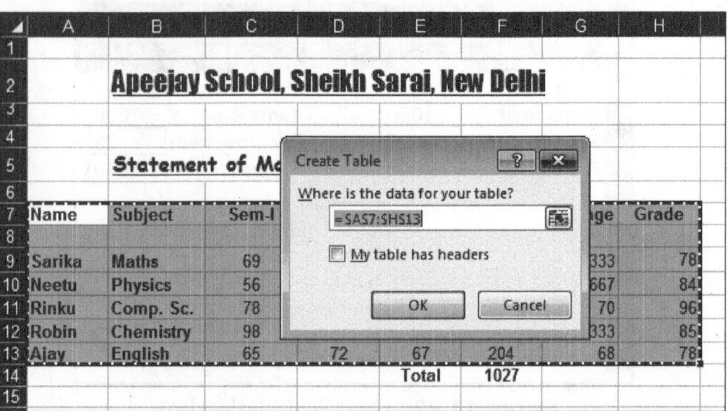

Figure 12.2 Create Table dialog box

5. Select the **My table has headers** check box, and then click OK.
6. The table will be created with the default style as shown in Figure 12.3.

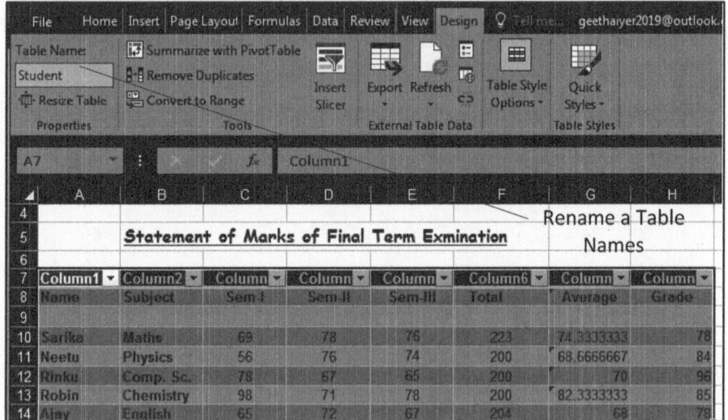

Figure 12.3 The Table will be created

☞ *Change the default name ("Table1) to something that is more relevant to the content.*

12.2.2 Import a List

You can also add data to an Excel worksheet from a word table by using Import External Data feature.

➡ **To import a list**

1. Select a cell to import data list in Excel.
2. Click the **Data** tab from **Get & Transform** group, click **Get External Data** drop-down list. Choose **From Text** command.
3. The **Import Text file** dialog box appears as shown in Figure 12.4, select the text file, and then click **Import**.
4. The **Text Import Wizard** step 1 of 3 dialog box appears as shown in Figure 12.5, select the desired setting in the Step of 1 of 3 wizard dialog box and click **Finish** button.

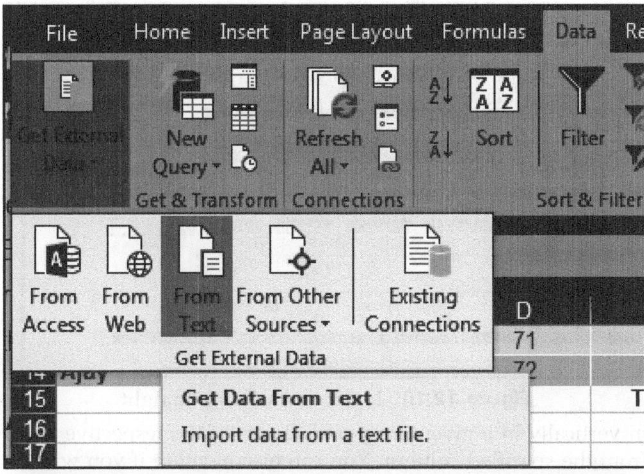

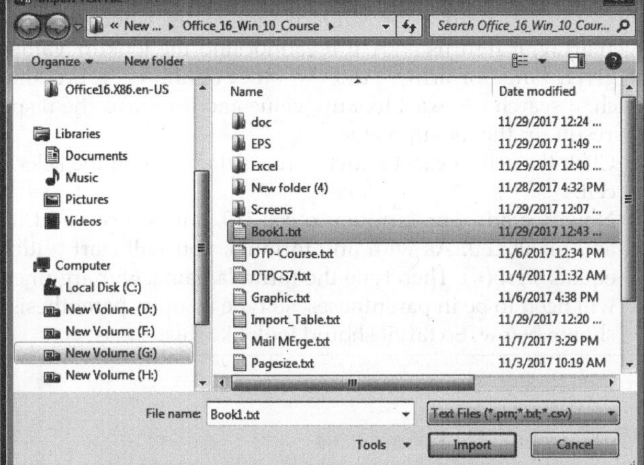

Figure 12.4 Import Text file dialog box

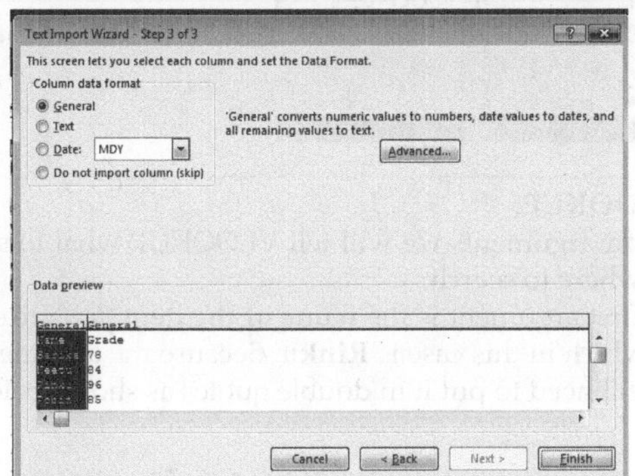

Figure 12.5 Text Import wizard dialog box

In the Step 1 of 3 first page of the **Text Import Wizard**, verify that **Delimited** is selected, and then select the table rows you want in the import has **Start import at row:** spinner box.

Click the check box **My data has headers**.

Click **Next >** button.

In the Step 2 of 3 first page of the **Text Import Wizard**, verify that **Delimiter** is selected, and then click the **Tab** check box by default.

In the Step 3 of 3 if you want to identify data formats for individual columns, click the column in the **Data preview** area, and then use the options in the **Column data format** section of the wizard to set options for the column.

Click **Finish**.

5. Again **Import Data** dialog box appears as shown in Figure 12.6.

Figure 12.6 Import Data dialog box

6. Click **Existing worksheet:** radio and then select the range.
7. Click OK to place the data in the current worksheet, at the location you initially selected.

12.2.3 Add Totals to Table

1. Select the table **Table Tools** contextual tab appears, click **Design** tab, then check the box for the **Total Row**, to add that row at the end of the table as shown in Figure 12.7.

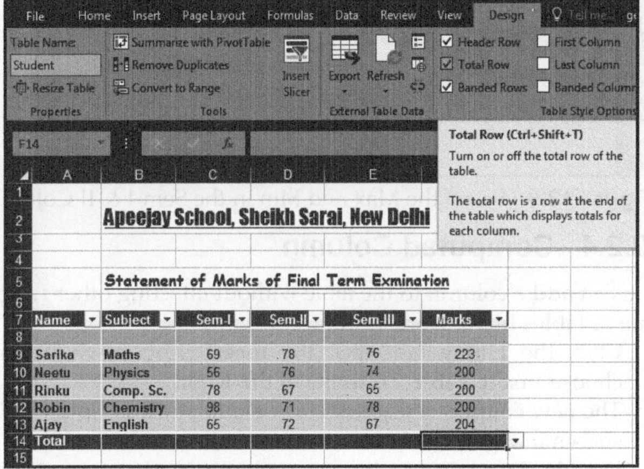

Figure 12.7 Select Table Row in the Design tab

2. Select the "**Marks**" column cell on the **Total Row**, click its arrow button and choose a function, e.g. choose **Sum** as shown in Figure 12.8.

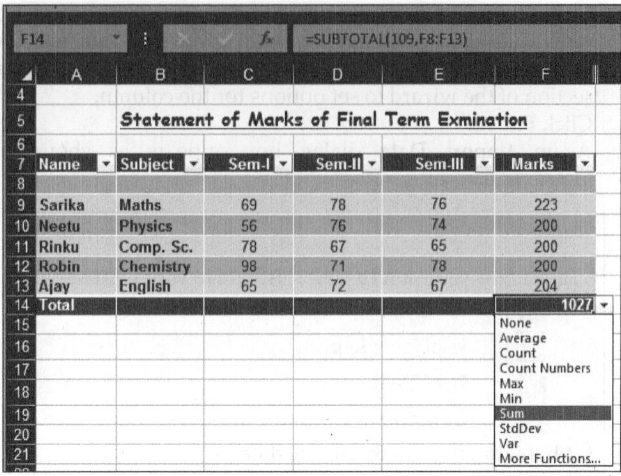

Figure 12.8 Select the function from the Marks column

☞ *The functions that you choose are entered into the formula as numbered sub-functions of the Subtotal function such as Average, Count numbers, Count, Max, Min, Std, Dev, Sum and Variance.*

3. The sum function for a column with numerical values, such as the "Marks" column to see the total marks.
4. You can use functions, such as **Max** and **Min** (sub-function) to show the range of values in a column e.g. to display the smallest and largest values in **Sem-II** and **III** column as shown in Figure 12.9.

	A	B	C	D	E	F
5		Statement of Marks of Final Term Exmination				
7	Name	Subject	Sem-I	Sem-II	Sem-III	Marks
9	Sarika	Maths	69	78	76	223
10	Neetu	Physics	56	76	74	200
11	Rinku	Comp. Sc.	78	67	65	200
12	Robin	Chemistry	98	71	78	200
13	Ajay	English	65	72	67	204
14	Total			67	78	1027

None / Average / Count / Count Numbers / Max / Min / Sum / StdDev / Var / More Functions...

Figure 12.9 Select the Max and Min in the Sem-I & II Column

12.2.4 Computed Column

You can add a column to the table without affecting other ranges, data or tables in the worksheet.

1. Click the **Home** tab, click the **Insert** drop-down list and choose **Insert Table Columns to the Right**.
2. The new column is inserted, the default named "Column1" as shown in Figure 12.10.
3. Double-click to select the new column header, type desired name you want to add a new column name.

12.2.5 Table Lookup

V in VLOOKUP stands for Vertical. It looks for the lookup_value

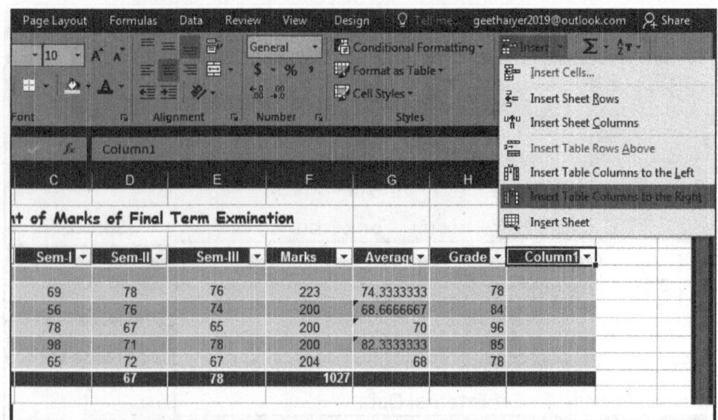

Figure 12.10 Insert new column to right

in vertically in a given array and results in the respective value from the specified column. You can also mention if you want to look for exact match.

Exact match returns the value if the lookup value exists in a given array, it returns #NA if it cannot find the lookup_value in the given range or array. And the other option is Approximate match, it search for exact lookup_value and it returns the respective result for the lookup value.

1. Click the cell to exact match returns the value in the selected cell.
2. Now, we add our formula to cell I10, but you can add it to any blank cell. As with any formula, you will start with an equals sign (=). Then type the formula name. Our arguments will need to be in parentheses, so type an open parenthesis as shown below. So far, it should look like this:

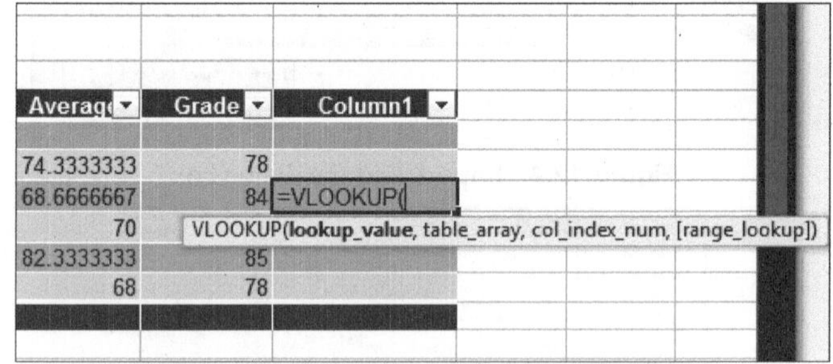

=VLOOKUP(

3. To add arguments we will tell VLOOKUP what to search for and where to search.
4. The first argument is the **name of the item** you are searching for, which in this case is **Rinku**. Because the argument is text, we will need to put it in double quotes as shown below:

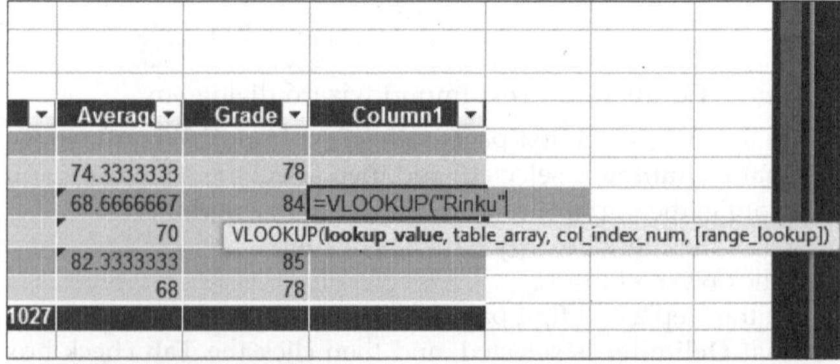

=VLOOKUP("Rinku"

5. The second argument is the cell range that contains the data. In this example, our data is in A9:F13. As with any function, you will need to use a comma to separate each argument as shown below:

☞ *It's important to know that VLOOKUP will always search the first column in this range. In this example, it will search column A for "Rinku". In some cases, you may need to move the columns around so the first column contains the correct data.*

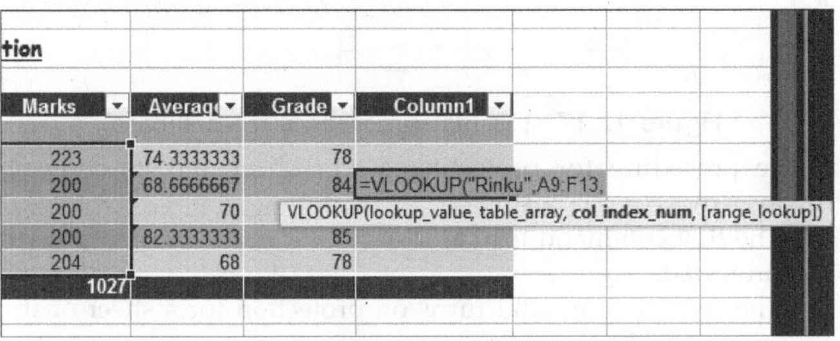

=VLOOKUP("Rinku", A9:F13,

6. The third argument is the column index number. The first column in the range is 1, the second column is 2, etc. In this case, we are trying to find the Marks are contained in the sixth column. This means our third argument will be 6: =VLOOKUP("Rinku", A9:F13, 6
7. The fourth argument tells VLOOKUP whether to look for approximate matches, and it can be either TRUE or FALSE. If it is TRUE, it will look for approximate matches. Because we are only looking for exact matches, the fourth argument should be FALSE. This is our last argument, and close the parentheses as shown below:

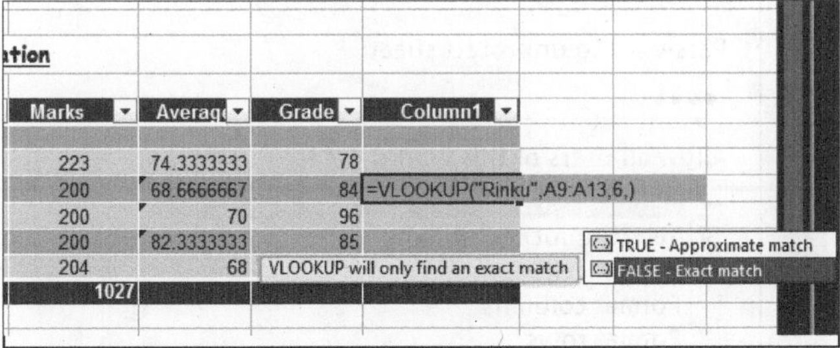

=VLOOKUP("Rinku", A9:F13, 6, FALSE)

When you press Enter, it should give you the answer, which is 200 Marks as shown in Figure 12.11.

Name	Subject	Sem-I	Sem-II	Sem-III	Marks	Average	Column1
Sarika	Maths	69	78	76	223	74.3333333	
Neetu	Physics	56	76	74	200	68.6666667	200
Rinku	Comp. Sc.	78	67	65	200	70	
Robin	Chemistry	98	71	78	200	82.3333333	
Ajay	English	65	72	67	204	68	
Total			67	78	1027		

Figure 12.11 The above argument for exact match given in the cell

12.2.6 Manage Data using Access

If you have large amounts of data, access is better for managing data; helping you keep it organized, easy to search data that may require more facilities in Access 2016.

1. Select **Access** from the start menu and you will be **Recent** backstage view of database template as shown in Figure 12.12.
2. In the **New** backstage view, select the category, such as **Personal**, to display a list of related template available on the Internet as shown in Figure 12.13.
3. Select the desired template tile to view a description of what that template have been used for. For example, here we select **Home Inventory**.

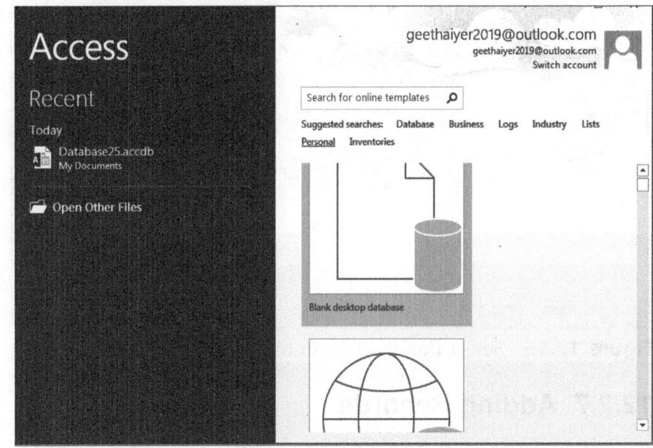

Figure 12.12 Access Recent backstage view

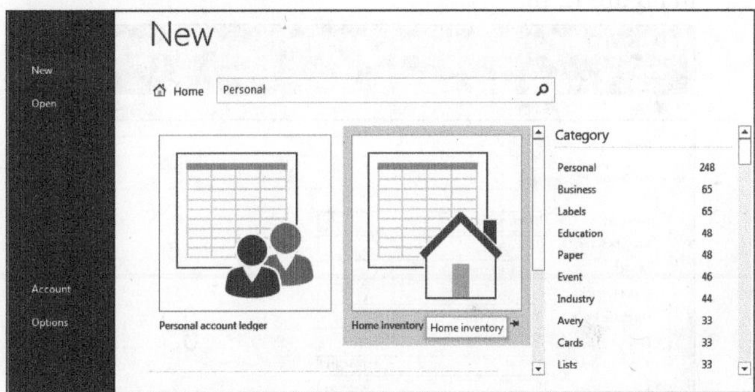

Figure 12.13 Selecting template from New backstage view

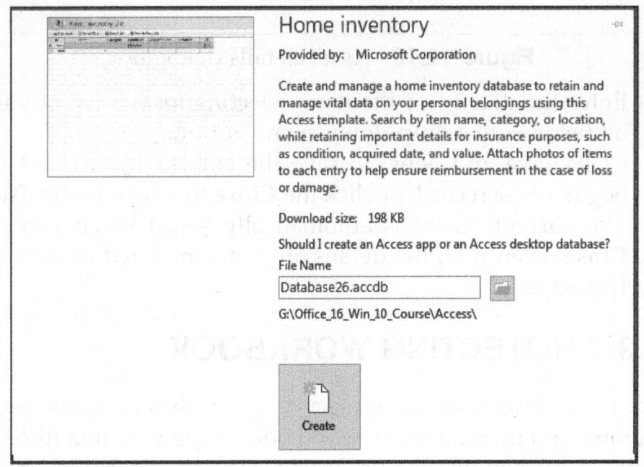

Figure 12.14 Select Create button to download the template

4. Select **Create** button to download that template which you want to use, specify a file name and select the desired location to save the template as shown in Figure 12.14.
5. Access prepares the template for use as a new database, but the database is opened with active content disabled.
6. A blank template appears, click **Enable Content** to enable the VBA macros in the template and make the database to ready for updating as shown in Figure 12.15.

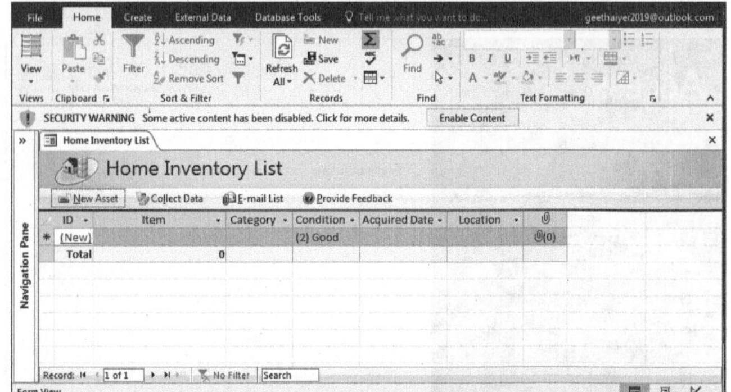

Figure 12.15 Select Enable content to update the blank template

12.2.7 Adding Records

1. Click the **New Asset** button to open the **Asset Details** dialog box, in which you can add a record to the database as shown in Figure 12.16.

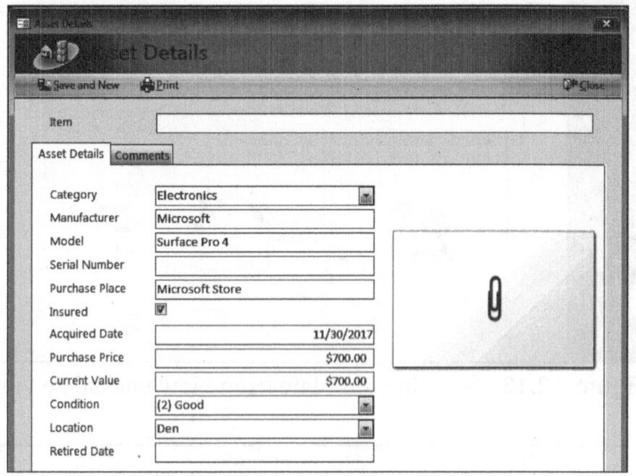

Figure 12.16 Asset Details dialog box

2. Enter the details for the item, selecting form a list of values on fields with a drop-down arrow button.
3. Click **Save and New**, to save the current record and then begin a new record, or click the **Close** to return to the list.
4. The current record is automatically saved when you click **Close**, even if all the details are not completed as shown in Figure 12.17.

12.3 PROTECTING WORKBOOK

With Excel 2016, you can protect cells, graphical objects, sheets, windows and even an entire workbook. To prevent unauthorized people from changing the protection status or the display of hidden information, you can also use the password facility.

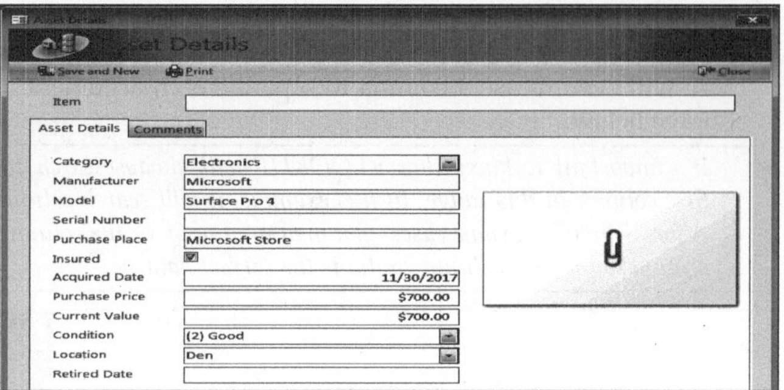

Figure 12.17 Details of records in the database

The procedure for protecting a worksheet and its contents involves two commands:

- The first command formats the cells or objects that you want protected.
- The second command turns on protection for a sheet or the entire workbook.

12.3.1 Protecting and Unprotecting Sheets

➡ **To turn on protection for a sheet:**

1. Under **Review** Tab, click **Changes** group and then click **Protect Sheet**. It will display **Protect Sheet** dialog box (Figure 12.18).
2. Here, In All<u>o</u>w all user of this worksheet to: list box, select the elements that you want users to be able to change.

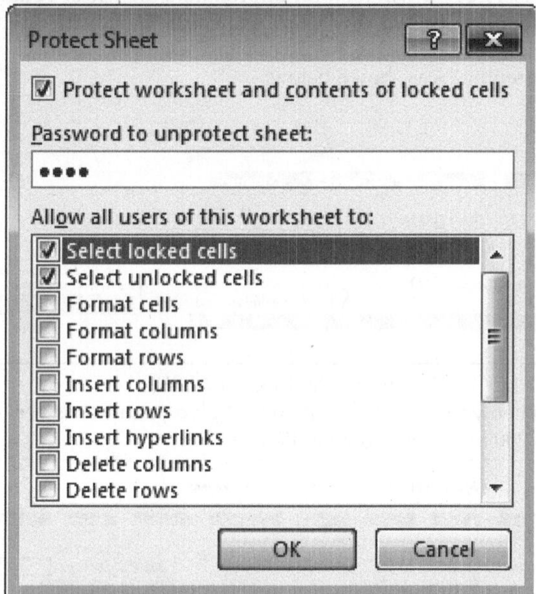

Figure 12.18 Protect Sheet dialog box

3. If you prefer, enter a password in the **Password to unprotect sheet:** text box.
4. **Confirm password** dialog box appears again type password to Re-enter password to proceed list box.
5. Click OK.

➡ **To unprotect the sheet:**

1. Under **Review** Tab, click **Changes** group and then click **Unprotect Sheet**. It will display **Unprotect Sheet** dialog box.

2. In this dialog box as shown in Figure 12.19, type the password, you have given to unprotect the sheet and then click OK.

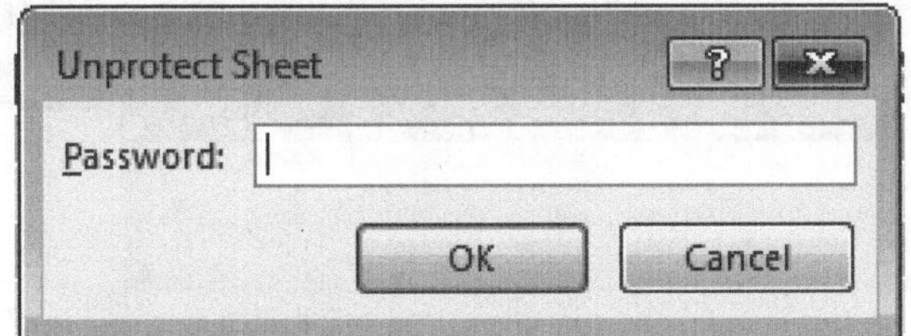

Figure 12.19 Unprotect Sheet dialog box

- **To protect the workbook:**

1. Under **Review** Tab, click **Changes** group and then click arrow next to **Protect Workbook**. It will display **Protect Structure and Windows** dialog box (Figure 12.20).

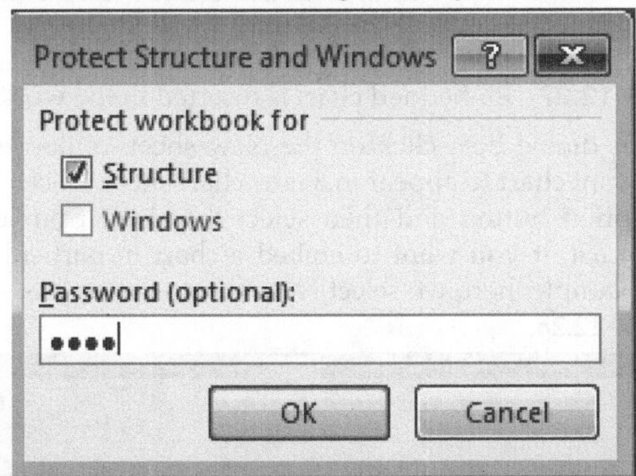

Figure 12.20 Protect Structure and Windows

2. In this dialog box, click on the **S**tructure check box if you want to protect the structure.
   Click on **W**indows check box if you want to keep workbook windows in the same size and position each time you open the workbook.
3. If you prefer, enter a password in the **P**assword (optional): text box.
4. Click OK.

12.3.2 Group of Sheets in a Workbook

Worksheets with a lot of content can sometimes feel overwhelming and even become difficult to read. Fortunately, Excel can organize data into groups, allowing you to easily show and hide different sections of your worksheet.

- **To group rows or columns:**

1. Select the rows or columns you want to group. In this example, we have selected columns E, F, and G as shown in Figure 12.21.
2. Click **Data** tab on the Ribbon on **Outline** group, then click the **Group** command as shown in Figure 12.21.
3. The selected rows or columns will be grouped. In our example, columns E, F, and G are grouped as shown in Figure 12.22.

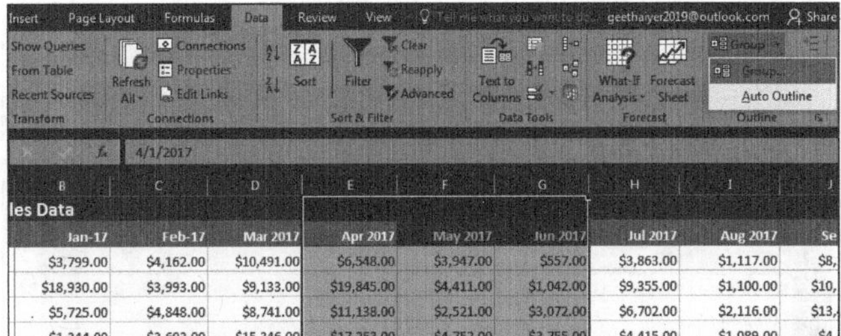

Jan-17	Feb-17	Mar 2017	Apr 2017	May 2017	Jun 2017	Jul 2017	Aug 2017
$3,799.00	$4,162.00	$10,491.00	$6,548.00	$3,947.00	$557.00	$3,863.00	$1,117.00
$18,930.00	$3,993.00	$9,133.00	$19,845.00	$4,411.00	$1,042.00	$9,355.00	$1,100.00
$5,725.00	$4,848.00	$8,741.00	$11,138.00	$2,521.00	$3,072.00	$6,702.00	$2,116.00
$1,344.00	$3,693.00	$15,346.00	$17,253.00	$4,752.00	$3,755.00	$4,415.00	$1,089.00

Figure 12.21 Select the columns to be group

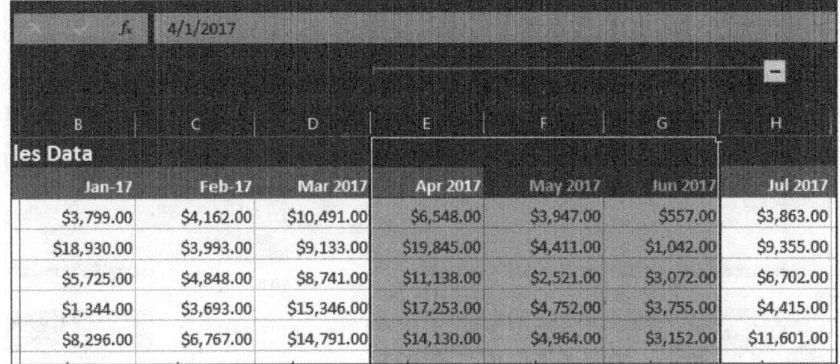

Jan-17	Feb-17	Mar 2017	Apr 2017	May 2017	Jun 2017	Jul 2017
$3,799.00	$4,162.00	$10,491.00	$6,548.00	$3,947.00	$557.00	$3,863.00
$18,930.00	$3,993.00	$9,133.00	$19,845.00	$4,411.00	$1,042.00	$9,355.00
$5,725.00	$4,848.00	$8,741.00	$11,138.00	$2,521.00	$3,072.00	$6,702.00
$1,344.00	$3,693.00	$15,346.00	$17,253.00	$4,752.00	$3,755.00	$4,415.00
$8,296.00	$6,767.00	$14,791.00	$14,130.00	$4,964.00	$3,152.00	$11,601.00

Figure 12.22 The columns get grouped

4. To ungroup data, select the grouped rows or columns, then click the **Ungroup** command.

➡ **To hide and show groups:**

1. To hide a group, click the minus sign, also known as the **Hide Detail** button as shown in Figure 12.22.
2. The group will be hidden. To show a hidden group, click the plus sign, also known as the **Show Detail** button as shown in Figure 12.23.

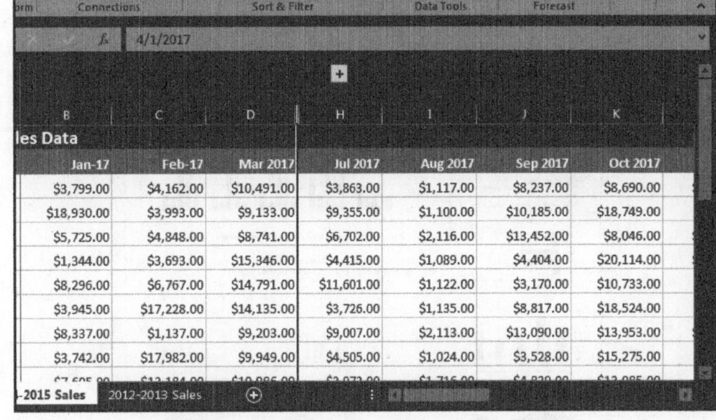

Jan-17	Feb-17	Mar 2017	Jul 2017	Aug 2017	Sep 2017	Oct 2017
$3,799.00	$4,162.00	$10,491.00	$3,863.00	$1,117.00	$8,237.00	$8,690.00
$18,930.00	$3,993.00	$9,133.00	$9,355.00	$1,100.00	$10,185.00	$18,749.00
$5,725.00	$4,848.00	$8,741.00	$6,702.00	$2,116.00	$13,452.00	$8,046.00
$1,344.00	$3,693.00	$15,346.00	$4,415.00	$1,089.00	$4,404.00	$20,114.00
$8,296.00	$6,767.00	$14,791.00	$11,601.00	$1,122.00	$3,170.00	$10,733.00
$3,945.00	$17,228.00	$14,135.00	$3,726.00	$1,135.00	$8,817.00	$18,524.00
$8,337.00	$1,137.00	$9,203.00	$9,007.00	$2,113.00	$13,090.00	$13,953.00
$3,742.00	$17,982.00	$9,949.00	$4,505.00	$1,024.00	$3,528.00	$15,275.00

Figure 12.23 The columns get hide

12.4 CREATING A CHART

➡ **To create a chart:**

1. Select the cells of which you want to create a chart, including the column titles and row labels. These cells will be the source data for the chart. In our example, we have select cells A1:F6 as shown in Figure 12.24.
2. From the **Insert** tab, click the desired **Chart** command. Alternatively, click **Recommended Chart** command as shown in Figure 12.25.

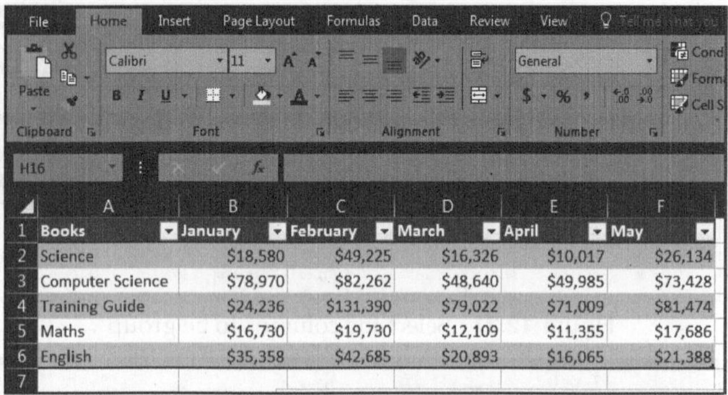

	A	B	C	D	E	F
1	Books	January	February	March	April	May
2	Science	$18,580	$49,225	$16,326	$10,017	$26,134
3	Computer Science	$78,970	$82,262	$48,640	$49,985	$73,428
4	Training Guide	$24,236	$131,390	$79,022	$71,009	$81,474
5	Maths	$16,730	$19,730	$12,109	$11,355	$17,686
6	English	$35,358	$42,685	$20,893	$16,065	$21,388

Figure 12.24 Select the data to create a chart

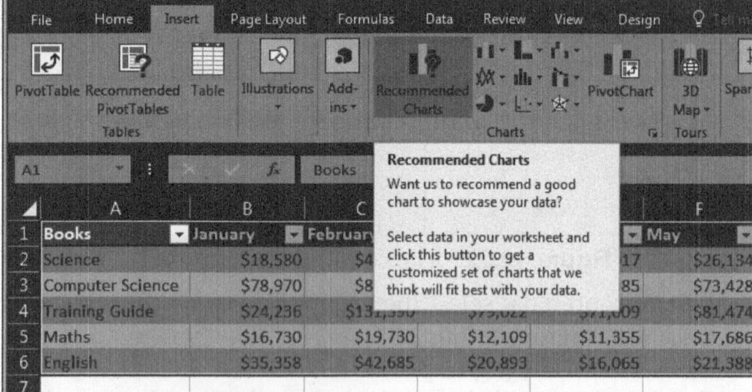

Figure 12.25 Selecting Recommended Chart

The **Insert Chart** dialog box appears with Recommended Charts tab available. In our example, we have selected the **Clustered Column** chart type as shown in Figure 12.26.

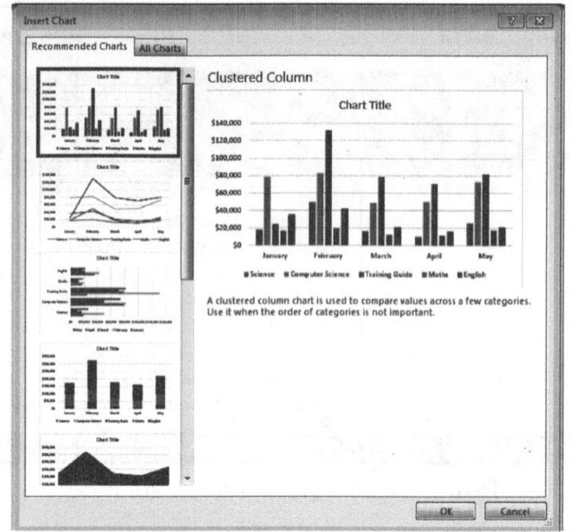

Figure 12.26 Insert Chart dialog box with recommended charts tab

4. The selected embedded chart inserted into the worksheet as shown in Figure 12.27.

12.4.1 Changing Location of a Chart

➡ **To change the location of a chart**

1. Click the embedded chart or the chart sheet whichever you want to move.
2. Under the **Design** tab, in **Location** group, click **Move Chart**. A **Move Chart** dialog box appears as seen in Figure 12.28.

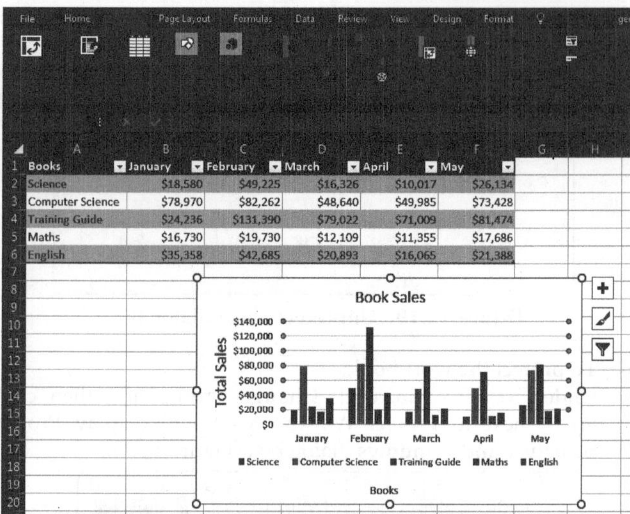

Figure 12.27 Embedded chart is inserted in the worksheet

3. In this dialog box, click on the New sheet: option button, if you want chart to appear in a new chart sheet. Click on Object in: option button and then select the sheet from the drop down list, if you want to embed a chart in particular sheet. For example, here we select New sheet of chart1 as shown in Figure 12.28.

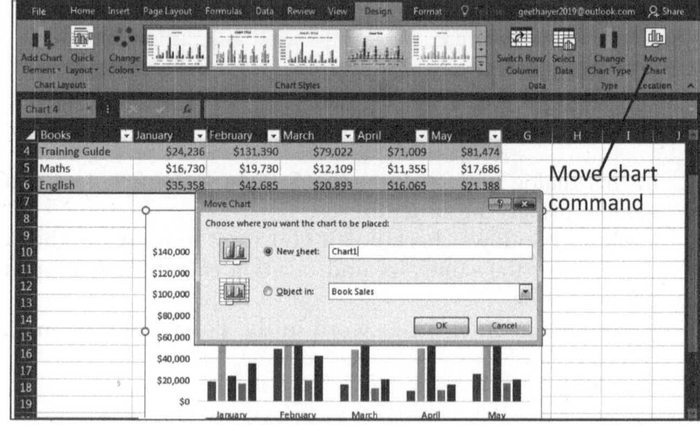

Figure 12.28 Move Chart dialog box

12.4.2 Sizing and Positioning a Chart

To change the size or proportion of chart, click the black handles along the borders (the pointer changes to a double-headed arrow). Now drag it until the chart is sized the way you want.

- To change the size of the chart without changing its proportions (that is the ratio of height to width) hold down the Shift key as you drag a corner handle.
- To align a chart with cell edges, hold down Alt key as you drag across where you want to set the chart.

In order to delete an embedded chart, just select the chart and press Del key.

12.4.3 Changing the Type of Chart

Excel 2016 offers you eleven different chart types and within each of these general types, you can select any sub-types. The easiest way to create chart is to select a chart type and sub-type you want. Thereafter, you may customize this chart according to your requirement.

➡ **To change the chart type:**

1. Under the **Design** tab, in **Type** group, click **Change Chart Type** command. A **Change Chart** dialog box showing different chart types appear as shown in Figure 12.29.

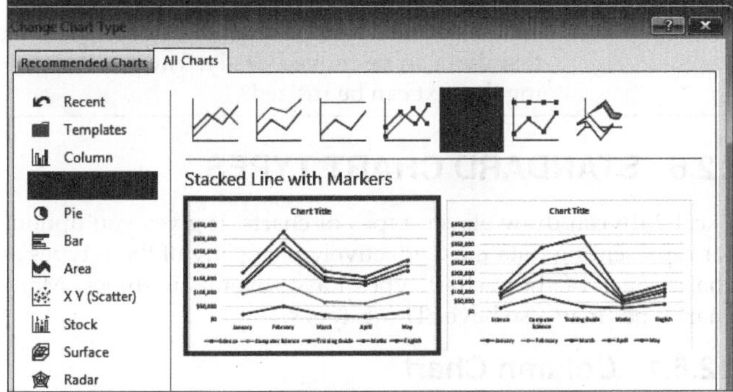

Figure 12.29 Change Chart Type dialog box

2. The **Change Chart Type** dialog box will appears as shown in Figure 12.30. Select a new chart type and layout, then click OK. In our example, we have selected Line chart.
3. Select a sub-type Line chart from the top list.
4. Click OK button. The selected chart type will appear. In our example, the line chart makes it easier to see trends in sales data over time.

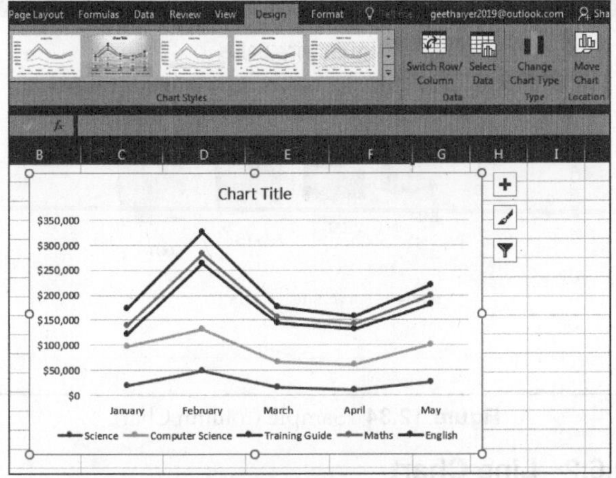

Figure 12.30 The selected Line chart appears

12.4.4 Changing Data Source

You can add data to an existing chart. You can even add new data series or data points to existing series or change the range of data used by a chart.

➡ **To change data source:**

1. Under the **Design** tab, in **Data** group, click **Select Data** command. Select **Data Source** dialog box appears as shown in Figure 12.31.
2. In this dialog box, make the following changes according to your need.

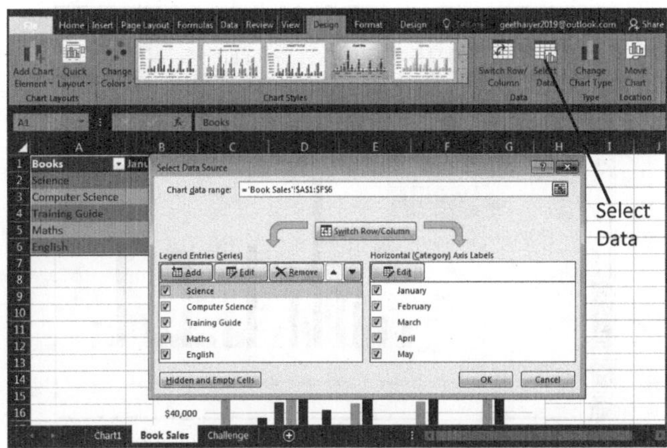

Figure 12.31 Data Source dialog box

Chart data range: This box displays the range of data that is plotted in the chart. If you want to change the range, click on the collapse Dialog button at the right end of this box. It will temporarily minimizes. Now select the new range and click this button again after you select the range.

Switch Row/Column: It switches the rows of worksheet from rows to the columns and vice versa.

Legend Entries (Series): It displays existing data series names.

Add: Click to add a new data series to the chart.

Edit: If you want to edit the existing range, click in this button to make changes to the data series

Remove: Click to remove the data series that you select in the Legend Entries (Series) box from the chart.

Horizontal (Categories) Axis Labels: Lists existing horizontal (category) axis labels.

Edit: Click to modify the horizontal (category) labels.

3. After making changes, click OK.

12.4.5 Inserting Chart Elements

Excel allows you to add chart elements such as Chart titles, legends, and data labels to make your chart easier to read. To add chart elements, click the Add Chart Element command on the Design tab, and choose the desired elements from the drop-down menu.

➡ **To insert chart elements:**

1. Activate the Chart to which you want to add a title.
2. To edit chart element, simple double click a **chart title** placeholder and being typing. Or
3. Click **Add Chart Elements** drop-down arrow in the **Chart Layouts** group. A list of elements appears, highlight the **Chart Title** option. A sub-menu appears as shown in Figure 12.32.
4. Click the **Centered Overlay** option to position the title in the center.

➡ **To Data Labels:**

1. Click **Add Chart Elements** drop-down arrow in the **Chart Layouts** group. A list of elements appears, highlight the **Data Labels** option. A sub-menu appears as shown in Figure 12.33. Or Click the shortcuts buttons place near chart as shown in Figure 12.33.

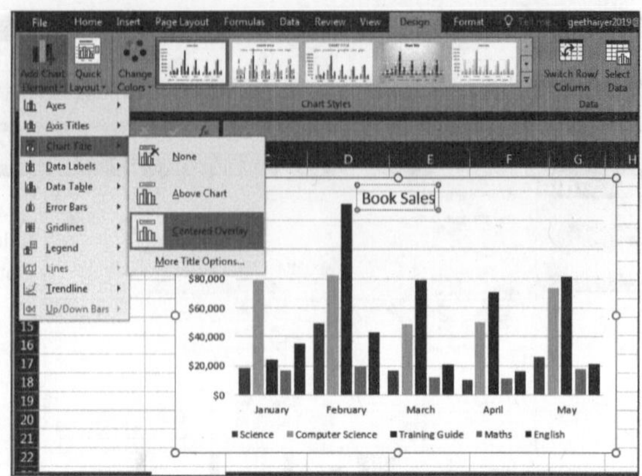

Figure 12.32 Inserting Chart Title element

2. Click the **Data Labels** check mark. Highlight Data Labels. A sub menu appears select the desired option from the list. In our example, we have select Inside base.
3. Similarly, you can other option such as Gridlines and Legends in the chart.

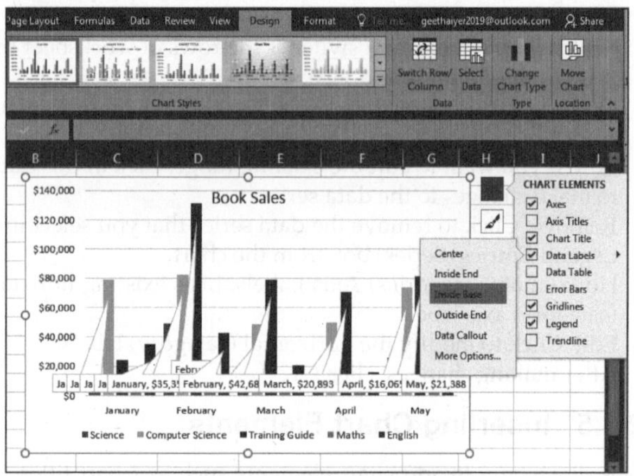

Figure 12.33 Add Data Labels

12.5 CHART TERMINOLOGIES

An Excel 2016 chart may contain objects that you may like to modify individually. Figure 12.1 shows some of these objects. Table 13.1 describes each object. Note that if you move mouse pointer over an object in a chart, a tip appears to give the description of the chart object.

Table 12.1 Parts of an Excel 2016 Chart

Object	**Description**
Axis (*x-axis* and *y-axis*)	The horizontal or x-axis along the bottom of charts is also referred to as *category* axis. The vertical or y-axis against which data points are measured is also referred to as *value* axis. This axis contains the scale against which data is plotted.
Data point	A single piece of data.
Data series	A collection of data points.
Legend	The name of each data series is used as a legend title.
Marker	An object that represents a data point in a chart such as bar, pie and symbols. Markers that belong to the same data series appear in the same shape, symbol and colour.
Plot area	The Rectangular area bounded by the two axes.
Text	Text associated with data points or free-floating text that can be moved easily. The box containing the text can be resized.

(Contd...)

12.6 STANDARD CHART TYPES

Excel 2016 can draw eleven types of charts. It gives you options for representing data most effectively using any of these types of charts. Each of these chart types have several sub-types. Many chart types may also have 3D sub-types.

12.6.1 Column Chart

A Column Chart typically displays the categories along the horizontal (category) axis and values along the vertical (value) axis. A sample *column chart* is shown in Figure 12.34. A column chart has the following sub-types – Clustered Column. Stacked Column. 100% Stacked Column. 3-D Clustered Column. 3-D Stacked Column. 3-D 100% Stacked Column. 3-D Column.

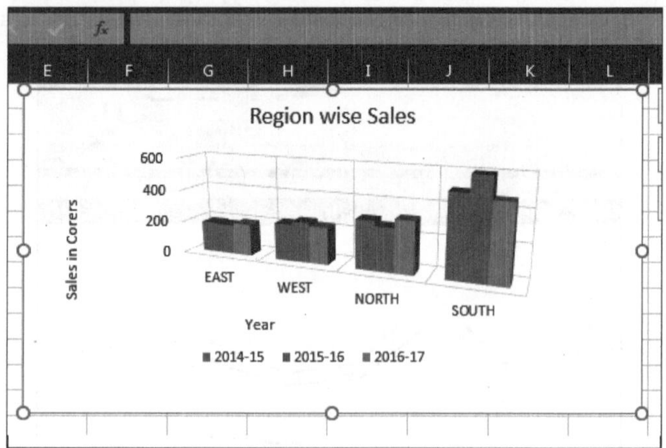

Figure 12.34 Sample Column Chart

12.6.2 Line Chart

A line chart compares trends over a period of time. Therefore, they are ideal for showing trends in data at equal intervals, such as months, quarters or years. A sample *line chart* is shown in Figure 12.35.

12.6.3 Bar Chart

Bar Charts illustrate comparisons among individual items. In a Bar Chart, the categories are organized along the vertical axis and the values are organized along the horizontal axis. A sample *bar chart* is shown in Figure 12.36. A Bar Chart has the following sub-types - Clustered Bar Stacked Bar 100% Stacked Bar 3-D Clustered Bar 3-D Stacked Bar 3-D 100% Stacked Bar.

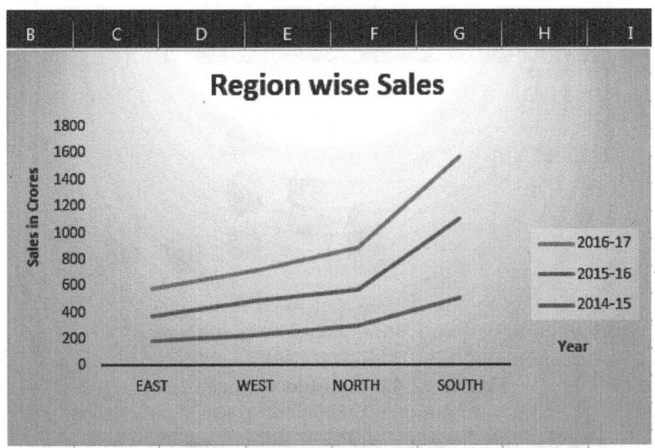

Figure 12.35 Sample Line Chart

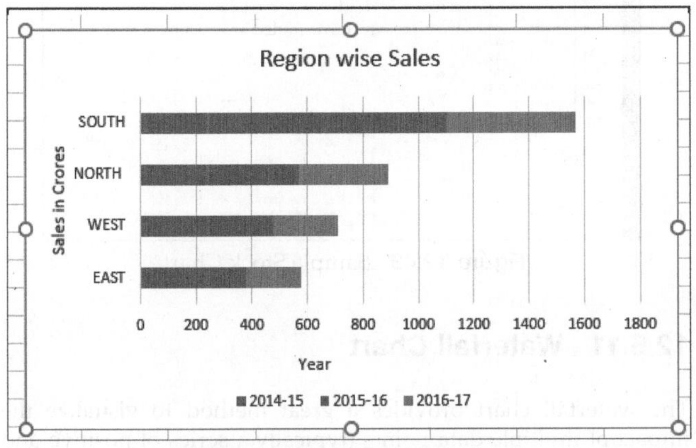

Figure 12.36 Sample Bar Chart

12.6.4 Pie Chart

Pie charts show the size of items in one data series, proportional to the sum of the items. The data points in a pie chart are shown as a percentage of the whole pie. To create a Pie Chart, arrange the data in one column or row on the worksheet. A sample *pie chart* is shown in Figure 12.37. A Pie Chart has the following sub-types -Pie 3-D Pie, Pie of Pie, and Bar of Pie.

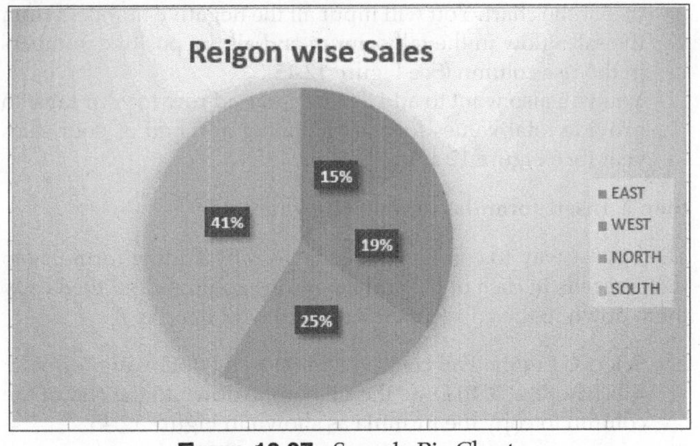

Figure 12.37 Sample Pie Chart

12.6.5 XY (Scatter) Chart

XY (Scatter) charts are typically used for showing and comparing numeric values, like scientific, statistical, and engineering data. A Scatter chart has two Value Axes – Horizontal (x) Value Axis Vertical (y) Value Axis. It combines x and y values into single data points and displays them in irregular intervals, or clusters. To create a Scatter chart, arrange the data in columns and rows on the worksheet. Place the x values in one row or column, and then enter the corresponding y values in the adjacent rows or columns. A sample *XY (scatter)* chart is shown in Figure 12.38. For example, there is a relationship between X (a person's salary) and Y (his/her car price).

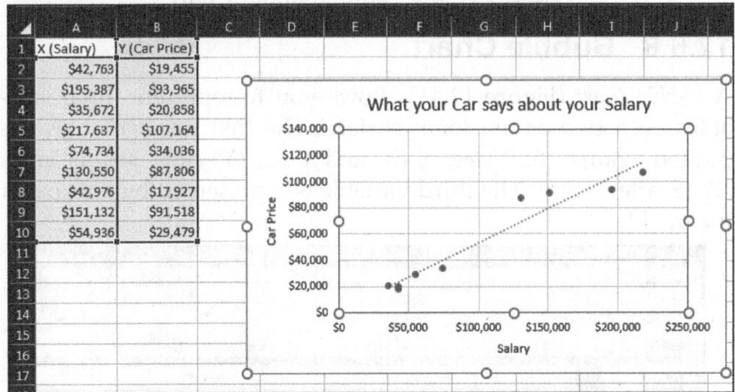

Figure 12.38 Sample XY(scatter) Charts

12.6.6 Area Chart

An area chart compares the continuous changes in volume of multiple data series. This type of chart sums the data from all the individual series to create the top line that encloses the area, giving the view of how different series contribute to total volume. Use this chart for sales and production figures of a company to show how volume changes over time and to emphasize the amount of volume to change. A sample *area chart* is shown in Figure 12.39.

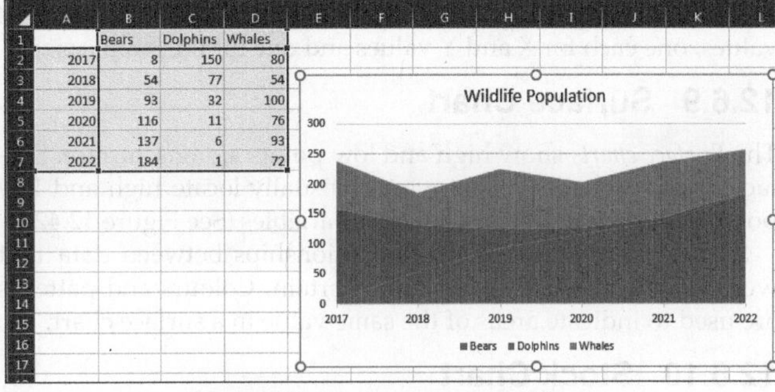

Figure 12.39 Sample Area Chart

12.6.7 Radar Chart

The *radar charts* are used to show the relationship between individual data series and between a specific series and the whole of the other (See Figure 12.40).

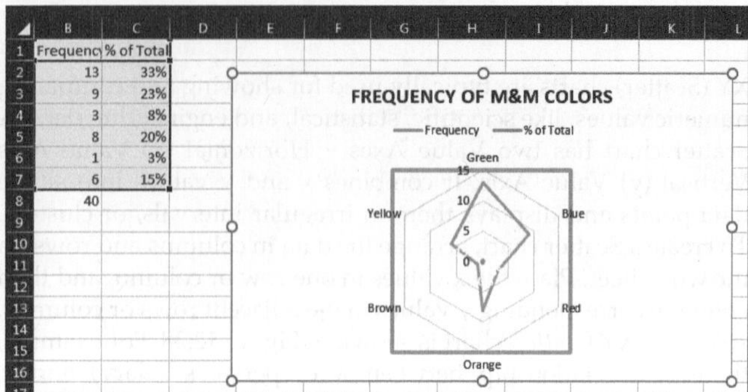

Figure 12.40 Sample Radar Chart

12.6.8 Bubble Chart

A *bubble chart* (Figure 12.41) allows you to represent three variables on a two-dimensional surface. The first two variables are plotted against the *Category* (X) and *Value* (Y) axes, just as in an XY (Scatter) chart. The third variable is represented by the size of the bubble.

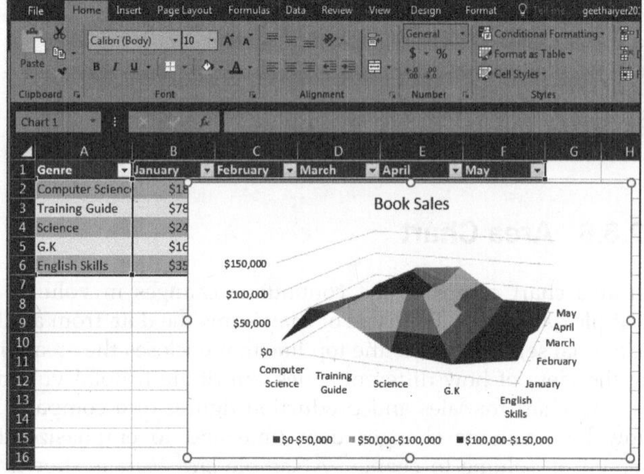

Figure 12.41 Sample Bubble Chart

To create a bubble chart, you need three rows or columns of values, one each for X and Y values and one for the bubble size.

12.6.9 Surface Chart

The *Surface charts* show high and low points along a surface. Surface charts are an excellent way to visually locate high and low points resulting from two changing variables (See Figure 12.42).

Surface charts can highlight relationships between data that would not otherwise be easy to ascertain. Colours and patterns are used to indicate areas of the same value in a surface chart.

12.6.10 Stock Chart

Stock charts display stock prices over time. You can display high, low and closing prices and volume of stocks traded (Figure 12.43). To create a Stock chart, arrange the data in columns or rows in a specific order on the worksheet. For example, to create a simple high-low-close Stock chart, arrange your data with High, Low, and Close entered as Column headings, in that order.

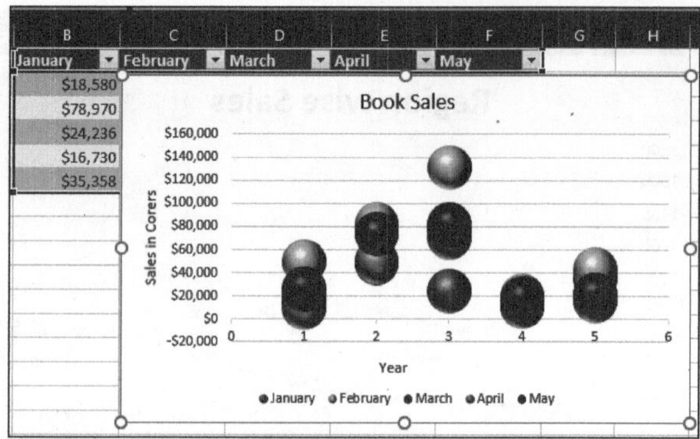

Figure 12.42 Sample Surface Chart

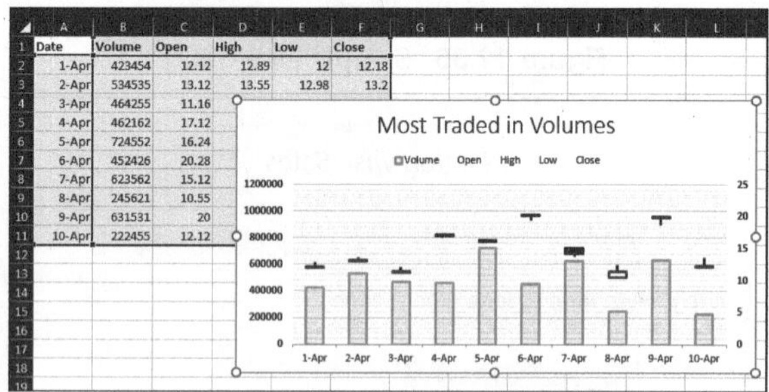

Figure 12.43 Sample Stock Chart

12.6.11 Waterfall Chart

The waterfall chart provides a great method to visualize the impact of multiple data points (typically a series of positive and negative values) as a running total.

Step 1 :Create a data table

Let us start with a simple table like annual sales numbers for the current year. You will see in the table below that the sales amounts vary for each month. Some months will have positive sales growth, while others will be negative. (See Figure 12.44)

1. Insert three additional columns to your Excel table to represent the movement of the columns on the waterfall chart. The base column will represent the starting point for the fall and rise of the chart. You will input all the negative numbers from the sales flow in the fall column and all the positive numbers in the rise column (See Figure 12.45).

   You will also want to add a Start and End row to your table to provide total values for the beginning and end of your sales year (See Figure 12.45).

Step 2: Insert formulas to complete your table

The easiest way to complete your table is by adding formulas to the first cells in each of the corresponding columns and then copy them down to the adjacent cells using the fill handle.

2. Select C4 in the Fall column and enter the following formula: =IF(E4<=0, -E4, 0) Drag the fill handle down to the end of the column to copy the formula as shown in Figure 12.45.

	A	E	F
1			
2	Sales 2017		
3		Sales Flow	
4	Start	6000	
5	Jan	2450	
6	Feb	-2100	
7	Mar	-1900	
8	Apr	2255	
9	May	-1137	
10	Jun	-1340	
11	Jul	2117	
12	Aug	1548	
13	Sep	1344	
14	Oct	1351	
15	Nov	-1750	
16	Dec	2852	
17	End		

Sheet1

Figure 12.44 Sales of every month

C4 =IF(E4<=0, -E4, 0)

	A	B	C	D	E	F
1						
2	Sales 2017					
3		Base	Fall	Rise	Sales Flow	
4	Start		0	6000	6000	
5	Jan	6000	0	2450	2450	
6	Feb	6350	2100	0	-2100	
7	Mar	4450	1900	0	-1900	
8	Apr	4450	0	2255	2255	
9	May	5568	1137	0	-1137	
10	Jun	4228	1340	0	-1340	
11	Jul	4228	0	2117	2117	
12	Aug	6345	0	1548	1548	
13	Sep	7893	0	1344	1344	
14	Oct	9237	0	1351	1351	
15	Nov	8838	1750	0	-1750	
16	Dec	8838	0	2852	2852	
17	End	11690				

Figure 12.45 Insert the Formula in C4 in the Fall column

3. Select D4 in the Rise column and enter the following formula: =IF(E4>0, E4,0) Copy the formula down to the end of the table using the fill handle as shown in Figure 12.46.
4. Select B5 in the Base column and enter the following formula: =B4+D4-C5.

Step 3: Build a stacked column chart

Now you have all the necessary data to build your waterfall chart.

Workbook Views | Show

D4 =IF(E4>0, E4,0)

	A	B	C	D	E	F
1						
2	Sales 2017					
3		Base	Fall	Rise	Sales Flow	
4	Start		0	6000	6000	
5	Jan	6000	0	2450	2450	
6	Feb	6350	2100	0	-2100	
7	Mar	4450	1900	0	-1900	
8	Apr	4450	0	2255	2255	
9	May	5568	1137	0	-1137	
10	Jun	4228	1340	0	-1340	
11	Jul	4228	0	2117	2117	
12	Aug	6345	0	1548	1548	
13	Sep	7893	0	1344	1344	
14	Oct	9237	0	1351	1351	
15	Nov	8838	1750	0	-1750	
16	Dec	8838	0	2852	2852	
17	End	11690				

Figure 12.46 Insert the Formula in D4 in the Rise column

5. Now, select the data to highlight in the chart. Include the row and column headers, and exclude the sales flow column as shown in Figure 12.47.

Chart 4

	A	B	C	D	E
1					
2	Sales 2017				
3		Base	Fall	Rise	Sales Flow
4	Start		0	6000	6000
5	Jan	6000	0	2450	2450
6	Feb	6350	2100	0	-2100
7	Mar	4450	1900	0	-1900
8	Apr	4450	0	2255	2255
9	May	5568	1137	0	-1137
10	Jun	4228	1340	0	-1340
11	Jul	4228	0	2117	2117
12	Aug	6345	0	1548	1548
13	Sep	7893	0	1344	1344
14	Oct	9237	0	1351	1351
15	Nov	8838	1750	0	-1750
16	Dec	8838	0	2852	2852
17	End	11690			

Figure 12.47 Select the data to highlight

6. Go to the **Insert** tab, click on the **Insert Column or Bar Chart** drop-down arrow in the **Charts** group, and then **Stacked Chart** as shown in Figure 12.48.

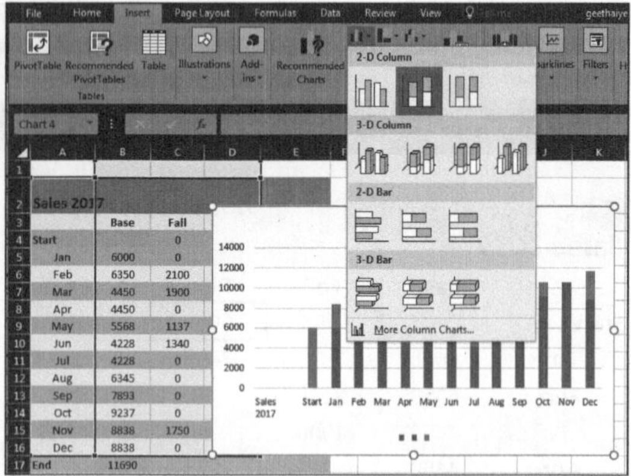

Figure 12.48 Selecting stacked chart and insert in the worksheet

Your stacked chart now appears in the worksheet, with all your data included, but it is not a waterfall chart. Next we will convert into the stacked column chart into a waterfall chart.

Step 4: Convert your stacked chart to a waterfall chart

7. Click on the Base series to select them. Right-click and choose **Format Data Series** from the list as shown in Figure 12.49.

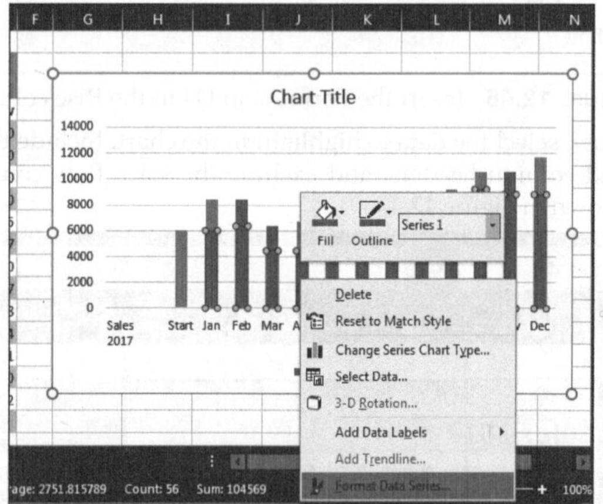

Figure 12.49 Selecting Format Data Series

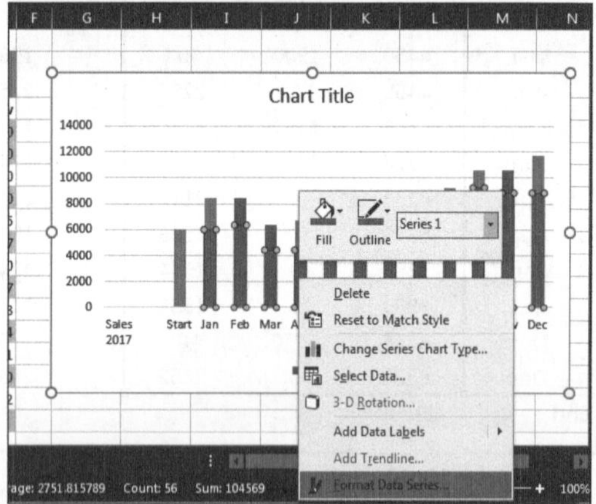

Figure 12.50 Selecting Format Data Series

8. The **Format Data Series** pane appears to the right of your worksheet. Click on the **Fill** and **Line** icon.
9. Select **No fill** in the **Fill** section and **No line** in the **Border** section as shown in Figure 12.50.
10. Now that the **Base** series is invisible, you should remove the **Base label** listed in the legend. Double click on **Base** in the legend, right-click on the selected label, and click **Delete** from the drop-down list.

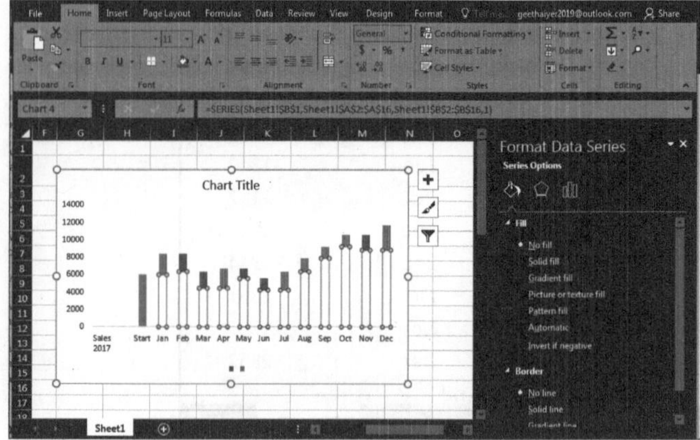

11. After making these changes, click on **Close** button to close the dialog box. You can see the waterfall chart as shown in Figure 12.51.

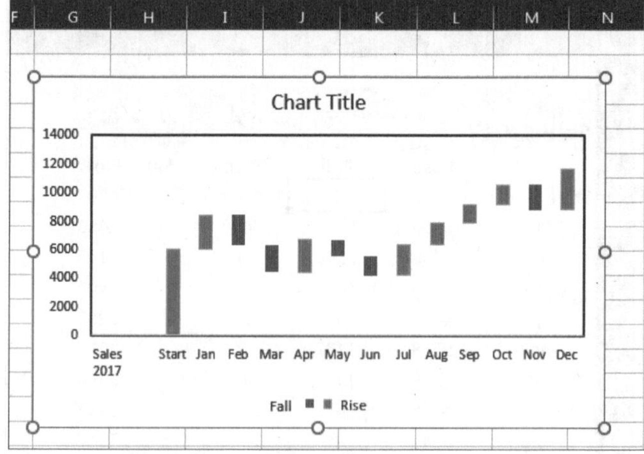

Figure 12.51 Waterfall chart in the worksheet

12.6.12 Box and Whisker Chart

Box and Whisker charts, also referred to as Box Plots are commonly used in statistical analysis. A box and whisker chart shows distribution of data into quartiles, highlighting the mean and outliers. The boxes may have lines extending vertically called 'whiskers'. These lines indicate variability outside the upper and lower quartiles, and any point outside those lines or whiskers is considered an outlier."

The box-and-whisker plot shows the minimum, first quartile, median, third quartile, and maximum of a set of data. Statisticians refer to this set of statistics as a five-number summary.

Each five-number summary as a box with "whiskers." The box is bounded on the top by the third quartile, and on the bottom by the first quartile. The median divides the box. How you lay out the chart determines the width of the box. The whiskers are error bars: One extends upward from the third quartile to the maximum, and the other extends downward from the first quartile to the minimum as shown image below.

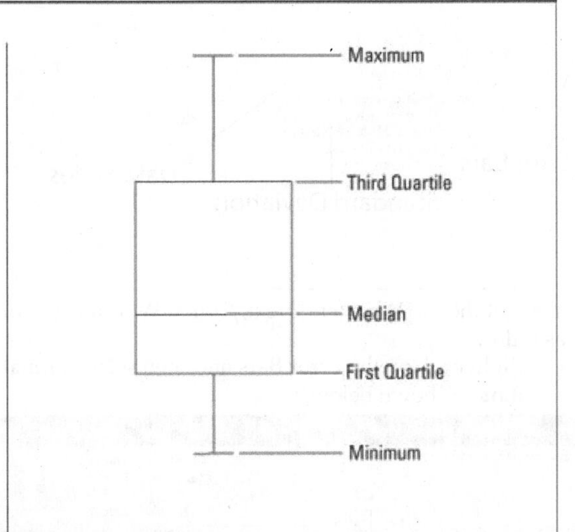

Preparation of Data

1. Create a data into a worksheet and start computing some statistics. The Figure 12.52 shows the worksheet and the statistics.

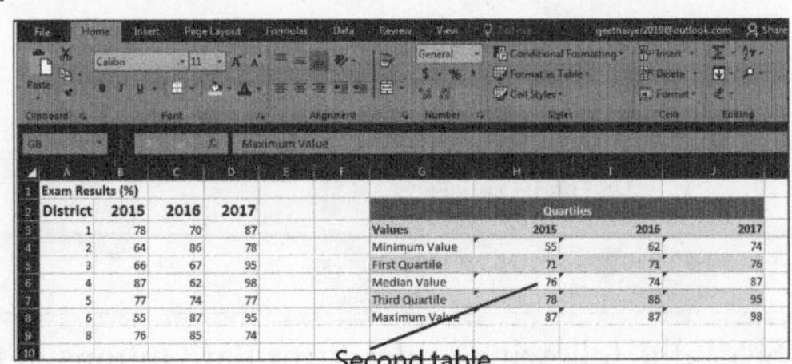

Exam Results (%)			
District	2015	2016	2017
1	78	70	87
2	64	86	78
3	66	67	95
4	87	62	98
5	77	74	77
6	55	87	95
8	76	85	74

Quartiles			
Values	2015	2016	2017
Minimum Value	55	62	74
First Quartile	71	71	76
Median Value	76	74	87
Third Quartile	78	86	95
Maximum Value	87	87	98

Figure 12.52 The data of worksheet and statistics

2. Now compute the following for each of the series – 2015, 2016 and 2017 using Excel Functions MIN, QUARTILE and MAX. The group of statistics holds the values for the five-number summary. You can use MIN to find the minimum value for each year, and MAX to find the maximum value. QUARTILE.INC computes the first quartile and the third quartile, and MEDIAN determines the median.
3. The resulting second table will be as shown in Figure 12.52 at the right side of the worksheet.
4. Again create a third table from the second table, computing the differences.
   Retain the first row – Minimum Value as it is.
   In the second row – compute values as First Quartile - Minimum Value.
   In the third row – compute values as Median Value - First Quartile.
   In the fourth row – compute values as Third Quartile - Median Value.
   In the fifth row – compute values as Maximum Value - Third Quartile.
5. You will get the third table as shown below.

Differences			
Values	2015	2016	2017
Minimum Value	55	62	74
Q1-Minimum Valu€	15.75	9	2.25
Median-Q1	5.25	3	10.75
Q3-Median	1.5	11.5	8
Max-Q3	9.5	1.5	3

From the third table create a box and whisker chart.

Creating a Box and Whisker Chart

Following are the steps to create a Box and Whisker chart.

1. Select the (i.e. difference data) in the worksheet as shown above. And
2. Insert a Stacked Column chart. The **Stacked column** chart appears as shown in Figure 12.53.
3. Click the **Design** tab on the Ribbon and then select **Switch Row/Column** command in the **Data** group as shown in Figure 12.53.

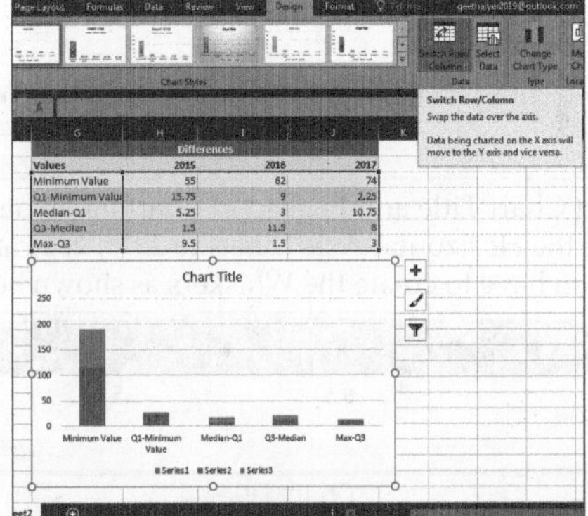

Figure 12.53 Inserted Stacked column chart and selecting Switch Row / Column command

4. After convert **Switch Row/Column**, the chart will appear as shown below.

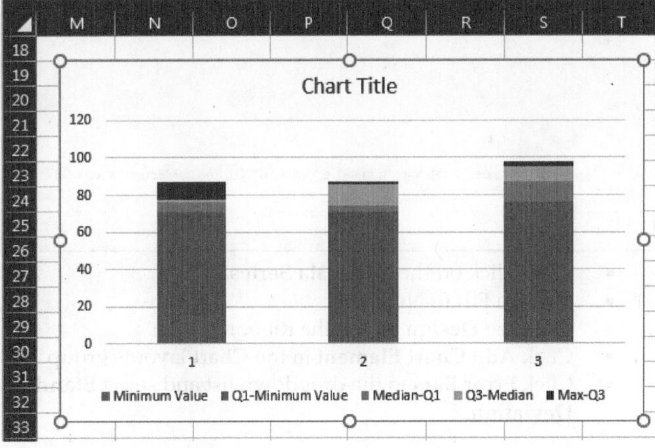

5. Right click on the bottom Data Series. Click **Fill** and select **No Fill.**

   The bottom Data series becomes invisible as shown below.

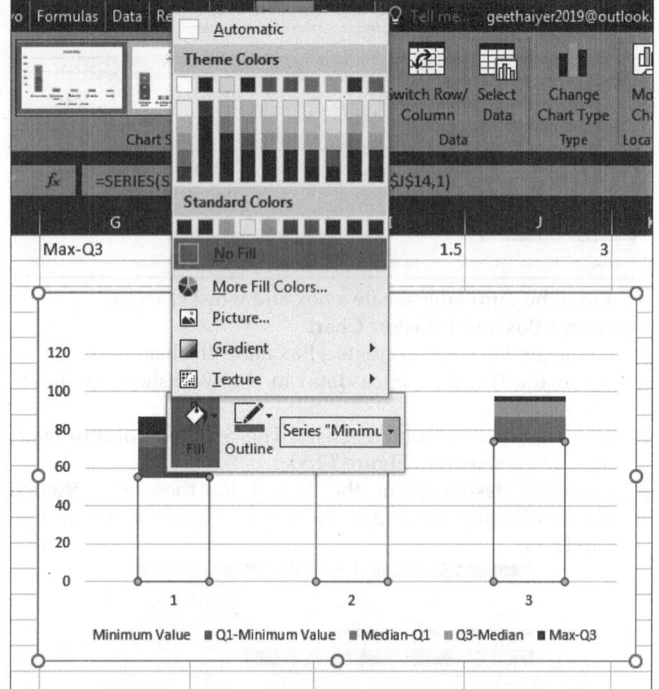

6. Deselect Chart Title and Legend in Chart Elements.
7. Change the Horizontal Axis Labels to 2015, 2016 and 2017.
8. Next, you have to create the Whiskers as shown below.

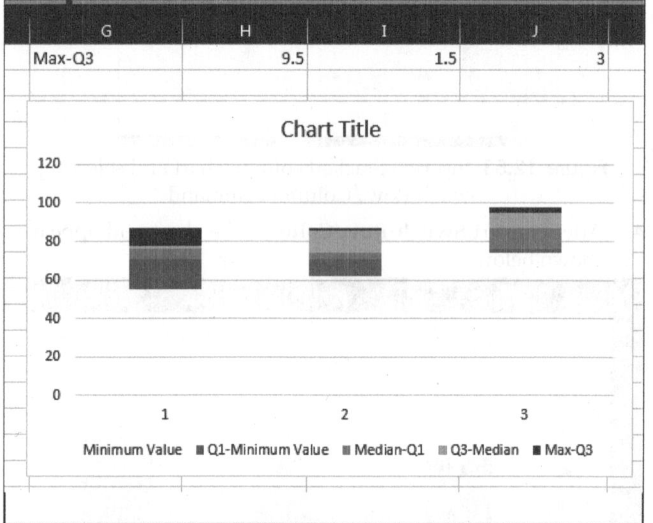

- Right click on the **Top Data Series.**
- Change **Fill** to **No Fill.**
- Click the **Design** tab on the Ribbon.
- Click **Add Chart Element** in the **Chart** layouts group.
- Click **Error Bars** in the dropdown list and select **Standard Deviation.**

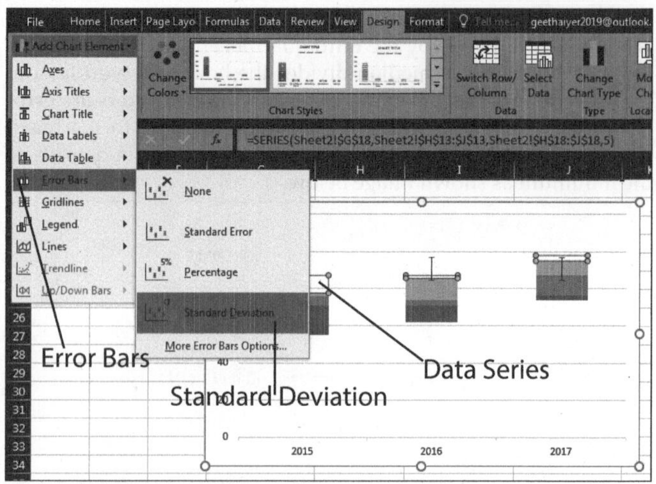

9. You got the top Whiskers. Next, format Whiskers (Error Bars) as follows
   - Right click on the Error Bars and then select **Format Error Bars** as shown below.

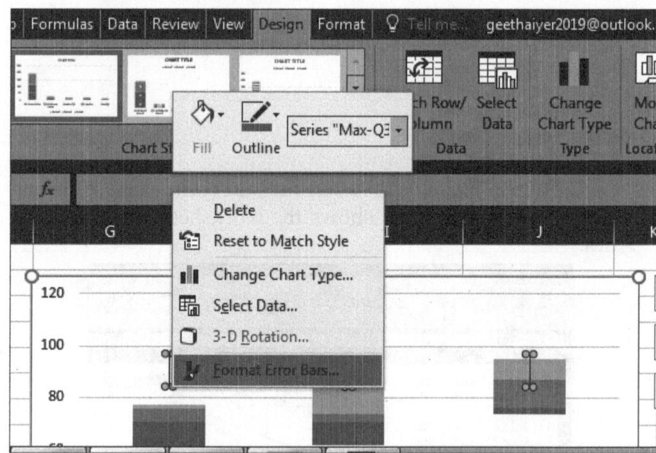

   - Select the following under **Error Bar Options** in the **Format Error Bars** pane as shown below.

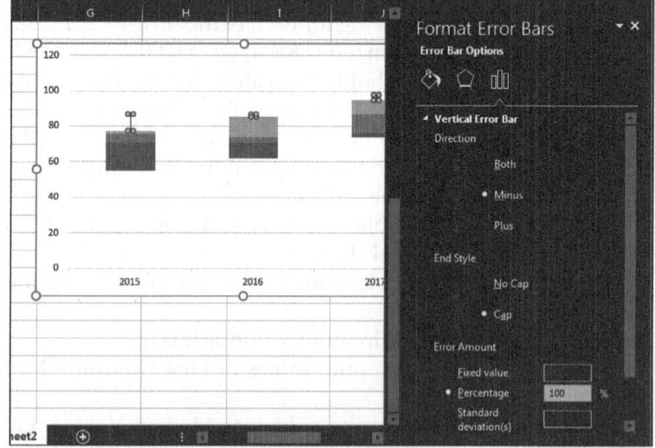

   - Select **Minus** under **Direction.**
   - Select **No Cap** under **End Style.**

- Select **Percentage** under **Error Amount** and type 100.

10. Click the Fill & Line tab under Error Bar Options in the **Format Error Bars** pane as shown below.

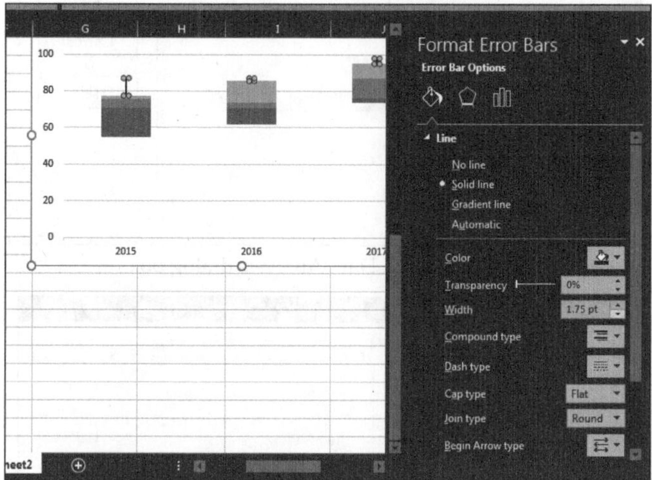

- Select **Solid line** under **Line.**
- Select the color as dark blue.
- Type 1.75 in the **Width** box.

11. Repeat the above given steps for the second lower bottom Series as shown below.

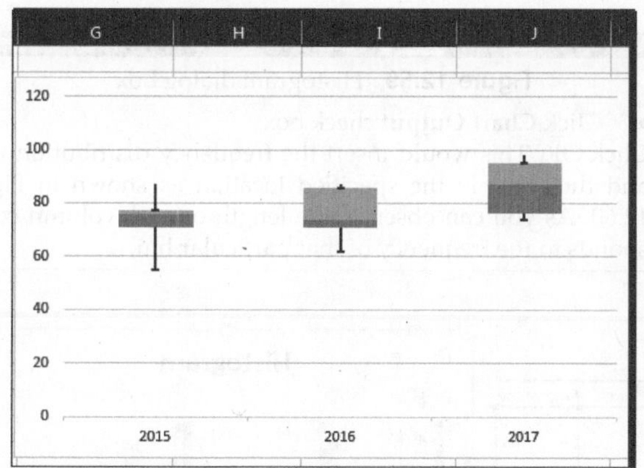

12. Next, format the boxes as follows and shown below Figure.
    - Right click on one of the Box series.
    - Click **Fill** and choose color as **light blue.**
    - Click **Outline** and choose the **color** as **dark blue.**

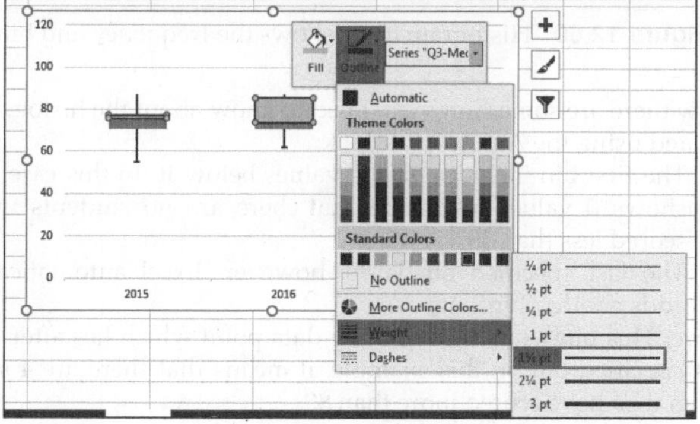

- Click **Weight** and select 1 1/2 pt.

13. Repeat the steps given above for the other Box series. After finished the Box and Whisker chart is shown in Figure 12.54.

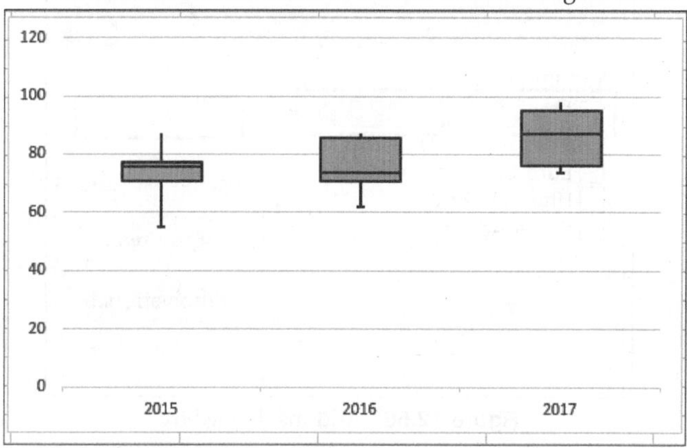

Figure 12.54 Box and Whisker chart

12.6.13 Histogram Chart

A Histogram is represented by rectangles with lengths corresponding to the number of occurrences of a variable in successive numerical intervals. The numerical intervals are called bins and the number of occurrences is called frequency.

Creating a Histogram in Excel

Histogram in Excel can be created in three ways:

- How to Install Data Analysis Toolpak in Excel.
- How to Create a Histogram in Excel using Data Analysis Toolpak.
- How to Create a Histogram in Excel using Frequency function.

How to Install Data Analysis Toolpak in Excel

To create a histogram in Excel, you first need to install the Analysis Toolpak add-in. This add-in enables you to quickly create the histogram by taking the data and data range (bins) as inputs.

1. Click **File** menu and choose **Options.**
2. In the **Excel Options** dialog box, select **Add-ins** in the navigation pane.
3. In the **Manage** drop-down, select **Excel Add-ins** and click **Go** as shown in Figure 12.55.

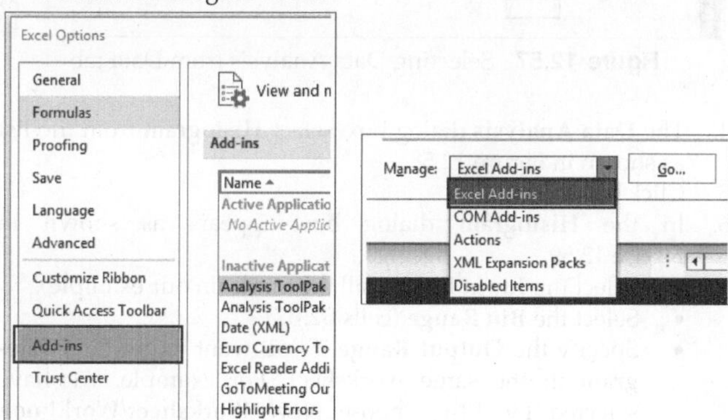

Figure 12.55 Select Add-ins in Manage drop-down list

4. In the Add-ins dialog box, select Analysis Toolpak and click OK as shown in Figure 12.56.

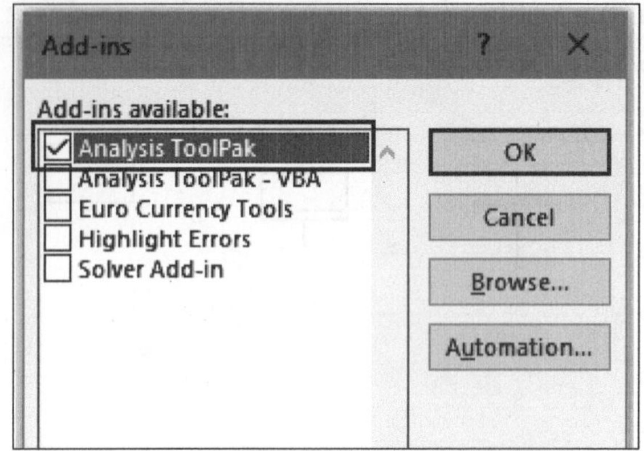

Figure 12.56 Add-ins dialog box

This would install the Analysis Toolpak and you can access it in the Data tab in the Analysis group.

5. Once you have the Analysis Toolpak enabled, you can use it to create a histogram in Excel.

➡ **To create a histogram using data analysis toolpak:**

1. Suppose you have a dataset as shown below. It has the marks (out of 100) of 17 students in a subject as shown in Figure 12.57.
2. To create a histogram using this data, we need to create the data intervals in which we want to find the data frequency. These are called bins. With the above dataset, the bins would be the marks intervals.
   You need to specify these bins separately in an additional column as shown below:
3. On the **Data** tab, in the **Analysis** group, click **Data Analysis** as shown in Figure 12.57.

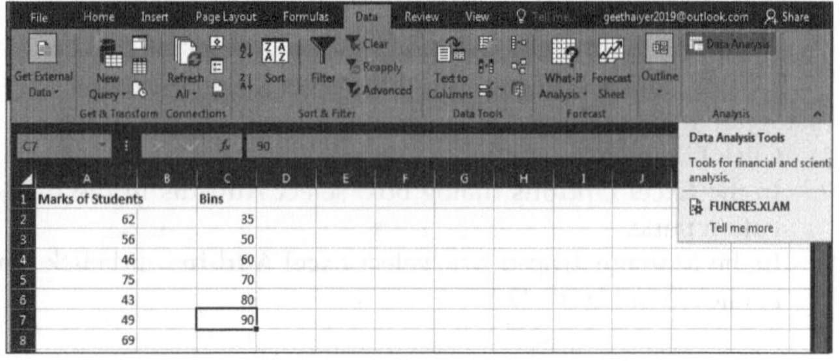

Figure 12.57 Selecting Data Analysis from Data tab

4. The **Data Analysis** dialog box, select **Histogram** from the list as shown in Figure 12.58.
5. Click OK.
6. In the **Histogram** dialog box appears as shown in Figure 12.59.
   - Select the **Input Range** (all the marks in our example)
   - Select the **Bin Range** (cells B2:B7)
   - Specify the **Output Range** if you want to get the **Histogram** in the same worksheet. For example, we have selected E9. Else, choose **New Worksheet/Workbook** option to get it in a separate worksheet/workbook.

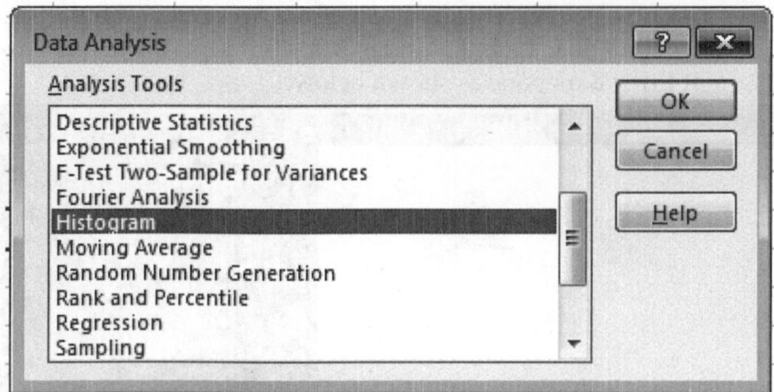

Figure 12.58 Data Analysis dialog box

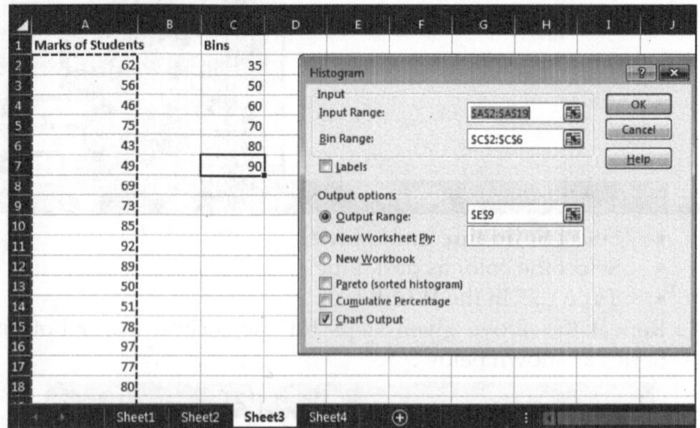

Figure 12.59 Histogram dialog box

- Click **Chart Output** check box.

7. Click OK. This would insert the frequency distribution table and the chart in the specified location as shown in Figure 12.60. As you can observe, the length of each column corresponds to the frequency of that particular bin.

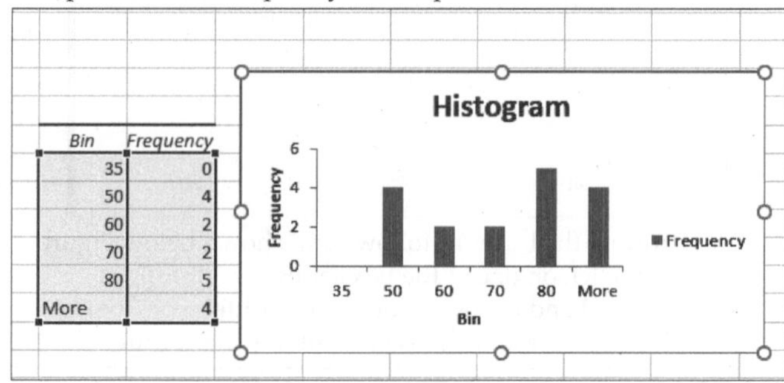

Figure 12.60 Histogram chart shows the frequency and bin value

Now there are somethings you need to know about the histogram created using the Analysis Toolpak:

- The first bin includes all the values below it. In this case, 35 shows 0 values indicating that there are no students who scored less than 35.
- The last specified bin is 80, however, Excel automatically adds another bin

More: This bin would include any data point which lies after the last specified bin. In this example, it means that there are 4 students who have scored more than 80.

12.7 USING SPARKLINES

Sparkline is a tiny chart in a worksheet cell that provides a visual representation of data. It is used to show trends in a series of values, such as seasonal increases or decreases or to highlight maximum and minimum values.

It is introduced in Excel 2010 to be a convenient alternative to charts. Unlike a traditional chart, a sparkline is placed inside a cell, allowing you to easily create a large number of sparklines.

☞ *Sparkline is a tiny chart that fits in a cell–to visually summarize trends alongside data. Sparklines show trends in a small amount of space. So, they are especially useful for dashboards or other places where you need to show a snapshot of your business in an easy-to-understand visual format.*

➡ **To create a sparkline:**

1. Select an empty cell or group of empty cells in which you want to insert sparklines.
2. Under the **Insert** tab, in the **Sparklines** group, click the type of sparkline that you want to create, such as Line, Column, or Win/Loss. (See Figure 12.61). For example, here we have selected Win/Loss option.

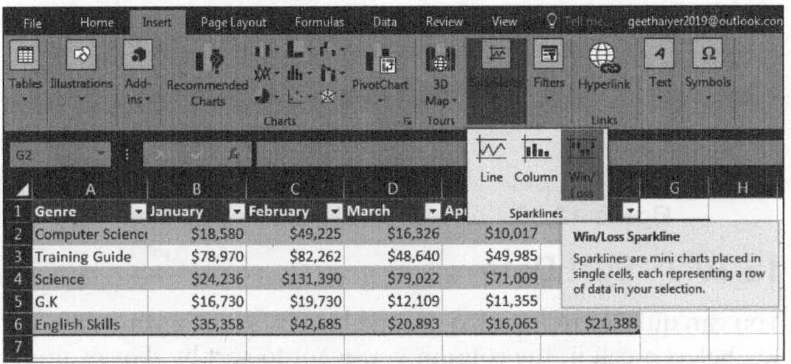

Figure 12.61 Selecting Sparkline command

3. It will display **Create Sparklines** dialog box as shown in Figure 12.62.

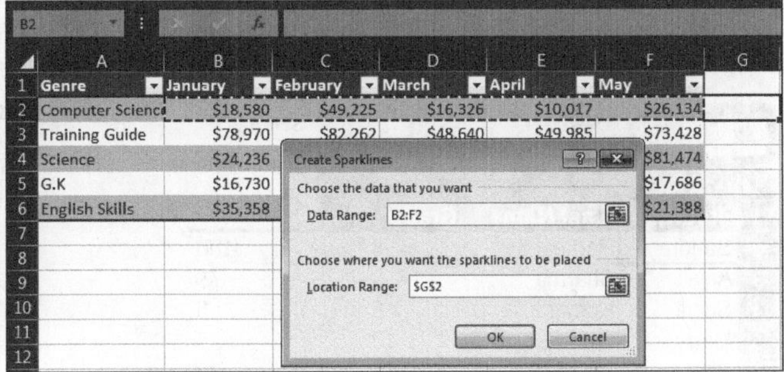

Figure 12.62 Create Sparklines dialog box

4. In this dialog box, type the range of the cells in the **Data Range:** box, or click the collapsable button to select the range that contains the data on which you want to create the sparkline.
5. Then click OK button.
   As you create a sparkline, **Sparkline Tools** become available and the **Design** tab is displayed as shown in Figures 12.63. You can use commands on this tab to modify the Sparkline, such as change the type, colour of a sparkline, showing high, low point as per your need.

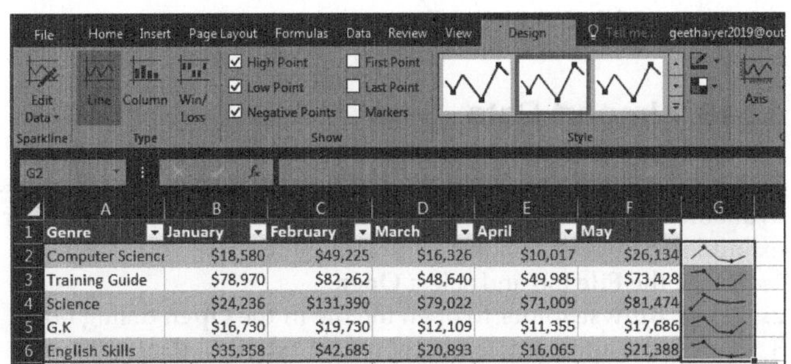

Figure 12.63 Design tab of Sparkline tools

6. In the **Design** tab in the **Show** group, click the check box **High Point** and **Low Point** to be emphasized with markers more readable.

12.8 PREVIEWING CHARTS

After creating a chart and before printing, it is a good practice to see the full page view (preview) of the chart.

☞ *In Excel 2016, you can preview and print your Excel files in one location—on the Print tab in the Microsoft Office Backstage view. To go back to your workbook and make changes before you print it, click the File tab.*

1. Activate the chart sheet.
2. Click the **File** tab, click on **Print** Option. The print backstage view options appears, click on **Print** command.
3. In this view, the properties of the default printer automatically appears in the left section and the preview of the chart sheet automatically appears in the right section.

12.9 TEMPLATES

1. Select the **File** tab and click the **New** button.
2. Select the desired Featured templates to view its contents and then click Create to open a document using the template.
3. Alternatively, select a category to review the templates from MS Office Online.
4. Choose a template to see the layout, then click **Create** button to download your desired template and open a document using that template as shown in Figure 12.64.

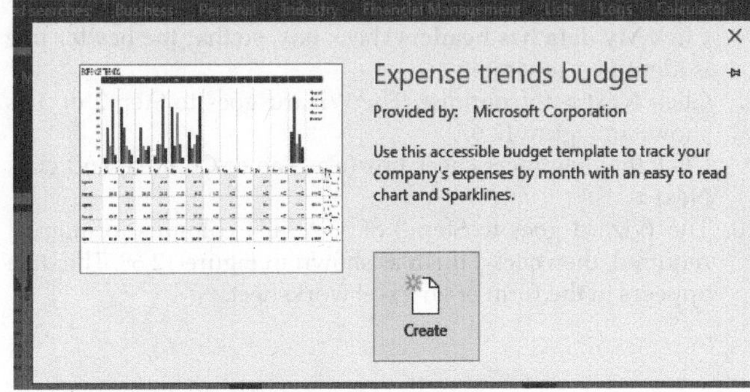

Figure 12.64 Select Create button to download template

12.10 MANAGE DATA

12.10.1 Import Data

You need to type the information in the worksheets if the data is available in another application such as access or text file. For example, to import data from a delimited text file:

1. Click the **File** tab and select **Open**.
2. Click **Browse** folder to open the file in the **Open** dialog box.
3. Select the appropriate file type (i.e Text Files) drop-down list.
4. Select the file in the contents pane which contains the data you wish to import as shown in Figure 12.65.

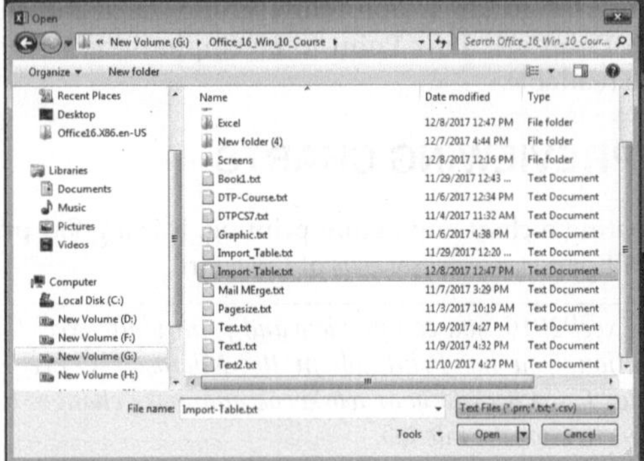

Figure 12.65 Select the file in the contents pane

5. Click **Open** button.
6. The **Text Import Wizard - Step of 1 of 3** dialog box appears which recognizes the delimited file as shown in Figure 12.66.

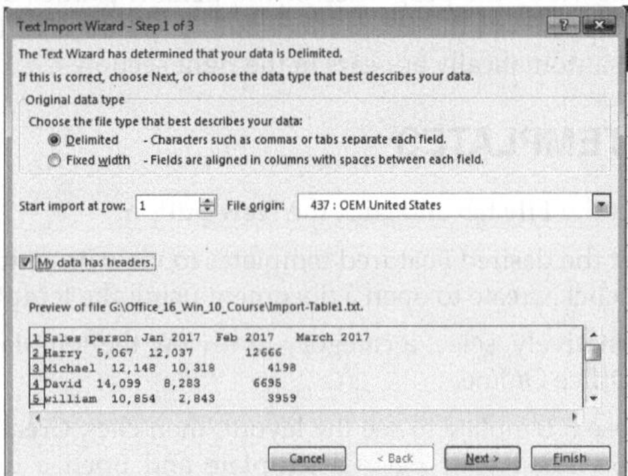

Figure 12.66 Text Import Wizard - Step 1 or 3

7. Click **My data has headers** check box, so that the header line is identified separately.
8. Click **Next >** to continue. The Wizard goes to Step 2 of 3 as shown in Figure 12.67.
9. Click the delimiters check box (e.g. Tab or Comma) and click **Next >**.
10. The Wizard goes to Step 3 of 3. Adjust columns formats, if required, then click **Finish** as shown in Figure 12.68. The data appears in the form of an Excel worksheet.

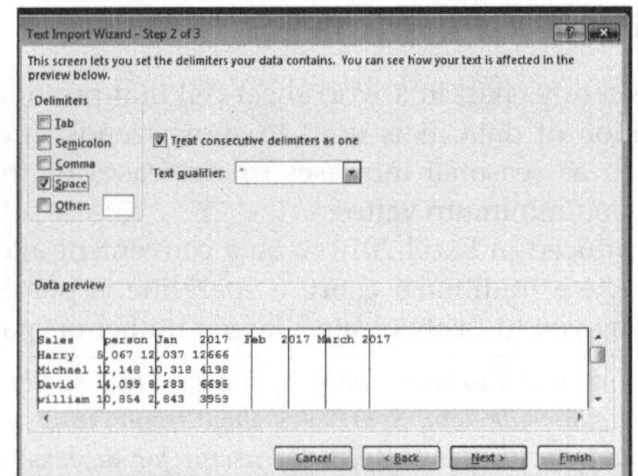

Figure 12.67 Text Import Wizard - Step 2 or 3

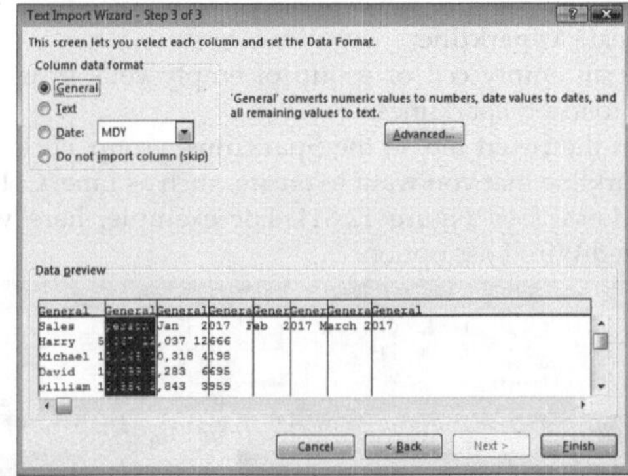

Figure 12.68 Text Import Wizard - Step 3 or 3

12.10.2 Sort Data

You can quickly reorganize a worksheet by sorting your data.

1. Select a cell in the column you want to sort by. For example, we have selected cell A1 as shown in Figure 12.69.

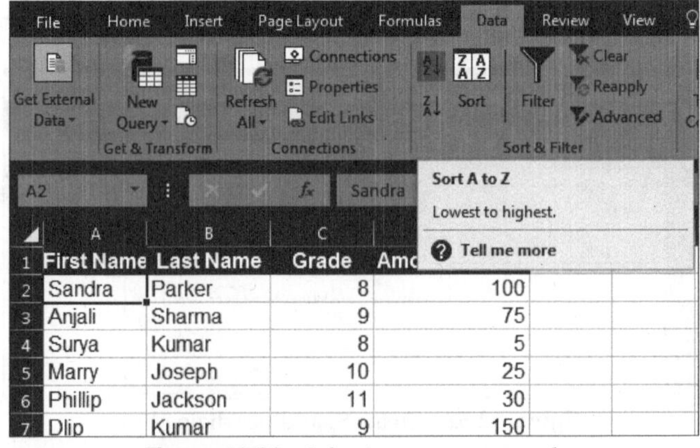

Figure 12.69 Selecting sort command

2. Select the **Data** tab on the Ribbon, then click the **A-Z** command to sort **A to Z**, or the **Z-A** command to sort **Z to A**. We have selected **A to Z**.
3. The worksheet will be sorted alphabetically by the selected column ascending order as shown in Figure 12.70.

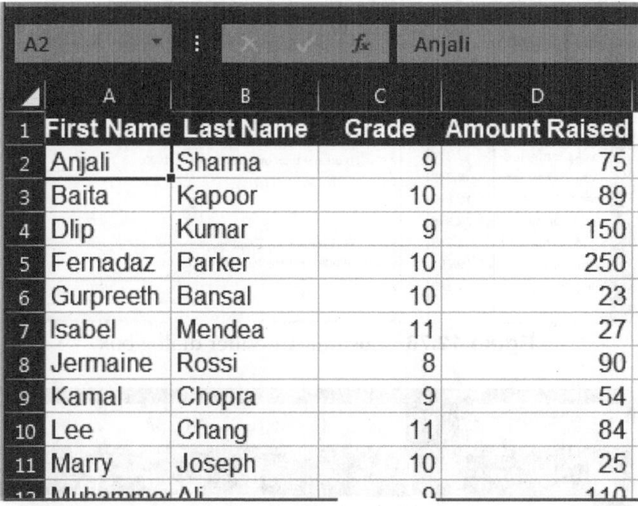

	A	B	C	D
1	First Name	Last Name	Grade	Amount Raised
2	Anjali	Sharma	9	75
3	Baita	Kapoor	10	89
4	Dlip	Kumar	9	150
5	Fernadaz	Parker	10	250
6	Gurpreeth	Bansal	10	23
7	Isabel	Mendea	11	27
8	Jermaine	Rossi	8	90
9	Kamal	Chopra	9	54
10	Lee	Chang	11	84
11	Marry	Joseph	10	25

Figure 12.70 The selected column sorted alphabetically

☞ *If you click in a single cell, Excel will select all the surrounding data and sort the rows of contiguous data into the required order.*

4. To sort by more than one value, click the **Sort** command to open **Sort** dialog box. The **Sort** dialog box appears as shown in Figure 12.71.

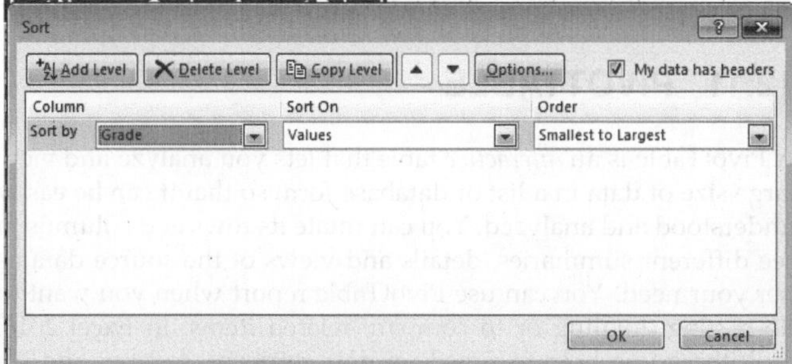

Figure 12.71 Sort dialog box

5. Choose the column you want to **Sort by**. In our example, we want to sort the Grade.
6. Decide the sorting order (either ascending or descending). In our example, we have selected Smallest to Largest.
7. Once you are satisfied with the selection, click OK button.
8. The selected **Grade** column sorted by **Smallest to Largest** Order as shown in Figure 12.72.

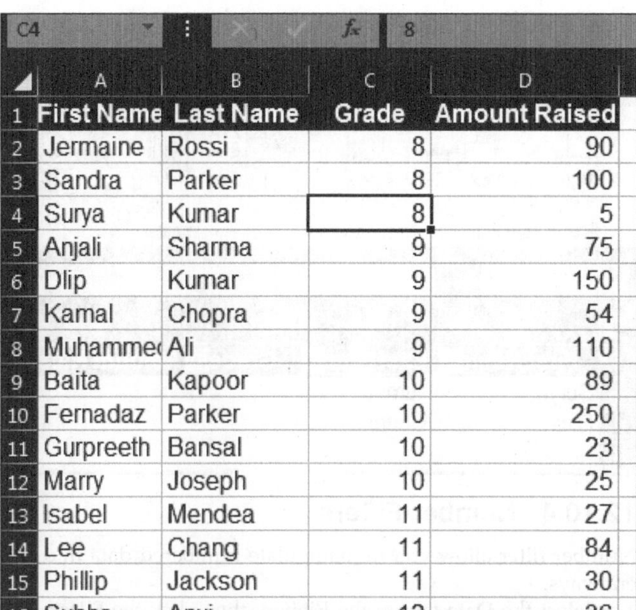

	A	B	C	D
1	First Name	Last Name	Grade	Amount Raised
2	Jermaine	Rossi	8	90
3	Sandra	Parker	8	100
4	Surya	Kumar	8	5
5	Anjali	Sharma	9	75
6	Dlip	Kumar	9	150
7	Kamal	Chopra	9	54
8	Muhammed	Ali	9	110
9	Baita	Kapoor	10	89
10	Fernadaz	Parker	10	250
11	Gurpreeth	Bansal	10	23
12	Marry	Joseph	10	25
13	Isabel	Mendea	11	27
14	Lee	Chang	11	84
15	Phillip	Jackson	11	30

Figure 12.72 Grade column sorted smallest to largest

12.10.3 Filters

You can filter the data to hide entries that are not of immediate interest.

1. Click a cell, select the **Data** tab and click the **Filter** command in the **Sort & Filter** group as shown in Figure 12.73.

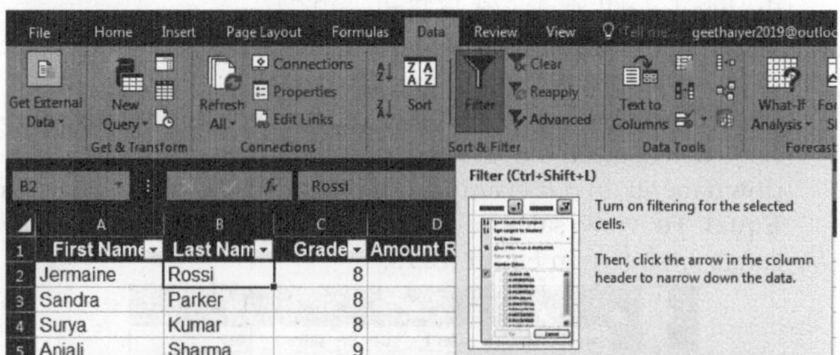

Figure 12.73 Select the Filter command

2. Click a filter icon, e.g. "Last Name", to display its **AutoFilter**.
3. Uncheck the **Select All** box, to deselect all entries, then select the specific entry you want, e.g. check "Kumar" as shown in Figure 12.74.

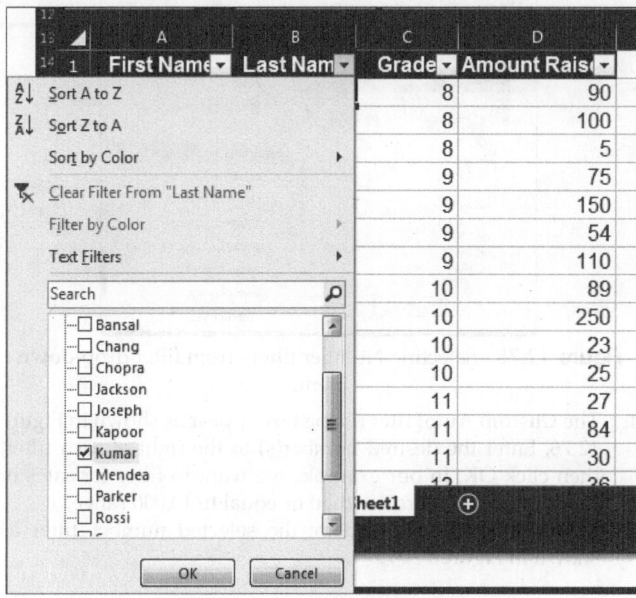

Figure 12.74 Select the Filter by Last Name

4. Click OK to apply the filter. Filter shows by Last Name as shown below.

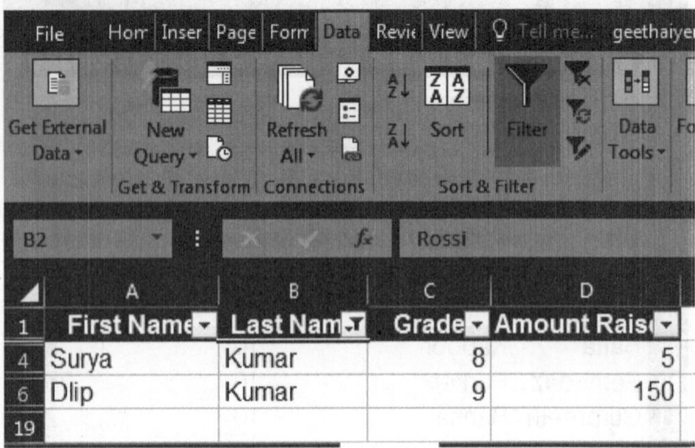

12.10.4 Number Filters

Number filter allow you to manipulate numbered data in different ways.

1. Select the **Data** tab on the Ribbon, then click the **Filter** command in the **Sort & Filter** group. A drop-arrow will appear in the header cell as shown in Figure 12.73.
2. Click the drop-down arrow for the column you want to filter. In our example, we will filter column B.
3. The **Filter** menu appear. Hover the mouse over **Number Filters**, then select the desired number filter from the drop-down menu. In our example, we will choose **Greater Than Or Equal To** view sales of Jan-18 between a specific number range as shown in Figure 12.75.

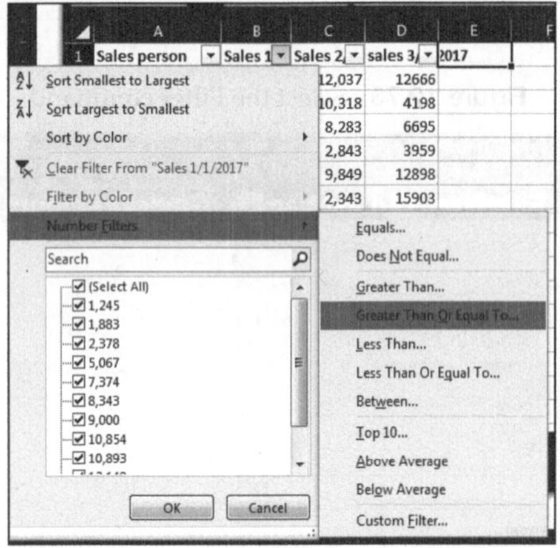

Figure 12.75 Selecting Number filters from filter drop-down menu

4. The **Custom AutoFilter** dialog box appear as shown in Figure 12.76. Enter the desired number(s) to the right of each filter, then click OK. In our example, we want to filter for sales of Jan-18 number(s) greater than or equal to 10,000 range.
5. The data will be filtered by the selected number filter as shown in Figure 12.77.

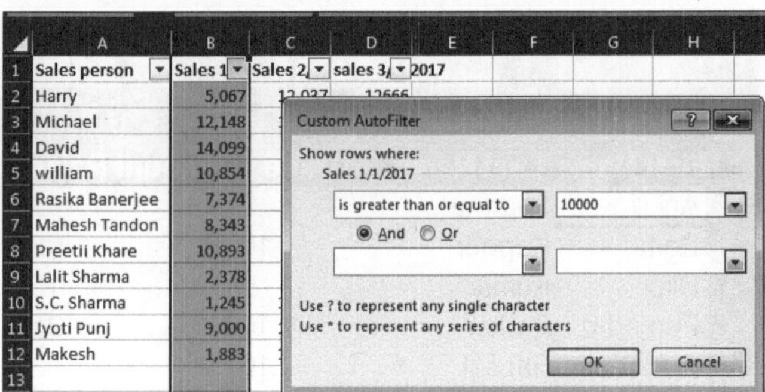

Figure 12.76 Custom Autofilter dialog box

B8 10893

	A	B	C	D	E
1	Sales person	Sales 1	Sales 2	sales 3/2017	
3	Michael	12,148	10,318	4198	
4	David	14,099	8,283	6695	
5	william	10,854	2,843	3959	
8	Preetii Khare	10,893	6,555	10993	
13					

Figure 12.77 Displays the selected records

12.11 PIVOTTABLE

A PivotTable is an *interactive* table that lets you analyze and view large size of data in a list or database form so that it can be easily understood and analyzed. You can rotate its rows and columns to see different summaries, details and views of the source data as per your need. You can use PivotTable report when you want to do sorting, totaling or to compare related items. In Excel 2016, multithreading help to speed up data retrieval, sorting, and filtering in PivotTables.

☞ *In Excel 2016, it is possible to fill down labels in a PivotTable so that you can more easily use the PivotTable. You can also repeat labels in PivotTables to display item captions of nested fields in all rows and columns.*

➡ **To create a PivotTable:**

1. Select the table or cells (including column headers) you want to include in the PivotTable as shown in Figure 12.78.
2. From the **Insert** tab, click the **PivotTable** command as shown in Figure 12.78.
3. The **Create PivotTable** dialog box appears as shown in Figure 12.79. Choose your settings, then click OK. In our example, here we use **Table1** as source data and place the PivotTable on a **New Worksheet**.

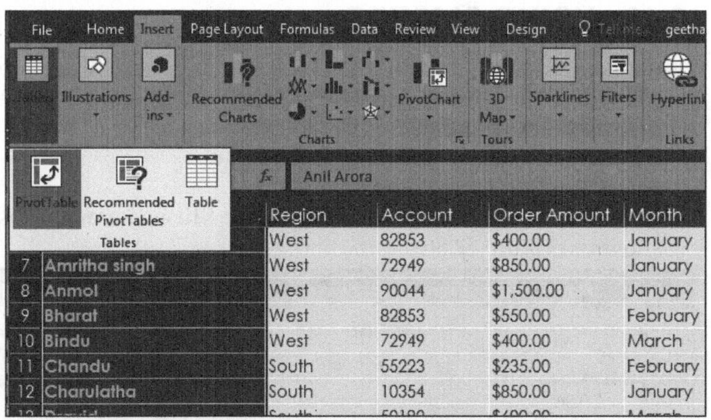

	Region	Account	Order Amount	Month
	West	82853	$400.00	January
7 Amritha singh	West	72949	$850.00	January
8 Anmol	West	90044	$1,500.00	January
9 Bharat	West	82853	$550.00	February
10 Bindu	West	72949	$400.00	March
11 Chandu	South	55223	$235.00	February
12 Charulatha	South	10354	$850.00	January

Figure 12.78 Displays the selected records

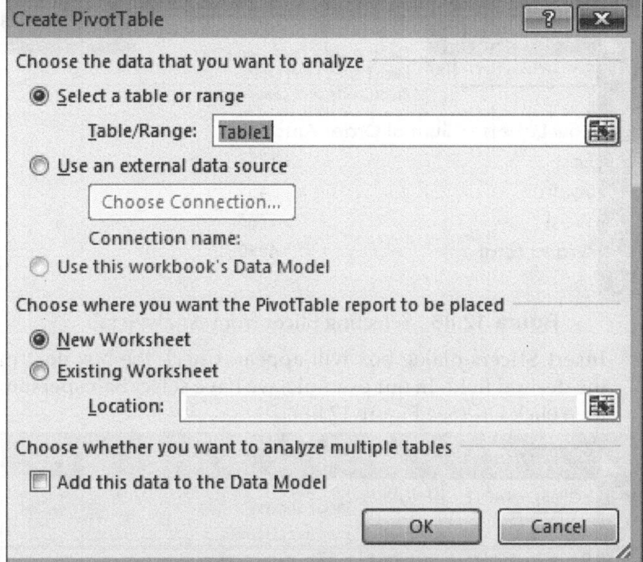

Figure 12.79 Create PivotTable dialog box

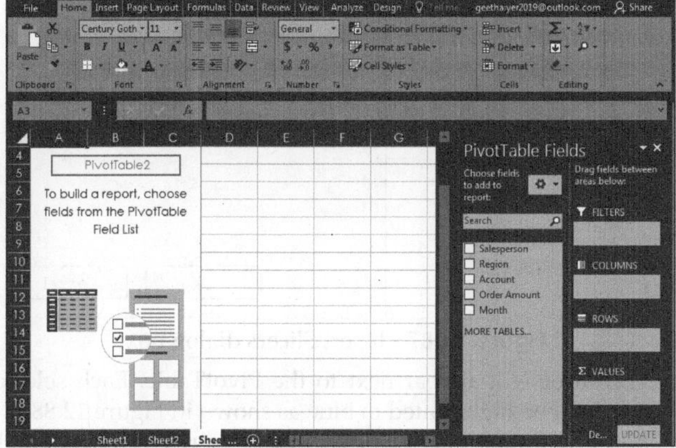

Figure 12.80 PivotTable Field List

4. A blank PivotTable and Field List will appear on a new worksheet as shown in Figure 12.80.
5. Once you create a PivotTable, you will need to decide which fields to add. In the **PivotTable Field List**, check the box for each field you want to add. In our example, check the **sales person** and **order Amount** fields to know the total amount sold by each salesperson.
   The selected fields will be added to one of the four areas below. The salesperson field has been added to the Rows area, and the order Amount has been added to values.
6. The PivotTable will calculate and summarize the selected fields. In our example, the PivotTable shows the amount sold by each salesperson as shown in Figure 12.81.

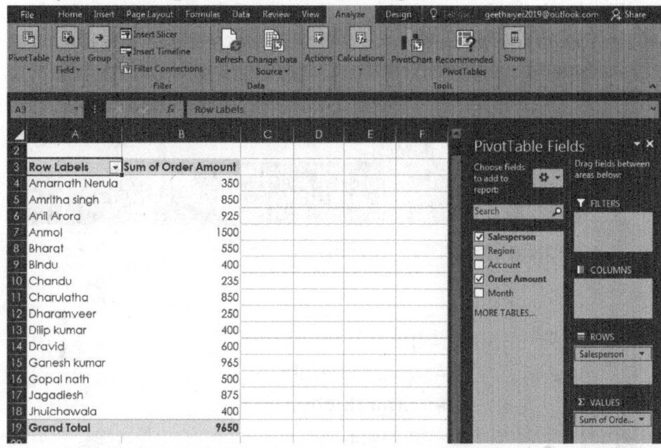

Row Labels	Sum of Order Amount
Amarnath Nerula	350
Amritha singh	850
Anil Arora	925
Anmol	1500
Bharat	550
Bindu	400
Chandu	235
Charulatha	850
Dharamveer	250
Dilip kumar	400
Dravid	600
Ganesh kumar	965
Gopal nath	500
Jagadiesh	875
Jhuichawala	400
Grand Total	**9650**

Figure 12.81 Summarize the selected fields

➡ **To add columns:**

1. In order to show multiple columns, you need to add a field to the Columns area.
2. Drag a field from the **Field List** into the **Columns** area. In our example, to add the **Month** field.
3. The PivotTable will include multiple columns. In our example, there is a column for each person's monthly sales, in addition to the grand total as shown in Figure 12.82.

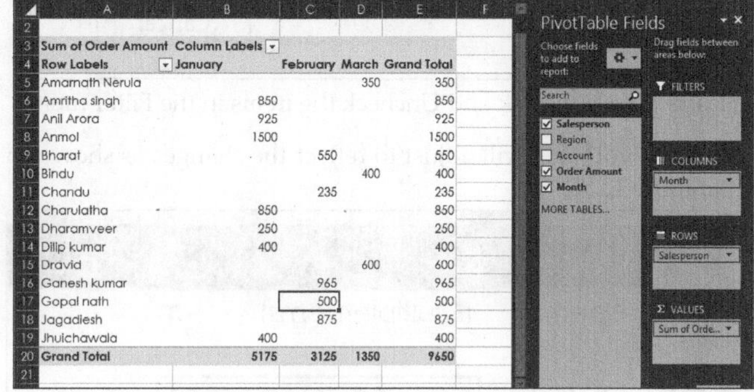

Sum of Order Amount	Column Labels			
Row Labels	January	February	March	Grand Total
Amarnath Nerula			350	350
Amritha singh	850			850
Anil Arora	925			925
Anmol	1500			1500
Bharat		550		550
Bindu			400	400
Chandu		235		235
Charulatha	850			850
Dharamveer	250			250
Dilip kumar	400			400
Dravid			600	600
Ganesh kumar		965		965
Gopal nath		500		500
Jagadiesh		875		875
Jhuichawala	400			400
Grand Total	**5175**	**3125**	**1350**	**9650**

Figure 12.82 To add columns

➡ **To add a filter:**

1. Drag a field from the **Field List** to the **Filters** area. In our example, we select the salesperson field as shown in Figure 12.83.
2. The **filter** will appear above the PivotTable. Click the **drop-down arrow**, then check the box next to **Select Multiple Items** as shown in Figure 12.83.

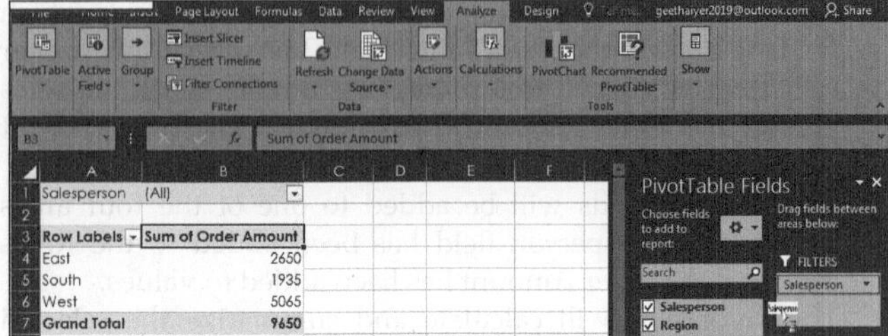

Figure 12.83 The filter appear in the PivotTable

3. Uncheck the box next to any items you do not want to include in the PivotTable. So, we have uncheck the boxes for a few salesperson, then click OK as shown in Figure 12.84.

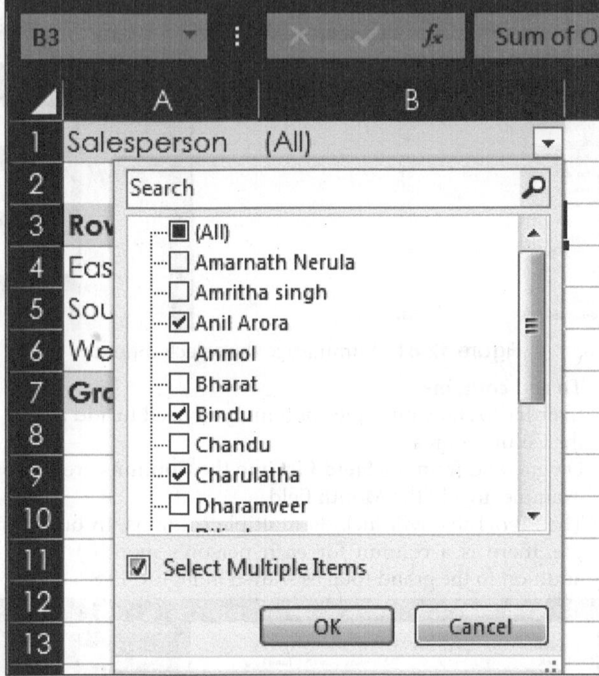

Figure 12.84 Check and Uncheck the items in the Filter menu

4. The PivotTable will adjust to reflect the changes as shown in Figure 12.85.

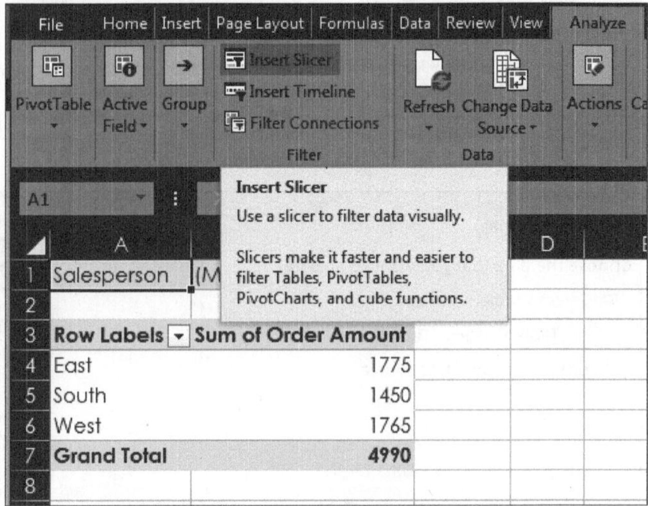

Figure 12.86 Selecting Slicer from Analyze tab

	A	B	C
1	Salesperson	(Multiple Items)	
2			
3	Row Labels	Sum of Order Amount	
4	East	1775	
5	South	1450	
6	West	1765	
7	Grand Total	4990	
8			

Figure 12.85 The select items reflect changes in the PivotTable

12.12 USING SLICERS

Slicers make filtering data in PivotTables even easier. Slicers are basically just filters but are easier and faster to use, allowing you to instantly pivot your data.

➡ **To add a Slicer in an existing PivotTable**

1. Select any cell in the PivotTable.
2. From the **Analyze** tab, click the **Insert Slicer** command as shown in Figure 12.86.
3. **Insert Slicers** dialog box will appear. Check the box next to the desired field. In our example, we have select **Salesperson**, then click OK (See Figure 12.87).

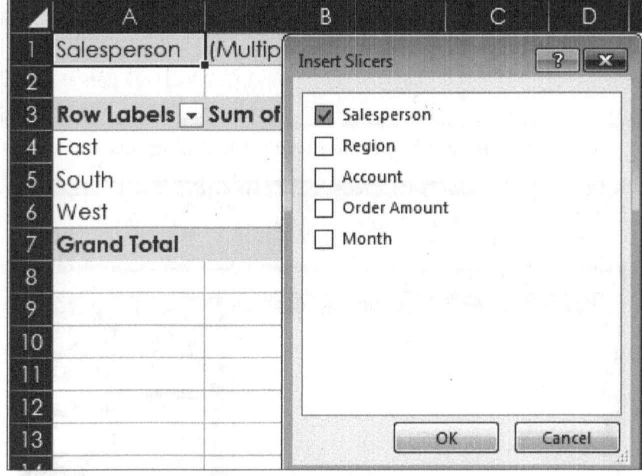

Figure 12.87 Insert Slicers dialog box

4. The slicer will appear next to the PivotTable. Each selected item will be highlighted in blue as shown in Figure 12.88.
5. Just like filters, only selected items are used in PivotTable. When you select or deselect an item, the PivotTable will instantly reflect the change.
   You can also click the **Filter icon** in the top-right corner of the slicer to select all items at once.

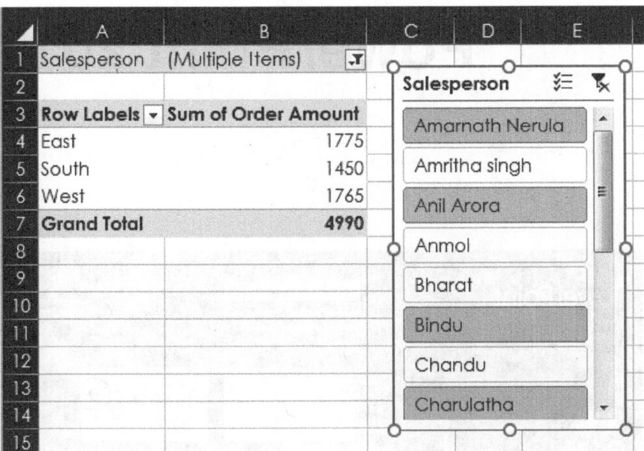

Figure 12.88 The slicer appear in the PivotTable

12.12.1 PivotCharts

PivotCharts are like regular charts, except they display data from a PivotTable.

➡ **To create a PivotChart:**

1. Select any cell in the PivotTable.

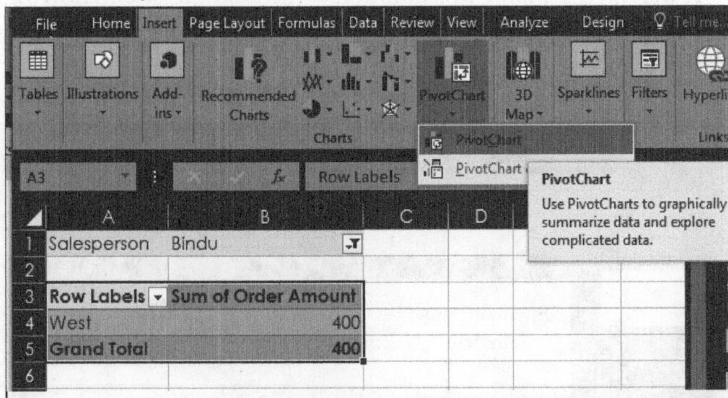

Figure 12.89 Select PivotChart

2. From the Insert tab, click the **PivotChart** command from **Charts** group as shown in Figure 12.89.
3. The **Insert Chart** dialog box will appear as shown in Figure 12.90. Select the desired **chart type** and **layout**, then click OK.
4. The PivotChart will appear as shown in Figure 12.91.

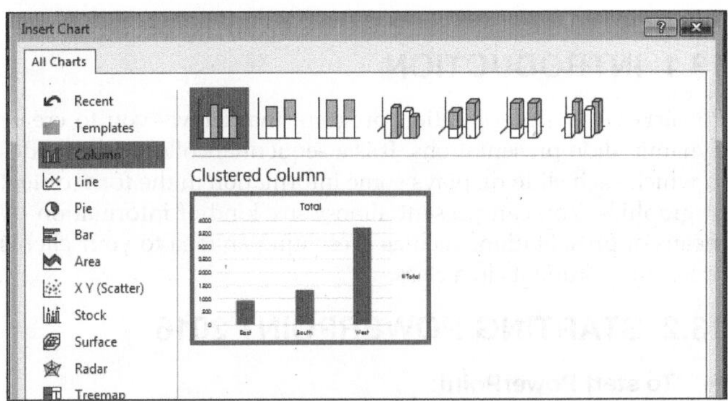

Figure 12.90 Insert Chart dialog box

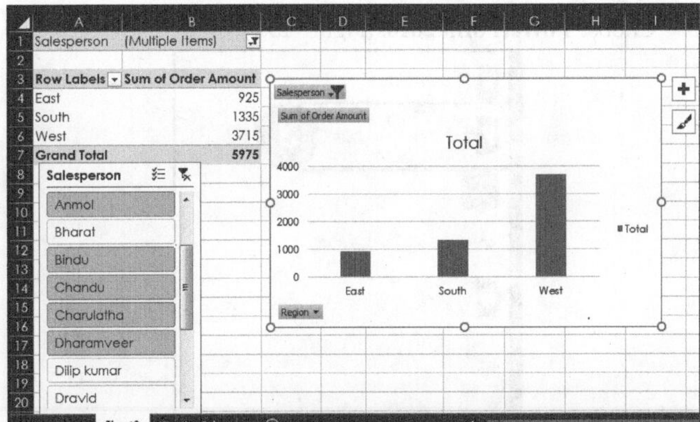

Figure 12.91 PivotChart chart in the worksheet

CHAPTER 13

PowerPoint 2016

13.1 INTRODUCTION

PowerPoint is a presentation program that allows you to create dynamic slide presentations. It is a sequential collection of slides in which each slide displays some information in the form of text or graphics. You can present almost any kind of information by means of presentation, such as presenting an idea to your clients or teaching students in a class.

13.2 STARTING POWERPOINT 2016

➡ **To start PowerPoint:**

1. Click the **Start** button on the Taskbar.
2. Highlight **All Programs** menu item and.
3. Choose **PowerPoint 2016**. (Figure 13.1).

Figure 13.1 Starting PowerPoint with the Start Button

When you open PowerPoint for the first time, the **Start Screen** will appear as shown in Figure 13.2. From here you will be able to create a new presentation, choose a template, and access your recently edited presentations. From the Start Screen, locate and select Blank Presentation to access the PowerPoint elements.

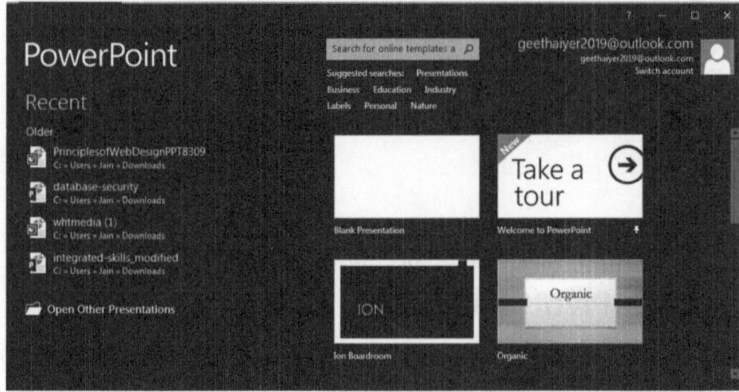

Figure 13.2 Start Screen

It displays a blank presentation with a single slide showing. The layout is simple, with a title at the top and a subtitle below. (Figure 13.3)

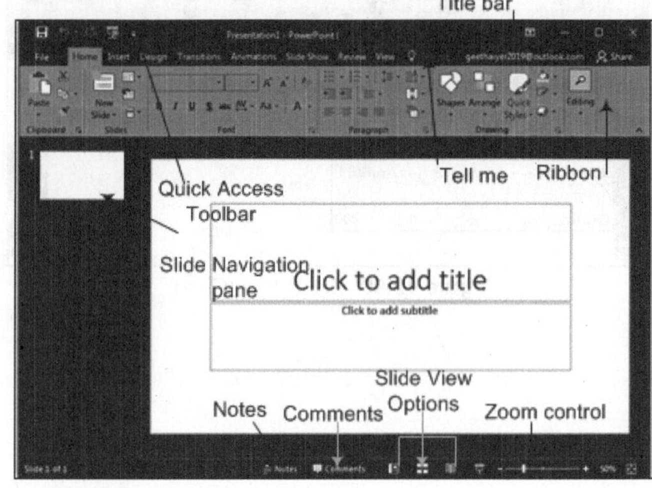

Figure 13.3 A blank Presentation displayed by PowerPoint

13.2.1 Understanding the Screen Elements

You will notice a close resemblance of the PowerPoint 2016 opening screen. The main elements of the PowerPoint window are as shown in Figure 13.3.

Title bar: The *Title bar* is at the top of the screen (Figure 13.3). It shows the title PowerPoint and the name of presentation. If you have not yet saved any presentation then it displays the default name for the presentation which is *Presentation1*.

Ribbon: Ribbon is displayed just below the title bar. In Ribbon, Commands are organized in logical groups, which are collected together under tabs (Figure 13.3).

Quick Access Toolbar: This toolbar is located by default at the top of PowerPoint 2016 window. By default, this toolbar displays the Save, Undo and Repeat buttons. You can customize the commands depending on the preference.

Minimize button: Shrinks the application window on the taskbar, you can click its button on the taskbar to reopen it.

Maximize button: A box at the right of a title bar that fills available space with the document or application.

Restore button: A double box at the right of a title bar that restores an application or document into a sizable window.

Close button: A box at the right of a title bar (X) that closes the window or dialog box.

Slide Navigation: The slide navigation pane allow you to view and organize the slides in the presentation.

Slide Pane: You can view and edit the selected slide.

Tell Me: The Tell me box works like a search bar to help you quickly find tools or commands you want to use.

Slide Number: You can quickly see the total number of slides in the presentation, as well as which slide you are working.

Notes: Click Notes to add notes to your current slide. Often called speaker notes, they can help you deliver or prepare for your presentation.

Comments: Reviewers can leave comments on any slide. Click comments to view comments from the current slide.

Slide View Option: There are four ways to view a presentation. Simply click a command to select the desired view.

13.2.2 The PowerPoint 2016 Interface

The new user interface is designed to help you to be more productive in PowerPoint, more easily find the right features for various tasks and also be more efficient.

Ribbon User Interface

PowerPoint uses a tabbed Ribbon system instead of traditional menus. The Ribbon contains multiple tabs, each with several groups of commands. For example, the **Font** group on the **Home** tab contains commands for formatting text in the document.

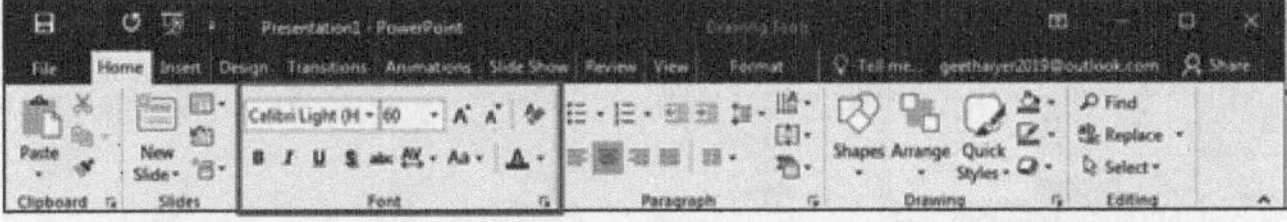

Some groups also have a small arrow in the bottom-right corner that you can click for even more options.

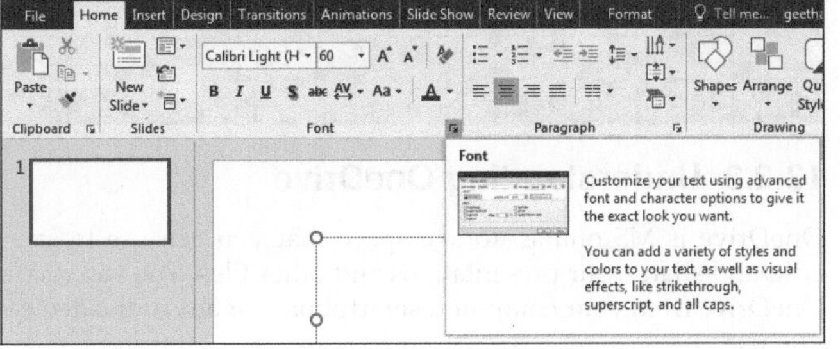

Showing and hiding the Ribbon

The Ribbon is designed to respond to current task, you can minimize it if you find that it takes up too much screen space. Click the Ribbon Display Options arrow in the upper-right corner of the Ribbon to display the drop-down menu.

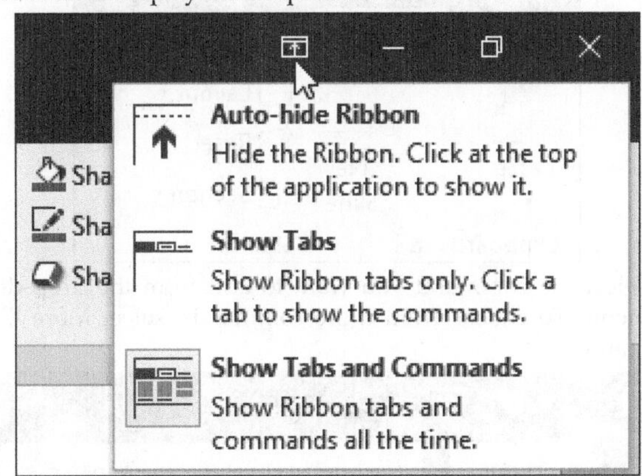

- **Auto-hide Ribbon:** Auto-hide displays your workbook in full-screen mode and completely hides the Ribbon. To show the Ribbon, click the Expand Ribbon command at the top of screen.
- **Show Tabs:** This option hides all command groups when they are not in use, but tabs will remain visible. To show the Ribbon, simply click a tab.
- **Show Tabs and Commands:** This option maximizes the Ribbon. All of the tabs and commands will be visible. This option is selected by default when you open PowerPoint for the first time.

Using the Tell me feature

Tell Me feature works just like a regular search bar: Type what you are looking for, and a list of options will appear. You can then use the command directly from the menu without having to find it on the Ribbon.

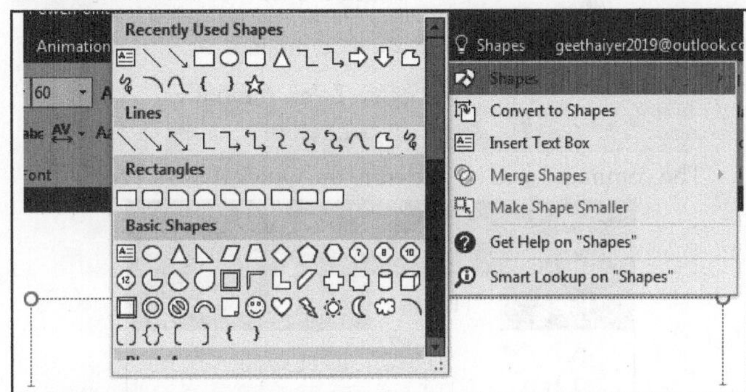

The Quick Access Toolbar

Quick Access Toolbar is located just above the Ribbon, it lets you to access common commands no matter which tab is selected. By default, it includes the Save, Undo, Redo, and Start From Beginning commands. You can add other commands depending on your preference.

➡ **To add commands to the Quick Access Toolbar:**

1. Click the drop-down arrow to the right of the Quick Access Toolbar.

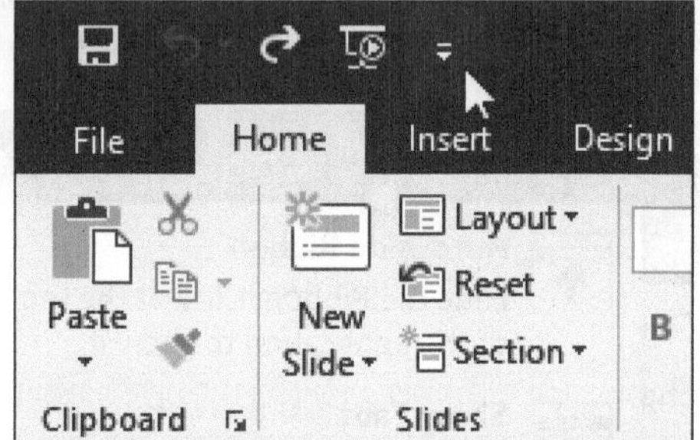

2. Select the command you want to add from the drop-down menu. To choose from more commands, select More Commands.

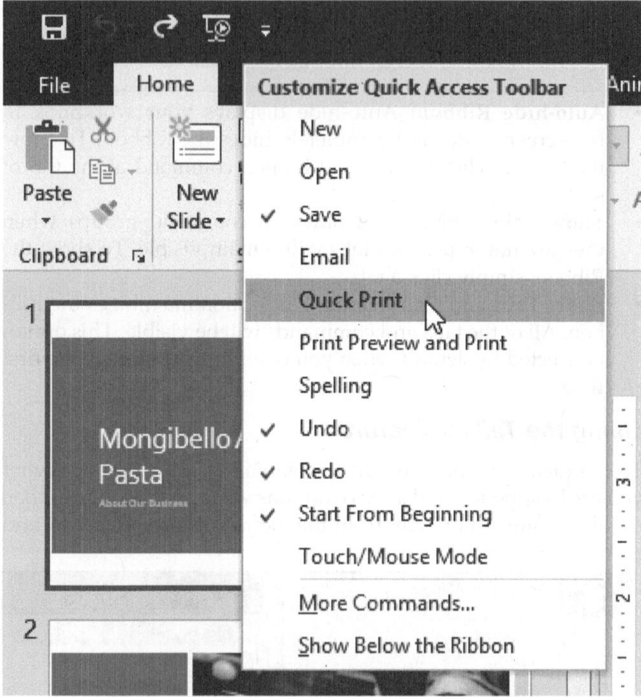

3. The command will be added to the Quick Access Toolbar.

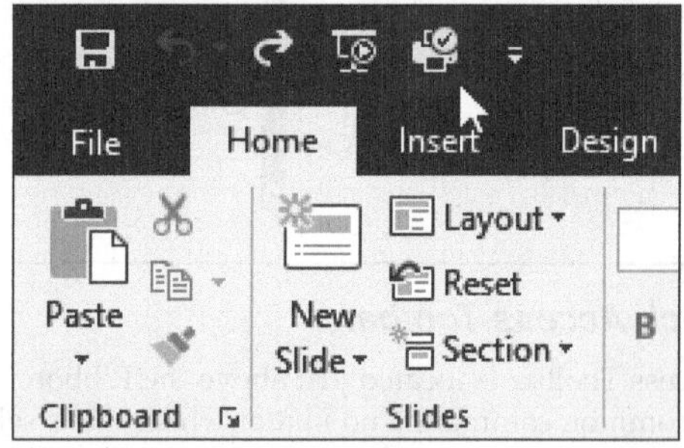

Zoom and other view options

PowerPoint has a variety of viewing options that change how your presentation is displayed. You can choose to view your presentation in Normal view, Slide Sorter view, Reading view, or Slide Show view. You can also zoom in and out to make your presentation easier to read.

Switching slide views

Switching between different slide views is easy to select the desired slide view command in the bottom-right corner of the PowerPoint window.

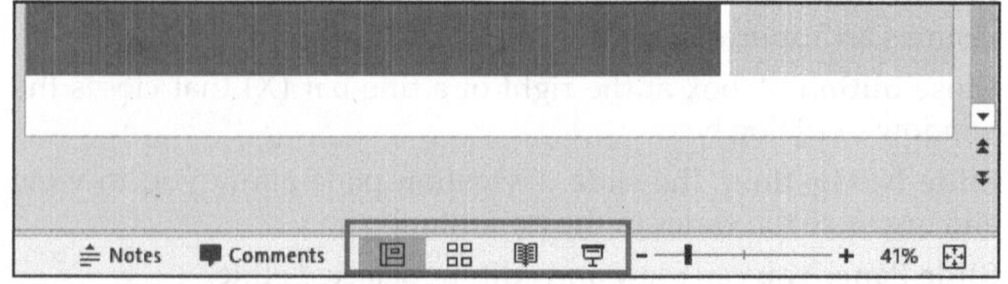

Zooming In and Out

To zoom in or out, click and drag the zoom control slider in the bottom-right corner of the PowerPoint window. You can also select the + or - commands to zoom in or out by smaller increments. The number next to the slider displays the current zoom percentage, also called the zoom level.

Backstage View

Backstage view gives you various options for saving, opening, printing, and sharing your presentations. To access Backstage view, click the **File** tab on the Ribbon. You can select the desired buttons to learn more about using Backstage view.

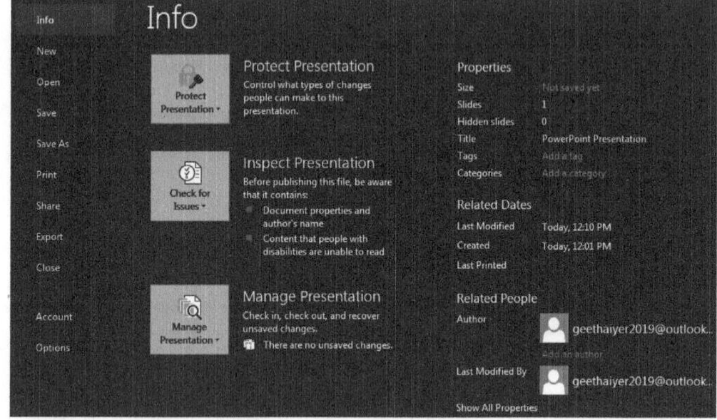

13.2.3 Understanding OneDrive

OneDrive is MS online storage space that you can use to save, edit, and share your presentations and other files. You can access OneDrive from your computer, smartphone, or any of the devices you use.

To get started with OneDrive, you need to set up a free MS account. Once you have a MS account, you will be able to sign in to Office. Just click Sign in the upper-right corner of the PowerPoint window.

Saving and Opening files

When you are signed in to your MS account, OneDrive will appear as an option whenever you save or open a file. You still have the option of saving files to your computer. However, saving files to your OneDrive allows you to access them from any other computer, and it also allows you to share files with friends and co-workers. For example, when you click **Save As**, you can select either **OneDrive** or **This PC** as the save location.

13.3 NEW FEATURES IN POWERPOINT 2016

PowerPoint 2016, brings some new features are:

PowerPoint Designer

With the new PowerPoint Designer, as soon as you insert an image, the Design Ideas panel opens at the right, offering several layout options for the graphical design of the current slide.

Morph Transition

PowerPoint 2016 adds a new transition type called Morph. This transition can help you make smooth animations, transitions, and object movements across the slides in the presentations.

13.3.1 Quick Shape Formats

Draw a shape on a slide and you will see an increase to the number of "preset" styles available. These styles expand your color and formatting options and save the time and effort it would take to create the effects manually.

13.3.2 Screen Recording

Perfect for demonstration, you can now include screen recordings in your presentation with just a few clicks. Just set up whatever you would like to record on your screen, then click **Insert** tab and choose **Screen Recording** and you will be able to select portion of your screen to record, capture and insert it directly into your presentation.

Collaboration and Sharing

Collaboration is integrated into Office 2016. Choose **Share** on the ribbon to share your presentation with others on SharePoint, OneDrive or another Online location.

Tell Me

One of the most new features is the "Tell Me" help tool. Just enter the words and phrases that describe the steps you want to do next and quickly get the features or actions you want to use.

Smart Lookup

The Smart Lookup feature, which is available in most of the Office 2016 programs. Just place your cursor on any word or highlight any phrase and right-click. Next, choose Smart Lookup form the drop-down list. The "insights" panel opens and displays information and images about the highlighted subject.

13.4 MANAGING SLIDES

As you add more slides to a presentation, it can be difficult to keep everything organized. Fortunately, PowerPoint offers tools to help you organize and prepare your slide show. It includes several different slide views, which are all useful for various tasks. The slide view commands are located in the bottom-right of the PowerPoint window. There are four main slide views:

13.4.1 Normal view

Normal view is the default and most often used view as shown Figure 13.4. This view displays one slide at a time in the Slide Area, and is used mainly for editing and creating slides, and shows PowerPoint's typical tri-pane interface that includes the **Slides Pane,** the **Slide Area,** and the **Notes Pane.**

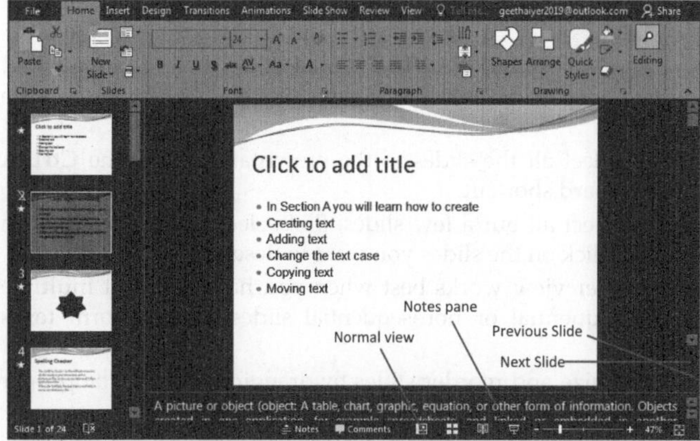

Figure 13.4 Normal view

➡ **To access Normal view:**

1. If you are not in Normal view, you can easily get to this view by choosing the **View** tab on Ribbon, and clicking the **Normal** button. Alternatively, you can click the **Normal** view button on the status bar.
2. To navigate to the next slide, you can use the vertical scrollbar on the Slide Area, or the **Next** and **Previous** buttons located at its bottom. You can also use the **Page Up** and **Page Down** keys on your keyboard to navigate between the slides.

13.4.2 Slide Sorter View

Slide Sorter view, you will see thumbnail sized representations of all slides in your presentation, as shown in Figure 13.5. This view is when you have to select multiple slides – you can quickly reorder, delete, or duplicate your slides. In addition, this view also clearly displays hidden slides.

➡ **To access Slide Sorter view:**

1. Click the **Slide Sorter** button on the Status Bar.
2. Click the **View** tab of the Ribbon, and click the **Slide Sorter** button on the **Presentations view** group.

Here are some guidelines for selecting slides in Slide Sorter view:

- To select a single slide, just click on the slide.

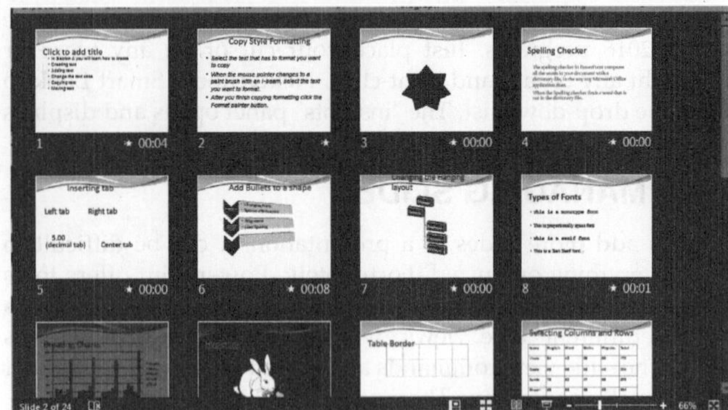

Figure 13.5 Slide Sorter view

- To select a range of slides, hold down the primary mouse button and drag across and over the slides like a marquee. Try to drag in a diagonal direction if you have more than one line of slides lined up.
- To select a contiguous range of slides, click the first slide, hold the **Shift** key on the keyboard and then click the last slide.
- To select multiple, non-contiguous slides, hold down the **Ctrl** key on your keyboard and then click the slides you want to select.
- To select all the slides in the presentation press the **Ctrl+A** keyboard shortcut.
- To select all but a few slides, first select all slides, and then **Ctrl** click on the slides you want to deselect.

Slide Sorter view works best when you have to select multiple slides (sequential or non-sequential slides) and perform tasks such as:

- Organize and reorder slides by dragging them in the proper sequence.
- Group slides into separate Sections.
- Easily copy, paste, or delete slides.
- Duplicate slides.
- Hide and show selected slides.
- Control transition effects that play when the presentation advances from one slide to the next.
- Set and adjust the slide timing of these transitions.
- **To change the slide order:**

1. Select the slide(s) you want to reorder, and drag them to a position where you want to place them.

To insert a new slide within Slide Sorter view, choose any of these three approaches:

1. **Use the Ribbon:**
   i. Place the cursor where you want to insert a new slide.
   ii. Select the **Home** tab of the Ribbon, and locate the **Slides** group.
   iii. Click the **New Slide** button.
2. Place the cursor where you want to insert a new slide, right-click and from the pop-up menu choose **New Slide** option.
3. Place the cursor where you want to insert a new slide and press the **Ctrl+M** shortcut key combination.

13.4.3 Notes Page View

The Notes Page is one of ten views available in PowerPoint 2016. This view shows you how your printed notes will appear. The Notes page shows the speaker notes that you add to the Notes pane for each slide. Each slide created contains its own Notes Page. You can print these pages out to use as a reference while delivering the presentation. These notes do not show on the screen during Slide Show view.

➡ **To access the Notes Page view:**

1. Click the **View** tab on the Ribbon, and click the **Notes Page** button on the **Presentations views** group as shown in Figure 13.6.

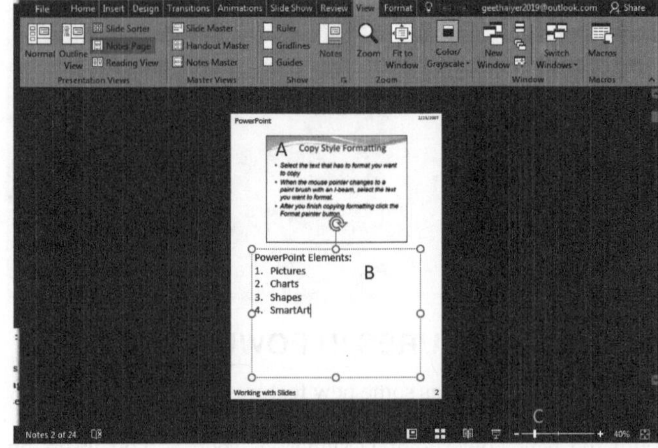

Figure 13.6 Notes page view

Here is a description of the various elements within Notes Page view:

A The large box on the top half of the page is a single slide that shows the same slide that you see in Normal view.

B The box located on the bottom half of the page is the Notes area -- this contains the same notes that are available within the Notes pane of Normal view. You can also add notes and edit them here -- changes made here show within the Notes pane of Normal view, and vice versa. Additionally, you can also format the text content here. Select the text that you want to format and right-click to bring up the Mini Toolbar.

C Remember that you can use the **Zoom** slider which is placed towards the right on the **Status bar** to get a better, zoomed-in view of any part of the Notes Page.

13.4.4 Slide Show View

Have you created all your slides -- and now you want to show it in front of an audience? In that case, the view that plays your presentation in full screen mode is Slide Show view, as shown in Figure 13.7.

➡ **To access Slide Show view:**

1. Click the **Slide Show** button on the **Status bar** to play the presentation from the active slide.
2. You can also access the Slide Show tab of the Ribbon. Then choose one of the following options:
   i. *From Beginning:* Starts the slide show from the first slide of the presentation. You can also use the **F5** Function key.

Copy Style Formatting

- Select the text that has to format you want to copy
- When the mouse pointer changes to a paint brush with an I-beam, select the text you want to format.
- After you finish copying formatting click the Format painter button.

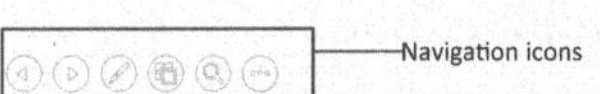

Figure 13.7 Slide Show view

ii. *From Current Slide:* Starts the slide show from the active slide. You can also use the **Shift+F5** shortcut key.

3. To exit Slide Show view, choose any of these options:
   i. Press the **Esc** (Escape) key.
   ii. Right-click on the slide, and choose the **End Show** option in the pop-up menu.

Remember that Slide Show view is a display view and no editing can be done on slides. If you hover your cursor over the bottom left area of the slide, you will find six watermarked navigation icons that you can see in Figure 14.6. These icons are explained below:

- *Previous Slide:* Click this icon to navigate to the previous slide (or press the P, Left Arrow, or Backspace keys).
- *Next Slide:* Click this icon to navigate to the next slide (or press the N, Right Arrow, or Spacebar keys).
- **Pen and Laser Pointer Tools:** Click on this button to bring up a menu, as shown in Figure 13.8 below.

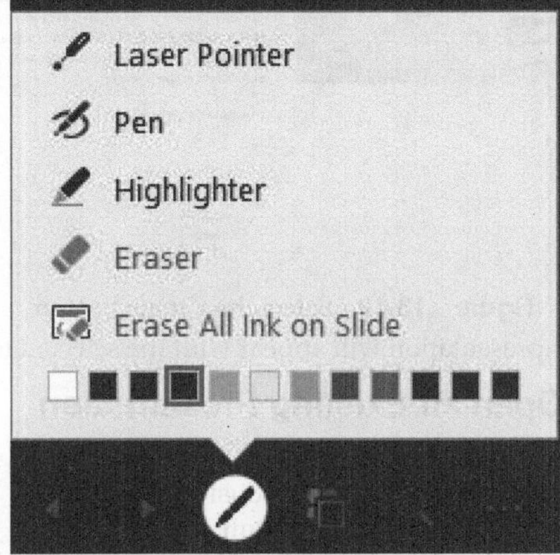

Figure 13.8 Pen options

- *Laser Pointer:* Directs the audience's eye with a bright colored point of light. You can set the Laser Pointer color within the Set Up Show dialog box – to access this dialog box, choose the Slide Show tab of the Ribbon, and then click the Set Up Slide Show button.
- *Pen:* Lets you draw or annotate with a pen.
- *Highlighter:* Works almost like a virtual highlighter pen.
- *Eraser:* Lets you erase any pen or highlighter marked areas (grayed out if there are no marked areas on the current slide).
- *Erase All Ink on Slide:* Removes all ink markings (grayed out if there are no marked areas on the current slide).
- *Ink Color:* Changes the pen color.

- *See All Slides:* Click on this button to bring up the whole slide deck and choose any slide.
- *Zoom into the slide:* With this tool you can zoom a part of the slide and then pan around.
- *More Options:* This icon, when clicked, opens a menu as below.

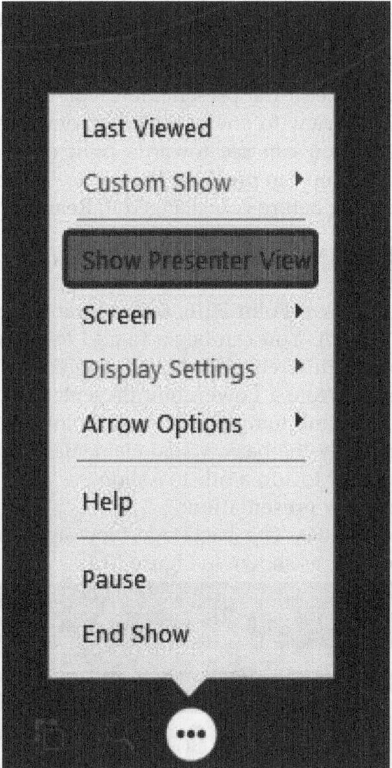

13.4.5 Reading View

Reading view is similar to Slide Show view in some ways because, in both views, the slide is shown in full-screen mode. However, in Reading view, you also see the PowerPoint title bar and the Status Bar at the top and bottom of the interface respectively, as you can see in Figure 13.9.

➡ **To access Reading view:**

1. Click the **View** tab on the Ribbon, and click the **Reading View** button on the **Presentations view** group.
2. Alternatively, you can also access **Reading** view from the **View** buttons on the right side of the **Status Bar** – just click the third button.

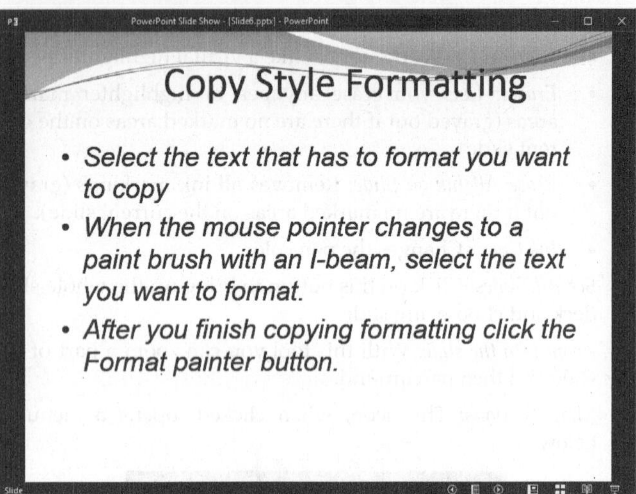

Figure 13.9 Reading view

If you want to edit the presentation, you can always switch from Reading view to one of the other views using the view buttons that you can see towards right on the Status Bar. Additionally, you can press the **Esc** key to go back to the view you were using before you changed to **Reading** view.

13.5 CREATING A PRESENTATION

When you start PowerPoint 2016, the program displays a blank title slide by default. You can begin to add text and pictures on that slide choose a different slide layout, apply a design etc.

If you want to create a PowerPoint presentation on your own, you can use the blank template in PowerPoint 2016. The blank template offers only the basic visual elements of a presentation, such as placeholder to add a title to a slide.

➡ **To create a new presentation:**

1. Click the **File** tab. The backstage view appears, displaying various options as shown in Figure 13.10.

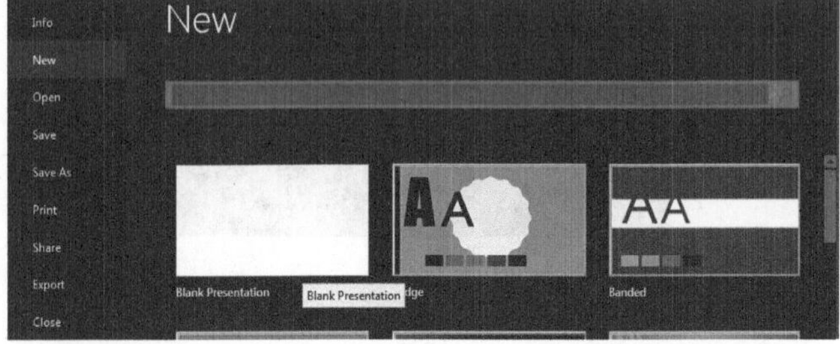

Figure 13.10 File backstage view with the New option selected

2. On the left side of the window, select the **New** option from the backstage view.
3. A new presentation is created with the name **Presentation1** as shown in Figure 14.3.

   You can see that a blank presentation contains a single slide with text boxes (placeholders) to enter a title and a subtitle. You can also apply different styles and background to it.

13.5.1 Create a New Presentation from a Template

A template is a predesigned presentation you can use to create a new slide show quickly. Templates often include custom formatting and designs, so they can save you a lot of time and effort.

➡ **To create a new presentation from a template:**

1. Click the **File** tab to access Backstage view, then select **New**.
2. You can click a suggested search to find templates or use the search bar to find something more specific. For example, we have search for the keyword **Presentations** as shown in Figure 13.11.

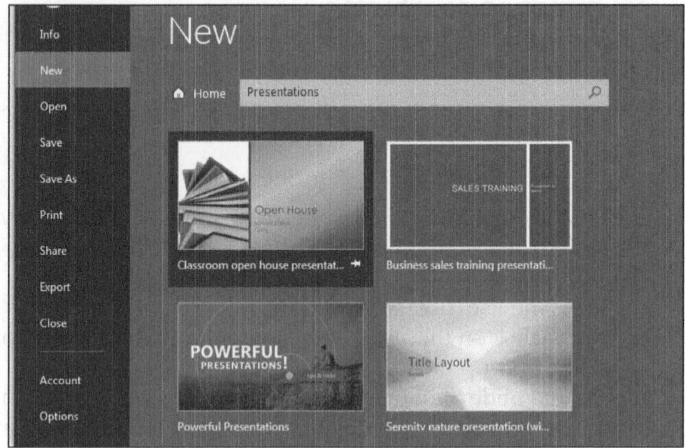

Figure 13.11 Selecting template from New backstage view

3. Select a desired template to review it.
4. Click **Create** to use the selected template and it get downloaded as shown in Figure 13.12.

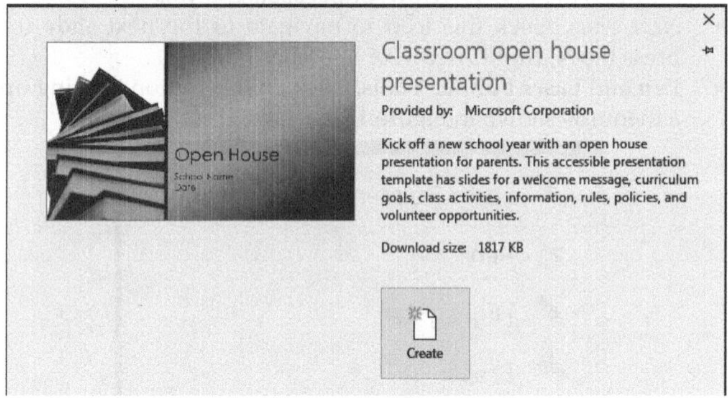

Figure 13.12 Select the Create button

5. A new presentation will appear with the selected template.

13.5.2 Open an Existing Presentation

In addition to creating new presentations, you will often need to open a presentation that was previously saved.

➡ **To open an existing presentation:**

1. Select the **File** tab to go to Backstage view, then click **Open** as shown in Figure 13.13.
2. Click **Browse**. Alternatively, you can choose **OneDrive** to open files stored on the OneDrive.
3. The **Open** dialog box will appear as shown in Figure 13.14.

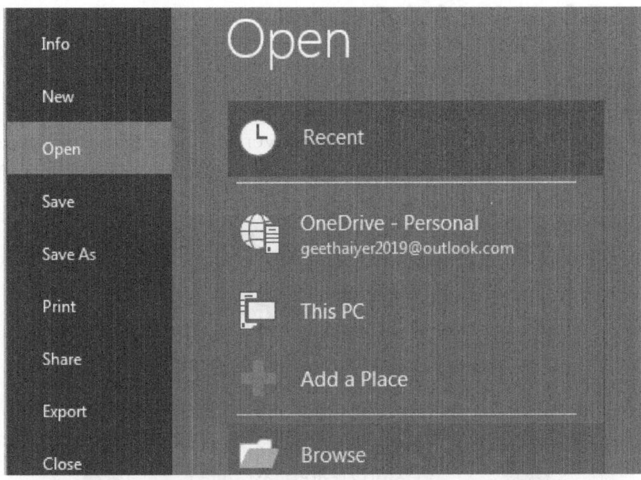

Figure 13.13 File backstage

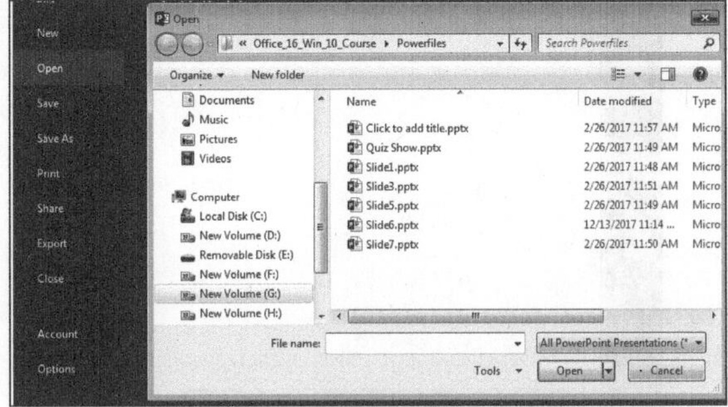

Figure 13.14 Open dialog box

4. Navigate the location of the folder where the file is located in the Address bar.
5. Click Open button to open the file.

13.5.3 Pin a Presentation

If you frequently work with the same presentation, you can pin it to Backstage view for easy access.

➡ **To pin a presentation:**

1. Select the **File** tab to go to Backstage view, then click **Open.** The **Recent** Presentations will appear as shown in Figure 13.15.

Figure 13.15 Pin a Presentation

2. Hover the mouse over the presentation you want to pin, then click the pushpin icon.
3. The presentation will stay in the Recent presentations list until it is unpinned. To unpin a presentation, click the push-pin icon again as shown in Figure 13.16.

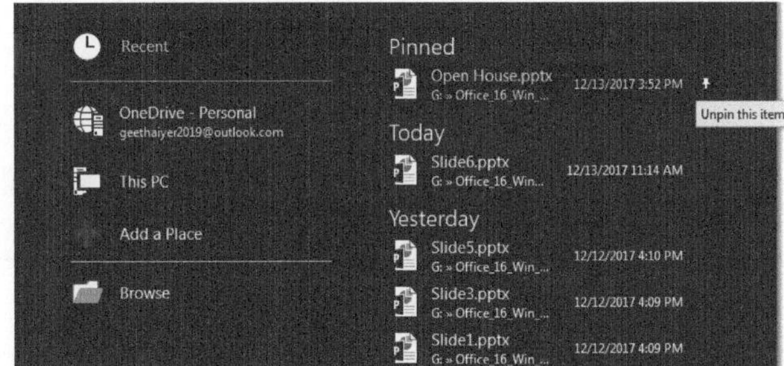

Figure 13.16 Pin a Presentation

13.5.4 Compatibility Mode

Sometimes you may need to work with presentations that were created in earlier versions of PowerPoint, like PowerPoint 2007 or PowerPoint 2010. When you open these types of presentations, they will appear in Compatibility Mode. If you want access to all PowerPoint 2016 features, you can convert the presentation to the 2016 file format. Note that converting a file may cause some changes to the original layout of the presentation.

➡ **To convert a presentation:**

1. Click the **File** tab to access Backstage view.
2. Click **Info** tab, click **Convert** command as shown in Figure 13.17.
3. The **Save As** dialog box will appear as shown in Figure 13.18. Select the **location** where you want to save the presentation, enter a **file name**, and click **Save.**

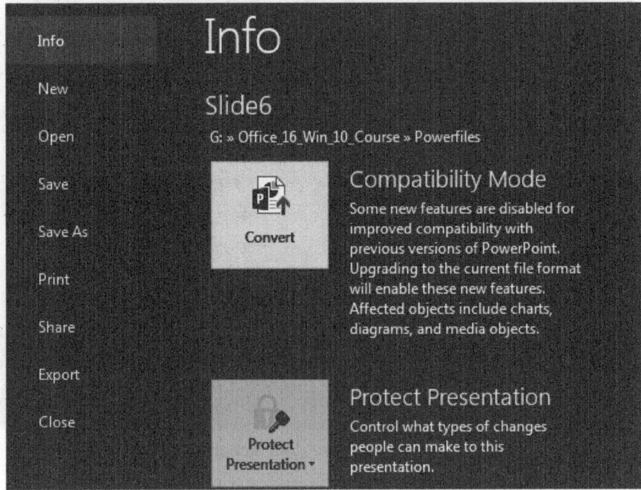

Figure 13.17 Select Convert command in Info tab

4. The presentation will be converted to the newest file type.

13.5.5 Saving the Presentation

It is important to save the presentation whenever you start a new file or make changes to an existing one. Saving can prevent the work from being lost.

PowerPoint offers two ways to save a file: **Save** and **Save As.** These options work in similar ways:

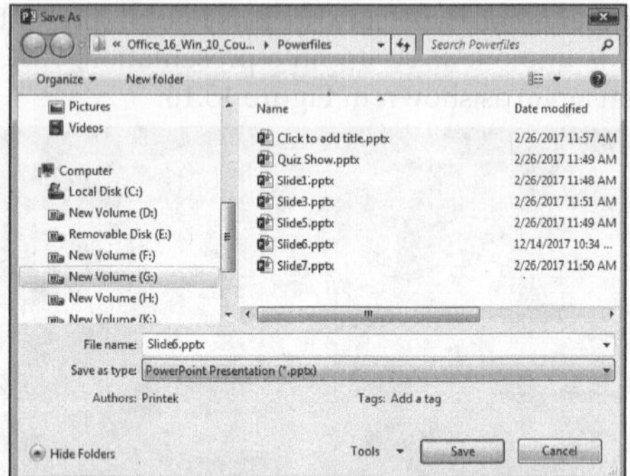

Figure 13.18 Save As dialog box

- *Save:* When you create or edit a presentation, you use the Save command to save your changes. When you save a file, you will only need to choose a file name and location the first time. After that, you can just click the Save command to save it with the same name and location.
- *Save As:* To use this command to create a copy of a presentation while keeping the original. When you use Save As, you will need to choose a different name and/or location for the copied version.

➡ **To save the presentation:**

1. Select the **Save** command on the Quick Access Toolbar.
2. If you are saving the file for the first time, the **Save As** pane will appear in Backstage view as shown in Figure 13.19.

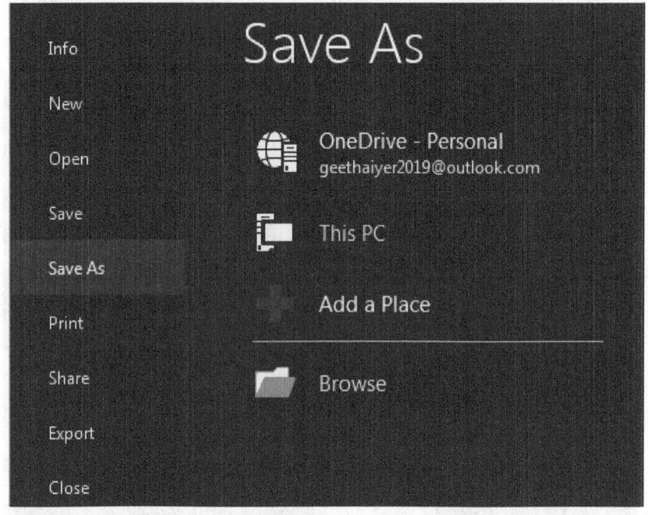

Figure 13.19 Save As backstage view

3. Click **Browse** to select a location on your computer. Alternatively, you can click **OneDrive** to save the file to your OneDrive.
4. The **Save As** dialog box will appear as shown in Figure 14.18. Select the location where you want to save the presentation.
5. Enter a file name for the presentation, then click **Save**.
6. The presentation will be saved. You can click the Save command again to save your changes as you modify the presentation.

13.5.6 Using AutoRecover

If you forget to save your changes or if PowerPoint crashes, you can restore the file using AutoRecover.

➡ **To use AutoRecover:**

1. Open PowerPoint. If autosaved versions of a file are found, the **Document Recovery** pane will appear as shown in Figure 13.20.

Figure 13.20 Document Recovery

2. Click to open an available file. The presentation will be recovered. Alternatively, select the **File** tab, click **Manage Presentation**, then choose **Recover Unsaved Presentations** as shown in Figure 13.21.

By default, PowerPoint autosaves every 10 minutes. If you are editing a presentation for less than 10 minutes, PowerPoint may not create an autosaved version. If you do not see the file you need, you can browse the autosaved files from Backstage view.

13.5.7 Exporting Presentations

By default, PowerPoint presentations are saved in the .pptx file type. However, if you need to use another file type, such as a PDF. It is easy to export your presentation from PowerPoint in a variety of file types. These are:

- **PDF:** Saves the presentation as a PDF document instead of a PowerPoint file.
- **Video:** Saves the presentation as a video.
- **Package for CD:** Saves the presentation in a folder along with the Microsoft PowerPoint Viewer, a special slide show player anyone can download.

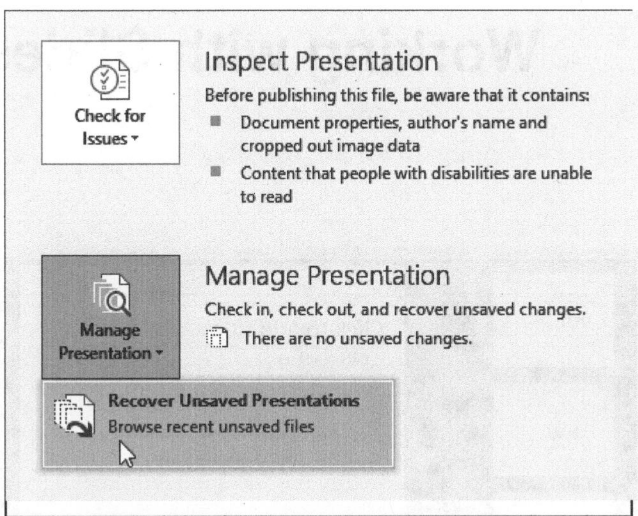

Figure 13.21 Recover Unsaved Presentations

- **Handouts:** Prints a handout version of your slides
- **Other file type:** Saves in other file types, including PNG and PowerPoint 97-2003.

➡ **To export a presentation:**

1. Select the file which you want to export a presentation.
2. Click the **File** tab to access Backstage view.
3. Click **Export**, then choose the desired option. In our example, we have select **Create PDF/XPS Document**. Then click **Create PDF/XPS** command as shown in Figure 13.22.
4. **Publish as PDF or XPS** dialog box appears as shown in Figure 13.23.

Figure 13.22 Selecting Create PDF / XPS

5. Select the location where you want to export the presentation, type a file name, then click **Publish**. The file get published in the Pdf format.

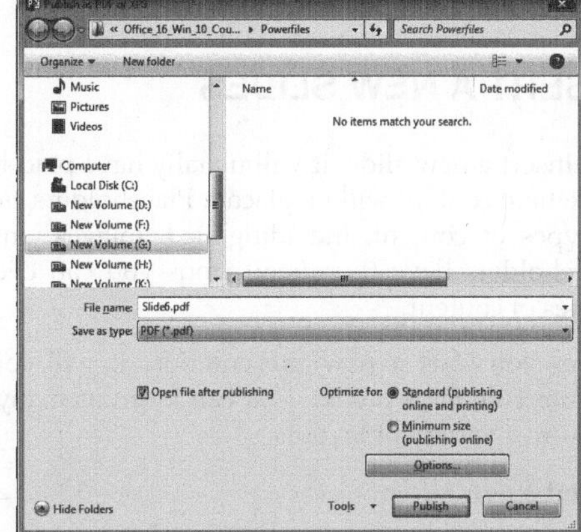

Figure 13.23 Publish as PDF / XPS dialog box

CHAPTER 14

Working with Slides

14.1 INTRODUCTION

PowerPoint presentation is set of slides. To begin creating a slide show, you will need to know the basics of working with slides. You will need to feel comfortable with tasks such as inserting a new slide, changing the layout of a slide, formatting text to a slide.

14.2 INSERT A NEW SLIDES

When you insert a new slide, it will usually have placeholders to show you where content will be placed. Placeholders can contain different types of content, including text, images, and videos. Many placeholders have thumbnail icons you can click to add specific types of content.

Whenever you start a new presentation, it will contain one slide with the Title Slide layout. You can insert as many slides as you need from a variety of layouts.

➡ **To insert a new slide:**

1. Click the **Home** tab, select **New Slide** drop-down arrow in the **Slides** group.
2. Choose the desired slide layout from the drop-down menu as shown in Figure 14.1.

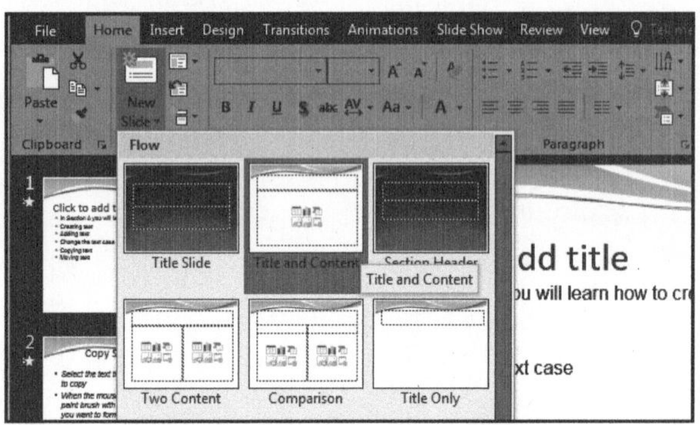

Figure 14.1 Selecting New Slide

3. The new slide will appear. Click any placeholder and begin typing to add text. You can also click an icon to add other types of content, such as a picture or a chart as shown in Figure 14.2.
4. To change the layout of an existing slide, click the **Layout** command, then choose the desired layout.

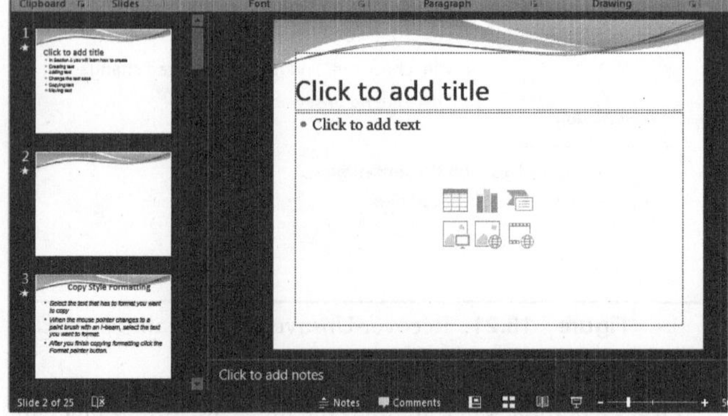

Figure 14.2 New slide with Title and content

14.2.1 Adding Text in a Placeholder

PowerPoint 2016 comes with predefined layouts you want to use, or you can add a blank slide and create a custom layout. Many of these layouts contain text placeholders for title, body and bulleted list.

1. After inserting a new slide, click anywhere within a placeholder to select it. The border indicates that the current placeholder is selected as shown in Figure 14.3.

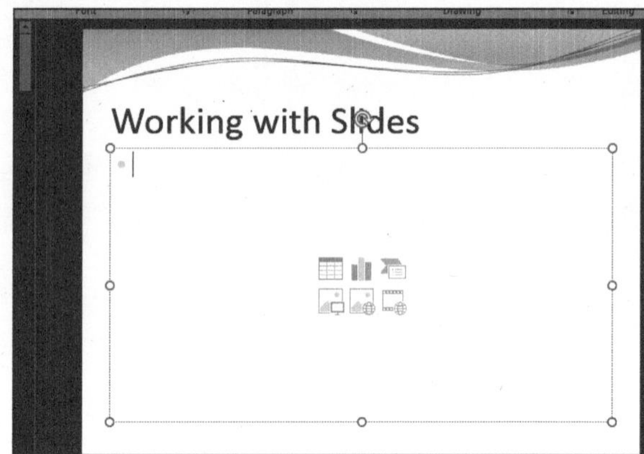

Figure 14.3 Add text to placeholder

2. The sample text disappears and an insertion point appears inside the placeholder, indicating that you can enter or type text.
3. If it is a bulleted-list placeholder, the sample text disappears and the bullet remains, with the insertion point positioned where the text will begin.
4. Type the text for the slide inside the selected placeholder and press Enter key.

5. In the case of bullets, press Enter key when you want to begin a new bulleted item. If the bulleted text is too long to fit on one line, PowerPoint automatically wraps the text to the next line and aligns the text.
6. When you finish entering text, deselect the object by clicking a blank area of the slide of the gray border around the slide.

14.2.2 Expand the Slide

1. If you continue to add items and you will see the text size and spacing adjusts to fit the text onto the slide.
2. Click the **AutoFit Options** button that appears when the slide fills, and click **Split Text Between Two Slides** as shown in Figure 14.4.

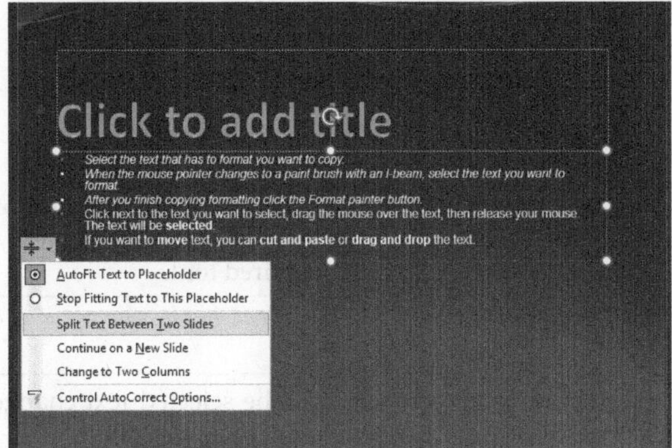

Figure 14.4 Expand the slide

3. A new slide is inserted, with the same layout and title as the original slide, and with the bulleted items shared between them.

14.2.3 Creating Text Outside a Placeholder

When you want additional text to appear on the slide, such as annotations or minor points that do not belong in a bulleted list, you can create a text box by using the Text Box button in the **Text** group on the **Insert** tab. You can create a text box in two ways:

- You can click the Text box button, click the slide where you want the text to appear, and then type.
- You can click the Text Box button, drag a box where you want the text to appear on the list, and then type. When the text reaches the right boundary of the box, the height of the box expands by one line so that the text can wrap. As you continue typing, the width of the box remains the same, but the height grows as necessary to accommodate all the text.

➡ **To create a text object:**

1. Click the **Insert** tab. In the **Text** group, click the **Text box** icon.
2. A new text box appears. Position mouse pointer at the place where you want to add text and then click it.
3. Click outside the text box to deselect it.

14.3 TEXT BASICS

You can copy text that appears in one place to another place. If you want to move text, you can cut and past or drag and drop the text.

➡ **To copy text:**

1. Select the text you want to copy.
2. On the **Home** tab, click **Copy** command or press **Ctrl + C** keys together.
3. Place the insertion point where you want the text to appear.
4. Click the Paste down pointing arrow and choose Paste command on the **Clipboard** group (or press Ctrl+V keys together.
5. The copied text will appear.

14.3.1 Moving Text

Moving text operation is similar to the copy text operation except that text is moved i.e. it is deleted from the original location and copied to a new place.

➡ **To move the text:**

1. Select the text you want to move,
2. Right-click and choose Cut from the shortcut menu or click the Cut button on the **Home** tab (or press Ctrl+X keys together).
3. Move to the new location, right-click, and choose Paste or click the **Paste** button on the **Home** tab (or press Ctrl+V keys together).
4. The text will appear in the new location.

☞ *Using Cut and Paste is the way to move text around between slides. Just select and cut the text, move to the appropriate slide, and paste it where you want it.*

14.3.2 Deleting Text

You can delete characters, words, or all the text in a text box. Using one of these methods:

- The Delete key erases the character to the right of the cursor.
- The Backspace key erases the character to the left of the cursor.

If you delete text accidentally, you can undo your action by clicking the Undo button on the Quick Access toolbar (or you can also press Ctrl+Z keys together).

14.3.3 Drag and Drop Text

1. Select the text you want to move, then click and drag the text to the desired location.
2. The text will appear in the new location as shown in Figure 14.5.

14.4 FORMATTING TEXT

Formatting Text can draw the audience's attention to specific parts of a presentation and emphasize important information. It has several options for adjusting your text, including size and color. You can also adjust the alignment of the text to change how it is displayed on the slide.

14.4.1 Aligning Text in a Slide

Alignment is the way text is placed between the margins of a page or a text box on a slide.

➡ **To align the text:**

1. Select the text, which you want to align.

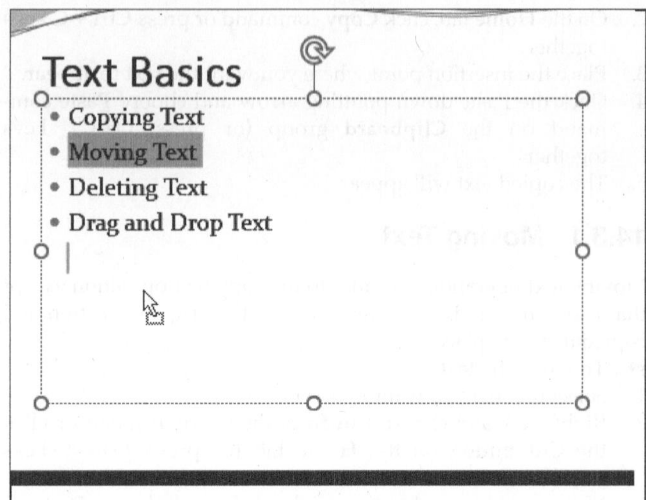

Figure 14.5 Drag and Drop text

2. On the **Home** tab, click the **Left**, **Center**, or **Right** alignment button on the **Paragraph** group. *Alternatively*, click the Paragraph Launcher dialog box and select the desired option in the alignment section. For example, we have select the center alignment as shown in Figure 14.6.

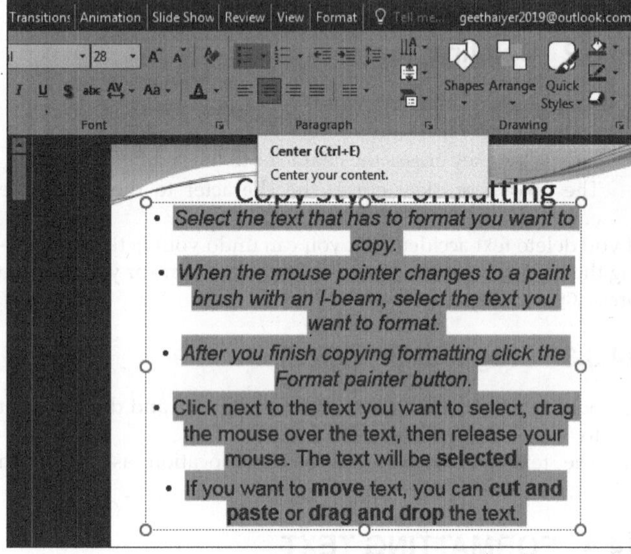

Figure 14.6 Selecting Center alignment

14.4.2 Changing Fonts

Fonts are also called *typefaces* in computer programs. There are groups of characters that share the same style or look.

➡ **To change the font of any text in a slide:**

1. Select the text you want to change.
2. Click the **Home** tab and choose **Font** drop-down list in the **Font** group. Select the desired font from the font list as shown in Figure 14.7. Or select the text, a mini toolbar appears. Select the font themes appears and choose the desired font you want to apply. Or

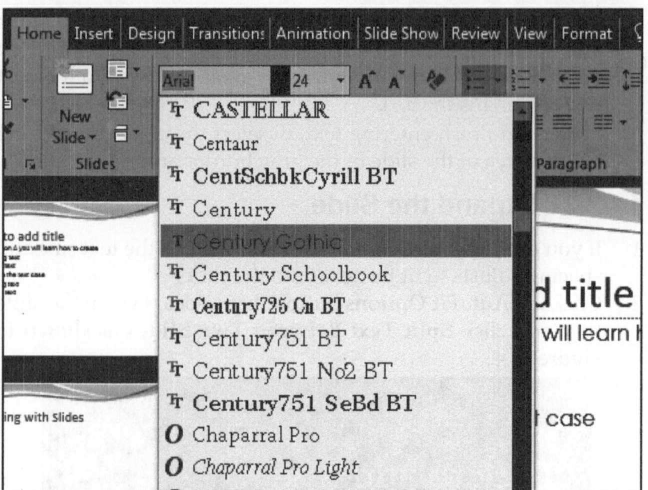

Figure 14.7 Selecting font command

Click the right mouse button and choose Font... from shortcut menu. The Font dialog box appears. Click **Latin text font** drop down list and select the required font.

☞ *Right type and size of font creates good impression on your audience.*

3. Click the font you want to use. The selected text changes to the selected font.

14.4.3 Changing the Text Size

Font size is measured in *points*, which is a height measurement, each point is 1/72 of an inch.

➡ **To change the size of text:**

1. Select the text you want to change.
2. On the **Home** tab, click the **Font size** drop-down list and choose desired font size. Or
   Select the text. A mini toolbar appears. Choose the desired font size you want to apply. Or click the right mouse button and choose Font... . In the **Font** dialog box that appears, click the **Size:** drop-down list and choose the desired size or type the size as shown in Figure 14.8. Or

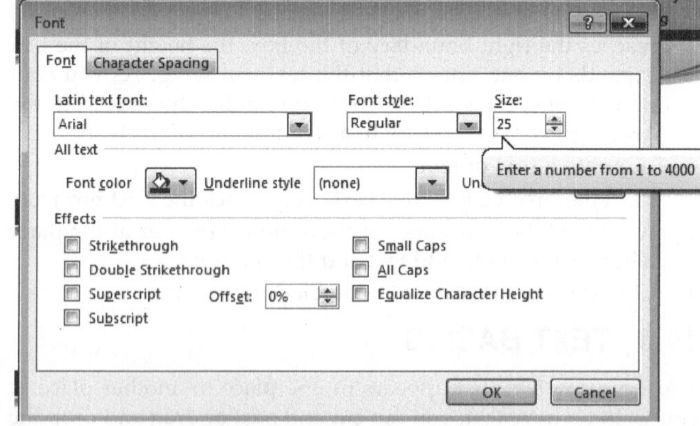

Figure 14.8 Font dialog box

3. Click the **Increase Font Size** and **Decrease Font Size** on the Ribbon command.

14.4.4 Adding Special Effects to Text

One of the easiest ways to make text stand out is to add special formatting effects to *characters, sentences,* or *paragraphs*. PowerPoint makes these tasks very easy.

➡ **To add special effect:**

1. Select text to which you want to apply special effect.
2. In the Font dialog box, the options Font style: box has the following:
   - Regular—The normal way the text appears.
   - Bold—The text appears bold or highlighted.
   - Italic—The text appears Italic.
   - Bold Italic—The text appears bold and Italic highlighted

   The All text has this option:
   - Font color— Specifies the color of the selected text. In the box, select the color. You can see the color under the bucket.
   - Underline style— Specifies whether selected text is underlined and the underline style. Click none to remove underlining.
   - Underline color— Specifies the color of the underline. This option remains unavailable until you apply an underline style.

   The Effect Areas has this option:
   - Strikethrough—Draws a line through the selected text.
   - Superscript—The text appears raised like x^2y
   - Subscript—The text appears lowered like H_20
   - Small caps—The selected text lowercase to small caps and reduces their size. It does not affect numbers, punctuation, non-alphabetic characters.
   - All caps—It converts lowercase to capitals.
   - Equalize Character Height—It reformats text effects to apply an even character height to text.

The font style and special effects of above explanation as shown in Figure 14.9.

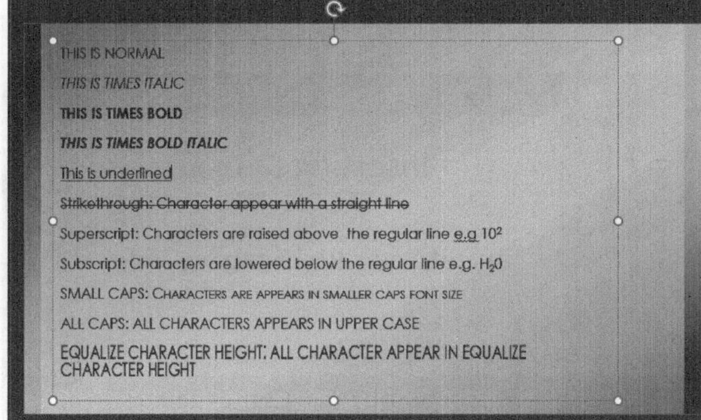

Figure 14.9 Font style and special effects applied in Font dialog box

14.4.5 Changing text color

➡ **To change the text colour:**

1. Select the text you want to change.
2. In the **Home** tab, click the **Font** group, click **Font Color** drop-down list. The font colors theme palette appears as shown in Figure 14.10.

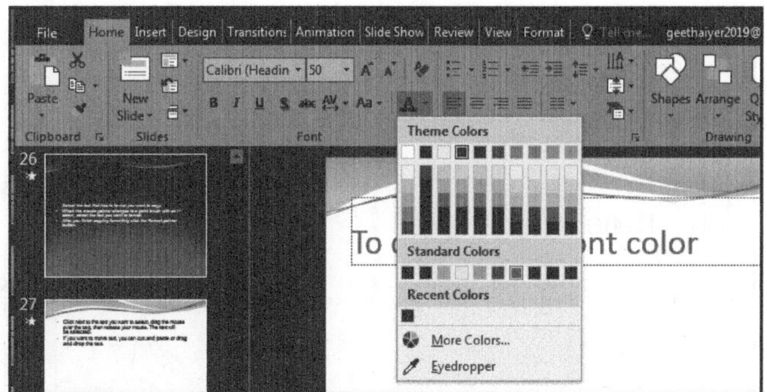

Figure 14.10 Selecting Font color in the home tab

3. Move the mouse pointer over the color, you can see the effect changes in the text. Choose the desired color you want to apply to the text.
4. The selected font color appears in the text.

14.4.6 Bullets and Numbering

➡ **To add bullets in the paragraph:**

1. Select the text or paragraphs you want to add bullet.
2. Click the **Bullet** command icon, in the **Paragraph** group. Click the arrow you want to choose the different bullet style. (See Figure 14.11) To customize the bullet sign, click Bullets and Numbering... command.

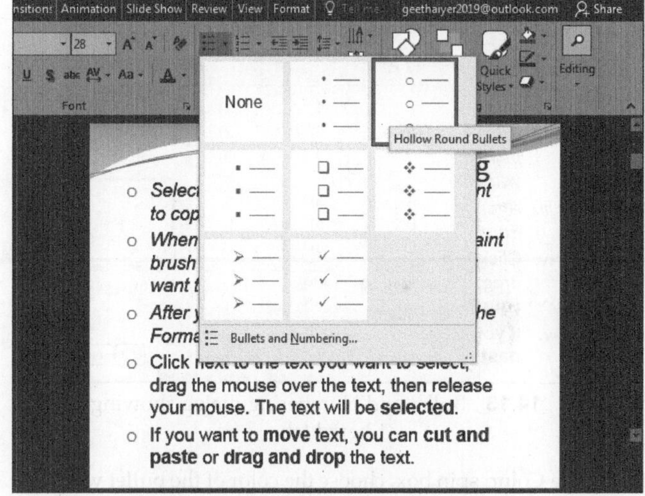

Figure 14.11 Selecting Bullet command

3. The **Bullets and Numbering** dialog box appears as shown in Figure 14.12. Click the **Bulleted** tab you want to modify.
4. You can select the Picture... button you can use the picture or motion clip file to use as a bullet.
5. In the Size: spin box, enter the bullet size you want as a percentage of the font size.
6. In the Color: spin box, choose the color of the bullet you want.

➡ **To add numbering in the paragraph:**

1. Select the text or paragraphs you want to add numbering.
2. Click the **Numbering** command icon, in the **Paragraph** group. Click the arrow to choose Bullets and Numbering... command. Or to customize the Number style, click Bullets and Numbering... command.

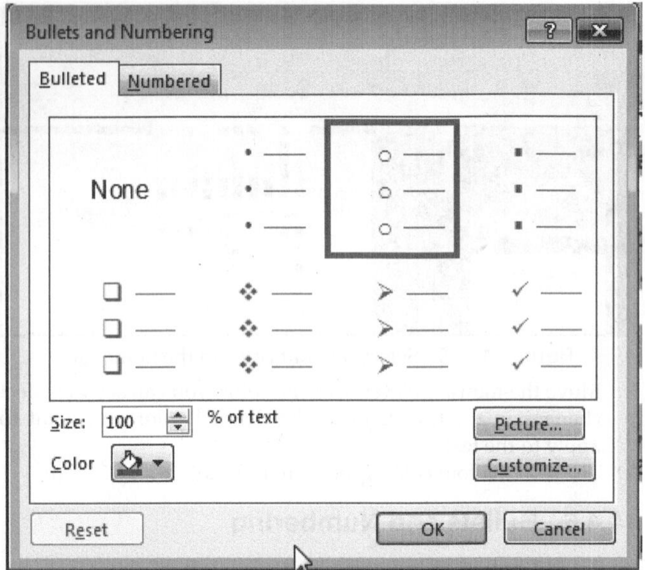

Figure 14.12 Bullets and Numbering dialog box

3. The **Bullets and Numbering** dialog box appears as shown in Figure 14.13. Click the Numbered tab you want to modify.
4. In the Size: spin box, enter the bullet size you want as a percentage of the font size.

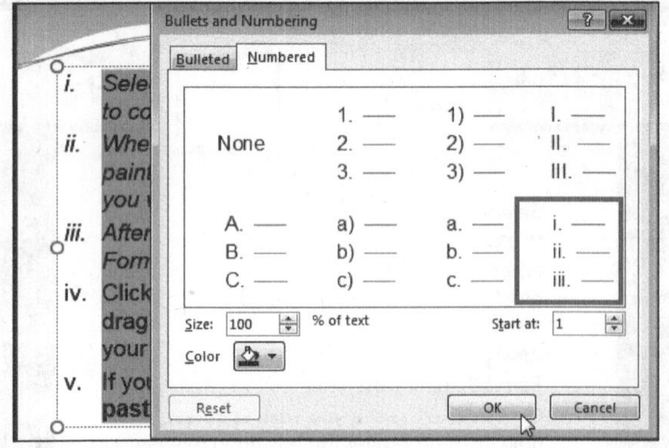

Figure 14.13 Bullet and Numbering dialog showing Numbered tab

5. In the Color: spin box, choose the color of the bullet you want.
6. In the Start at: spin box, choose the number of letter to use in the list.

14.4.7 Removing Bullets and Numbering

➡ **To remove bullets and numbering:**

1. Select the text or placeholders you want to remove bullets and number form.
2. On the **Home** tab, in **Paragraph** group, choose the bullet down arrow, a bullet palette list appears, choose **None**. Or You can press Backspace to remove bullet or numbering from an item in a list. PowerPoint automatically adjusts the number sequence of a numbered list.

14.4.8 Tabs

The function of a tab is to help you align text in your documents. The tab is a small marker that tells the text where you want to stop. PowerPoint gives you the option of choosing four different tab stops: left, right, center and decimal tabs.

Setting Tabs

You can set your own tabs or use the defaults. The available tab types are:

➡ **To set tabs on the ruler:**

1. Choose the type of tab you want by clicking in the tab selection box at the left of the horizontal ruler until the tab type appears. Table 14.1 shows how the different tab icons appear. If ruler is not displayed, click the **View** tab, click the **Ruler** check box in the **Show** group.
2. Move the pointer to the ruler bar and click the point at which you want to add the tab. (Figure 14.14)

Table 14.1 Different types of tab types

Button	Tab Type	Description
	Left tab	The text left aligned at the tab
	Right tab	The text right aligned at the tab
	Center tab	The text is center aligned at the tab
	Decimal tab	The decimal point where the numbering is aligned

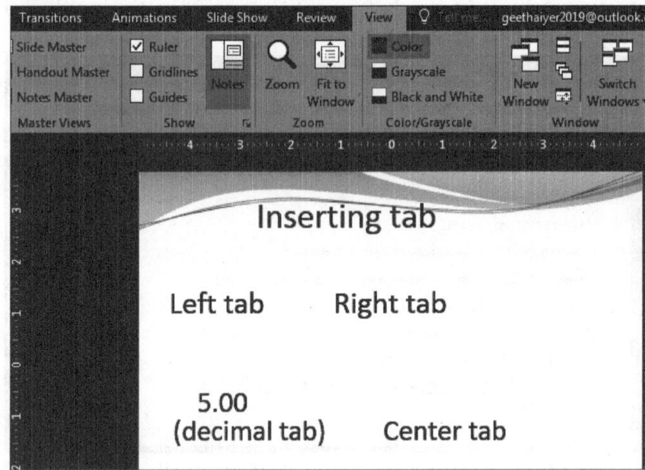

Figure 14.14 Different types of tabs placed on the ruler

14.4.9 Set Paragraph Indents

Using the ruler involves changing the indention of specific text or paragraphs.

➡ **To change indent:**

1. In the slide pane, select the text you want to set an indentation for.

2. If the ruler is not displayed, click **View** tab and choose **Ruler** in the **Show** group.
3. To set the indent for the first line of a paragraph, drag the upper indent marker.
4. To set the left indent for other lines in a paragraph, drag the lower indent marker. The rectangular part of the lower indent marker also moves with it as shown in Figure 14.15.

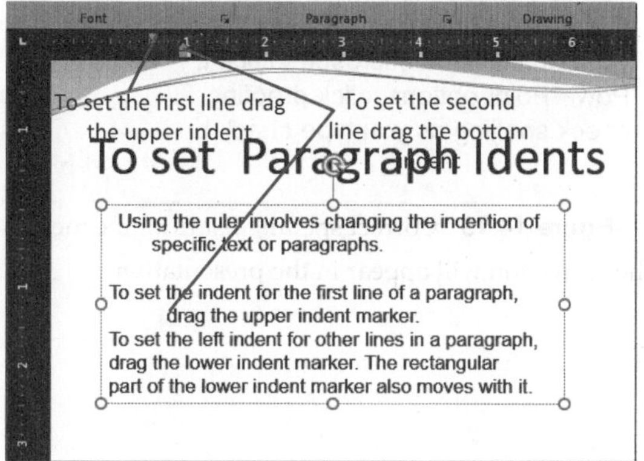

Figure 14.15 To set indent in the paragraph

5. To maintain the relationship between the first line and the rest of the paragraph, move both markers by dragging the rectangular part of the lower marker.

14.4.10 Adding Background Colour

The slide background is a rectangle that completely fills the page you set by choosing File, Page Setup. You can apply the same formatting styles to the background that you can apply to any other drawing objects.

➡ **To change background:**

1. Click the **Design** tab and choose **Format Background** in **Customize** group. On the right side the **Format Background** settings pane appears as shown in Figure 14.16.
2. Click the desired settings you want to apply as a background. For example, here we have select Pattern fill as shown in Figure 14.16.

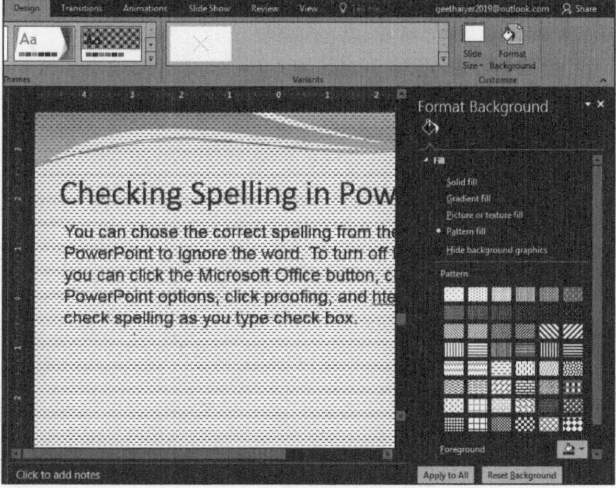

Figure 14.16 Selecting pattern fill in the Format Background settings

3. Choose the required pattern fill and choose the **Foreground** drop-down arrow to fill a color.
4. Click **Apply to All** button. The selected pattern appears in the background in your presentation slide.

14.4.11 Using the Spelling Checker

PowerPoint's spelling checker checks the spelling of the entire presentation–all slides, outlines, notes pages, and handout pages. The spelling checker in PowerPoint compares all the words in your document with a dictionary file, in the way any MS-Office application does. When the spelling checker finds a word that is not in the dictionary file, it highlights the word in your slide and displays the word in the Spelling pane, as shown in Figure 15.17. You can stop using the spelling checker at any time by clicking the Close button in the Spelling dialog box.

➡ **To check the spelling in a presentation file:**

1. Click the **Review** tab. In the **Proofing** group, click **Spelling** command. The Spelling pane on the right as shown in Figure 14.17.

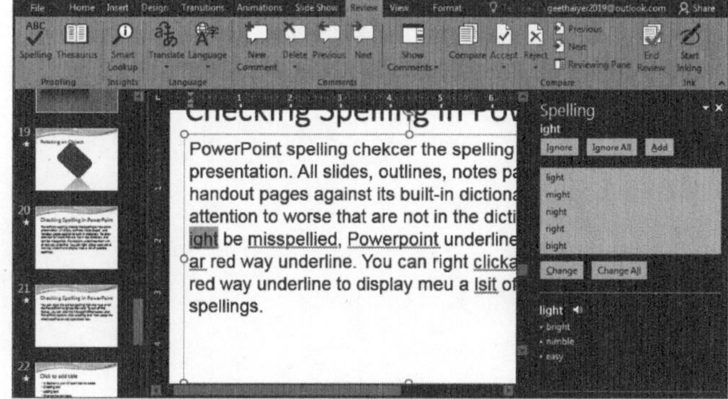

Figure 14.17 Spelling pane appears

2. The list of misspell words highlight in the Suggestions box. Select the correct spelling and click **Change** to correct the error.
3. PowerPoint will move through each error until you have reviewed them all. After the last error has been reviewed, a dialog box will appear confirming that the spelling check is complete. Click OK (See Figure 14.18).

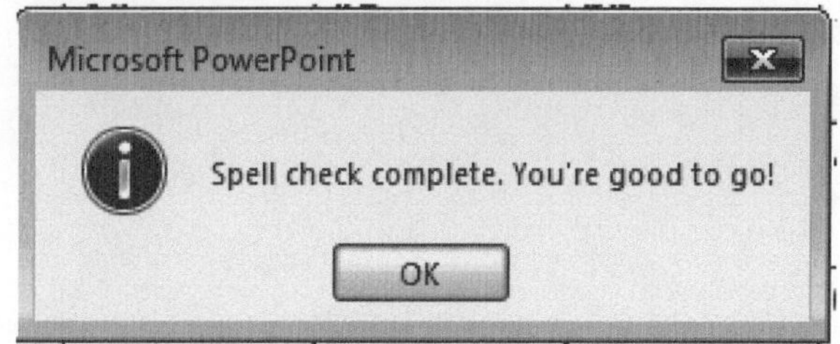

Figure 14.18

Ignoring Spelling Errors

The spell check is not always correct. It may sometimes think a word is spelled incorrectly when it is not. This often happens with people's names and proper nouns, which may not be in the dictionary. If says something is an error, you can choose not to change it using one of three options:

Ignore	This will skip the word without changing it.
Ignore All	Ignores this word every time you find it.
Change	Changes the original word by replacing it with the word in the Change to: box.
Change All	Changes every occurrence of this word to the word in the Change to: box.
Add	Adds this word to the dictionary so the speller does not stop here any more.

Automatic Spell Check

By default, PowerPoint automatically checks your presentation for spelling errors, so you may not even need to run a separate check using the Spelling command. These errors are indicated by red wavy lines.

➡ **To use the automatic spell check feature:**

1. Right-click the underlined word. A menu will appear.
2. Click the correct spelling from the list of suggestions as shown in Figure 14.19.

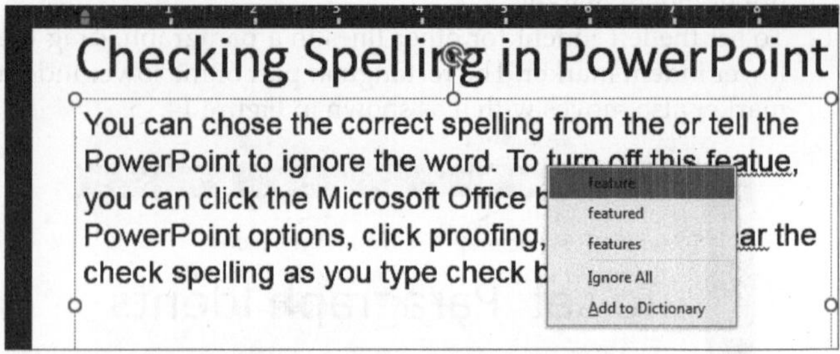

Figure 14.19 Correct spelling list from the menu

3. The correction will appear in the presentation.

Working with Tables and Objects

15.1 INTRODUCTION

Information presented in a tabular form enables you to communicate effectively with your audience. For example, a table can be used to compare sales figures for previous year and the current year. By using tables you can show information in a form that can be quickly grasped by your audience. You can place a graphic on any slide, if the slide contains a graphics placeholder and also animate text and objects such as clip art, shapes, and pictures.

15.2 INSERTING A TABLE SLIDE

You can insert a Table in a slide in two different ways. These are:

- Create a new slide which is specifically made to contain a table.
- Insert a table in the existing slide.

➡ **To create a new slide with table:**

1. Click the **Insert** tab, click the **Table** drop-down arrow as shown in Figure 15.1.

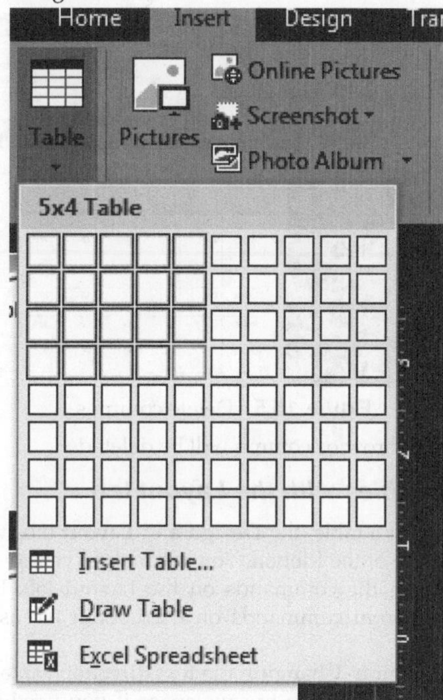

Figure 15.1 Selecting rows and columns in table command

2. Hover the mouse over the grid of squares to select the desired number of **columns** and **rows** in the table. In our example, we have insert a table with four rows and five columns. Or
   You can also insert a table by clicking the **Insert Table** command in a **placeholder**.
3. The table will appear on the current selected side as shown in Figure 15.2.

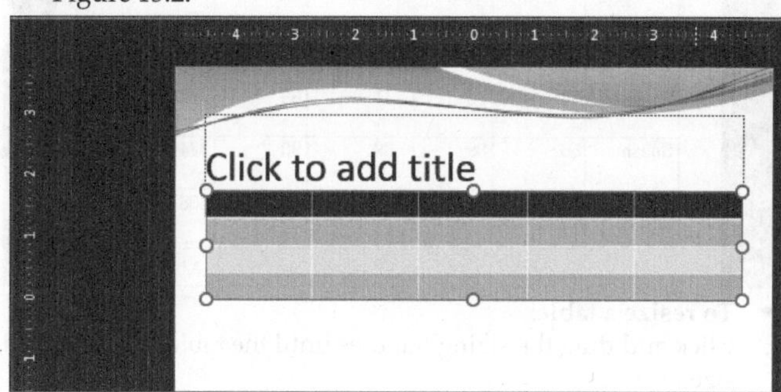

Figure 15.2 The table is inserted

15.2.1 Entering Text in a Table

When you create a new table, an empty table appears on the slide as shown in Figure 15.2. When you insert a table, the insertion point flashes in the first cell in the upper left corner of the table. The text you type appears at the insertion point. After entering the text in the table and to exit the editing mode, click anywhere outside the table. Or

1. Click anywhere in the table, and begin typing to add text.
   You can use the **Tab** key or the **arrow keys** on the keyboard to navigate through the slide.

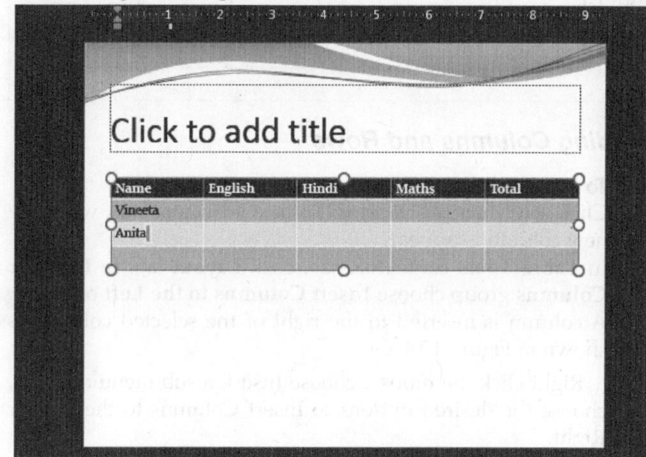

Figure 15.3 Entering text in a table

15.2.2 Editing a Table

Powerpoint includes several options for customizing tables, including moving and resizing as well as adding rows and columns.

➡ **To move a table:**

1. Click and drag the edge of a table to move it to a new location on a slide as shown below.

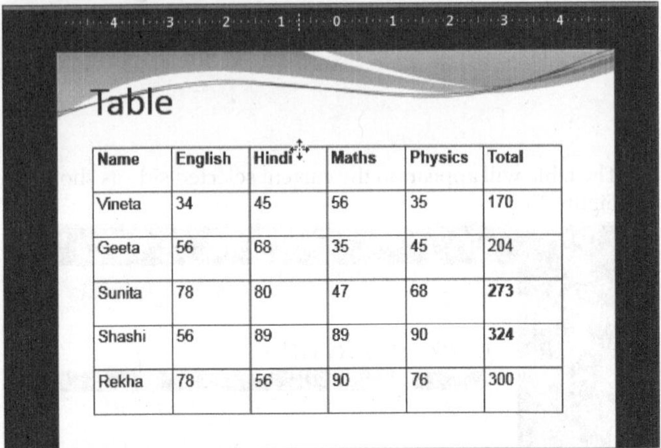

Table

Name	English	Hindi	Maths	Physics	Total
Vineta	34	45	56	35	170
Geeta	56	68	35	45	204
Sunita	78	80	47	68	273
Shashi	56	89	89	90	324
Rekha	78	56	90	76	300

➡ **To resize a table:**

1. Click and drag the sizing handles until the table is the desired size.

Table

Name	English	Hindi	Maths	Physics	Total
Vineta	34	45	56	35	170
Geeta	56	68	35	45	204
Sunita	78	80	47	68	273
Shashi	56	89	89	90	324
Rekha	78	56	90	76	300

Adding Columns and Rows

➡ **To insert a column:**

1. Click anywhere in the column next to where you want the new column to appear.
2. In **Table Tools** contextual tab, click **Layout** tab. In **Rows & Columns** group choose **Insert Columns to the Left** or **Right**. A column is inserted to the right of the selected column as shown in Figure 15.4. Or

   Right click the mouse, choose Insert, a sub menu appears, choose the desired options to Insert Columns to the Left or Right.

➡ **To insert a row:**

1. Click anywhere in the row next to where you want the new row to appear.
2. In **Table Tools** contextual tab, click **Layout** tab. In **Rows & Columns** group choose **Insert Rows to the Above** or **Below**. A row is inserted to the above or below of the selected row. Or

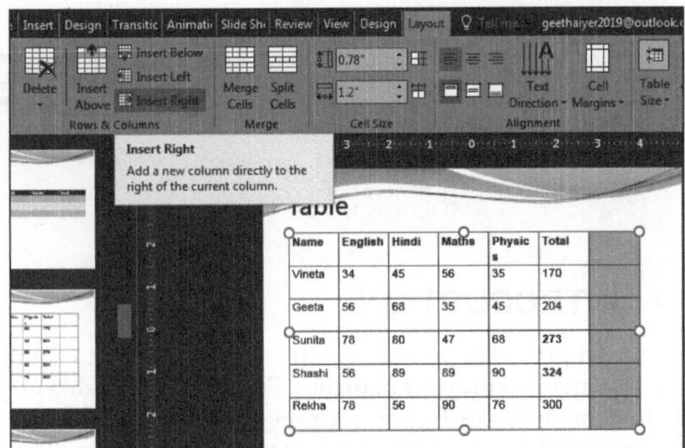

Figure 15.4 Adding columns to right

Right click the mouse, choose Insert Rows Above or Insert Rows Below. A row is inserted above or below of the selected row.

Deleting Columns and Rows

➡ **To delete columns/rows, do this:**

1. Select the columns/rows you want to delete.
2. In **Table Tools** contextual tab, click **Layout** tab. In **Rows & Columns** group choose **Delete Columns** or **Rows**. Or right click the mouse, choose Delete Rows or Columns as shown in Figure 15.5.

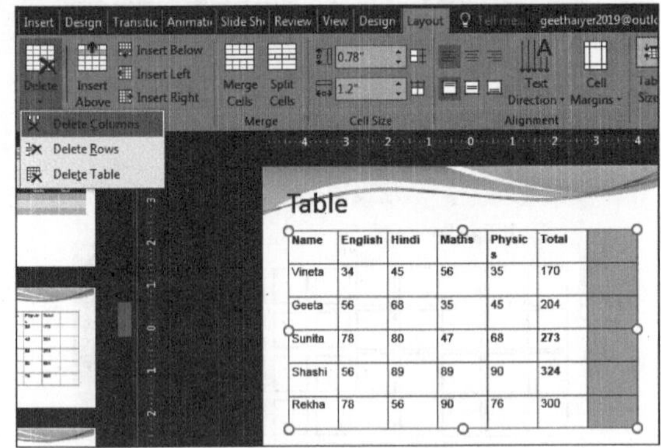

Figure 15.5 Delete columns

3. The selected row or column will be deleted.

Modifying tables with the Layout tab

When you select a table, the **Design** and **Layout** tabs will appear on the right side of the Ribbon. You can make a variety of changes to a table using the commands on the Layout tab. Figure 15.6 shows the different commands on the Layout tab as discussed below:

(A) **Text Direction**–Changing the text direction can add style to the table. It also help to save space if you need to fit more columns in the table.

(B) **Text Alignment**–By changing the text alignment, you can control where the text is located within cells.

(C) **Distribute Rows and Columns**–To keep the table looking neat and organized, you may want to distribute the rows or columns equally, which makes them all the same size.

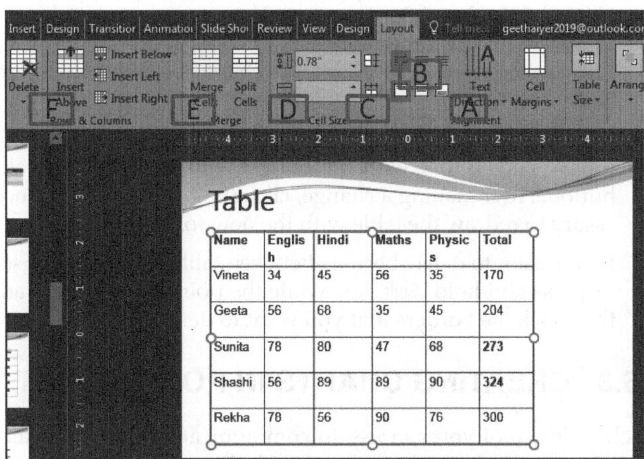

Figure 15.6 Different Layout tab commands

(D) **Cell Size**–You can type a desired row height and column width of the cells. If you prefer, you can click the AutoFit command to automatically adjust the cells based on their content.

(E) **Merge and Split Cells**–Some table require Layout that does not fit the standard grid. In these cases, you may need to merge or split cells.

(F) **Add or Remove Rows and Columns**–You can insert or delete rows and columns in your table as needed.

15.2.3 Changing a Table Style

PowerPoint makes it easy to change the look and feel of your tables. For example, you can quickly apply different table styles and customize the table borders.

➡ **To apply a table style:**

1. In **Table Tools** contextual tab, click **Design** tab.
2. In the **Table Style** group, click the **More** drop-down arrow to see a available table style gallery opens as shown in Figure 15.7.

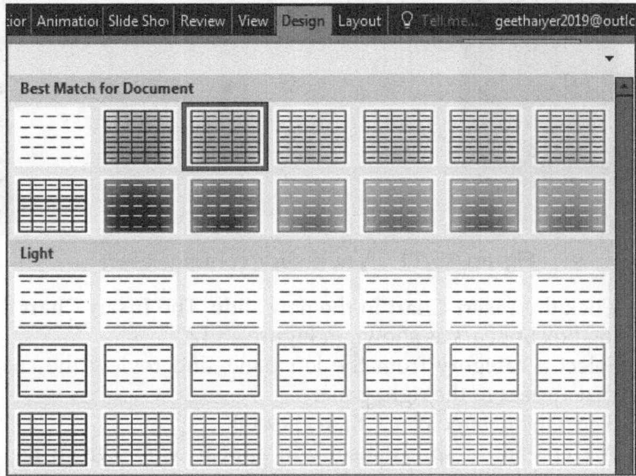

Figure 15.7 Selecting table style in the Table Style group

3. Select the desired table style you want to apply. The selected table style is applied in the table as shown in Figure 15.8.

To clear the table style, click the **More** button and then click **Clear Table.**

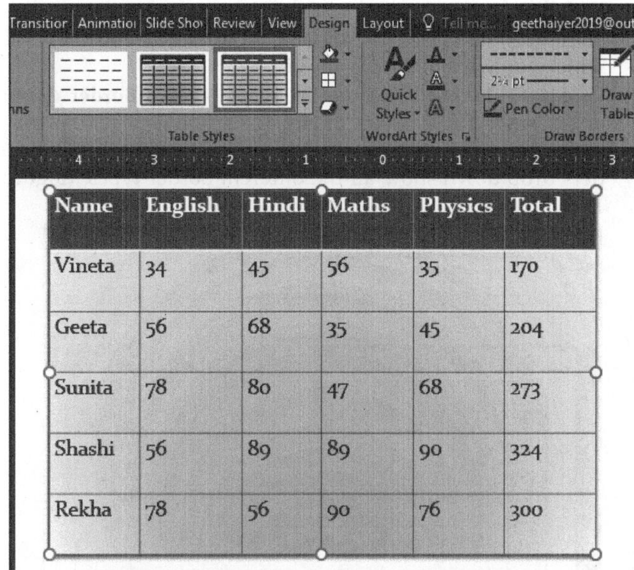

Figure 15.8 The selected table style appear

Change Table Style Options

You can apply a table style to specific parts of your table by selection options in the **Table style Options** group.

➡ **To apply a table style options:**

1. Click the table that you want to change the table style option.
2. In **Table Tools** contextual tab, click **Design** tab. In the **Table Style Options group** there are six options:
   - To emphasize the first row of the table, select the **Header Row** check box.
   - To emphasize the last row of the table, select the **Total Row** check box.
   - To have alternating striped rows, select the **Branded Rows** check box.
   - To emphasize the first column of the table, select the **First Column** check box.
   - To emphasize the last column of the table, select the **Last Column** check box.
   - To have alternating striped columns, select the **Branded Column** check box.
3. Select the desired options you want to apply in the table and click the options in the check box.

15.2.4 Adding Borders and Fills

PowerPoint establishes default borders around cells and the table itself, on the current presentation template. You can change borders separating cells, columns and rows or around the entire table.

Changing Table Borders

You may specify a variety of ways for border formatting in a table. You can choose:

1. The Pen style (solid line, dashed line, dotted line, etc.)
2. The Pen weight (1/4 point to 6 points)

3. The Pen colour.

➡ **To select the table cells that you want to add or change the table border:**

1. Select the entire table, or the cells, columns, or rows around which you want to specify the border.
2. Under **Table Tools**, on the **Design** tab, click **Border** down arrow in the **Table Styles** group. The actual name of this button changes depending on what was last selected. The borders drop down show all the different border types. (Figure 15.9)

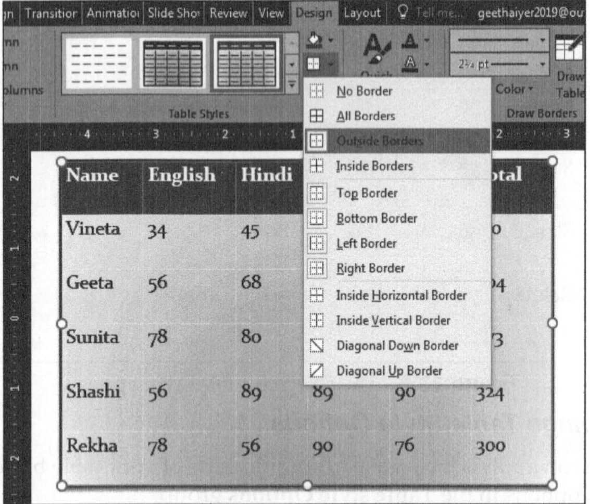

Figure 15.9 Selecting table border

3. Click the border you want. The selected portion of the table changes to reflect the new border type.
4. If you want to change the border line style, first you must select to **No Border** and then choose **Pen Style**. The **Pen Style** palette drop down menu appears as shown in Figure 15.10.

Figure 15.10 Borders Style drop down list appears

5. Click the border style you want. The mouse pointer changes to pen style. Click the table row or column line. You can see the selected portion of your table changes to the new border style.
6. If you want to change the border width or border color, repeat steps 2 to 4 with the border width and border color button. After making a change, click the Border button if necessary to redraw the table with the new formatting.
7. If you want to delete borders between table cells, click Eraser, or press and hold Shift key while the pointer is a pencil, and then click the borders that you want to delete.

15.3 CREATING CHARTS IN POWERPOINT

A chart is a tool you can use to communicate data graphically. Including a chart in a presentation makes it easy to visualize comparisons and trends.

Charts that you create will be embedded in PowerPoint 2016, and the chart data is stored in an Excel 2016 worksheet that is incorporated in the PowerPoint file.

15.3.1 Insert a Chart in a Presentation

➡ **To insert a chart in a slide:**

1. Click the **New slide** in the **Slides** group. It display the slides after which you want to add the chart slide. Or click the **Insert** tab, on the **Illustrations** group, click the **Chart** icon.
2. The new slide appears. In the center of the slide contains *table, chart, Media clips, SmartArt* etc. as shown in Figure 15.11.

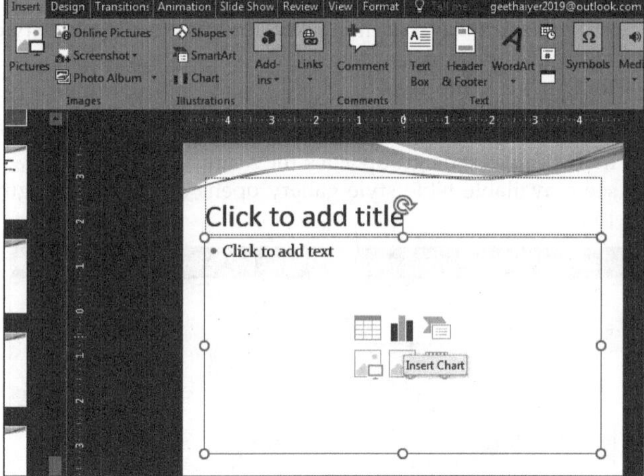

Figure 15.11 A new slide contains chart

3. Click the **Insert Chart** in the new slide. The **Insert Chart** dialog box appears as shown in Figure 15.12.
4. Select a **category** from the left pane, and review the charts that appear in the right pane.
5. Select the desired chart, then click OK.
6. A chart and a spreadsheet will appear as shown in Figure 15.13. The data that appear in the spreadsheet is **placeholder source data**. You will replace with your own information. The source data is used to create the chart.

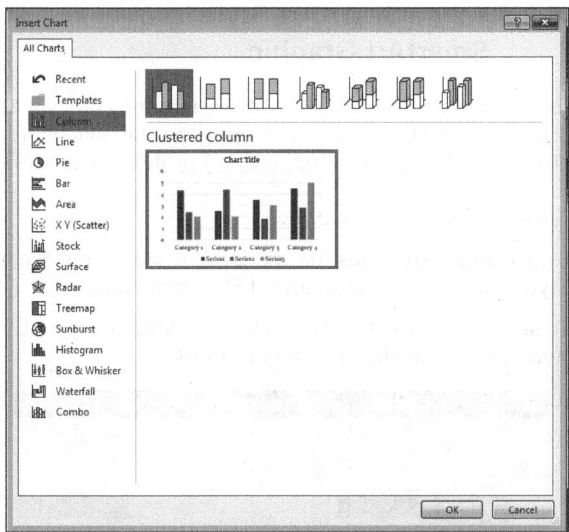

Figure 15.12 Insert Chart dialog box

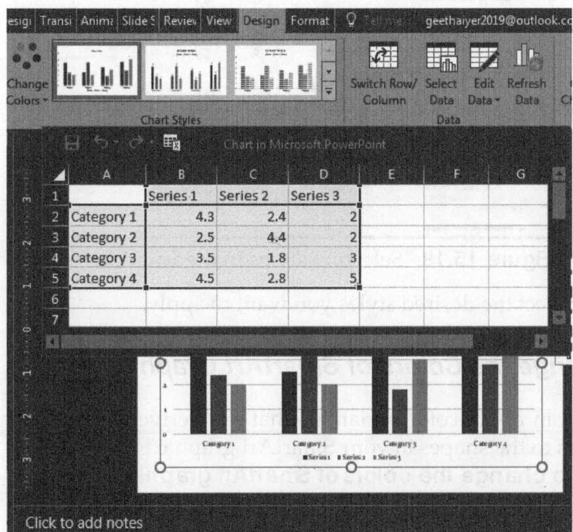

Figure 15.13 Sample Data graphically displayed

7. Enter data in the worksheet. When you are done, click X to close the spreadsheet as shown in Figure 15.14.

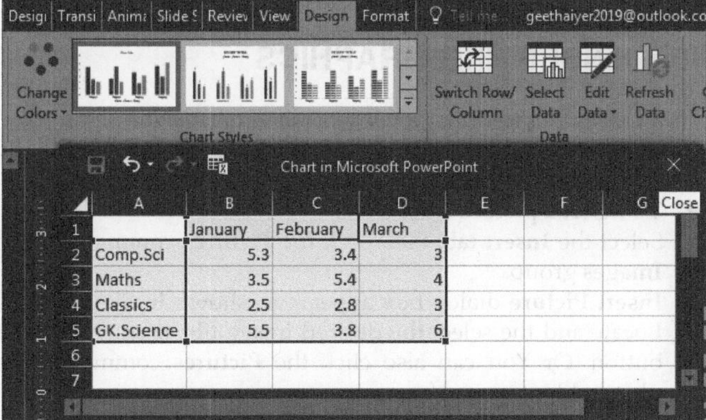

Figure 15.14 Enter data in the worksheet

The chart will be completed.

15.3.2 Creating charts with existing Excel data

If you already have data in an existing Excel file you want to use for a chart, you can transfer the data by copying and pasting it. Just open the spreadsheet in Excel, select and copy the desired data, and paste it into the source data area for your chart.

You can also embed an existing Excel chart into your PowerPoint presentation. This may be useful when you know you will need to update the data in your Excel file and want the chart to automatically update whenever the Excel data is changed.

15.3.3 Changing Data in an Existing Chart

If you create a chart for your presentation and then the data used in the chart changes, you can update the data so that the chart is accurate.

➡ **To add a chart in an existing slide:**

1. Select the chart that you want to change.
2. Under **Chart Tools**, on the **Design** tab, in the **Data** group, click **Edit Data** as shown in Figure 15.15.

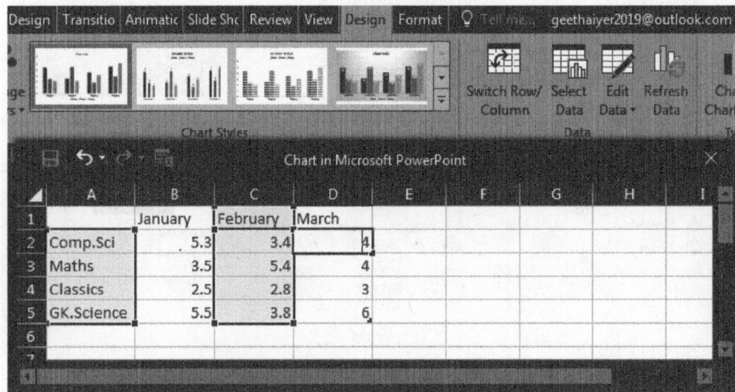

Figure 15.15 Edit data in an existing slide

3. Chart in Microsoft PowerPoint windows opens, you can change the data.

15.4 CREATING A SMARTART GRAPHIC

A SmartArt graphic is a visual representation of your information that you can quickly and easily create, choosing from among many different layouts, to effectively communicate your message or ideas.

When you create a SmartArt graphic, you are prompted to choose a type of SmartArt graphic, such as Process Hierarchy, Cycle or Relationship. A type is similar to a category of SmartArt graphic, and each type contains several different layouts. After you choose a layout, it is easy to change the layout for your SmartArt graphic. Most of your text and other content, colors, styles, effects, and text formatting are automatically carried over to the new layout.

15.4.1 Insert SmartArt Graphic

➡ **To insert a SmartArt graphic:**

1. Click the **Insert** tab, in the **Illustrations** group, click **SmartArt**. Click the **New slide** in the **Slides** group. It display the slides after which you want to add the SmartArt slide as shown in Figure 15.16.
2. **Choose a SmartArt Graphic** dialog box appears as shown in Figure 15.17. Click the type and layout that you want.

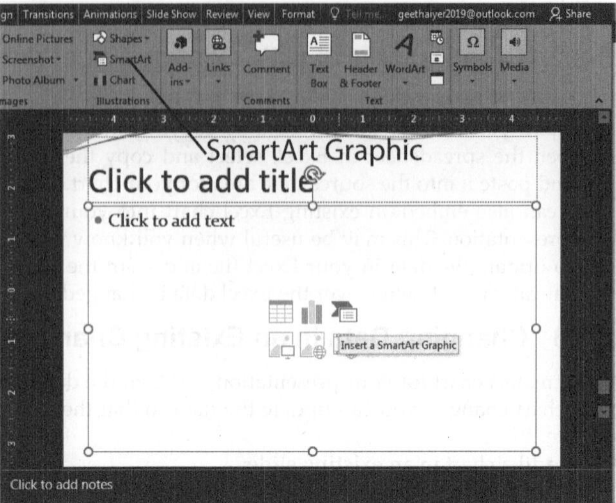

Figure 15.16 Insert SmartArt Graphic

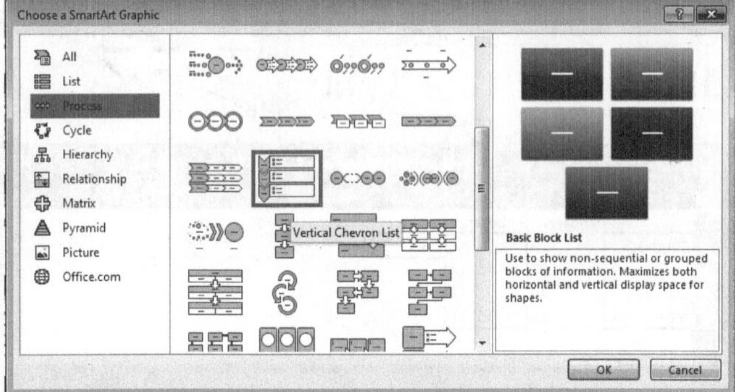

Figure 15.17 SmartArt Graphic dialog box

3. Enter your text by doing one of the following:
   - Click in a shape in your SmartArt graphic, and then type the text.
   - Click [Text] in the Text pane, and then type your text. (Figure 15.18)
   - Copy text from other program, click [Text], and then paste into the Text pane.

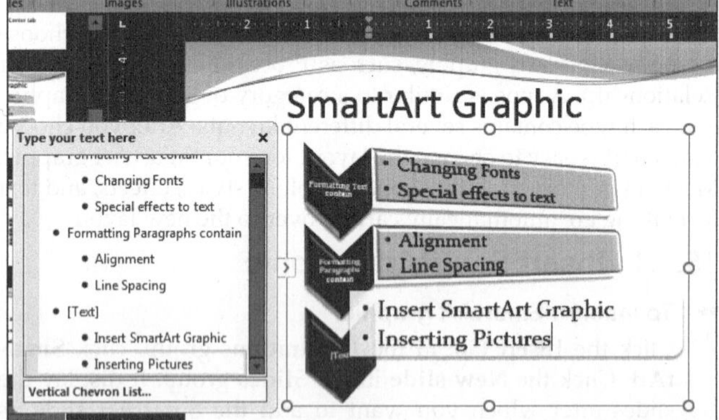

Figure 15.18 Type a text in the SmartArt graphic placeholder

15.4.2 Apply a SmartArt Style to a SmartArt Graphic

A SmartArt Style is a combination of various effects, such as line style, bevel, or 3-D, that you can apply to the shapes in your SmartArt graphic to create a unique and professionally designed look.

1. Click your SmartArt graphic.
2. Under **SmartArt Tools**, on the **Design** tab, in the **SmartArt Styles** group, click the SmartArt Style that you want.
3. To see more SmartArt Styles, click the **More** button. A list of styles appears as shown in Figure 15.19.

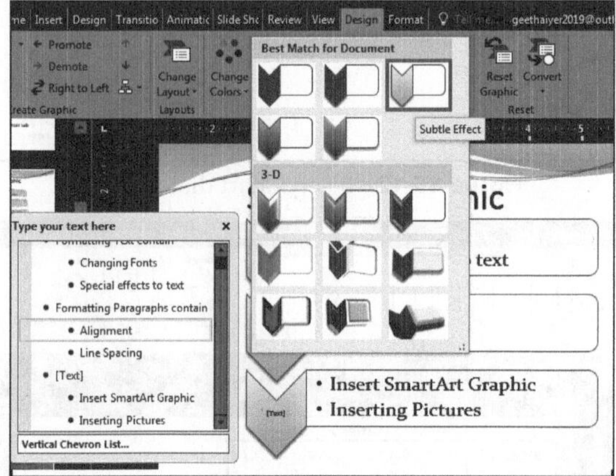

Figure 15.19 Selecting styles in the SmartArt Styles

4. Select the desired styles you want to apply.

Change the Colors of SmartArt Graphic

You can apply color variations that are derived from the theme colors to the shapes in your SmartArt graphic.

➡ **To change the colors of SmartArt graphic:**

1. Click your SmartArt graphic.
2. Under **SmartArt Tools**, on the **Design** tab, in the **SmartArt Styles** group, click **Change Colors**.
3. Click the color variation that you want.

15.5 INSERTING GRAPHICS

Adding pictures can make your presentations more interesting. You can insert a picture from a file on your computer onto any slide.

➡ **To insert a picture from a file:**

1. Select the **Insert** tab, then click the **Pictures** command in the **Images** group.
2. **Insert Picture** dialog box appears as shown in Figure 15.20. Locate and the select the desired image file, then click Insert button. Or You can also click the **Pictures** command in a placeholder to insert images.

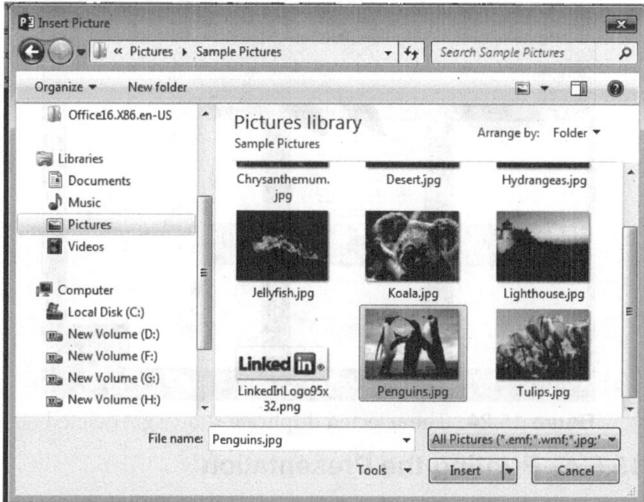

Figure 15.20 Insert Picture dialog box

Figure 15.21 The picture appear in the slide

3. The Picture will appear on the current selected slide as shown in Figure 15.21.

15.5.1 Modifying Pictures

PowerPoint makes it easy to modify pictures in your presentations such as resizing, select and rotate pictures.

➡ **To select a picture:**

1. Simply click to select a picture. A solid line will appear around a selected picture.

➡ **To resize a picture:**

1. Click and drag the corner sizing handles until the picture is the desired size.

15.5.2 Rotating and Flipping Objects

You can change the position of shapes by rotating or reversing them. Reversing a shape is also referred to as creating a mirror image or flipping. You can rotate a single object or a group of objects around its own centre.

➡ **To rotate a picture:**

1. Click and drag the arrow above an image to rotate it right or left. Or select the object, by clicking mouse pointer on it.
2. Click the **Drawing Tools** tab, in the **Arrange** group. Choose **Rotate** at the right side of the Selection pane. Click the down arrow and choose one of the following options:
   - Click **More Rotation Options...** from the list. The **Format Picture** navigation pane appears, click the **Rotation** spinner box to the set the angle of rotation as shown in Figure 15.22.

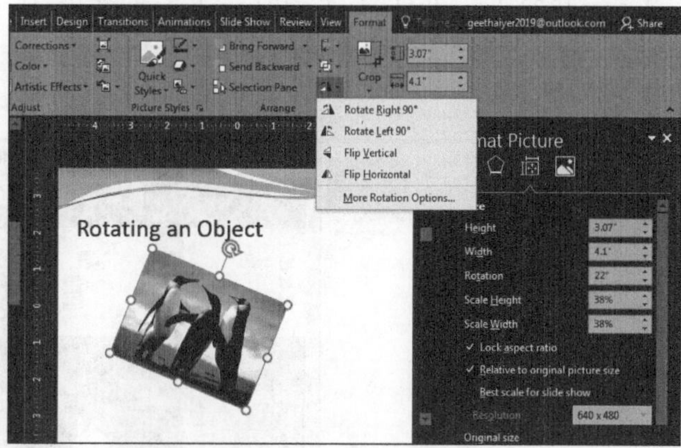

Figure 15.22 Select rotation command in the Format Picture navigation pane

   - To rotate the shape 90 degrees to the right, click **Rotate Right 90°** as shown in Figure 15.22.
   - To rotate the shape 90 degrees to the left, click **Rotate Left 90°** Or
   - Drag the rotation handle in the direction that you want to rotate the shape. Or
3. When the object is in the desired angle position, release the mouse button. The object appears in its new rotated position as shown in Figure 15.22.

Flipping an Object

Flipping means to turn an object by 180°, either horizontally or vertically (leading to a *lateral/vertical* inversion respectively).

➡ **To flip an object:**

1. Select the object(s) to be flipped.
2. Click the **Drawing Tools** tab, in the **Arrange** group. Choose Rotate at the right side of the Selection pane. Click the down arrow and choose one of the following options.
   - Flip Horizontal — Mirrors the object left to right (lateral inversion)
   - Flip Vertical — Rotates the object 180 degrees top to bottom (vertical inversion).
3. Click Flip Horizontal or Flip Vertical. The object is turned accordingly.

15.5.3 Duplicating and Deleting Slides

To add a slide that contains the content of an existing slide in a presentation, you can duplicate the slide. You can duplicate i.e. copy or delete selected slides in slide sorter view also.

➡ **To duplicate the slides:**

1. Switch to **Slide Sorter View.** Select the slide or slides you want to duplicate.
2. On the **Home** tab, in the **Slides** group, click **New Slide** down arrow and choose **Duplicate Selected Slides.**
3. Figure 15.23 shows the Slides (i.e. 9) have been duplicated.

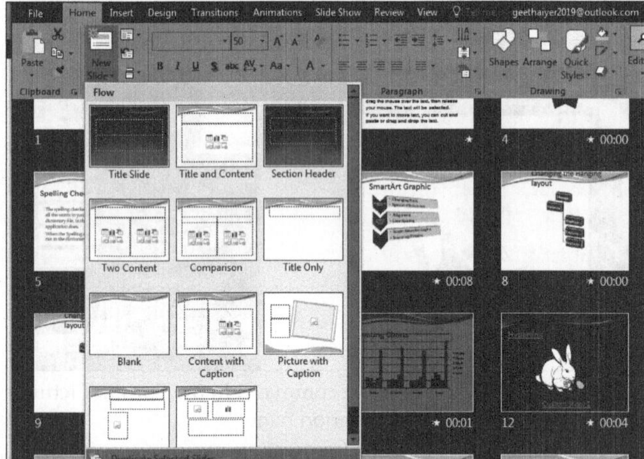

Figure 15.23 The selected slides (i.e. 9) have been duplicated

➡ **To delete the slides, do this:**

1. Select the slide or slides you want to be delete.
2. On the **Home** tab, in the **Slides** group, click **Delete Slide** Or Right-click the slide and choose **Delete slide.**
3. Figure 15.24 shows you the duplicate selected slides i.e. slide 9 get deleted.

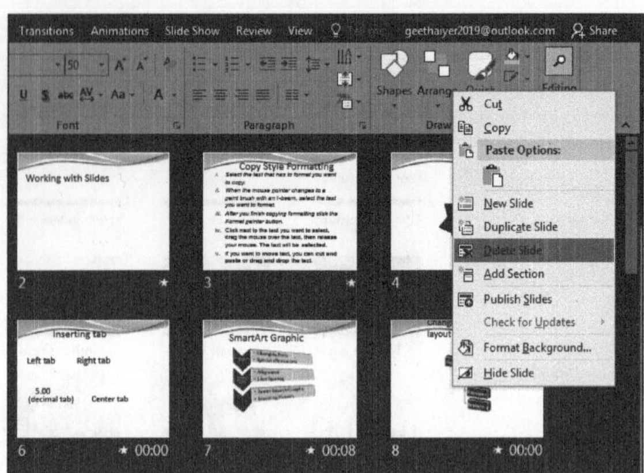

Figure 15.24 The selected duplicate slide 9 get deleted

15.5.4 Printing the Presentation

In PowerPoint 2016, you can either print all the slides or the current slide of a presentation. In addition, you can decide how many slides you want to print on a single page.

➡ **To print a presentation:**

1. Open the presentation that you want to print.
2. Click the **File** tab on the ribbon, click **Print** tab. The **Print** backstage view appears as shown in Figure 15.25.

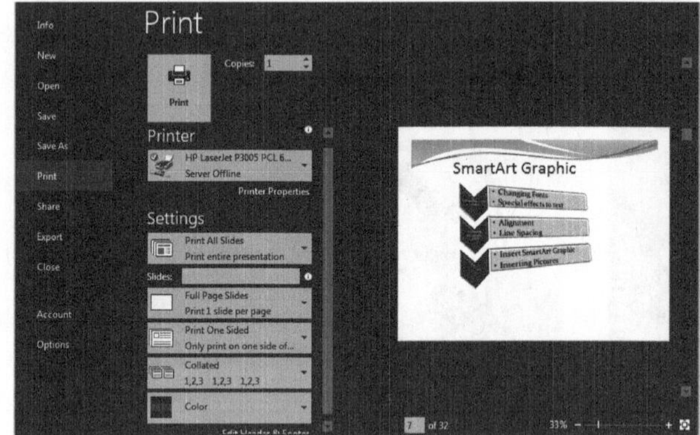

Figure 15.25 Print backstage view settings

3. The name of the currently selected printer is shown under **Printer** drop-down arrow. To print the presentation on a different printer, select the desired printer from the **Printer** drop-down list.
4. Specify the number of copies you want to print, for each slide in the **Copies:** spinner box.
5. The **Settings** drop down list has the option which allows you to select the pages you want to print.

   Print All Slides–Choose Print All Slides option to print the entire presentation at one time.

   Current slide–Choose the Current slide option, to print the slide shown on the monitor.

   Custom Range–Choose to print the selected slides, and enter the corresponding slide numbers in the **Slides:** edit box e.g., to print slide 3 and 6 through 8, enter 3,6-8 in the Slides edit box.

   Custom Show–Prints a certain custom show you have set up. Each custom shows you have created appears on the list.

Print Hidden Slides–If any slides are hidden (do not display during a slide show), they can be printed by checking the *Print Hidden Slides* check box.

6. **Collate**–Specify if you want to arrange while printing multiple copies. When you choose collate option, each set is printed completely from first page to the last page. Then the next set is printed.
7. **Full Page Slides**–You can choose from one of four print layouts: Full, Page Slides, Notes Pages, Outline, and Handouts
8.. **Preview Pane**–You can see a preview of how your presentation will look when printed.
9. **Slide Selection**–You can click the arrows to view a different slide in the preview pane.
10. **Zoom Control**–You can click the zoom to page button on the right to zoom in and out of the preview pane. Click and drag the slides to use the **Zoom Control**.
11. Click the **Color** button, and select the color setting for the printouts:
    - **Color**—This is default. When you use this settings with a black-and-white printer, it results in slides with grayscale or black backgrounds.
    - **Grayscale**—To print in grayscale, select the grayscale check box.
    - **The Pure black & white option**—converts all colours in the presentation to either black or white. Prefer this option if you need to print on a printer that cannot print gray shades.
12. After you have done the desired settings, click **Print**.

CHAPTER 16

Customizing Your Presentation

16.1 POWERPOINT THEME

Theme is a group of design settings. It includes color settings, font and effect settings and also a background settings to the presentation. Themes can also be applied to tables, SmartArt graphics, shapes, or charts in your slides. When you apply a theme to a presentation, the slide master and theme color of the new templates replaces the slide master, of the original presentation. After you apply a theme you find that each slide you add has the similar look. PowerPoint 2016 comes with a wide variety of professionally designed templates.

16.1.1 Applying Themes

All themes included in PowerPoint are located in the **Themes** group on the **Design** tab. Themes can be applied or changed at any time.

➡ **To apply a Theme:**

1. Open the presentation you want to apply a different design.
2. Click the **Design** tab, in the **Theme** group, click More button. A list of themes gallery as seen in Figure 16.1 appears.

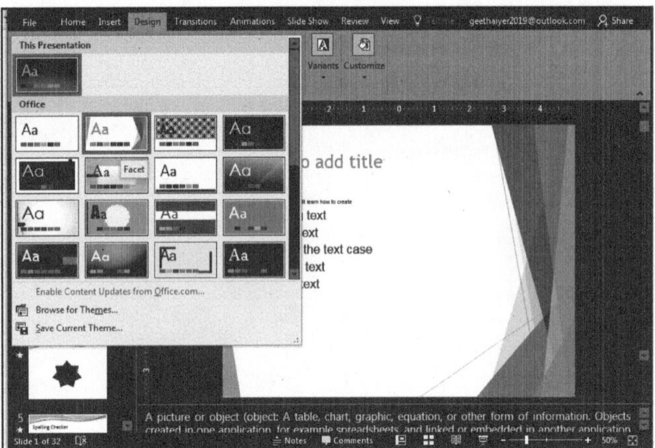

Figure 16.1 Applying different Theme design

3. Select the desired theme design you want to use or any presentation whose design you want to change.
4. You can also apply to *All slides, Selected slides.* Right-click the Themes and choose the desired option to apply.
5. Once you have applied theme, you can also select a **variant** for that theme from the **Variants** group. Variants use different theme colors while preserving a theme's overall look as shown in Figure 16.2.
6. After apply the selected theme you can Save the Current Theme.

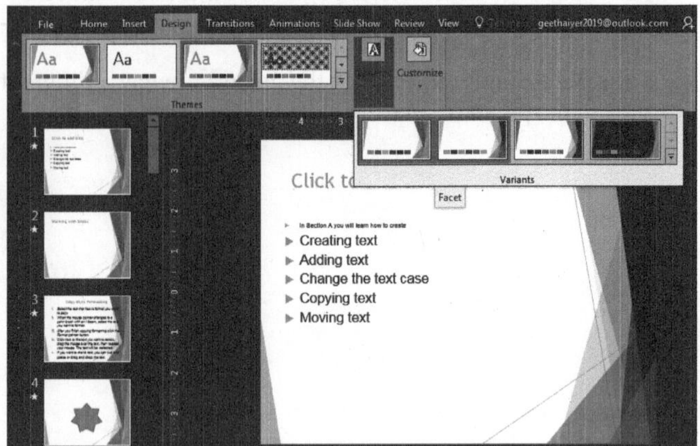

Figure 16.2 Selecting variant theme colors

16.1.2 Slide Master View

Slide Master view is a special feature in PowerPoint that allows you to quickly modify the slides and slide layouts in your presentation. From there, you can edit the slide master, which will affect every slide in the presentation. You can also modify individual slide layouts, which will change any slides using those layouts.

Slide Master view can help you to create a consistent, professional presentation without a lot of effort. You could use Slide Master view to change in your presentation, but there are some of its most common uses.

- **Modify backgrounds**–Slide Master view makes it easy to customize the background for all of your slides at the same time.
- **Rearrange placeholders**–If you find that you often rearrange the placeholders on each slide, you can save time by rearranging them in Slide Master view instead. When you adjust one of the layouts in Slide Master view, all of the slides with that layout will change.
- **Customize text formatting**–Instead of changing the text color on each slide individually, you could use the Slide Master to change the text color on all slides at once.
- **Create unique slide layouts**–If you want to create a presentation that looks different from regular PowerPoint themes, you could use Slide Master view to create your own layouts.

➡ **To add a slide master:**

1. Click the **View** tab, in the **Master Views** groups, click **Slide Master.**
2. The presentation will switch to **Slide Master view,** and the **Slide Master** tab will be selected on the Ribbon.
3. In the left navigation pane, scroll up and select the **first slide.** This is the **slide master** as shown in Figure 16.3.

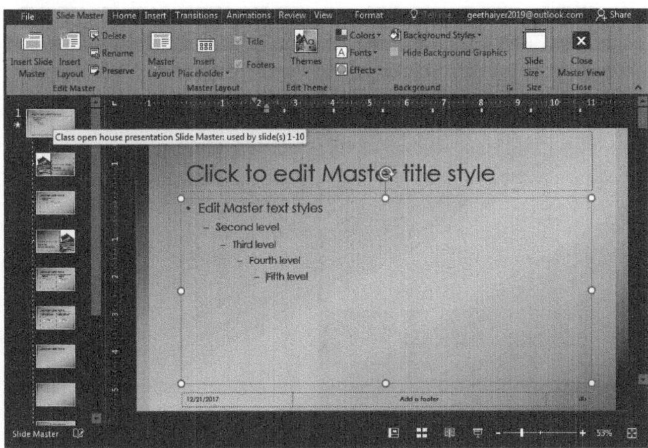

Figure 16.3 PowerPoint Slide Master

4. Make the desired changes to the slide master. For example, we insert a picture of the Greenfood logo.
5. Move, resize or delete slide objects as needed. For example, we have resize the logo and move it to the bottom right corner as shown in Figure 16.4.
6. After you insert the logo, click the **Close Master View** command on the **Slide Master** tab as shown in Figure 16.4.

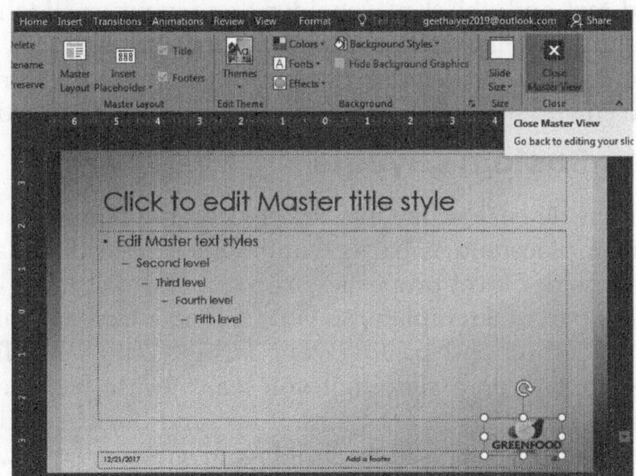

Figure 16.4 Insert the picture of Logo

7. The change will appear on all slides of the presentation.

16.1.3 Customizing text formatting

You can also customize the text formatting from slide master view, including the font, text size, and alignment.

➡ **To change the text formatting:**

1. Select the master title style on the slide master.
2. Right-click the menu and choose the desired font type, for example, we have selected Arial.
3. Each title placeholder is connected to the master title style on the slide master. The change title font appears in the other slides of master slide.
4. When you are finished, click the **Close Master View** command on the slide.

☞ *Instead of customizing individual placeholders, you could change the theme fonts for a presentation. From the Slide Master tab, click the Fonts command in the Background group, then select the desired fonts.*

16.1.4 Using Notes Pages

Notes Pages act like a manuscript for your presentation. You would write the text you want to discuss during the course of a presentation, for each slide.

You can also type and format your notes as you work in Normal view, but to see how your notes pages will be printed and to see the full effect of any text formatting, such as font colors, switch to **Note page view**.

To customize your Notes Pages, you can change the following:

- Size and position of the slide image.
- Add page numbers, date, header or footer.
- Add text and graphics to individual Note Pages or to the Notes Masters, so that they appear on each Notes Page.

Creating Notes

PowerPoint offers two ways for preparing Notes Pages. These are as follows:

- You can prepare the Notes Pages after you have finished making the slides.
- You can create each of the Notes Pages as you are working on each individual slide.

➡ **To create notes using Notes Pages:**

1. Click the **View** tab, in the **Presentation Views** click **Notes page**.
2. In the **Notes Page View**, you see the entire **Notes page**. Click the placeholder to begin entering the text for your Note. And there is a picture of the slide at the bottom (See Figure 16.5).

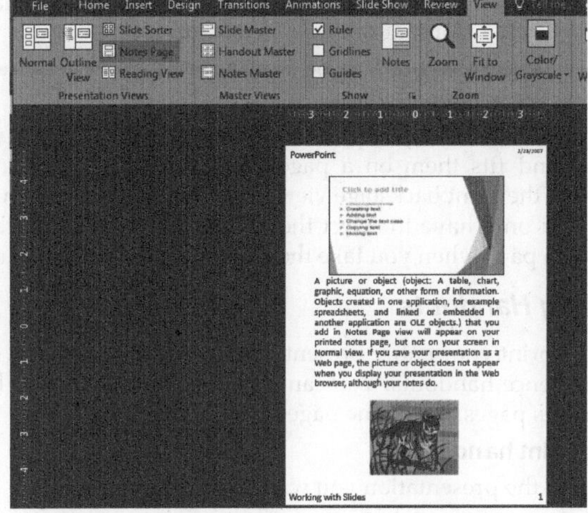

Figure 16.5 Notes Page view to see full effect

16.1.5 Printing the Notes Pages with Slide Thumbnails

1. Open the presentation for which you want to print notes pages with slide thumbnails.

2. Click the **File** tab. The backstage view appears, click **Print** tab. The **Print** backstage view appears.
3. Under **Settings**, click the arrow next to **Full Page Slides**, and then under **Print Layout**, click **Notes Pages.** (See Figure 16.6)

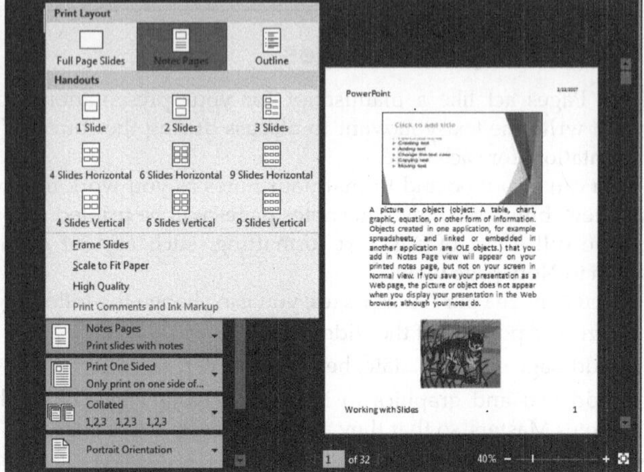

Figure 16.6 Selecting Notes pages in the Print layout

4. To specify the page orientation, click the arrow next to Portrait Orientation, and then click **Portrait** Orientation or **Landscape** Orientation from the list.
5. Click print.

16.1.6 Using Handouts for Presentation

Handout lets you include two, three, six or nine small images of the slides in your presentation. You can select the format when you print them.

Handouts can be created in the following two ways:

- Print the Handouts using the standard PowerPoint format, i.e. two, three, six or nine slide on a page format.
- The Handout format can be customized to your requirement using the handout master.

If you make Handouts, PowerPoint shrinks the slides you have created and fits them on a page, according to the option you choose in the print backstage view. To use standard Handout formats, you only have to select the number of slides you want to print on a page when you take the printouts for the Handouts.

Printing Handouts

You can print your entire presentation – the slides, outline, notes and audience handouts. You can also print specific slides, handouts, notes pages, or outline pages.

➡ **To print handouts:**

1. Open the presentation you want to print.
2. Click the **File** tab, the backstage view appears.
3. To click one or multiple slides per page in handout format, under **Handouts**, click the number of slides you want per page, and whether you want them to appear in order vertically or horizontally. (See Figure 16.7)
4. After applying the desired option, click print.

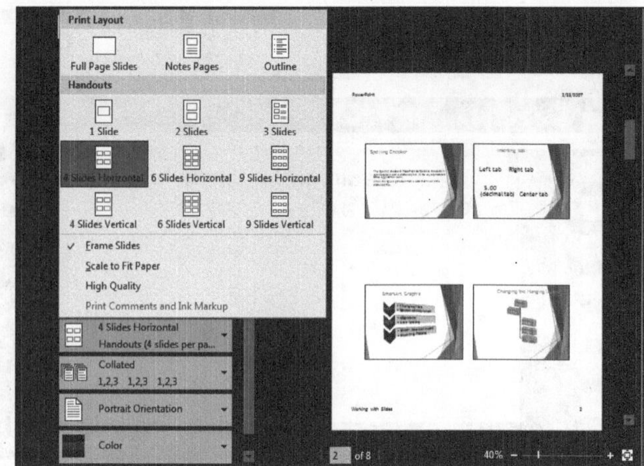

Figure 16.7 Selecting slides per page in handout format in the File tab

16.2 OVERVIEW OF LAYOUTS

You can use layouts to arrange objects and text on slide. A layout is one part of a slide master that defines positioning information for content that will appear on a slide. Layouts contain placeholders, such as titles and bulleted lists, and slide content such as SmartArt graphics tables, charts, shapes and clip art. While you can add text and object placeholder to a layout or slide master, you cannot add placeholders directly to a slide.

PowerPoint 2016 includes five built-in, standard layouts. You can also create custom layouts that meet your specific needs.

16.2.1 Custom Layouts

You can create custom layouts that specify the number, size and location of placeholder, background content and optional slide and placeholder level properties. You can also distribute custom layouts as part of a template, so you no longer have to wait valuable time cutting and pasting your layouts onto new slides or deleting content on a slide that you want to use with new and different content. There are types of text and object-based placeholders that you can add to build your custom layout. These include:

- Content
- Text
- Picture
- Chart
- Table
- Diagram
- Media
- Clip Art

16.2.2 Insert a New Slide Layout

To insert a new slide layout, go to the Slide Master view, add a new layout, add text-specific and object-specific placeholders and then save the presentation as a template file.

➡ **To insert a new slide layout:**

1. Click the **View** tab, in the **Master Views**, click **Slide Master**.
2. In the pane that contains the slide master and layouts, click a location below the slide master where you want to add the new layout.
3. On the **Slide Master** tab, in the **Edit Master** group, click **Insert Layout**. A new layout slide is inserted.

4. To add a placeholder, on the **Slide Master** tab, in the **Master Layout** group, click the arrow next to **Insert placeholder**, and then click a placeholder you want to insert. For example, here we have select Picture placeholder as shown in Figure 16.8.

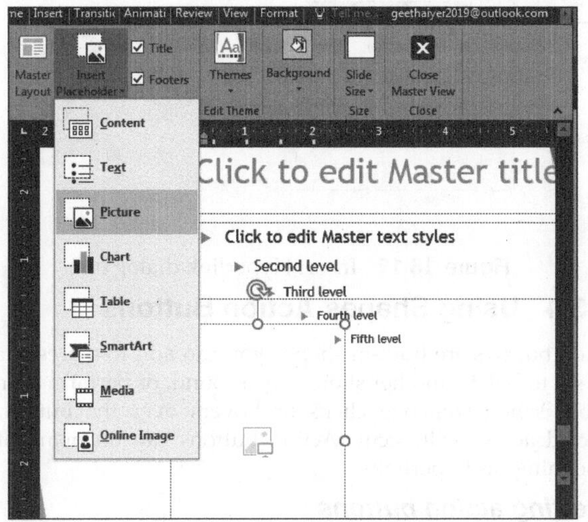

Figure 16.8 Selecting Placeholder in the Master layout group

5. Click and drag to draw the placeholder on the slide.

➡ **To rename a custom layout:**

When you are done designing your custom layout, you will give it a unique name so it will be easy to find.

1. From the **Slide Master** view, select the desired layout, then click the **Rename** command.
2. Rename Layout dialog box will appear as shown in Figure as shown in Figure 16.9.

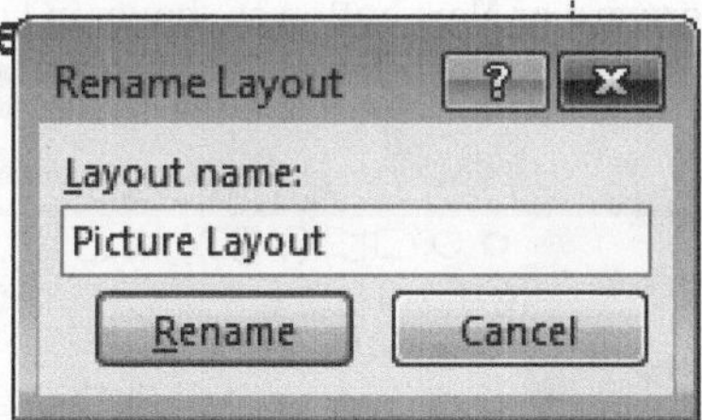

Figure 16.9 Rename Layout slide

➡ **To use a custom layout:**

Once you have created a custom slide layout, it is easy to add a new slide with that layout or apply it to an existing slide.

1. If you are currently in **Slide Master view**, click the **Close Master View** command on the **Slide Master** tab.
2. From the **Home** tab, you can insert a new slide with the custom layout or apply it to an existing slide. For example, we have select the **Layout** command and apply the new style to slide.
3. The custom slide layout will be applied. It also allows you to add new placeholders to existing slide layouts.

16.3 CREATING AND PRESENTING A CUSTOM SHOW

By creating custom shows in PowerPoint 2016, there are two kinds of custom shows: basic and hyperlinked. A basic custom show is a separate presentation or a presentation that includes some of the slides of the original. A hyperlinked custom show is a quick way to navigate to one or more separate presentations.

16.3.1 Basic Custom Shows

Use a basic custom show to give separate presentations to different groups in your organization. For example, if your presentation contains a total of five slides, you can create a custom show named "Custom 1" that includes just slides 1, 3 and 5. You can create a second custom show named "Custom 2" that includes slides 1, 2, 4 and 5. When you create a custom show from a presentation, you can always run the entire presentation in its original sequential order.

16.3.2 Creating a Basic Custom Show

➡ **To create a basic custom show:**

1. Click the **Slide Show** tab, in the **Start Slide Show** group, click **Custom Slide Show** down arrow and then select **Custom Shows...** .

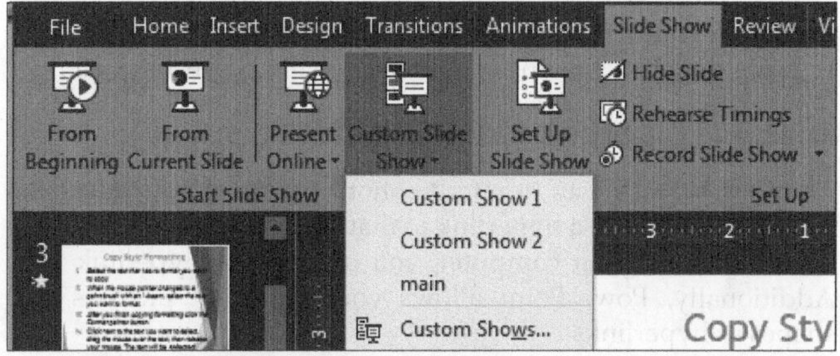

2. **Custom Shows** dialog box appears as shown in Figure 16.10. Click **New...** button. The **Define Custom Show** dialog box appears as shown in Figure 16.11.

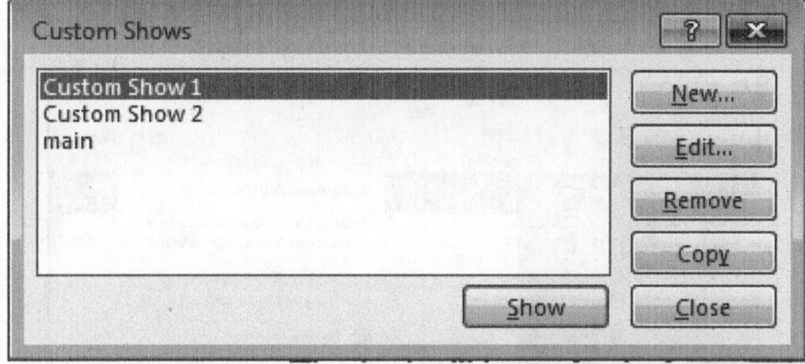

Figure 16.10 Custom Shows dialog box

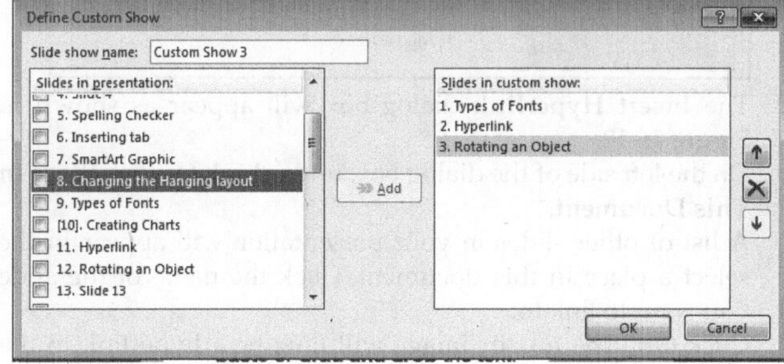

Figure 16.11 Define Custom Shows dialog box

3. Under **Slides in presentation:** click the slides that you want to include in the custom show and then click **Add >>**

☞ *To select multiple sequential slides, click the first slide, and then hold down* Shift *key while you click the last slide that you want to select. To select non-sequential slides, hold down* Ctrl *key while you click each slide that you want to select.*

4. To change the order in which slides to be appear, under **Slides in custom show:** click a slide, and then click one of the arrow to move the slide up or down in the list.
5. Type a name in the **Slide show name box:** and then click OK. To create additional custom shows with any slides in your presentation, repeat steps 1 through 5.

☞ *To create a graceful ending to a slide show you can add a blank slide at the end of presentation. Click File tab, and then choose Options tab. The PowerPoint Options dialog box appears. Click Advanced Page, under Slide Show click End with black slide check box. If you do not include the black slide option, then PowerPoint will reappear first slide after the last slide.*

6. To Preview a custom show, click the name of the show in the **Custom shows** dialog box, and then click **Show** button.

16.3.3 Hyperlink Custom Shows

To create a quick way to refer to another slide in your presentation, you can create a hyperlink to that slide. If you need to access a file stored on your computer, you can create a hyperlink to it. Additionally, PowerPoint allows you to format pictures and shapes as hyperlinks.

➡ **To insert a hyperlink to another slide:**

1. Right-click the selected text or image, then click **Hyperlink**. Or click the **Hyperlink** command in the **Links** group on the **Insert** tab as shown below.

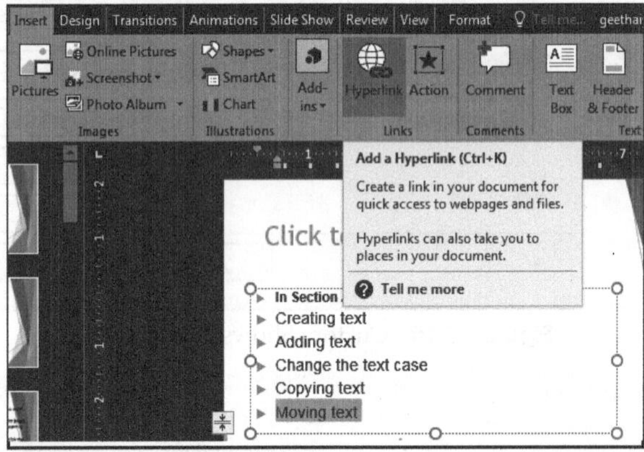

2. The **Insert Hyperlink** dialog box will appear as shown in Figure 16.12.
3. On the left side of the dialog box, under **Link to:** click **Place in This Document**.
4. A list of other slides in your presentation will appear in the select a place in this document. Click the name of the slide you want to link to.
5. Click OK. The text or image will now be a hyperlink to the slide you select.

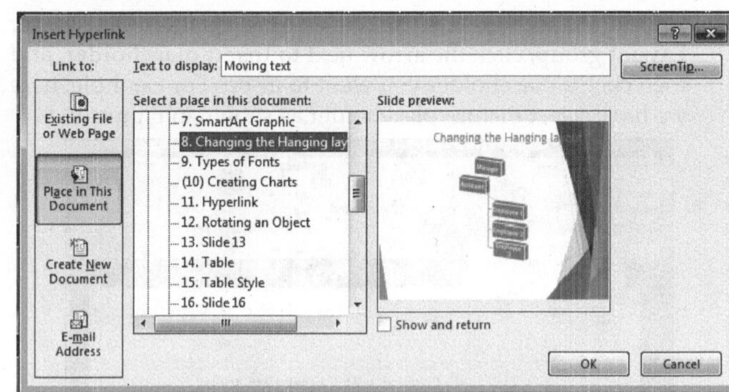

Figure 16.12 Insert Hyperlink dialog box

16.3.4 Using Shapes Action Buttons

Action buttons are built-in shapes you can add to a presentation and set to link to another slide, play a sound, or perform a similar action. When someone clicks or hovers over the button, the selected action will occur. Action buttons can do many of the same things as hyperlinks.

Inserting action buttons

You can insert action buttons on one slide at a time, or you can insert an action button that will show up on every slide. The second option can be useful if you want every slide to link back to a specific slide, like the title page or table of contents.

➡ **To insert an action button on one slide:**

1. Click the **Insert** tab, click **Shapes** command in the **Illustrations** group. A drop-down menu will appear with the action buttons located at the very bottom.
2. Select the desired action button. For example, we have selected **Forward or Next** button as shown in Figure 16.13.

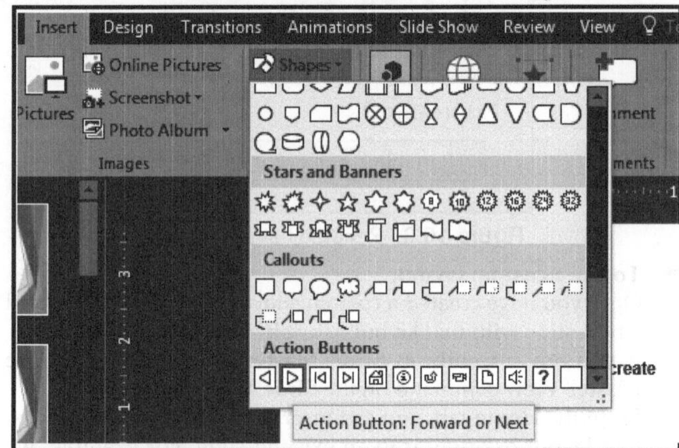

Figure 16.13 Selecting Action button

3. Click and drag the Insert the button onto the slide by clicking the desired location. The **Action Settings** dialog box will appear as shown in Figure 16.14.
4. Select the **Mouse Click** or **Mouse Over** tab. Selecting the **Mouse Click** tab means the action button will perform its action only when clicked. Selecting the **Mouse Over** tab will make the action button perform its action when you move the mouse over it.

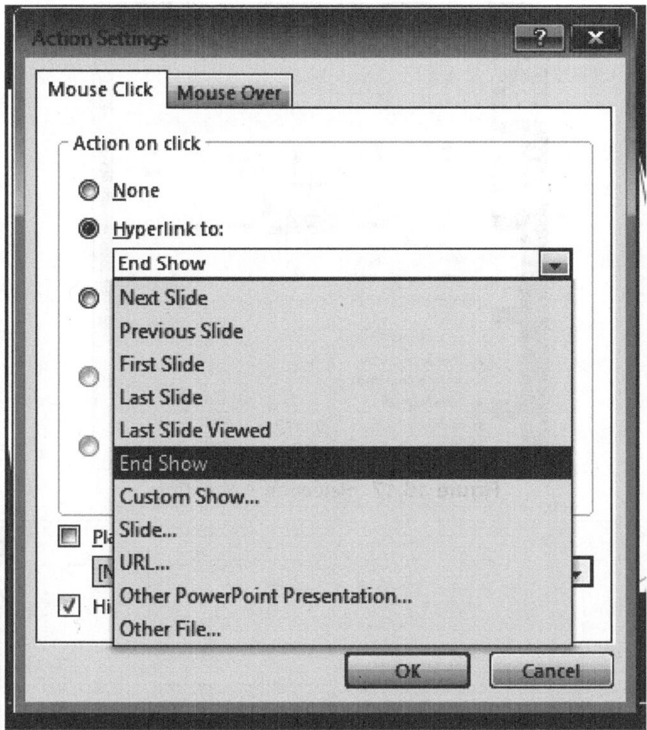

Figure 16.14 Action settings dialog box

5. In the **Action on click** section, select **Hyperlink to:**, then click the drop-down arrow and choose an option from the menu. For example, we have selected **End Show** as shown in Figure 16.14.
6. Check the **Play Sound** box if you want a sound to play when the action button is clicked. Select a sound from the drop-down menu. When you are done, click OK button as shown below.

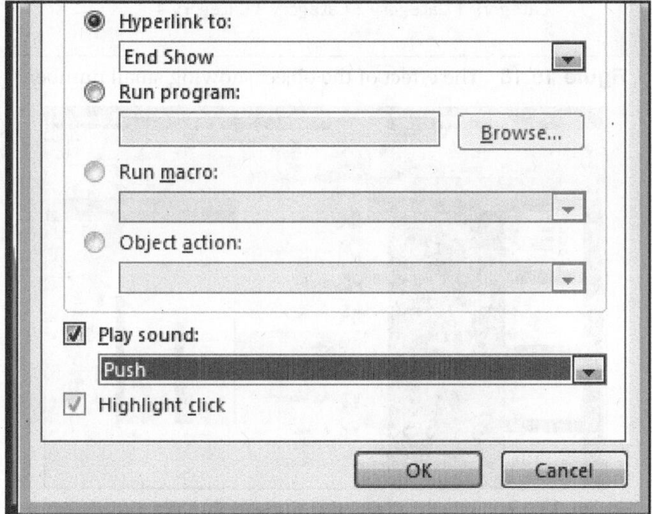

➡ **To test an action button:**

After you create an action button, you should test it.

1. Click the **Slide Show** tab.
2. In the **Start Slide Show** group, click **From Current Slide**. Alternatively, press **Shift+F5** keys together as shown below.

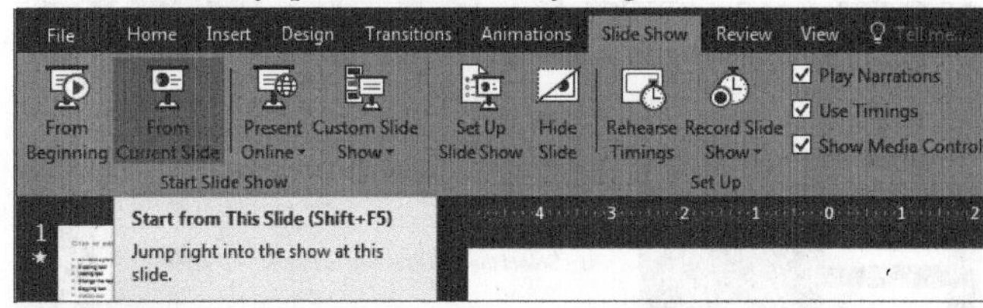

3. Click your action button. The Slide Show comes back to Normal view slide.

➡ **To edit an action button:**

1. Select the action button.
2. Click the **Insert** tab.
3. In the **Links** group, click the **Action** command. The Actions Settings dialog box will appear.
4. Edit the action or hyperlink, then click OK.

16.3.5 Add Transitions between Slides

Slides transitions are the animation-like effects that occur in the slide show view, when you move from one slide to the next. You can control the speed of each slide transition effect, and you can also add sound.

➡ **To add transitions to slides:**

1. Select the slide(s) you want to add a transition effect.
2. Click the **Transitions** tab. In the **Transition to This slide** group, click down arrow and then select the effect that will be applied during the slide show. For example here we select *Exciting* under *curtains*. (Figure 16.15)

Figure 16.15 Selecting Transition effect to Slide

3. You can use the **Apply To All** command in the **Timings** group to apply the same transition to all slides in the presentation.
4. Select the Sound option to give sound transitions to your slide show from the **Sound:** drop-down list in the **Timings** group.
5. The Advance section has two options for transition:
   - On mouse click check box–if you want the transition to take place on clicking the mouse.
   - Automatically after–in this case the transition takes place automatically after the time you specify in the *seconds* box.
6. In the **Duration** field in the **Timing** group, enter the desired time for the transition. For example, we have decrease the time to half a second–or 00.18 to make the transition faster.
7. Click preview command to preview the current transitions effect in the **Preview** group on the **Transitions** tab.
8. Click the **Play animations** command in the **Slide Navigation** pane as shown in Figure 16.16.

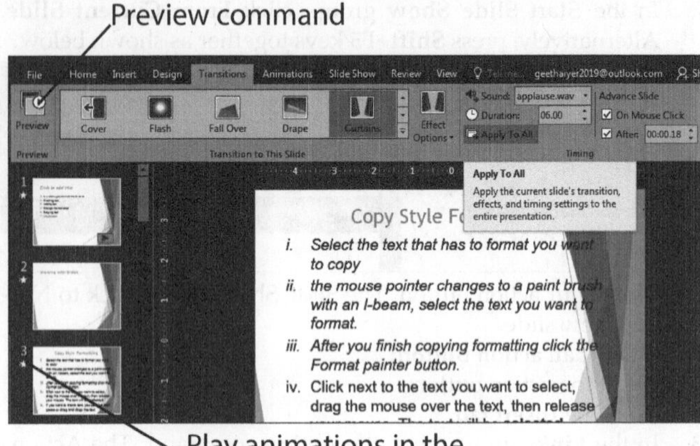

Figure 16.16 Preview a transition

➡ **To modify the transition effect:**

1. You can quickly customize the look of a transition by changing its direction.
2. Select the slide with the transition you want to modify.
3. Click the **Effect Options** command and choose the desired option. These options will vary depending on the selected transition.
4. The transition will be modified, and a preview of the transition will appear.

➡ **To remove a transition:**

1. Select the slide with the transition you want to remove.
2. Choose **None** from the **Transition to This Slide** group. The transition will be removed.

16.4 ANIMATETEXTAND OBJECTS

In PowerPoint, you can animate text and objects such as clip art, shapes, and pictures. Animation or movement –on the slide can be used to draw the audience's attention to specific content or to make the slide easier to read.

16.4.1 Using Animations

➡ **To apply an animation to an object:**

1. Select the object you want to animate.
2. On the **Animations** tab, click the **More** drop-down arrow in the **Animation** group.
3. A drop-down menu of animation effects will appear. Select the desired effect as shown in Figure 16.17.
4. The effect applied to the object as shown in Figure 16.18. The object will have a small number next to it to show that it has an animation. In the Slide pane, a star symbol also will appear next to the slide as shown in Figure 16.17.

16.4.2 Animation Effects

Some effects will have options you can change.

➡ **To set animation effects:**

1. In the **Animations** tab, click **Effects Options** drop down arrow in the **Animation** group. The list of animation effects appears as shown in Figure 16.19.

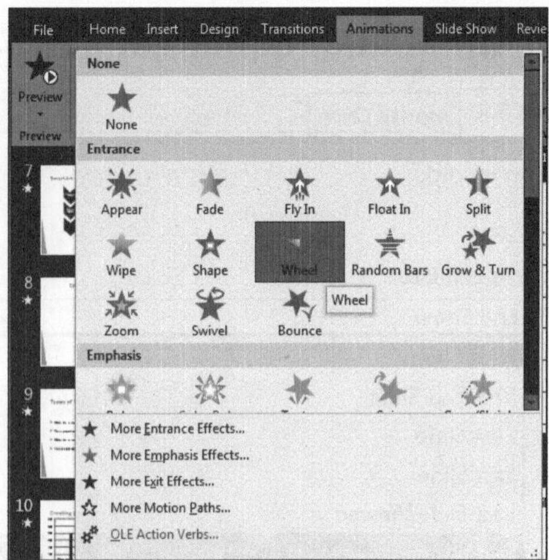

Figure 16.17 Selecting Animations

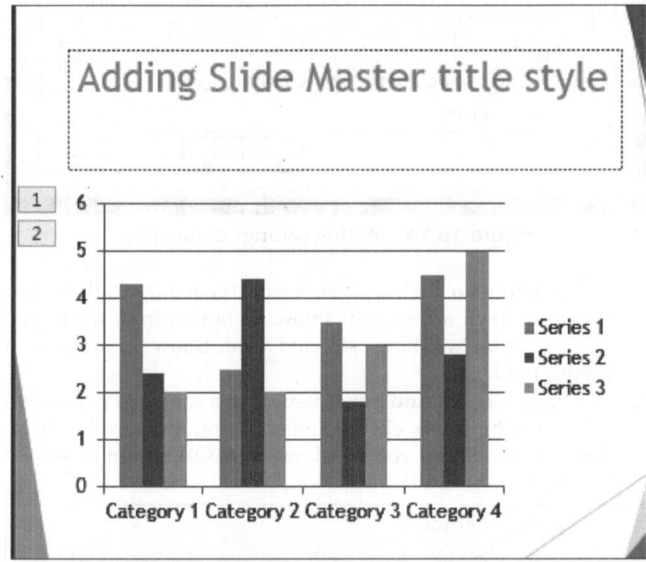

Figure 16.18 The effect of the object showing small number

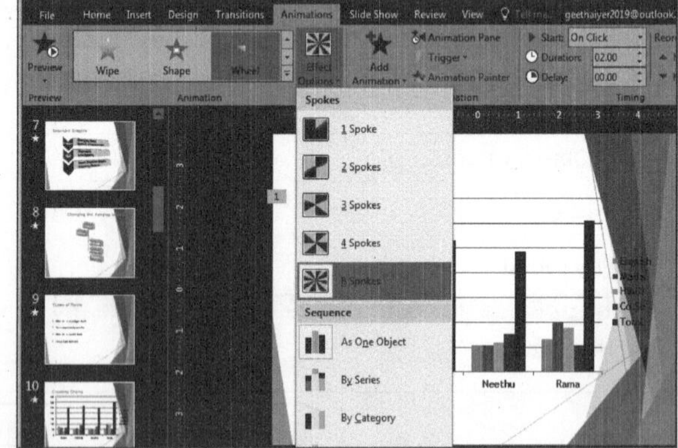

Figure 16.19 Selecting Effect options in the Animation group

2. Click the desired effect options. For example here we select **Spokes** effect to animate.

3. After you apply the effect, immediately it animates the selected effect option in the slide.
4. Select the desired sequence of the object by *As One Object, By Series, By Category, By Element in Series* and *Element in Category.*
5. Click the **Animation pane** command in the **Advanced Animation** group. The Animation pane will open on the right of the window. It will show all of the effects for the current slide in the order in which they will appear. Click the **Play From** the effects for the current slide to play. (See Figure 16.20)

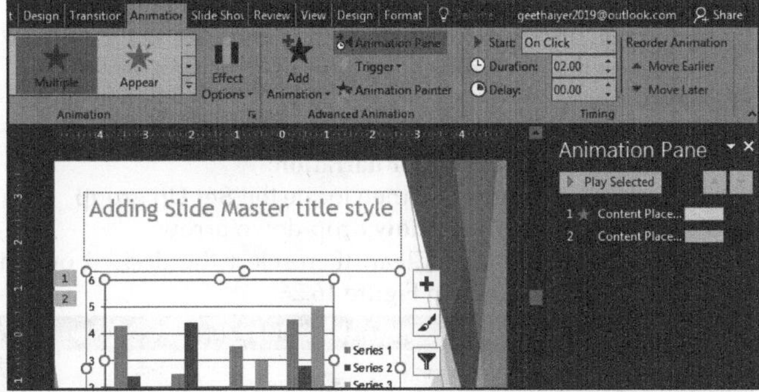

Figure 16.20 Animation pane showing effects of current slide

➡ **To remove an animation:**

1. Select the small number located next to the animated object.
2. Press the **Delete** key. The animation will be deleted.

16.5 RUNNING A SLIDE SHOW

When you develop a slide show in Slide Sorter view, you can get a preview of transition effects for all slides. But to see the transitions full-screen and to see animated or bulleted text slides, you must select the presentation as a slide show.

16.5.1 Starting the Slide Show

When you view a slide show, you have following options:

1. Click **Slide Show** tab in the **Start Slide Show group**, choose Slide Show from beginning or press Shift+F5 keys together.
2. In the Slide show, go to next slide, press N or click the Backspace key to go to the previous slide.

➡ **To set a slide show option:**

1. Click **Slide Show** tab in the **Set Up** group, choose **Set Up Slide Show** icon. The **Set Up Show** dialog box appears as shown in Figure 16.21.
2. To show all slides in your presentation, Click All in the Show slides section.
3. To show a specific group of slides from your presentation, enter a starting and ending slide in From: and To: edit boxes.
4. To start a custom slide presentation that derives from another presentation, click Custom Show: drop down list and then click the presentation that you want to view as a custom show.
5. After selecting the desired settings, click OK.

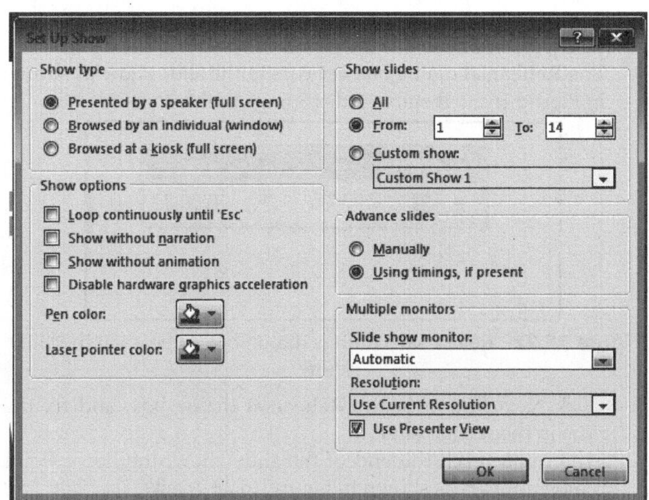

Figure 16.21 Set Up Show dialog box

Giving Special Show

PowerPoint offers three special slide show types. These are available on the Set Up Show dialog box (Figure 16.21).

1. Click Presented by a speaker (full screen): It is the traditional, full-screen slide show.
2. Click Browsed by an individual (window): Runs the slide show in a standard window.
3. Click Browsed at a kiosk (full screen): It displays a full screen as a self running show which restarts after 5 minutes.

Set Up Show Options

Use the options in the Show options section to specify how you want sound files, narrations, or animation to run in your presentation. The options are:

- Click the check box, to play a sound file or animation continuously, select the Loop continuously until press Esc key.
- To show a presentation without playing an embedded narration, select the show without narration check box.
- To show a presentation without playing an embedded animation, select the Show without animation check box.
- When you deliver your presentation before audience, you can write on your slides. Specify an ink color, in the Pen color: list, select an ink color.

16.6 REHEARSING AND RECORDING THE PRESENTATION

PowerPoint offers several tools that can help you rehearse your slide show. You can even record a copy with voice over narration, allowing viewers to watch the presentation on their own.

16.6.1 Rehearsing Slide Show Timings

Rehearsing timings can be useful if you want to set up a presentation to play at a certain speed without having to click through the slides.

➡ **To rehearse timings:**

1. On the **Slide Show** tab, in the **Set Up** group, click **Rehearse Timings** to start the show in rehearsal mode.

2. It starts a full-screen slide show in which you can rehearse your presentation.
3. The **Rehearsal** dialog box appears in the slide show as shown in Figure 16.22. It starts slide timings in the first slide.

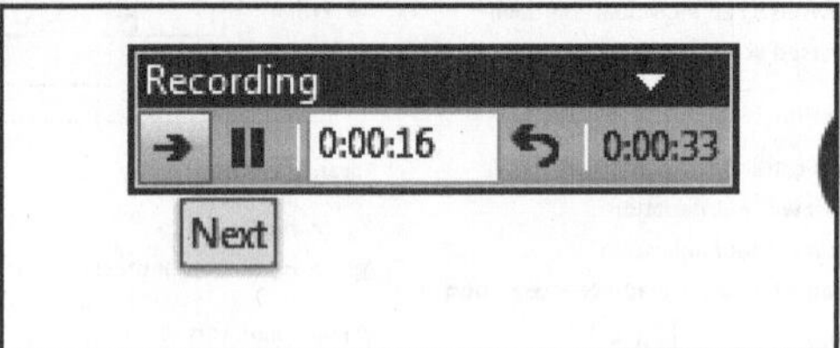

Figure 16.22 Rehearsal Timings dialog box appears in the slide show

4. Click **Next** button in the **Rehearsal** dialog box, and fix the time in the second slide.
5. When you reach the end of the slide show, the PowerPoint dialog appears as shown in Figure 16.23. It asks *The Total time for the slide show was 0:00:42. Do you want to keep the new slide timings to use when you view the slide show?* Yes or No. Click Yes to accept the timings or No to try again.

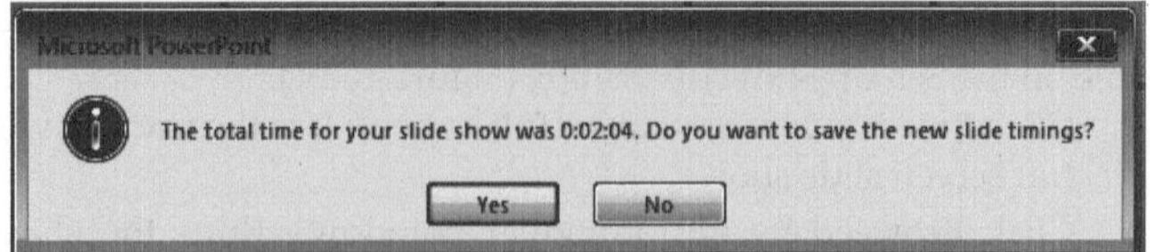

Figure 16.23 Total time of presentation

6. The amount of time you spend on each slide is recorded and you can save those timings to run the show automatically in the future.

16.6.2 Recording your Slide Show

The Record Slide Show feature is similar to the Rehearse Timings feature, but it is a bit more comprehensive. If you have a microphone for your computer, you can record voiceover narration for the entire presentation.

➡ **To record a slide show:**

1. From the **Slide Show** tab, select the **Record Slide Show** drop-down arrow, then choose either **Start Recording from Beginning** or **Start Recording from Current Slide...** as shown in Figure 16.24.

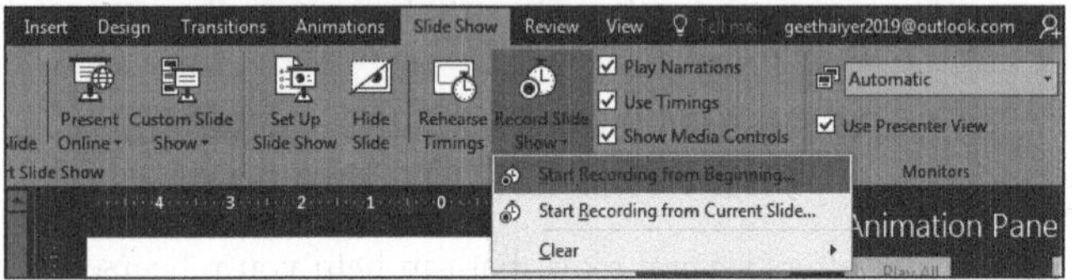

Figure 16.24 Selecting Start Recording from Beginning

2. A **Record Slide Show** dialog box will appear as shown in Figure 16.25. Select the desired options, then click **Start Recording.**

☞ *Remember, you can only record narration, if you have a microphone attached to your computer.*

3. Your presentation will appear in full-screen view. Make sure to speak clearly into the microphone if you are recording narration.

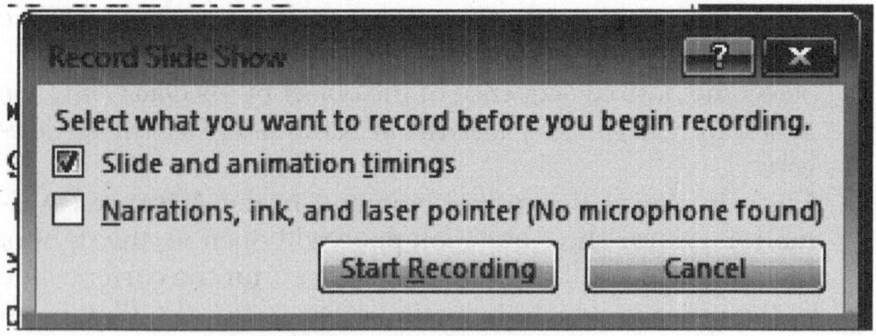

Figure 16.25 Record Slide Show

4. When you are ready to move to the next slide, click the **Next** button on the **Recording** toolbar or use the right arrow key.
5. When you reach the end of the show, PowerPoint will close the full-screen view.

➡ **To remove slide timings or narration:**

1. Click the **Slide Show** tab, then locate the **Set Up** group.
2. Click the **Record Slide Show** drop-down arrow.
3. Hover the mouse over Clear, then select the desired option from the list as shown in Figure 16.26.

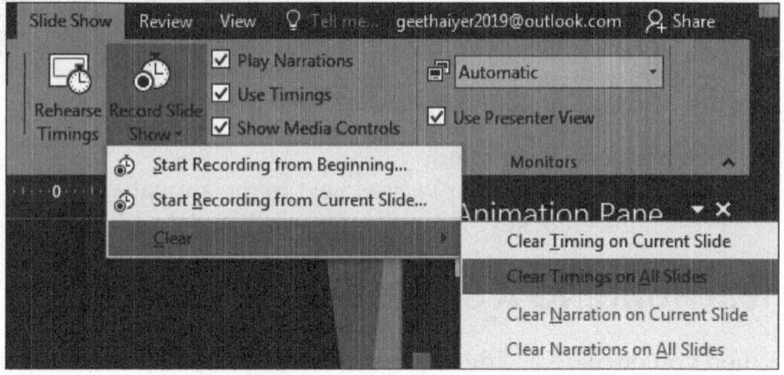

Figure 16.26 Clear record options list

16.7 PACKAGEFORCD

Packaging your PowerPoint 2016 presentation to a CD makes your presentation ready to view on any computer. Often the available computer does not have PowerPoint 2016 installed. Packaging for CD includes the PowerPoint Viewer so that your presentation can be played on any computer, even those that do not have PowerPoint 2016 installed.

➡ **To package a presentation for CD:**

1. With the presentation open, select the **File** tab, choose **Export**, select **Package Presentation for CD** and then **Package for CD** as shown in Figure 16.27.

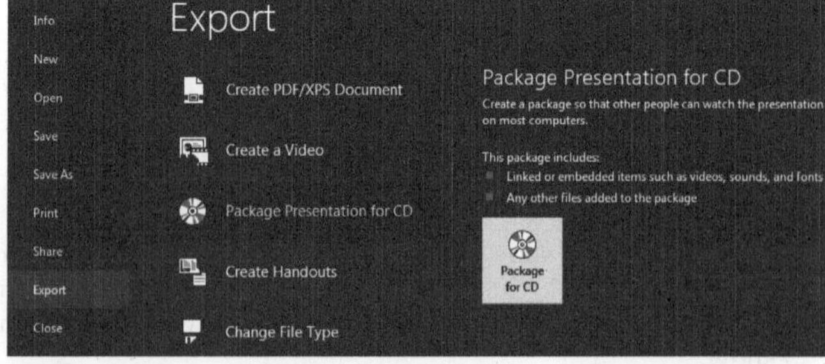

Figure 16.27 Selecting Package for CD in the Export backstage view

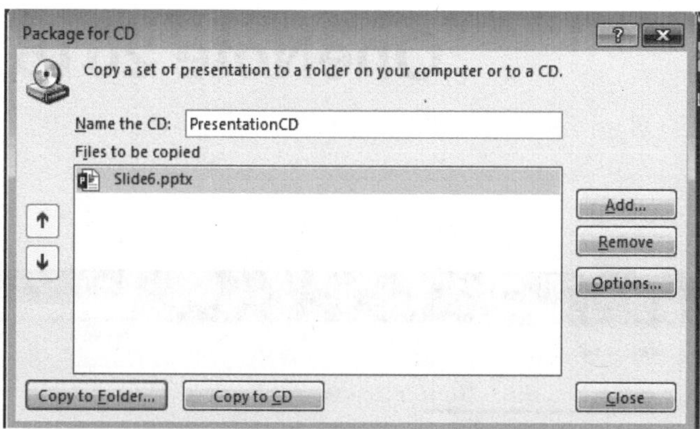

Figure 16.28 Package for CD dialog box

2. Package for CD dialog box appears as shown in Figure 16.28, type a name for the CD, in the **Name the CD:** list box. For example, we have select the default name **PresentationCD.**
3. Click the **Add...** button to add multiple presentations on the CD.
4. The **Add Files** dialog box appears, select the files and then click the Add button.
5. The selected presentation files add to the Files to be copied section of the Package for CD dialog box.
6. Click **Copy to Folder...** as shown in Figure 16.28.
7. **Copy to Folder** dialog box appears as shown in Figure 16.29, to edit the folder name and location, select the **Folder name:** and **Location:** list box, then click OK.
8. The **Package for CD** dialog box closes and a message box opens to confirm the inclusion of linked files in the package containing your presentation as shown in Figure 16.30.

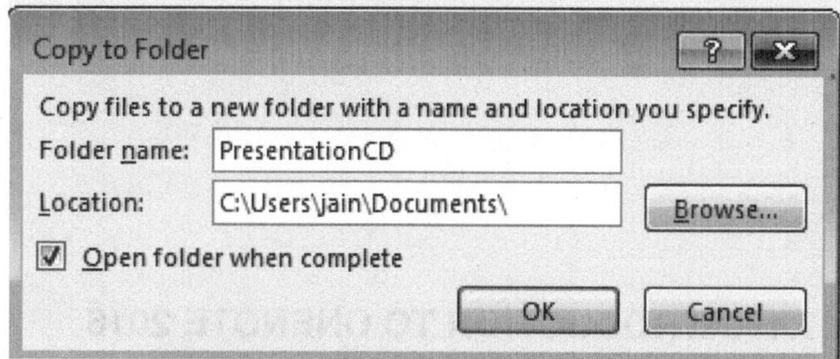

Figure 16.29 Copy to Folder dialog box

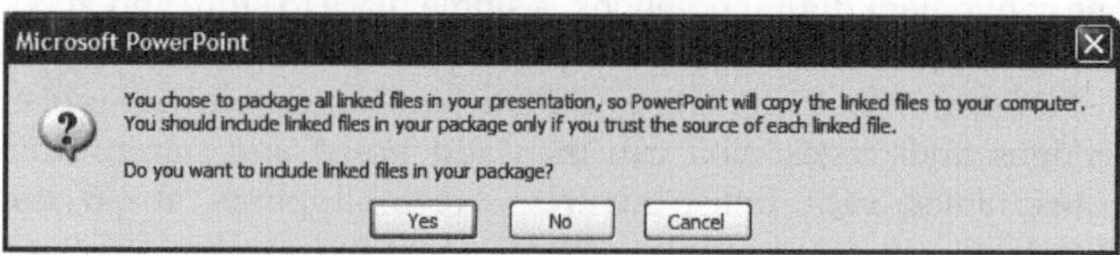

Figure 16.30 Message box opens to confirm the inclusion of linked files in your package

9. Click the **Yes** button in the message box.
10. The presentation files are added to the folder, along with all the files needed to run the PowerPoint Viewer.
11. Confirm that you have everything you need, then go back to the Package for CD dialog (see step 2) and this time select Copy to CD. You will be prompted to insert a blank CD, and the files will be added.
12. After the files have been copied to the CD, the **Package for CD** dialog box re-appears. Click the **Close** button on the **Package for CD** dialog box.

CHAPTER 17

OneNote 2016

17.1 INTRODUCTION TO ONENOTE 2016

MS OneNote is a personal information management application – PIM for short –designed to help you gather notes of all kinds into one convenient digital notebook. a single place to store and access information about school, work, and your personal life. It takes just a few minutes to create a new OneNote notebook with tabbed sections and pages. You can then add typed and handwritten notes, tables, files, links, pictures, screen clippings, audio, and video.

17.1.1 Why Use OneNote?

OneNote is the ultimate virtual notebook that enables users to create notes in various formats, share those notes, sync those notes with the cloud, and collaborate with others. You can easily create typed, handwritten, audio and video notes, and search those notes. You do not have to worry about forgetting to save those notes because everything is saved automatically as you work.

➡ **To start OneNote:**

1. Click Start button.
2. Highlight All Programs and select OneNote 2016.
3. OneNote start up and opens with the **Quick Notes** tab selected, and displaying an advice page headed "OneNote: one place for all of your notes" as shown in Figure 17.1.

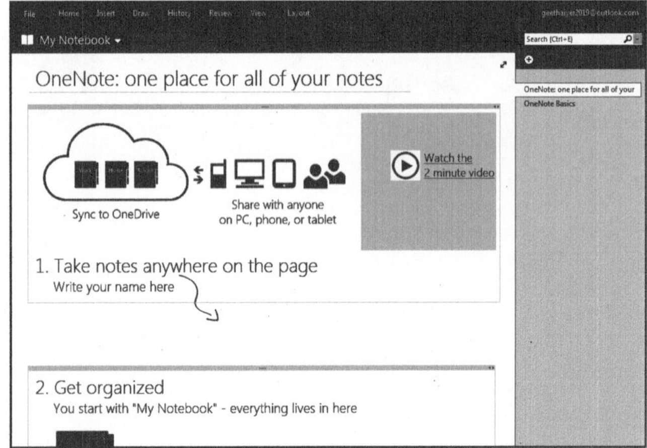

Figure 17.1 Quick Notes

4. In the right side pane, select the page item entitled "OneNote Basics" to see the second page as shown in Figure 17.2.
   This describes the many benefits of the OneNote applications such as:
   - **Remember everything**–Add tags to any notes, make checklists and to-do lists.

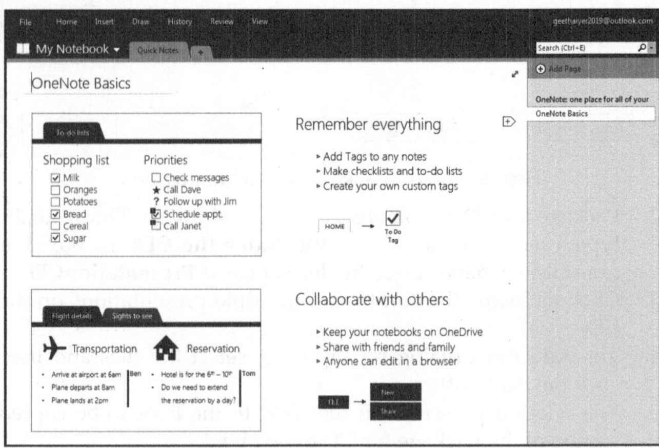

Figure 17.2 OneNote Basics page

- **Collaborate with others**–The ability to share your notebooks and collaborate with others on the notebooks content with colleagues, friends, and family via OneDrive.
- **Keep everything in Sync**–Store all of your notes on the cloud for access from anywhere, and on any device, via OneDrive.
- **Clip from the web**–Save screenshots of any item you find of interest on any web page.
- **Organize with tables**–Create data tables that can be converted for your Excel spreadsheets.
- **Write notes on slides**–Send PowerPoint slides or Word documents to OneNote and Annotate with a stylus on your tablet.
- **Integrate with Outlook**–Add Outlook tasks from OneNote.
- **Add Excel Spreadsheets**–Keep track of your finances, and budgets, or anything you want to track.
- **Brainstrom without clutter**–Share only the essentials in notes to focus on the important matters.
- **Take Quick Notes**–Quickly jot down thoughts and ideas as they occur to you.

☞ *The first time OneNote starts, a folder named "OneNote Notebooks" gets added to your Documents folder.*

17.1.2 OneNote 2016 Interface

The OneNote 2016 Interface is different from previous version of OneNote. The following Illustrates the interface and where OneNote features are located as shown in Figure 17.3.

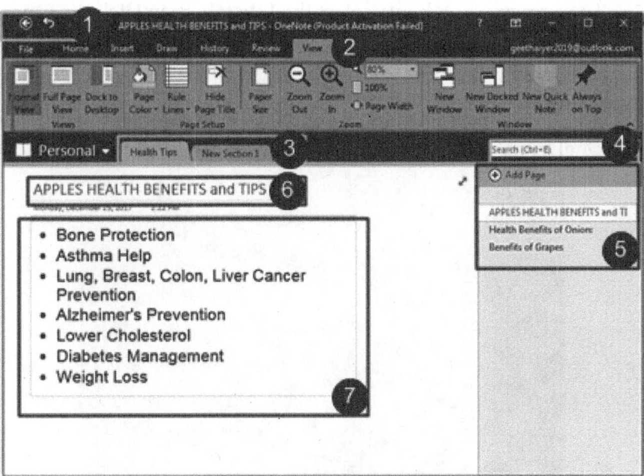

Figure 17.3 OneNote 2016 Interface

Quick Access Toolbar

The Quick Access Toolbar is a small toolbar at the top left of the application window that you can customize to contain buttons for the functions that you use most often.

Customize the Quick Access Toolbar

➡ **To customize Quick Access toolbar:**

1. Click the drop-down arrow on the far right
2. Click any **listed command** to add it to the Quick Access Toolbar as shown in Figure 17.4.

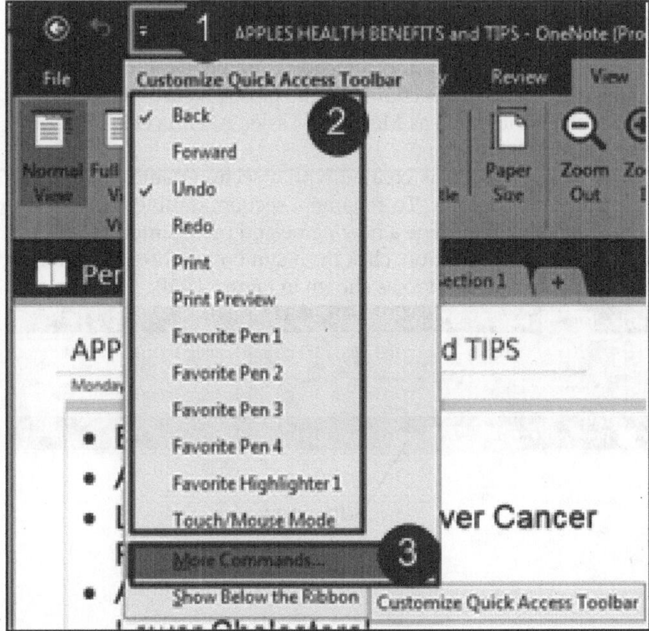

Figure 17.4 Quick Access Toolbar More commands

3. Click **More Commands** to choose from a comprehensive list of commands.
4. **OneNote Options** dialog box appears as shown in Figure 17.5, select a command from the list by clicking on it.

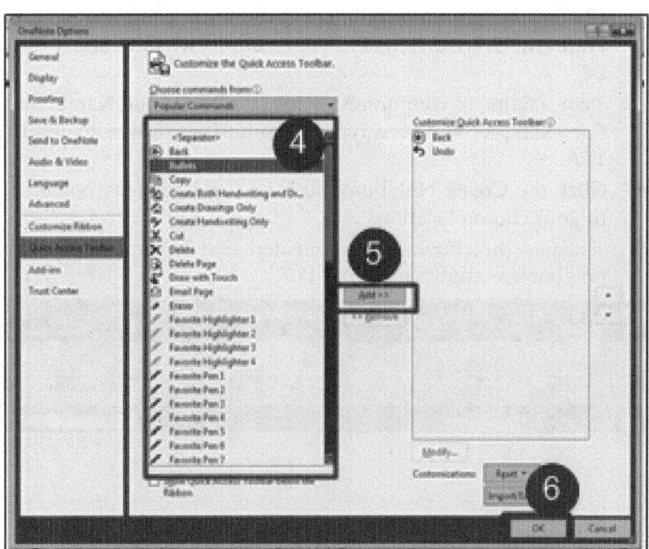

Figure 17.5 OneNote Options dialog box

5. Click the **Add** button
6. Repeat steps 4 & 5 to add additional commands.
7. Click the OK button to confirm your selection as shown in Figure 17.5.

The Ribbon

The ribbon is a panel that contains functional groupings of buttons and drop-down lists organized by tabs. The ribbon is designed to help you quickly find the commands that you need to complete a task.

17.1.3 Creating a New Notebook

You can create multiple notebooks. Within a notebook you can create multiple sections and multiple pages to each section.

Notebook

Notebooks are like binders that store your information in a central location.

➡ **To open new Notebook:**

1. Click **File** tab, then click **New** backstage view as shown in Figure 17.6.

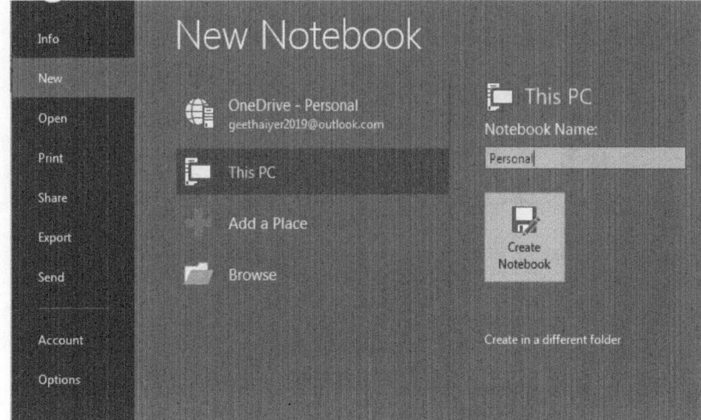

Figure 17.6 New Notebook backstage view

2. Choose where you put the notebook, such as in the cloud on your **OneDrive** or **This PC**. For example, we have select **This PC**.
3. Type a name of your notebook into the **Notebook Name:** box. For example, we have type "Personal" as shown in Figure 17.6.
4. Click the **Create Notebook** button to add the new notebook to your chosen location.
5. The new notebook will be created and become the active notebook as shown in Figure 17.7.

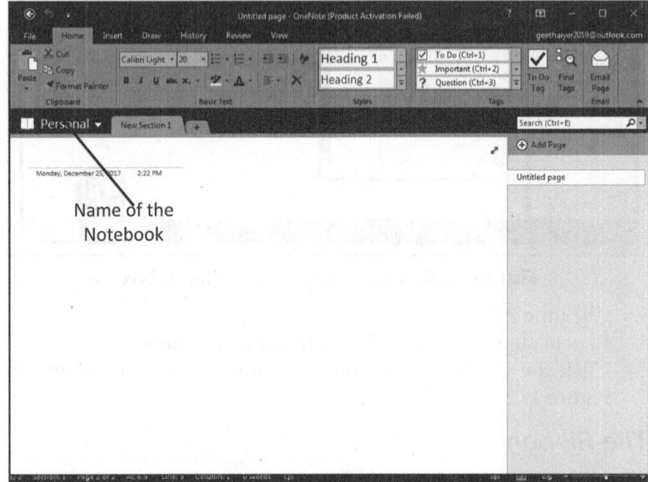

Figure 17.7 New Notebook

17.1.4 Opening and Closing Notebooks

You can open and close notebooks as needed. Notebooks stay open until you close them. As you add and work with more notebooks, they tend to clutter the list or sidebar.

Open a notebook using the Open Notebook window. Depending on the notebook's location, you may need to navigate to the particular notebook you want to use.

1. To close the notebook, select the **File** tab, it come back to **Info** backstage view, click the **Settings** drop-down arrow and choose **Close** as shown in Figure 17.8.

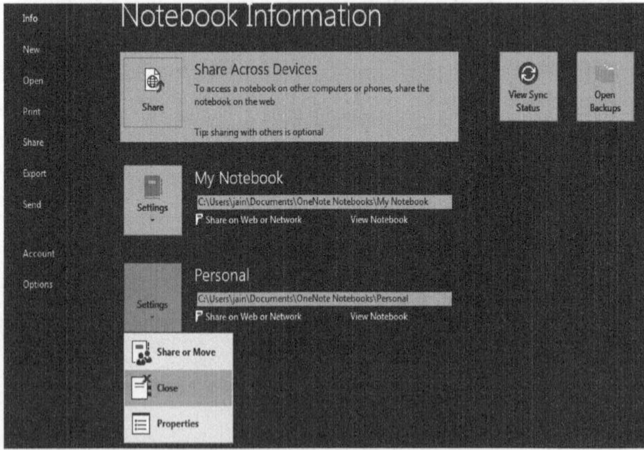

Figure 17.8 Close a Notebook

2. To re-open a notebook, select the **File** tab, then click the **Open** command, and choose the name of the notebook in the **Recent** items and select the file as shown in Figure 17.9. Alternatively, click the **Browse** button to navigate the file documents folder on your computer. Or you can Open from OneDrive.

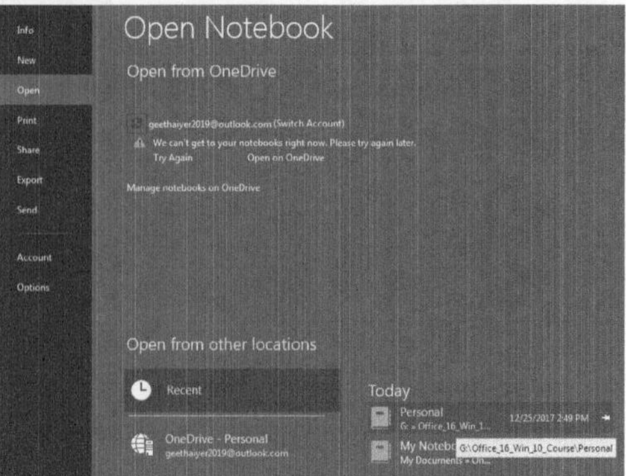

Figure 17.9 Open a Notebook document

Close Notebooks with the Shortcut Menu

You can quickly close a notebook using the shortcut menu without having to display the **Notebook Information** window in Backstage View. The context menu offers commands related specifically to notebooks, such as syncing and sharing.

1. Click the Notebooks list.
2. Right-click over the notebook you want to close.
3. Click **Close this Notebook.**

17.1.5 Add Sections

A OneNote is organized into sections and pages, and it is easy to make them colorful. Sections are the tabs in your noteboook that create categories such as Meetings, Tasks, Agenda etc.

➡ **To add sections:**

1. A new notebook is created with a section named "**New Section 1**" by default. To rename a section, double-click its current name, then type a new name and press **Enter**.
2. To add a new section, click the + symbol on the small tab next to the last section tab as shown in Figure 17.10.

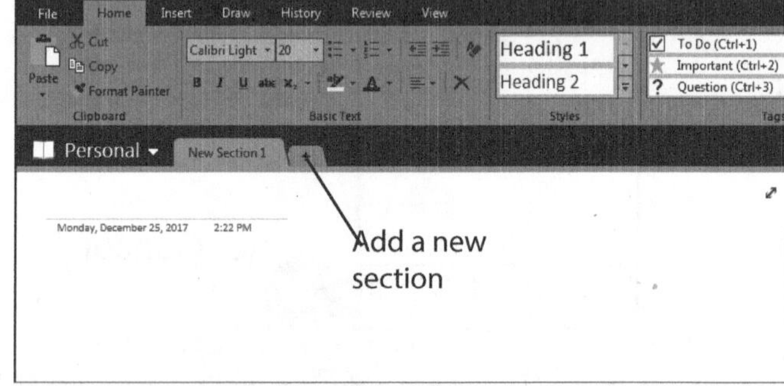

Figure 17.10 Add a new section

3. Right-click the section tab, a sub menu appears select Rename it get automatically colored, to distinguish them from other sections as shown in Figure 17.11.

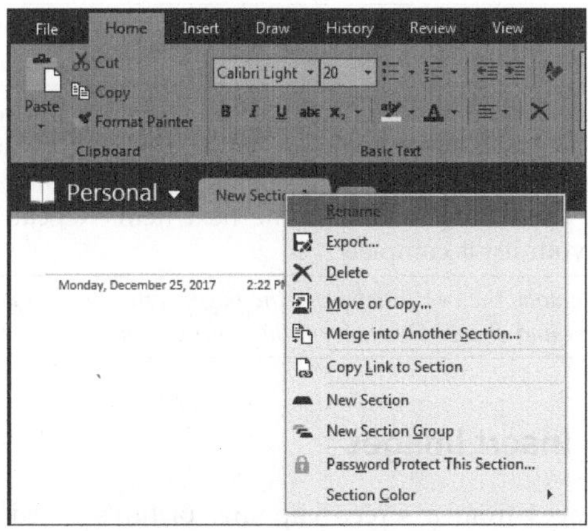

Figure 17.11 Rename a notebook

➡ **To move a section:**

1. Left-click and hold a section tab with your mouse.
2. While holding the section, drag the section left or right of the other sections. You will see a small rectangle with arrow mouse pointer showing where the section will be placed as shown in Figure 17.12.

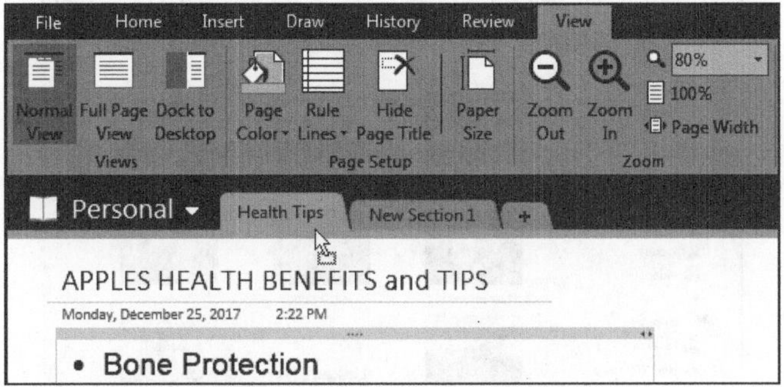

Figure 17.12 Move a section

3. When the section is where you want to place it, let go of the left-click on your mouse.

➡ **To Delete a section:**

1. Right-click on a section name.
2. Click **Delete** as shown in Figure 17.11.

17.1.6 Add Pages

A new section is created with a blank page header by default. Page hold the notes in your sections for your noteboook. To rename a page, click the header area at the top of the page, then type a page title and press Enter.

➡ **To add pages:**

1. Click on the section where you want to add a page, click the Add Page (+) button at the right side pane.
2. At the top of the page Untitled Page appears as shown in Figure 17.13.
3. Type the new page name in the Highlighted area above the line as shown in Figure 17.13.
4. See the page name now appear in the pages pane, and on the OneNote window title bar as shown in Figure 17.14.

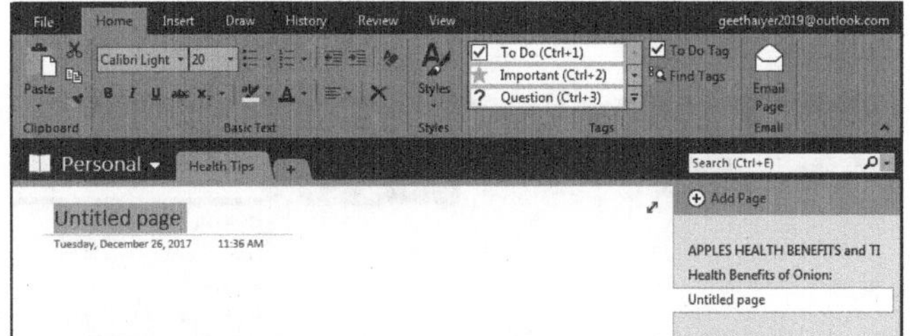

Figure 17.13 Add pages in the notebook

☞ *To change a section color, right-click the section tab then choose Section Color from the menu, and pick a color.*

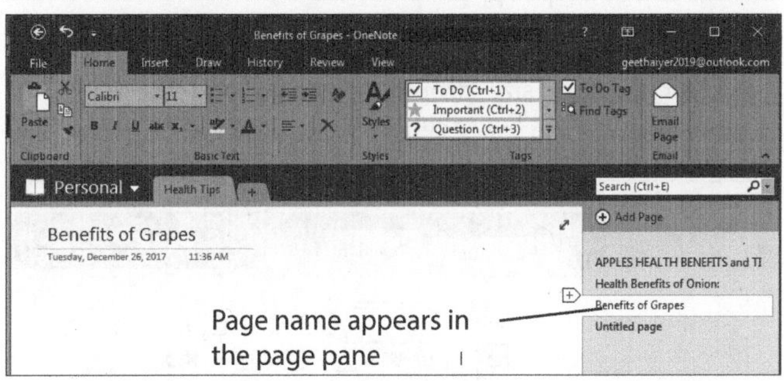

Figure 17.14 Type a page title and it add pages pane

➡ **To move a page:**

1. **Left-click and hold** a page tab with your mouse.
2. While holding the page, drag the page up or down of the other pages. You will see a **right arrow and a line showing** where the page will be placed as shown in Figure 17.15.

Figure 17.15 Move a page

3. Release the mouse button where you want to place it the page.

➡ **To Delete a page:**

1. Right-click on a page name.
2. Click **Delete.**

17.1.7 Make Notes

Notes in OneNote are contained in frames. After a page is named, a note frame with a blinking cursor appears automatically below the title. You can start a new note by clicking anywhere on a page and typing. The basic tools for formatting text in OneNote are similar to those found in other applications.

1. Open Notebook and choose a section within a notebook then click anywhere on a page and simply start typing as shown in Figure 17.16.

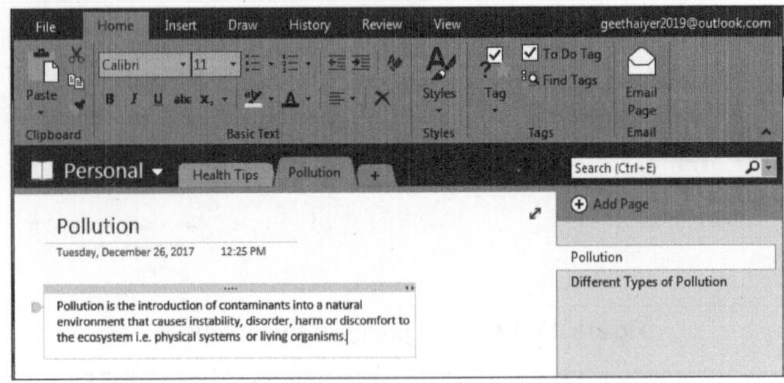

Figure 17.16 Start Typing in note container

2. The text you type appear within a note container box.
3. Double-click on the text in a note container to see formatting options appears as shown in Figure 17.17.
4. Select the font size drop-down arrow and the select the desired font size. For example, we have selected **Bold** style as shown in Figure 17.17.

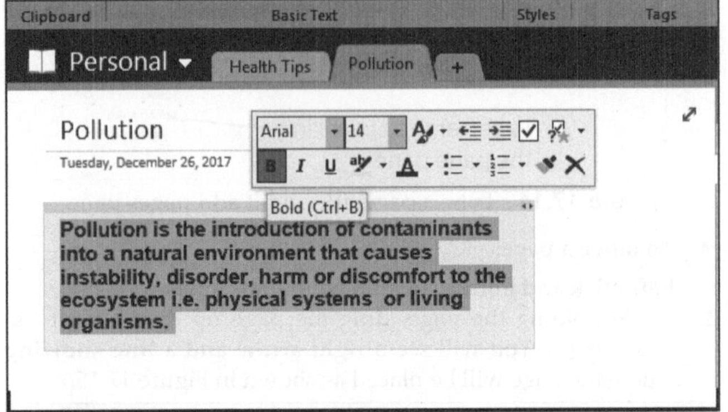

Figure 17.17 Selecting Bold style from the pop-up menu

☞ *To convert handwritten notes to text, choose the Draw tab, then select Ink to Text from the Convert group. Your note now appears as text in a note container.*

5. Click on the header bar of a note container to drag your notes around the page.
6. To enter bulleted list, select the text, a format pop-menu appears, select the bullets drop-down arrow.
7. The bulleted list appears as shown in Figure 17.18, select the desired bullet from the **Bullet Library** list. Or

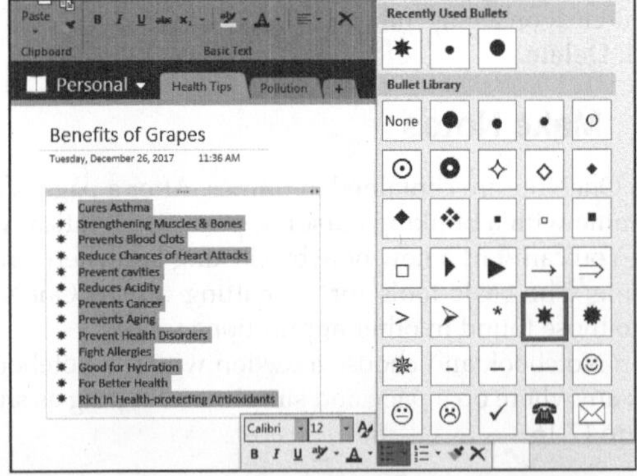

Figure 17.18 Selecting Bullet list from the Bullet Library

☞ *Drag the handle at the top right-hand side of a note container to make the container wider.*

8. If you want numbering list, select the numbering drop-down arrow to the desired number style. Or Type 1. (a numbered one followed by a period) then press the Spacebar.
9. Then press **Enter** and type the next item. Repeat this step until your list is complete.

☞ *To remove the container from the page, right-click on a note container and choose Delete from the context menu.*

17.1.8 Insert Images

Insert images from a screen clipping, pictures saved on your machine, online pictures, or a scanned image.

➡ **To insert images:**

1. Click the **Insert** tab and click the **Pictures** command in the **Images** group.
2. The **Insert picture** dialog box appears as shown in Figure 17.19, navigate the file in the address bar.

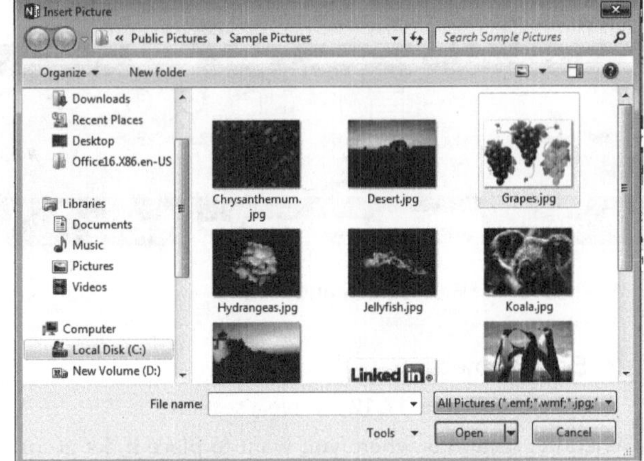

Figure 17.19 Insert Picture dialog box

3. Select the desired file in the contents pane, and then click **Insert** button.
4. The image is inserted in the current page in your OneNote notebook as shown in Figure 17.20.

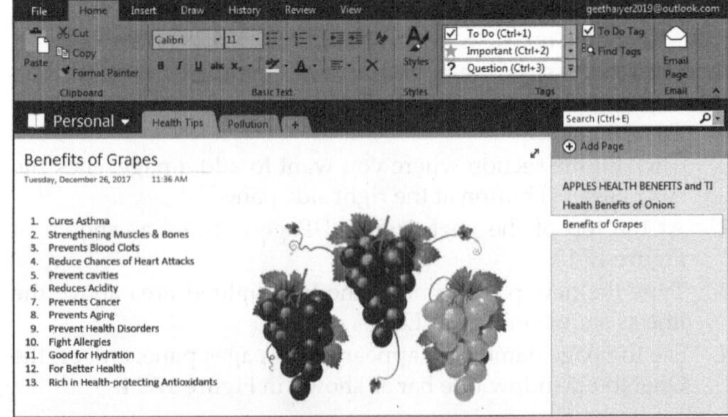

Figure 17.20 The image is inserted in OneNote notebook

☞ *Pictures are inserted in note containers which can be adjusted with their grab handles to resize inserted images.*

➡ **To insert screen clipping:**

1. Click the **Insert** tab, click the **Screen Clipping** command.
2. An overlay layer appears on your screen so you can drag the cursor to select an area to clip for your notebook page as shown in Figure 17.21.

Figure 17.21 Overlay layer of the image

3. The screen clipping area of the image inserted in the notebook as shown in Figure 17.22.

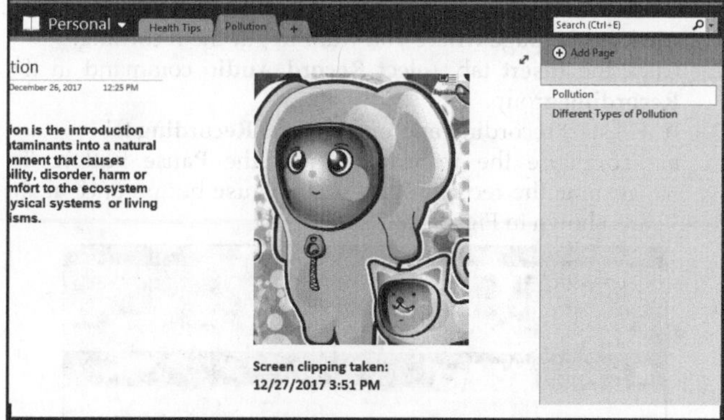

Figure 17.22 Screen clipping image

17.1.9 Capture Snippets

As your browse the internet you can add or save links to interesting snippets, or websites of interest, on a page in your OneNote notebook.

1. Select the page in the notebook where you want to add a link.
2. Click the **Insert** tab, click the **Link** command in the **Links** group.
3. The **Link** dialog box appears as shown in Figure 17.23. Enter the **Text to display:** on the link, then type or paste the URL Address in the **Address:** text box.

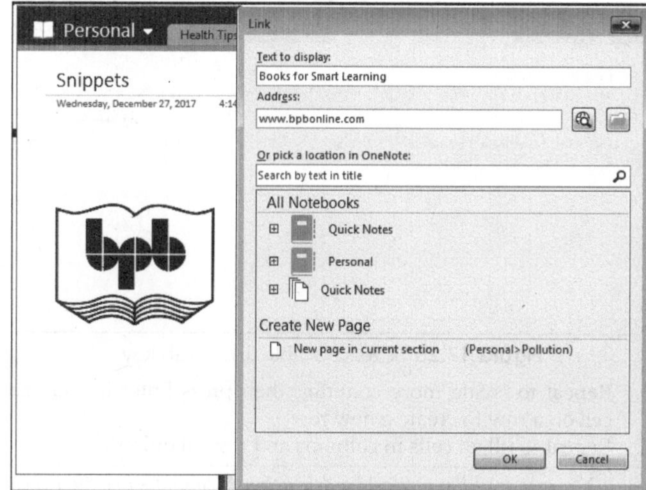

Figure 17.23 Links dialog box

4. Click OK button. The selected links appears in the note container box as shown in Figure 17.24.

☞ *You can right-click on a link in your notebook and choose Edit Link from the context menu, to reopen the Link dialog and modify the link.*

Figure 17.24 Address link container box

17.1.10 Create Tables

Tables are used in OneNote to organize information. A table with a specific number of rows and columns can be inserted on a page. Another way to create a table in to start typing a note and then press Tab to insert a new column and Enter to insert a new row.

➡ **To create a table using only the keyboard:**

1. Click an empty area of the page then press Tab key to create a table column.
2. Type a text, as context for the first column cell (heading), then press Tab again to create another column heading as shown in Figure 17.25.

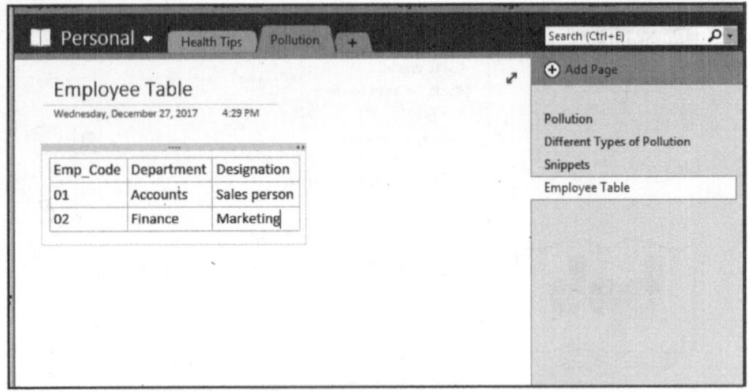

Figure 17.25 Create a table using Tab key

3. Repeat to create more columns, then press Enter in the last cell on a row to create a new row.
4. Repeat to fill all cells in columns and rows required.

☞ *You can drag the vertical borders between columns to adjust each column width.*

➡ **To create a table using the Ribbon:**

1. Select the **Insert** tab, then click the **Table** down-arrow command.
2. In the **Insert Table** palette appears as shown in Figure 17.26, move the cursor over the grid box to select desired row and column boxes.

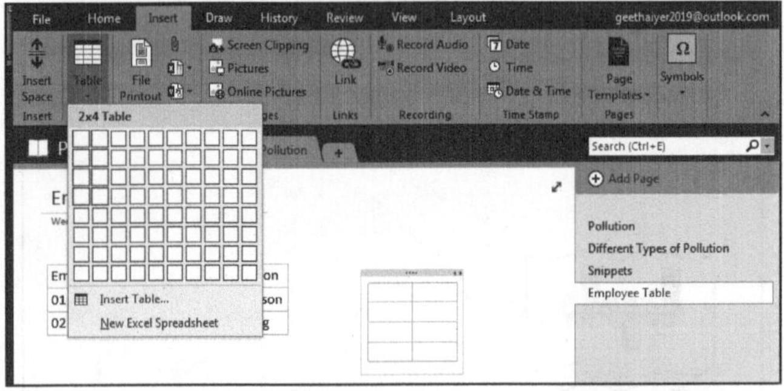

Figure 17.26 Insert Table palette

3. The table is inserted in your page and the **Table Tools, Layout** tab appear where you can change the table properties. Select the Shading color to heading as shown in Figure 17.27.

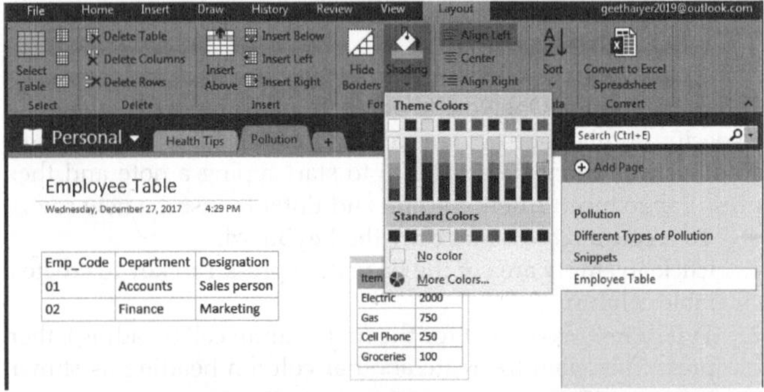

Figure 17.27 Table Layout options

You can also right-click on any table and choose the **Table** item from the context menu to also find the **Layout** options.

4. Add text to the cells to complete the table data as shown in Figure 17.27.

☞ *You can use the Convert to Excel Spreadsheet button to export a table to the Excel application.*

5. To sort a column into alphabetical order, click anywhere in the column to select it, then click **Sort** down-arrow to select **Sort Ascending** as shown in Figure 17.28.

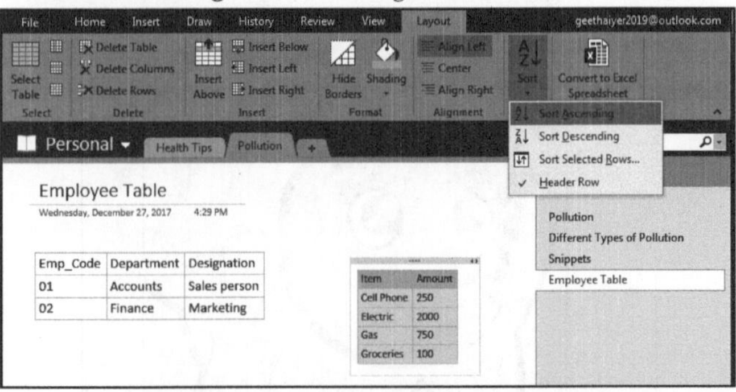

Figure 17.28 Selecting Sort command

17.1.11 Record Audio

OneNote gives you the capability to record audio and video directly in your notes while retaining the ability to enter text.

☞ **Note:** *To record audio, you will need a microphone. To record video, you will need a web camera.*

➡ **To Record Audio:**

1. Click on the page where you want to put the recording.
2. Click the **Insert** tab, select **Record Audio** command in the **Recording** group.
3. It will start recording and open up the **Recording** tab.
   a. To pause the recording, press the **Pause** button. To resume the recording press the **Pause** button once again as shown in Figure 17.29.

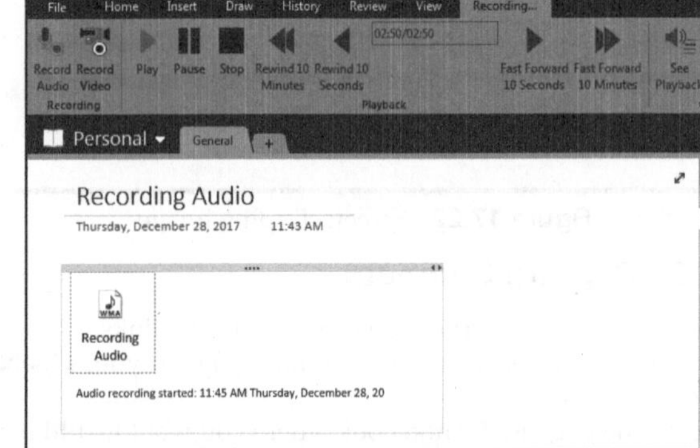

Figure 17.29 Showing Recording tab to insert audio

   b. To stop the recording, press the **Stop** button when you finish your audio note message.
4. After pressing the Stop button, the Recording tab will change to the **Playback tab** as shown in Figure 17.30.
5. Click the **Play** command to listen to your recorded audio as shown in Figure 17.30.

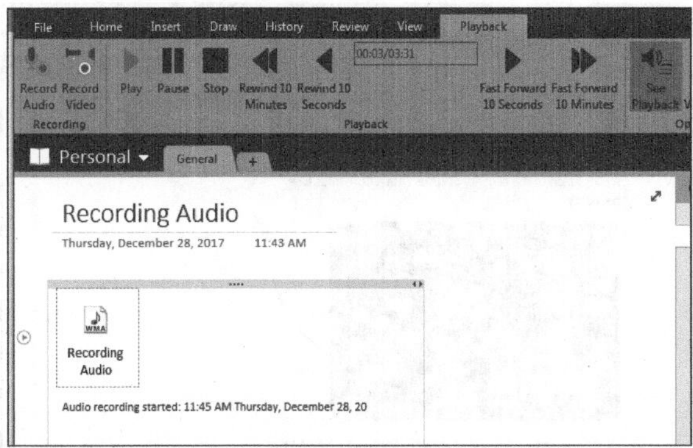

Figure 17.30 Showing Playback tab to play the audio

➡ **To Record Video:**

1. Click on the page where you want to put the video recording.
2. Click the **Insert** tab, select **Record Video** command in the **Recording** group.
3. It will start recording and open up the Recording tab and preview video window as shown in Figure 17.31.

Figure 17.31 Recording video

   a. To pause the recording, press the **Pause** button. To resume the recording, press the **Pause** button again.
   b. To stop the recording, press the **Stop** button.

4. After pressing the Stop button, the Recording tab will change to the **Playback tab** as shown in Figure 17.31.
5. Click the **Play** command to watch your recorded video as shown in Figure 17.31.

17.1.12 Page Templates

Page Templates give you pre-formatted pages that consist of backgrounds, colors, to-do lists,calendars, and other functional content.

1. Click the **Insert** tab, then click the **Page Templates** command in the **Pages** group and choose the **Page Templates** item to open a "**Templates**" pane as shown in Figure 17.32.
2. Click a category to expand to discover available templates, for example, expand the **Planners** category.
3. Now, select any available template to add a page in OneNote, for example, we have select **Simple To Do List** as shown in Figure 17.32.
4. To **Do List page** appears, you can rename the title as Grocery Items and add the list items in the list.

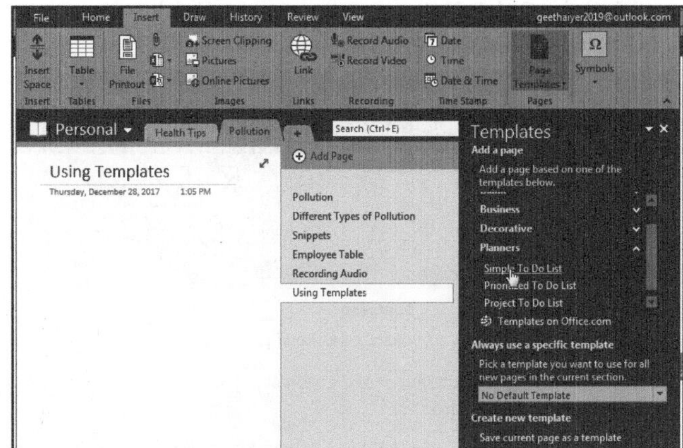

Figure 17.32 Templates pane

5. After adding the items, click the **X** button on the "Templates" pane to close the pane.

17.1.13 Quick Notes

Great ideas come from articles you read, or videos you watch, and associations you make when you are doing other work. You can capture those ideas in OneNote by creating a quick note. When you create a new quick note, OneNote opens a small window where you can enter your note and format its text.

➡ **To create a quick notes:**

1. Press **Window key + N** keys together to open a quick note window as shown in Figure 17.33.
2. Type or write the note's text in the quick note window as shown in Figure 17.33.

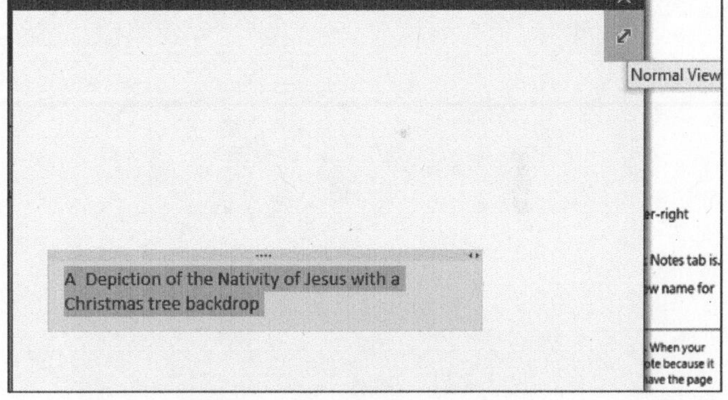

Figure 17.33 Quite note window

3. To format a quick note, click the Auto-hide ribbon button (the three dots) at the center of the quick note window's title bar to display the ribbon as shown in Figure 17.33.
4. Use the buttons on the Ribbon tabs to format your quick note's contents. For example, we have select the font size command as shown in Figure 17.34.

➡ **To open a quick note in its OneNote page:**

1. Click the **Normal View** button (the two-headed arrow) in the upper-right corner of the quick note.
2. Launch OneNote, then click the down-arrow beside your notebook name to see the notebook list menu.

3. Select the **Quick Notes** item to see your Quick Note save in OneNote as shown in Figure 17.35.

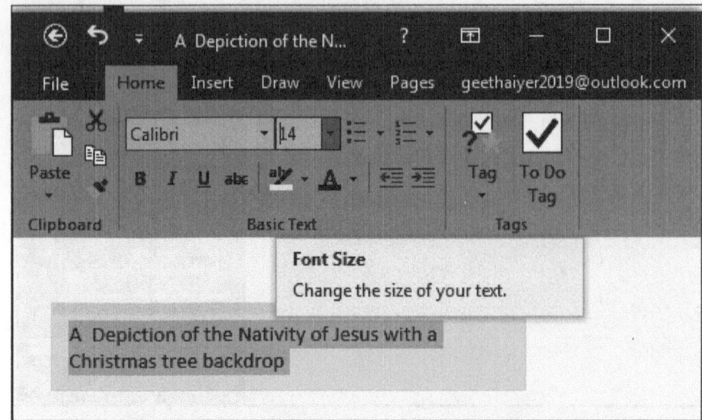

Figure 17.34 Select font size to format the contents

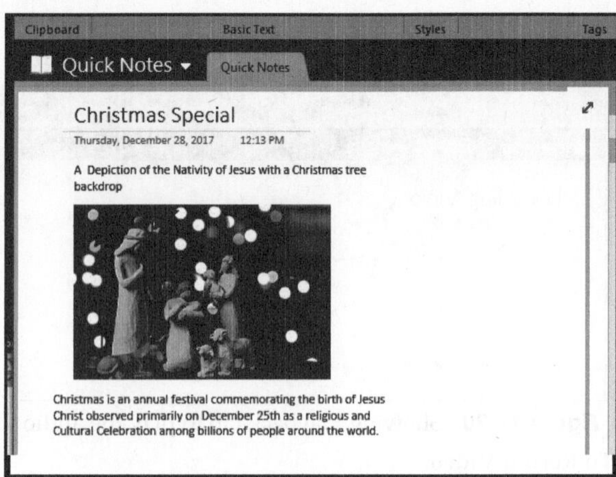

Figure 17.35 Selecting Quick Notes in the OneNote

CHAPTER 18

Internet

18.1 INTRODUCTION TO INTERNET

The Internet has been in a state of continuous evolution since the late 1960s. Some simplified descriptions of the Internet, are "a large computer network" or "network of networks", "an instantaneous and global messaging system". The Internet is making it easier for people to communicate with one another using computers. The most popular way of communication on the Internet is the electronic mail (e-mail).

Internet is an immensely complex combination of thousands of technologies and dozens of services used by tens of millions of people around the world each day. Internet is thus, a network of networks. Figure 18.1 shows a Web of computers which is laid around the globe. The Internet is a network of thousands of computer networks. Every network and every computer in these networks exchange information according to certain rules called *protocols*. These different computers and different networks are united with the common thread of two protocols, i.e., Internet Protocol (IP), and Transmission Control Protocol (TCP).

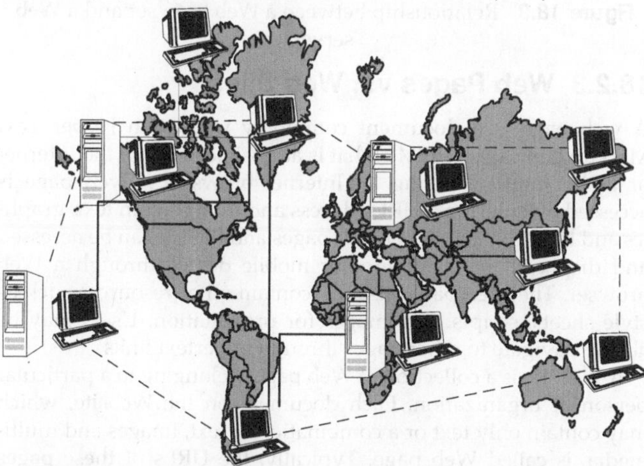

Figure 18.1 Internet as the network of computers connected with one another all over the world

18.1.1 Applications of Internet

With the help of Internet you can:

- Exchange messages using e-mail (Electronic mail).
- Transfer files as well as software.
- Browse through information on any topic on web.
- Communicate in real time (chat) with others connected to the Internet.
- Search databases of government, individuals and organizations.
- Read news available from leading news groups.
- Send or receive animation and picture files from distant places.
- Set up a site with information about your company's products and services.

18.1.2 Advantages/ Disadvantage of Internet

Advantages of Internet

1. We can send and receive information through email service. Your messages are delivered instantly to people anywhere in the world.
2. We can gather information for new job openings. We can also apply online for jobs.
3. Any kind of information on any topic under the sun is available on the Internet. The 'search engine' on the Internet can help you to find data on any subject that you need.
4. You can also shop online. There are many online stores and sites that can be used to look for products as well as buy them using your credit card.
5. This is one of the most happening and fun things to do via the Internet. You can download innumerable, games, music, videos, movies and a host of other entertainment software from the Internet.

Disadvantages of Internet

1. There are hundred of vendors selling products of various brands. We get confused with too many choices.
2. We feel helpless when the internet connection is down.
3. We always remain engaged with many online activities such as checking emails, socializing, chatting, online shopping, business-deals, etc.
4. If you use the Internet, you may be facing grave danger as your personal information, such as name, address, credit and card number, etc. can be accessed by other culprits to make your problem worse.
5. Virus is nothing but a program which disrupts the normal functioning of your computer systems. Computer attached to the Internet are more prone to virus attacks and they can end up into crashing your whole hard disk.

18.2 INTERNET SERVICES

18.2.1 World Wide Web

The World Wide Web, or simply "the Web" is a global information system that is the fastest-growing area of the Internet. In other words World Wide Web is a series of servers that are interconnected through hypertext. *Hypertext* is a method of presenting information in which certain text are highlighted, that, when selected, displays more information on that particular topic (See Figure 18.2).

The Web, like all Internet services, is based on the interaction and transfer of data between special server computers (Web servers) and your PC (using Web browser software such as Internet Explorer from Microsoft).

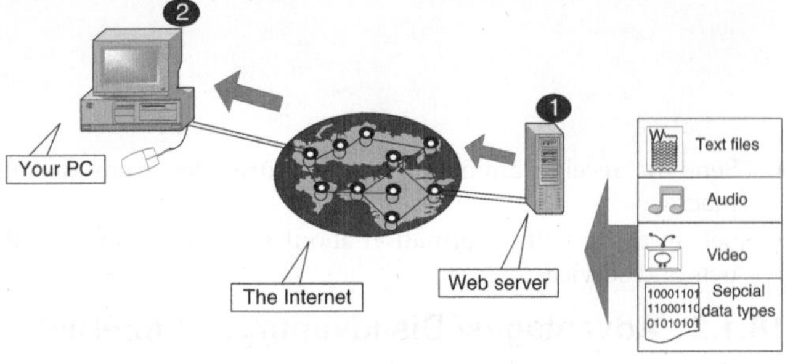

Figure 18.2 Some data types available on the Web

How it Works?

1. The World Wide Web is the fastest growing and most innovative part of the Internet. When you browse the Web, you view multimedia pages composed of text, graphics, sound and video. The Web used hypertext links that allow you to jump from one place to another on the Web. The language that allows you to use hypertext links and to view Web pages is called Hypertext Markup Language, more commonly knows as HTML.
2. The Web works on client/server model in which client software–known as Web browser–runs on a local computer. The server software runs on a Web host. To use the Web, you first make an Internet connection, and then launch your Web browser.
3. In a Web browser, you type the Uniform Resource Locator (URL) for a location you want to visit or click on a link that will send you to the desired location. The names for Web locations are URLs. Your Web browser sends the URL request using HTTP (Hypertext Transfer Protocol), which defines the way the Web browser and the Web server communicate with one another.
4. URLs contain several parts. The first part–the http://–details which Internet protocol to use. The second part– the part that usually has a www in it–Sometimes tells what kind of Internet resource is being contacted. The third part –such as satishibm.com, can vary in length and identifies the Web server to be contacted. The final part identifies a specific directory on the server and a home page, document or other Internet object.
5. The request is sent to the Internet. Internet routers examine the request to determine which server to send the request to. The information just to the right of the http://in the URL tells the Internet on which Web server the requested information can be found. Routers send the request to that Web server.
6. The Web server receives the request using the HTTP protocol. It is told which specific document is being requested.
7. When the server find the requested home page, document, or object, it sends that home page, document, or object back to the Web browser client. The information is then displayed on the computer screen in the Web browser.

18.2.2 Web Browser

A Web browser is a software application program that resides on your PC and can display text, images, and multimedia data found on different Web pages. It allows you to specify a Web page, navigate using links, and "bookmark" your favorite Web pages. The commonly used web browsers are Internet Explorer and Netscape Navigator and Mozilla Firefox. The relationship between Web server and Web browser is shown in Figure 18.3.

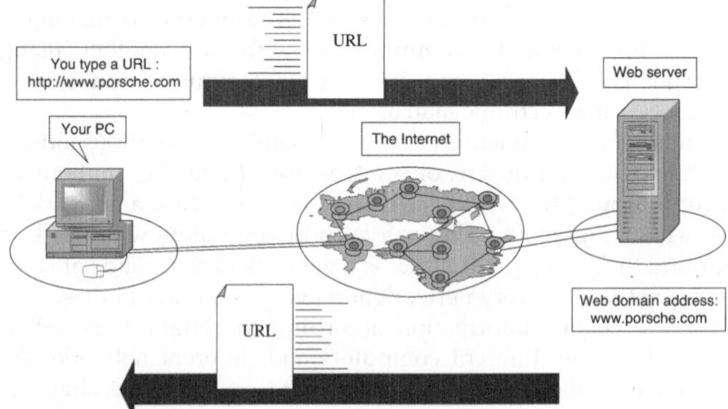

Figure 18.3 Relationship between a Web browser and a Web server

18.2.3 Web Pages vs. Web Sites

A web page is a document commonly written in Hyper Text Markup Language (HTML) that is accessible through the Internet or aother network using an Internet browser. A web page is accessed by entering a URL address and may contain text, graphics and hyperlinks to other web pages and files. It can be accessed and displayed on a monitor or mobile device through a Web browser. The Web pages usually contain other resources such as style sheets, scripts and images for presentation. Users may be able to navigate to other pages through hypertext links.

A Website is a collection of Web pages belonging to a particular person or organization. Each document on the Website, which may contain only text or a combination of text, images and multimedia, is called Web page. Typically, the URLs of these pages share a common prefix, which is the address of the home page of the site. The home page is the "front door" of the site. The URL of the home page also server as the URL of the Website. For example,
http://www.microsoft.com/ms.htm is a Website.

18.2.4 Uniform Resource Locator (URL)

URL stands for Uniform Resource Locater, which means it is a uniform (same throughout the world) way to locate a resource (file or document) on the Internet. The URL specifies the address of a file and every file on the Internet has a unique address. Web software, such as your browser, use the URL to retrieve a file from the computer on which it resides.

The actual URL is a set of four numbers separated by periods. An example of this would be 202.147.23.8 but as these are difficult for humans to use, addresses are represented in alphanumeric form that is more descriptive and easy to remember. Thus, the URL of my site which is URL 209.164.80.192 can also be written as www.simplygraphix.com. The Internet Domain Name System translates the alphanumerical address to numeric.

For example, the URL of my company site is:

`http://www.simplygraphix.com/`

and a typical page on this site would be:

`http://www.simplygraphix.com/portfolio/4.html`

The above URL consist of:

- Protocol: http
- Host computer name: www
- Domain name: simply graphic
- Domain type: com
- Path: /portfolio
- File name 4.html

Protocols

In addition to the http protocol (mentioned above), there are a few other protocols on the Internet.

- **File:** Enables a hyperlink to access a file on a local system.
- **FTP:** Used to download files from remote machines.
- **Gopher:** Helps in accessing a gopher server.
- **mailto:** Calls SMTP (the Simple Mail Transport Protocol) and enables a hyperlink to send an addressed e-mail message.
- **telnet:** Provides the means for a hyperlink to open a telnet session on a remote computer.

18.2.5 Benefits of Search Engines

Search engine provide ways of finding information on the Internet. There is a wide variety of search engines and features.

Variety–An Internet search can generate a variety of sources of information. The variety allows anyone searching for information to choose the types of sources they would like to use, or to use a variety of sources to gain a greater understanding of a subject.

Precision–The ability to provide refined or more precision results. Putting quotations marks around a set of words will bring up results with the exact same words, excluding others. Some search engine, such as Google or Yahoo, enable you to specify the type of web sources to be searched.

Organization–Internet search engines help to organize the Internet and individual websites. Search engines aid in organizing the vast amount of information that can be scattered in various places on the same web page into an organized list that can be used more easily.

18.2.6 Commerce on the Internet

The term covering all commercial activity on the Internet, including auctioning, placing orders, making payments, transferring funds and collaborating with trading partners, Internet commerce is not a synonym for electronic commerce (e-commerce) but one of its subsets.

Internet Commerce is the use of the Internet for creating and completing business transactions. It also includes:

- **The sales and marketing cycle**–For example, by analysing online feedback to ascertain customer's needs.
- **Identifying new markets**–Through exposure to a global audience through the World Wide Web.
- **Developing Customer Relationships**–Achieving loyalty through ongoing email interaction.
- **Assisting potential customers with their purchasing decision**–For example, by guiding them through product choices in an intelligent way.
- **Providing round-the-clock points of sale**–Making it easy for buyers to order online, irrespective of location.
- **Supply chain management**–Supporting those in the supply chain, such as dealers and distributors, through online interaction.

Internet Commerce also provides business a growing, dynamic channel for efficient delivery of goods and services to consumers: business-to-consumer. In business-to-consumer, goods to consumers online in a more personalized, dynamic environment. Businesses-to-consumer will increasingly include the delivery of digital goods–software, electronic media, and information. Consumers will also look more frequently to the Internet for the delivery of services, including ticketing, reservations, and financial services. In short, Internet commerce–business-to-business and business-to-consumer-will dramatically impact the way goods and services are managed, bought and sold form manufacturer to consumer.

18.2.7 Impact of the Internet on Society

The Internet has caused a great revolution in the society, allowing people from all over the world to communicate their ideas and feelings. The Internet has also changed the way society treats people. It has allowed minor groups much more power than they had in real life. There are many changes to society because of the Internet; whether such changes enhance or ruin our life is up to us.

Now a days, Internet availability is not limited to computers and laptops. Even mobile phonew with internet facility at affordable process helping indirectly the Internet to reach maximum number of users.

Some of the changes on the society are given in the following sections:

Unlimited Knowledge–We increasingly use the World Wide Web as a universal reference library. Type any keyword into a search engine you will find a host of sites with information on that topic.

Virtual relationships–One major impact that the Internet has had on society is in transforming the field of personal relationships. The new breed of online dating sites allow people to meet at a distance, chat in real time or by e-mail, exchange photographs, even talk to each other with voicemails.

Chat rooms are another popular way for meeting people from all round the world online.

Remote Intervention–The Internet and multimedia have the potential to transform healthcare by removing the need for doctor and patient to be in the same room.

E-mail–The impact on e-mail is the most important method for communicating and developing relationships.

18.2.8 Use of Search Engines

Search engines are programs that search documents for specified keywords and returns a list of the documents where the keywords were found. A search engine is really a general class of programs, however, the term is often used to specifically describe systems like Google, Bing and Yahoo! Search that enable users to search for documents on the World Wide Web.

There are some uses of search engines. These are:

- **Full Text Search Engine:** Full Text Search Engine retrieves information from internet, establish database and retrieve the records according to user's query. It can be divided into two parts: first one has its own crawler. Another one is to hire other search engine's database.
- **Directory Search Engine:** We cannot call it a true search engine. It retrieves all the entries of directory listing.
- **META Search Engine:** It provides search results from multiple search engines simultaneously according to user's query.
- **Vertical Search Engine:** Vertical Search Engine focuses on specific search field.

18.3 METHODS OF CONNECTING TO THE INTERNET

18.3.1 Broadband Connections

A high speed Internet connection with at least 256 Kbps speed is termed as a Broadband connection. A channel may be broadband if it sends a signal without modulation on a carrier. The signal covers the whole range of frequency that medium can carry. The broadband term is now hijacked by the Internet Service Provider. Hence the term broadband is used for high speed Internet access. It services at a high-speed internet access of minimum 512 Kbps and upto a maximum of 100 Mbps.

A customer's basically used land line phone for providing this service. He can use his telephone for a normal telephone call even while he is browsing Internet. There is no separate telephone charges for the connection to the Internet. The access to the Internet will be around 8 times faster than a normal dial up access. The advantage are:

(i) Cost (ii) Speed (iii) No setup time (iv) Always On

18.3.2 Wi-Fi Connections

Wireless Internet access, sometimes referred to as a "hot spot," is a local area network run by radio waves rather than wires. Wireless Internet access is broadcast from a central hub, which is a hard-wired device that actually brings in the Internet connection. The hub, located at the main computer system or server, broadcasts Internet connectivity to clients, which is basically anyone within receiving range who is equipped with a wireless LAN card.

Wireless Internet access is very convenient in the home, it can be even more so in the workplace. A wired network cannot only be very time consuming to install throughout a building, it is also very expensive. Ethernet cables used to connect client machines might need to be routed through walls, ceilings, and floors. In the past, this disadvantage was sometimes overlooked due to the advantages of greater security and faster data transfer speeds through Ethernet cables.

These advantages of Wireless LANs can be installed in virtually minutes by nearly anyone. They are extremely inexpensive, and can have data transfer rates that rival hard-wired Ethernet LANs. Furthermore, Wi-Fi Protected Access II (WPA2) encrypts all traffic on the LAN, addressing the problem of eavesdropping.

One of the most popular applications for wireless Internet access is the public hot spot. Internet cafes are one example of places where one can sit with a laptop and sip coffee while cruising the Internet, checking e-mail, or doing research. Cell phones and Personal Digital Assistants (PDAs) equipped with Web browsers can also utilize wireless Internet access points through public hot spots.

Some localities provide free wireless Internet access for residents and visitors. Since wireless LANs use radio waves that distort over long distances, the radius of the signal is limited. The further from the hub, the weaker the signal. Therefore cities that provide access will cover a specific area within the city where people can park to gain access.

Technology for wireless LANs is improving constantly. When designing a new wireless network, the person setting up the network should be sure to get network cards, a hub, and a wireless modem that support the latest protocols and security measures. Instructions should be followed carefully when configuring wireless Internet access.

18.3.3 Satellite Broadband

Satellite is the ultimate option for people living in remote areas and who cannot receive any other form of broadband internet. It requires the installation of a special satellite dish. There are mainly two types of connections: one-way connections and two-way connections. In the one-way connection, you will be able to receive data, but for sending data, you will need a dial-up modem through a telephone line or IDSN line. In the two-way connection, data is both sent and received through the satellite dish, though it is more expensive. Satellite transmission may be affected by weather conditions. The cost of installing and running satellite broadband can be quite expensive as compared with other types of broadband.

18.3.4 Cellular

Cellular technology provides wireless Internet access through cell phones or mobile telephone. It is a type of short-wave analog or digital telecommunication in which a subscriber has a wireless connection from a mobile phone to a relatively nearby transmitter. The speeds vary depending on the provider, but the most common are 3G and 4G speeds. A 3G is a term that describes a 3rd generation cellular network obtaining mobile download speeds of around 100 Mbps. 4G is the fourth generation of cellular wireless standards. The download speeds of 4G up to 1Gbps.

18.4 INTERNET PROTOCOLS

The internet Protocol (IP) is the primary network protocol used on the Internet, developed in the 1970s. On the Internet and many other networks, IP is often used together with the Transport Control Protocol (TCP) and referred to interchangeably as TCP/IP. IP supports unique addressing for computers on a network. Most networks use the Internet Protocol version 4 (IPv4) standard that features IP addresses four bytes (32 bits) in length. The newer Internet Protocol version 6 (IPv6) standard features addresses 16 bytes (128 bits) in length.

The Internet Protocol (IP) is a network-layer (Layer 3) protocol that contains addressing information and some control information that enables packets to be routed. IP is documented in RFC 791 and is the primary network-layer protocol in the Internet protocol suite. Along with the Transmission Control Protocol (TCP), IP represents the heart of the Internet protocols.

18.4.1 TCP/ IP

TCP is a set of rules (protocol) used along with the Internet Protocol (IP) to send data in the form of message units between computers over the Internet. While IP takes care of handling the actual delivery of the data, TCP takes care of keeping track of the individual units of data (called packets) that a message is divided into packets for efficient routing through the Internet.

For example, when an HTML file is sent to you from a Web server, the Transmission Control Protocol (TCP) program layer in that server divides the file into one or more packets, numbers the packets, and then forwards them individually to the IP program layer. Although each packet has the same destination IP address, it may get routed differently through the network.

TCP is a connection-oriented protocol, which means that a connection is established and maintain until the message or messages to be exchanged by the application program at each end have been exchanged. TCP is responsible for ensuring that a message is divided into the packets that IP manages and for reassembling the packets back into the complete message at the other end. In the Open Systems Inter-connection (OSI) communication model, TCP is present in layer 4, the Transport layer.

18.4.2 FTP

The File Transfer Protocol (FTP) service allows an Internet user to move a file from one computer to another on the Internet. A file may contain any type of digital information such as text document, image, artwork, movie, sound, software, etc. Hence, anything that can be stored on a computer can be moved with FTP service. Moving a file from a remote computer to individual (ones own) computer is known as *downloading* the file and moving a file from one's own computer to a remote computer is known as uploading the file.

☞ *FTP is an* ***interactive*** *system. The FTP client that comes with Windows NT or 2000 is a character-based client.*

Numerous FTP servers present all over the world allow users anywhere on the Internet to log in and download the files which are placed on them. The main competitor for FTP is HTTP (Hyper Text Transfer Protocol) and the day is not very far when sites would run HTTP servers instead of the FTP servers. It is so because HTTP servers can do whatever FTP server can do and do it more efficiently.

One problem with downloading files over the Internet is that some files are so large that it can take a tremendous amount of time to download them. As a way to speed up file transfers and save space on the FTP server, files are commonly *compressed.* Many different methods are used to compress files. After the files have been downloaded, you will need to run the decompression software such as PKUNZIP to decompress the files to use them.

18.4.3 HTTP

The *Hypertext Transfer Protocol* (HTTP) is a set of rules for exchanging files (text, graphics, images, sound, video and other multimedia files) on the WWW. It is an access method to access web pages used on the Internet. The HTTP generally works in combination with WWW.

☞ *The http is responsible for accessing hypertext documents on WWW.*

Your web browser is an HTTP client, sending requests to server machines. When the user enters a file request in the browser program by either opening a web file (typing in a URL) or clicking on a hypertext link, the browser builds an HTTP request and sends it to an HTTP program in the destination server machine, which receives the request and after any necessary processing returns the requested file.

18.5 E-MAIL

E-mail is a method of sending messages, voice, video and graphics over digital communication link, such as the Internet any where in the world at very cost-effective rate. Technically, e-mail is a type of client/server application that provides a routed, stored message service between any two e-mail accounts. Because all modern computers can be connected to the Internet, users can send e-mail over the Internet to any location that has telephone or wireless digital service.

18.5.1 Starting Outlook

The Microsoft Outlook program provides the email and time management functions in Office 2016. To start the application:

1. Click **Start** menu, choose **All programs** and then select **Outlook 2016**.
2. The first time you start Outlook, it helps you to define the email accounts you want to manage using this application as shown in Figure 18.4.

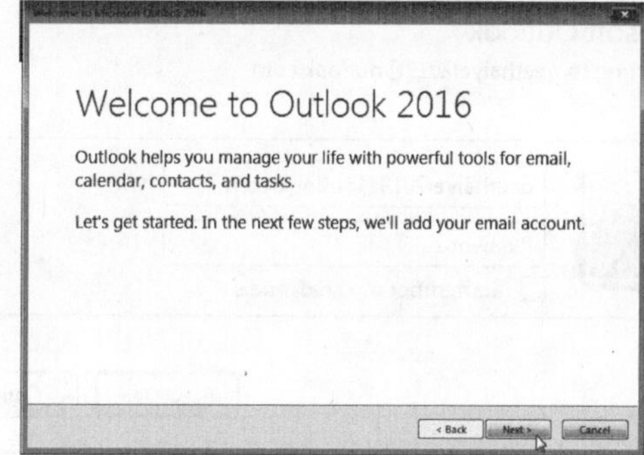

Figure 18.4 Welcome screen

3. Click **Next** to get started, select **Yes** to set up Outlook to **Add an email account**, then click **Next** again as shown in Figure 18.5.
4. In this dialog box, type the name in the **Your Name:** text box and type e-mail address in the **E-mail Address:** text box. After that Type password in the **Password:** text box and in the **Re-type Password:** text box confirm the password. Then click **Next >** button as shown in Figure 18.6.

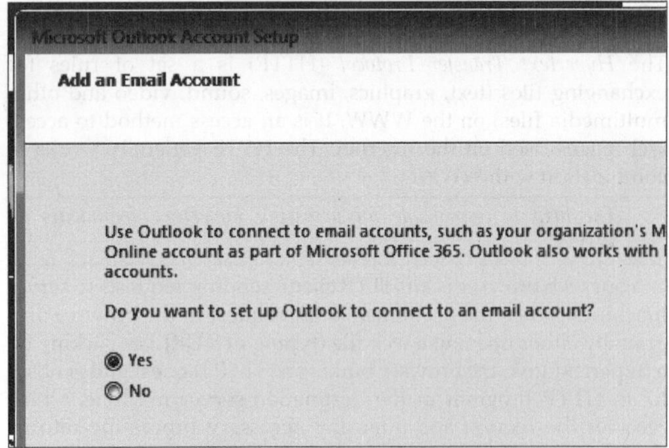

Figure 18.5 Add an email account

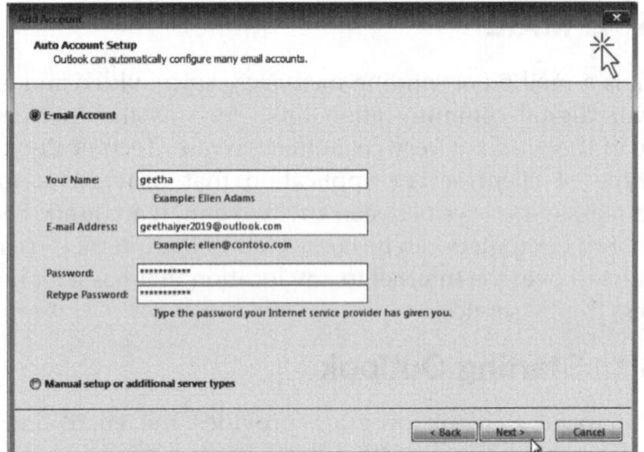

Figure 18.6 Add Account Settings

5. The wizard establishes the network connection, and searches for the server settings that support your email account.

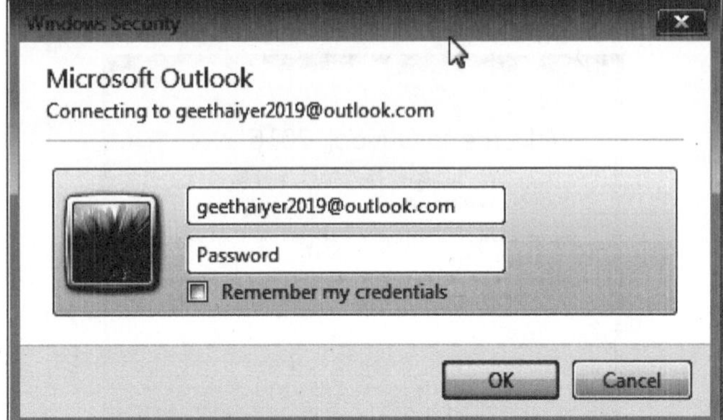

Figure 18.7 Enter the password for email

6. When you account has been located, the wizard then asks you to enter your password for that account as shown in Figure 18.7, and then click **Next >** button.
7. Finally, the wizard logs on to your account on the server and you can click **Finish** to see your email account is ready for use as shown in Figure 18.8.

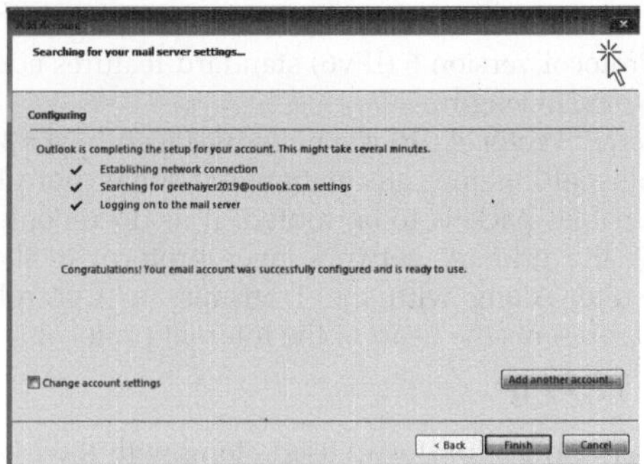

Figure 18.8 Finish an email account

18.5.2 Your First Messages

Outlook opens with the Inbox, showing your first email messages, e.g. a welcome message from the Outlook team as shown in Figure 18.9.

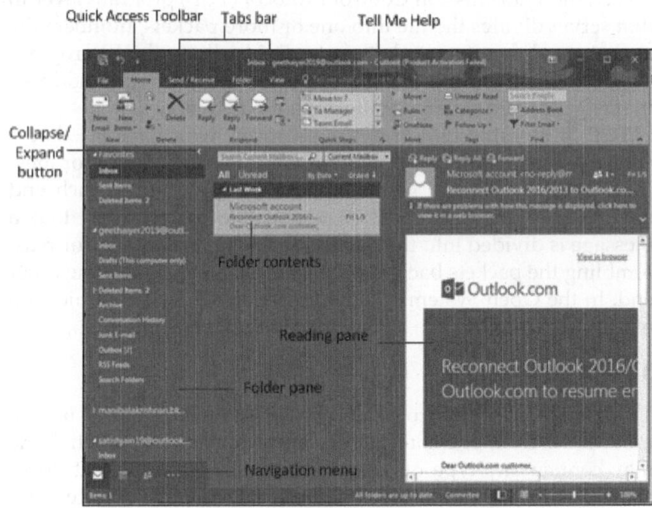

Figure 18.9 First messages of email

You can click the button at the top right of the Folder pane to collapse (or expand) that pane, to provide more space to display message content.

18.5.3 Turn Off Reading Pane

1. Select the **View** menu in the **Layout** group choose **Reading Pane** drop-down arrow and select **Off** option as shown in Figure 18.10.
2. Messages will be left unread until opened and displayed in a list grouped list.

☞ *Unread message appear in bold, coloured font. Messages that have been opened in a regular font.*

3. Double-click on any message to open the message and display its contents.
4. Select **File** and then **Close** from the list in the backstage view to close the message window, or just click the window's **X** close button.

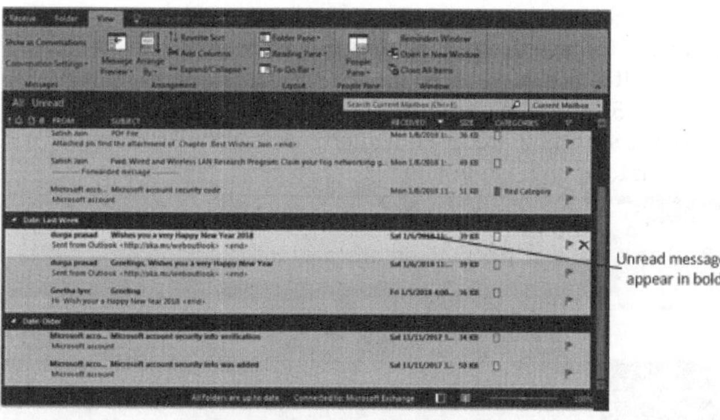

Figure 18.10 Reading pane

18.5.4 Create a Message

One of the most common task for Outlook users is sending and receiving e-mail. The mail message window, like other item windows in Outlook 2016, features the new Ribbon in place of menus and toolbars.

➡ **To create a new e-mail message and type the e-mail address:**

1. In the **Home** Tab, under the **New** group, click **New E-mail** as shown in Figure 18.11.

☞ *Shortcut key to open New mail message is* Ctrl + N *or* Ctrl + Shift + M *keys pressed together.*

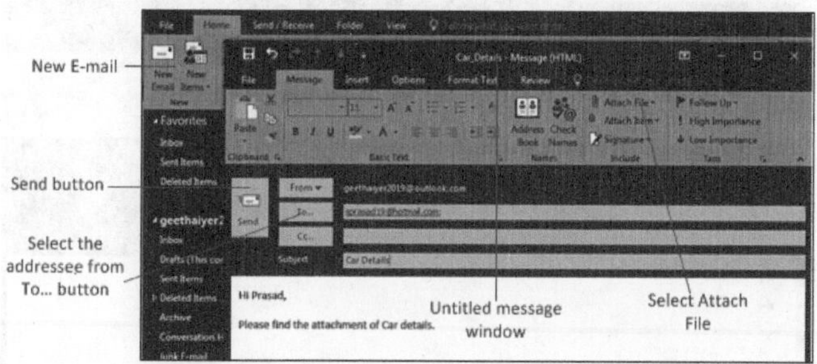

Figure 18.11 Creating new e-mail message

2. Outlook 2016 opens an Untitled Message window.
3. In this window, enter the recipient addresses in the **To...** text box (See Figure 18.11). If you want to enter multiple recipient addresses, you can separate it by a semicolon and one space.
4. If you want to send a copy of the message to someone besides the recipient, enter the address in the **Cc...** text box.
5. The new message window's title bar appears. It displays Untitled - Message (Plain Text) until you enter text on the Subject line. The subject line then appears in the title bar of the message window.
6. Type the body of the message in the message window below the subject line.
7. If required, click **Attach File** and select any files to attach.
8. Then click **Send** icon to send the message.

18.5.5 Insert a Signature

You can create a signature to add to the emails you send.

1. Select the **Insert** or **Message** tab click **Signature** drop-down arrow to select **Signatures** command in the **Include** group as shown in Figure 18.12.

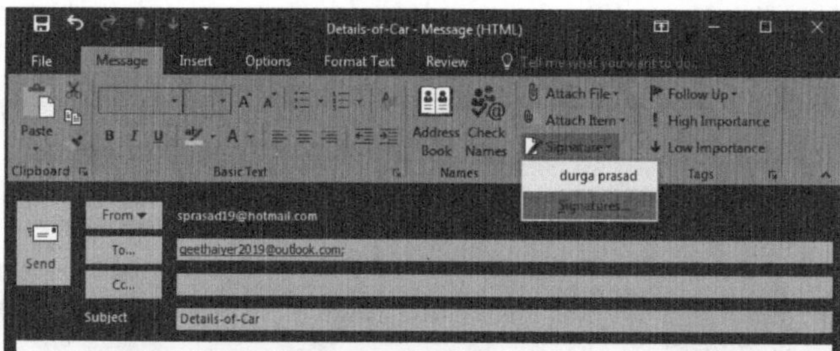

Figure 18.12 Insert a signature

2. The **Signatures and Stationery** dialog box appears 18.13, click the **New** button. The **New Signatures** dialog box appears as shown in Figure 18.13.

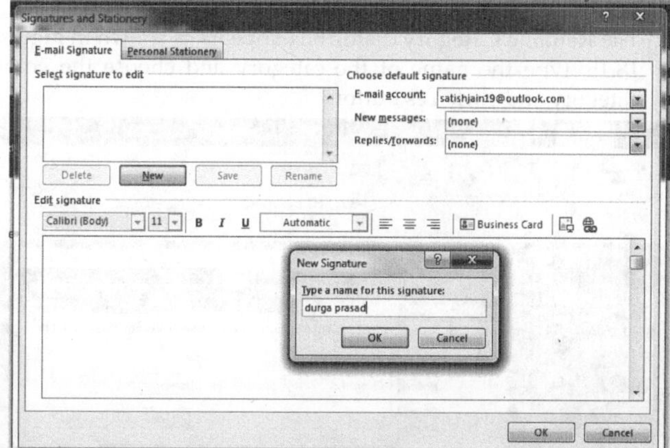

Figure 18.13 Signatures and Stationery showing New Signatures dialog box

3. **Type a name for the signature:** list box and click OK. The signature appears in the **Select signature to edit** list box.
4. Add the signature text and click OK to save it by name.
5. Position the cursor where you want to insert a signature, then click Signature again and select the name of the signature you want to insert as shown in Figure 18.14.

18.5.6 Message Tags

You can use tags to sort and organize messages.

1. Select a message, then select the **Home** tab.

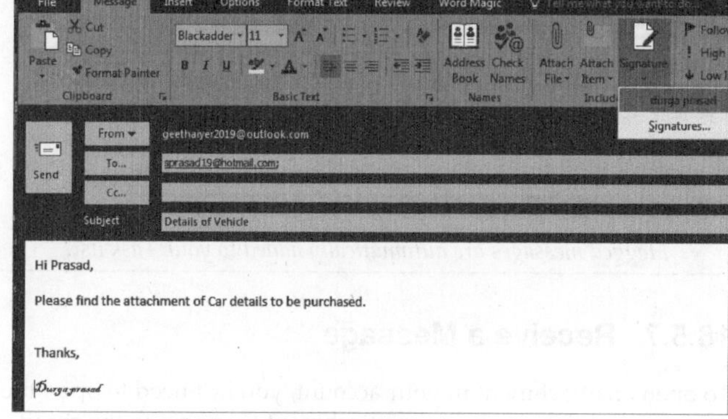

Figure 18.14 Inserting a signature

2. Click **Unread/Read** to toggle the read status of the selected message in the **Tags** group.

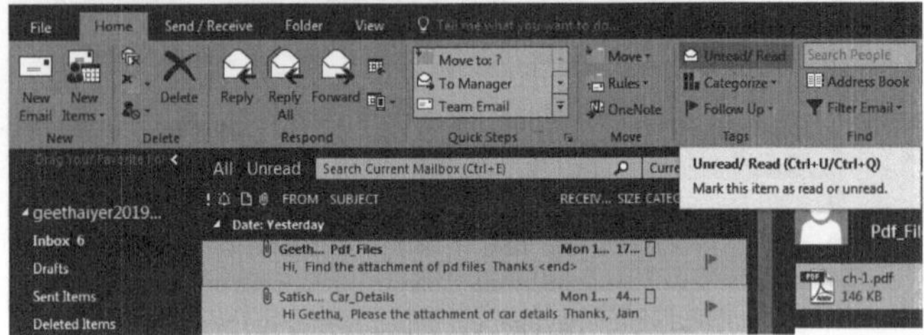

3. Click **Categorize** drop-down arrow to choose a color to associate with the selected message.

☞ *Email accounts that use an IMAP connection do not have the Categorize tag for their messages.*

4. The **Rename Category** dialog box appears as shown in Figure 18.15, type the name of the category and choose the color category and click **Yes** button.

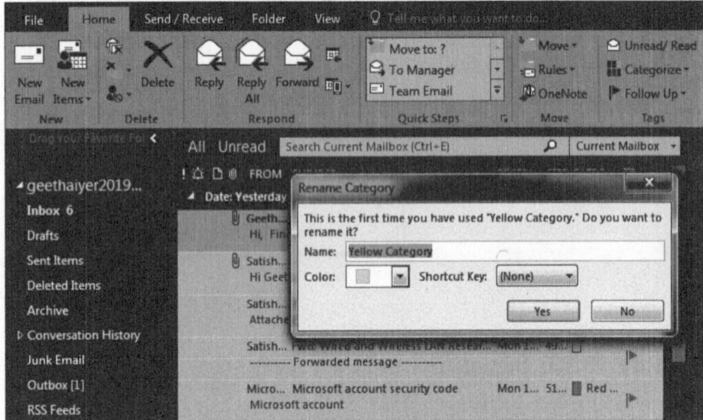

Figure 18.15 Rename category

5. The first time you select a specific color, you will be asked if you want to rename it, or assign, it a shortcut key.
6. Click the **Follow Up** button on the **Home** tab to assign a reminder flag to the selected message as shown below.

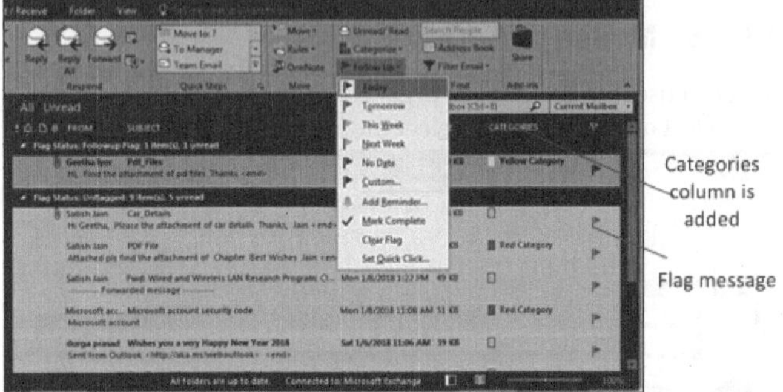

☞ *Flagged messages are automatically added to your Task list.*

18.5.7 Receive a Message

To open an attachment in your account, you just need to open the message and then click on the attachment icon next to the email's message. Some viruses can be sent via an attachment, so it is important to have up-to-date antivirus software if you are downloading attachments.

1. Click **Send/Receive** tab, and click **Send/Receive All Folders.**
2. Make sure you are in your inbox. Select the Mail which you want to open as shown in Figure 18.16.

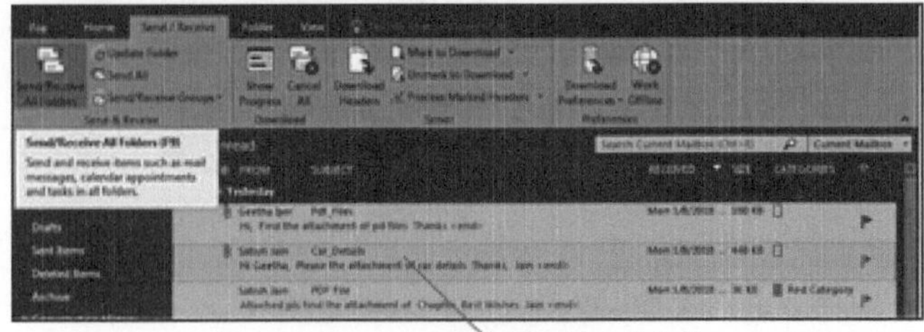

Figure 18.16 Selecting the Mail

3. The selected mail will be downloaded and displayed in the Inbox. Or Double-click the message title to display the contents as shown in Figure 18.18.
4. An email with an attachment will have a paperclip icon next to it to show that there is something attached to the email you have received.
5. Click the arrow button next to the icon to open a drop-down menu. Click **Preview** option to view the attachment file as shown in Figure 18.17.

Figure 18.17 Selecting the Preview option

6. The attachment file get opened, click the **Back to message** button to close the preview, then close the message window to return to Outlook as shown in Figure 18.18.

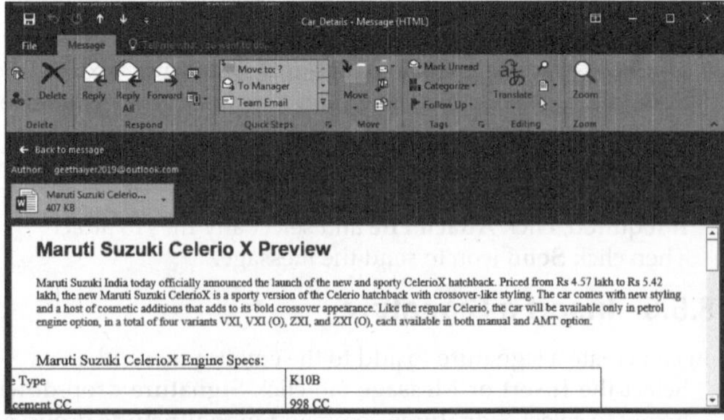

Figure 18.18 Back to message button to close the preview

☞ *You can choose the Open option to open the attachment with the program associated with the attachment's file type, such as the Word program for a doc file.*

18.5.8 Save All Attachments

To save all the attachments at once:

1. Open the message, right-click on any attachment icon in the Reading pane and select the **Save All Attachments...** option as shown in Figure 18.19.

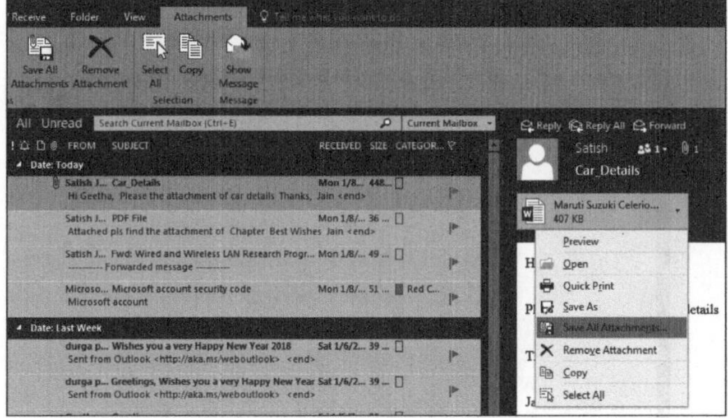

Figure 18.19 Selecting Save All Attachments

2. The following commands are listed in the context menu, which is displayed when you right click:
   - **Preview:** It enables a preview of the attached file in the reading pane.
   - **Open:** It opens the attached document.
   - **Quick Print:** It sends the currently selected attachment to the default printer for printing.
   - **Save As:** It Opens the Save Attachment dialog box, where you can specify the appropriate location and file name to save the attached item.
   - **Save All Attachments:** It saves all the attachments included with an e-mail message on your computer system.
   - **Remove Attachment:** It removes the currently selected attachment from an e-mail message.
   - **Copy:** It copies the currently selected attachment. You can place the copy of the attachment at a desired location on your system using the Paste command.
   - **Select All:** Selects all the attachments included in an e-mail message.
3. The list of attachments is displayed in the **Save All Attachments** dialog box as shown in Figure 18.20.
4. Click OK button. The **Save Attachment** dialog box appears, select the folder where you want to save the download file and then click **Save** button to save the file as shown in Figure 18.21.

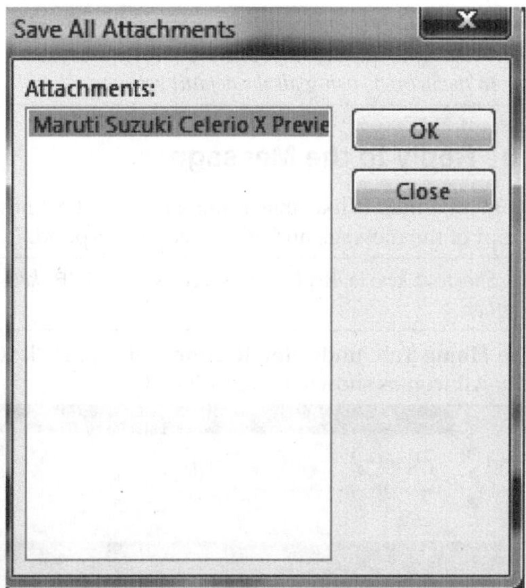

Figure 18.20 Save All Attachments dialog box

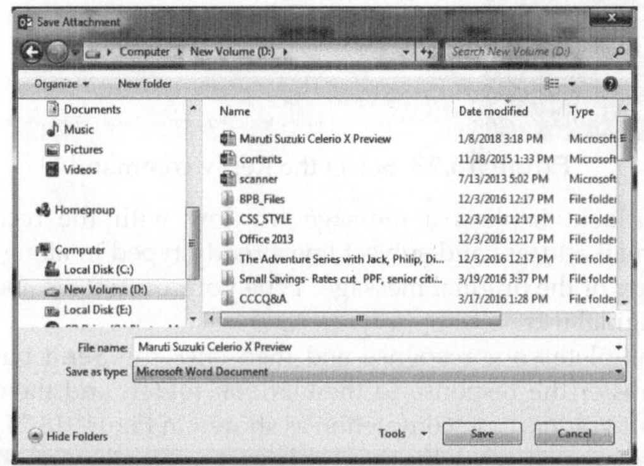

Figure 18.21 Save Attachments dialog box

18.5.9 Print the Message

1. From the message, select the **File** tab, click **Print** option.
2. Click the **Print Options** to change the printer or adjust the print settings, e.g. the number of copies you want.
3. The **Print** dialog box appears as shown in Figure 18.22.

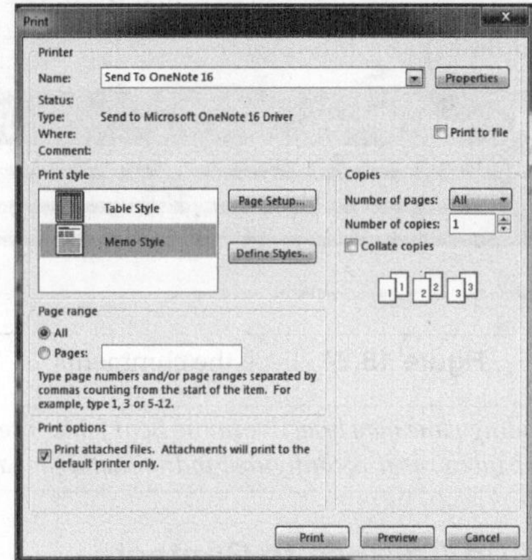

Figure 18.22 Print dialog box

4. Check the Print attached files box if you want to print any attachments in the **Print Options** section.
5. Click the **Print** button.

☞ *The print preview shows how the message will appear on the page. Right-click on a message and select Quick Print to send the message to the printer, using all the default settings.*

18.5.10 Reply to the Message

Replying to an e-mail is like answering a letter – it acknowledges your receipt of the message and allows you to respond.

☞ *The Shortcut key to Reply a message is* Ctrl + R *keys pressed together.*

1. In the **Home** Tab, under the **Respond** group, click **Reply** or **Reply All** icon as shown in Figure 18.23.

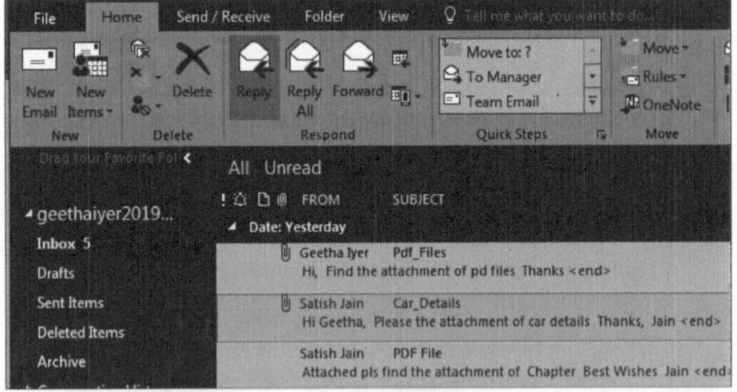

Figure 18.23 Select the Reply command

2. Outlook displays a message window with the recipient's e-mail address and subject line already typed in along with a copy of the original message. Type your comments above the original text.
3. Complete your response and then click the **Send** button to transfer the response to the Outlook folder, and then to the Sent Folder upon completion as shown in Figure 18.24.

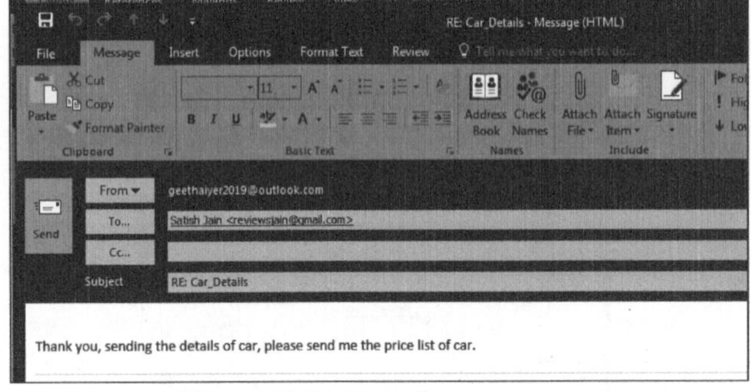

Figure 18.24 Type the comments

☞ *The Reading pane may be active in the Sent folder even if switched off in the inbox, as it is configured individually for each folder.*

18.5.11 Add Address to Contacts

Whenever you receive an email, you can add the email address of the sender to your Outlook Contacts list.

1. Right-click the email address and select **Add to Outlook Contacts** as shown in Figure 18.25.

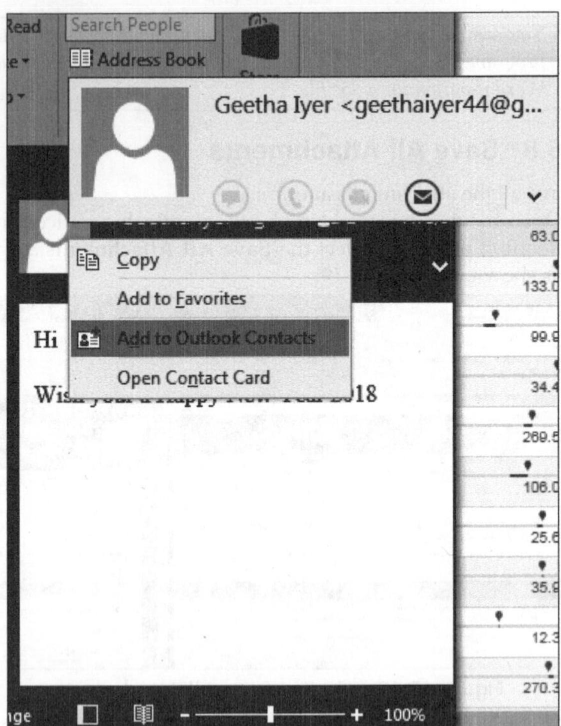

Figure 18.25 Selecting Add to Outlook contacts

2. The dialog box open to review the data that has pre-entered, and include any extra type of information you entered.
3. Click **Save** to record the details in the Contacts list as shown in Figure 18.26.

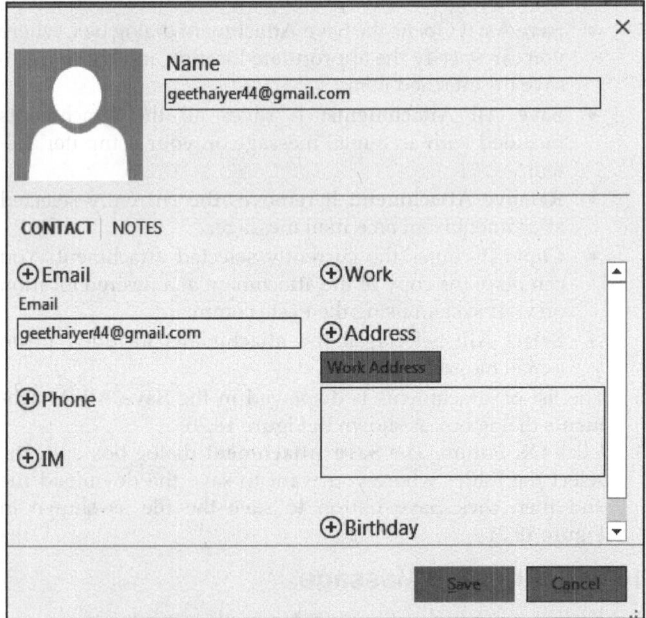

Figure 18.26 Save the record details in contacts list

4. To review the new additions in the Contacts list, click Edit button to add further details if required.

18.5.12 RSSFeeds

Subscribing a RSS Feed enables you to get all summaries of updated news of favourite web sites automatically. It stands for Short for Really Simple Syndication or Rich Site Summary, RSS revolutionized the way that users interact with content online.

Instead of checking back every day to any particular site to see if it is been updated, RSS feeds give users the ability to simply subscribe to the RSS feed, much like you would subscribe to a newspaper, and then read the updates from the site, delivered via RSS feeds.

1. When you find an RSS feed you would like to subscribe to on a website, you need to copy the URL address (See Figure 18.27).

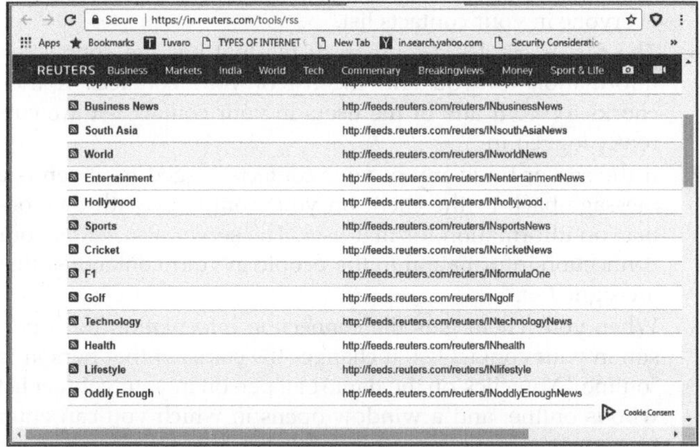

Figure 18.27 List of websites to subscribe RSS feed

2. Right-click on the **RSS Feeds** folder, to open its context menu, then choose to **Add a New RSS Feed...** as shown below.

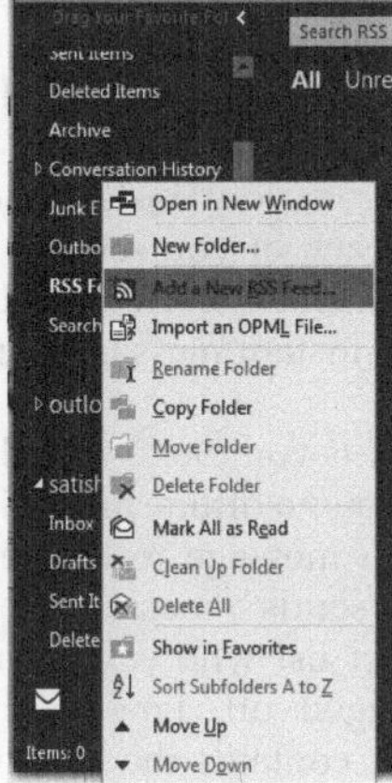

3. The **New RSS Feed** dialog box appears as shown in Figure 18.28, press **Ctrl+V** to paste in the copied URL, then click **Add** button.
4. A dialog box asks you confirm whether you want to add the feed – click the **Advanced** button as shown below.

Figure 18.28 New RSS Feed dialog box

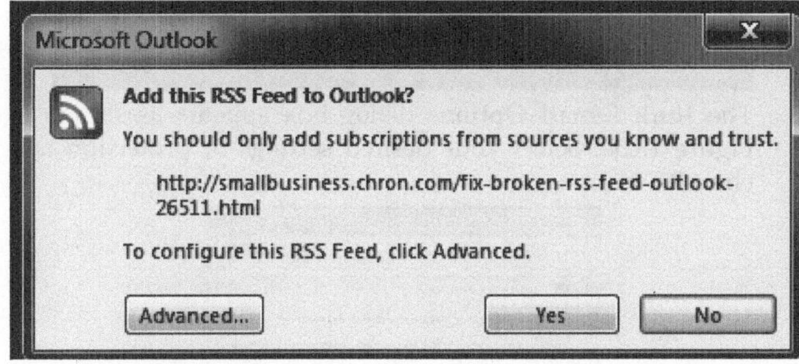

5. The **RSS Feed Options** dialog box appears as shown in Figure 18.29. Enter an **RSS Feed Name** and select any required configuration changes, then click **OK** to close the options.

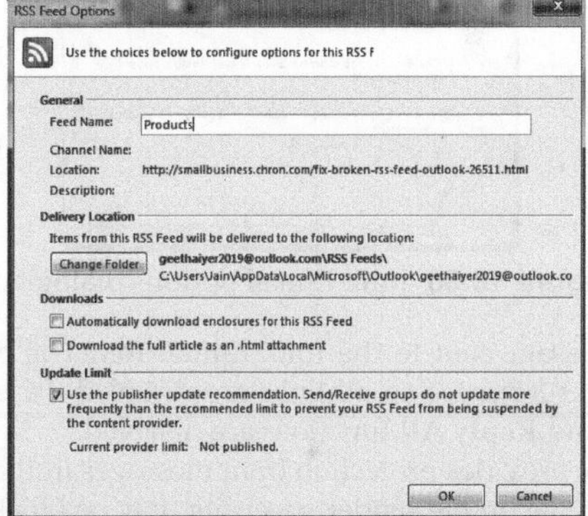

Figure 18.29 RSS Feed options dialog box

6. Now, click **Yes** to confirm you want to add the feed, and see the feed item appears in the Outlook.

18.5.13 Spam and Phishing

Use the Symantec Spam Quarantine service, to filter unwanted emails. The service scans all incoming email before delivering it, identifies potential spam using a series of tests, and filters them to the Spam Quarantine server.

The Outlook Junk Email filter identifies spam as messages are received, and moves to the Junk E-mail folder. To adjust the settings:

1. From the **Home** tab, select the **Junk** button in the **Delete** group, then click **Junk E-mail Options...**.

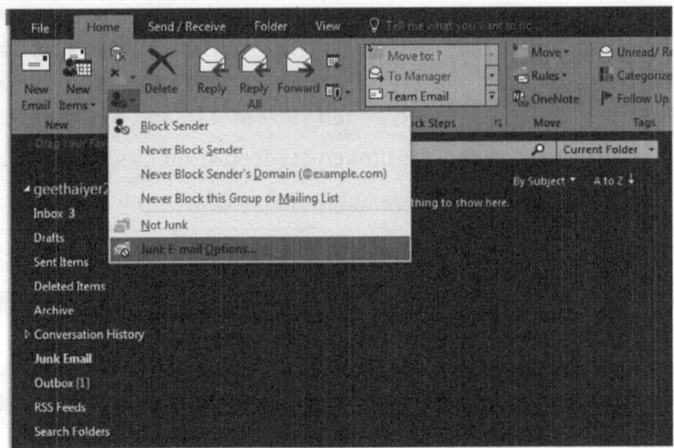

2. The **Junk E-mail Options** dialog box appears as shown in Figure 18.30. Select your desired settings of protection and click **OK** button.

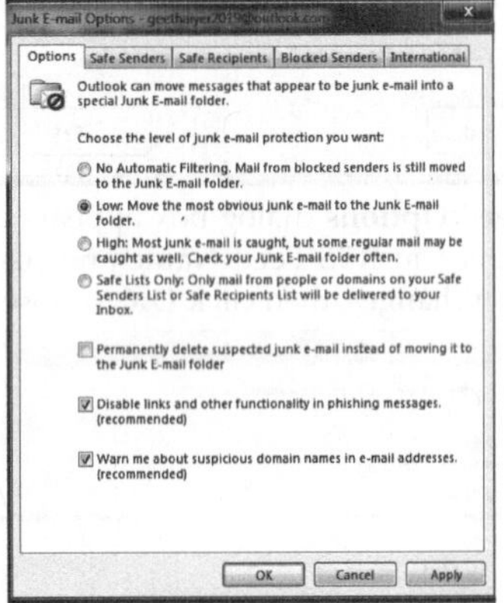

Figure 18.30 Junk E-mail options dialog box

Any message sent to the Junk E-mail folder is converted to plain-text format, and all links are disabled. In addition, the **Reply** and **Reply All** functions are disabled.

3. Outlook provides protection from messages in the Inbox.
4. Links to file on the sender's website may be blocked, links to websites may be disabled, and you may not be allowed to use the **Reply All** functions.
5. To explore how Outlook handles potentially damaging messages, visit the website **emailsecuritycheck.net** Submit an email address, and respond to the confirming email.

☞ *Do not respond in any way to messages that you think may be spam. Even clicking on an Unsubscribe link will confirm that your address is a genuine email account, and this may get it added to lists of validated account names.*

18.6 USING INSTANT MESSAGING

Instant Messaging (IM) is a form of electronic communication enabling ad hoc collaboration through sending and receiving messages across a network connection. Some of the popular and widely used instant messenger programs available today. Steps given below will make you to understand exactly what happens with an instant-messaging service:

1. You go to download page i.e. http://www.google.com/talk/ or http://www.skype.com and get a free software client for your computer.
2. You install the software and open the client.
3. The client tries to connect to the server. It uses a proprietary protocol for communication.
4. Once the client is connected to the server, you can enter your name and password to log in to the server. If this is your first time on, you can sign up for an account and immediately begin using it. When server verifies your name and password, you are logged in.
5. The client sends connection information (IP address and number of the port assigned to the client) to server of the computer you are using. It also provides user with names of everyone in your contacts list.
6. The server creates a temporary file that has the connection information for you and the list of your contacts. It then checks to see if any of the users in your contact list are currently logged in.
7. If the server finds any of your contacts logged in, it sends a message back to the client on your computer with the connection information for that user. The server also sends your connection information to the people in your contact list that are signed on.
8. When your client gets the connection information for a person in your contact list, it changes the status of that person to "online." You click on the name of a person in your contact list who is online, and a window opens in which you can enter text into. You enter a message and click "send" or hit return to communicate with that person.
9. Because your client has the IP address and port number for computer of the person that you sent the message to, your message is sent directly to the client on that person's computer. In other words, the server is not involved at this point. All communication is directly take place between the two clients.
10. The other person gets your instant message and responds. The window that each of you sees on your respective computers expands to include a scrolling dialog of the conversation. Each person's instant messages appears in this window on both computers.
11. When conversation is complete, you close the message window. Eventually, you go offline and exit. When this happens, your client sends a message to the server to terminate the session. The server sends a message to the client of each person on your contact list who is currently online to indicate that you have logged off. Finally, the server deletes the temporary file that contains the connection information for your client.

Some of the popular Instant Messenger are Yahoo Messenger, MSN Messenger, Rediff Bol, Google Talk and Skype.

18.7 MOBILE ADHOC NETWORKS

A MANET (Mobile Adhoc Network) is a self-configuring network of mobile devices connected by wireless links. Each device in a MANET is free to move independently in any direction, and will therefore change its links to other devices frequently. Each must forward traffic unrelated to its own use, and therefore be a router. The primary challenge in building a MANET is equipping each device to continuously maintain the information required to properly route traffic.

MANETs usually has a routable networking environment on top of a Link Layer ad hoc network.

The growth of laptops and 802.11/Wi-Fi wireless networking have made MANETs a popular research topic since the mid- to late 1990s. Many academic papers are evaluating protocols and abilities for mobile adhoc networks based on the packet drop rate, the overhead introduced by the routing protocol, and other measures.

18.7.1 Types of MANET

There are three types of MANETs. These are as follows:

(a) **Vehicular Ad Hoc Networks (VANETs):** VANETs are used for communication among vehicles and between vehicles and roadside equipment.
(b) **Intelligent Vehicular Ad Hoc Networks (InVANETs):** InVANETs have built-in artificial intelligence that helps vehicles to behave in intelligent manners during vehicle-to-vehicle collisions, accidents, drunken driving etc.
(c) **Internet Based Mobile Ad-hoc Networks (iMANET):** MANETs are ad-hoc networks that link mobile nodes and fixed Internet-gateway nodes. In such type of networks normal ad-hoc routing algorithms do not apply directly.

18.8 WHAT IS SECURITY?

Computer security is the process of preventing and detecting unauthorized use of your computer. Prevention measures help you stop unauthorized users (hackers) from accessing any part of your computer system. Detection helps you to determine whether or not someone attempted to break into your system, if they were successful, and what they may have done.

Our computers have become an extension of everything we do from banking and investing to shopping and communicating with others through email or chat. You may not consider your communications "top secret", most likely you do not want strangers reading your email, using your computer to attack other systems, sending forged email from your computer, or examining personal information stored on your computer.

18.8.1 Need of Computer Security

We need Computer security, because hackers have the ability to watch all your actions on the computer, or cause damage to your computer by reformatting your hard drive or changing your data. A hacked computer can be used to:

1. Record keystrokes and steal passwords.
2. Send spam and phishing emails.
3. Harvest and sell email address and passwords.
4. Infect other systems.
5. Hide programs that launch attacks on other computers.
6. Distribute child pornography.
7. Generate large volumes of traffic, slowing down the entire system.

Some key steps that everyone can take include:

1. Use good, cryptic passwords that cannot be easily guessed and keep your passwords secret.
2. Make sure your computer, devices and applications are current and up to date.
3. Make user your computer is protected with up-to-date anti-virus and anti-spyware software.
4. Do not click or unknown or unsolicited links or attachments, and do not download unknown files or programs onto your computer or other devices.

18.8.2 Inbuilt PC Security

Security in computer systems deals with protecting the various resources and information of a computer system against destruction and unauthorized access.

Tools

Before getting to the details of securing your PC, it will be very helpful to look at the inbuilt security and privacy tools available in Windows 7. These tools are as under:

(a) User Account Password
(b) User Account Control
(c) Parental Control
(d) Firewall
(e) Windows Defender programs
(f) Biometric Service
(g) Data encryption
(h) Internet Explorer's anti-phishing and anti-spam features

User Account Password In Windows 7, we have to assign a password to each user account on the computer. This prevents unauthorised users from accessing the system and it enables you to lock your computer.

User Account Control User Account Control is used to help you to stay in control of your PC. This tool asks you to confirm certain actions that could harm your system. If you have an administrator account, click **Yes** to continue; if you have a standard account, you must enter an administrator's user name and password to continue.

Parental Controls Windows 7's Parental Controls provides tools to protect children from inadvertently running certain programs, playing unsuitable games, and using the computer at inappropriate times.

Windows Firewall Windows 7 comes with the Windows Firewall feature turned on. This prevents intruders from accessing your computer while you are online.

Windows Defender Windows Defender is an antispyware program. It continuously monitors system settings to prevent the installation of known spyware and to alert you the presence of spyware-like activity.

Biometric Service Windows Biometric Service provides support for fingerprint biometric devices so that you can use a fingerprint reader to log on to your computer and to enter administrative credentials in response to UAC elevation prompts.

☞ *Spyware is a software program that installs on your computer without your knowledge or consent. This program surreptitiously gathers data from your computer, steals your passwords, displays advertisements, and hijacks your Web browser.*

Data encryption *BitLocker Drive Encryption* encrypts entire hard drives and makes the data completely inaccessible to a thief. In Windows 7, BitLocker To Go can also be used to protect removable storage drives, such as portable hard drives and USB flash drives.

Internet Explorer's anti-phishing and anti-spam Security improvements in Internet Explorer include restrictions on ActiveX controls, a SmartScreen phishing filter, and InPrivate Filtering and InPrivate Browsing to prevent information about your browsing habits from being tracked.

18.9 NETWORK SECURITY CONCEPTS

18.9.1 Virus

A computer virus is a kind of malware program which, when run, get replicated by inserting copies of itself into another computer programs, data files of the hard drive. When the replication process of virus get succeeds, the affected areas are called as "infected".

Computer viruses can be considered as small software programs which are designed to spread from one computer to another through an interface program.

Some type of harmful activity, performed by virus on infected hosts, are:

- stealing hard disk space
- stealing CPU time
- accessing information
- corrupt or delete data on your computer
- erase everything on your hard disk, etc.

So, one can say the viruses are self-replicating computer programs that install themselves without the user consent.

Computer virus can also execute instructions which cause harm, that is why computer viruses affect security (See Figure 18.31).

Common Types of Viruses are:

- **Resident Viruses:** This type of virus is a permanent virus that dwells in the RAM memory and then interrupt all of the operations which are executed by the system. Examples: CMJ, Meve, etc.
- **Multipartite Viruses:** It is distributed through infected media and usually get hide in the memory.
- **Direct Action Viruses:** In this virus replicate and when a specific condition is met, the virus comes into an action and infect files present in the directory or folder which are specified in the AUTOEXEC.BAT file PATH.
- **Overwrite Viruses:** In this, virus deletes the information contained in the files. Examples: Way, Trj.Reboot.
- **Boot Virus:** It affects the boot sector of a floppy or hard disk.
- **Macro Virus:** It infect files which are created by using certain applications or programs which contain macros.
- **Directory Virus:** It change the paths which indicate the location of a file. So, when you are executing a program infected by a virus, you are actually running a virus program, as the original file and program have been previously moved by the virus.
- **Polymorphic Virus:** These kinds of virus encrypt itself by using different algorithms and encryption keys every time they infect a system.
- **File Infectors:** In this virus infects the program or executable files and when the programs are run, the virus gets activated, thus produces the damaging effects.
- **Network Virus:** It spread through a Local Network Area (LAN), and sometimes throughout the internet.
- **E-mail viruses:** It travels as an attachment to e-mail messages, and replicates by mailing to dozens of people in the victim's e-mail address book.

Figure 18.31 Computer virus

There are three types of viruses

- **Boot Sector Virus:** It install itself on the beginning track of a hard drive.
- **File infector:** It attach themselves to a program file.
- **Macro Virus:** Infect data file.

Characteristics of Computer Virus

- It requires a host program as a carrier.
- It gets activated by an external action.
- It is able to replicate.

Computer viruses can spread through many ways, which are:

- Email
- Removable hardware
- Downloading
- By attaching itself to file or boot records, etc.

Damage Caused by Virus

- It gives you fake pop ups which tell you to buy non-existent antivirus software.
- Some can monitor what you are doing.
- Slow down your computers performance
- Steal files from your computer, passwords, bank account details.

Viruses are extremely dangerous - be aware of using the internet.

18.9.2 Worms

It is a standalone malware computer program which replicates itself, so that it can spread to other computers, through computer network. Computer worm does not need to attach itself to an existing program, unlike virus; but it harms to network, by consuming the bandwidth.

Worms are mainly created or designed to spread, but not to change the systems through which they pass. Worms such, as the Morris worm and Mydoom are payload (It is an action done by a program apart from the act of spreading in itself and causes damage to the operating system or even to the BIOS), which cause major disruption by increasing the network traffic.

To minimize the threat of worms, try to keep computers' operating system, other software up-to-date, avoid opening of unrecognized or unexpected emails, install firewall and keep your antivirus software updated.

Worms can also install backdoors (a secret method, of bypassing normal authentication in a product, computer system, cryptosystem or algorithm etc. and is used for securing the unauthorized remote access to a computer) on computers (See Figure 18.32).

Figure 18.32 Computer Worm

The characteristics of a worm are

- It is self-contained.
- It can replicate
- It is activated by creating Process

How worm spread

Worms are autonomous agents who are capable of propagating themselves without the use of other program or intervention or action by a user.

Damage cause by worm

- Disrupt services
- Create system management problems
- It can scan for passwords and send information back to attacker.

Different types of Computer Worm

- **Email Worms:** It spread through infected email messages as an attachment or a link.
- **Instant Messaging Worms:** It spread by sending links to the contact list of instant messaging applications.
- **Internet Worms:** It scan all available network resources by using local operating system services, it will connect and gain access to computer if it is found to be vulnerable.
- **IRC Worms:** It spread through IRC chat channels, which sends infected files or links to an infected website.

18.9.3 Trojan Horse

A Trojan horse, is a malicious computer program which misrepresents itself to appear useful or interesting just to persuade a victim to install it. Typically, an individual e-mail use a Trojan in the form of a joke program, which appears to be useful but that actually does damage. So, in Trojan horse, code is hidden in a program such as game or spreadsheet which looks safe to run but has hidden side effect.

It can be employed by cyber-thieves and hackers to get the access to users' systems, by tricking some form of social engineering on systems. Once Trojans get activated, then it can enable cyber-criminals to spy and steal your sensitive data, gain backdoor access to your system. Trojans cannot self-replicate themselves.

Trojan can:

- Delete the data
- Block the data
- Modify the data
- Copy the data

Types of Trojan

Trojans are classified according to the type of actions:

- **Backdoor:** It gives remote control to the malicious users of an infected computer.
- **Exploit:** These are the program which contain data or code and it takes an advantage of a vulnerability within application software which is running on your computer.
- **Rootkit:** These are designed to conceal certain objects or activities in your system. It prevents malicious programs to get detected.
- **Trojan-Banker:** It is designed to steal the account data for online banking systems, e-payment systems, and credit or debit cards.
- **Trojan-DDoS:** It conduct DoS (Denial of Service), which is done by sending multiple requests from your and several other infected computers, the attack then overwhelm the target address.
- **Trojan-Downloader:** It automatically download and install new versions of malicious programs onto your computer.
- **Trojan-Dropper:** It is used by hackers to install Trojans and / or viruses for preventing the detection of malicious programs.

How Trojan Horses Spread

They generally spread through e-mail.

Limitations

Since Trojan Horse malware is not technically viral, it cannot self-replicate and requires a user interaction to function.

Protection against Trojans

By installing anti-malware software, on either PCs, laptops, Macs, tablets, and smartphones; one can get protection against Trojans.

18.9.4 Spams

Spam is flooding the Internet with many copies of the same message. The most common form of spam is unwanted e-mail.

18.10 CYBER CRIME

Any criminal activity that uses a computer either as an instrument, target or a means for perpetuating further crimes comes within the ambit of cyber crime".

A generalized definition of cyber crime may be "*unlawful acts wherein the computer is either a tool or target or both*". The computer may be used as a tool in the following kinds of activity financial crimes, sale of illegal articles, pornography, online gambling, intellectual property crime, e-mail spoofing, forgery, cyber defamation, cyber stalking. The computer may however be target for unlawful acts in the following cases unauthorized access to computer/computer system/computer networks, theft of information contained in the electronic form, e-mail bombing, data didling, salami attacks, logic bombs, Trojan attacks, internet time thefts, web jacking, theft of computer system, physically damaging the computer system.

18.10.1 Reasons for Cyber Crime

(a) *Capacity to store data in comparatively small space* :The computer has unique characteristic of storing data in a very small space. This affords to remove or derive information either through physical or virtual medium makes it much more easier.

(b) *Easy to access* : The problem encountered in guarding a computer system from unauthorized access is that there is every possibility of breach not due to human error but due to the complex technology. By secretly implanted logic bomb, key loggers that can steal access codes, advanced voice recorders; retina imagers etc. that can fool biometric systems and bypass firewalls that can be utilized to get past many a security system.

(c) *Complex* : The computers work on operating systems and these operating systems in turn are composed of millions of codes. Human mind is fallible and it is not possible that there might not be a lapse at any stage. The cybercriminal take advantage of these lacunas and penetrate into the computer system.

(d) *Negligence* : Negligence is very closely connected with human conduct. It is therefore very probable that while protecting the computer system there might be any negligence, which in turn provides a cyber criminal to gain access and control over the computer system.

(e) *Loss of evidence* : Loss of evidence is a very common and obvious problem as all the data are routinely destroyed. Further collection of data outside the territorial extent also paralyses this system of crime investigation.

18.10.2 Prevention of Cyber Crime

You should keep following things in mind before you use the Internet.

(a) To prevent cyber stalking avoid disclosing any information pertaining to oneself. This is as good as disclosing your identity to strangers in public place.

(b) Always avoid sending any photograph online particularly to strangers and chat friends as there have been incidents of misuse of the photographs.

(c) Always use latest and updated anti-virus software to guard against virus attacks.

(d) Always keep backup volumes so that one may not suffer data loss in case of virus contamination.

(e) Never send your credit card number to any site that is not secured, to guard against frauds.

(f) Always keep a watch on the sites that your children are accessing to prevent any kind of harassment or depravation in children.

(g) It is better to use a security programme that gives control over the cookies and send information back to the site as leaving the cookies unguarded might prove fatal.

(h) Web site owners should watch traffic and check any irregularity on the site. Putting host-based intrusion detection devices on servers may do this.

(i) Use of firewalls may be beneficial.

(j) Web servers running public sites must be physically separate protected from internal corporate network.

18.11 DATA SECURITY AND PROTECTION

It means protecting data, either from destructive forces and unwanted actions of an unauthorized users.

Data protection is an attempt of ensuring the security of computer-processed data from an unauthorized access, any kind of destructive user actions, and from computer failure.

18.11.1 Concept

Data security technology includes:

- **Disk encryption:** It refers to encryption technology which encrypts data on a hard disk drive.
- **Backups:** It is done to ensure that the data which is lost can be recovered from another source.
- **Data masking:** It is the process of masking specific data within a database in order to ensure that the data security is maintained and the sensitive information is not exposed to unauthorized user.
- **Data erasure:** It is a software-based overwriting method which completely destroys all electronic data which resides on a hard drive, and ensure that no sensitive data is leaked.

With increasing use of computer-based information systems, a concern for the protection of computer-processed data is increasing day by day. Design of entry and display of data, sequence control, user guidance, and data transmission functions can affect the security of the data which is being processed.

Data protection mainly deal with two general problems.

1. Data must be protected from an unauthorized access, which is actually a problem of data security.
2. Data must be protected from errors by an authorized system users.

Design techniques which are needed to achieve data security and prevent user errors are different.

18.11.2 Creating Strong Password

Passwords gives the first line of protection against any unauthorized access to your computer. The stronger your password, the more protected your computer is from hackers and malicious software.

What makes a password strong (or weak)?

A strong password must:

- be eight characters long (characters: uppercase A-Z, lower case a-z, Numbers 0-9, Symbols which found on the keyboard and spaces ' ~ ! @ # $ % ^ & * ( ) _ - + = { } [ ] \ | : ; " ' < > , . ? /)
- not contain user, real or company name.
- not contain a complete word.
- be different from previous passwords.

Example of strong password: 12@a!08

18.11.3 Identify Secure Website

While visiting a website it may ask for sensitive information such as credit card numbers or your social security number, the first step you can take to secure your privacy is to create a strong password. Always try to verify that any information you enter on this site is transmitted and stored properly, as once information is entered online, is transmitted as plain text which can be to intercept by any one.

To avoid this, make sure that the website is encrypted over a secure connection.

- **HTTPS:** Secure website's URL begin with "https" rather than "http". "s" in this stands for secure and is using SSL (Secure Sockets Layer) connection. Information will be encrypted before being sent to a server.
- **THE LOCK ICON:** It is displayed somewhere in the window of your web browser and gives you detailed information on the security status of the website.

18.11.4 Clear Cookies

Follow the simple steps to delete Cookies in Internet Explorer

1. Press Start
2. Click on Control Panel
3. Double click on the Internet options
4. Under the General Tab, Click Delete
5. The Delete Browsing History dialog box will appear.
6. Click the 'cookies' checkbox.
7. Click the delete button present at the bottom of the dialog box.
8. You will be taken back to the Internet properties dialog box.
9. Click "OK".

18.11.5 How to Delete Cookies in Chrome

1. At the top right side of browser toolbar, click on the Chrome icon.
2. Click on **Settings.**
3. Scroll down to the bottom.
4. Click "**Show advanced settings**".
5. Under "**Privacy**", Click on "**Content Settings**", option.
6. Under "**Cookies**", Click on "**All cookies and site data**", option.
7. Full list of all your cookies appears.
8. Click REMOVE ALL to clear all your cookies or pick a particular website and clear your cookies from that site.

18.12 DISCOVER NETWORK

Computer network is a group of two or more computers that connect with each other to share a resource. Sharing of devices and resources is the purpose of computer network. You can share printers, fax machines, scanners, network connection, local drives, and other resources.

18.12.1 Networking Components

There are multiple components that go into computer networks, but not all of these are needed in every type of network. An understanding of the various components that are available can help you design the right network for your home or business environment.

18.12.2 Hubs

A hub is a device where data arrives from one or more nodes (computers in a network) and is forwarded to one or more other nodes. Figure 18.33 shows a hub.

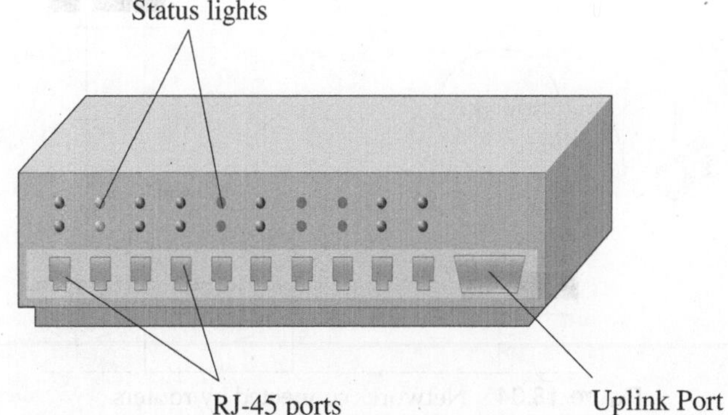

Figure 18.33 A hub

Hubs generally have 4 to 24 RJ-45 ports for twisted-pair cabling and one or more uplink ports for connecting the hub to other hubs. Also, hubs have indicator lights to indicate the status of the port link status, collisions and so on.

Hubs receive signals from each station (node) and repeats the signals to all other stations connected to the hub. Some hubs, called active hubs, also amplify the signal before transmitting it to other nodes. Hence hubs are also known as *multiport repeaters*.

18.12.3 Switches

Switch is a telecommunication device grouped as one of computer network components. Switch is like a Hub but built in with advanced features. It uses physical device addresses in each incoming messages so that it can deliver the message to the right destination or port. It selects a path or circuit for sending a data unit to its next destination. In smaller networks, switch is not required. It is required in large internetworks, where there can be many possible ways of transmitting a message from a sender to destination. The purpose of the switch is to select the best possible path.

18.12.4 Routers

Routers are devices (computers) containing software that help in determining the best path out of the available paths, for a particular transmission (See Figure 18.34). They consist of a combination of hardware and software. The hardware includes the physical interfaces to the various networks in the internetwork. The two main pieces of software in a router are the operating system and the routing protocol.

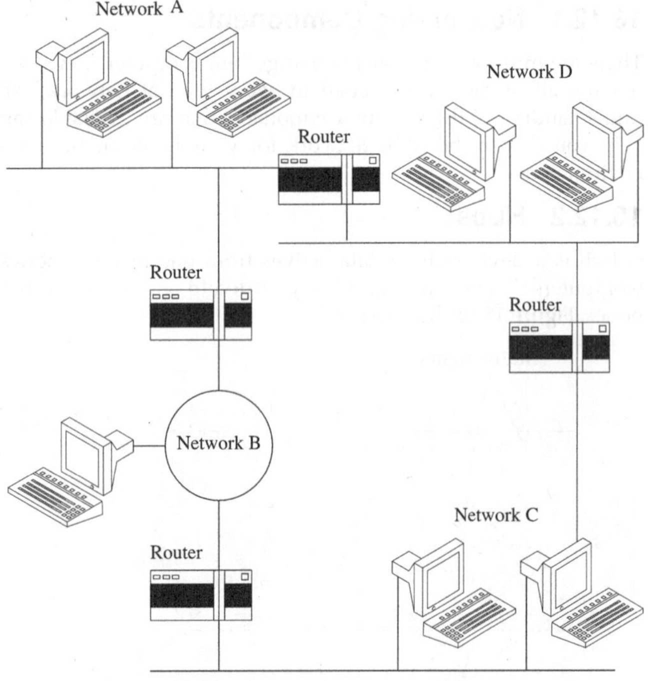

Figure 18.34 Networks connected by routers

☞ *A router between two LANs receives messages from both networks, checks their destinations, and transmits the messages to the required LAN. Since messages are stored in the routers system before re-transmission, routers are said to implement a store-and-forward technique.*

Routers use logical and physical addressing to connect two or more logically separate networks. They accomplish this connection by organizing the large network into logical network segments or subnetworks. Each of these subnetworks is given a logical address. This allows the networks to be separate but still access each other and exchange data when necessary. Data is grouped into packets, or blocks of data. Each packet, in addition to having a physical device address, has a logical network address.

18.12.5 Bridges

Bridges are devices (computers) that can transmit data between two heterogeneous LANs. Bridges divide a large network into smaller segments. They also filter data and keep the traffic separate for each segment. When a packet enters a bridge, it reads the address contained in the frame and compares that address with a table (containing addresses of all the nodes in both the segments). When the bridge finds a match, it sends the packet to the destination segment (See Figure 18.35).

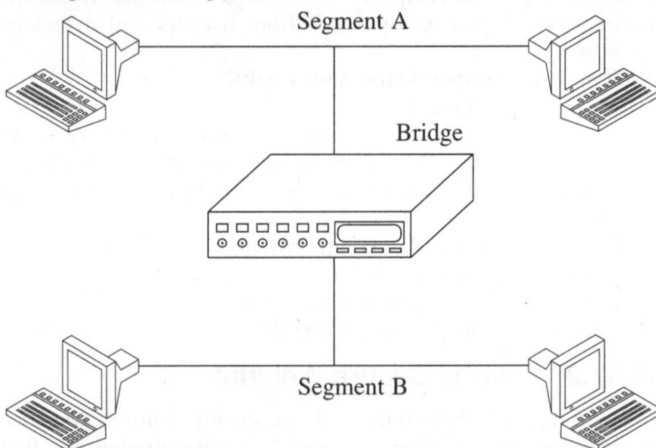

Figure 18.35 The bridge connecting two segments of PCs

A bridge operates in the following manner:

(a) A bridge receives all the signals from both segment A and B (See Figure 18.35).

(b) The bridge reads the addresses and discards (filters) all signals from segment A that are addressed to segment A, because they need not cross the bridge.

(c) Signals from segment A addressed to a computer on segment B are transmitted to segment B.

(d) The signals from segment B are treated in a similar way. Only those signals that are meant for segment A are retransmitted.

18.12.6 Modems

A modem enables you to connect your computer to the available internet connection over the existing telephone line. Like NIC, Modem is not integrated with a computer motherboard. It comes as separate part which can be installed on the PCI slots found on motherboard.

A modem is not necessary for LAN, but required for internet connection such as Broadband and Wi-Fi. There are some types of modems, which differs in speed and transmission rate. Standard PC modem or Dial-up modems (56Kb data transmission speed), Cellular modem (used in a laptop that enables to connect while on the go), cable modem (500 times faster than standard modem) and DSL Modems are the most popular.

18.12.7 Cables and Connectors

Cable is one way of transmission media which can transmit communication signals. The wired network topology uses special type of cable to connect computers on a network. There are a number of solid transmission Media types, which are listed below.

Twisted pair wire

It is classified as Category 1, 2, 3, 4, 5, 5E, 6 and 7. Category 5E, 6 and 7 are high-speed cables that can transmit 1Gbps or more.

Coaxial cable

Coaxial cable more resembles like TV installation cable. It is more expensive than twisted-pair cable but provide high data transmission speed.

Fiber-optic cable

It is a high-speed cable which transmits data using light beams through a glass bound fiber. Fiber-optic cable is high data transmission cable comparing to the other cable types. But the cost of fiber optics is very expensive which can only be purchased and installed on governmental level.

Connectors

Connectors normally called "Input and Output connectors" (or I/O for short), are interfaces for linking devices by using cables. They generally have a male end with pins protruding from it. This plug is meant to be inserted into a female part (also called a socket), which includes holes for accommodating the pins. However, there are "hermaphroditic" plugs which can act as either male or female plugs, and can be inserted into either one.

The pins and holes in connectors are usually linked to the electric wires which form the cable. The pin layout describes which pins couple with which wires.

Input/output connectors

The computer's motherboard has a certain number of input-ouput connectors located on the "rear panel as shown figure below." Most motherboards have the following connectors:

Serial port: It uses a DB9 connector, for connecting older devices;

Parallel port: It uses a DB25 connector, mainly for connecting old printers.

USB ports: (1.1, low-speed, or 2.0, high-speed), for connecting more recent peripherals.

RJ45 connector: (called the LAN port or Ethernet port), for connecting the computer to a network. It interfaces with a network card built into the motheboard.

VGA connector (called SUB-D15): It used for hooking up a monitor. This connector interfaces with the built-in graphics card.

Jacks (Line-In, Line-Out and microphone), for connecting speakers or a hi-fi sound system, as well as a microphone. This connector interfaces with the built-in sound card.

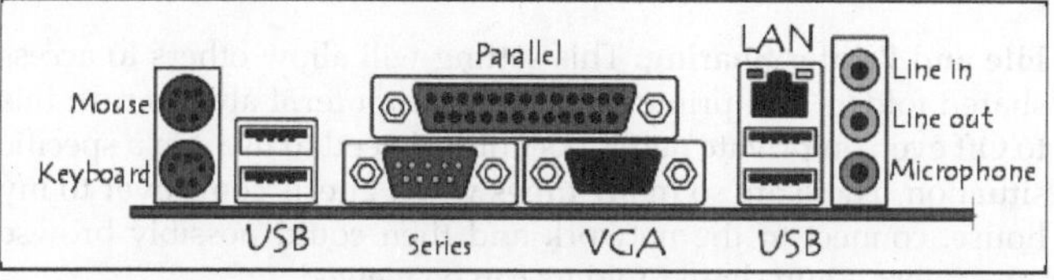

18.12.8 Network Interface Card

Network adapter is a device that enables a computer to talk with other computer/network. Using unique hardware addresses (MAC address) encoded on the card chip, the data-link protocol employs these addresses to discover other systems on the network so that it can transfer data to the right destination.

An adapter card that plugs into the system bus of a computer and allows the computer to send and receive signals on a network. A network interface card (NIC) is also known as a network adapter card or simply a network card. (See Figure 18.36)

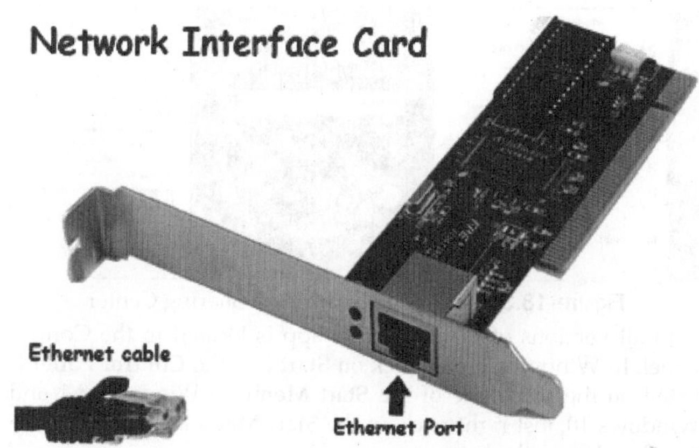

Figure 18.36 Network card

There are two types of network cards: wired and wireless. The wired NIC uses cables and connectors as a medium to transfer data, whereas in the wireless card, the connection is made using antenna that employs radio wave technology. All modern laptop computers incorporated wireless NIC in addition to the wired adapter.

Network Card Speed

Network Interface card, one of the main computer network components, comes with different speeds, 10Mbps, 100Mbps, and 1000Mbps, so on. Recent standard network cards built with Gigabit (1000Mbps) connection speed. It also supports to connect slower speeds such as 10Mbps and 100Mbps. However, the speed of the card depends on your LAN speed. For example, if you have a switch that supports up to 100Mbps, your NIC will also transfer a data with this same speed even though your computer NIC has still the capability to transfer data at 1000Mbps (1Gbps).

18.12.9 Network Sharing Center

The Network and Sharing Center provides connectivity between your computer and the Internet, a network, or another computer. With the Network and Sharing Center, you can gain access to network resources and functionality, whether you are in the same location as the network or in a remote location. Connections are created, configured, and monitored from the Network and Sharing Center.

With each connection you define in the Network and Sharing Center you can create a link between your computer and another computer or network. Outgoing connections contact a remote access server by using a configured access method (local area network [LAN], wireless networking, dial-up modem, ISDN line, cable or DSL modem, and so on) to establish a connection with a remote network.

Opening Network & Sharing Center

The first step is to open the **Network and Sharing Center**. The quickest way to by clicking on **Start** and typing in **network and.** This will instantly bring up the app in the list as shown in Figure 18.37.

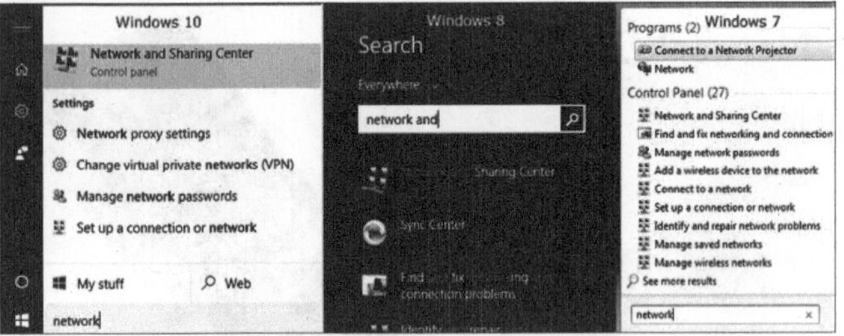

Figure 18.37 Opening Network & Sharing Center

In all versions of Windows, the app is located in the Control Panel. In Windows 7, just click on **Start** and the **Control Panel** is listed on the right side of the **Start Menu**. In Windows 8.1 and Windows 10, just right-click on the **Start Menu** and choose **Control Panel** from the list.

In the **Control Panel**, you can click on the **Network and Internet** category, and then click on **Network and Sharing Center**. If you are in icon view, just click directly on **Network and Sharing Center** as shown in Figure 18.38.

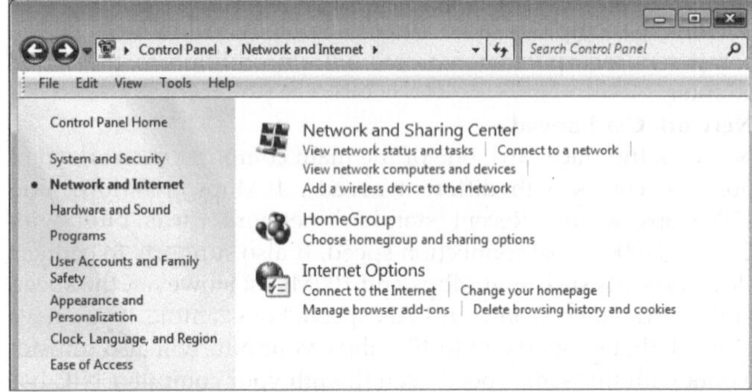

Figure 18.38 Select Network and Sharing Center in Network and Internet category

After, click Network and Sharing center you can see the active network and networks, the network type, the type of access as shown in Figure 18.39. Here you will find the options for changing your network adapter settings, a link to all network sharing settings, and wizards for setting up new connections or troubleshooting problems.

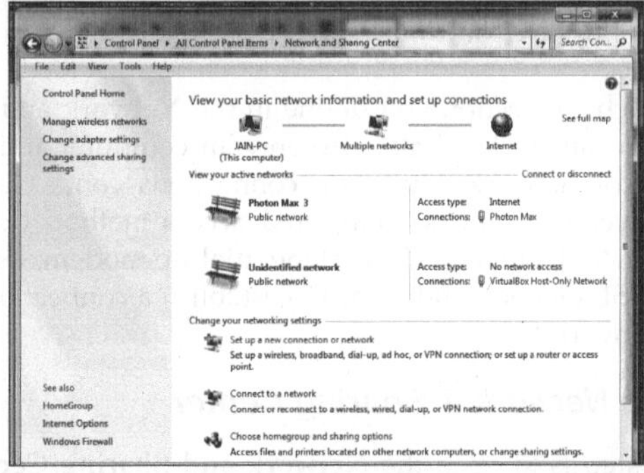

Figure 18.39 View and basic network information and set up connection

To access your network sharing settings, click or tap the "**Change advanced sharing settings**" link on the left column.

Advanced Sharing Settings

Here we fill find advanced sharing options, which are configured for each network profile. A separate network profile is created for each network we use as shown in Figure 18.40. For different profile we have different sharing options depending on the network we are connected to.

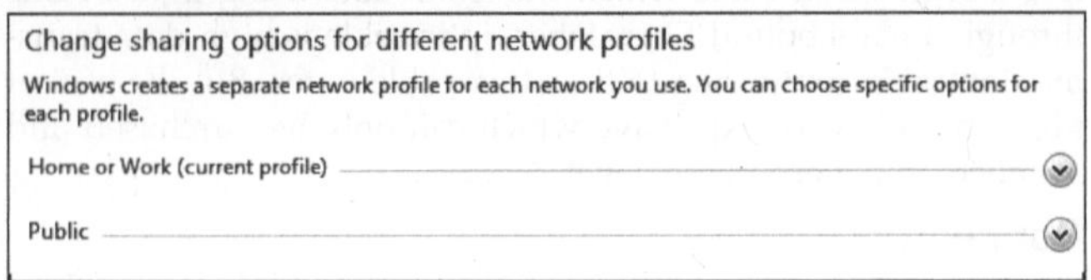

Figure 18.40 Different Network profiles

Network Discovery: The first option is "**Network discovery**". This setting is turned on for private networks by default and it means that your computer can be seen by other computers and vice versa. When you open Windows Explorer, you might see the name of another computer connected to your network under Network Locations. Keep in mind that if we disable Network discovery, we do not disable other forms of sharing (See Figure 18.41).

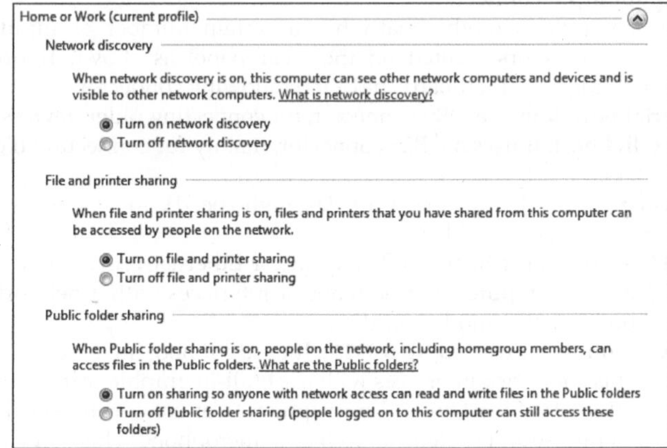

Figure 18.41 Work profile part I

File and Printer Sharing: This setting will allow others to access shared folders and printers on your computer. I always turn this to Off even on private networks unless I need to use it in a specific situation. There are so many times when guests come over to my house, connect to the network and then could possibly browse my system. Only shared folders can be viewed.

Public Folder Sharing: This option turned off unless you specifically need to share data with another computer. The reason is that it is very easy to accidentally save files into these publicly shared folders without realizing it, which will then be accessible by anyone on the network. A very useful feature when you need it, but a big privacy risk otherwise.

Media Streaming: This is another option you should keep disabled until you need to use it. This basically turns your computer into a DLNA server so that you can stream music, movies and pictures to other devices on the network like an Xbox One, etc. When enabled, it opens up quite a few ports in your firewall also.

When media streaming is on, people and devices on the network will be able to access pictures, music and videos on our computer. Also, our computer will be able to find media resources on the network. In Media streaming options we will be able to name our media library, choose on which networks to share, and what type of media to share as shown in Figure 18.42.

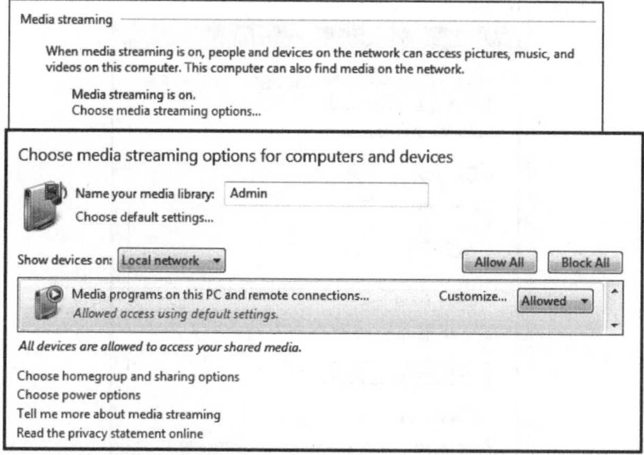

Figure 18.42 Media Streaming Options

File Sharing connections: This options allows us to protect share connections using a 128-bit encryption, or 40 or 56-bit encryption for legacy devices (See Figure 18.43).

Password Protected Sharing: The Password protected sharing option means that only users which have a user account and password on our computer can access our shared files and printers, and Public folder. If you want to give other users access, you have to turn off this option (See Figure 18.45).

HomeGroup connections: The HomeGroup connections option is only available in the Home Network profile. It determines how authentication works for HomeGroup resources. HomeGroup is a simple way to manage sharing and authentication on Home networks running Windows 7. If all computers in the HomeGroup have been configured with the same usernames and passwords, we should choose the "Allow Windows to manage homegroup connections" option (See Figure 18.43).

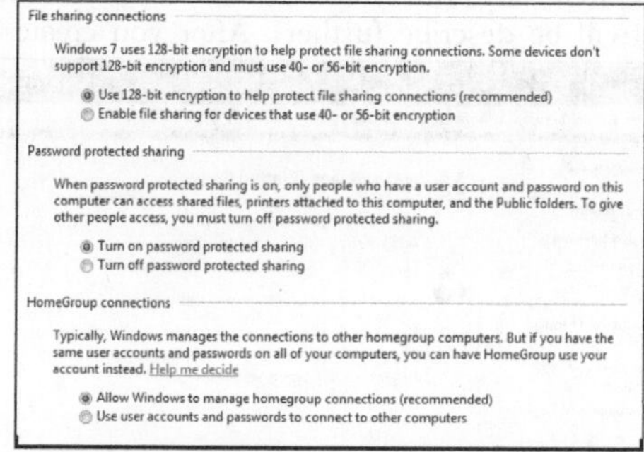

Figure 18.43 Work profile part II

18.12.10 Sharing Files and Folders

To share files and folders between computers on a network the computers must all belong to the same workgroup and the 'File and Printer Sharing' service must be enabled on all the participating computers.

Sharing Permissions

For shares, the only permissions available are:

- Full control: Users may perform all duties of the Change and Read permissions (listed in the following items), including taking ownership.
- Permissions for Read.
- Read: Users can view the contents of the share, read files, and run programs.

Individuals can also be denied access to a shared folder.

Creating Shares

➡ **To share a drive perform the following steps:**

1. Open 'Windows Explorer' navigate to the Folder that you want to share, do not open the folder just have its icon visible.
2. Right-click the folder and select **Properties** as shown in Figure 18.44. Or click **Properties** from the toolbar. The **Properties** dialog box appears, select **Sharing** tab you want to share the folder. (Figure 18.44).

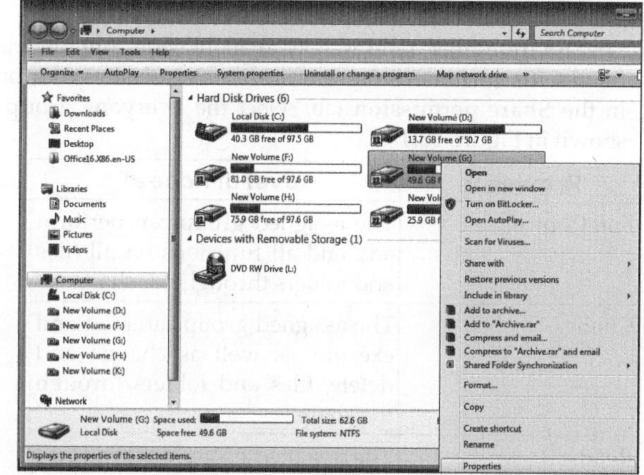

Figure 18.44 Select Properties

4. The **Foldername Properties** window appears, select **Sharing** tab. Click **Advanced Sharing** button in the **Advanced Sharing** section then click OK button as shown in Figure 18.45.

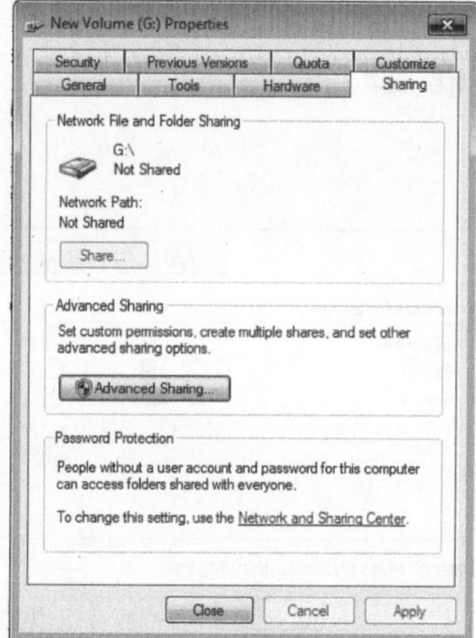

Figure 18.45 Sharing Tab

5. The **Advanced Sharing** dialog box appears as shown in Figure 18.46, tick the **Share this folder.**

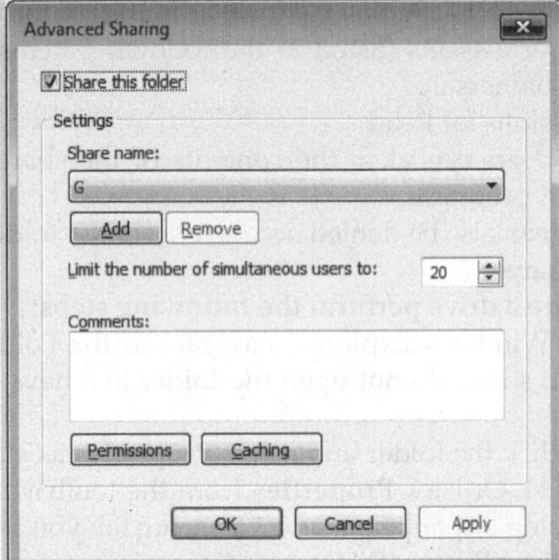

Figure 18.46 Advanced Sharing dialog box

6. The '**Share name:**' field is now available and automatically filled with the folder's name. Click the **Permissions** button.
7. In the **Share permission** tab, select the **Everyone** group as shown in Figure 18.47.

Permission	Level of Access
Full Control	The assigned group can perform any and all functions on all files and folders through the share.
Change	The assigned group can read and execute, as well as change and delete, files and folders through the share.
Read	The assigned group can read and execute both files and folders, but has no ability to modify or delete anything through the share.

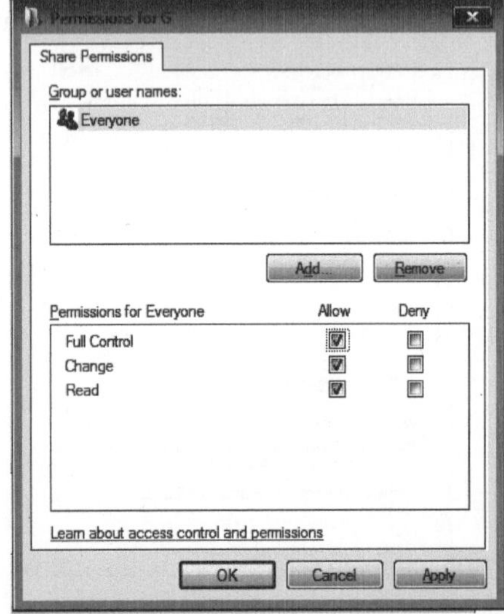

Figure 18.47 Share Permission tab

8. In the **Permission for Everyone** section, you can assign different levels of permission for different users and groups. At the share level, there are the following types of permission:
9. Click '**Apply**' then 'OK' to close the window.
10. Click **OK** button to close the **Advanced sharing** tab. The **Network File and Folder sharing** section being shared as shown in Figure 18.48.

Figure 18.48 The selected get shared

18.12.11 Join Homegroup

HomeGroup is a new feature of Windows. This feature makes it easy to share resources among your computers at home. These "resources" can include printers as well as files from your documents, pictures, music, and video libraries. Other people cannot change the files that you share, unless you give them permission to do so.

When you set up a computer with Windows, a HomeGroup is created automatically. But you can also create a HomeGroup manually (will be describe further). After you create or join a

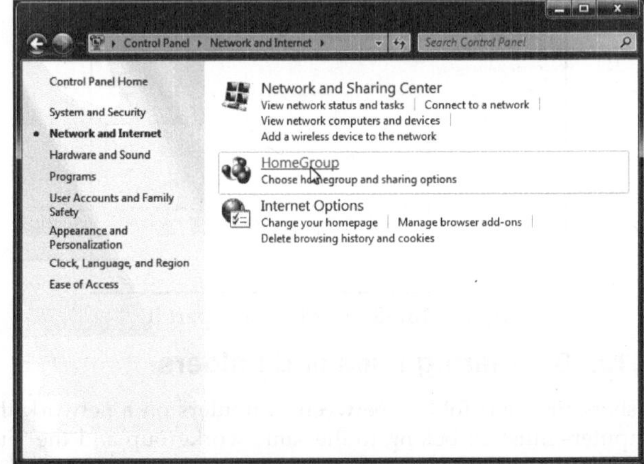

Figure 18.49 Network and Internet window

HomeGroup, you can select the libraries that you want to share. You can prevent specific files or folders from being shared, and you can share additional libraries later. You can help protect your HomeGroup with a password, which you can change at any time.

➡ **To create a HomeGroup:**

1. In **Control Panel** window, click the **Network and Internet Category**.
2. Then in **Network and Internet** window, click **HomeGroup** from the right pane of the window as shown in Figure 18.49.
3. It will display another window called **HomeGroup window** as shown in Figure 18.50.

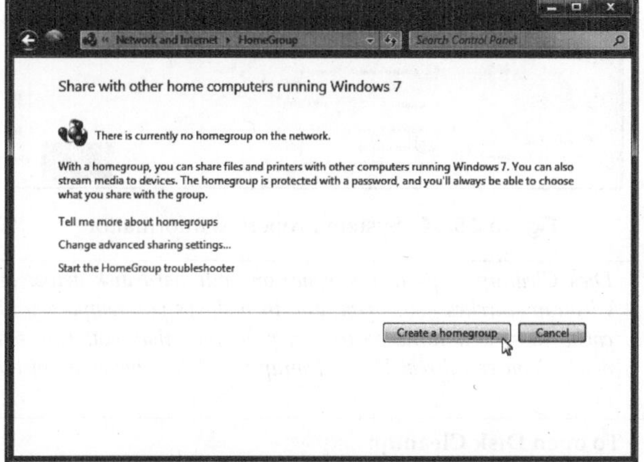

Figure 18.50 HomeGroup window

4. In this window, On the **Share with other home computers running Windows** 7 page, click **Create a homegroup** (Figure 18.51).
5. After that the **Create a Homegroup Wizard** appears (Figure 18.52).

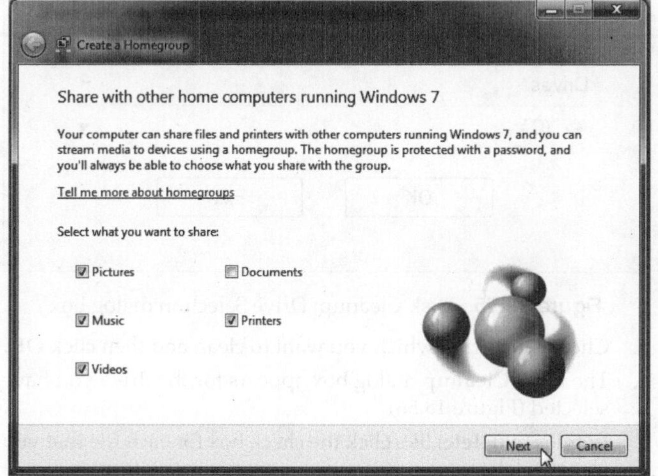

Figure 18.51 Create a HomeGroup Wizard

6. In Figure 18.51, click the check box for each type of file you want to share with the homegroup.
7. Then click **Next** button.
8. Click **Next** button. Windows 7 creates the homegroup.
9. Next window of the **Create a HomeGroup wizard** displays the homegroup password (Figure 18.52).

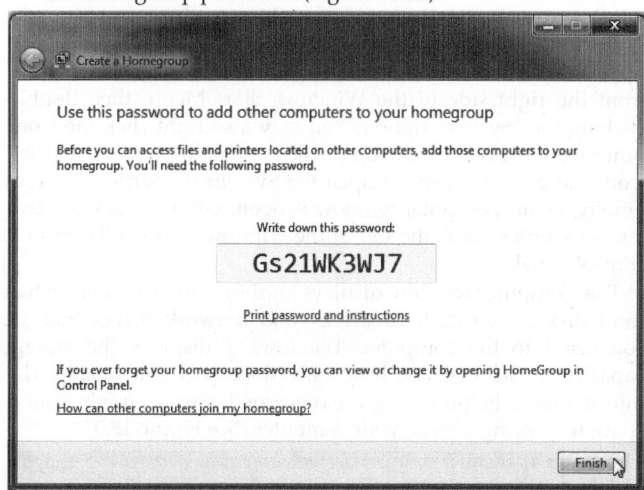

Figure 18.52 HomeGroup password in a HomeGroup wizard

10. Write down the homegroup password and then click **Finish** button.
11. After creating a homegroup, you can now join your computer to other Windows 7 computers to the HomeGroup so that you can access shared libraries and printers.

• **To add computer to homegroup:**

1. In the **HomeGroup** window, click **Join** now, and then complete the wizard.

18.12.12 Network Troubleshooting

Troubleshooting is the process of identifying, planning and resolving a problem, error or fault within a software or computer system. It enables the repair and restoration of a computer or software when it becomes faulty.

Network troubleshooting is primarily done by network engineers or administrators to repair or optimize a network. It is generally done to recover and establish network or Internet connections on end nodes/devices.

Finding and resolving problems and establishing Internet/network connection of a computer/device/node:

- Configuring a router, switch or any network management device.
- Installing cables or Wi-Fi devices.
- Updating firmware devices on router switch.
- Removing viruses.
- Adding, configuring and reinstalling a network printer.

Network troubleshooting can be a manual or automated task. When using automated tools, network management can be done using network diagnostic software.

18.13 SYSTEM & SECURITY

18.13.1 System Properties

In Windows 7, you can look up information about your computer in two primary locations. One is the Computer window and the other is the System Control panel.

You can open the Computer window by selecting "Computer" from the right side of the Windows Start Menu. The Computer window can also be displayed by clicking the "Computer" option in the left sidebar of any open window on the desktop. You can open the System control panel by first selecting "Control Panel" from the right side of the Windows Start Menu, then double-clicking the "System" option. You may also right-click the Computer icon if it is available on the desktop and select "Properties" from the pop-up menu to open the System properties window. Finally, if the Computer window is open, you can click on "System properties" near the top of the window to open the System control panel.

The Computer window displays hard disk information such as local disks, external hard drives, and network drives that are connected to the computer. Windows 7 displays the storage capacity of each disk and how much disk space is available. This information is helpful if you are concerned you are running out of space for storing files on your computer (See Figure 18.53).

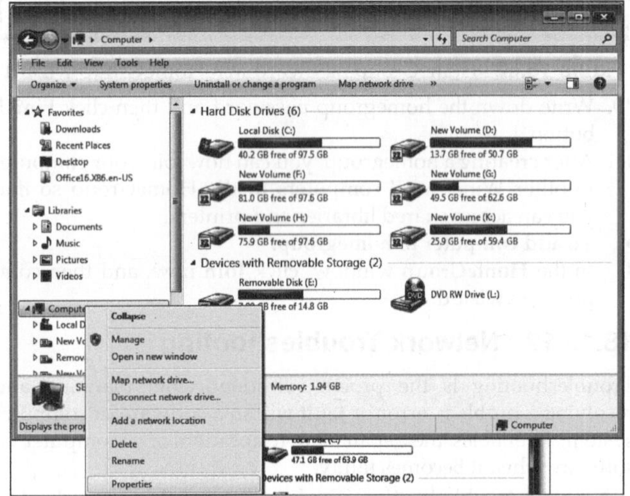

Figure 18.53 Computer window

The System control panel allows you to view more detailed system information, but does not include information about connected hard disks. This information includes the CPU model and speed, the amount of RAM installed, the current operating system, and other information. The System control panel is useful for checking if your computer meets the system requirements for a specific application (See Figure 18.54).

18.13.2 Clean up Your Disk

Scandisk is a PC tool available in Windows operating system. It is a diagnostic and repair program that scans the data on your hard drive clean. By using this hard drive clean-up tool, you can increase the speed of your PC, as this will enable faster access to files and folders.

Disk Cleanup

You can use Disk Cleanup to free up space on your hard disk by removing temporary Internet files, removing installed components and programs that you no longer use, and emptying the Recycle Bin.

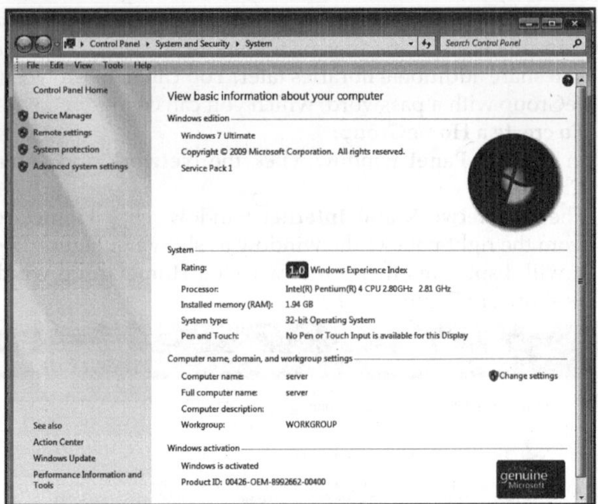

Figure 18.54 System Properties information

☞ *Disk Cleanup helps to free space on your hard disk drive. Disk Cleanup searches your drive, and then shows you temporary files, cache files, and unnecessary program files that you can safely delete. You can direct Disk Cleanup to delete some or all of those files.*

➡ **To open Disk Cleanup:**

1. Click **Start** button, highlight **All Programs**, highlight **Accessories**, highlight **System Tools** and then choose **Disk Cleanup**.
2. **Disk Cleanup: Drive Selection** dialog box appears as seen in Figure 18.55.

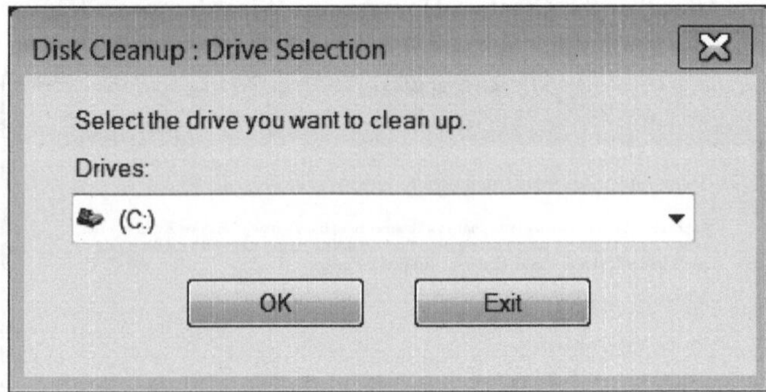

Figure 18.55 Disk Cleanup: Drive Selection dialog box

3. Choose the drive which you want to clean and then click **OK**.
4. The **Disk Cleanup** dialog box appears for the drive you have selected (Figure 18.56).
5. In **Files to delete:** list, click the check box for each file that you want to delete.
6. Then click **OK**.

18.13.3 Windows Update

Windows Update is a free Microsoft service that is used to provide updates like **service packs** and **patches** for the Windows

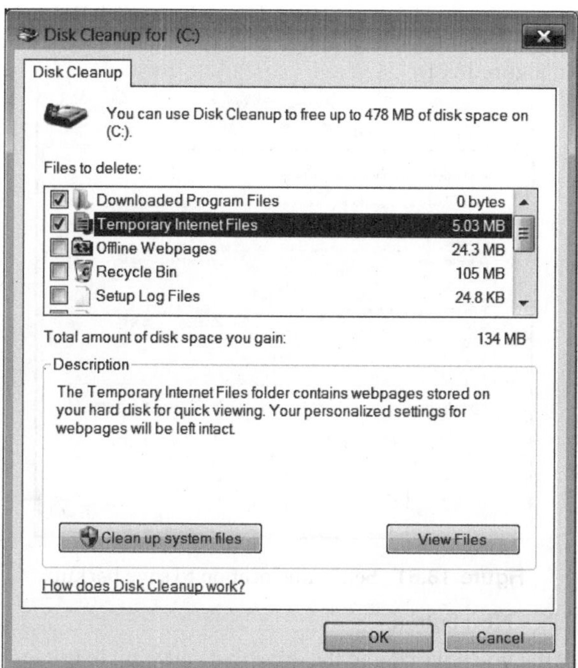

Figure 18.56 Disk Cleanup dialog box for a specific drive

operating system and other software. It is also used to update **drivers** for popular **hardware** devices. And is it also to keep Windows and several other programs updated. Updates often include feature enhancements and security updates to protect Windows from malware and malicious attacks.

- To access Windows update depends on which Windows operating system you are using:
  (i) **Windows 10:** Windows update is built-in and a part of System settings, available from the Start menu.
  (ii) Windows 8, Windows 7 and Windows Vista: Windows update is integrated as a **Control Panel** applet and is accessible from within Control Panel.

➡ **To change windows update settings in Windows 7, 8 and vista.**

1. Click **Start** menu and choose **Control Panel.**
2. Click on the **System and Security** link. From the System and Security window, choose the **Windows Update** link as shown in Figure 18.57.
3. Once **Windows Update** opens, click the **Change Settings** link on the left as shown in Figure 18.58.
4. The window shows *Choose how Windows can install updated.* The settings you see on the screen right now control how Windows Update will look for, receive and install updates from Microsoft as shown in Figure 18.59.
   The important updates options you have:
   - *Install updates automatically (recommended):* Choose this option to have Windows Update automatically check for, download, and install important security patches.
   - *Download updates but let me choose whether to install them:* Choose this to have Windows Update automatically check for and download important updates but not install them. You will have to explicitly choose to install the updates either from Windows Update or during the next shutdown process.

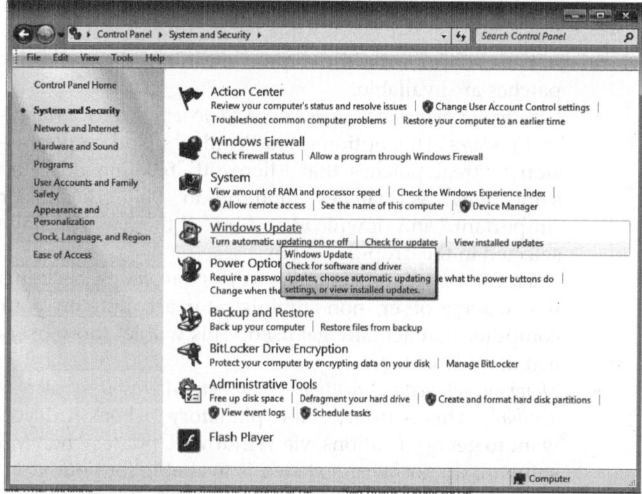

Figure 18.57 Select Windows Update link

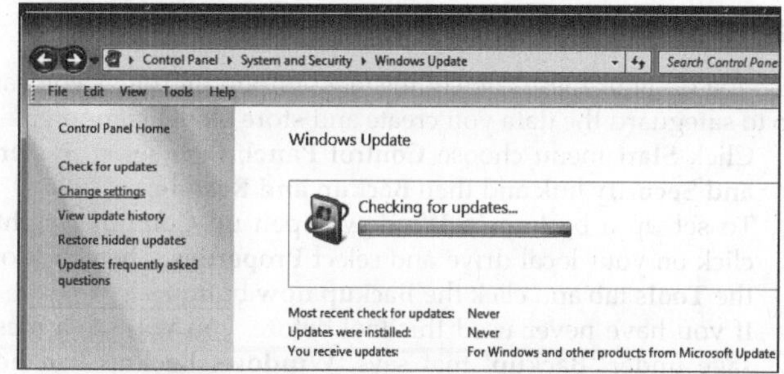

Figure 18.58 Select Change Settings

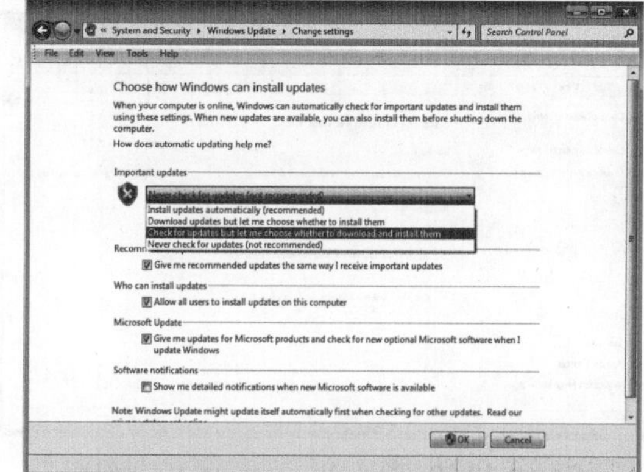

Figure 18.59 Choosing setting for updates

- *Check for updates but let me choose whether to download and install them:* With this option, Windows Update will check for and notify you of available updates but you will need to manually approve the download and installation of them.
- *Never check for updates (not recommended):* This option disables Windows Update completely in Windows 8, 7, or Vista. When you choose this, Windows Update would not even check with Microsoft to see if important security patches are available.
- *Give me recommended updates the same way I receive important updates:* This option gives Windows Update permission to treat patches that Microsoft "recommends" the same way as patches thought to be "critical" or "important," and download and install them as you have selected in the drop-down box.
- *Allow all users to install updates on this computer:* Check this if you have other, non-administrator accounts on your computer that actually get used. This will let those users install updates too.
- *Show me detailed notifications when new Microsoft software is available:* This is pretty self-explanatory - check it if you want to get notifications, via Windows Update, when MS software do not have installed is available for your computer.

5. Click OK to save the changes.

18.13.4 Backup and Restore Data

Backing up your files is one of the most important things you can do to safeguard the data you create and store on the computer.

1. Click **Start** menu choose **Control Panel**, then select **System and Security** link and then **Backup and Restore.**
   To set up a backup in Windows open up Computer right-click on your local drive and select **Properties**. Then click on the **Tools** tab and click the **Backup now** button.
2. If you have never used this tool before, you will see a message under **'Backup'** that says **'Windows Backup had not bee setup'**. Click the link labelled **Set up backup** to the right of that message as shown in Figure 18.60.

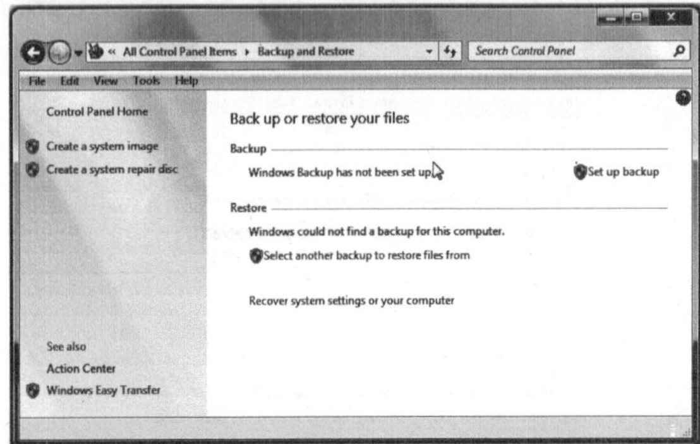

Figure 18.60 Back up or restore your files

3. The **Set up backup** *shows where you want to save your backup.* Windows will search for a suitable drive to store the backup or you can also choose a location on your network. If you backup to a network location you might need the password to the share.

If you plugged in your **External** hard drive, click **Refresh**. For example, here we have select the **Expansion Drive** as shown in Figure 18.61.

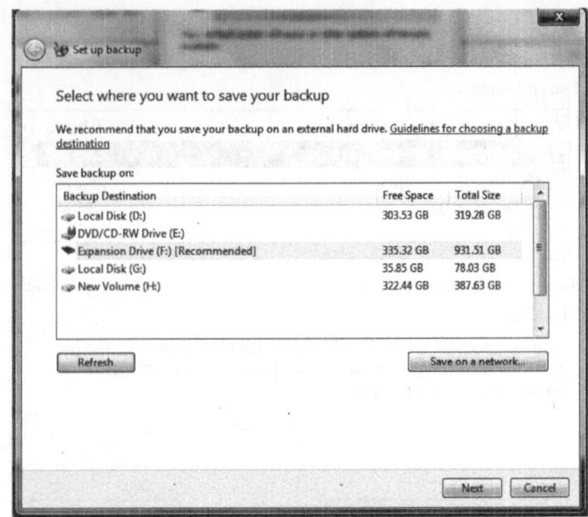

Figure 18.61 Select the location to save backup

4. Click **Next** button.
5. After you have chosen the drive that you want to use for your backup, the program will ask you to identify what you want to back up. The default selection is to let Windows choose for you, and create a disk image at the same time. For example, here we have select **Let me choose** as shown in Figure 18.62 .

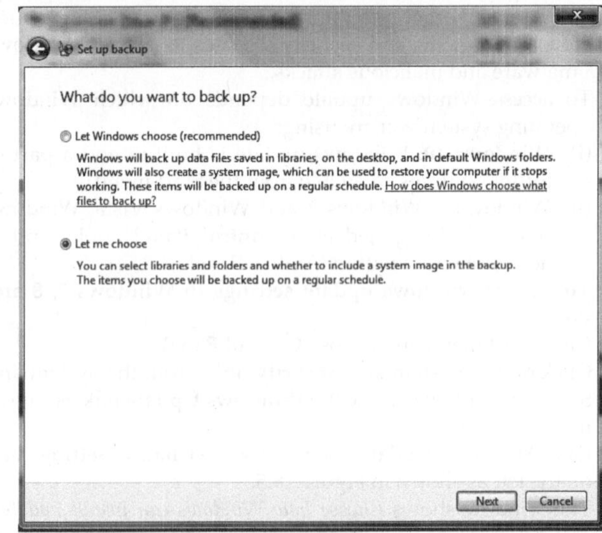

Figure 18.62

6. Select the files and folder to include in the backup.
7. Now review the backup job and make sure everything looks correct. Before you run your backup, you will probably want to take a look at the default schedule that Windows has set up for you, to confirm that your computer is going to be on at that time of day. If you want to adjust it, click **Change Schedule** and then set it to something more suitable to your schedule as shown in Figure 18.63.

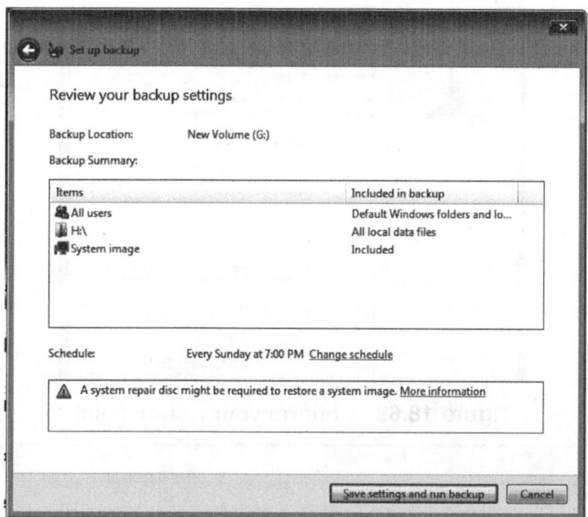

Figure 18.63 Review your backup settings

8. Click **Save settings and run backups.** The first backup will be a somewhat lengthy process, but future backups will be quicker, as they will back up only files that have been added or changes since your previous backup. While it runs you can monitor the progress as shown in Figure 18.64.

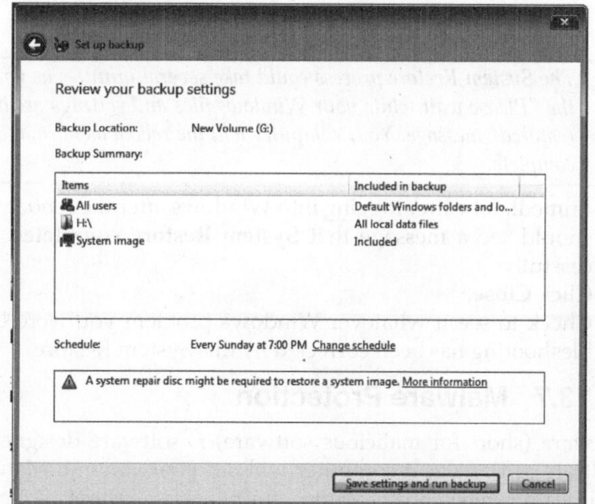

Figure 18.64 Review your backup settings

9. Click the **View** Details button to see exactly what is being backup during the process.
10. When the backup is complete you will see the two backup files and image folder if you create one.

18.13.5 Restoring from Backup

1. To restore all of your backed-up data, click **Restore my files** as shown in Figure 18.65.
2. You can browse for folders on the left side, look for the folder name of your backup.
3. Select the folder, and then click **Add folder** from the browse the backup for folders or drives as shown in Figure 18.66.

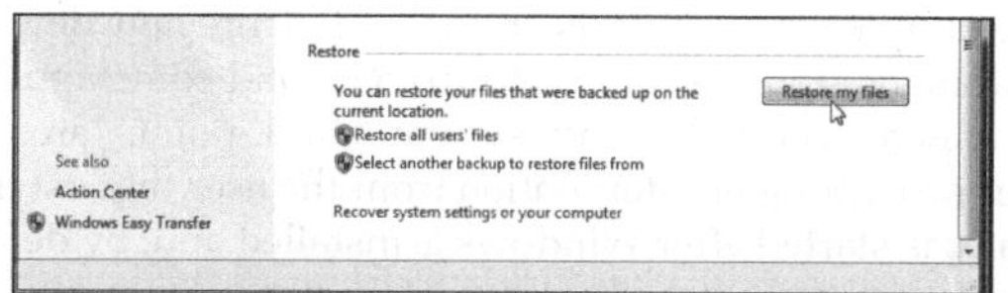

Figure 18.65 Select Restore my files

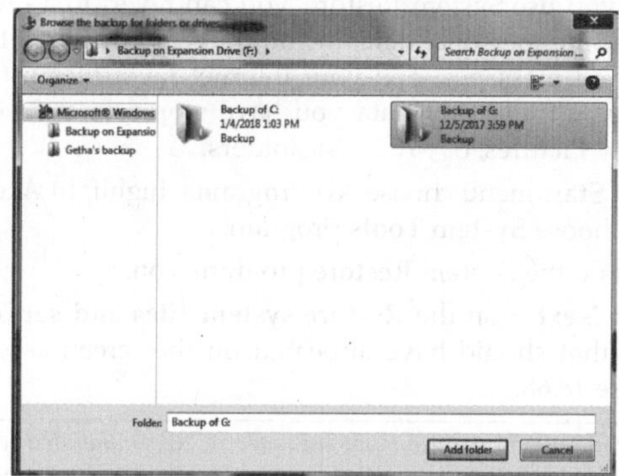

Figure 18.66 Add folder

4. Once you have added the folder to your restore list, click **Next** and choose Whether you want the files restored to the original location or to a new location. Finally, click **Restore** to bring back all of your data.
5. Progress of the restoration will vary depending on the size of the data and location it is restoring from (See Figure 18.67).

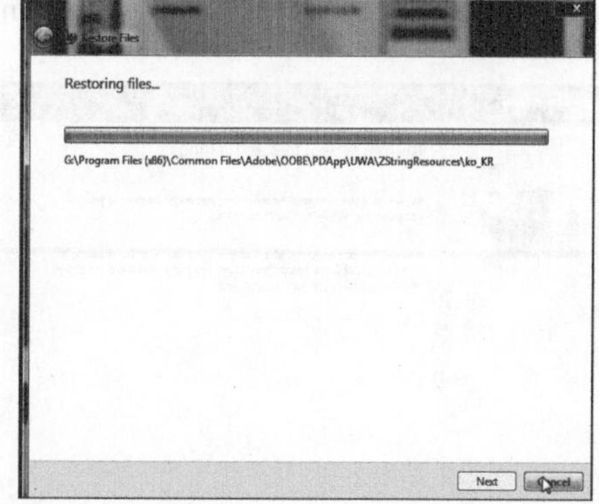

Figure 18.67 Progress of restoration

18.13.6 System Restore

The System Restore tool in Windows is one of the helpful utilities available to fix a major problem in Windows. It is a recovery tool for Windows that allows you to reverse certain kinds of changes made to the operating system. System Restore is used to return important Windows files and settings such as drivers, registry keys, system files, installed programs etc.

System Restore automatically tracks changes to your computer and creates restore points before major changes take place. To create a restore point, System Restore takes a full snapshot of the registry and some dynamic system files.

For example, restore points are created before new device drivers, automatic updates, unsigned drivers, and some applications are installed. These healthy system check-points are created without prompting or intervention from the user the first time the computer is started after Windows is installed and, by default, on a daily basis after that. You can also manually create restore points.

When you use System Restore, you can revert to a saved state without losing personal data, including Word documents, e-mail settings and messages, and your Internet favourites list. System Restore won't lose any data you have stored in the My Documents, My Pictures, or My Music folders.

1. Click **Start** menu choose **All Programs**, highlight **Accessories** and choose **System Tools** program.
2. Click on the **System Restore** program icon.
3. Click **Next >** on the **Restore system files and settings** window that should have appeared on the screen as shown in Figure 18.68.

☞ *If you have two options on this screen, Recommended restore and Choose a different point, select the Choose a different restore point option before clicking Next > unless you are absolutely sure that the preselected restore point is the one you want to use.*

4. Choose the restore point that you want to use.

   Any restore points that you manually created, scheduled restore points that Windows automatically created, and any created automatically during the installation of certain programs will be listed here. You cannot use System Restore to undo Windows changes to a date that a restore point does not exist for.

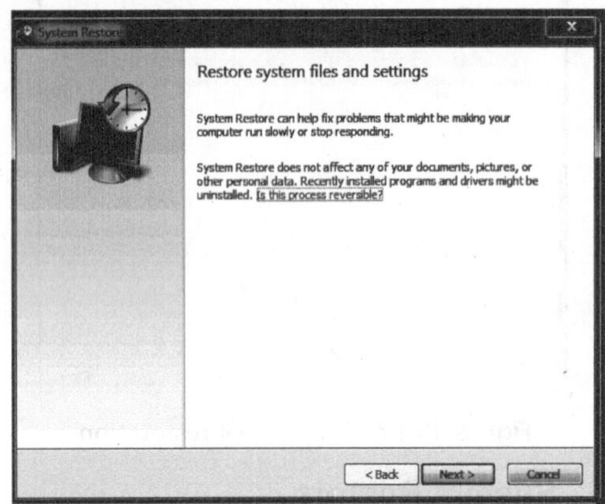

Figure 18.68 Restore system files and settings

5. Click Next >.
6. Click **Finish** on the **Confirm your restore point** window to begin the System Restore as shown in Figure 18.69.
7. Click **Yes** to the *Once started, System Restore cannot be interrupted. Do you want to continue?* dialog box as shown in Figure 18.70.
8. System Restore will now restore Windows to the state that was recorded in the restore point you chose in Step 4.

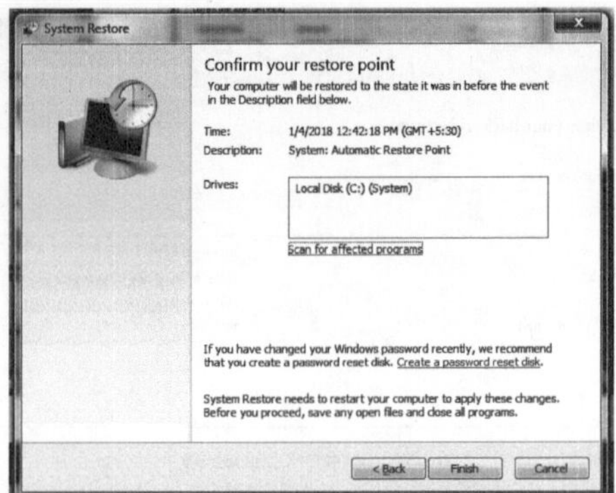

Figure 18.69 Confirm your restore point

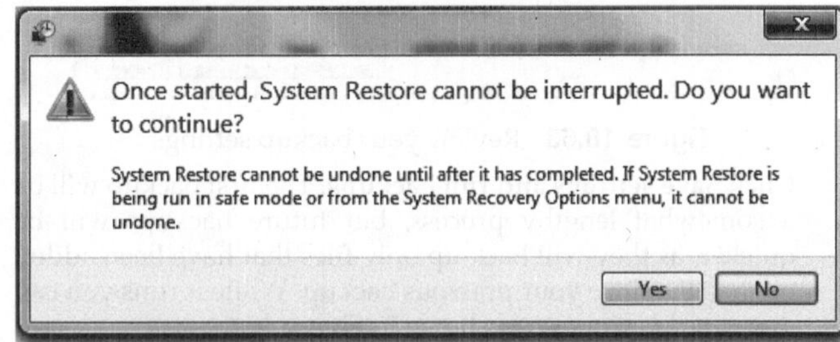

Figure 18.70 System Restore Confirm message

☞ *The System Restore process could take several minutes as you see the "Please wait while your Windows files and settings are being restored" message. Your computer will the reboot as normal when complete.*

9. Immediately after logging into Windows after the reboot, you should see a message that **System Restore completed** successfully.
10. Click **Close**.
11. Check to see if whatever Windows problem you were troubleshooting has been corrected by this System Restore.

18.13.7 Malware Protection

Malware (short for malicious software) is software designed to infiltrate or damage a computer without your consent. Malware includes *computer viruses, worms, trojan horses, spyware, scareware* and more. It can be present on websites and emails, or hidden in downloadable files, photos, videos, freeware or shareware. (However, it should be noted that most websites, shareware or freeware applications do not come with malware.) The best way to avoid getting infected is to run a good anti-virus protection program, do periodic scans for spyware, avoid clicking on suspicious email links or websites.

- *Virus:* Malware programs that can reproduce itself and infect other computers.
- *Spyware:* It surreptitiously monitors and collects information from your computer or browsing habits without your consent – usually for advertising purposes. It can also gather info from your address book, and even your passwords and credit card numbers.

- *Scareware:* You are surfing the net and suddenly an official-looking screen pops up warning you there is a problem on your computer, such as: Your computer may be infected with harmful spyware programs. Immediate removal is required. To scan, click Yes. You are not sure if it is real or not, so what do you do? Be careful, this might be scareware. If there is any doubt, you can close your browser immediately by pressing ALT+F4. This will prevent any scareware from loading.

So you can install anti-virus and anti-spyware utilities on your computer that will seek and destroy the malicious programs they find on your computer. So join the fight against badware and install some protective utilities on your hard drive. There are plenty of free tools available to help you remove it.

The following software runs continuously in the background, helping to protect your computer from infection:

1. *Microsoft Security Essentials:* Provides real-time protection for your home PC that guards against viruses, spyware, and other malicious software.
2. *AVG FREE:* Anti-Virus software from Grisoft that automatically protects computers from viruses by providing timely virus database updates and protection.
3. *Sandboxie:* Create a secure partition on your computer for safer web browsing with this free program. This is a great tool for more advanced users.

18.13.8 Windows Firewall

A firewall can either be software-based or hardware-based and is used to help keep a network secure. Its primary objective is to control the incoming and outgoing network traffic by analysing the data packets and determining whether it should be allowed through or not, based on a predetermined rule set. A network's firewall builds a bridge between an internal network that is assumed to be secure and trusted, and another network, usually an external (inter)network, such as the Internet, that is not assumed to be secure and trusted. All messages entering or leaving the intranet pass through the firewall, which examines each message and blocks those that do not meet the specified security criteria.

Many personal computer operating systems include software-based firewalls to protect against threats from the public Internet. Many routers that pass data between networks contain firewall components and, conversely, many firewalls can perform basic routing functions.

There are several types of firewall techniques:

- ***Packet filter:*** Firewalls filter packets that attempt to enter or leave a network and either accept or reject them depending on the predefined set of filter rules.
- ***Application gateway:*** The application gateway technique employs security methods applied to certain applications such as Telnet and File Transfer Protocol servers.
- ***Circuit-level gateway:*** A circuit-level gateway applies these methods when a connection such as Transmission Control Protocol is established and packets start to move.
- ***Proxy server:*** Proxy servers can mask real network addresses and intercept every message that enters or leaves a network.
- ***Stateful Inspection or Dynamic Packet Filtering:*** This method compares not just the header information, but also a packet's most important inbound and outbound data parts. These are then compared to a trusted information database for characteristic matches. This determines whether the information is authorized to cross the firewall into the network.

Many firewalls use two or more of these techniques in concert. A firewall is considered a first line of defence in protecting private information. For greater security, data can be encrypted.

CHAPTER 19

Time Management

19.1 OUTLOOK CALENDAR

Outlook 2016 calendar is used to organize your daily activities and to remind you of important tasks and events. Using the calendar effectively can help you stay organized, on time, and on task. You can schedule and track appointments, meetings, and events, and block time as a reminder to yourself to take care of tasks.

1. To open the Calendar click the **Calendar** button on the **Navigation bar** i.e., select the Calendar link (or icon) in the bottom left corner of the main window. (See Figure 19.1).

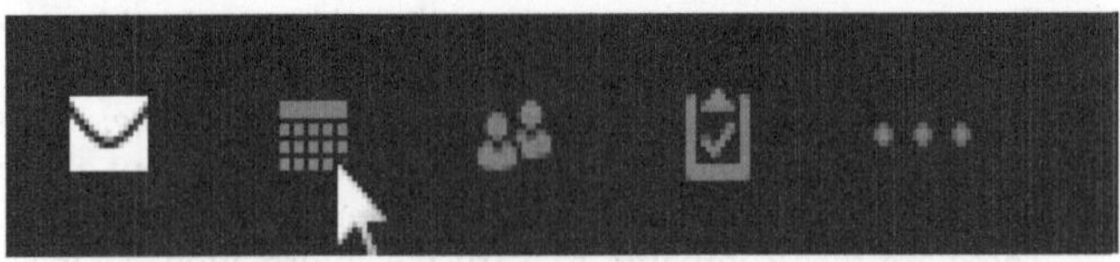

Figure 19.1 Calendar button on Navigation toolbar

2. Outlook calendar will be displayed as shown in Figure 19.2.

Figure 19.2 Current calendar display

3. Now click the **Mail** button on **Navigation bar**, and select your email account as shown in Figure 19.3.

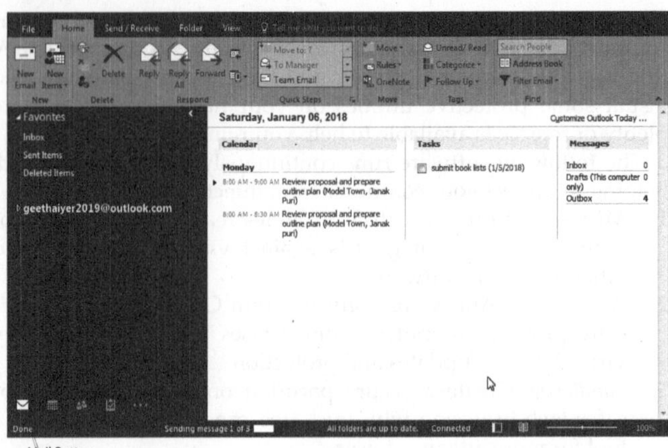

Figure 19.3 Email account is displayed using Navigation bar > Mail button

19.2 SCHEDULE AN APPOINTMENT

Appointments are blocks of time you schedule for only yourself (as opposed to meetings, to which you invite other Outlook users). An appointment has a specific start time and end time (as opposed to an event, which occurs for one or more full 24-hour periods). Events are day-long blocks of time that you schedule on your Outlook calendar, such as birthdays, payroll days, or anything else occurring on a specific day but not at a specific time. In all other respects, creating an event is identical to creating an appointment, in that you can specify a location, indicate recurrence, indicate your availability, and attach additional information to the event item. You can schedule an appointment by entering a subject and time in an appointment window or directly on the calendar.

To schedule an event, you need to provide only the date. You can schedule an event in an appointment window, or directly on the calendar. To schedule an event do the following:

1. Open the Calendar and select the day for the appointment as shown in Figure 19.4. In the left column, select your desired date from the small month view in the top left; it will become highlighted (the current date is highlighted/outlined as well). The area to the right will display the Day view by the hour (if not, select the Day button towards the top, rather than Week or Month).
2. Open a new appointment window by clicking on the **New Appointment** button. (See Figure 19.5). It will open a New appointment window.

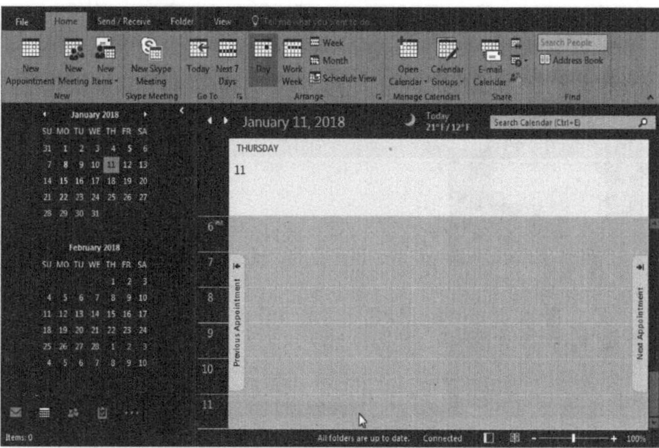

Figure 19.4 Calendar showing day of appointment

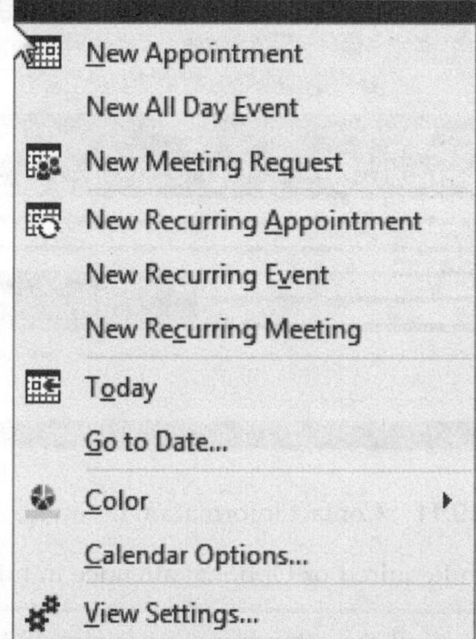

Figure 19.5 New appointment menu

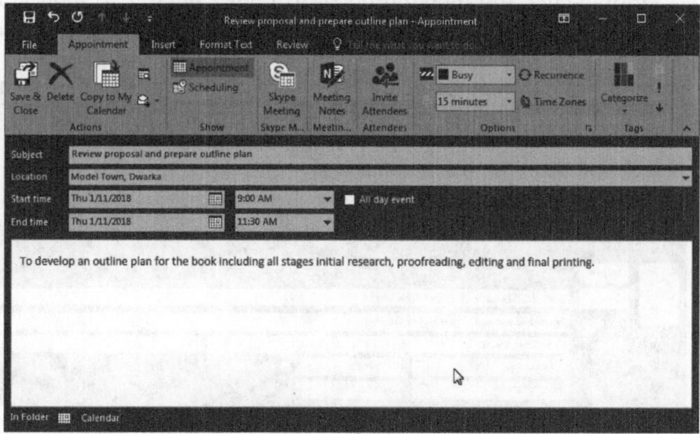

Figure 19.6 New appointment window

3. In the Subject box, enter an identifying name for the event.
4. In the Location box, enter the event location.
5. In the Start and End time row select start and end time by clicking on the down arrow and select a new value. Enter any additional information as you would for an appointment. Then save and close the event by clicking on Save & Close button. (See Figure 19.6).

19.3 CHANGE APPOINTMENT DETAILS

The appointment added to the calendar shows the subject, start time, duration and location. Move the mouse over the appointment area to see more details.

1. Single click the calendar at the appointment area and you can edit the text of the subject title. Double click the appointment to open the appointment editor form, add or change any of the details.
2. Click **Save & Close.**
3. You can drag the appointment block to change the start or finish times. When you release the mouse button, Outlook displays an editable bar that spans the selected time.
4. In the editable bar, enter an identifying name for the appointment. When you begin typing, Outlook creates an appointment with the default availability and reminder time. When an appointment is being edited on the calendar, it has sizing handles on the top and bottom.
5. If you want to change the appointment time span, drag the top or bottom sizing handle and press **Enter** key or click away from the bar to create the appointment.

19.4 RECURRING APPOINTMENTS

A recurring calendar item can happen at almost any regular interval, such as every Tuesday and Thursday, every other week, or the last weekday of every month. Configuring a recurrence creates multiple instances of the item on your calendar at the time interval you specify. You can set the item to recur until further notice, to end after a certain number of occurrences, or to end by a certain date. The individual occurrences of the recurring item are linked. When making Configure calendar item options changes to a recurring item, you can choose to update all occurrences or only an individual occurrence of the appointment. Recurring items are indicated on the calendar by circling arrows.

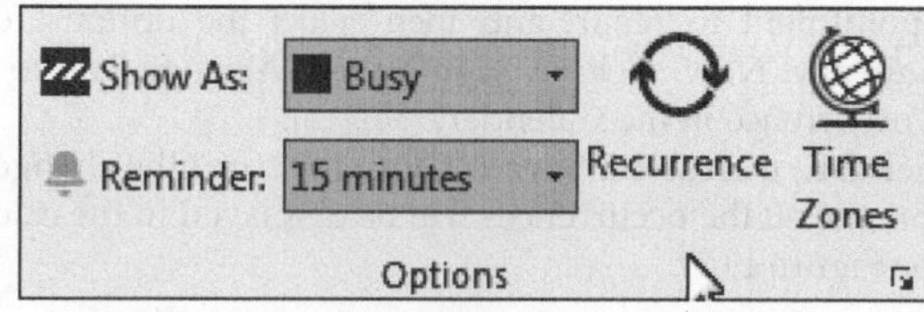

Figure 19.7 Appointment Recurrence menu

You can also maintain Privacy in your calendar. You can tag a calendar item as Private if you want to ensure that the details aren't displayed when you share your calendar or send calendar information to other people. Private items are indicated on the calendar by a lock, and identified to other people as Private Appointment rather than by the subject.

Make an existing appointment recurring, do the following:

1. Open the appointment that you want to set to recur and click **Recurrence.** (See Figure 19.7). It will display Appointment Recurrence dialog box as shown in Figure 19.8.

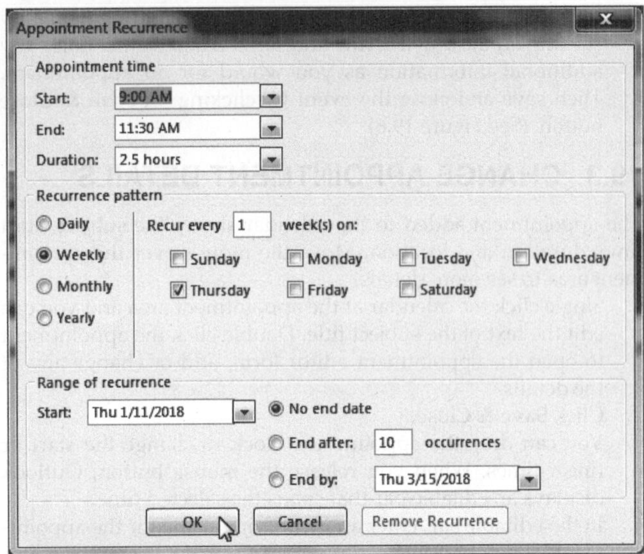

Figure 19.8 Appointment Recurrence dialog box

Figure 19.9 All the occurrences are displayed in the calendar

2. Specify frequency and the period of recurrence. Click the frequency - Daily, Weekly, Monthly, Yearly - that you want the appointment to recur, and then select the options for the frequency. Now click on **Month** from **Arrange Tab** to show all occurrence in the Calendar.
3. Click **OK**, then select **Save & Close** to record the changes.
4. Note the all the occurrences will be displayed in the calendar. (See Figure 19.9).

19.5 CREATE A MEETING

A meeting is a calendar event that you send to other people. You create a meeting the same way you do an appointment, but you invite attendees and may add a resource such as a conference room.

1. Double-click the appointment entry in the calendar, and click the **Invite Attendees button** in the **Attendees group**. (See Figure 19.10).
2. On the Invitation message form , click the **To** button to open the contacts list. Enter contact information for the people you want to invite to the meeting. (See Figure 19.11).

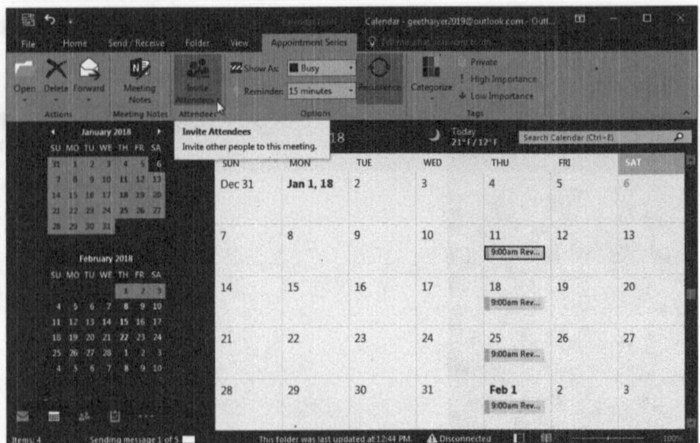

Figure 19.10 Invite Attendees button in the Attendees group

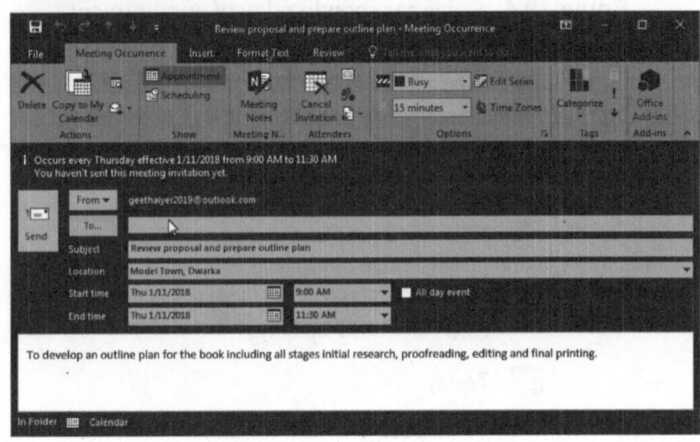

Figure 19.11 Contact information for invitee people

3. Select each Required or Optional attendee in turn, then click OK.
4. After adding all the attendees (See Figure 19.12), Click the **Send** button to send the invitation to each of them. You can double-click the meeting entry in your calendar to view the current status, which will show no response received. The invitation will also be received in the organizer's Inbox.

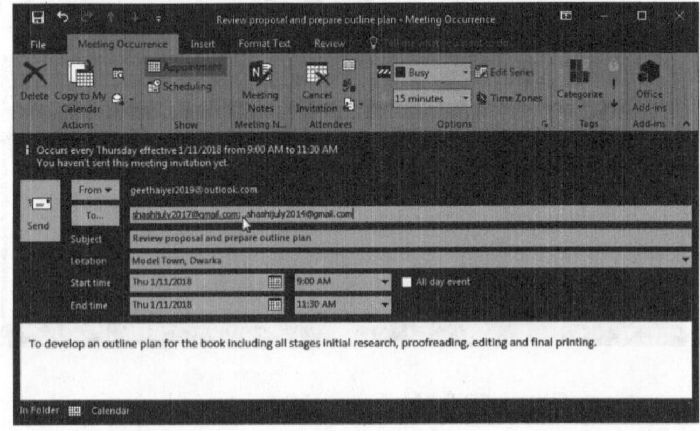

Figure 19.12 A dialog box after adding all attendees

19.6 RESPOND TO AN INVITATION

When you receive a meeting request from another Outlook user, the meeting appears on your calendar with your time scheduled as Tentative. Until you respond to the meeting request, the organizer doesn't know whether you plan to attend. You can respond to a meeting request in one of these four ways:

- **Accept the request** : Outlook deletes the meeting request and adds the meeting to your calendar.
- **Tentatively accept the request** : This option indicates that you might be able to attend the meeting but are undecided. Outlook deletes the meeting request and shows the meeting on your calendar as tentatively scheduled.
- **Propose a new meeting time** : Outlook sends your request to the meeting organizer for confirmation and shows the meeting with the original time on your calendar as tentatively scheduled.
- **Decline the request** : Outlook deletes the meeting request and removes the meeting from your calendar.

If you don't respond to a meeting request, the meeting remains on your calendar with your time shown as tentatively scheduled and the meeting details in gray font rather than black. When accepting or declining a meeting, you can choose whether to send a response to the meeting organizer. If you don't send a response, your acceptance will not be tallied, and the organizer will not know whether you are planning to attend the meeting. If you do send a response, you can add a message to the meeting organizer before sending it.

To respond to a meeting request :

1. In the meeting window, in the Reading Pane, or on the shortcut menu that appears when you right-click the meeting request, click Accept, Tentative, or Decline.
2. Choose whether to send a standard response, a personalized response, or no response at all.

19.7 ADD HOLIDAYS

Holidays are a type of event, and it can be useful to have them on your calendar so you can plan around days that you might not be working or that businesses might be closed. Instead of creating events on your calendar for individual holidays, you can have Outlook add them for you. When adding holidays to the calendar, you can choose from 112 countries or regions, and four religions. You can add multiple sets of holidays to your calendar, so if you work with clients or colleagues in another location, you can add those holidays to your calendar so you can anticipate scheduling issues. By default no holidays or special events are shown in the Calendar.

To add holidays to your Outlook calendar, follow these steps:

1. Open the Outlook Options dialog box and display the Calendar page, select **File** > **Options**. (See Figure 19.13).
2. In the **Calendar** options section, click the **Add Holidays** button to open the Add Holidays to Calendar dialog box. You can add holidays from a specific location or religion to your calendar. (See Figure 19.14).

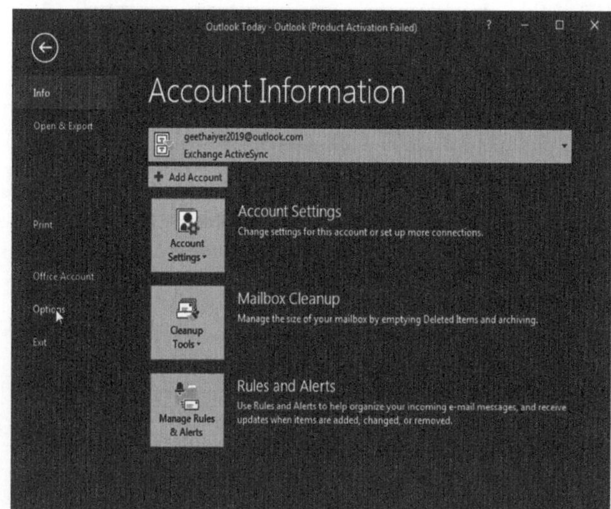

Figure 19.13 The Outlook Options dialog box

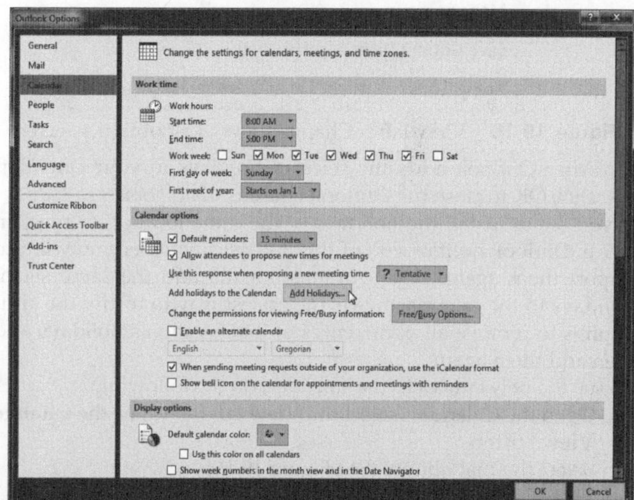

Figure 19.14 The Calendar options section with Add Holidays button

3. Select the check boxes to select the country or countries whose holidays you want to add to your calendar, and then click **OK** (See Figure 19.15). A progress dialog box is displayed for a very brief period which after display disappears. When the Holidays for the selected region (country) is finished, a confirmation message is displayed. The time may vary depending on how many countries you have selected. When you see the confirmation box, click **OK** to close it.

The entries for the selected country or countries are then imported into your calendar and National Holidays for the countries you checked will show up in your Outlook Calendar.

Figure 19.15 Add Holidays to Calendar dialog box

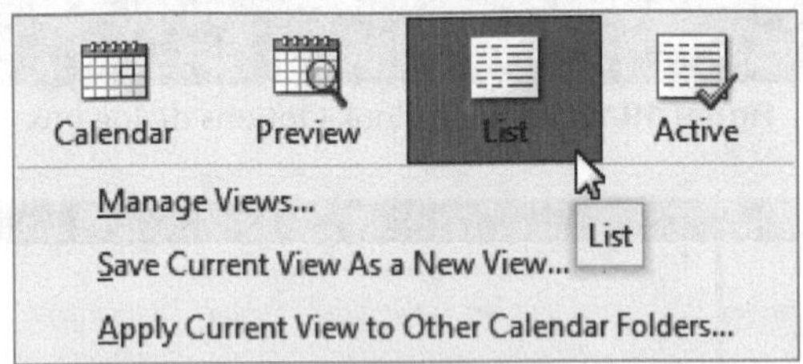

Figure 19.16 View tab > Change View >List option selected

4. After Outlook adds the selected holidays to your calendar, click OK to close the Outlook Options dialog box.

If you try to install the holidays of the same location or religion twice, Outlook notifies you of this and asks whether you want to import them again. If you unintentionally add the same set of holidays to the calendar twice, the easiest way to rectify the situation is to remove all occurrences of that location's holidays and then add them again.

To see the new entries in the calendar, do the following:

1. Open the Calendar, select the **View tab** then click the **Change View** button.
2. Select the **List** option. (See Figure 19.16).
3. The calendar contents will be displayed in START date order (See Figure 19.17).

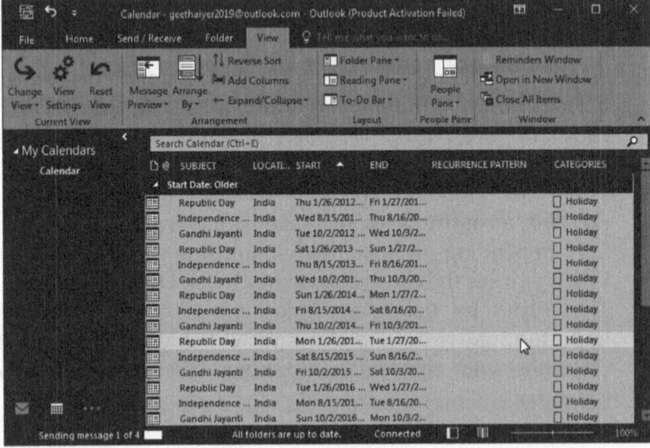

Figure 19.17 Calendar content displayed

If you have more than one country inserted, you can right-click **Location** then choose **Group By** to remove the entire events for one country. To remove a set of holidays from your calendar, follow these steps:

1. Search the calendar for category: holiday. Narrow the search to a specific location or holiday by adding search criteria if necessary, to locate the holidays you want to remove. Outlook highlights the search terms in the results.
2. Select individual holidays you want to remove; or click any holiday in the list to activate the list, and then press Ctrl+A to select all the holidays in the search results. Then press the Delete key.

19.8 REPORT FREE/ BUSY TIME

When creating an appointment or event, you indicate your availability (referred to as Free/Busy time) by marking it as Free, Working Elsewhere, Tentative, Busy, or Out of Office. The appointment or event is color-coded on your calendar to match the availability you indicate.

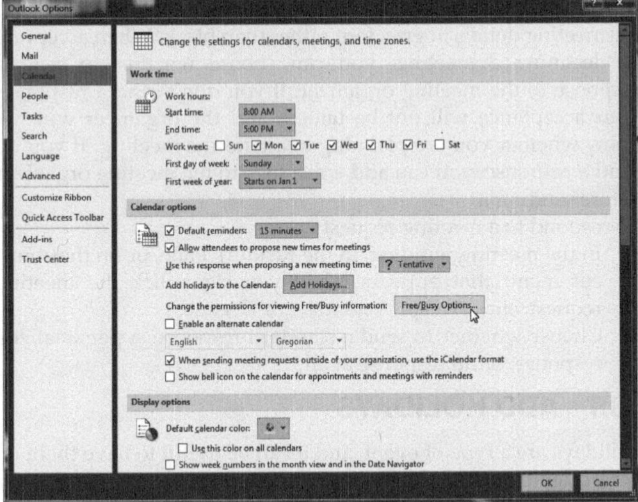

Figure 19.18 Free/Busy Options button in the Calendar Options

If free/busy information is available for meeting attendees, the status is indicated by the standard free/busy colors and patterns that match the legend at the bottom of the page. If no information is available Outlook shows the time with gray diagonal stripes.

Free/ busy time is available only for attendees in your organization or another connected organization, or attendees that share free/busy information through a web service. Outlook can help you choose the most suitable times to hold meetings, based on reports from the proposed attendees, giving details of their availability:

1. Open Outlook and select **File** > **Options** > **Calendar** > **Free/Busy Options** button. (See Figure 19.18).
2. Click the **Free/Busy Options** button in the Calendar Options category. It will display Internet Free/Busy Options dialog box (See Figure 19.19).
3. Check the box for **Publication at location**, and provide the address for a networked folder or drive that is accessible by all potential attendees, then Click **OK**.

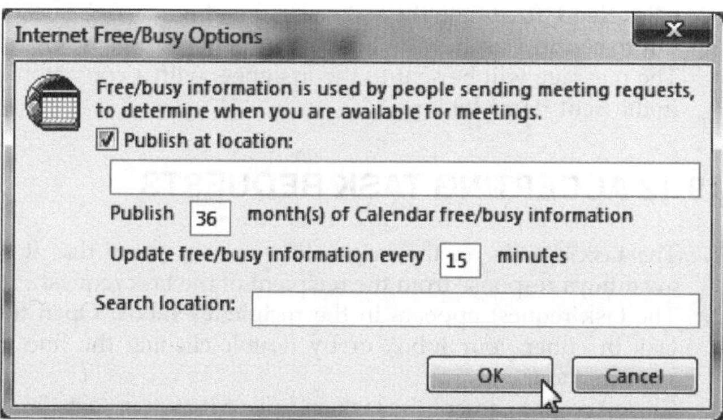

Figure 19.19 Internet Free/Busy Options dialog box

19.9 SCHEDULE A MEETING

A primary difficulty when scheduling a meeting is finding a time that works for all the people who need to attend it. Scheduling meetings through Outlook is significantly simpler than other methods of scheduling meetings, particularly when you need to accommodate the schedules of several people. Outlook displays the individual and collective schedules of people within your own organization, and of people outside of your organization who have published their calendars to the Internet. You can review attendees' schedules to locate a time when everyone is available, or have Outlook find a convenient time for you.

You can use the reported free/busy information to help set up a new meeting. You can use Scheduling to set up a new meeting or to revise the timing for an existing meeting.

1. Create a meeting again with initial details then click **Scheduling** to show free/busy times.
2. From options tab, choose AutoPick Next. (See Figure 19.20).

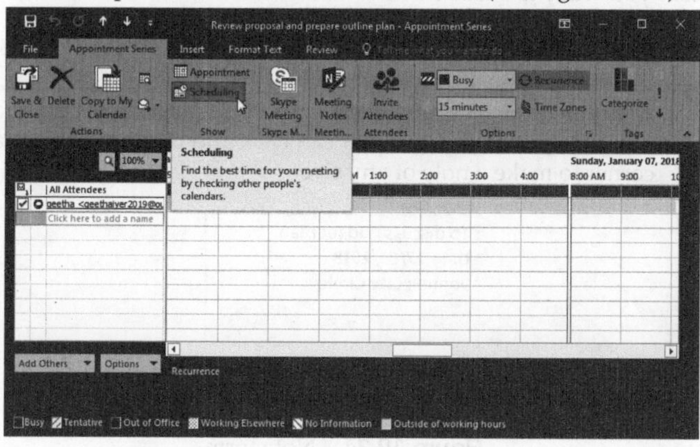

Figure 19.20 A dialog box to schedule a meeting

3. Click **Send** to add the revised details to the calendar and send updated invitation to all the attendees.

19.10 CREATING TASKS

A *task* is an activity that should be completed by a specified date and time which you can assign to yourself, another Outlook user, or a group of users. Tasks can be recurring if they are performed at regular intervals. You can attach files to tasks you send to other users.

Many people keep a list of things to do - on paper, in a spreadsheet, or by using a combination of paper and electronic methods. In Outlook, you can combine your various lists into one list, enhanced with reminders and tracking.

If you create a task, you initially own the task. Only a task's owner can make changes to the task. This means that the owner can modify the properties (the percent complete, the status, the start date, and so on) of all tasks that the owner creates and owns. When a task is assigned to someone else and that person accepts the task, the assignee becomes the owner of the task. The creator can then view the task's properties, but can no longer change them - only the current owner can make those changes.

Outlook can create and manage implicit tasks as follow-ups of other Outlook items. It can also create explicit tasks, which can be assigned to others. To create implicit task do the following:

1. Right-click an Outlook item, select **Follow up** and select the **Flag Message** option. (See Figure 19.21)

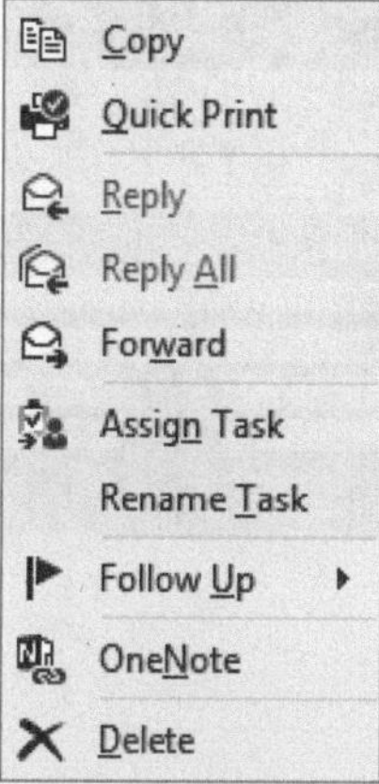

Figure 19.21 In Follow up drop-down menu the Flag Message option selected

2. The follow-up item is added to the Tasks folder and also appears on the To-Do-List.

To create an explicit task:

1. To display the Task folder, Click the ellipsis (...) on the Navigation bar and select Tasks. Click on New Item button > Task > New Task (See Figure 19.22).
2. Click Type a new task in the Tasks folder, or the To-Do-List. (See Figure 19.23)
3. In the Subject box, type a name for the task. If you have got a lot to enter, keep the subject short, and then add the details in the task body.
4. If there is a fixed start or end date, set the Start date or Due date.
5. Set the task's priority by using Priority. You can choose a "High," "Normal" or "Low" priority.
6. If you want a pop-up reminder, check Reminder, and set the date and time.
7. Click **Task** > **Save & Close**.

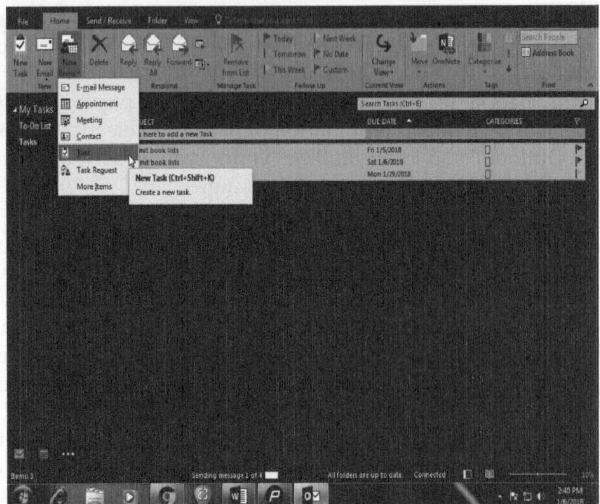

Figure 19.22 New Item button > Task > New Task selected

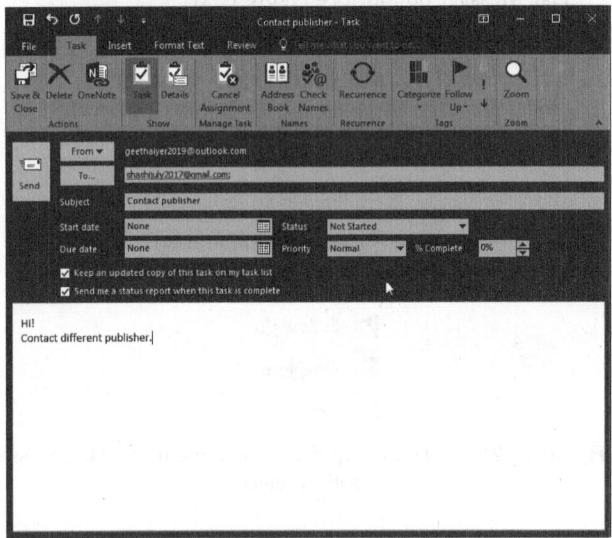

Figure 19.23 New task selected

Microsoft Outlook 2016 organizes your emails, calendars, contacts, tasks, and to-do lists, all in one place. It all starts with your email account. From there you can start working with emails, turning them into tasks or appointments, and storing the people you interact with in your contacts, so you never have to remember an email address or phone number.

19.11 ASSIGNING TASKS

The main benefit of using Outlook to assign tasks is that you can receive status reports on assigned tasks and view these status reports in your Tasks folder. Also, the activities of sending task requests and processing responses to those requests is automated. To assign an existing task, do the following

1. To assign a task to another user, click **Assign Task** in the **Manage Task group** once you have created the Task. Once accepted, the assignee will become the Owner of the task.
2. Click **To** and select a name or names from the Address Book.
3. Click **Send**, to initiate the task-assignment request, then click **OK** to confirm the new ownership.
4. The message will be sent to the assignee, with a copy stored in the **Sent Items** folder

19.12 ACCEPTING TASK REQUESTS

1. The task details on the originating system show that it is awaiting a response from the recipient of the task request.
2. The task request appears in the recipient's Inbox. Open the task in either your Inbox or by double-clicking the line in your calendar.
3. Click **Accept** to accept the task and place it in your task list.
4. Add a Priority or Category, if needed.
5. Click **Decline** to delete the task from your Calendar. As a courtesy, be sure to send a message giving a reason.

19.13 FINISHING A TASK

When you have finished a task that has been assigned to you, select the task and click the Mark Complete button on the Ribbon. This will remove the task from your to-do bar and calendar.

19.14 OUTLOOK NOTES

Notes are the electronic equivalent of paper sticky notes. Use notes to jot down questions, ideas, reminders, and anything you would write on paper. You can leave notes open on the screen while you work. This is convenient when you are using notes for saving information you might need later, such as directions or text you want to reuse in other items or documents. To create a note, do the following:

1. Click the **New Note** button on the Home tab, or press Ctrl+Shift+N to start a new note.
2. Type the text in the note. (See Figure 19.24). The notes are of a standard initial size, but you can click and drag an edge or a corner to make a note of any size.

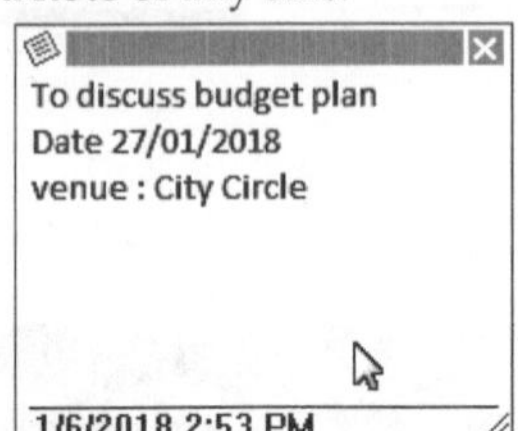

Figure 19.24 Note form

3. You can leave the note open while you work, and drag it to any location on your screen for easier viewing.
4. To close the note, click the [X] close button.

To change the view settings of your Notes folder, do the following:

1. Select the **View** tab and click **List** to allow more space for the note titles. (See Figure 19.25).
2. Right-click a note to copy or print it, to forward it to another user, or to delete it.

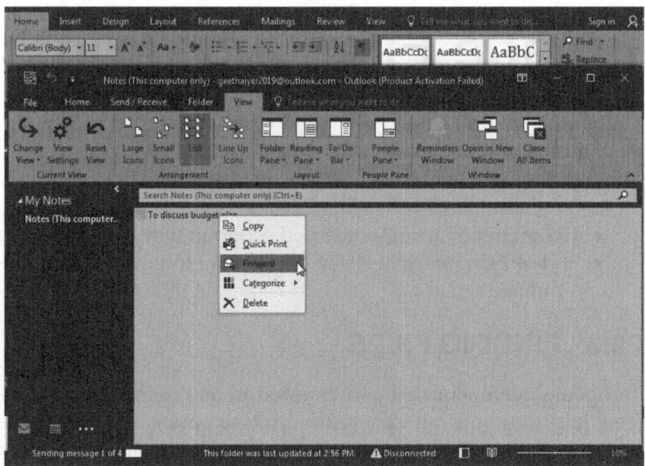

Figure 19.25 View setting of Note folder

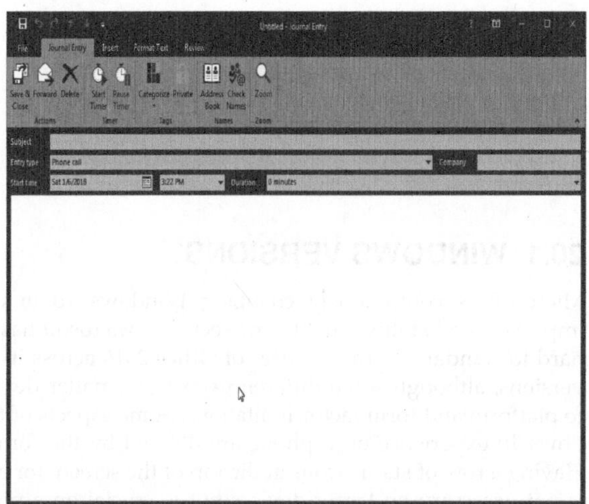

Figure 19.26 Journal Entry

19.15 JOURNAL

Microsoft Outlook has a tracking feature to track your work activities in your work day, it is called *Journal*. Journal is a type of project log book. Journal automatically records actions that you choose which relate to specific contacts and puts the actions in a Timeline view. You can use Journal to track Microsoft Outlook items, such as e-mail messages or meetings. It can also track other Microsoft Office files, such as Word documents or Excel workbooks. Journal keeps a record of any interaction that you want to remember - even something that is not located on your computer, such as a phone conversation or a paper letter that you mailed or received. To find Journal do the following:

1. On the **Navigation Bar**, click **ellipsis (...)** > **Folders** > **Journal**. (Or just press Ctrl+8).
2. You can work with your existing Journal entries or create new ones from the Folder pane. Select the **Journal Entry** then enter your activity details. (See Figure 19.26).
3. Click **Save & Close** to see the entry on the Timeline. (See Figure 19.27). The Timeline view shows when each item and document was created, saved, sent, received, opened, and modified. When you change the time fields used to display items on the timeline, the location and duration of the items may change on the timeline.

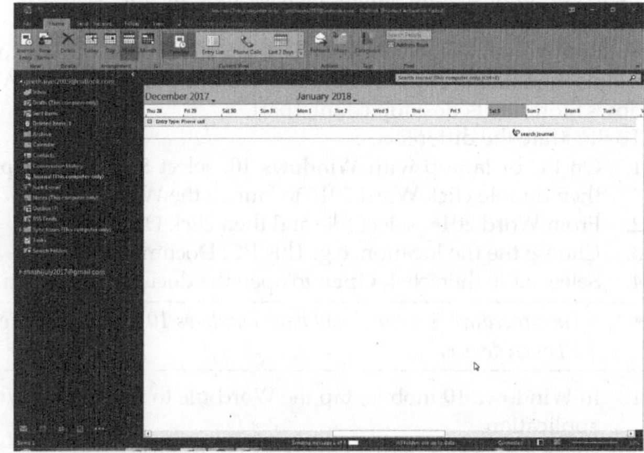

Figure 19.27 Journal Entry on Timeline

CHAPTER 20

Manage Files and Fonts

20.1 WINDOWS VERSIONS

Microsoft is continuously changing Windows 10 in order to improve its reliability, quality and security. Microsoft has worked hard to standardize the features of Office 2016 across its various versions, although some differences exit on smaller devices due to platform and form factor limitations. Some aspects of the Windows 10 experience on a phone are defined by the form factor. Having a row of status icons at the top of the screen, for example, is not necessary on larger devices but is crucial on a phone, for quickly checking cellular signal strength and remaining battery life. Windows 10 platform is designed to run on more than just PCs. For phones and small tablets, that means Windows 10 Mobile. The version of Windows 10 that runs on mobile devices is built on the same core code as Windows 10 for desktop PCs, and it runs the same universal apps, delivered through the same Windows Store, as its desktop counterpart.
To illustrate the differences:

1. On PC or laptop with Windows 10, select **Start** > **All apps**, then double click Word 2016 to launch the Word application.
2. From Word 2016, select File and then click **Open**.
3. Choose the file location, e.g. This PC, Documents,
4. Select a file then click **Open** to open the document for editing.

☞ *The procedure is same if you have windows 10 in Tablet mode on a Touch device.*

1. In Windows 10 mobile, tap the Word tile to launch the Word application.
2. Select a file from the Today list, or tap Browse.
3. Choose a location app, e.g. tap This Device.
4. Select the folder and tap the check button to open that folder.
5. Select a document, then tap the check button to open the selected document - ready for editing.

20.2 LIBRARY LOCATION

In the Windows 10 environment, the Documents Library is the default location for saving new files. When saving a document for the first time, you must specify a filename, the file type, and a place where you can access the document. The filename should help users find and identify the file, and the file location should be convenient for the file's future users. You can save files to portable storage devices such as a flash drive, to your computer's hard drive, to a network location, or to OneDrive. The Save As command enables users to save their work to the cloud and access the document quickly from any computer or tablet.
Office 2016 allows you to reopen a document you have saved previously in a library location, from any office apps:

1. From within an app, select File and choose **Open**. Now you can choose the appropriate location of the document you want to reopen:
   - **Recent** : Recently worked document will be shown here
   - **OneDrive**: Document stored on cloud will be shown here
   - **This PC**: This will show document stored on your computer.

20.3 FINDING FILES

To open a document that is not stored in one of the offered top-level locations you can choose the Browse option to look for the document or search the document by name. For example, to track a document named "cyber safety" in office 2016, do the following:

1. Open Word 2016 and select **File** > **Open** and click on **Browse** option. A dialog box will be displayed as shown in Figure 20.1.

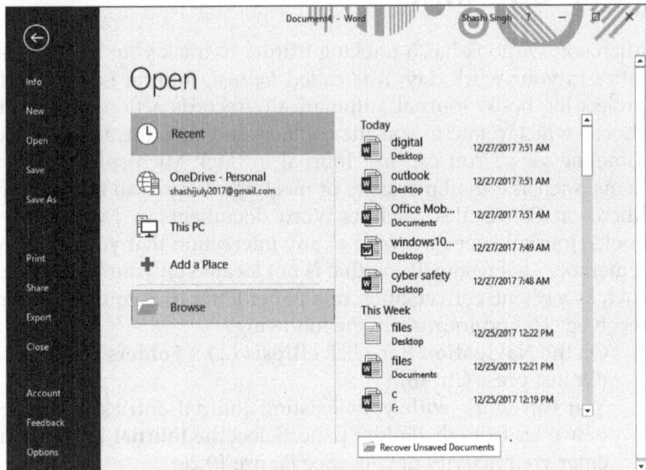

Figure 20.1 Word 2016 File > Open

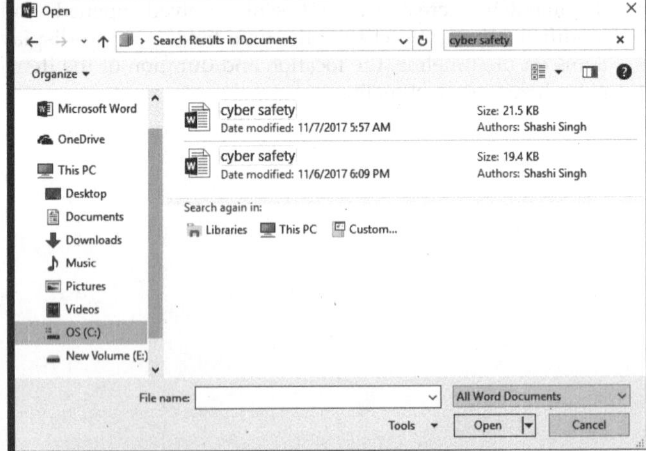

Figure 20.2 Matching document for the search term is displayed

2. Click on the Search box located in the top right corner and type the search term say "*cyber safety*". It will display the matching documents that contain the specified word in their titles or in their content. See Figure 20.2.
3. Right-Click a file, and select **Open file location**, to see the folder where it is stored (See Figure 20.3). Now click on **Open** button or double-click the file to open it in Word.

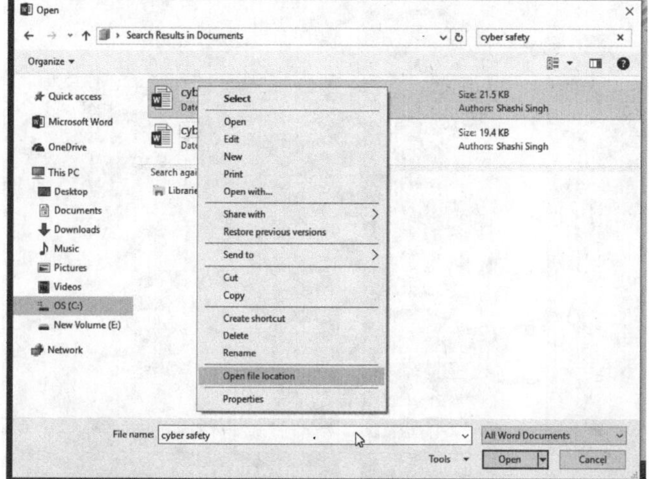

Figure 20.3 Dialog box showing Open file location

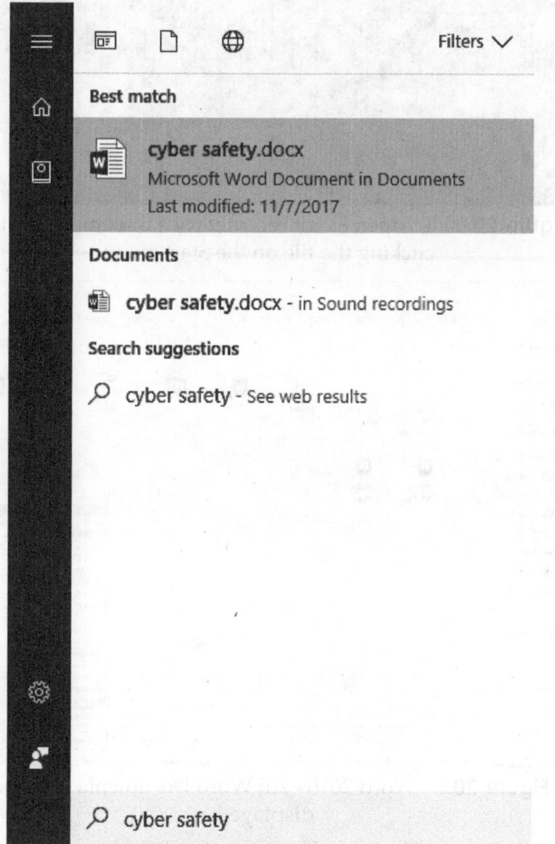

Figure 20.4 Windows 10 Search box

You can also locate documents using operating system Search facility. To use operating system Search facility do the following:

1. In Windows 10, click the Search box and type the search term say "*cyber safety*" as shown in Figure 20.4. It will display matching documents, applications and other files.

You can also locate documents directly in File Explorer. To locate documents directly in File Explorer, do the following:

1. In File Explorer select **This PC** and type the search term to automatically invoke Search as shown in Figure 20.5.

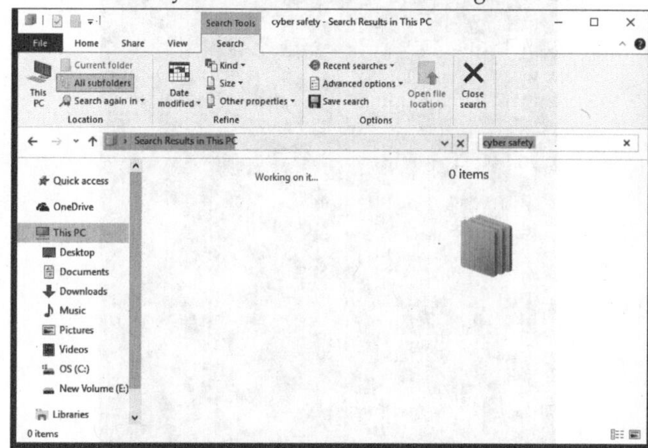

Figure 20.5 Search using File Explorer

☞ *Although Word 2016 is used in these examples, but you can use same search procedures for documents in other Office applications such as Excel 2016 and PowerPoint 2016 also.*

20.4 RECENT DOCUMENTS

You can also open the documents that you worked previously. To open list of recently used documents do the following:

1. Select **File** > **Open** then **Recent** and click an entry in the Recent list to open it. (See Figure 20.6).

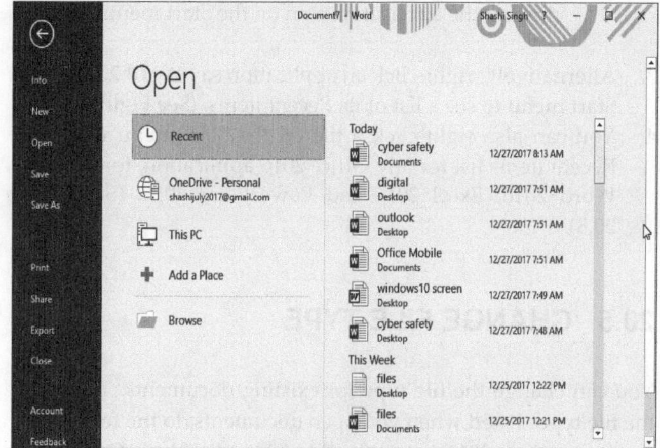

Figure 20.6 To open list of recently used document using File > Open

2. You can also right-click on the application icon on the taskbar to display the "Jump list", which shows recent items.

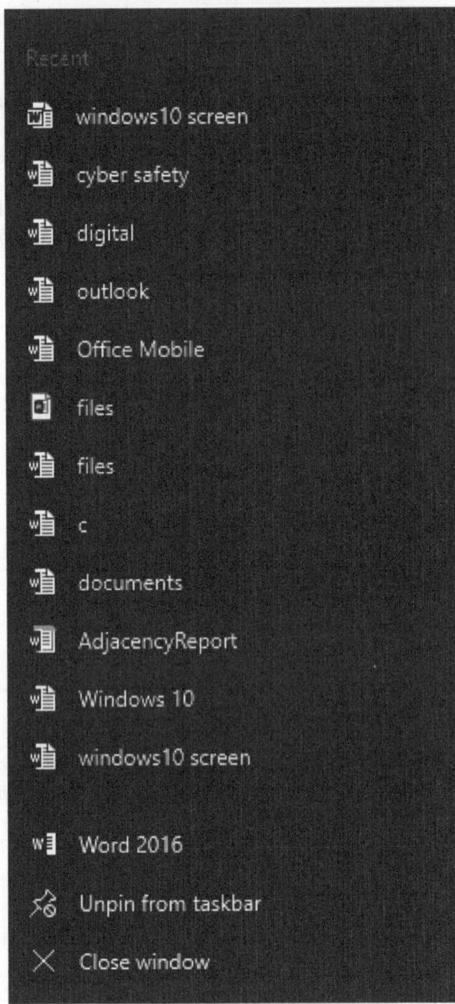

Figure 20.7 To open list of recently used document by right clicking the application icon on the Start menu

3. Alternatively, right-click an application say Word 2016 on the Start menu to see a list of its Recent items. (See Figure 20.7).
4. You can also right-click a tile on the Start menu to see the Recent items list for any Office 2016 application, for example, Word 2016, Excel 2016 and PowerPoint 2016. (See Figure 20.8).

20.5 CHANGE FILE TYPE

You can change the file type for existing documents. To change the file types listed when you open documents do the following:

1. From Word 2016, select the **File** tab and click on **Open**. Now select the file location, say Documents.
2. Choose the file type or group of types, say All Word Documents. The specified file type will be displayed. See Figure 20.9.

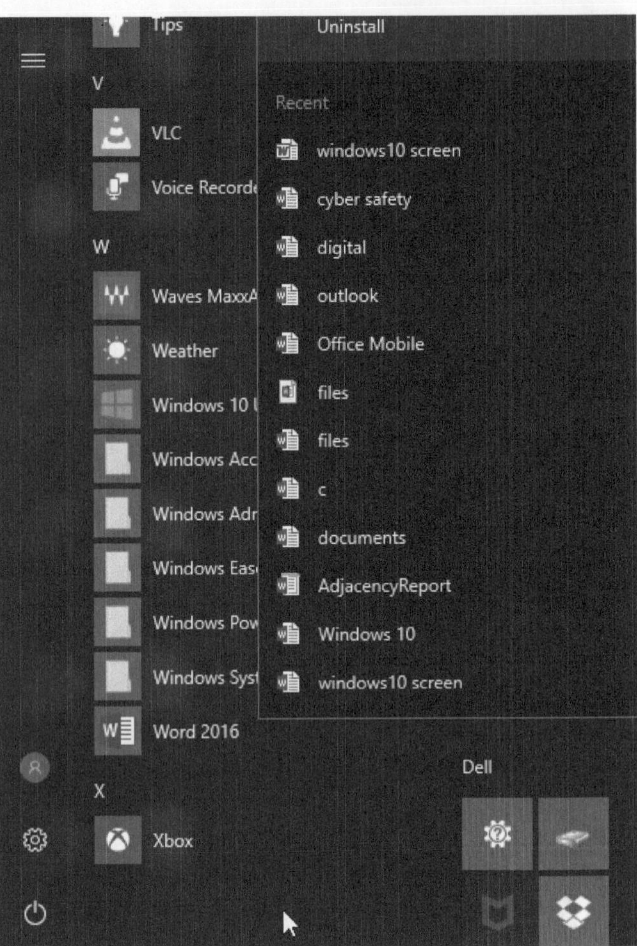

Figure 20.8 To open list of recently used document by right clicking the tile on the Start menu

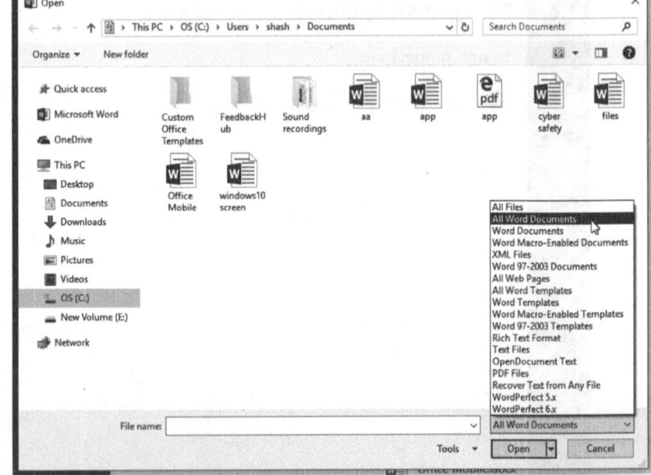

Figure 20.9 Word 2016 - All Word Documents file types displayed

You can also see files with their extensions. To show the file name extension for the documents do the following:

1. Open File Explorer and click on **View** Tab and check the box : File name extensions as shown in Figure 20.10.

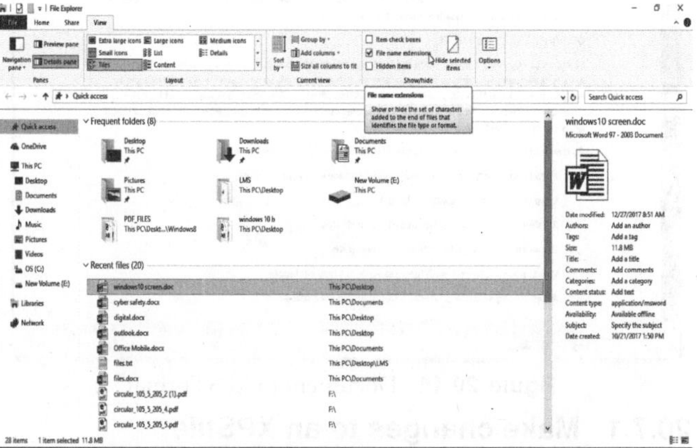

Figure 20.10 File Explorer to show file name extension for the documents

20.6 XML FILE FORMAT

Office 2016 uses file formats based on XML. The XML formats are automatically compressed and can be upto 75% smaller, saving disk space and reducing transmission sizes and times when you send files via email or across the internet. Files are structured in a modular fashion, which keeps different data components in the file separate from each other. This allows files to be opened, even if a component within the file is damaged or corrupted. The XML file format is applied to Word 2016, Excel 2016 and PowerPoint 2016. This XML file types include:

Application	XML file type	Extension
Word	Document	.docx
	Macro enabled XML file type for Word	.docm
	Word template	.dotx
	Macro enabled word template	.dotm
Excel	Workbook	.xlsx
	Macro enabled XML file type	.xlsm
	Excel Template	.xltx
	Macro enabled excel template	.xltm
	Non-XML binary workbook	.xlsb
	Macro-enabled add-in	.xlam
PowerPoint	Presentation	.pptx
	Macro enabled PowerPoint show	.pptm
	Template	.potx
	Macro-enabled Template	.potm
	Macro-enabled add-in	.ppam
	show	.ppsx
	Macro-enabled show	.ppsm

File format helps you to identify the type of content specific file contains. For example, .xltm means excel file which has macros installed on it. You can change the file format to previous versions to support your co-workers who are still working with older versions of Microsoft Office applications.

20.7 SAVE AS PDF or XPS

Sometimes you allow other users to view and print your document without making any changes in it. These could include resumes, legal documents or newsletter etc. Office 2016 provides two in-built file formats.

Portable Document Format (PDF)

PDF preserves document formatting and enables file sharing. When the PDF format file is viewed on-line or printed, it retains the format that you intended. The PDF format is also useful for documents that will be reproduced using commercial printing methods. PDF is accepted as a valid format by many agencies and organizations.

XML Paper Specification (XPS)

XPS also preserves document formatting and protects the data content. However, it is not widely used. The XPS format ensures that, when the file is views on-line or printed, it retains the exact format you intended.

Microsoft Office 2016 enables you to save your word document in PDF format so that user who has free Adobe reader can read your document. XPS is a competitive product from Microsoft, which also provides a free XPS viewer.

All the Office 2016 applications include the capability to save documents or reports in the PDF and XPS formats. To save an Office document in either format do the following:

1. Open the document in the appropriate application say open Word document using Word 2016 as shown in Figure 20.11.

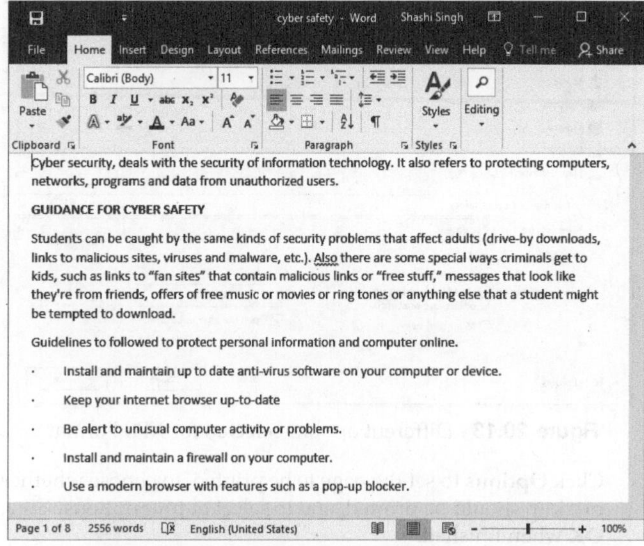

Figure 20.11 Document opened in Word 2016

2. Click the **File** tab.
3. Click **Save As**. A Save As dialog box appears. Select the location and folder to store the new copy.

4. In the File Name box, enter a name for the file, if you haven't already. In the Save as type list, click **XPS Document** (See Figure 20.12). If you want the file to open in the selected format after saving, select the Open file after publishing check box. If the document requires high print quality, click Standard (publishing on-line and printing). If the file size is more important than print quality, click Minimum size (publishing on-line). (See Figure 20.13).

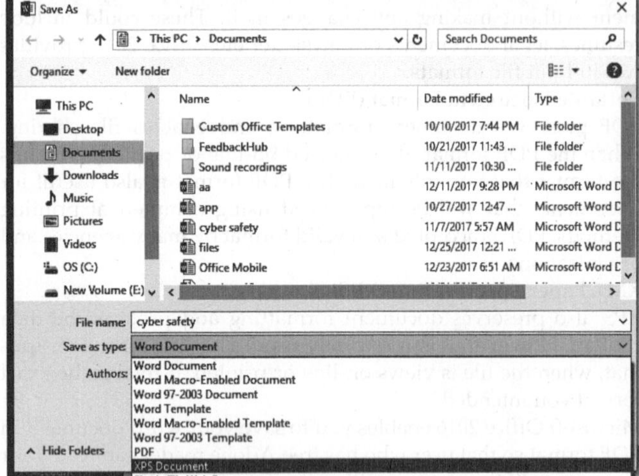

Figure 20.12 Saving document in XPS Format

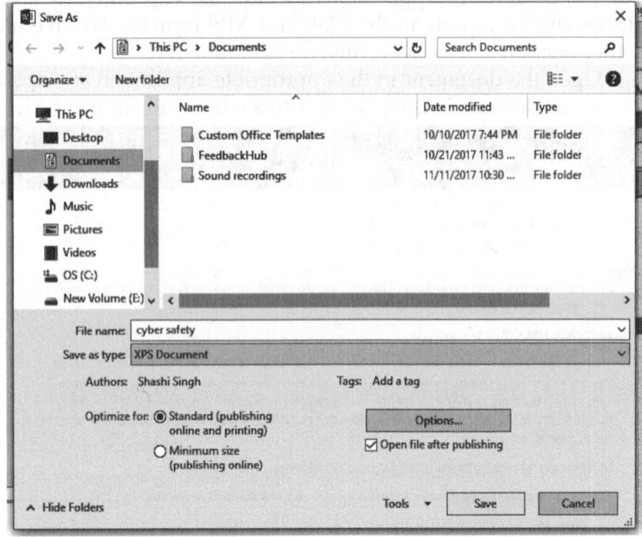

Figure 20.13 Different options selected for XPS Format

5. Click **Options** to set the page to be printed, to choose whether markup should be printed, and to select output options. Click **OK** when finished.
6. Click Save. The document is saved and then displayed using chosen format. (See Figure 20.14).

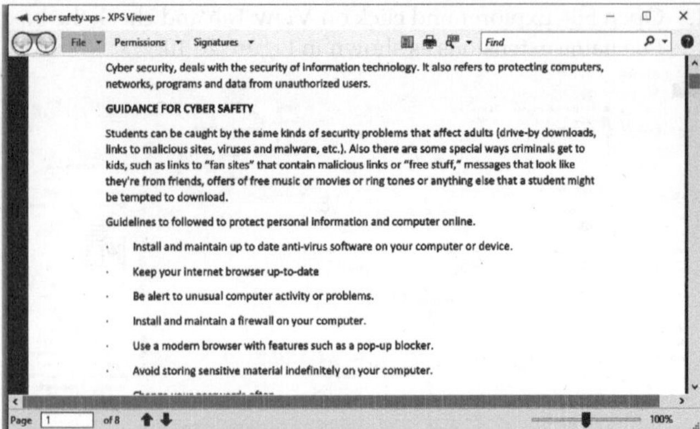

Figure 20.14 Document in XPS Format

20.7.1 Make changes to an XPSfile

Because the purpose of XPS files is to keep them from being changed, you cannot easily convert or save a XPS file into another file format if you don't have the source file.

To change the XPS file, open the original Office file in your Office program, make your changes, and then save the file in XPS format again.

20.8 FONTS IN OFFICE 2016

There are a number of fonts provided with Office 2016 such as Calibri, Arial, Comic Sans MS, Century, Impact, Times New Roman, Verdana etc. You can preview text using these and all other Windows fonts. To preview text using different available fonts do the following:

1. First select the text you want to preview. Now from **Home** Tab, click on the down arrow on the Font box.
2. Scroll the list to choose the required font and move the mouse pointer over the font name to see the immediate preview using that font (See Figure 20.15).
3. Click the desired font name to put the changes into effect. This helps indicate how the text will appear.

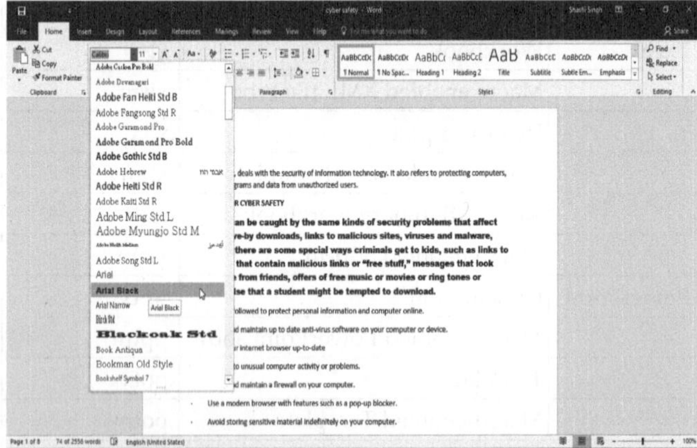

Figure 20.15 Preview of selected font

By default, when you create a new blank document, the text you start typing will be a Normal style using a font of Calibri with a size of 11. This is a commendable choice, but it might not be right for you. You can change that default. Change its styling to be the way you want it. For example, you could change the font size, the font family and even the colour. To change your Word 2016 default font style and size do the following:

1. Open any document or create a new document. Let us create a new document. You can see as shown in Figure 20.16, default font style is Calibri and size is 11.

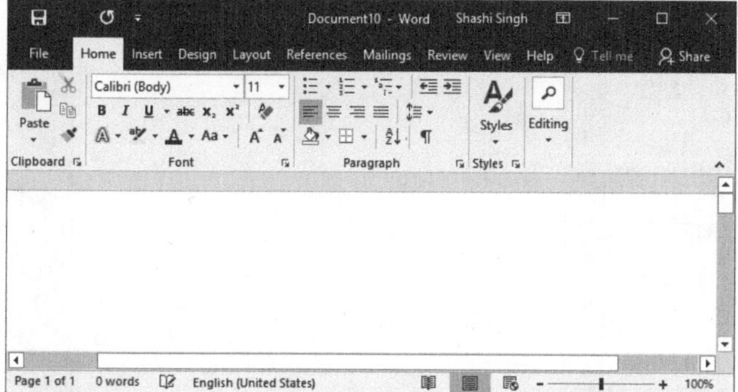

Figure 20.16 New document showing default font style and size

2. Click the **Home** tab in the top left corner. Font dialog box will appear.
3. Select your desired Font style for example, Arial and Size as 12 as shown in Figure 20.17.

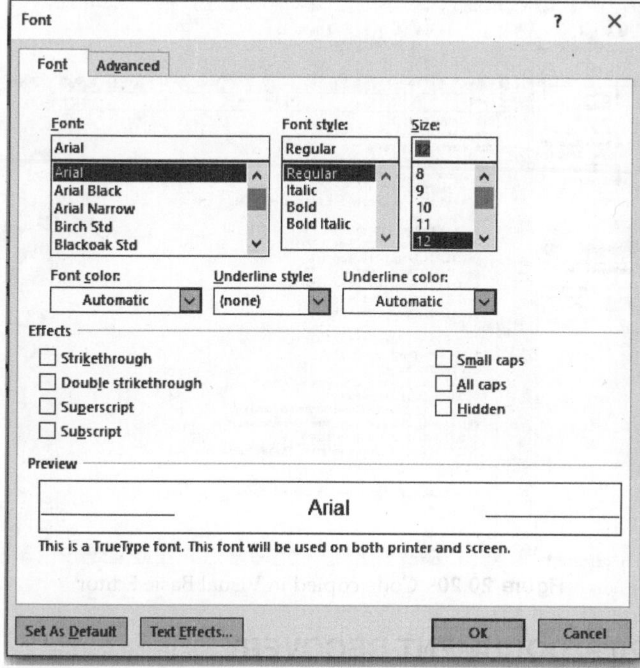

Figure 20.17 Font dialog box with Font style Arial and size 12

4. Click Set as Default in the bottom left corner from Font dialog box.
5. Select the radio button "**For this document only**" in the dialog box that appears.
6. Click **OK** to confirm your changes. (See Figure 20.18).

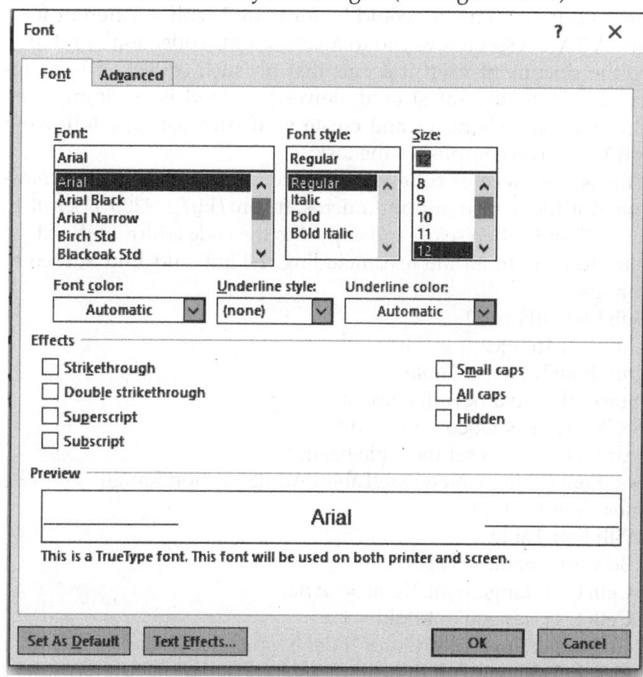

Figure 20.18 Confirm your changes dialog box

20.8.1 Create and Run ListAllFonts

When you are creating a document on your system, it is easy to know what fonts are being used the list of fonts is limited to those available on the system. If you receive a document from a different person, however, the other person's system may have different fonts installed than you do. This means that their Word document could be formatted with fonts you don't even have on your system. Today there are literally hundreds of sites where you can find and download free fonts for your personal use, some even for business use.

With the help of a macro available from Microsoft, you can create a document that provides a sample of every font on your system. Macros are little snippets of Visual Basic for Applications code, and they get stored with the Normal.dot file of your installation of Word. Therefore, you have access to this (and any other macro) whenever you need to list your fonts. All you do is go to the View and select Macros, and then View Macros. When you click Run, the macro will provide you with a list of every font in your computer.

If you want to generate a list of fonts used within a document (as opposed to a list of fonts available on a system), you have a couple of choices. First of all, you can open the Word document in a text editor and look around in the parts of the document you don't normally see in Word. Near the end of the file you should see a list of fonts used in the document. If you do this, however, you should be very careful to not make any changes to the Word document while it is open in your text editor. Doing so can easily make the document no longer usable in Word.

A Word-based solution is to simply look through each character in a document and check out what font is used to format the character. A character-by-character approach is necessary because each character could be formatted with a different font, and VBA doesn't allow you to access a fonts collection in relation to the document itself it seems that no such collection is maintained. Thus, the safest (and slowest) method is to simply step through each character and create your own list. The following VBA macro accomplishes the task:

This is the piece of code you need to add to your Word's Normal.dot file. (visit support.microsoft.com/kb/209205) Scroll to ListAllFonts, then select and copy it to the code editor in Word, be sure to include all the text including the Sub and End Sub commands.

```
Sub ListAllFonts()
Dim J As Integer
Dim FontTable As Table
'Start off with a new document
Set NewDoc = Documents.Add
'Add a table and set the table header
Set FontTable = NewDoc.Tables.Add(Selection.Range, FontNames.Count + 1, 2)
With FontTable
 .Borders.Enable = False
 .Cell(1, 1).Range.Font.Name = "Arial"
 .Cell(1, 1).Range.Font.Bold = 1
 .Cell(1, 1).Range.InsertAfter "Font Name"
 .Cell(1, 2).Range.Font.Name = "Arial"
 .Cell(1, 2).Range.Font.Bold = 1
 .Cell(1, 2).Range.InsertAfter "Font Example"
End With
'Go through all the fonts and add them to the table
For J = 1 To FontNames.Count
 With FontTable
 .Cell(J + 1, 1).Range.Font.Name = "Arial"
 .Cell(J + 1, 1).Range.Font.Size = 10
 .Cell(J + 1, 1).Range.InsertAfter FontNames(J)
 .Cell(J + 1, 2).Range.Font.Name = FontNames(J)
 .Cell(J + 1, 2).Range.Font.Size = 10
 .Cell(J + 1, 2).Range.InsertAfter "ABCDEFG abcdefg 1234567890"
 End With
Next J
FontTable.Sort SortOrder:=wdSortOrderAscending
End Sub
```

So here is what you do. First, copy all of the code text above (shown formatted in Courier) to the Clipboard. Then, in Word, select View, and then View Macros.

Write a name for the macro in the Macro Name edit box say ListAllFonts, do not give spaces in the names here. Then click Create. Word will open the Normal.dot file and enter the Visual Basic editor at this point (See Figure 20.19).

Here, select everything in the Normal - New Macros(Code) window and delete it, so that you have nothing in the window at all. You will be bringing everything you need from this blog entry.

Then, copy the code above into the window. It will then look as shown in Figure 20.20.

This is the final window. Now select File, Close and Return to Microsoft Word, and then you are back in the normal Word environment.

Reselect View Macros, click the macro name "ListAllFonts", and then click Run to execute the macro code. A new document is created, displaying all font names and examples in the form of a table. (See Figure 20.21).

Save the new document, to store the table of font names and examples.

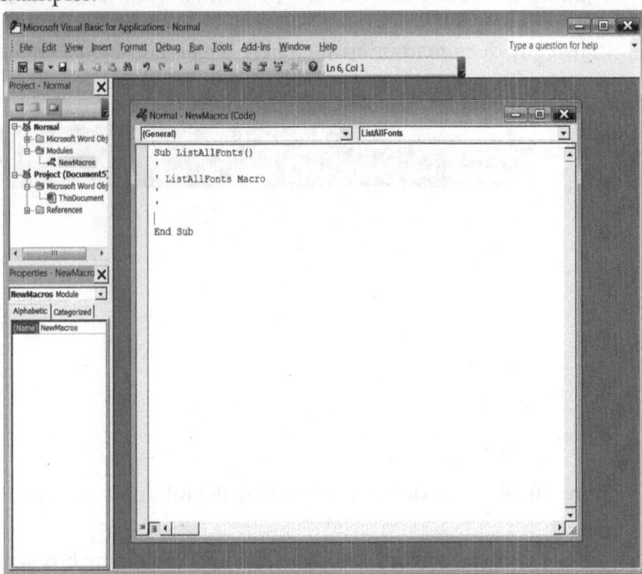

Figure 20.19 Word with Visual Basic editor

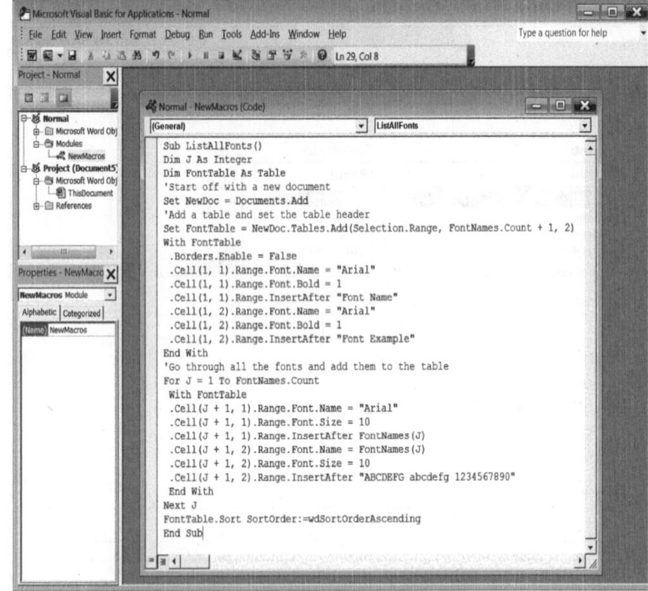

Figure 20.20 Code copied in Visual Basic Editor

20.9 DOCUMENT RECOVERY

Many of us have experienced a situation where we have created a Word document and then accidentally closed it out without saving it. The next time you start the application concerned, the Document Recovery feature will recover as much as possible.

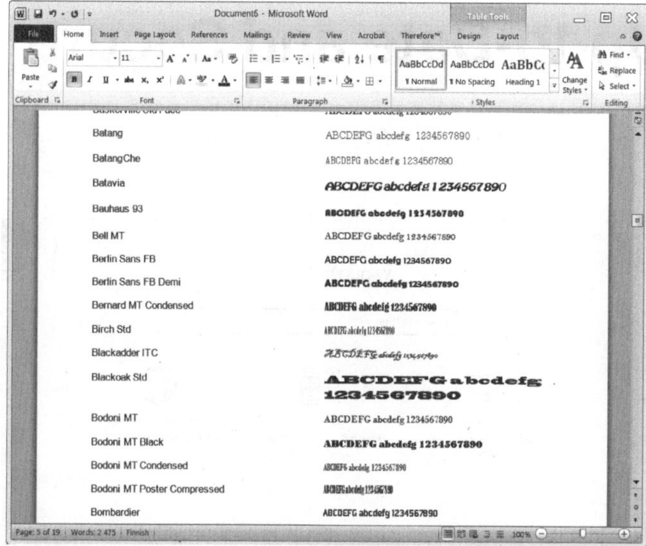

Figure 20.21 Document displaying all font names and examples

Restart Word to look for the recovered document. End all Word related processes. Restart Word and then see if the missing file is displayed in the Document Recovery task pane. By default, Word searches for Auto-Recover files each time it starts. Double click the Auto-Recover files one by one. If you find your lost Word file, save it immediately.

1. Open the program (e.g. Word) and click on **Recover Unsaved Document** as shown in Figure 20.22.

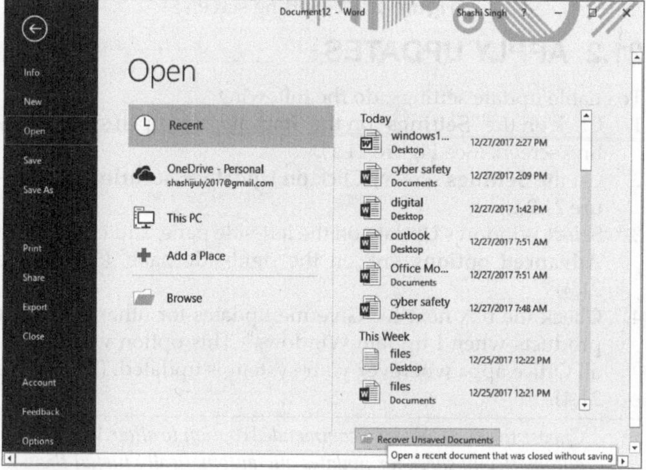

Figure 20.22 Program showing Recover unsaved Document

2. An open dialog box will be displayed (See Figure 20.23). Choose the required document.
3. Select **File** > **Save As** to save the document.

Another situation you might find yourself in: accidentally closing out of a previously saved document but failing to save the latest changes. Microsoft Word will help you recover up to the last 10 minutes of your work. You can also change the amount of time you would like Word to save a recoverable copy of your work.

1. Click the **File** tab > **Manage Documents**.
2. Locate and click on the latest autosave version to recover the latest changes made to your document. Don't forget to Save your recovered Word document.

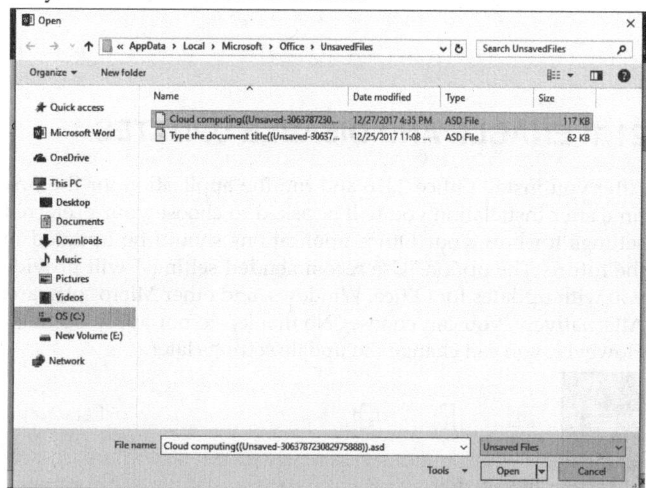

Figure 20.23 Open dialog box showing unsaved documents

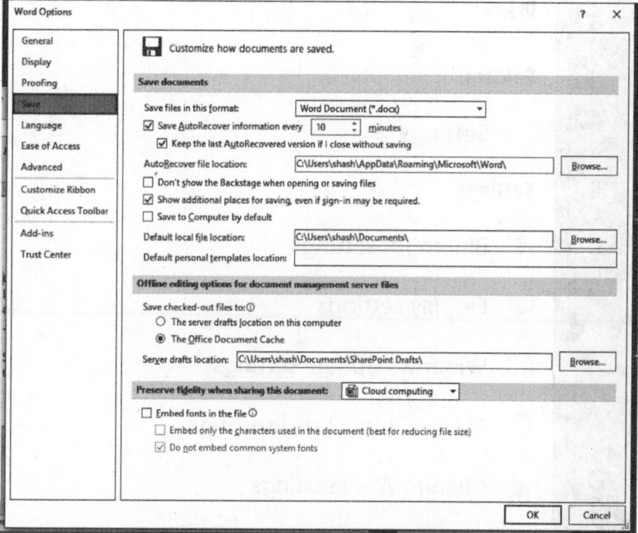

Figure 20.24 Word Options dialog box

Change the save Auto-Recover information time

If you would like change the frequency with which Microsoft Word automatically saves a recoverable copy of your document, follow the steps below. The default time is set to 10 minutes.

1. Click the **File** tab > **Options**. In the Options dialog box click the Save option located on the left side. Click the **Save** option in the Word Options dialog box. (See Figure 20.24)
2. Under Save documents change the minutes to how often you would like Word to save a recoverable version of your document.
3. Change Auto-Recover time in Word. When finished click **OK**.

CHAPTER 21

Up-to-Date and Secure

21.1 ENABLE AND DISABLE UPDATES

After you install Office 2016 and run the application for the first time after installation you will be asked to choose your preferred settings for how your Office applications should be updated in the future. The option "Use recommended settings" will provide you with updates for Office, Windows, and other Micro software. Alternatively, you can choose "No thanks" to not apply updates. However, you can change the update settings later.

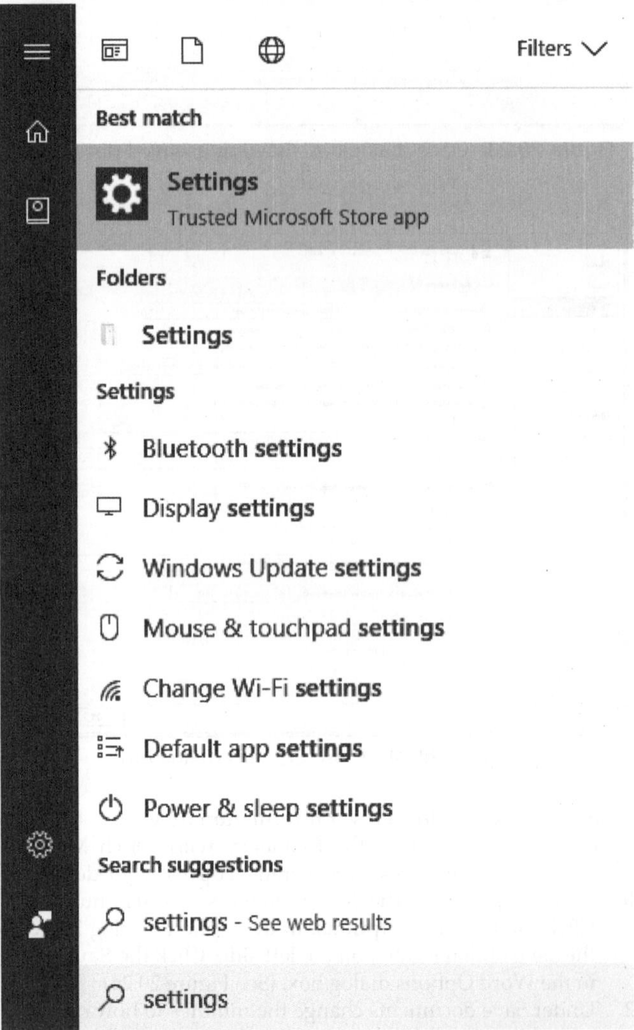

Figure 21.1 Start menu > Setting option selected

Figure 21.2 Setting screen

21.2 APPLY UPDATES

To enable update settings, do the following:

1. Click on the "**Settings**" on the **Start** menu to open system Setting screen. (See Figure 21.1).
2. On the **Settings** screen, Click on **Update & security**. (See Figure 21.2).
3. Select Windows Update on the left-side pane, and click on the **Advanced options** link on the right-side pane. (See Figure 21.3).
4. Check the box next to "Give me updates for other Microsoft products when I update Windows". This option will update all Office apps wherever your system is updated. (See Figure 21.4).

☞ *Choose the Automatic (recommended) option to allow Windows to automatically check for updates and automatically install them.*

To disable update settings, do the following:

1. Open Settings panel. (Right click on Windows 10 desktop and from the context menu select Display Settings. Click the return arrow in the upper left corner to go to Settings panel.)
2. Click on **Update & security**.
3. Select **Windows Update** on the left-side pane, and click on the **Advanced options** link on the right-side pane.

4. Uncheck the box next to "Give me updates for other Microsoft products when I update Windows". This action will stop other Microsoft products including Office 2016 from automatically updating when you update Windows.

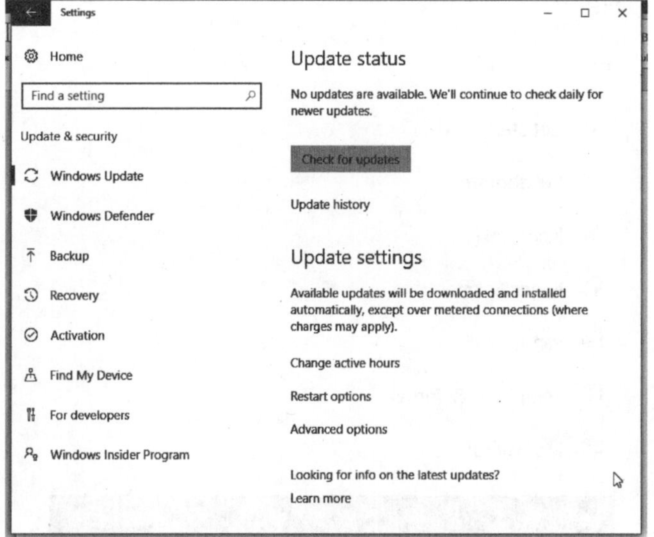

Figure 21.3 Windows Update > Advanced options link

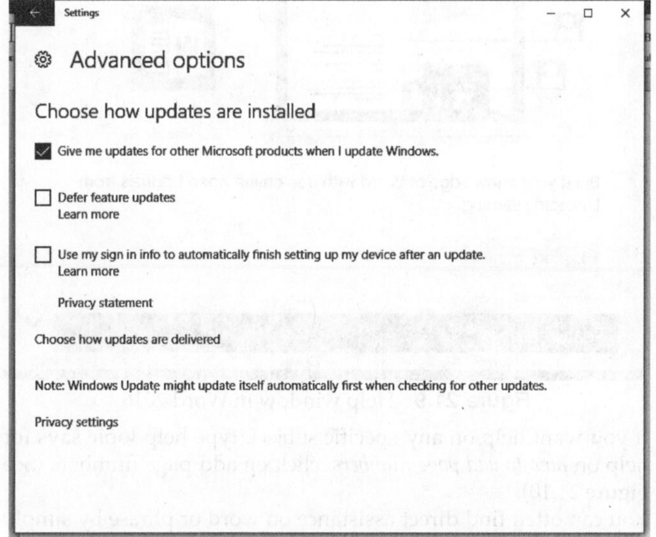

Figure 21.4 Check the box next to "Give me updates" option selected

Enable or Disable Automatic Office 2016 Updates

1. Open any Office 2016 application, such as Word.
2. Click on the **File** tab.
3. Select the **Account** tab on the left-side pane. On the right-side pane, locate the Office Updates section. (See Figure 21.5.)
4. Click on **Update Options** button, to open a menu offering various settings options. (See Figure 21.6.)
5. Choose the **Update Now** option to apply all available updates immediately. It will display following screen as shown in Figure 21.7.

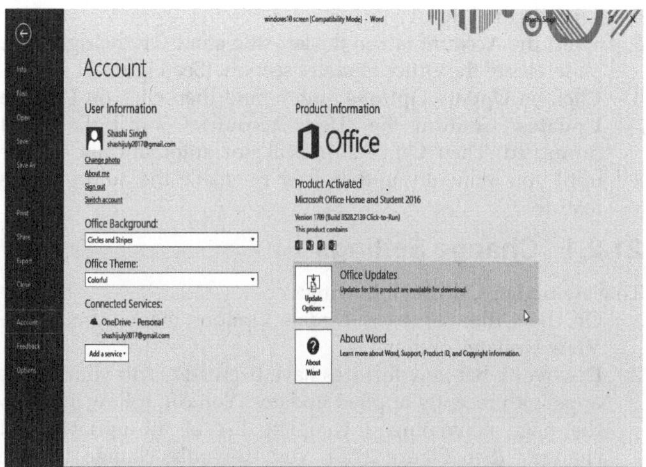

Figure 21.5 Word 2016 File > Account option selected

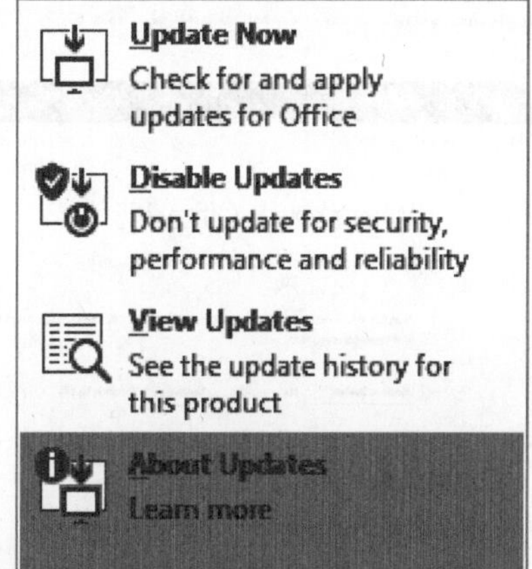

Figure 21.6 Menu offering various update options

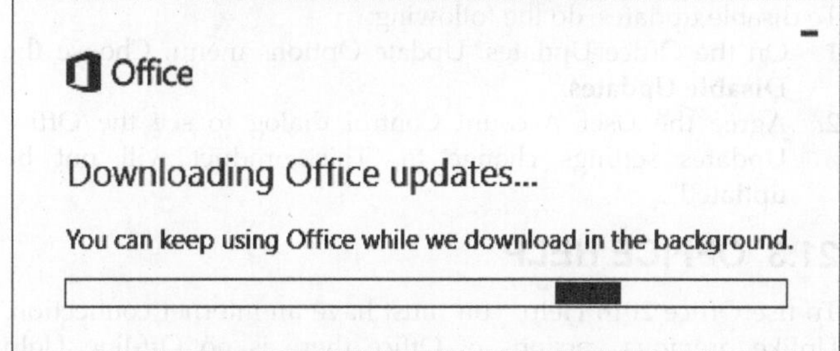

Figure 21.7 Update now option in progress

If you are using the new Microsoft Office 2016 on Windows, you may find it automatically updates every now and then when the network is available on your computer. That's because Microsoft Office 2016 comes with the auto update feature, which is enabled by default, so that it will automatically update without informing you. The auto update feature saves users from manually updating. However, constant updates may make the drives or applications on some computers not perform well, so that some users may want to disable auto updates feature and stop Office 2016 from updating.

1. Open any Office 2016 application, such as Word.

2. Click on the **File** tab.
3. Select the **Account** tab on the left-side pane. On the right-side pane, locate the Office Updates section. (See Figure 21.5.)
4. Click on **Update Options** button, and then click on **Disable Updates**. Confirm the "User Account Control dialog" if prompted. Then Office 2016 will not automatically update until you manually update it or re-enable the auto updates feature.

21.2.1 Change Settings

To view updates, do the following:

1. On the Office Updates, Update Options menu, choose the **View Updates** option.
2. Discover what new features have been added to your Office apps with recently applied updates. You can follow a link to the page containing a complete list of all updates and changes. (See Figure 21.8). You can only change Update Options if you have Administrator privileges on the System.

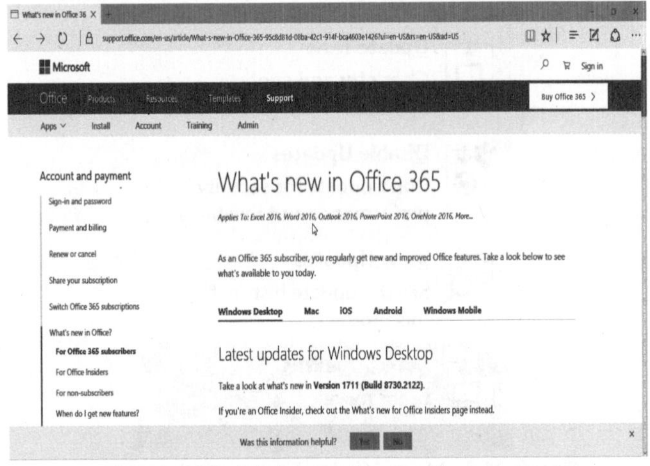

Figure 21.8 Update now option in progress

To disable updates, do the following:

1. On the Office Updates, Update Options menu, Choose the **Disable Updates**.
2. Agree the User Account Control dialog to see the Office Updates settings change to "This product will not be updated".

21.3 OFFICE HELP

To use Office 2016 Help, you must have an internet connection. Unlike previous versions of Office there is no Off-line Help option. You can access the product Help in four different ways:

- You can access Help from the **File** menu. In any Office application, click File and in the top right corner, click the familiar **?** button.
- Or use the **F1** function key anytime to open the Help Viewer window for the Office application you are working on.
- Just type your query in the "**Tell me what to do**" box. From the search results, you can quickly get to features you want to use or actions you want to perform. For help content on your search phrase, click the option Get Help on "search phrase".
- You can also add a help shortcut to your Quick Access Toolbar if you want to be able to get to it easily.

If you need assistance for any Office 2016 application, you can call upon the Office Help feature. Open Word 2016 application, press F1 to see Help window as shown in Figure 21.9.

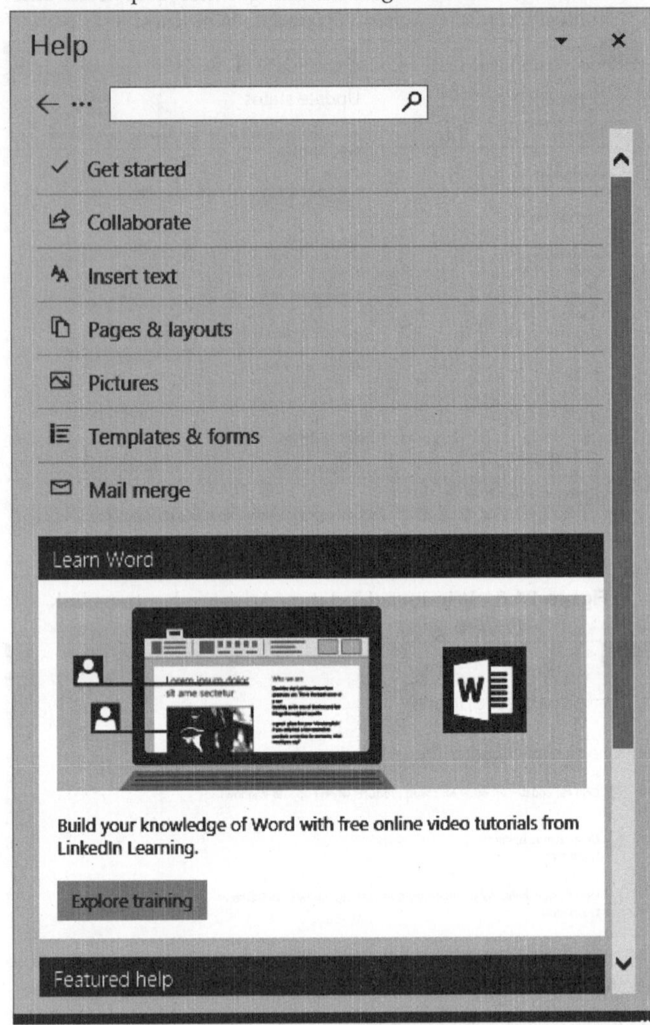

Figure 21.9 Help window in Word 2016

If you want help on any specific subject, type help topic says for help on *how to add page numbers*, click on add page numbers (See Figure 21.10).

You can often find direct assistance on word or phrase by simply clicking on "**Tell me what to do**" (See Figure 21.11), and type what you want to know, such as commands you can't find or options you want to configure.

Open a document in Word, then type "*word count*" into Tell Me box to see an instant document analysis. (See Figure 21.12).

You can also add a help shortcut to your Quick Access Toolbar. Here's how:

1. Select **File** > **Options** > **Quick Access Toolbar**.
2. Under the drop-down where it says Choose commands from, select All Commands.
3. Select Help from the list of commands to add to the Quick Access Toolbar.
4. Click **Add**. (See Figure 21.13).

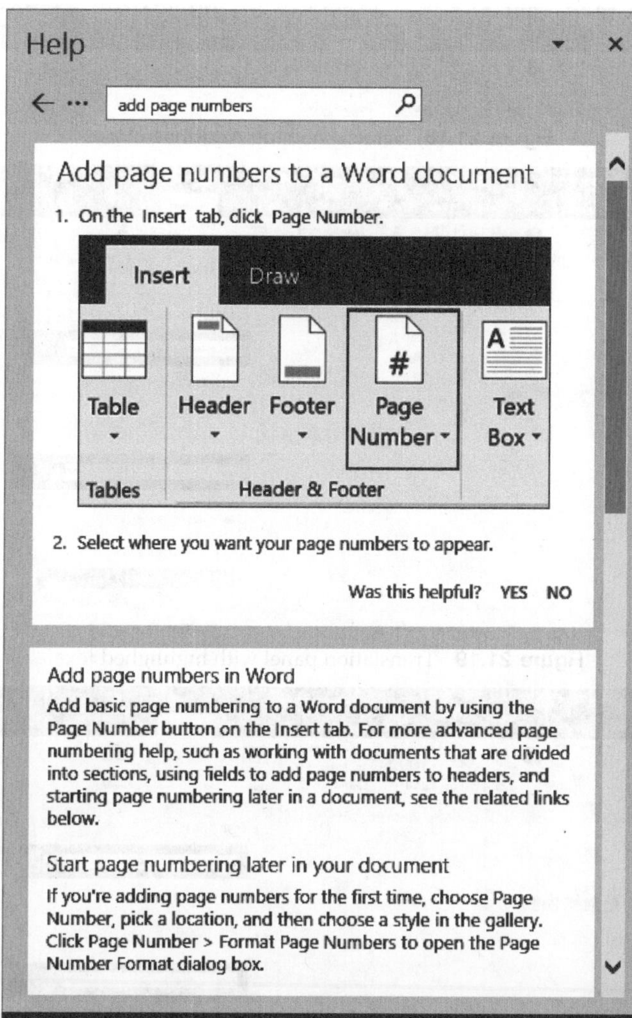

Figure 21.10 Help window showing help for the specific topic

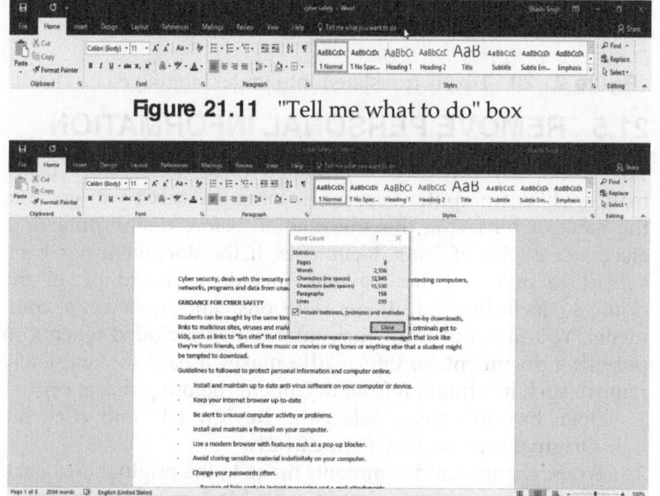

Figure 21.11 "Tell me what to do" box

Figure 21.12 Explore help using "Tell me what to do" box

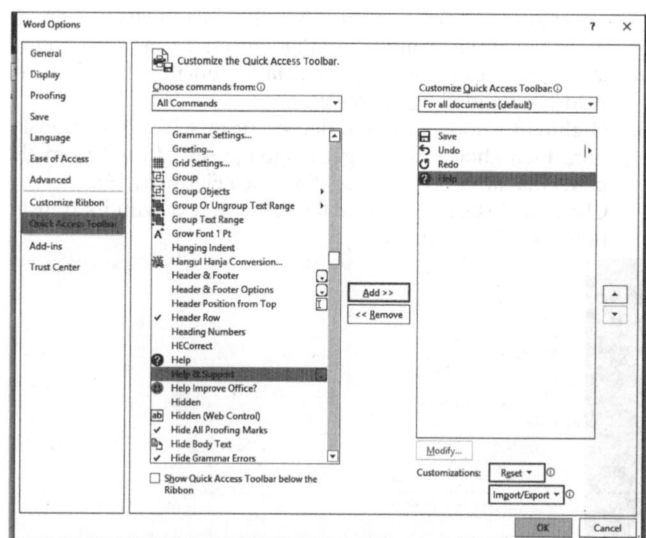

Figure 21.13 Word Options box to add the Quick Access Toolbar

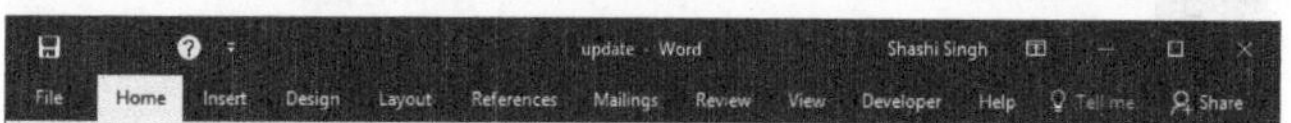

Figure 21.14 Quick Access Toolbar in the upper-left corner added

5. When you are done, click **OK**. The shortcut to help will be added to your Quick Access Toolbar in the upper-left corner. (See Figure 21.14).

21.4 DEVELOPER TAB

The developer tab in Microsoft Word provides users with the option to write and run macros, use ActiveX controls and XML commands, create applications in Microsoft Office, to employ "Add-ins" and more. Add-ins (or add-ons) are programs that add complimentary features to Microsoft Office applications. The developer tab is not readily available on the ribbon in Word by default, but can be added at any time through the options menu. To enable the Developer tab in a Word 2016 Office application, do the following:

1. Open the application and Click on the "**File**" tab and select "**Options**". The Options dialog box will be displayed. (See Figure 21.15).
2. Click on "**Customize Ribbon**".
3. Under Customize the Ribbon and under Main Tabs, place a checkmark next to "**Developer**" (See Figure 21.16).
4. Click on **OK** button. The Options dialog box will close, and the developer tab will now be available on the ribbon until you either disable the developer settings or until you reinstall a Microsoft Office application on your computer.
5. You can now see that your Options change has been applied, and the Developer tab is now added to the title bar as shown in Figure 21.17.
6. Click the **Add-ins** button. This lets you control Add-In programs and templates. In Word 2016 the *blue* boxes button was added to let you go to the Office On-line Store to look for more Add-Ins. (See Figure 21.18). Click the Store link to download Add-Ins to increase available functional features.

7. Select any **Add-in**, then Click **Insert** to include its functionality in the application for example, insert Translator to allow language translation. The Translator functionality is a free Add-in provided by Microsoft.
8. Highlight some text in the document to select it for translation, then choose the target language say *"Hindi"* from the panel that appears for translation. (See Figure 21.19).
9. Click on "**Insert**" to replace the selected text with its translation. (See Figure 21.20).

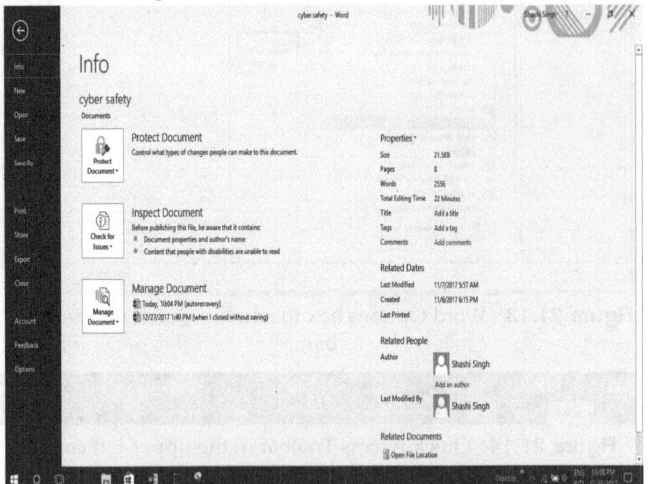

Figure 21.15 File tab > Options

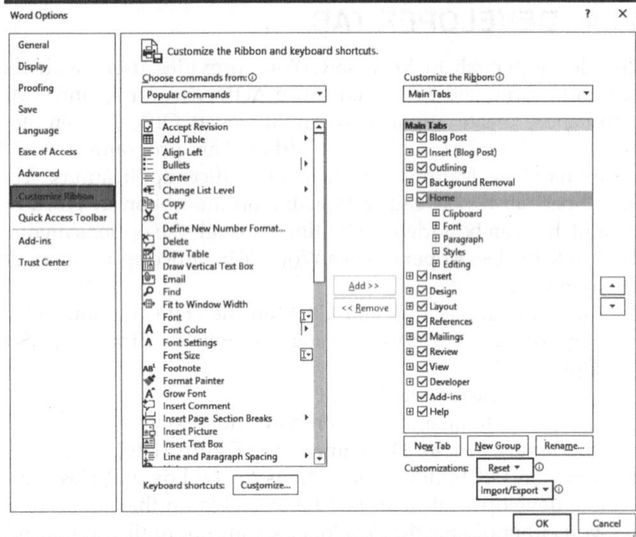

Figure 21.16 Option dialog box with Developer box checked

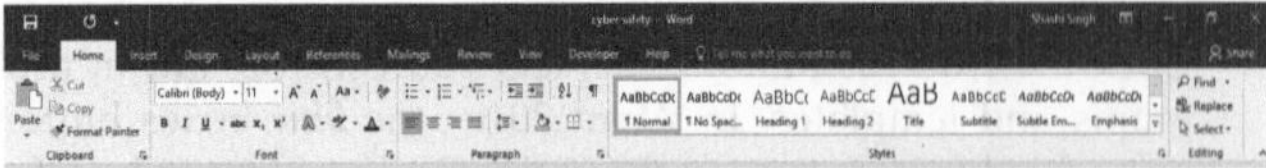

Figure 21.17 Developer tab added to the Title bar

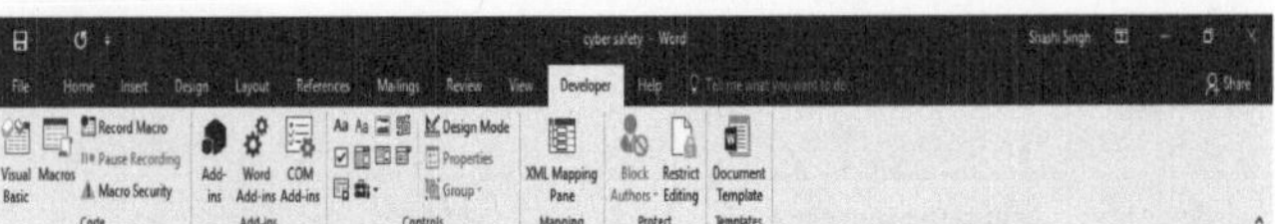

Figure 21.18 Screen showing Add-ins button

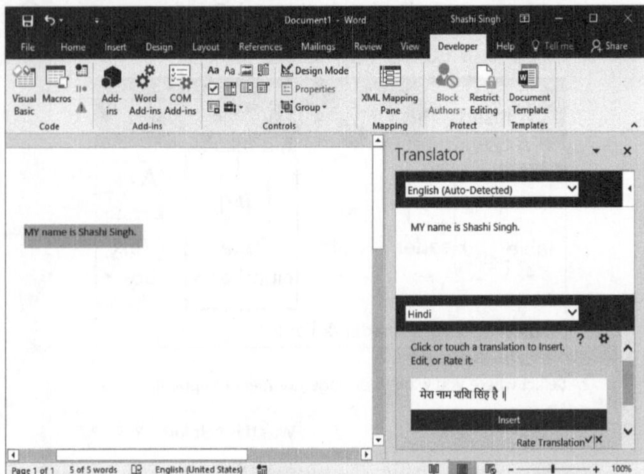

Figure 21.19 Translation panel with highlighed text

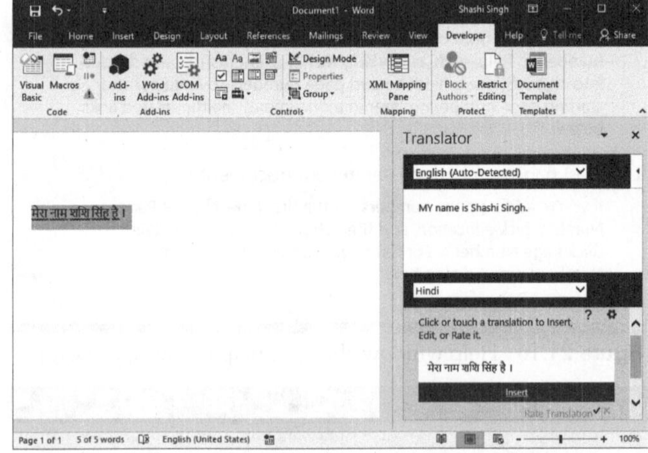

Figure 21.20 Text is translated into target language i.e., Hindi

21.5 REMOVE PERSONAL INFORMATION

To protect any sensitive information from accidentally being made public, Computer Services recommends that you get into the habit of removing this information before distributing final electronic copies of your documents. If the document has been subject to revision, the file may include a record of all the changes, including additions, deletions, and reviewer's comments. You may not want such information included when you publish a document, so Office 2016 makes it easy to completely remove such information from documents before publication:

1. Open the document. Select the **Review** tab, and click the "**Original**" option. (See Figure 21.21).
2. To see changes and comments made to the original text, click the down-arrow and select "**Simple Markup**".

3. Select **File** > **Save As**, enter a new filename then Save a copy of a document. Note that do not make changes to master document. It is best to work with a copy of document, to avoid the possibility of accidently removing too much information.
4. Click the **File** tab. With Info highlighted on the left, you will see the file properties on the right that show, for example, the author of the file. (See Figure 21.22).
5. Click the **Check for Issues box** and then **Inspect Document** in the drop-down menu (See Figure 21.23). The Document Inspector window appears.

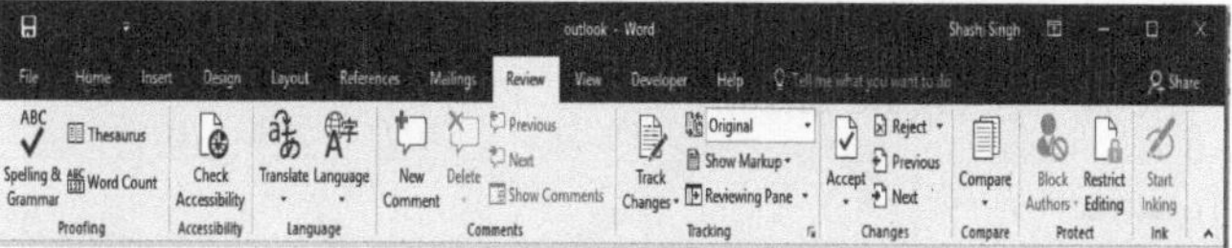

Figure 21.21 Screen with Review tab with Original option selected

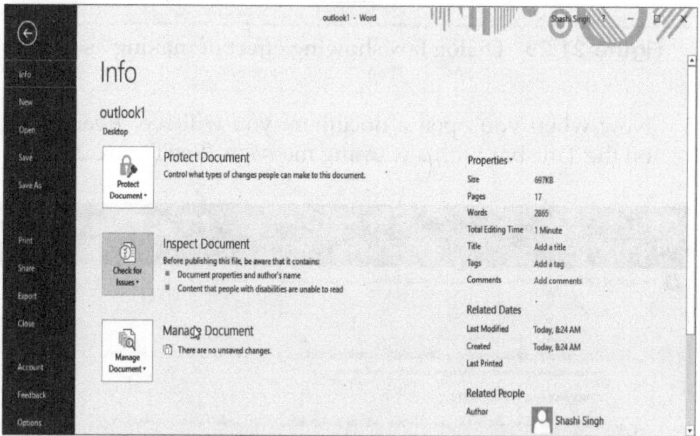

Figure 21.22 File > Info > Check for issues button

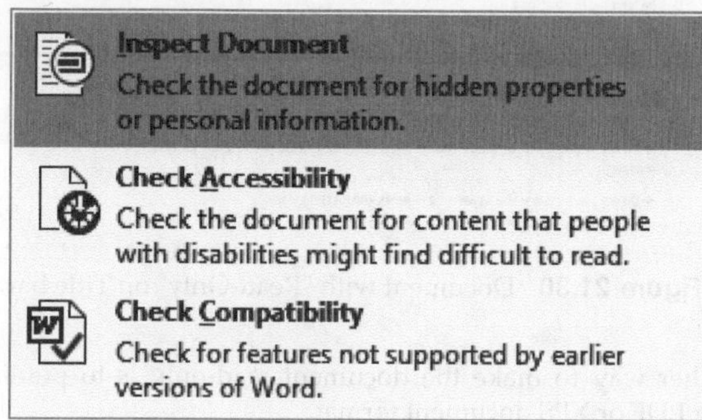

Figure 21.23 Inspect Document drop-down menu

6. Check the boxes against the document content you want to examine or leave all items checked then click the "**Inspect**" button. (See Figure 21.24). If you are using Microsoft Word, select at a minimum, the following options:
   - Comments, Revisions, and Versions
   - Document Properties and Personal Information
   - Invisible Content
   - Hidden Text
7. The system will search for items that pertain to the categories you selected. If it finds any items, you will be prompted to remove them. Click **Remove All** to delete the information. (See Figure 21.25)
8. To finish, click **Close**.
9. If you are prompted to save the document changes when you close the file, click **Save**.

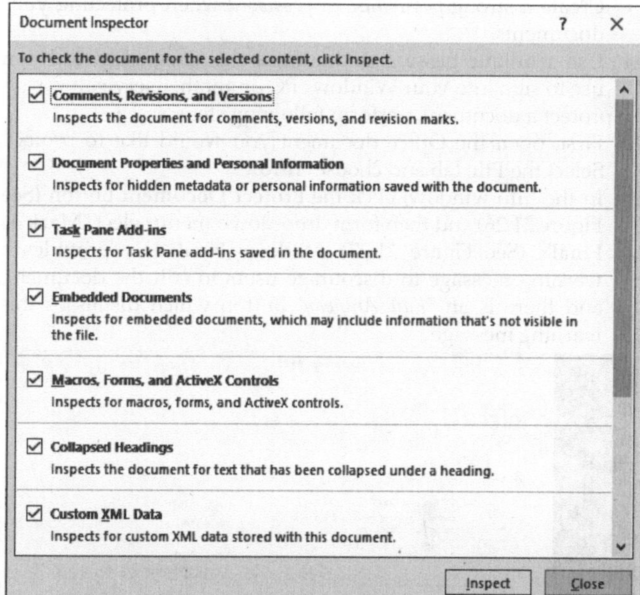

Figure 21.24 Document Inspector with all items checked

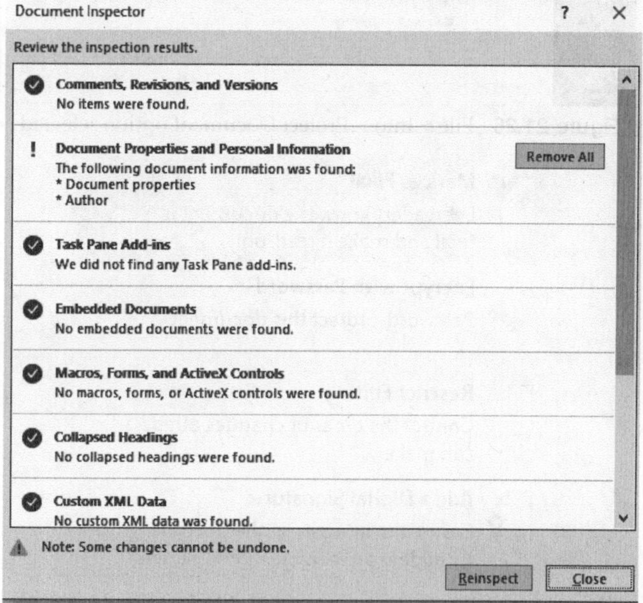

Figure 21.25 Document Inspector with Review the Inspection Resources

21.6 PROTECT YOUR DOCUMENTS

When you send out a document you might want other people should not make unauthorized changes to the content. You can prevent people from viewing or modifying documents by protecting your document with a password. When password protecting your documents keep in mind some essential tips:

- Create a strong *passphrase* or *password* when protecting your documents.
- Use a unique password, don't use the same password you use to sign into your Windows PC or another service.

To protect a document, perform following steps:

1. First, open the Office document you would like to protect. Select the **File** tab and choose "**Info**".
2. In the Info window, click the **Protect Document** button (See Figure 21.26) and then form drop-down menu select "**Mark as Final**". (See Figure 21.27). Mark as Final only provides a warning message to discourage users to edit the document, and there is an "*Edit Anyway*" button which dismisses this warning message.

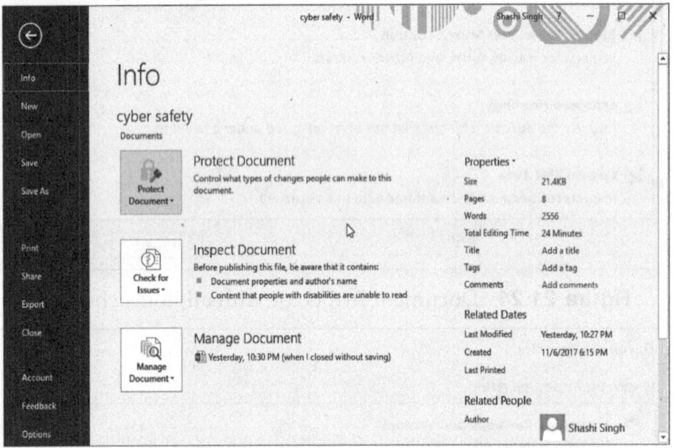

Figure 21.26 File > Info > Protect Document option selected

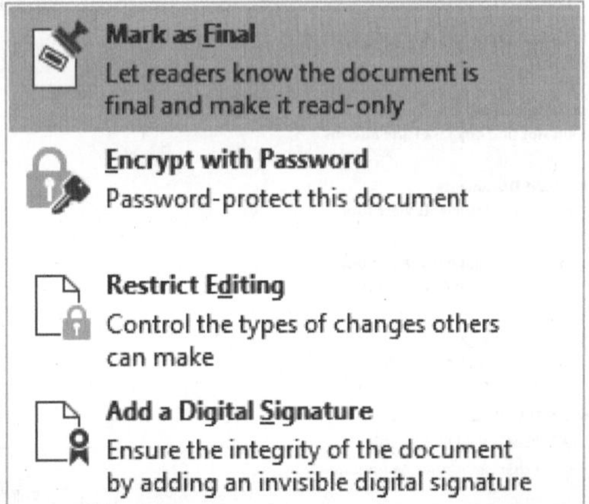

Figure 21.27 Drop-down menu with Mark as Final selected

3. A dialog box will be displayed with a message "This document will be marked as final and saved", Click **OK** button to confirm. (See Figure 21.28).

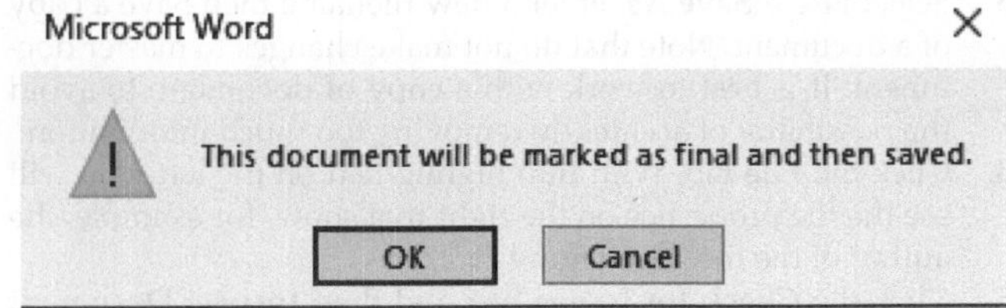

Figure 21.28 A dialog box with a warning message

4. The effects of making as final will be explained in the dialog box. (See Figure 21.29).

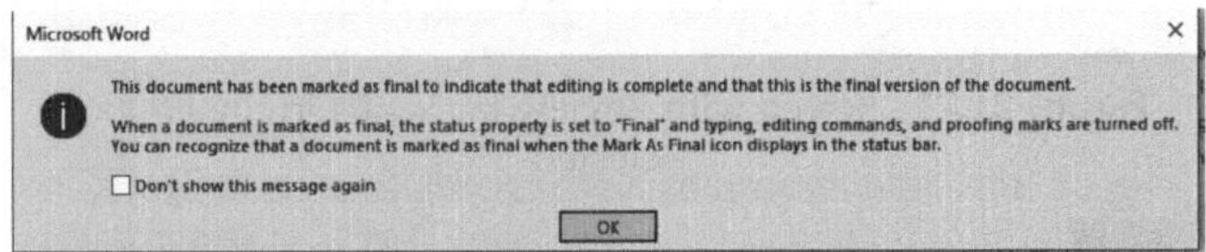

Figure 21.29 Dialog box showing effect of making as final

5. Now when you open a document you will see "Read-Only" on the Title bar with a warning message. (See Figure 21.30).

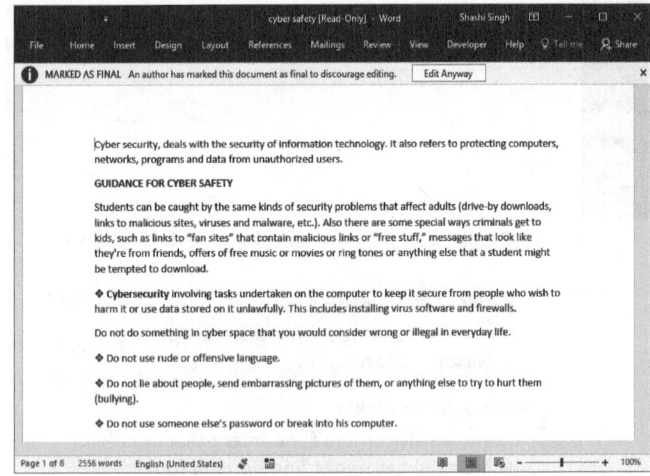

Figure 21.30 Document with "Read-Only" on Title bar

Another way to make the document read-only is to publish it using PDF or XPS document format.

21.6.1 Encrypt with Password

Alternatively, you can encrypt a document to restrict unauthorize access.

1. Click the **File** tab, click **Info**, then select the **Protect Document** button. Now Click **Encrypt with Password** from the drop-down that appears. (See Figure 21.31).

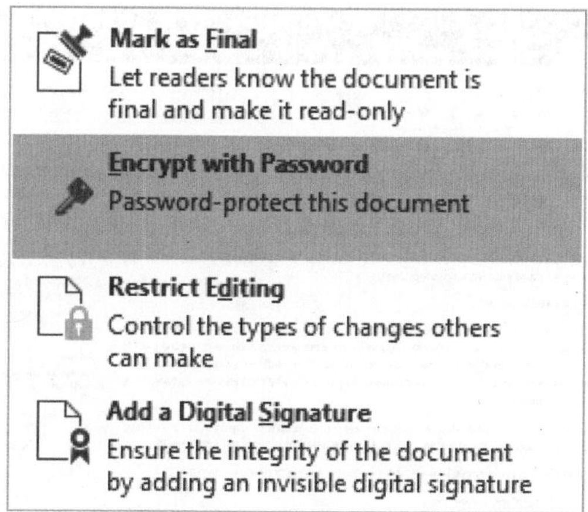

Figure 21.31 File tab > Info > Protect Document > Encrypt with Password

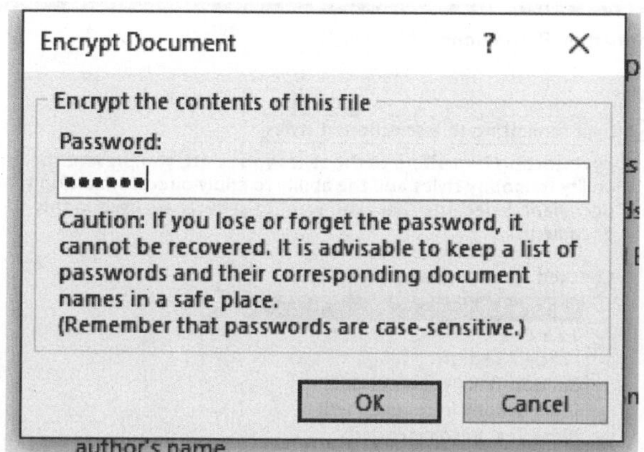

Figure 21.32 Encrypt Document password dialog box

2. Enter your password then click **OK**. (See Figure 21.32).
3. Enter the password again to confirm it and click **OK** in the dialog box that appears. (See Figure 21.33).

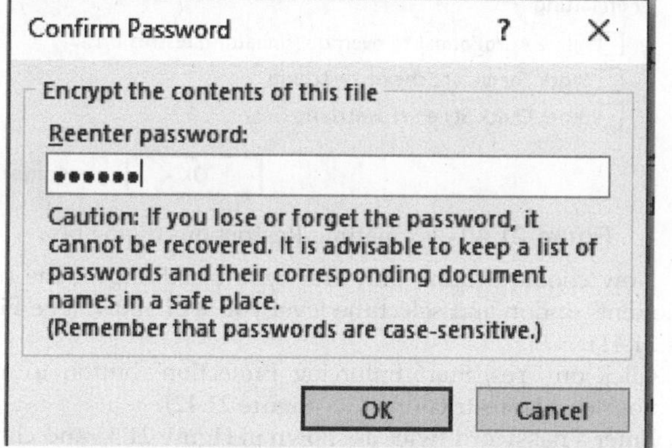

Figure 21.33 Confirm password dialog box

4. With encryption applied, no one will be able to review or change the document without the correct password as indicated in the document Info page. (See Figure 21.34). Microsoft Word will now indicate the document is protected.

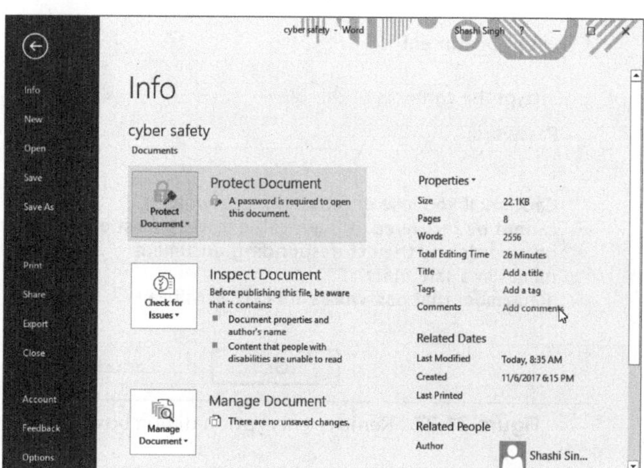

Figure 21.34 Protect Document in the document info page

5. The contents are not altered, but when you close the document, you will still be prompt to save the changes. (See Figure 21.35).
6. Now, when you open the document, you will be prompted to enter your password to access its contents. Also note that Passwords are case-sensitive. In other words, you have to enter the correct combination of upper- and lowercase letters to successfully enter the password. After entering password, click on **OK** button. (See Figure 21.36).

Figure 21.35 Save changes dialog box

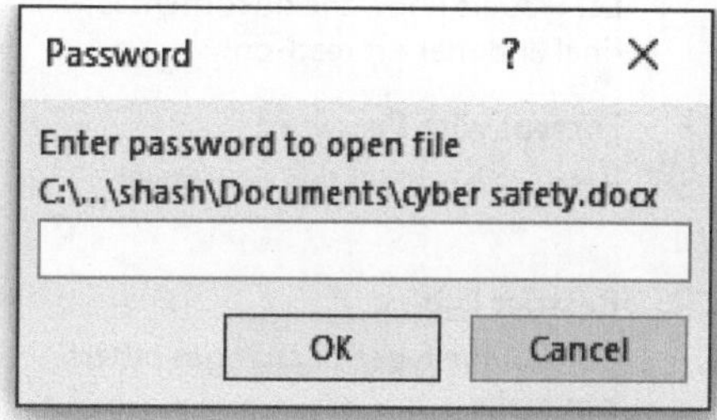

Figure 21.36 Enter password dialog box to open the document

21.6.2 Remove the Encryption

- Open the document, then select **Encrypt with Password** again, delete the existing password and click **OK**. (See Figure 21.37).

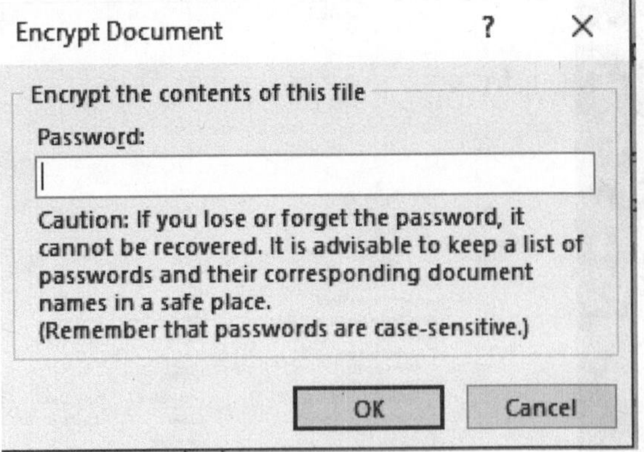

Figure 21.37 Remove encryption dialog box

21.7 RESTRICT PERMISSION

You can also apply specific levels of protection using Restrict Permission. To apply restrict permission do the following:

1. Working with a copy of your document, select the **File** tab and choose "**Info**".
2. In the Info window, click the **Protect Document** button and then form drop-down menu select "**Restrict Editing**". (See Figure 21.38).
3. The Restrict Editing pane appears, with three options as shown in Figure 21.39.
4. Choose "Limit formatting to a selection of styles" option and click on "**Settings**" link, to specify styles in your document. (See Figure 21.40). Check the styles you wish to allow, then click the **OK** button to close the Formatting Restrictions dialog box.

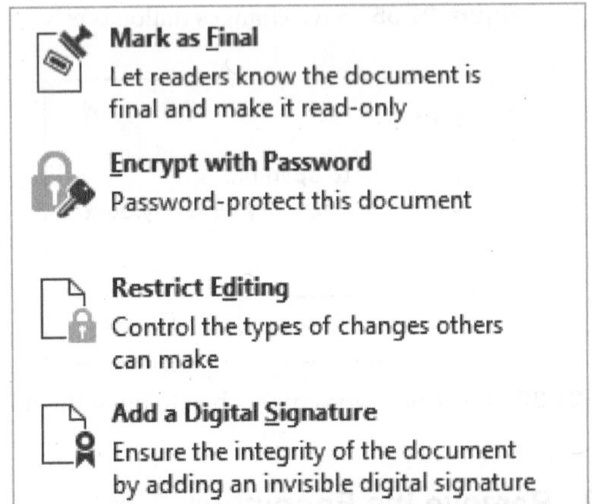

Figure 21.38 File tab > Info > Protect Document > Restrict Editing

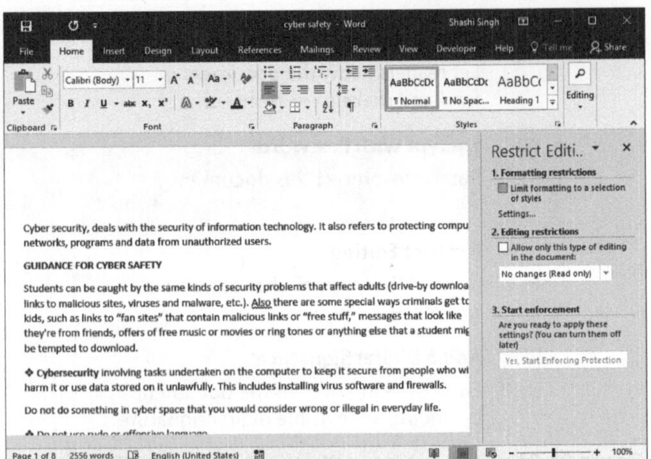

Figure 21.39 Restrict Editing pane with three options

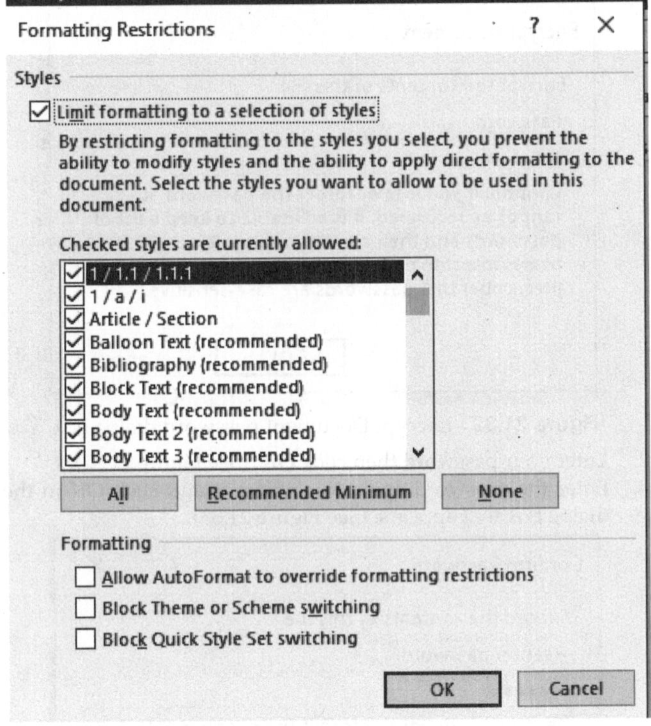

Figure 21.40 Formatting Restrictions dialog box

5. Now choose "Allow only this type of editing in the document" option and select the level you will allow. (See Figure 21.41).
6. Click on "Yes, Start Enforcing Protection" button to apply your chosen restrictions. (See Figure 21.42).
7. Enter a password twice as shown in Figure 21.43 and click on **OK** button.
8. Other users can only read the document, they cannot make any modification in it.

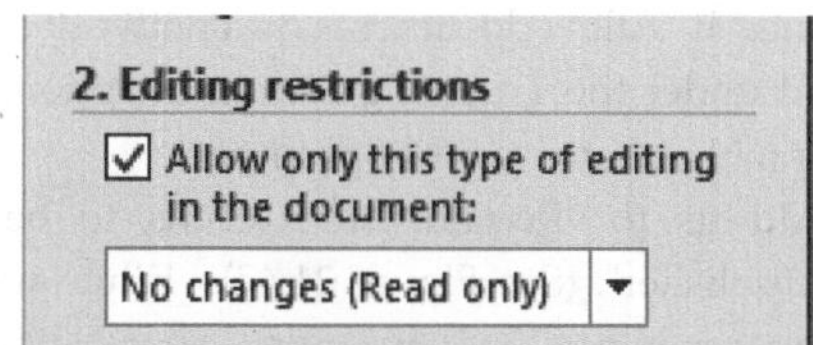

Figure 21.41 Editing Restrictions dialog box

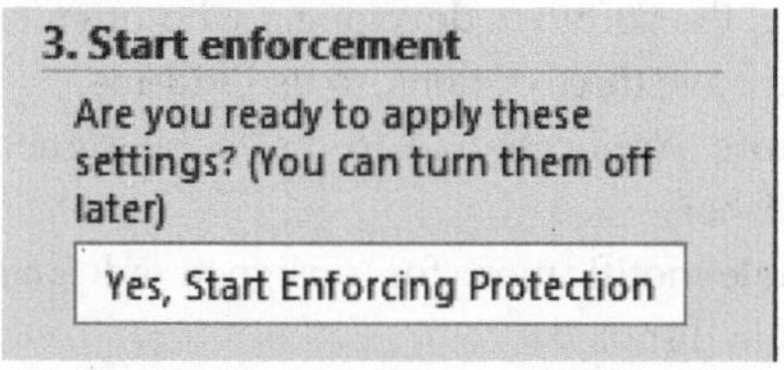

Figure 21.42 Start Enforcing Protection dialog box

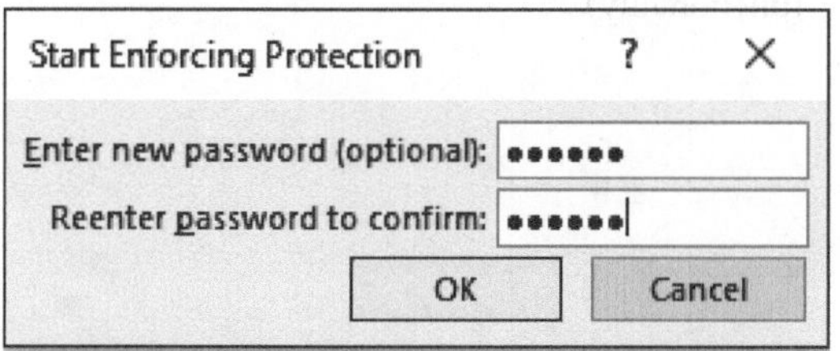

Figure 21.43 Start Enforcing Protection dialog box for accepting password

21.7.1 Remove the Restriction

- Open the document, then click "**Stop Protection**" button in the Restrict Editing pane. Now enter the password in the Unprotect document box (See Figure 21.44) and click on **OK** button to enable the document without restrictions.

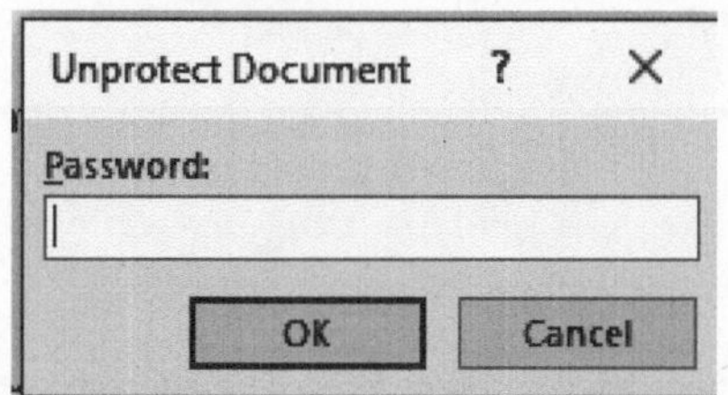

Figure 21.44 Unprotect document dialog box

21.8 TRUST CENTER

The Trust Center contains security and privacy settings for office applications. Microsoft Office Trust Center settings include security features to help prevent these attacks. The Trust Center is found in the Options Tab of Microsoft Office applications, including Outlook, Word, Excel and PowerPoint. To get to the Trust Center do the following:

1. Go to the **File** tab and select **Options**, and then **Trust Center**. (See Figure 21.45).
2. Click the "**Trust Center Settings**" button to see the Trust Center controls. Choose "**Macro Settings**" to see options to Disable or Enable certain macros. (See Figure 21.46).

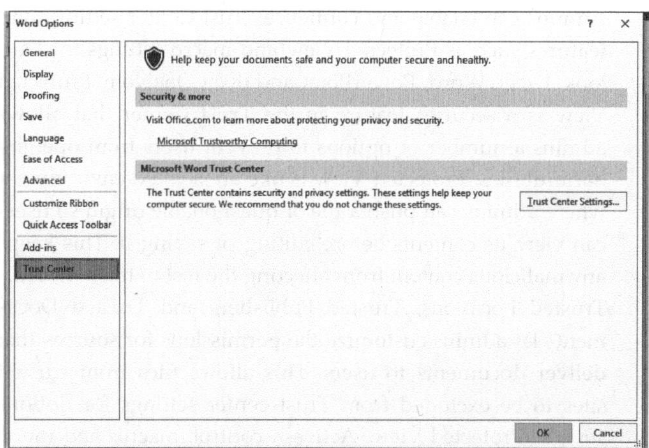

Figure 21.45 File > Options> Trust Center

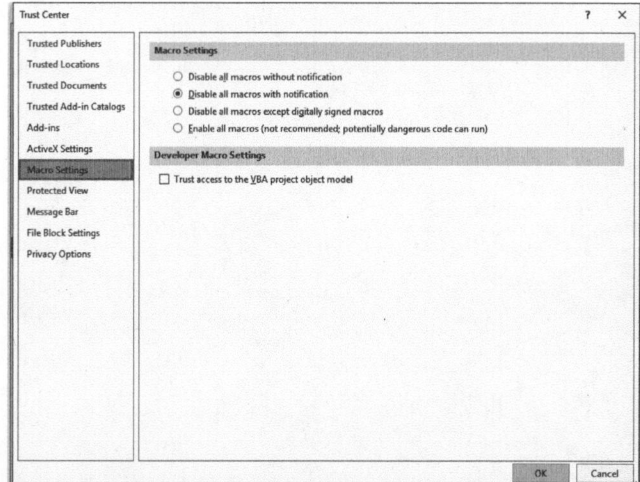

Figure 21.46 Trust Center with Macro settings

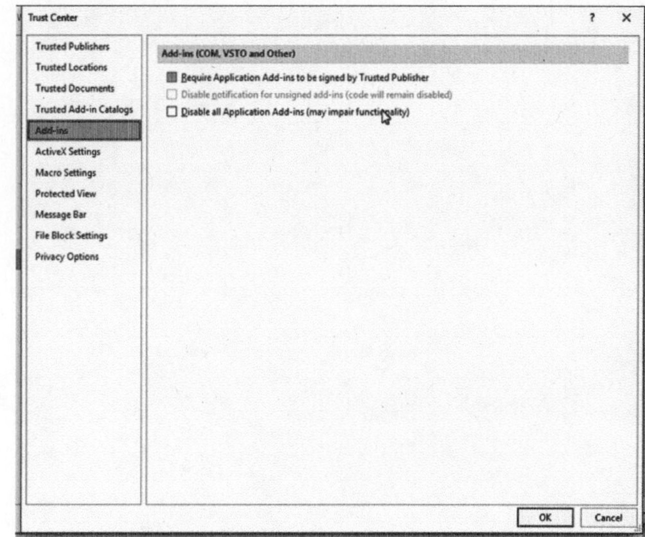

Figure 21.47 Trust Center > Add-ins

Admins can enable and configure Trust Center settings and features such as Protected View and macro settings for Outlook, Excel, Word, PowerPoint and even OneNote. Protected View is a security feature in the Trust Center that allows admins a number of options to prevent users from opening harmful files. Protected View is like an isolated environment where admins can push a file of questionable origin so users can view its contents before editing or saving it. This keeps any malicious content from affecting the rest of the network. Trusted Locations, Trusted Publishers and Trusted Documents let admins customize the permissions for sources that deliver documents to users. This allows files from trusted sites to be excluded from Trust center settings for options such as Protected View, Active-X control, macros and more. For instance, if "Allow documents on a network to be trusted" is enabled under the Trusted Documents option, documents will open without any security prompts.

4. Select Add-ins to "Require all Add-ins to be signed by Trusted Publisher". (See Figure 21.47). While working with add-ins, you may need to learn more about digital signatures and certificates, which authenticates an add-in, and trusted publisher, the software developers who often create add-ins. Here you have three options, to use add-ins.
   - Require Application Add-ins to be signed by Trusted Publisher.
   - Disable notification for unsigned add-ins (code will remain disabled).
   - Disable all Application Add-ins (may impair functionality).

CHAPTER 22

More Office Apps 10

22.1 OFFICE TOOLS

When you click on Start and expand Microsoft Office 2016 Tools folder, it displays Office 2016 Language Preference and Office 2016 Upload Center as describe in following sections:

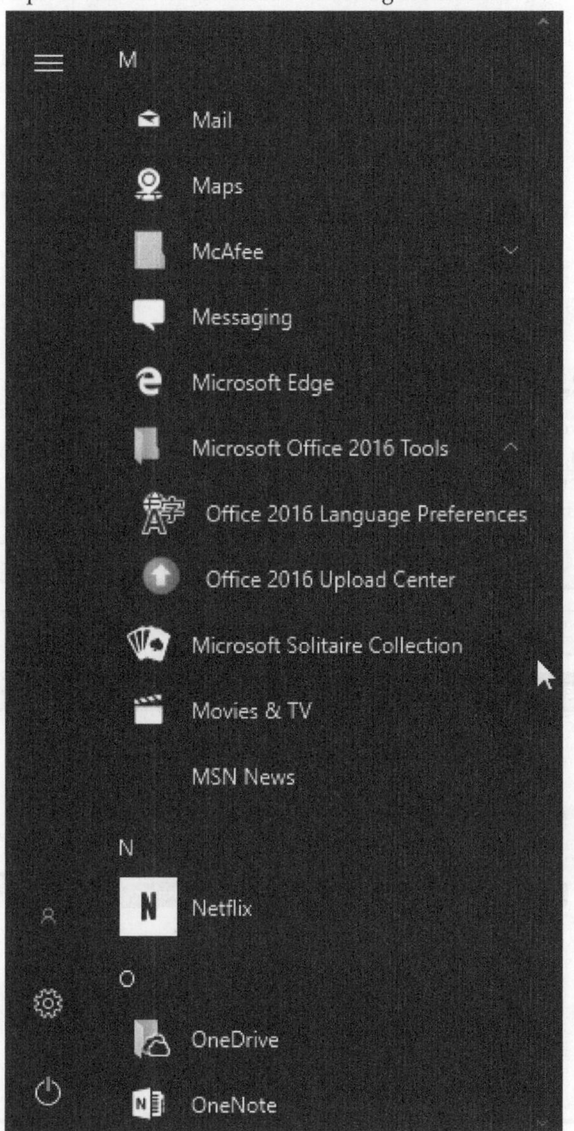

Figure 22.1 Start menu > Microsoft Office 2016 Tools > Office 2016 Language Preferences selected

22.1.1 Office 2016 Language Preference

The Office 2016 setup procedure will by default, automatically install the language version that matches your system location. You can install additional languages for your system in Windows Settings, then choose your preferred Display Language for Office with the Language Preferences app.

1. Click on **Start** menu > **Microsoft Office 2016 Tools** folder and select **Office 2016 Language Preferences** to launch the app as shown in Figure 22.1.
2. A Microsoft Office Language Preferences dialog box will be displayed as shown in Figure 22.2. Click the arrow button to open the drop-down languages menu and select the language you want to install. (See Figure 22.3).
3. Now, Click on **Add** button to see the language appear in the Editing Language list.

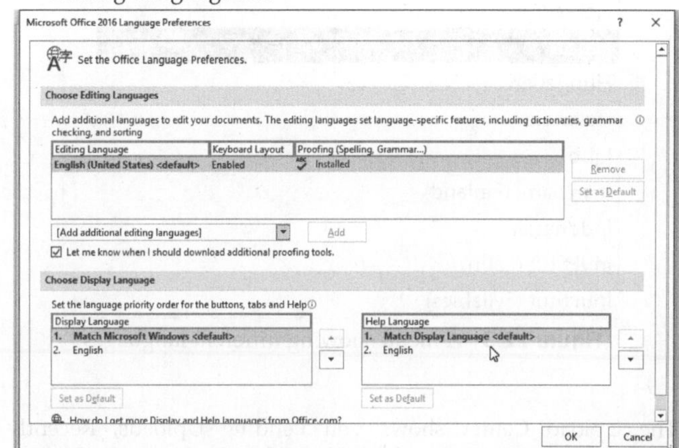

Figure 22.2 A Microsoft Office Language Preferences dialog box

22.1.2 Upload Center

Microsoft Office Upload Center now gives you a way to see the state of files you are uploading to a server, in one location. When you upload a file to a web server, Microsoft first saves that file locally to the Office Document Cache before it starts the upload, which means that you can save changes and immediately continue working even when you are offline or have a bad network connection. The Microsoft Office Upload Center lets you keep track of how uploads are progressing, and whether any files need your attention. Microsoft Office Upload Center applies to Excel 2016, Word 2016, and PowerPoint 2016. This is helpful in the following situations:

- You have opened a file from a server, and the server goes offline. You can save the file, knowing that it will be uploaded when the server goes back online.

- An error occurs during the upload. You are alerted immediately, so that you can fix the problem and resume the upload quickly.

To open the Upload Center using the Windows Start menu:

1. Click the **Start** menu.
2. Click **Microsoft Office Tools**.
3. Click **Microsoft Office Upload Center** to open the app. (See Figure 22.4).

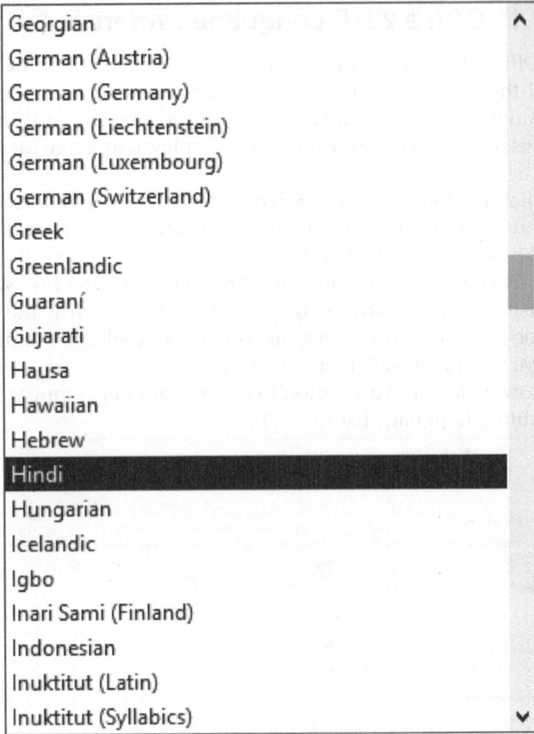

Figure 22.3 A menu showing different languages

The Upload Center shows you Pending Uploads, Recently Uploaded files and All Cached Files. When you open the Upload Center, the default screen shows you any files that are currently pending upload to the server. Work with all files in the Upload Center:

- To upload all files that are pending upload in the Upload Center, click **Upload All**.
- To pause all uploads, click **Pause Uploads**. To resume all uploads click **Resume Uploads**.
- To make changes to notifications, and how the Office Document Cache is managed, click **Settings**.
- To work with a specific file in the Upload Center, click Actions or Resolve adjacent to the file, and then select what you want to do from the menu.
- You can also select the file that you want to work with and access file actions through the Actions menu in the toolbar, and through the context menu for each file.

4. Select the document in the list, then click its **Actions** button for options.
5. Choose the Open Site option to find the document in its online location. See Figure 22.5.

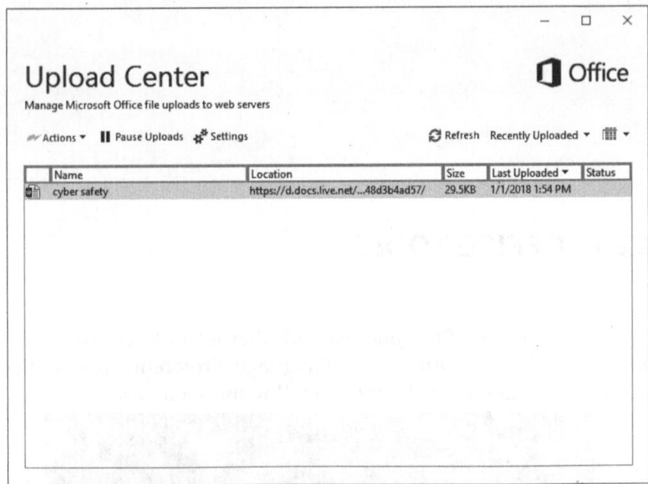

Figure 22.4 An Upload Center screen showing file

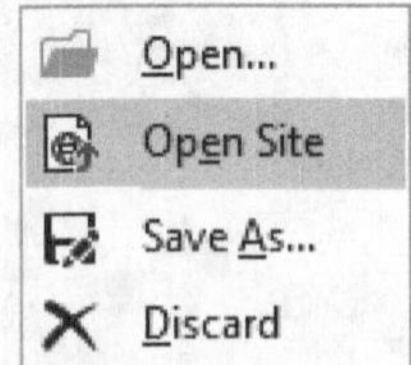

Figure 22.5 Open Site option selected from the menu

22.2 OFFICE ONLINE

If you have a Microsoft Account and associated OneDrive, you can use the Office Online apps to create or access your Office documents from a browser, and share files with other users online.

1. Open your browser and visit site "*onedrive.live.com*". If you are signed in to your Microsoft Account, your OneDrive "Files" view appears as shown in Figure 22.6.

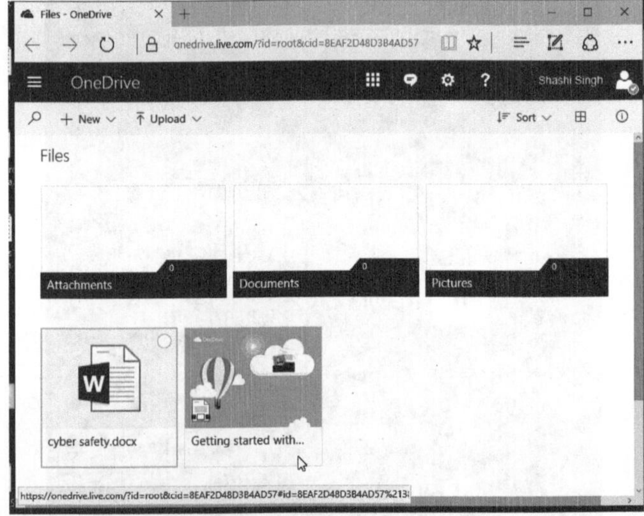

Figure 22.6 OneDrive "Files" view

2. Open a folder and select an existing Word document - to see it opens within your browser.

3. You can edit the document much like with Microsoft Word app. If you have the Word app installed on your device, and require more than the limited functionality that Word Online provides, you can select "EDIT IN WORD".

22.3 OFFICE FOR ANDROID

The Microsoft Office Mobile apps have the familiar look and feel of Office with an intuitive touch experience designed for Android phones and tablets.

- View, edit, and create documents on the go.
- Get quick access to your files in the cloud whenever you need them.
- Your Office documents maintain the same formatting across your PC and mobile devices.
- Easily share your documents with others by just emailing an attachment or a hyperlink.

Microsoft has produced versions of Word, Excel, PowerPoint, Outlook and OneNote for Android devices.

1. Go to Google Play Store on your Android device and search for "Microsoft office" to see the available apps. (See Figure 22.7).

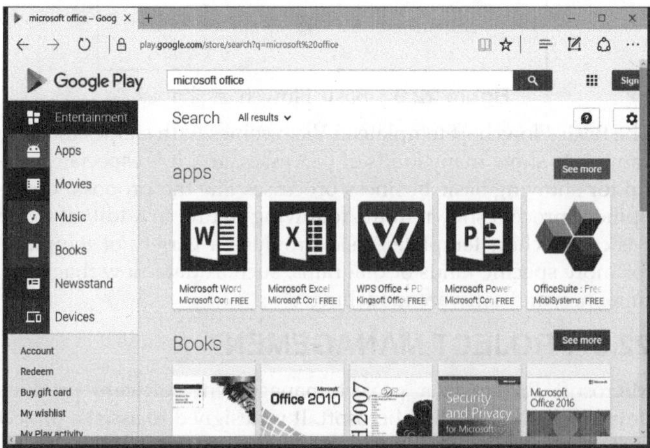

Figure 22.7 Google play store to search Microsoft office apps

2. Click the app you want to install such as the Microsoft app.
3. When the installation process is complete, click on Word icon. It lets you create template to create a new document or open existing document on your Android device.
4. Click on **Sign In** button and enter your Microsoft Account details to access your existing documents on your OneDrive. Now select location, folder and file to open from the back-stage screen that appears.
5. A copy of the file downloads to your Android device. Now you can open Word app for viewing or editing and save the file.

22.4 SWAY STORYTELLING

Sway is for 'digital storytelling', and it fits in very well with some recent trends like responsive design and interactive stories. Think of it as a way of collecting content -- anything from photos to maps to tweets to music to charts and even PDFs, Excel spreadsheets and PowerPoint presentations -- and having it arranged almost automatically into a professionally presented, nicely laid-out, dynamic result that you can see in a browser, that fits to the screen size for whatever device you view it on.

☞ *Sway - a presentation tool in the Office suite.*

All the content in your Sway is laid out in cards, which you use to add or organise chunks of information. Cards are how you organise chunks of content. There are cards for grouping content into stacks, lists, grids and slideshows, but there are also cards for specific content types. Cards let you embed anything you can put in an iframe, from a SoundCloud audio track to a 3D model from Sketch frame to a Google Map section. You can also add a chart. So you can place a whole variety of media content on a Sway card to illustrate your story with pictures, video and graphics.

The functionality of Microsoft's digital storytelling app are discussed below:

- Quickly create interactive and accessible web content without needing to be a web developer.
- Create and / or share Sways with the rest of the web.

Sway is not intended to be a replacement for PowerPoint, but provides an alternative way to quickly present ideas in a story. There are a number of similarities between PowerPoint and Sway:

- Both are part of Microsoft Office.
- Both can be used to create rich presentations.
- Both support multimedia including video, audio and images.
- Both feature customisable templates

Sway is distinguished from PowerPoint by some key differences:

- Sway is an online presentation and storytelling app that's free for anyone with a Microsoft account. Sways can live on the web and you can view them in a browser. PowerPoint is licensed and on desktop.
- Sway is better suited to integrating online content. Sway makes your presentation dynamic. You need to be online to view a Seay presentation. PowerPoint is better for offline usage, including printouts and presentations featuring static media such as charts and graphs.

22.5 VISIO DIAGRAMS

Microsoft Visio is a diagramming and vector graphics application and is part of the Microsoft Office family. Microsoft made Visio available in two editions: Standard and Professional. The Standard and Professional editions share the same interface, but the Professional edition has additional templates for more advanced diagrams and layouts, as well as capabilities intended to make it easy for users to connect their diagrams to data sources and to display their data graphically. The Professional edition features three additional diagram types, as well as intelligent rules, validation, and subprocess (diagram breakdown). (See Figure 22.8).

Visio Online is a new way to view, edit, and share Visio diagrams on the web. Start with a basic diagram to express common ideas, such as depicting a plan, making a proposal, or describing a sequence of steps in a process. It's simple and easy to create first-class diagrams with commonly-used diagram types and rich shape sets. To collaborate with team members and stakeholders, view and add comments and share the diagram with others.

Visio helps you visually communicate complex information from multiple data sources:

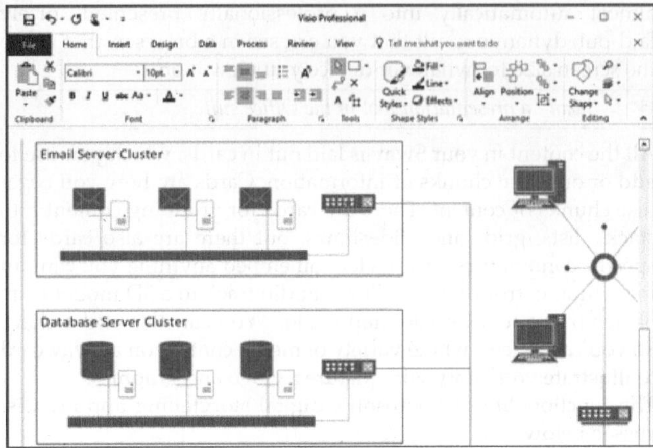

Figure 22.8 Visio Professional edition

- Quickly create professional flow charts, timelines, process maps, organizational charts etc.
- Keep diagram data points current by connecting diagram elements directly to data sources.
- Use data graphics to simplify and enhance the visualization of complex information.
- View and share the most up-to-date Visio diagrams from nearly anywhere with Visio Online.

Flowcharts are diagrams that show the steps in a process. Basic flowcharts are easy to create and, because the shapes are simple and visual, they are easy to understand (See Figure 22.9). When you open the Basic Flowchart template, the Basic Flowchart Shapes stencil opens too. Each shape on the stencil represents a different kind of step in a process . Here are some of the most common shapes:

- **Start/End**: Use this shape for the first and last step of your process.
- **Process**: This shape represents a typical step in your process. This is the most frequently used shape in almost every process.
- **Decision**: This shape indicates a point where the outcome of a decision dictates the next step. There can be multiple outcomes, but often there are just two - yes and no.
- **Subprocess** : Use this shape for a set of steps that combine to create a sub-process that is defined elsewhere, often on another page of the same document. This is useful if the diagram is very long and complex.
- **Document** : This shape represents a step that results in a document.
- **Data**: This shape indicates that information is coming into the process from outside, or leaving the process. This shape can also be used to represent materials and is sometimes called an Input/Output shape.
- **On-page reference** : This small circle indicates that the next (or previous) step is somewhere else on the drawing. This is particularly useful for large flowcharts where you would otherwise have to use a long connector, which can be hard to follow.
- **Off-page reference** : When you drop this shape onto your drawing page, a dialog box opens where you can create a set of hyperlinks between two pages of a flowchart or between a sub-process shape and a separate flowchart page.

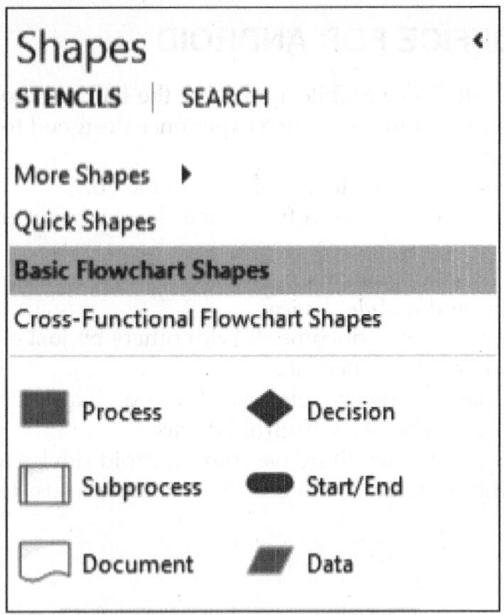

Figure 22.9 Basic Flowchart shapes

The Basic Flowchart template in Visio comes with shapes that you can use to show many kinds of processes, and it is especially useful for showing basic business processes like the proposal development process shown in the following figure. In addition to the Basic Flowchart template, Visio provides a variety of templates for more specific kinds of diagrams, such as data flow diagrams, timelines, and software modelling.

22.6 PROJECT MANAGEMENT

Microsoft Project is a project management software product, developed and sold by Microsoft. It is designed to assist a project manager in developing a plan, assigning resources to tasks, tracking progress, managing the budget, and analysing workloads.

Microsoft Project Management helps you get started quickly and execute projects with ease. Built-in templates, familiar scheduling tools, and access across devices increase productivity for project managers and teams.

- **Built-in templates** : Built-in, customizable templates use industry best practices to help you get started on the right path-so there's no need to create project plans from scratch.
- **Project planning** : Familiar scheduling features like Gantt charts and prepopulated pulldown menus help reduce training time and simplify the project planning process. The application creates critical path schedules, and critical chain and event chain methodology third-party add-ons also are available. Schedules can be resource levelled, and chains are visualized in a Gantt chart.
- **Out-of-the-box reports** : Share reports across your organization to keep everyone on the same page. Reports include everything from burndown charts to financials; and are available across devices.

- **Multiple timelines** : Quickly view all project activities, from tasks to upcoming milestones. Customize timelines to represent specific data and easily share them with project stakeholders. The timeline view allows the user to build a basic Visio-style graphical overview of the project schedule. The view can be copied and pasted into PowerPoint, Word, or any other application.
- **Access across devices** : Microsoft Project & Portfolio Management is available on Windows, iOS, and Android devices, so team members can update tasks on their device of choice and view timelines and reports on the go.
- Microsoft Project can recognize different classes of users. These different classes of users can have differing access levels to projects, views, and other data. Custom objects such as calendars, views, tables, filters, and fields are stored in an enterprise global which is shared by all users.
- **User controlled scheduling** : User-controlled scheduling offers flexible choices for developing and managing projects.
- Project 2016 adds a new Reports section, backwards-compatibility with Project Server 2013, better integration with other Microsoft products, and improved appearance of user interface items.

22.6.1 Switching Task

MS Project by default sets tasks to be manually scheduled. Scheduling is controlled in two ways:

- **Manual Scheduling** : This is done to quickly capture some details without actually scheduling the tasks. You can leave out details for some of the task with respect to duration, start and finish dates, if you don't know them yet.
- **Automatic Scheduling** : This uses the scheduling engine in MS project. It calculates value such as task durations, start date and finish dates automatically. It takes into accounts all constraints, links and calendars.

22.7 BUSINESS PRODUCTS

Microsoft offers an additional range of high-end Office-related products specifically designed for business customers.

22.7.1 Microsoft Exchange Server

Microsoft Exchange is a hosted messaging solution that gives users access to email, calendar, contacts, and tasks from PCs, the web, and mobile devices. Some of its features are giver below:

- Users can retrieve contact lists from a local directory service such as Microsoft Exchange Server
- Microsoft Office can show if other people are working on the same document.
- All communication between the clients takes place through a Skype for Business Server. This makes communications more secure, as messages do not need to leave the corporate intranet, unlike with the Internet-based Windows Live Messenger. The server can be set to relay messages to other instant messaging networks, avoiding installation of extra software at the client side.
- A number of client types are available for Microsoft Lync, including mobile clients.
- Allows sharing files.

22.7.2 SharePoint Online

Microsoft SharePoint is a browser-based collaboration, document management platform and content management system. It is a central web-based portal. Using SharePoint, you can manage your colleague's and your own documents, social activities, data, and information.

SharePoint 2016 is Microsoft's document management and collaboration tool with a software-as-a-service strategy at its core. Like SharePoint 2013, the product is offered in the cloud as part of the Office 365 suite and is known as SharePoint Online; the online premises version is known as SharePoint Server 2016. Features in SharePoint 2016 include:

- **Access services**: Users can support Office 365 apps or download Excel features to pivot Access tables. Microsoft also improved related item control where users can add new items.
- **Compliance features**: The In-Place Hold Policy Center and the Compliance Center enable administrators to build policies and apply them against their SharePoint environment. The updated features allow users to delete documents from their OneDrive for Business sites.
- **Document library accessibility**: Users can use landmarks for a page to make it easier to navigate, keyboard shortcuts for document tasks, announcements for upload progress, improved callout readings and updates to the help documentation.
- More durable links.
- Microsoft's newest version of SharePoint includes new and improved security features focused on encryption and information rights management.
- It allows groups to set up a centralized, password-protected space for document sharing.
- Documents can be stored, downloaded and edited, then uploaded for continued sharing.

22.7.3 OneDrive for Business

As its name indicates, OneDrive for Business is designed for organizations. It allows a company to provide cloud storage to its employees and manage its usage from a central location. Here you can store, share, and sync your work files. You can update and share your files from any device with OneDrive for Business. You can even work on Office documents with others at the same time. OneDrive for Business is different from OneDrive, which is intended for personal storage separate from your workplace.

22.7.4 Skype for Business

Skype for Business is hosted communications service that connects people anytime anywhere. It is used by corporate for instant messaging, audio/video calls and web conferences.

Difference between Skype and Skype for Business

Skype allows users to communicate with any other Skype user for free via IM, voice, video and screen sharing, and conference calls for up to 25 people. With Skype you can get a phone number and make PSTN calls that you pay for by the minute. Skype can be used for business but it best for small organizations or startups.

Skype for Business allows for advanced call routing and handling that most businesses require. You can setup hunt groups, delegates, advanced forwarding options, and auto attendants, most of which is needed in a large enterprise setting. Skype for Business can also replace conferencing services, it allows for up to 250 users on single conference call. Skype for Business allows you to record your meetings, and gives you special meeting controls for presenters and a meeting hall for attendees. Skype for Business gives you enterprise-grade security, allows you to manage employee accounts, and is integrated into your Office apps. Also, Skype for Business has real-time availability that's integrated with your calendar which means your Outlook calendar will automatically update your Skype for Business presence, showing co-workers when you're available for calls or IMs and when you're not. Skype for Business is made for larger organizations looking to replace their current phone system with a cloud-based PBX. It has all the same functions as a traditional office phone system but because it is software and cloud-based it allows for their team and users to be mobile and connected using multiple forms of communication.

22.7.5 Yammer

Yammer is a private microblogging and collaboration platform for enterprise social networking. The Yammer collaboration platform allows you to integrate business applications via Open Graph. Yammer provides a simple way for your team to collaborate, share knowledge, and engage everyone across your company. Yammer groups can now be more easily managed through dynamic group membership that updates automatically as people join, leave or move within organizations.

22.7.6 Power BI

Power business intelligence BI is a cloud-based business analytics service that enables anyone to visualize and analyze data with greater speed, efficiency, and understanding. It connects users to a broad range of data through easy-to-use dashboards, interactive reports, and compelling visualizations that bring data to life.

22.7.7 Microsoft Dynamics CRM

Customer Relationship Management (CRM) is a system for managing a company's interactions with current and future customers. It often involves using technology to organize, automate, and synchronize sales, marketing, customer service, and technical support. CRM can help reduce costs and increase profitability by organizing and automating business processes that nurture customer satisfaction and loyalty.

Microsoft Dynamics CRM is a customer relationship management software package developed by Microsoft. Dynamics CRM also offers full mobile support for using CRM apps on mobiles and tablets.

Microsoft Dynamics CRM is offered in two categories

CRM Online

CRM Online is a cloud-based offering of Microsoft Dynamics CRM where all the backend processes (such as application servers, setups, deployments, databases, licensing, etc.) are managed on Microsoft servers. CRM Online is a subscription-based offering which is preferred for organizations who may not want to manage all the technicalities involved in a CRM implementation.

CRM On-Premise

CRM on-premise is a more customized and robust offering of Microsoft Dynamics CRM, where the CRM application and databases will be deployed on your servers. This offering allows you to control all your databases, customizations, deployments, backups, licensing and other network and hardware setups. Generally, organizations who want to go for a customized CRM solution prefer on-premise deployment as it offers better integration and customization capabilities.

From the functional standpoint, both the offerings offer similar functionalities; however, they differ significantly in terms of implementation.

- CRM Online is a cloud-based solution provided by Microsoft in which all the servers and databases are managed by Microsoft. CRM On-Premise solution provided by Microsoft in which the servers and databases are managed by the customer.
- You can get started with an online offering in a matter of few days. You pay for the users and used space on-the-go. Setting up an on-premise offering needs technical skills as well as sufficient time to setup the CRM instance and get it running.
- CRM Online supports relatively less customizations and extensions. CRM On-Premise supports relatively more customization and extensions.
- CRM Online does not give the ability to perform manual data backup and restore options, since the database is hosted on Microsoft servers. However, Microsoft performs daily backups of the database. CRM on-premise gives complete ability to manage your database.
- CRM Online provides inbuilt capabilities of features such as insights, social listening, analytics, etc. CRM on-premise has extra costs for these features.
- CRM Online supports automatic updates to future version. CRM on-premise updates need to be installed by the administrator.

APPENDIX

Tips and Tricks in Excel 2016

A.1 EXCEL 2016 MAIN WINDOW

1. **File tab:** It provides access to the *Backstage* view, which contains tools for common tasks such as creating, opening, saving, sharing, and printing workbooks. You can also use the *File* tab's tools to sign in to or out of your Microsoft Account, set program options, set a workbook password, and inspect your workbook for personally identifiable information. (Figure A.1)

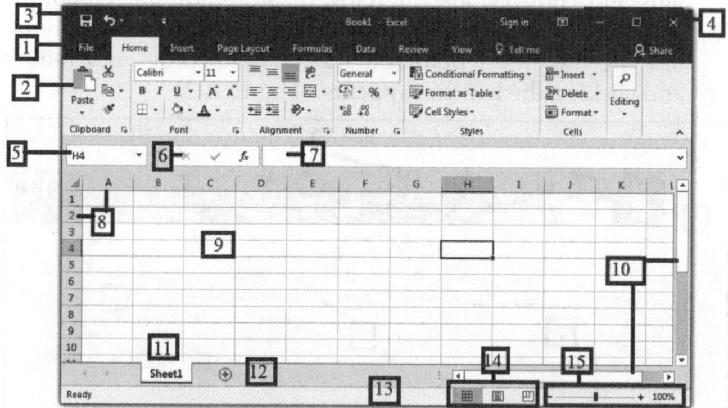

Figure A.1 Excel 2016 Main Window

2. **Ribbon:** A set of controls near the top of the program window that provides access to tools for adding, editing, and formatting worksheet contents.
3. **Quick Access Toolbar:** A set of buttons at the top left corner of the program window, above the Ribbon, which provides one-click access to commonly used features. When you install Excel 2016, the *Quick Access Toolbar* has four buttons: *Save, Undo, Redo*, and *Customize Quick Access Toolbar*. You can add, remove, and reorder the toolbar buttons as needed.
4. **Workbook window controls:** Controls at the top right corner of the program window lets you to minimize, maximize, restore, or close the workbook window. The *Maximize* and *Restore* buttons are two states of the same control and never appear at the same time.
5. **Name box:** A box above the header for worksheet column A. The name box displays the address of the active cell, the dimensions of a selected cell range while the left mouse button is held down, or the name of a selected range of cells. Typing a cell address into the name box and pressing **<Enter>** selects the cell you identified.
6. **Insert Function button:** Click the **Insert Function** button to display the *Insert Function* dialog box, which lets you search for functions, select a function to use in your formula, and identify the inputs (arguments) to be used in the formula.
7. **Formula bar:** Displays the contents of the active cell, whether it is a value typed directly into the cell or a formula. Clicking in the formula bar lets you edit the cell's contents, after which you can press <Enter> to accept the change or press *<Esc>* to cancel the change.
8. **Column and row headers:** Letters and numbers that identify horizontal rows and vertical columns in a worksheet. Excel identifies rows using numbers along the left edge of the worksheet and columns using letters along the top edge of the worksheet.
9. **Cell range and active cell:** The active cell, which Excel identifies by changing its border to dark green, is the cell currently selected for editing. A cell range is a collection of cells that have been highlighted by using the mouse or keyboard. A cell range may contain many cells, but there is only one active cell at a time.
10. **Scroll bars:** The horizontal scroll bar lets you to move left and right within a worksheet without changing the active cell. Similarly, the vertical scroll bar lets you to move up and down within a worksheet.
11. **Sheet tab bar:** A set of indicators at the bottom right corner of the program window that represent the sheets within a workbook. Excel displays the sheet tab of the active worksheet with a white background, bold text, and an underline.
12. **New Sheet button:** A button that, when clicked, inserts a new worksheet to the right of the active sheet.
13. **Status bar:** A section of the bottom edge of the program window that displays program information such as when a background save is in progress, when the workbook is recalculating, and summary calculations for values in selected cell ranges.
14. **View controls:** There icons between the status bar and zoom controls change how a worksheet is displayed. *Normal* displays the worksheet as a simple grid, *Page Layout* displays the worksheet headers and footers, and *Page Break Preview* shows which worksheet content will appear on which printed page. The dashed lines in *Page Break Preview* show automatic page breaks; the solid lines show manual page breaks.
15. **Zoom controls:** A set of controls to increase or decrease the worksheet magnification. Clicking the *Zoom Out* button (looks like a minus sign) makes the worksheet's contents 10% smaller; clicking the *Zoom In* button (looks like a plus sign) makes the worksheet's contents 10% bigger. Dragging the slider on the bar between the buttons lets you change the zoom level more rapidly. The zoom level appears at the bottom right corner of the program window; clicking that number displays the *Zoom* dialog box.

A.1.1 New Features

- **Get Help using Tell me what you what you want to do:** Click the Tell me what you want to do text on the Ribbon or press **Alt + Q** and start typing a description of what you want to do in Excel. The program displays a list of topics related to the task you describe; clicking a link displays the *Help* file on that topic. Press **<F1>** to open Help directly.
- **Use new charts:** Six new chart types are included in Excel 2016; *waterfall* (shows how resources, usually money in an account, varies over time), histogram (summarizes the number of values that fall into certain ranges, or bins), *Pareto* (combines a column chart with a line chart to show how much each category contributes to the whole), *box-and-whisker* (plot shows the average, maximum, minimum, and median (or middle) values for a data series), *tree map*, and *sunburst*(show how much sets of categories and subcategories of data contribute to a whole).
- **Add a handwritten equation:** Previous versions of Excel let you to create an equation using a built-in-template, such as the Pythagorean theorem, or by designing your own using common patterns. In Excel 2016, you can use your finger or a stylus on a touch-sensitive device to write an equation by hand and add it to the workbook.
- **Forecast data using exponential smoothing:** Exponential smoothing is a forecasting technique that gives higher weights to recent values in data series. By comparison, standard linear regression models give equal weight to every value. Under exponential smoothing, sales from last month would be more important than sales from two years ago when forecasting future values.
- **Add tables to the Excel Data Model:** Several advanced features introduced in Excel 2016 take advantage of the Excel Data Model. The Data Model is in internal representation of Excel tables and other data sources in your workbook. If two tables have a value in common, such as a customer identification number in a customer list that is also in a table of orders, you can define a relationship between the tables and combine their values in PivotTables.
- **Create forecast sheets:** Users are able to create separate worksheets by using line charts and the new exponential smoothing techniques described earlier.
- **Bring in data using Power Query:** This feature adds many more capabilities for bringing data into Excel from a variety of sources including text files, databases, and the web. You can use Power Query to control which tables or parts of tables to import into Excel and manage updates when the data source changes.

A.1.2 Ribbon

- **Tab:** Displays a range of tools based on a common theme. For example, the *Home* tab displays the most commonly used tools, and the *Formulas* tab presents tools for entering and auditing formulas using built-in functions and analytical tools.
- **Group:** Contains a focused collection of tools on a Ribbon tab. The *Review* Tab's *Comments* group, for example, contains tools for adding, deleting, and reviewing cell comments.
- **Dialog box expander:** Provides access to a dialog box that contains tools related to a Ribbon group. For example, clicking the dialog box expander at the bottom right corner of the **Home** Tab's, *Font* group opens the *Formal Cells* dialog box and displays its *Font* tab.
- **Contextual tab:** Displays one or more Ribbon tabs that contain tools related to a selected worksheet object. When an image is selected, a *Design* contextual tab with image-management tools appears.
- **Gallery:** Contains a set of ready-made formats that can be applied to a worksheet object such as an image, shape, or Excel table. Galleries also include menu items which you can click to create, modify, and delete custom styles. When you hover your mouse pointer over a style in a gallery, Excel 2016 shows a live preview of your worksheet's appearance if the style were applied.
- **Ribbon display options:** Enables you to display the Ribbon tabs and controls, just the tabs, or auto-hide the Ribbon. If you auto-hide the Ribbon, you can display it temporarily by moving you mouse pointer to the top of the program window and clicking the bar that appears. (Figure A.2)

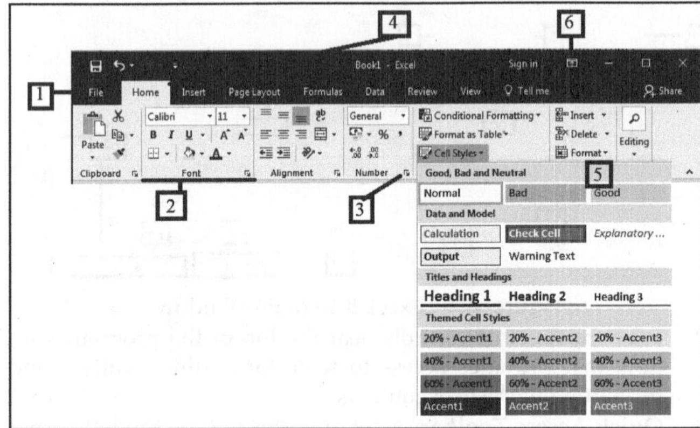

Figure A.2 Ribbon

A.1.3 Document File Formats

Excel 2016 lets you to work with files in a wide range of formats, including workbook file and text files in which values are separated by commas. In Office 97 and later, all Excel workbooks were capable of running macros (stored procedures written using visual Basic for Applications). Starting with Office 2007, Excel files could be either normal workbooks or macro-enabled workbooks. The following table summarizes the most commonly used file types in Excel 2016.

Extension	Description
.xlsx	Excel 2007 or later workbook
.xlsm	Excel 2007 or later macro-enabled workbook
.xltx	Excel 2007 or later template or regular workbooks

(Contd...)

.xltm	Excel 2007 or later template for macro-enabled workbooks
.xls	Excel 97-2003 workbook
.xlt	Excel 97-2003 workbook template
.ods	OpenDocument Spreadsheet file

A.2 MICROSOFT ACCOUNTS

Excel 2016, part of the Microsoft Office 2016 program suite, provides many ways to share files and collaborate by using the Internet. For example, most Excel 2016 users can take advantage of online file storage and web-based Office Online programs through One-Drive (formerly Sky-Drive). You can access these services through a Microsoft Account, which also works for Xbox Live, Office 365 (the online subscription edition of Microsoft Office), Skype, and other Microsoft services.

- **Sign up for a Microsoft Account:**

1. In a web browser, visit www.onedrive.com.
2. Click **Sign up**.
3. Select either **OneDrive** or **OneDrive for Business**.

- **Sign in to your Microsoft Account from Excel 2016:**

1. Near the top right corner of an Excel workbook window, click **Sign in**.
2. Type you email address or phone number in the Name box and click **Next**.
3. Type your password in the Password box and click **Sign in**.

A.2.1 Entering & Editing Cell Data

- **To enter data into a cell:**

1. Click a cell to select it.
2. Type the value you want to appear in the cell.
3. Press **<Enter>** to accept the value and move one cell down. Or

   Press **<Tab>** to accept the value and move one cell to the right.

- **To edit cell contents:**

1. Click the cell you want to change, type a new value, and press **<Enter>** or **<Tab>** OR
1. Double-click the cell you want to change.
2. Click within the cell's contents, and use the keyboard to edit the value.
3. Press **<Enter>** when you are done. OR
1. Click the cell you want to change.
2. Click in the **Formula Bar** to position the insertion point within the cell's contents, edit the value, and press **<Enter>**.
3. Cancel cell data entry or edits:
4. While editing a cell, press **<Esc>**.

- **To enter data into multiple cells:**

1. Select the cells into which you want to enter the value.
2. Type the value (Excel displays what you type in the active cell).
3. Press **<Ctrl>** + **<Enter>**.

- **To enter data onto multiple sheets:**

1. Hold down the **<Ctrl>** key.
2. Click the sheet tabs where you want to enter the data.
3. On the active worksheet, select the cells into which you want to enter the value, type the value (Excel displays what you type in the active cell).
4. Press **<Ctrl>** + **<Enter>**.

- **To extend a data series using the fill handle:**

1. Select a range of cells that contains numbers or dates.
2. At the bottom right corner of the selections, drag the fill handle to extend the series.
3. Dragging the fill handle down (or to the right for values in a row) increase the values, whereas dragging up or to the left decreases the values.

- **To enter a data series using Fill > Series:**

1. Click the cell that contains the first value in the series.
2. On the **Home** tab, in the **Editing** group, click **Fill** and then click **Series**.
3. In the **Series** dialog box, select whether the series should extend down (columns) or to the right (rows).
4. Select the type of series (linear increases or decrease values by a set amount).
5. Select the date unit (if appropriate), and whether the values represent a trend.
6. Then enter a step value (the amount the series values increase or decrease) and a stop value.
7. Click OK.

- **To find value in a worksheet:**

1. On the **Home** tab, in the **Editing** group, click **Find & Select**.
2. Click **Find** (or press **<Ctrl>** + **<F>** to display the **Find** tab of the **Find and Replace** dialog box.
3. Type the value to find in the **Find what** box.
4. Click **Options** to display additional options such as defining a format to search for, where and how to look, whether to match the case of the text in the *Find what* box, or to match only cells that contain just the value in the *Find what* box.
5. Click **Find All** to select all cells with the value or **Find Next** to highlight the next cell that contains the value.

- **To replace values in a worksheet:**

1. On the **Home** tab, in the *Editing* group, click **Find & Select**.
2. Click **Replace** (or press **<Ctrl>** + **<H>**) to display the *Replace* tab of the *Find and Replace* dialog box.
3. Type the value to change in the *Find what* box, and type the replacement value in the *Replace* with box.
4. Click **Options** to display additional options such as defining a format to search for, where and how to look, whether to match the case of the text in the *Find what* box, or to match only cells that contain just the value in the *Find what* box.
5. Click either **Replace All** to change all occurrences of the value, or **Find Next** and then Replace to replace the next occurrence of the value.

A.2.2 Undo & Redo Changes

- **To Undo a change:**

1. On the *Quick Access Toolbar*, click **Undo** or press **<Ctrl>** + **<Z>**.
2. To undo multiple changes at once, click the Undo button's down arrow and click the last item into the list of actions you want to undo. This will unto the action you clicked and every action on the list above it.

- **To redo a change:**

1. On the *Quick Access Toolbar*, click **Redo** or press **<Ctrl>** + **<Y>**.
2 To redo multiple changes at once, click the Redo button's down arrow and click the last item in the list of actions you want to redo. This will redo the action you clicked and every action on the list above it.

A.2.3 Managing Cells, Rows, Columns

- **To select a cell range:**

1. Click a cell at a corner of the range you want to select.
2 Hold down the left mouse button, and drag the mouse pointer to highlight the additional cells.

- **To select noncontiguous cell ranges:**

1. Select the first cell range to include in the overall selection and hold down **<Ctrl>** while you select a new cell range.
2. Repeat as described until all cells are selected.

- **To copy data in a cell range:**

1. Select the cells that contain the data to be copied and either press **<Ctrl>** + **<C>** or, on the **Home** tab, in the **Clipboard** group, click **Copy.**

- **To cut data in a cell range:**

1. Select the cells that contain that data to be cut and either press **<Ctrl>** + **<X>** or, on the **Home** tab, in the **Clipboard** group, click **Cut.**

- **To paste data:**

1. Select the cell where you want to paste your data or the cell at the top left corner of the range where you want to paste the data.
2. Then either press **<Ctrl>** + **<V>** or, on the **Home** tab, in the **Clipboard** group, click **Paste.**

- **To control paste options:**

1. Copy the data you want to paste, and either select a cell range or click the cell at the top left corner of the range where you want the pasted data to appear.
2. Then, on the **Home** tab, in the **Clipboard** group, click the **Paste** button's down arrow.
3. From the palette of icons that appears, click the option you want to use when pasting your data. OR
1. Copy and paste your data into a cell range, click the **Paste Options** action button that appears at the button right corner of the pasted range.
2. Click the icon representing the option you want to apply.

- **To move a cell range:**

1. Select a cell range.
2. When the cells still selected, move your mouse pointer over the edge of the range until it changes to a four-way arrow.
3. With the mouse pointer in position, drag the cells to the new location.
4. If the moved range overlaps with cells that contain data, a confirmation dialog box will appear.
5. Click **OK** to replace the values, or click **Cancel** to stop the process.

- **To insert cells:**

1. Select a cell range of the size you want to insert.
2. Right-click any select cell and then click **Insert.**
3. In the **Insert** dialog box, select the option that represents how you want the surrounding cells to move to make room for the inserted cells, then click **OK.**

- **To delete cells:**

1. Select the cells you want to delete.
2. Right-click any selected cell and then click **Delete.**
3. In the **Delete** dialog box, select the option that represents how you want the surrounding cells to move to accommodate the deleted cells.
4. Click OK.

- **To select rows or columns:**

1. Click the row header of the row you want to select or the column header of the column you want to select. OR
2. Hold down **<Ctrl>** and click the headers of the rows or columns you want to select. OR
3. Hold down **<Shift>**, click the first row or column header you want to select, and then click the last row or column header in the range you want to select.

- **To insert rows or columns:**

1. Right-click a row or column header, and then click **Insert**. Or
2. Select a number of rows or columns, right-click any selected row or column header, and then click **Insert.**

- **To delete rows or columns:**

1. Select the rows of columns you want to delete.
2. Right-click any selected row or column header.
3. Click **Insert.**

- **To hide rows or columns:**

1. Select a contiguous range of rows or columns.
2. Right-click the header of any selected row or column, and then click **Hide.**

- **To unhide rows or columns:**

1. Select the rows or columns on either side of the hidden rows or columns.
2. Right-click any selected row or column header, and then click **Unhide.**

- **To apply Font & Cell Formatting:**

1. Click the **Font** control's down arrow to select a font to apply to the selected cells.
2. Click the **Font Size** control's down arrow to select a font size to apply to the selected cells or type the desired font size in the **Font Size** box.
3. Press **<Enter>.**
4. Click either **Increase Font Size** or **Decrease Font Size** to change the size of the text in the selected cells.
5. Click **Bold**, **Italic**, or **Underline** to apply the desired formatting to the selected cells.
6. Click the **Borders** button's down arrow to select a border pattern to apply to the selected cells.
7. Click **More Borders** to display the **Border** tab of the *Format Cells* dialog box.
8. To change the selected cells' background color, click the **Fill Color** control's down arrow and select a color from the palette. To change the color of text in the selected cells, click the **Font Color** control's down arrow and select a color in the palette.
9. Click **Align Left**, **Center**, or **Align Right** to align text with the left edge, center, or right edge of the selected cells.
10. Click **Top Align**, **Middle Align**, or **Bottom Align** to align text with the top edge, middle, or bottom edge of the selected cells.

11. Click **Orientation** to change how text is rotated within the cell. To display the Alignment tab of the Format Cells dialog box, click Orientation and then click Format Cell Alignment.
12. Click **Wrap Text** to increase a cell's vertical size to fits its contents within its current width by displaying text on more than one line.
13. Click **Decrease Indent** or **Increase Indent** to change the distance of a cell's contents from the left border.
14. The *Merge & Center* options combine multiple cells from a row into a single cell. Click **Merge & Center** to center the contents within the merged cell, or click the down arrow and select **Merge Across** to leave the text left-aligned, **Merge Cells** to merge cells in multiple rows, or **Unmerge Cells** to split a merged cell (i.e. undo a merge).

A.3 CREATING FORMULAS

Terms to remember

- **Formula:** A statement that calculates a value in a worksheet cell.
- **Function:** A built-in calculation that combines values in a specific way, such as by finding the sum of all values in a cell range.
- **Argument:** A value used in a formula (also the input).
- **Output:** The result of a formula.
- **Returns:** A verb describing the act of a formula generating a result, or output.

  Example: The formula = 3 + 4 returns an output of 7.

  Syntax: The structure of a function, specifying the number and order of arguments (inputs) it requires to return a result.

Order of Operations

Excel 2016 follows mathematical conventions when determining the order of operations used in a calculation. That order is:

1. Parentheses ()
2. Negation, such as (-3)
3. Percentage (%)
4. Exponentiation (^, e.g., 2^3 is written as 2^3)
5. Multiplication and division (* and /)
6. Addition and subtraction (+ and -)

Example: 3 + 9 * 7 = 66, where 9 * 7 = 63, and 3 + 63 = 66. If two operations on the same level, such as multiplication and division, occur outside parentheses, Excel performs them in left-to-right order. One example could be 9 * 7/3 = 21. You can change the order of operations by using parentheses, so (3 + 9) * 7 = 84, where 3 + 9 = 12, and 12 * 7 = 84.

- **To create a formula:**

1. Type an equal sign followed by the values, cell references, or functions to be used in the calculation.

- **Refer to cells & cell ranges in formulas:**

1. Worksheet cells are identified by their column letter and then their row number.

   Example: The top left cell in a worksheet is in column A and row 1, so its cell address is A1.
2. You can also refer to cell ranges, or collections of cells. To identify a cell range, type the address of the cell at the top left corner of the range, followed by a colon, and then type the address of the cell at the bottom right corner of the range.

   Example: The reference for the first five cells in columns A and B would be A1:B5.
3. Create relative, absolute & mixed references:
4. When you type a cell reference with just the column letter and row number (e.g., A1), that reference can change when you copy its formula to another cell.

   Example: Copying the formula = **A1 + A2** and pasting it one cell to the right would create the formula = **B1 + B2**. The destination cell is one column to the right of the original cell, so Excel changes the formula's references based on that difference.
5. To create an absolute reference, one that doesn't change when you copy a formula, type a $ before the column and row designators.

   Example: The formula = **A1*A2** won't change, regardless of the cell you copy it to.
6. To create a mixed reference, where either rows or columns are absolute, add a $ before the element you want to remain the same.

   Example: The cell reference **A$1** allows changing columns, and **$A1** allows changing rows.

A.3.1 To create Formulas Using Functions

Functions are predefined recipes for performing specific calculations. For example, rather than add a series of numbers and divide by the number of values to find the average, you can use the *AVERAGE* function to calculate the result you want.

A.4 FUNCTION CATEGORIES

Excel 2016 divides functions into several categories, which helps you discover the function you need for a particular task. Clicking a category button in the **Formulas tab's Function Library** group displays a list of the functions available in that category.

1. **Insert Function:** Opens a dialog box of the same name, where you can search for the function you need and enter the values or arguments required to perform its calculation.
2. **Recently Used:** Displays functions you have used recently.
3. **Financial:** Displays functions related to financial data, such as *PMT* to calculate periodic payments at a given interest rate, *FV* to calculate the future value of an investment with recurring payments at a fixed interest rate, or NPER to calculate the total number of periods for an investment.
4. **Logical:** Includes functions that let you test for certain conditions and return a **TRUE** or **FALSE** results.

   Example: You can use the *IFERROR* function to display either the formula's result or, if the formula generates an error, a custom message.
5. **Text:** Includes functions such as **LEFT** and **RIGHT**, which return the leftmost or rightmost characters in a cell's text, or *UPPER* and *LOWER*, which change a cell's text to all uppercase or all lowercase letters.
6. **Date & Time:** Contains functions related to dates and times, such as the MONTH function, which returns the month component of a date, or *MINUTE*, which returns the minute component of a time.
7. **Lookup & Reference:** Displays functions that let you find values within a worksheet, such as *VLOOKUP*, and define links to other files and web resources, such as *HYPERLINK*.

8. **Math & Trig:** Includes functions that perform mathematical and trigonometric calculations, such as finding the square root of a number using **SQRT** or finding the sine of an angle using **SIN**.
9. **More Functions:** A drop-down list that includes the following additional categories: *Statistical, Engineering, Information, Compatibility,* and *Web*. The *Compatibility* category gathers functions that have been replaced with newer versions in Excel 2016 but are still available to allow backward compatibility with earlier versions. The other categories contain advanced functions used in the field name.

- **To insert a function:**

1. Start creating the formula where you want to insert the function, and then take one of the following steps:
   a. Type the first letters of the function name and either finish typing its name or click the function on the AutoComplete list that appears and press <Tab>.
   b. Click **Insert Function.**
   c. Select the function you want to add.
   d. On the *Formulas* tab of the Ribbon, in the *Function Library* group, click the category of the function you want to add, then click the function name.

- **To get help using function argument ToolTips:**

1. Start creating a formula and enter the name of the function followed by a left parenthesis (i.e., = **SUM()**.
2. In the function ToolTip that appears below the cell that contain the formula, position the mouse pointer over the function name.
3. In the ToolTip, when the function name's text changes to a blue, underlined format, click it to display the relevant Help file.

- **To add an AutoSum function:**

1. Select a cell below a column of numbers.
2. On the **Home** tab of the Ribbon, in the **Editing** group, click **AutoSum** to add a **SUM** formula, or click the AutoSum button's down arrow to select another function.

A.4.1 Using Tables in Formulas

Tables give formal structure to lists of data in a worksheet, with unique names for the table as a whole and for each column.

Example: A table named Table1 (the default name for the first table you create in a workbook) could have columns named *Data, StoreNumber*, and *Sales*.

You could summarize the table's data using formulas, PivotTables, or charts. When you create tables, Excel automatically updates your formulas, PivotTables, or charts when you add a row of data. If you add data to a worksheet outside a table, you must edit the summary's settings reflect the new values.

- **To create a table:**

1. Click any cell in a data list.
2. On the **Home** tab, in the **Styles** group, click **Format as Table.**
3. In the gallery that appears, click the style you want to apply.

	A	B	C	D
1	Year ▾	Month ▾	State ▾	Sales ▾
2	2016	January	Virginia	Rs. 2,62,576
3	2016	January	Maryland	Rs. 3,86,812
4	2016	January	Delaware	Rs. 4,93,331
5	2016	February	Virginia	Rs. 2,58,931
6	2016	February	Maryland	Rs. 2,71,657
7	2016	February	Delaware	Rs. 1,56,634
8	2016	March	Virginia	Rs. 2,14,184
9	2016	March	Maryland	Rs. 2,24,570
10	2016	March	Delaware	Rs. 2,00,946

4. In the Format As Table dialog box, verify that Excel has identified the correct cell range.
5. Check the **My table has headers** box if appropriate.
6. Click OK.

Refer to a table column in a formula:

1. Start creating a formula in a cell, such as = AVERAGE().
2. In the parentheses, type the name of the table or start typing it and select it from the suggestions list.
3. Type a left square bracket [, click the name of the column you want to summarize, and then type a right square bracket]: = AVERAGE(Sales16[Sales]).
4. Finish editing your formula and pres <Enter>.

A.4.2 Summary & Statistical Functions

Spreadsheets store numerical data efficiently, so it makes sense that Excel includes literally hundreds of summary and statistical functions you can use to analyze and summarize your data. The functions in this section all take values, cell ranges, or combinations of the two as arguments.

Example: The formula = **SUM(14, 15, C8:C10)** would add 14 to 15, and then add the values in the cell range **C8:C10** to that total.

Each of the following functions follow the same syntax, **Function(number1, [number2]...).**

- **function:** Name of the function.
- **number1:** Required argument consisting either of a number or the address of a cell or cell range that contains numbers.
- **number2 and subsequent number argument:** Additional ranges to be included in the summary.

The following functions are the most commonly used summary and statistical functions:

- **SUM:** Adds the values in all named cells.
- **PRODUCT:** Multiplies the values in all named cells.
- **AVERAGE:** Finds the arithmetic average, or mean, of the values in all named cells.
- **MEDIAN:** Finds the middle value in the value list when the values are sorted into ascending numerical order. If there is an even number of values, the middle two values are averaged.

- **MODE.SNGL:** Finds the most common value in the set.
- **MIN:** Finds the minimum value in the set, ignoring logical values and text.
- **MINA:** Finds the minimum value in the set, including logical values and text.
- **MAX:** Finds the maximum value in the set, ignoring logical values and text.
- **MAXA:** Finds the maximum value in the set, including logical values and text.
- **STDEV.P:** finds the standard deviation of the values in the set by using a sample of values from the set.
- **VAR.P:** Finds the variance of the values in the set by using all values in the set.
- **VAR.S:** Finds the variance of the values in the set by using a sample of values from the set.

  Example: You could find the sum of all sales to customers in Virginia or calculate the average value of months with sales under Rs.250,000 (see the table show here).

	A	B	C	D
1	Year	Month	State	Sales
2	2016	January	Virginia	Rs. 2,62,576
3	2016	January	Maryland	Rs. 3,86,812
4	2016	January	Delaware	Rs. 4,93,331
5	2016	February	Virginia	Rs.,931
6	2016	February	Maryland	Rs. 2,71,657
7	2016	February	Delaware	Rs. 1,56,634
8	2016	March	Virginia	Rs. 2,14,184
9	2016	March	Maryland	Rs. 2,24,570
10	2016	March	Delaware	Rs. 2,00,946

- **To find the sum of data that meets one condition:**

1. In a worksheet cell, create a formula the form =SUMIF (**range, criteria, [sum_range]**), where:
   - Range represents the cells that contain the values to be evaluated using the formula's criteria.
   - Criteria represents the rule used to evaluate whether to include a value in the summary.
   - Sum_range is an optional argument that identifies the cells that contain the numerical values to be included in the summary, if they are different from the cells identified by the range argument.
2. Press <Enter>.
3. Given the sample data in the table shown in this section, the formula = *SUMIF(C:C10, "Virginia", D2:D10)* would return Rs.735,691.

- **To find the average of data that meets one condition:**

1. In a worksheet cell, create a formula of the form =*AVERAGEIF*(**range, criteria, [average_range]**), where:
   - *range* represents the cells that contain the values to be evaluated using the formula's criteria.
   - *criteria* represents the rule used to evaluate whether to include a value in the summary.
   - *average_range* is an optional argument that identifies the cells that contain the numerical values to be included in the summary, if they are different from the cells identified by the range argument.
2. Press <Enter>.

   Given the sample data in the table shown in this section, the formula

   a. =AVERAGE(B2:B10, "March", D2:D10) would return Rs. 213,233.

A.4.3 Counting Values in Cell Ranges

In addition to summarizing values in a range using SUM, AVERAGE, or another arithmetic function, you can count the number of values of specific types that appear in a range. The basic COUNT family to functions all follows the syntax of *function(value1, [value2]...)*, where:

- *value1* is a cell reference or range.
- *value2* and subsequent value arguments are optional arguments that refer to subsequent cell ranges.

  The basic COUNT functions are:
  - **COUNT:** Counts the number of cells that contain numbers:
  - **COUNTA:** Counts the number of cells in a range that are not empty
  - **COUNTBLANK:** Counts the number of cells I a range that are blank.

  You can also use the conditional versions of COUNT, COUNTIF, and COUNTIFS to count values that meet one or more criteria.

- **To count cells that contain data that meets one condition:**

1. In a worksheet cell, create a formula of the form =**COUNTIF(range, criteria)**, where:
   - range represents the cells that contain the values to be evaluated using the formula's criteria.
   - criteria represent the rule used to evaluate whether to include a value in the summary.
2. Press <Enter>.
3. Given the sample data in the table shown in the **Summary & Statistical Functions** section, the formula =**COUNTIF(D2:D10, "<300000")** would return 7.

A.4.4 Performing Financial Calculations

Principal & Interest Payments

Financing a private purchase or business venture requires you to repay the loan over time. A fully amortized loan, one that is paid in full at the end of the term, requires periodic payments that are often made on a monthly basis. The PMT function calculates the periodic payment required to pay off a loan over the time frame you specify. Each payment has an interest and principal component, which can be calculated using the *IPMT* and *PPMT* functions, respectively.

Use the PMT function:

In a worksheet cell, create a formula of the form **=PMT(rate, nper, pv, [fv], [type])** rate, where:

- rate is the annual interest rate, which should be divided by the number of payments per year.
  Example: For a loan with a 4.8% interest rate and monthly payments, the rate would be 4.8%/12.
  - *nper* is the number of payments.
  - *pv* is the present value, or principal, of the loan.
  - *fv* is an optional argument for the future value of the loan. Most loans are paid in full (fully amortized) at the end of the payment period, so this value can usually be omitted.
  - *type* is an optional argument for when the payment is due. If omitted or 0, the payment is due at the end of the period (almost always true); if 1, the payment is due at the start of the period.

  Example: = PMT(4.8%/12, 360, 350000) returns the value -Rs.1,836.33. The formula returns a negative value because it represents cash you owe.

  It is common practice to multiply the PMT function's result by -1 or to make the principal amount negative in order to display the result as a positive number.

Use the IPMT & PPMT functions:

The *IPMT* and *PPMT* functions use the same *rate, nper, pv, fv,* and type arguments along with the per argument.

In a worksheet cell, create a formula of the form = IPMT(rate, per, nper, pv, [fv], [type]) or =PPMT(rate, nper, pv, [fv], [type]), where:

- *per* is the period for which you are calculating the interest and principal components of the payment.
  Example: =IMPT(4.8%/12, 12, 360, 350000) returns -Rs.1,380.41, and =PPMT(4.8%/12, 12, 360, 350000) returns -Rs.455.92. Adding Rs.1,380.41 + Rs.455.92 (the absolute values of the payment) gives you Rs.1,836.33, which corresponds to the result of the PMT function.

	A	B	C
1	Interest Rate	4.80%	
2	Periods per Year	12	
3	Total Payment Periods	360	
4	Loan Principal	Rs. 3,50,000.00	
5			
6	Monthly Payment	Rs. 1,836.00	=PMT(B1/B2, -1*B4)
7	Period of Payment	12	
8	Interest Component	Rs. 1,380.41	#DIV/0!
9	Principal Component	Rs. 455.92	Rs.PPMT(B1/B2, B7, B3, -1*B4)

Calculating Present Value

The PV function calculates the present value of a series of payments given the number of payments, the amount of each payment, and the interest rate you want to assume.

- **To use the PV function:**

1. In a worksheet cell, create a formula of the form =PV(rate, nper, pmt, [fv], [type]), where:
   - *rate* is the annual interest rate, which should be divided by the number of payments per year.
     Example: For a loan with 6% interest rate and monthly payments, the rate would be 6%/12.
   - *nper* is the number of payments.
   - *pmt* is the amount of each payment (this value must remain constant).
   - *fv* is an optional argument for the future value of the loan. Most loans are paid in full (fully amortized) at the end of the payment period, so this value can usually be omitted.
   - *type* is an optional argument for when the payment is due. If omitted or 0, the payment is due at the end of the period (almost always true); if 1, the payment is due at the start of the period.

   Example: =PV(6%/12, 60, 1000), which calculates the present value of 60 monthly payments of Rs.1,000 each and assumes a 6% annual interest rate, returns a value of -Rs.51.725.56.

   As with the PMT function, PV returns a negative value because it assumes the money is leaving your account. The formula's result is less than the nominal sum of the payments, Rs.60,000, because future payments are discounted at a 6% annual rate.

A.4.5 Auditing Formulas

When you create a formula, you rely on the formula's inputs to be present and of the type you expect. For example, you can't divide a value by zero. If an error does occur, such as when you leave a cell blank or try to divide a value by zero, Excel displays an error value. The following list describes the most common error codes and their likely causes.

- **#DIV/0!:** Indicates a divide by zero error. This error occurs when you refer to a cell that is blank or that contains a zero value.
- **#N/A!:** Indicates that a value is not available for the formula. This error occurs when required data is missing from a from a function such as VLOOKUP.
- **NAME?:** Indicates that Excel doesn't recognize the name of a function or can't identify a named range, or if text was entered into a function's argument list without enclosing it in double quotes.
- **####:** Indicates the column isn't wide enough to display the value it contains. To fix the error, widen the column until the value appears.
- **#NULL!:** Indicates that a cell range doesn't doesn't return a value the function needs for its calculation. To fix the error, verify that your range reference is correct.
- **#NUM!:** Indicates that Excel expected a number but found a nonnumerical value instead. One common cause of this error is when currency values are entered using symbols and commas, such as Rs.2,500. To fix this error, either refer to a cell that is formatted as a numerical data type or enter the number without any punctuation.
- **#REF!:** Indicates that cells referred to by the formula have been deleted or had their contents replaced by pasting other cells on top of them. To fix the error, edit the cell references or re-create the formula.
- **#VALUE!:** Indicates that a formula is attempting to perform mathematical operations on text values. To avoid this error, ensure all cells to which the formula refers contain numbers or use a function such as SUM that can perform its calculations when the data supplied includes nonumerical values.

A cell that might contain an error or inconsistency, such as formula that excludes cells next to the range your formula summarizes or a cell that contains a formula that is different from the formulas in adjoining cells, is marked by a dark-green indicator at the top-left corner of the cell.

- **To change error-indicator options in Excel:**

1. On the **File** tab, click **Options**.
2. In the **Excel Options** dialog box, click the **Formulas** category.
3. Use the controls in the Error Checking and Error checking rules sections of the Formulas page to set the error-checking options.
4. Click OK.

- **To show worksheet formulas:**

1. On the **Formulas** tab, in the **Formula Auditing** group, click **Show Formulas**.

2. **To check a worksheet for errors:**

1. On the **Formulas** tab, in the **Formula Auditing** group, click **Error Checking**.
2. In the **Error Checking** dialog box, do any of the following:
   - Click Help on this error to display the help file for the error displayed.
   - Click Show Calculation Steps to display the Evaluate Formula dialog box.
   - Click Ignore Error to exclude the error from the error-checking operation.
   - Click Edit in Formula Bar to display the formula in the formula bar.
   - Click Previous to view the previous error.
3. Click Next to view the next error.
4. When you have reached the last error, Excel displays a dialog box indicating there are no more errors.
5. Click OK to close that dialog box.

- **To trace the source of an error:**

1. Click a cell that contains an error.
2. On the **Formulas** tab, in the **Formula Auditing** group, click the **Error Checking** button's down arrow, and then click **Trace Error**.

- **To move through a formula step-by-step:**

1. Perform any of these steps:
   - Click Evaluate to summarizes the next expression in the formula.
   - Click Step In to display the result of the underlined expression.
   - Click Step Out to return to the formula evaluation.
   - Click Restart to step through the formula again.
   - Click Close to exit the Evaluate Formula dialog box.

- **To create a link to a cell or cell range not on the current worksheet:**

1. If necessary, open the workbook that contains the outside data you want to use in your formula.
2. Start creating the formula where you want to use data in cells in another worksheet or workbook.
3. Display the external worksheet, and select the cells that contain the data to include in the formula.
4. Finish entering the formula and press <Enter>.

- **To define Excel Tables:**

1. Excel tables give formal structure to lists of data in a worksheet, with unique names for the table as a whole and each column.
   Example: A table named Table1 (the default name for the first Excel table you create in a workbook) could have columns named *Date, Store Number*, and *Sales*.
   You can summarize the Table's data using formulas, PivotTables, or charts. Excel automatically updates your formulas, PivotTables, or charts when you add a row of data to a table. If you add data to a worksheet outside a table, you must edit the summary's settings to reflect the new values.

- **To create a table:**

1. Click any cell in a data list.
2. On the **Home** tab, in the *Styles* group, click **Format as Table**.
3. In the gallery that appears, click the style you want to apply.
4. In the Format As Table dialog box, verify that Excel has identified the correct cell range for the table, check the My table has headers box if appropriate, and click **OK**.

- **To add a row to a table:**

1. In a worksheet cell in the row directly below the table's last row, enter a new value. A new row will be added to the table.

OR

1. Click the cell at the right end of the last row in the table. Press **<Tab>** to create a new row.

- **To add a column to a table:**

1. In a worksheet cell in the column directly to the right of the table's last column, enter a new value. A new column will be added to the table.

- **To select a table column:**

1. Position the mouse pointer over the header of the table column you want to select.
2. When the pointer changes to a downward-pointing black arrow, click the header.

- **To select a table row:**

1. Position the mouse pointer over the left edge of the leftmost cell in the row you want to select.
2. When the pointer changes to a rightward-pointing black arrow, click the cell.

- **To delete a table column:**

1. Position the mouse pointer over the header of the table column you want to delete.
2. When the pointer changes to a downward-pointing black arrow, right-click the header, point to **Delete**, and then click **Table Columns**.

- **To delete a table row:**

1. Position the mouse pointer over the left edge of the leftmost cell in the row you want to delete.
2. When the pointer changes to a rightward-pointing black arrow, right-click the cell, point to **Delete**.
3. Click **Table Rows**.

- **To rename a table:**

1. Click any cell in the table.
2. On the **Design** contextual tab of the Ribbon, in the **Properties** group, type a new value in the **Table Name** box, then press <Enter>.

- **To format a table:**

1. Click any cell in the table.

2. On the **Home** tab of the Ribbon, in the **Styles** group, click **Format as Table.**
3. Click the style you want to apply.

- **To add a total row:**

1. Click any cell in the table.
2. On the **Design** contextual tab of the Ribbon, in the **Table Style Options** group, check the **Total Row** box.

- **To Change a total row cell's summary operation:**

1. Click any cell in a table total row.
2. Click the down arrow that appear and then click the operation you want to apply or click **More Functions** to display the **Insert Function** dialog box.

- **To Refer to a table column in a formula:**

1. Start creating a formula in a cell, such as = **AVERAGE().**
2. In the parentheses, type the name of the table or start typing it and select it from the suggestions list.
3. Type a left square bracket [, click the name of the column you want to summarize, and then type a right square bracket] to close the column reference.
4. Finish editing your formula, then press **<Enter>**.

- **To convert a table into a cell range:**

1. Click any cell in the table.
2. On the **Design** contextual tab of the Ribbon, in the Tools group, click **Convert to Range.**
3. In the confirmation dialog box that appears, click **Yes.**

A.5 MANAGING WORKBOOKS & WORKSHEETS

- **To create a new workbook:**

1. From within an existing workbook, press **<Ctrl>** + **<N>**. OR
1. Click the **File** tab of the Ribbon.
2. Click **New.**
3. Click the template you want to use.
4. Click **Create.**

- **To open an existing workbook:**

1. Click the **File** tab of the Ribbon and then click **Open**, or press **<Ctrl>** + **<O>.**
2. Click a file listed in the **Recent file** list. OR
1. Click **OneDrive, This PC**, or **Browse**, navigate to the folder the contains the file, and double-click it.

- **To save a workbook for the first time:**

1. On the **Quick Access Toolbar**, click **Save.** OR
1. Click the **File** tab of the Ribbon and then click **Save**, or press **<Ctrl>** + **<S>.**
2. On the *Save As* page of the Backstage view, click **OneDrive, This PC**, or **Browse.**
3. In the **Save As** dialog box, navigate to the folder where you want to save the file.
4. Type a name for the file in the *File name* box, then click **Save.**

- **To save a workbook under a new name or folder:**

1. Click the **File** tab of the Ribbon and then click **Save As**, or press **<F12>.**
2. In the **Save As** dialog box, navigate to the folder where you want to save the file.
3. Type a name for the file in the **File** name box, then click **Save.**

- **To close a workbook:**

1. Do one of the following:
   a. Click **Close** at the top right corner of the program window.
   b. Click the **File** tab of the Ribbon and then click **Close.**
   c. Press **<Ctrl> + <W>.**
2. If you have unsaved changes, in the dialog box that appears after you start to close the workbook, click Save to save the changes or **Don't Save** to discard all unsaved changes.

- **To print a worksheet:**

1. Click the **File** tab of the Ribbon and then click **Print**, or press **<Ctrl>** + **<P>.**
2. Set print options including the number of copies, printer, orientation, and paper size.
3. Click **Print.**

- **To verify files using the Compatibility Checker:**

1. Click the **File** tab of the Ribbon.
2. On the **Info** page of the Backstage view, click **Check for Issues** and then **Check Compatibility.**
3. In the results dialog box, if desired, click **Select versions to show** and then click the versions for which you want to check feature compatibility.
4. If desired, click **Copy to New Sheet** to save the compatibility report to a worksheet in the current workbook.
5. Click OK.

- **To display a worksheet:**

1. On the sheet tab bar, click the worksheet's tab.

- **To add a worksheet:**

1. Click the **Home** tab of the Ribbon. Then, in the **Cells** group, click the **Insert Cells** button's down arrow and then click **Insert Sheet.** OR
2. Click **New Sheet**, which is just to the right of the sheet tabs.

- **To rename a worksheet:**

1. Double-click the sheet tab you want to rename, type a new name for the worksheet, and press <Enter>.

- **To reposition a worksheet:**

1. On the sheet tab bar, click and drag the sheet tab to its new location.

- **To copy a worksheet within a workbook:**

1. On the sheet tab bar, right-click the sheet tab of the worksheet you want to copy, and then click **Move or Copy.**
2. In the Before sheet panel, click the name of the worksheet you want the copied worksheet to appear before.
3. Check the **Create a copy** box.
4. Click **OK.**

- **To move a worksheet to another workbook:**

1. Open the workbook to which you want to move the worksheet.
2. Display the worksheet you want to move.
3. On the sheet tab bar, right-click the sheet tab of the worksheet you want to move, and then click **Move** or **Copy.**
4. In the **Move or Copy** dialog box, click the **To book** down arrow and either click the target workbook or click (**new book**) to create a new workbook.
5. In the **Before sheet** panel, click the name of the worksheet you want the moved worksheet to appear before.
6. Click OK.

- **To copy a worksheet to another workbook:**

1. Open the workbook to which you want to copy the worksheet.
2. Display the worksheet you want to copy.
3. On the sheet tab bar, right-click the sheet tab of the worksheet you want to copy, and then click **Move or Copy**.
4. In the **Move or Copy** dialog box, click the **To book** down arrow and either click the target workbook or click (**new book**) to create a new workbook.
5. In the **Before sheet** panel, click the name of the worksheet you want the copied worksheet to appear before.
6. Check the **Create a copy** box.
7. Click OK.

- **To change a worksheet's tab color:**

1. Right-click the sheet tab, point to **Tab Color**, and click the color to apply to the sheet tab.

- **To delete a worksheet:**

1. Right-click the sheet tab, and then click **Delete**.
2. If the worksheet contained data, click **Delete** in the confirmation dialog box that appears.

A.6 SORTING & FILTERING DATA

- **To sort data in ascending or descending order:**

1. Click any cell in the column by which you want to sort your data.
2. On the **Home** tab, in the **Editing** group, click **Sort & Filter**.
3. Click either **Sort Smallest to Largest** or **Sort Largest to Smallest**.

- **To sort data using a custom sort order:**

1. Click any cell in the data list you want to sort.
2. On the **Home** tab, in the **Editing** group, click **Sort & Filter**, and then click **Custom Sort**.
3. In the **Sort** dialog box, click the **Sort by** control's down arrow and select the column by which to sort.
4. Click the **Sort On** control's down arrow and select the cell contents (e.g., values or cell color) by which to sort.
5. Click the **Order** control's down arrow, and then click **Custom List**.
6. In the **Custom Lists** dialog box, either:
   a. Click the existing custom list you want to use.
   b. Type the new list, with each item separated by a comma, in the List entries box, and click **Add**.
7. Click OK to close the **Custom Lists** dialog box.
8. Click OK to close the **Sort** dialog box and sort your data.

A.7 PIVOT TABLES

Excel 2016 lets you to create powerful summaries, but a basic worksheet isn't that flexible. It can take a long time to rearrange data into exactly the order you want, even if you use tables, filters, and other techniques.

Example: Suppose you have a table that contains customer order information (See Table A.1.

You can filter the table and change the summary functions in the Total row, but it's difficult and time-consuming to change the data's arrangement.

A PivotTable lets you rearrange your data quickly, creating exactly the summaries you need.

Example: You might organize sales data by month, customer, and product (See Figure A.2)

Table A.1 Customer Order Information

Order ID	Customer	Months	Product	Total
1	A	January	Wrap	Rs. 3,400.00
2	B	January	Boxes	Rs. 1,800.00
3	C	January	Bags	Rs. 750.00
4	D	February	Wrap	4,200.00
5	E	February	Boxes	2,100.00
6	F	February	Bags	Rs. 400.00
7	G	March	Boxes	Rs. 2,400.00
8	H	March	Wrap	Rs. 1,900.00
9	I	March	Bags	Rs. 800.00

Table A.2 Organize sales data by month, customer and product

Sum of Total	Column Labels			
Row Labels	Bags	Boxes	Wrap	Grand Total
= January	Rs.750.00	Rs.1,800.00	Rs.3,400.00	Rs.5,950.00
	A	Rs.750.00	Rs.3,400.00	Rs.4,150.00
	B	Rs.1,800.00	Rs.1,800.00	
= February	Rs.400.00	Rs.2,100.00	Rs.4,200.00	Rs.6,700.00
	D	Rs.2,100.00	Rs.2,100.00	

(Contd...)

	E	Rs.400.00	Rs.400.00	
	F	Rs.4,200.00	Rs.4,200.00	
=March	Rs.800.00	Rs.2,400.00	Rs.1,900.00	Rs.5,100.00
	G	Rs.1,900.00	Rs.1,900.00	
	H	Rs.800.00	Rs.2,400.00	Rs.3,200.00
Grand Total	Rs.1,950.00	Rs.6,300.00	Rs.9.500.00	Rs.17,750.00

Table A.3 Data organized by customer, product and month

Sum of Total	**Column Labels**				
Row Labels	January		February	March	G.Total
=A	Rs.4,150.00	Rs.2,100.00	Rs.6250.00		
	Bags	Rs.750.00	Rs.750.00		
	Boxes	Rs.2,100.00	Rs.2,100.00		
	Wrap	Rs.3,400.00	Rs.3,400.00		
=B	Rs.1,800	Rs.400.00	Rs.1,900.00	Rs.4,100.00	
	Bags	Rs.400.00	Rs.400.00		
	Boxes	Rs.1,800.00	Rs.1,800.00		
	Wrap	Rs.1,900.00	Rs.1,900.00		
=C	Rs.4,200.00	Rs.3,200.00	Rs.7,400.00		
	Bags	Rs.800.00	Rs.800.00		
	Boxes	Rs.2,400.00	Rs.2,400.00		
	Wrap	Rs.200.00	Rs.4,200.00		
Grand Total	Rs.5,950.00	Rs.6,700.00	Rs.5,100.00	Rs.17,750.00	

If you would rather see the same data organized by customer, product, and month, you can change the PivotTable arrangement in a few seconds (See Figure A.3).

As you can see, changing the field's order changes the PivotTable's emphasis. There is no single best arrangement for any data set. Instead, you should explore your data by creating multiple configurations and writing down the field orders that convey the message you want to deliver.

A.7.1 Creating & Pivoting Pivot Tables

PivotTables are dynamic workbook objects that let you to reorganize your data, but they draw their data from a static source such as a worksheet data list, a table, or an external data source in which the contents are arranged as a table. Once you link to a data source, you can create your PivotTable and organize your data to discover the information you need.

A PivotTable's organization is determined by the order of fields in the Columns, Rows, and Values areas of the PivotTable Fields pane. If you have a single field in one of those areas, then it defines the arrangement. If you have more than one field in an area, such as Quarter and Month in the Rows area, then the PivotTable displays a header for each quarter, followed by values for each month within that quarter. That pattern continues for each of the four quarters in the year.

- **To arrange data for use in a PivotTable:**

1. Arrange your data in a list so that each column contains a specific type of data (e.g., Productid) and each row contains values relating to an instance of the object described by the list (e.g., a product).
2. If necessary, add headers to the top of each column to identify the data summarized by those columns.
3. Ensure there are no blank rows or blank columns within the data list and no extraneous data in the cells surrounding the list. The right column and bottom row should be blank, and the left column and top row should either be the edge of the worksheet or should be blank as well.

- **To create a table:**

1. Click any cell in a data list.
2. One the **Home** tab, in the **Styles** group, click **Format as Table.**
3. Click the style you want to apply from the gallery that appears.
4. In the **Format as Table** dialog box, verify that Excel has identified the correct cell range, check the **My table** has **headers** box if appropriate, and click **OK**.

- **To open the Create PivotTable dialog box:**

1. Click the cell you want to identify as the top-left cell of the PivotTable.
2. On the **Insert** tab, in the **Tables** group, click **PivotTable.**

- **To refresh PivotTable data:**

1. Click any cell in the PivotTable.
2. On the **Analyze** contextual tab, in the **Data** group, click the main body of the **Refresh** button to refresh data for the current **PivotTable**. OR.
3. Click the **Refresh** button's down arrow, and then click **Refresh All** to update all PivotTables that draw data from the same source as the current PivotTable.

- **To Pivot a PivotTable:**

1 Open the PivotTable Fields pane (**Show or hide the Field List** in the **Managing Pivot Tables** section), and take any of the following actions:

- Drag a field from the Field List to one of the *Values, Rows, Columns,* or *Filters* areas to add that field's values and organization level to the PivotTable.
- Drag a field from one area of the PivotTable to another (e.g., the *Columns* area to the Rows area).
- Drag a field from one position in an area to another.
- Drag a field from one of the *Values, Rows, Columns,* or *Filters* area to the Field List to remove the field from the PivotTable.

A.7.2 Creating and Manipulating Pivot Charts

Just as charts let you summarize your data visually, Pivot Charts let you create dynamic visual summaries of your data.

Example: You could create a PivotChart that displays a column for a company's quarterly sales and then add the Months field to the PivotChart to show how each month contributed to the quarter's total sales.

- **To create a PivotChart:**

1. Click any cell in the data source you want to summarize using a PivotChart.
2. On the **Insert** tab, in the **Charts** group, click the **PivotChart** button's down arrow, and then click **PivotChart**.
3. In the **PivotChart Fields** pane, drag fields to the Legend (Series), Axis (Category), and Values areas.

- **To create a PivotChart from an existing PivotTable:**

1. Click any cell in the body of the PivotTable.
2. On the **Insert** tab, in the **Charts** group, click the type and subtype of chart you want to create.

- **Pivot a PivotChart:**

1. Display the *PivotChart Fields* pane, and do any of the following:
   - Drag a field from the Field List to any of the areas at the bottom of the pane to add the field to the PivotChart.
   - Drag a field from one of the four areas at the bottom of the pane to the Field List to remove the field from the PivotChart.
   - Drag a field to a new area, or to a new position within an area, to change the PivotChart's arrangement.

- **To apply a style to a PivotChart:**

1. Click the PivotChart.
2. On the **Design** contextual tab, in the **Chart Styles** group, click the gallery's **More** button.
3. In the gallery, click the style you want to apply to the PivotChart.

- **To change a PivotChart's layout:**

1. Click the PivotChart.
2. On the **Design** contextual tab, in the **Chart Layouts** group, click the **Quick Layout** button.
3. In the button list that appears, click the layout you want to apply.

- **To change a PivotChart's chart type:**

1. Click the PivotChart.
2. On the **Design** contextual tab, in the **Type** group, click **Change Chart Type**.
3. In the **Change Chart Type** dialog box, click the new chart type for your chart.
4. In the gallery of subtypes, click a new subtype for your chart.
5. Click **OK**.

- **To add a trendline to a PivotChart:**

1. Click the PivotChart.
2. On the **Design** contextual tab, in the **Chart Layouts** group, click the **Add Chart Element**.
3. In the button list that appears, point to *Trendline,* and then click the type of trendline you want to create:
   - **None:** Removes any trendlines from the chart.
   - **Linear:** Uses existing data to draw a single line that minimizes the distance between the line and each data point, assuming a linear data distribution.
   - **Exponential:** Uses existing data to draw a single line that minimizes the distance between the line and each data point, assuming an exponential distribution.
   - **Linear Forecast:** Draws a linear trendline and extrapolates the trendline several periods into the future.
   - **Moving Average:** Draws a trendline where each point reflects the last few data values; a moving average of three periods would display the average of the last three measurements.
   - **More Trendline Options:** Displays the Format Trendline pane, which contains tools you can use to change the characteristics of the trendline.

A.7.3 Printing PivotTables

1. Click any cell in the PivotTable.
2. Press **<Ctrl>+<A>**. OR
1. On the **Analyze** contextual tab, in the **Action** group, click the Select button, and then click **Entire PivotTable.**
2. On the **File** tab, click **Print**. OR
3. Press **<Ctrl>+<P>**.
4. Select a printer, and then change settings as needed for the print job.
5. Click **Print**.

- **To print headers at the top of each printed page:**

1. Click any cell in the PivotTable.
2. On the **Analyze** contextual tab, in the **PivotTables** group, click the **Options** button.
3. In the **PivotTable Options** dialog box, click the **Printing** tab.
4. On the **Printing** page of the dialog box, check the **Repeat** row labels on each printed page box.
5. Click OK.

- **To print each item on its own page:**

1. Click any cell in the PivotTable.
2. On the **Analyze** contextual tab, in the **Active Field** group, click the **Field Settings** button.
3. In the **Field Settings** dialog box, click the **Layout & Print** tab.
4. On the **Layout & Print** tab, check the **Insert** page break after each item box.
5. Click OK.

- **To print a PivotChart:**

1. Click the PivotChart.
2. On the **File** tab, click **Print**. OR
1. Press **<Ctrl>+<P>**.
2. Verify that Printed Selected Chart appears in the Settings control.

3. Select a printer, and then change settings as needed for the print job.
4. Click **Print**.

A.7.4 Filter Data Using Slicers

Excel tables, lets you to organize data and summarize it within the table or create PivotTables, provide a wide range of filtering tools through each column's filter arrows. While those filters are powerful, it's difficult to determine at a glance what rule you have applied and what set of values is visible. While using the filter arrows is ideal for when you are analyzing data alone, slicers let audiences remind themselves of the filter's criteria and made presentations easier to understand.

- **To Filter a worksheet using a slicer:**

1. Click any cell in an Excel table.
2. On the **Insert** tab of the ribbon, in the **Filters** group, click **Slicer.**
3. In the **Insert Slicers** dialog box, check the boxes next to the columns for which you want to create a slicer.
4. Click **OK.**
5. In the slicer, click the value you want to display within the table column.

- **To select multiple values in a slicer:**

1. Display a slicer.
2. On the command bar of the slicer, click the **Multi-Select** button. OR
1. Press <Alt>+<S>.
2. Click individual values within the slicer to hide or display them within the table.

- **To clear a slicer filter:**

1. On the command bar of the slicer, click the **Clear Filter** button. OR
2. Press <Alt>+<C>.

A.8 WHAT-IF ANALYSIS

Planning business activities requires you to make guesses, or forecasts, about the future. While there is no way to be sure what the future will bring, you can create alternative data sets, called scenarios, to explore possible future outcomes. Scenarios identify new values for worksheet cells without changing the original data until you apply the scenario. You can apply one or several scenarios at a time to explore the impact of those assumptions on your formulas.

Because scenarios change a worksheet's values, you should always create a backup copy of your original workbook before adding your scenarios.

- **To open the Scenario Manager dialog box:**

1. On the **Data** tab of the ribbon, in the **Forecast** group.
2. Click What-If Analysis.
3. Click Scenario Manager.

- **To create a scenario:**

1. In the **Scenario Manager** dialog box, click **Add.**
   - In the **Scenario** name box, type a scenario name.
   - Click in the **Changing cells** box, and the select the cells to change.
   - Click OK.
2. In the **Scenario Values** dialog box, enter new values for the selected cells.
3. Click OK.
4. Click **Close** to close the **Scenario Manager** dialog box.

- **To apply a scenario:**

1. In the **Scenario Manager** dialog box, click the scenario you want to display.
2. Click **Show.**
3. Click another scenario, and click **Show** to display it. OR
1. Click **Close.**
2. If you save a workbook while a scenario is displayed, the scenario values replace your original data.

- **Remove a scenario you just displayed:**

1. Press <Ctrl>+<Z> to undo the action. OR
1. On the **Quick Access** Toolbar, click the **Undo** button's down arrow.
2. Click the action to remove the scenario.

Using the **Undo** button's down arrow reverses every change made since you displayed the scenario.

A.8.1 Calculating Target Values Using Goal Seek

Determining how much one values contributes to a total, such as the percentage of sales a particular product represents for your company, is simply a matter of dividing the sales for your product by your company's total revenue. If an office supply store sells Rs. 5,000 of custom letterhead each month as part of total sales of Rs. 25,000, you know the share of letterhead sales is 20%.

But suppose you want letterhead sales to be 23% of the total. You can't simply increase letterhead sales to Rs 5,750, which 23% of Rs 25,000, because total sales would increase to Rs 25,750, and you would fall short. Rather than use trial and error to find the required input for a formula to return a desired result, you can use Goal Seek and have Excel do the work for you.

- **To calculate a value using Goal Seek:**

1. Set up a worksheet with a value and summary formula that includes the changing value, such as the arrangement shown in the **Goal Seek** example.
2. On the **Data** tab of the ribbon, in the **Forecast** group, click **What-If Analysis**, and then click **Goal Seek.**
3. In the **Goal Seek** dialog box, in the **Set** cell box, type the address of the cell that contains the formula you want to produce a specific result.
4. In the **To** value box, enter the formula's target value, such as 30%.
5. In the By changing cell box, enter the address of the cell with the value you want to change to example, that cell is B2.
6. Click OK.